AI and the Transformation of Academic Work in Higher Education

Rany Sam
https://orcid.org/0000-0003-3266-5974
National University of Battambang, Cambodia

IGI Global
Scientific Publishing
Publishing Tomorrow's Research Today

Vice President of Editorial | Melissa Wagner
Director of Acquisitions | Mikaela Felty
Director of Book Development | Jocelynn Hessler
Production Manager | Mike Brehm
Cover Design | Jose Rosado

Published in the United States of America by
IGI Global Scientific Publishing
701 East Chocolate Avenue
Hershey, PA, 17033, USA
Tel: 717-533-8845 | Fax: 717-533-7115
Website: https://www.igi-global.com E-mail: cust@igi-global.com

Library of Congress Cataloging-in-Publication Data

LCCN: 2026032956 (CIP Data Pending)
ISBN13: 9798260032046
EISBN13: 9798260032060
British Cataloguing in Publication Data
A Cataloguing in Publication record for this book is available from the British Library.

This book is dedicated to all educators, researchers, academic leaders, and students whose commitment to knowledge, innovation, and lifelong learning continues to shape the future of higher education.

It is also dedicated to scholars around the world who embrace change with integrity, curiosity, and a shared commitment to advancing teaching, research, and academic excellence in the age of artificial intelligence. Your dedication to responsible scholarship and the pursuit of knowledge inspires meaningful progress for future generations.

On a personal note, I dedicate this work with profound gratitude to my family, whose unwavering love, encouragement, patience, and understanding have been my greatest source of strength throughout this journey. Their constant support has made this achievement possible.

May this volume encourage thoughtful dialogue, responsible innovation, international collaboration, and a shared vision for a future in which artificial intelligence enhances, rather than replaces, the human values at the heart of higher education.

Rany Sam
Editor

Editorial Advisory Board

Table of Contents

Foreword xv

Preface xviii

Acknowledgment xxi

Chapter 1
Artificial Intelligence and the Transformation of Academic Work: Teaching, Research Productivity, and the Future of the Academic Profession 1
Borey Be, University of Cambodia, Cambodia
Nayheak Khun, Ministry of Labour and Vocational Training, Cambodia

Chapter 2
Artificial Intelligence and the Transformation of Academic Work: A Policy Analysis and Institutional Case Study From India 31
Rajesh Prasad, Ajay Kumar Garg Engineering College, India

Chapter 3
AI in Learning and Education: Implications for Faculty Careers in Higher Education 61
Sanjeev Kumar, Lovely Professional University, India
Pardeep Kumar, Lovely Professional University, India

Chapter 4
Can AI Improve Faculty Organisational Commitment and Reduce Turnover Intention? Evidence From Private Higher Education Institutions 85
Ritu Arora, Chandigarh University, India
Azmee Zaheer, Chandigarh University, India

Chapter 5
Professional Development for Academicians in the Age of Artificial Intelligence 115
Kritikka Kunte, Ajeenkya D.Y. Patil University, India
Sunil Sankathala, Ajeenkya D.Y. Patil University, India
Krutika Patre, Ajeenkya D.Y. Patil University, India
Susanta Das, Ajeenkya D.Y. Patil University, India

Chapter 6
Professional Development for Academicians in the Age of Artificial Intelligence: A Multidimensional Framework for Academic Identity, Competence, and Institutional Transformation 137
Winter Seshoka, University of Limpopo, South Africa

Chapter 7
Reimagining Doctoral Research in the Age of AI: Strengthening Scholar–Supervisor Collaboration and Enhancing Research Quality 167
Kesavan Dhanapal, SRM Institute of Science and Technology, India
S. Sivaprakkash, Central University of Tamil Nadu, India
Rafia Banu, B.S. Abdur Rahman Crescent Institute of Sciences and Technology, India
Naveenraj Xavier, SRM Institute of Science and Technology, India

Chapter 8
Enhancing Research Supervision in Cambodian Teacher Education: The Academic Profession and Professorial Roles in the Age of AI 197
Da Bou, Graduate School, National University of Battambang, Cambodia
Chan Hum, National University of Battambang, Cambodia
Sopha Soeung, National Institute of Education, Cambodia
Rany Sam, National University of Battambang, Cambodia

Chapter 9
AI-Enhanced Academic Careers in Cambodia: Rethinking Professorial Roles, Evaluation, and Identity in a Digitally Transformed Higher Education 231
Sovanna Huot, Department of Education, National Institute of Education (NIE), Phnom Penh, Cambodia
Phearun Tep, Department of English, University of Delhi, New Delhi, India

Chapter 10
The Moroccan Academic Profession in the Age of Rankings and AI-Driven Evaluation: Professorial Appointments, Careers, and Daily Realities 261
Kenza Ennida, National School of Commerce and Management, Sidi Mohamed Ben Abdellah University, Morocco
Mehdi Chaoui Roqai, National School of Commerce and Management, Sidi Mohamed Ben Abdellah University, Morocco
Saif Allah Allouani, National School of Business and Management, Sidi Mohammed Ben Abdellah University, Fez, Morocco

Chapter 11
The Dialectics of Digital Transformation AI Ethics, Academic Freedom: Policy Praxis in Indonesian Universities.. 295
Amirul Mukminin, Universitas Jambi, Indonesia
Kasinyo Harto, Universitas Islam Negeri Raden Fatah, Palembang, Indonesia
Lenny Marzulina, Universitas Islam Negeri Raden Fatah, Palembang, Indonesia
Dian Erlina, Universitas Islam Negeri Raden Fatah, Palembang, Indonesia
Rina Antasari, Universitas Islam Negeri Raden Fatah, Palembang, Indonesia
Fridiyanto Fridiyanto, UIN Sulthan Thaha Saifuddin Jambi, Jambi, Indonesia
Edi Surya Negara, Universitas Bina Darma, Indonesia
Ella Masita, Universitas Jambi, Indonesia

Chapter 12
An Empirical Study From Odisha State of India for Studying the Knowledge and AI Literacy of Pre-Service Teachers 327
Arakhita Behera, Regional Institute of Education (NCERT), Ajmer, India
Ajay Kumar Singh, Department of Humanities and Social Sciences, Graphic Era (Deemed to be) University, Dehradun, India
Rahul Ranjan, RIE (NCERT), Mysuru, India
Kiranbala Behera, Department of Rural Development, Ravenshaw University, Cuttack, India

Compilation of References 359

About the Contributors 415

Index 427

Detailed Table of Contents

Foreword xv

Preface xviii

Acknowledgment xxi

Chapter 1
Artificial Intelligence and the Transformation of Academic Work: Teaching, Research Productivity, and the Future of the Academic Profession 1
Borey Be, University of Cambodia, Cambodia
Nayheak Khun, Ministry of Labour and Vocational Training, Cambodia

The rapid growth of artificial intelligence (AI) is changing academic work in higher education. It is reshaping teaching, research, and professional identity. This chapter explores how AI affects workload, professional skills, autonomy, and identity among faculty. It shows that AI can increase work demands while also requiring new skills. The chapter also discusses the importance of governance, institutional policies, and ethical frameworks in guiding responsible AI use. It stresses the need for transparency, accountability, and participatory decision-making. Professional development is essential to build digital literacy, ethical awareness, and flexible teaching practices. Drawing on research from different fields and global contexts, the chapter calls for human-centred, fair, and sustainable approaches to AI in higher education. It provides practical insights for university leaders, policymakers, and researchers who aim to balance innovation with ethical responsibility and protect the future of the academic profession.

Chapter 2
Artificial Intelligence and the Transformation of Academic Work: A Policy Analysis and Institutional Case Study From India 31
Rajesh Prasad, Ajay Kumar Garg Engineering College, India

The study focuses on the topic of the artificial intelligence (AI) use in academic activity and faculty practice in Indian higher education, employing the mixed-method approach of policy analysis and a comprehensive case study. The analysis will also be based on the national policy documents as well as the information on the survey and interviews, collected via a chosen institution of higher learning. It examines how AI-led reforms can be perceived and experienced at different levels. The findings indicate that although the policy frameworks are very favourable to

AI-enabled transformation, they are not yet fairly implemented, and are mediated by the institutional ability and readiness of the faculty. Empirical data shows that AI tools are used to teach and support research, but this application is associated with the increased demand on performance and the aggravation of academic labour. The research also indicates the differences in access to the digital infrastructure and reveals the new ethical issues regarding the surveillance, academic honesty and algorithmic discrimination.

Chapter 3
AI in Learning and Education: Implications for Faculty Careers in Higher Education 61
Sanjeev Kumar, Lovely Professional University, India
Pardeep Kumar, Lovely Professional University, India

Artificial intelligence (AI) is transforming the learning and education, shapes teaching and learning methods, methods of evaluating learning, and the overall higher education. The AI provides opportunities and challenges to members of the faculty that have significant career growth implications, professional identity implications and instructional role implications. The effectiveness of the teaching process, adapting learning to the individual student, and stimulating research can be enhanced through artificial intelligence (intelligent tutoring systems), automated grading, adaptive learning, and data-driven analytics. However, there are other aspects of these developments, such as the faculty allowing new competencies in the context of AI literacy, digital pedagogy, and technology use ethics. The integration of AI may also be similar to the allocation of the ancient functions, where mentorship, the right to think critically, and the application of the human judgment can be put in the field where the AI devices will not be able to achieve the results of the complex thought.

Chapter 4
Can AI Improve Faculty Organisational Commitment and Reduce Turnover Intention? Evidence From Private Higher Education Institutions 85
Ritu Arora, Chandigarh University, India
Azmee Zaheer, Chandigarh University, India

The fast adoption of Artificial Intelligence within private higher learning institutions has immensely changed the academic and administrative processes, thus impacting that of the faculty and organisational performance. This paper will discuss how perceptions of AI by the faculty members, in terms of perceived AI usefulness, perceived AI-driven workload reduction, perceived AI-based decision fairness, and perceived AI-enabled organisational support influence organisational commitment and turnover intention. Quantitative and cross-sectional research design was adopted and 520 respondents' private universities in India were sampled and primary data were obtained. Structural Equation Modeling was used to analyse the data to evaluate the measurement and structural relationships. The results reveal that the existence of positive attitudes to AI as helpful, equitable, supporting, and workload-saving has a strong positive impact on the organisational commitment and indirectly on the turnover intentions of faculty members.

Chapter 5
Professional Development for Academicians in the Age of Artificial Intelligence 115
Kritikka Kunte, Ajeenkya D.Y. Patil University, India
Sunil Sankathala, Ajeenkya D.Y. Patil University, India
Krutika Patre, Ajeenkya D.Y. Patil University, India
Susanta Das, Ajeenkya D.Y. Patil University, India

Intelligent tutoring systems, adaptive learning platforms, automated grading systems, & Gen AI applications are some of the tools used in universities to enhance educational practices. This chapter examines the connection between AI and higher education and puts the idea in its professional growth of academicians in the era of AI. It talks about the increasing applications of AI technologies in learning and teaching practices and how such tools can be used to facilitate data-driven decision making and customized learning. Another point that the chapter discusses is the changing of academic roles and the need to impart new digital competencies in educators. Some of the most important aspects of professional growth are AI literacy, digital pedagogical skills, data literacy, ethical awareness, institutional training programs, and lifelong learning. The chapter concludes that effective implementation of AI in higher education is hinged on the constant learning and development of the institution and the capacity of the teachers to learn in fast changing technological environments.

Chapter 6
Professional Development for Academicians in the Age of Artificial Intelligence: A Multidimensional Framework for Academic Identity, Competence, and Institutional Transformation........ 137
Winter Seshoka, University of Limpopo, South Africa

AI is reshaping not only teaching and research in higher education but also academic identity, governance, and professional development. Yet little is known about AI-responsive professional development (PD) that addresses academic careers, appointments, and evaluation. This chapter develops a multidimensional, theoretically grounded PD framework based on TPACK, Human-AI Collaboration Theory, Transformational Learning Theory, and Digital Ethics. It analyses how AI transforms academic identities, institutional structures, and career pathways, with a comparative perspective on developed versus developing contexts. The chapter then identifies seven structural gaps in current PD models: fragmentation, technocentrism, one-size-fits-all approaches, inequity, time constraints, policy-practice disconnects, and lack of collaboration. In response, the ACADEME-AI Professional Development Framework is introduced, integrating four dimensions: Knowledge & Competence, Relational & Agency, Identity & Transformation, and Digital Ethics.

Chapter 7
Reimagining Doctoral Research in the Age of AI: Strengthening Scholar–Supervisor Collaboration and Enhancing Research Quality 167
Kesavan Dhanapal, SRM Institute of Science and Technology, India
S. Sivaprakkash, Central University of Tamil Nadu, India
Rafia Banu, B.S. Abdur Rahman Crescent Institute of Sciences and Technology, India
Naveenraj Xavier, SRM Institute of Science and Technology, India

Doctoral research is increasingly shaped by the everyday presence of artificial intelligence, influencing how scholars think, write, manage uncertainty, and engage with supervision. This chapter examines the cognitive, emotional, and relational shifts that arise as doctoral students enter research with early clarity, structured thinking, and AI-supported confidence rather than prolonged ambiguity. While this transformation can reduce anxiety and sustain momentum, it also raises critical questions about independence, originality, and research quality. Drawing on doctoral education literature and supervisory perspectives, the chapter argues that fear-driven and prohibition-based institutional responses weaken trust and obscure learning processes. Instead, it reframes AI as part of the contemporary scholarly infrastructure requiring interpretive guidance. A collaborative research quality model is proposed to demonstrate how autonomy, methodological integrity, transparent supervision, and intellectual maturation can be strengthened through guided AI integration.

Chapter 8
Enhancing Research Supervision in Cambodian Teacher Education: The Academic Profession and Professorial Roles in the Age of AI 197
Da Bou, Graduate School, National University of Battambang, Cambodia
Chan Hum, National University of Battambang, Cambodia
Sopha Soeung, National Institute of Education, Cambodia
Rany Sam, National University of Battambang, Cambodia

This chapter investigates the impact of supervisory procedures used by Cambodian teacher educators on research outputs and student teachers' views within the framework of current educational changes in Cambodia. A quantitative survey was used to collect data from 106 teacher educators and 337 student teachers in Teacher Education Colleges (TECs). The data collected were subjected to ANOVA and Regression analysis. The results reveal that CS has a major positive role in student teachers' research skills, as shown by a positive coefficient ($\beta = 0.858$, Sig.

= 0.037) in the era of AI. On the other hand, MS has potential, although it shows a non-significant negative effect (β = -0.108, Sig. = 0.716). AS and TS, on the other hand, are not very satisfactory. In particular, TS has a substantial negative connection with research findings (β = -0.826, Sig. = 0.030). The results suggest the necessity to revise supervisory procedures and analyze transformative supervision to improve the effectiveness of instruction.

Chapter 9
AI-Enhanced Academic Careers in Cambodia: Rethinking Professorial Roles, Evaluation, and Identity in a Digitally Transformed Higher Education 231
Sovanna Huot, Department of Education, National Institute of Education (NIE), Phnom Penh, Cambodia
Phearun Tep, Department of English, University of Delhi, New Delhi, India

This chapter investigates the impacts of AI on the transformation of academic evaluation, professorial roles, and professional identity within Cambodia's higher education system and beyond. Artificial intelligence (AI) impacts higher education systems around the world, from teaching and learning to research and assessment. In Cambodia, the modernization of higher education is intertwined with digitization and quality-assurance reforms, in which AI technologies strongly shape the academic profession. It reviews 136 articles on AI in higher education, labor, digital governance, and professional identity in Cambodia, using the PRISMA framework. The chapter discusses research, teaching, and administrative opportunities and challenges, as well as issues such as algorithmic bias, the digital divide, autonomy, reliance on metrics, and academic evaluation. This chapter offers a nuanced and pragmatic approach to the integration of AI in Cambodia's higher education system, grounded in ethical policies and fair evaluation and academic governance that support capacity building and collaboration.

Chapter 10
The Moroccan Academic Profession in the Age of Rankings and AI-Driven Evaluation: Professorial Appointments, Careers, and Daily Realities............... 261
Kenza Ennida, National School of Commerce and Management, Sidi Mohamed Ben Abdellah University, Morocco
Mehdi Chaoui Roqai, National School of Commerce and Management, Sidi Mohamed Ben Abdellah University, Morocco
Saif Allah Allouani, National School of Business and Management, Sidi Mohammed Ben Abdellah University, Fez, Morocco

This chapter proposes a theoretically grounded, empirically informed analysis of how successive waves of reform and the growing reliance on digital metrics and rankings are reshaping professorial appointments, academic careers and professional identities in Moroccan public universities. Framing Morocco as a Global South case of "AI-adjacent" and datafied governance, it draws on documentary analysis, secondary survey data and bibliometric indicators to examine the incorporation of bibliometric measures into recruitment and promotion, the everyday consequences for teacher-researchers' workload, autonomy and status, and the scenarios this trajectory opens for the future integration of AI-based evaluation tools. The chapter contributes to debates on the academic profession in the age of AI by highlighting the specific vulnerabilities and opportunities of a middle-income, reform-oriented system.

Chapter 11
The Dialectics of Digital Transformation AI Ethics, Academic Freedom: Policy Praxis in Indonesian Universities.. 295
Amirul Mukminin, Universitas Jambi, Indonesia
Kasinyo Harto, Universitas Islam Negeri Raden Fatah, Palembang, Indonesia
Lenny Marzulina, Universitas Islam Negeri Raden Fatah, Palembang, Indonesia
Dian Erlina, Universitas Islam Negeri Raden Fatah, Palembang, Indonesia
Rina Antasari, Universitas Islam Negeri Raden Fatah, Palembang, Indonesia
Fridiyanto Fridiyanto, UIN Sulthan Thaha Saifuddin Jambi, Jambi, Indonesia
Edi Surya Negara, Universitas Bina Darma, Indonesia
Ella Masita, Universitas Jambi, Indonesia

The chapter critically assesses the dialectics of AI integration, ethical governance, and academic freedom in higher education institutions in Indonesia. Adopting the methodology of a systematic critical qualitative review informed by the PRISMA principles, the paper brings together the analytical approaches of "What's the Problem Represented to Be?" and theories of algorithmic governance, digital colonialism, and epistemic justice. As results of analysis show, AI integration entails the emergence of opaque algorithmic governance undermining epistemic independence, entrenchment of digital colonial dependency, and, most importantly, a notable gap between regulatory aspirations and reality. In this regard, there is a need for the development of Pancasila-based AI governance models, Institutional AI Ethical Review Committees vested with powers from faculties, mandatory safeguards of data sovereignty, and AI literacy programs informed by local context.

Chapter 12
An Empirical Study From Odisha State of India for Studying the Knowledge and AI Literacy of Pre-Service Teachers 327
Arakhita Behera, Regional Institute of Education (NCERT), Ajmer, India
Ajay Kumar Singh, Department of Humanities and Social Sciences, Graphic Era (Deemed to be) University, Dehradun, India
Rahul Ranjan, RIE (NCERT), Mysuru, India
Kiranbala Behera, Department of Rural Development, Ravenshaw University, Cuttack, India

Artificial Intelligence (AI) is used by all stakeholders in most educational organizations. AI is thought to improve student engagement, personalize the learning process, and increase administrative effectiveness in educational processes. This paper explores and examines the awareness of AI and its different approaches among pre-service teachers (PSTs) in Odisha state of India. A systematic evaluation process is undertaken to achieve the mentioned objective. It conducts a survey of 150 PSTs who were randomly selected from three public B.Ed. colleges in Khordha district of this state. The descriptive analysis and Chi-square test were used to investigate AI literacy scale. It noted that PSTs pursue different programmes to increase their efficiency in AI application at institute level. There appeared an insignificant gap in the AI competency literacy among PSTs. It demonstrates the value of in-person group instruction and experiential, hands-on training for improving PSTs' AI literacy.

Compilation of References 359

About the Contributors 415

Index 427

Foreword

It is both an honor and a privilege to introduce ***AI and the Transformation of Academic Work in Higher Education***, a timely and thought-provoking volume that addresses one of the most profound developments shaping contemporary higher education. Artificial intelligence (AI) is redefining the ways universities teach, conduct research, evaluate academic performance, govern institutions, and engage with society. As AI continues to evolve at an unprecedented pace, it presents not only extraordinary opportunities for innovation but also complex questions concerning ethics, academic integrity, professional identity, human agency, and the future purpose of higher education.

This volume arrives at a pivotal moment. Around the world, universities are navigating rapid digital transformation while striving to preserve the enduring values that define higher education: intellectual freedom, critical inquiry, scholarly rigor, ethical responsibility, and service to society. The challenge before us is no longer whether AI should become part of higher education. That transformation is already well underway. The more important question is how institutions can harness AI responsibly to enrich teaching, strengthen research, improve decision-making, and expand access to knowledge while ensuring that human judgment, creativity, and academic integrity remain at the center of educational practice.

One of the greatest strengths of this edited volume lies in its breadth, diversity, and international perspective. Bringing together distinguished scholars from Cambodia, India, Indonesia, South Africa, and other academic communities, the book reflects a rich exchange of ideas across different higher education systems, policy environments, and cultural contexts. Despite differences in institutional traditions and technological readiness, the contributors reveal a shared commitment to understanding how AI can advance educational excellence while addressing the ethical, social, and organizational challenges accompanying digital transformation.

The chapters collectively offer a comprehensive examination of the changing nature of academic work. They explore AI-enabled teaching and learning, faculty development, academic identity, research productivity, doctoral supervision, institutional leadership, governance, academic careers, organizational commitment, AI literacy, digital competencies, academic evaluation, ethical governance, and policy innovation. By integrating empirical research, conceptual analyses, systematic reviews, and practical frameworks, the contributors move beyond discussions of AI as a technological tool to examine its broader implications for the future of the academic profession and the sustainability of higher education.

Particularly noteworthy is the book's inclusion of perspectives from developing and emerging higher education systems. International debates on AI frequently emphasize experiences from highly resourced institutions, often overlooking the realities, innovations, and aspirations of universities operating in rapidly changing educational environments. This volume helps address that imbalance by presenting valuable evidence and thoughtful analyses from diverse national contexts. In doing so, it demonstrates that meaningful scholarship and innovative practice emerge from every region of the world and that global dialogue is strengthened when multiple voices are represented.

The editors deserve special recognition for their scholarly vision and leadership in bringing together this outstanding collection. Developing an edited volume of this scope requires intellectual commitment, international collaboration, and careful editorial coordination. The result is a coherent and balanced work that bridges theory, research, policy, and practice while offering meaningful insights for a wide range of readers. The contributors likewise deserve sincere appreciation for sharing their expertise and advancing our collective understanding of one of the defining issues facing higher education today.

As Rector of the National University of Battambang, I have witnessed the growing importance of digital innovation in strengthening teaching, research, institutional governance, and international collaboration. Universities today are expected not only to prepare graduates for an increasingly AI-driven world but also to cultivate ethical leaders, critical thinkers, and responsible citizens capable of addressing complex global challenges. Meeting these expectations requires institutions to embrace technological innovation while safeguarding the human values that have long defined academic excellence. AI should therefore be regarded not as a substitute for educators and scholars but as a transformative partner that enhances human capability, expands intellectual possibilities, and supports the advancement of knowledge when implemented with wisdom, responsibility, and integrity.

Beyond its scholarly contributions, this volume provides valuable guidance for university leaders, policymakers, faculty members, researchers, doctoral supervisors, graduate students, and educational practitioners seeking to navigate the opportunities and challenges of AI-enabled transformation. Its evidence-informed analyses and practical recommendations will support informed decision-making, encourage responsible innovation, and stimulate future research across disciplines and national boundaries.

I am confident that *AI and the Transformation of Academic Work in Higher Education* will become an important reference for scholars and institutions seeking to understand the evolving relationship between artificial intelligence and the academic profession. More importantly, I hope this volume will inspire continued international collaboration, thoughtful policy development, and innovative research that place human dignity, academic excellence, ethical leadership, and the public mission of higher education at the heart of technological progress.

I warmly congratulate the editors and contributing authors on this significant scholarly achievement. I commend this outstanding volume to readers around the world and trust that it will make a lasting contribution to the advancement of higher education in the age of artificial intelligence.

H.E. Sok Khorn
National University of Battambang, Cambodia

Preface

Artificial Intelligence (AI) has emerged as one of the most transformative forces shaping the future of higher education. Across universities worldwide, AI is redefining teaching, learning, research, assessment, academic leadership, institutional governance, and scholarly communication. These developments offer unprecedented opportunities to enhance educational quality, expand research capacity, and support evidence-informed decision-making. At the same time, they raise important questions concerning academic integrity, ethics, professional identity, data privacy, algorithmic bias, digital equity, and the evolving role of educators in an increasingly AI-enabled academic environment.

Recognizing both the opportunities and the challenges presented by AI, we developed ***AI and the Transformation of Academic Work in Higher Education*** to provide a comprehensive, internationally informed examination of how AI is reshaping the academic profession. Rather than viewing AI solely as a technological innovation, this volume examines its broader implications for faculty work, institutional leadership, policy development, academic careers, research supervision, professional development, governance, and educational transformation. Throughout the volume, the contributors demonstrate that the future of higher education depends not only on technological advancement but also on the enduring importance of human judgment, ethical responsibility, critical thinking, collaboration, and lifelong learning.

One of the defining strengths of this edited volume is its international and interdisciplinary perspective. The contributors represent universities and research institutions across Cambodia, India, Indonesia, South Africa, and other regions, bringing together diverse perspectives that reflect different higher education systems, institutional priorities, and stages of digital transformation. Although these contexts differ considerably, the chapters collectively demonstrate that higher education institutions around the world face common opportunities and shared challenges in adopting AI responsibly while strengthening faculty capacity, institutional resilience, and academic excellence.

This volume brings together conceptual analyses, empirical investigations, systematic reviews, policy studies, and practical frameworks that address a wide range of contemporary issues. Readers will find discussions of AI-enabled teaching and learning, faculty career development, academic identity, organizational commitment, professional development, doctoral supervision, AI literacy, academic evaluation, institutional governance, ethical AI, digital transformation, and policy innovation. Together, these contributions offer both theoretical insights and practical guidance for educators, researchers, university leaders, policymakers, and graduate students seeking to understand and respond to the rapidly evolving landscape of higher education.

CHAPTER OVERVIEW

The book is organized into twelve chapters, each examining AI from a complementary perspective. The opening chapters explore AI's influence on faculty careers, institutional policy, and the changing nature of academic work. Subsequent chapters examine professional development, academic identity, organizational commitment, doctoral supervision, and research quality in AI-enabled environments. The later chapters broaden the discussion by addressing academic governance, ethics, AI literacy, digital transformation, and national experiences from Cambodia, India, Indonesia, and South Africa. Collectively, these chapters demonstrate that effective AI integration requires not only technological capability but also sound governance, ethical leadership, institutional readiness, and continuous professional learning.

Throughout the editorial process, our goal has been to produce a volume that bridges research, policy, and practice. We hope the evidence, perspectives, and recommendations presented throughout this book will support informed decision-making, stimulate interdisciplinary collaboration, and encourage the responsible integration of AI across higher education institutions. More importantly, we hope this collection contributes to ongoing international dialogue on how AI can strengthen the academic profession while preserving the fundamental values that define higher education.

Producing an international edited volume is a collaborative endeavor that depends on the dedication and expertise of many individuals. We extend our sincere appreciation to all contributing authors for sharing their scholarship and enriching this volume with diverse perspectives and rigorous research. We are equally grateful to the reviewers, whose constructive feedback strengthened the quality, clarity, and coherence of the chapters. Finally, we express our sincere gratitude to the editorial and production team at IGI Global for their professionalism, guidance, and unwavering support throughout every stage of the publication process.

We hope that ***AI and the Transformation of Academic Work in Higher Education*** will serve as valuable resources for researchers, faculty members, university leaders, policymakers, doctoral students, and educational practitioners. Above all, we hope this volume inspires continued research, international collaboration, and thoughtful dialogue on how artificial intelligence can be integrated responsibly to advance higher education while safeguarding academic excellence, ethical integrity, and human-centered learning for generations to come.

The Editors
Rany Sam

Acknowledgment

The completion of ***AI and the Transformation of Academic Work in Higher Education*** has been made possible through the collective expertise, dedication, and collaboration of many individuals and institutions. As editor, I extend my sincere gratitude to everyone whose contributions have made this volume possible.

First and foremost, I express my deepest appreciation to all contributing authors for their outstanding scholarly work. Their willingness to share their expertise, research, and diverse perspectives has resulted in a volume that advances understanding of how artificial intelligence is transforming academic work, institutional leadership, and the future of higher education. The international collaboration represented in this book reflects the value of scholarly exchange across disciplines, institutions, and countries and demonstrates the importance of addressing global educational challenges through collective academic effort.

I am equally grateful to the anonymous reviewers for their careful evaluations, constructive feedback, and thoughtful recommendations. Their expertise and commitment to academic excellence have significantly strengthened the quality, rigor, and coherence of the chapters and have contributed substantially to the scholarly value of this publication.

My sincere appreciation is also extended to the editorial and production team at IGI Global Scientific Publishing for their professionalism, guidance, and unwavering support throughout every stage of the publication process. Their commitment to maintaining the highest standards of academic publishing has been instrumental in bringing this volume to completion.

I would also like to acknowledge the universities and research institutions represented by the contributing authors. Their continued support for research, innovation, international collaboration, and knowledge dissemination has created an environment in which scholarly work of this nature can flourish.

Special thanks are extended to colleagues, research collaborators, and students whose insightful discussions, constructive feedback, and intellectual engagement have enriched the development of this volume. Their encouragement and exchange of ideas have inspired many of the perspectives presented throughout these chapters.

On a personal note, I wish to express my heartfelt gratitude to my family for their unwavering encouragement, patience, understanding, and constant support throughout this editorial journey. Their confidence in my work has been a continual source of strength and motivation.

It is my sincere hope that ***AI and the Transformation of Academic Work in Higher Education*** will make a meaningful contribution to the growing body of scholarship on artificial intelligence in higher education. I hope this volume will stimulate further interdisciplinary research, encourage international collaboration, inform evidence-based policy and institutional practice, and support educators, researchers, university leaders, and policymakers in navigating the opportunities and challenges presented by AI. Above all, I hope it helps shape a future in which technological innovation and human values work together to strengthen the academic profession and advance the mission of higher education.

Rany Sam
Editor

Chapter 1
Artificial Intelligence and the Transformation of Academic Work:
Teaching, Research Productivity, and the Future of the Academic Profession

Borey Be
http://orcid.org/0000-0002-0719-7497
University of Cambodia, Cambodia

Nayheak Khun
http://orcid.org/0009-0006-9240-2235
Ministry of Labour and Vocational Training, Cambodia

ABSTRACT

The rapid growth of artificial intelligence (AI) is changing academic work in higher education. It is reshaping teaching, research, and professional identity. This chapter explores how AI affects workload, professional skills, autonomy, and identity among faculty. It shows that AI can increase work demands while also requiring new skills. The chapter also discusses the importance of governance, institutional policies, and ethical frameworks in guiding responsible AI use. It stresses the need for transparency, accountability, and participatory decision-making. Professional development is essential to build digital literacy, ethical awareness, and flexible teaching practices. Drawing on research from different fields and global contexts, the chapter calls for human-centred, fair, and sustainable approaches to AI in higher

DOI: 10.4018/979-8-2600-3204-6.ch001

education. It provides practical insights for university leaders, policymakers, and researchers who aim to balance innovation with ethical responsibility and protect the future of the academic profession.

1. INTRODUCTION

Higher education systems worldwide are undergoing a profound transformation as artificial intelligence (AI), particularly generative AI systems such as ChatGPT, become embedded across teaching, research, administration, and academic evaluation. Unlike earlier waves of educational technology that primarily digitized or automated existing academic practices, contemporary AI systems increasingly participate in knowledge production, pedagogical mediation, and institutional decision-making. AI thus operates not merely as a technical instrument but also as a sociotechnical force that actively reshapes how academic work is organized, evaluated, and governed (Butson & Spronken-Smith, 2024; Dwivedi et al., 2023; Leonardi, 2025).

Academic work has traditionally been understood as a constellation of interrelated practices, teaching, research, and service, anchored in disciplinary knowledge, peer evaluation, collegial governance, and normative commitments to scholarly integrity. Academic professionalism relies on interpretive judgment, reflexivity, and collective self-regulation rather than standardized automation. Teaching has involved relational pedagogy and contextualized assessment; research has depended on methodological rigor and epistemic accountability; and service has reflected commitments to institutional and societal engagement. These practices have been underpinned by assumptions about human agency as the central driver of academic value.

The integration of AI unsettles these assumptions. Automated and semiautomated systems now support or perform tasks such as curriculum design, assessment feedback, literature review, data coding, and performance monitoring (Branda et al., 2025; S. Chen & Cheung, 2025). As AI-generated outputs circulate within academic systems, the boundary between human and machine agency becomes increasingly blurred. This raises critical questions about authorship, originality, accountability, and the distribution of responsibility within academic work. More broadly, it challenges established understandings of what constitutes legitimate academic contribution and how such contributions should be evaluated.

Empirical research has documented the rapid uptake of generative AI across higher education, driven by perceived usefulness, efficiency gains, and social influence within academic communities (Abdaljaleel et al., 2024; Be, 2026; Grassini et al., 2024; Habibi et al., 2023). Academics report using AI to support teaching preparation, feedback generation, research writing, and administrative tasks, often without formal institutional guidance. Moreover, studies consistently reveal the ambivalence and anxiety surrounding AI adoption. Concerns related to academic integrity, ethical responsibility, the erosion of critical thinking, and professional displacement are widely reported among both faculty and students (Abuadas & Albikawi, 2026; Budhathoki et al., 2024; Eke, 2023).

These tensions highlight that AI adoption in higher education is not a purely technical process but a socially negotiated practice shaped by institutional norms, power relations, and governance arrangements. The acceptance of AI is mediated by trust in institutions, perceptions of fairness and legitimacy, and the clarity of ethical boundaries (Barus et al., 2025; Bunduchi et al., 2025). When governance frameworks are weak or ambiguous, academics are often left to manage ethical risks individually, intensifying professional uncertainty and moral burden. AI thus becomes intertwined with broader transformations in academic labor conditions, workload intensification, and performance-based accountability.

Importantly, the effects of AI on academic work are uneven across global contexts. Much of the literature focuses on well-resourced institutions in the Global North, where AI adoption is supported by robust digital infrastructure, policy frameworks, and professional development. Emerging research from developing and transitional higher education systems, however, reveals distinct challenges related to infrastructure gaps, limited regulatory capacity, uneven staff preparedness, and fragile governance mechanisms (Ahmad Malik et al., 2025; Ayyash & Salah, 2025). In such contexts, AI adoption often outpaces institutional readiness, exacerbating existing inequalities within and between universities and amplifying anxieties among academic staff.

From a theoretical perspective, analyzing academic work in the age of AI requires moving beyond instrumental or technologically deterministic accounts. Sociotechnical and posthumanist approaches emphasize that AI systems are embedded within institutional cultures, organizational structures, and professional norms that shape how technologies are interpreted, enacted, and contested (Babanoğlu et al., 2025; Wang & Wang, 2025; Yurdunkulu et al., 2025). From this perspective, AI does not simply replace academic labor; rather, it reconfigures it by redistributing expertise, reshaping roles, and redefining what counts as a valuable academic contribution.

Framed within this critical and relational lens, the chapter examines how AI mediates academic work across teaching, research, workload, professional identity, and evaluation. By synthesizing interdisciplinary scholarship from education, sociology, information systems, and AI ethics, this chapter seeks to illuminate not only what AI does in universities but also how it reshapes the meaning, values, and sustainability of academic work itself. In doing so, it positions AI as a catalyst for rethinking the academic profession and invites renewed attention to governance, ethics, and human-centered approaches in an increasingly algorithmic higher education landscape.

2. HIGHER EDUCATION SYSTEMS AND THE CHANGING CONDITIONS OF ACADEMIC WORK

Over the past three decades, higher education systems worldwide have undergone profound structural transformations shaped by massification, marketization, internationalization, and digitalization. Universities have increasingly been repositioned as competitive, performance-oriented organizations operating within quasimarket environments. These shifts have been accompanied by the rise of managerial governance, audit cultures, and metric-based accountability systems that prioritize efficiency, visibility, and measurable outcomes. Artificial intelligence does not enter higher education as a form of neutral or external innovation; rather, it is layered onto these already transformed systems, functioning less as a disruptive rupture than as an accelerator of existing trends in academic labor, governance, and evaluation (Butson & Spronken-Smith, 2024; Caamaño-Gordillo et al., 2025).

Within contemporary higher education, academic work is being increasingly evaluated through quantifiable indicators such as publication counts, citation metrics, journal rankings, grant income, student satisfaction scores, and completion rates. Extensive research has demonstrated that these metric-driven regimes reshape academic behavior by privileging what is measurable over what is pedagogically, intellectually, or socially meaningful. As a result, academic roles become fragmented, workloads intensify, and definitions of scholarly value narrow toward standardized outputs (Branda et al., 2025; Di Plinio, 2025). These conditions create a fertile environment for the adoption of AI-enabled technologies, which promise efficiency, scalability, and real-time monitoring aligned with managerial imperatives.

Digitally mediated higher education systems rely on increasingly complex infrastructures, including learning management systems, research information systems, bibliometric databases, and analytics dashboards. AI enhances these infrastructures through predictive analytics, automated classification, and algorithmic evaluation, enabling institutions to process and compare large volumes of academic data at unprecedented speed. While such systems are often justified as evidence-based tools for improving quality and decision-making, they also reconfigure power relations within universities. Authority over academic judgment shifts from collegial, peer-based processes toward algorithmically mediated managerial oversight, reducing opportunities for contextual interpretation and professional discretion (Hadan et al., 2026).

These infrastructural transformations also influence expectations surrounding academic productivity and responsiveness, reshaping how academic work is coordinated and evaluated within universities.

The changing conditions of academic work are also deeply uneven. Access to AI tools, training opportunities, and institutional support varies widely across institutions, disciplines, and regions. Early-career academics, adjunct faculty, and scholars in resource-constrained settings often face heightened precarity as performance expectations increase without corresponding investment in capacity-building or workload protection (Adu, 2025; Alhwaiti, 2023). In contrast, well-resourced institutions and senior academics are better positioned to leverage AI for enhanced productivity, visibility, and competitive advantage. These disparities contribute to the stratification of academic labor and reinforce inequalities within global knowledge economies. These developments contribute to changing forms of academic coordination and evaluation within increasingly data-driven institutional environments

Crucially, these transformations are not technologically inevitable. They are shaped by policy choices, institutional priorities, and governance arrangements that determine how AI is integrated into higher education systems. AI can function as a supportive infrastructure that enhances pedagogical innovation and scholarly capacity or as a mechanism that deepens managerial control and labor precarity. Understanding this dual potential requires an analytical lens that captures the interaction between structural conditions, technological mediation, professional practice, and governance.

To synthesize these dynamics, the following subsection introduces a conceptual framework of AI-mediated academic work in higher education. As presented in Table 1, the framework integrates macro-level structural and policy conditions, institutional AI infrastructures, transformations in teaching and research practices, shifts in workload and professional identity, and the governance and ethical mechanisms through which these changes are institutionalized. This framework provides the analytical foundation for the sections that follow, guiding the examination of how AI reshapes academic work across teaching (Section 3), research productivity (Section 4), professional identity and autonomy (Section 5), governance and evaluation (Section 6), and pathways toward sustainable and ethical AI integration (Section 7).

Table 1. Conceptual Framework of AI-Mediated Academic Work in Higher Education

Dimension	Core Components	Key Processes	Implications for Academic Work
Macro-Level: Structural & Policy Context	Massification, marketization, digitalization, performance-based funding, national AI and higher education policies	Policy alignment, regulatory gaps, strategic prioritization of AI	Sets conditions under which AI is adopted; shapes institutional expectations and constraints
Institutional AI Infrastructures	Learning management systems, research information systems, analytics dashboards, generative AI tools	Datafication, automation, algorithmic mediation	Enables efficiency and monitoring while embedding managerial logics into academic work
Teaching Practices	AI-supported pedagogy, assessment automation, learning analytics, student support systems	Pedagogical redesign, feedback acceleration, surveillance	Shifts academic roles from content delivery to learning design; alters student-teacher relations
Research Practices & Productivity	Generative AI for literature review, writing, data analysis; bibliometric platforms	Acceleration of output, metrication, visibility optimization	Redefines research productivity; intensifies publication pressure and strategic compliance
Academic Workload & Labor Conditions	Task redistribution, continuous availability, reskilling demands	Work intensification, temporal fragmentation, boundary blurring	Increases workload pressure; challenges work–life balance and well-being
Professional Identity & Agency	Academic autonomy, expertise, ethical judgment, professional values	Reskilling and deskilling, identity negotiation, moral labor	Reconfigures what it means to be an academic in AI-mediated environments
Governance & Evaluation Mechanisms	Performance appraisal systems, promotion and tenure criteria, algorithmic decision-making	Standardization, ranking, predictive evaluation	Institutionalizes AI through metrics; shifts power from collegial judgment to managerial oversight
Ethical & Governance Frameworks	AI ethics principles, institutional policies, accountability structures	Transparency, fairness, data protection, human oversight	Mitigates risks of bias, surveillance, and inequity; builds institutional trust
Professional Development & Capacity Building	AI literacy, ethical training, pedagogical innovation programs	Reflexive practice, collective learning, professional empowerment	Supports sustainable AI adoption and protects professional integrity
Outcomes: Sustainable & Ethical Academic Work	Human-centric AI use, equitable evaluation, resilient academic profession	Feedback loops between practice, governance, and identity	Ensures AI enhances rather than undermines academic work and autonomy

3. AI AND THE TRANSFORMATION OF TEACHING PRACTICES

The integration of artificial intelligence into higher education is reshaping teaching practices in ways that extend far beyond the introduction of new instructional tools. In AI-mediated learning environments, pedagogy is increasingly reorganized through sociotechnical arrangements in which human and nonhuman actors jointly participate in the design, delivery, and evaluation of learning. Generative AI systems now contribute to content creation, feedback provision, learning analytics, and student support, transforming teaching from a predominantly human-centered activity into a distributed practice mediated by algorithmic systems (Chan & Tsi, 2024; Guan et al., 2025). This transformation challenges foundational assumptions about pedagogy, assessment, and academic authority while raising critical questions about professional responsibility and educational values.

Pedagogical Redesign in AI-Mediated Learning

One of the most visible impacts of AI in higher education is the redesign of pedagogical practices. Generative AI tools are being increasingly used by academics to support lesson planning, instructional material development, adaptive learning pathways, and personalized feedback. Empirical studies across disciplines report generally positive attitudes toward these tools, particularly with respect to efficiency gains, scalability in large classes, and the potential for differentiated instruction (Adiguzel et al., 2023; Kong et al., 2024; Schmidt et al., 2025). For educators operating under conditions of heavy teaching loads and limited resources, AI offers pragmatic solutions for managing routine instructional tasks.

However, these efficiencies are accompanied by a redistribution of pedagogical responsibility. Rather than simply delivering content, educators must now design learning environments that anticipate, regulate, and critically integrate AI use. This includes making deliberate decisions about when AI is permitted, constrained, or explicitly incorporated into learning activities. Pedagogical redesign increasingly emphasizes process-oriented learning, inquiry-based tasks, and reflective engagement in response to the availability of AI-generated outputs. Designing such learning experiences requires substantial intellectual and emotional labor, including curriculum reconfiguration, assessment realignment, and continuous experimentation, the forms of work that are often underrecognized within institutional workload models.

Moreover, pedagogical adaptation to AI is uneven across disciplines and institutional contexts. Fields with strong traditions of standardized assessment or content transmission may experience greater disruption, while disciplines emphasizing interpretation, practice, or contextual reasoning may adapt more readily. In institutions lacking clear pedagogical guidance or professional development, educators are often left to navigate AI integration individually, reinforcing disparities in teaching quality and professional confidence.

Assessment Practices and Academic Integrity

Assessment has emerged as the most contested domain of AI-mediated teaching. Generative AI fundamentally destabilizes conventional assumptions about authorship, originality, and individual performance, rendering traditional take-home assignments and written examinations increasingly vulnerable to automation. In response, many institutions have expanded the use of AI detection tools, plagiarism software, and remote proctoring technologies, positioning AI simultaneously as a pedagogical aid and a surveillance mechanism (Cotton et al., 2024; Eke, 2023).

However, growing evidence highlights the technical limitations, biases, and ethical risks associated with AI detection systems. False positives, a lack of transparency, and disproportionate impacts on multilingual and nontraditional students have raised serious concerns about fairness and trust (Abuadas & Albikawi, 2026; Farrokhnia et al., 2024). As a result, many educators are shifting toward alternative assessment practices that foreground learning processes rather than final outputs. These include oral examinations, in-class problem-solving, portfolio-based assessment, reflective writing, and iterative project work.

For instance, several universities initially attempted to restrict or prohibit AI-generated content in coursework because of concerns about plagiarism, authorship, and academic integrity (Cotton et al., 2024; Eke, 2023). However, these restrictions proved difficult to enforce because students could access generative AI tools independently outside institutional systems. In response, some educators redesigned assessment strategies by introducing oral examinations, in-class writing activities, reflective journals, and process-based assignments that require students to explain and defend their reasoning rather than simply submit polished written outputs. Research further indicates that concerns regarding AI detection systems are growing, particularly because false positives may disproportionately affect multilingual students and nontraditional writers (Farrokhnia et al., 2024). These developments illustrate how AI is reshaping institutional assumptions about evidence of learning, originality, and authorship in higher education.

Academic authority and epistemic mediation

AI-mediated teaching practices also involve reconfiguring academic authority and epistemic control. Traditionally, educators have occupied a privileged position as disciplinary experts and gatekeepers of legitimate knowledge. Generative AI disrupts this hierarchy by providing students with immediate access to explanations, examples, and synthesized knowledge, often presented in authoritative and fluent language (Babanoğlu et al., 2025; Wang & Wang, 2025).

This shift does not eliminate academic authority but transforms it. Educators are increasingly called upon to function as epistemic guides and ethical mediators. Their role involves helping students interrogate AI-generated outputs, evaluate credibility, understand bias, and situate knowledge within disciplinary and societal contexts. Teaching critical AI literacy thus becomes a core pedagogical responsibility, encompassing not only technical understanding but also ethical reasoning and reflexive judgment.

This transformation places new demands on professional identity. Educators must reconcile expectations to embrace innovation with responsibilities to safeguard academic standards and intellectual rigor. However, institutional recognition of these evolving roles remains limited, particularly in systems where teaching quality is evaluated through standardized metrics and student satisfaction surveys that inadequately capture epistemic and ethical labor.

Student-Teacher Relations in AI-Mediated Classrooms

The integration of AI also reshapes student–teacher relations by altering expectations of support, responsiveness, and availability. AI-mediated tools can enhance accessibility and confidence, particularly for students who are reluctant to seek help directly from instructors or who benefit from immediate feedback (Baidoo-Anu et al., 2024). For some learners, AI functions as a supplementary tutor, reducing barriers to engagement and participation.

Recent studies suggest that some students feel more comfortable interacting with AI chatbots than seeking direct assistance from lecturers, particularly in large classes or multilingual learning environments (Baidoo-Anu et al., 2024; Chan & Hu, 2023). While AI-mediated support may increase confidence and accessibility for some learners, it also changes expectations surrounding academic responsiveness and feedback. Educators increasingly report pressure to provide immediate feedback comparable to AI-generated responses, even though meaningful pedagogical engagement often requires sustained dialog and contextual understanding (Lee et al., 2022). These developments demonstrate that AI not only supplements student support but also gradually reshapes relational dynamics in higher education classrooms.

Moreover, the normalization of AI assistance risks recalibrating students' expectations of academic labor. Educators may be perceived as secondary or reactive sources of support, potentially eroding relational dimensions of teaching such as mentorship, dialog, and care. These relational aspects remain central to meaningful learning but are difficult to quantify or automate (Chan & Tsi, 2024). For academics, managing these shifting relationships involves boundary work and emotional labor, as they negotiate availability, trust, and pedagogical responsibility in AI-rich environments. These transformations are deeply shaped by institutional governance, professional recognition, and evaluative regimes that determine which forms of pedagogical labor are visible and valued.

4. REDEFINING RESEARCH PRODUCTIVITY IN AI-SUPPORTED ACADEMIC WORK

Research productivity has long functioned as a central mechanism through which academic work is evaluated, rewarded, and governed within higher education systems. Publications, citations, grants, and research visibility serve not only as indicators of scholarly contribution but also as key determinants of career progression, institutional reputation, and resource allocation. In AI-supported research environments, artificial intelligence reshapes not only how research is conducted but also how scholarly value is defined, measured, and legitimized. Generative AI tools promise efficiency gains across literature review, data analysis, and manuscript preparation, yet they simultaneously intensify publication pressure and entrench metric-driven evaluation regimes that structure contemporary academic labor (Branda et al., 2025; Caamaño-Gordillo et al., 2025).

AI and the Reconfiguration of Research Practices

Generative AI tools are being increasingly integrated into multiple stages of the research process, including literature searching, conceptual mapping, data coding, translation, and academic writing. Empirical studies report growing acceptance of AI-assisted research, particularly for routine, repetitive, or language-intensive tasks, where AI is perceived as enhancing efficiency and accessibility (Dwivedi et al., 2023; Madanchian & Taherdoost, 2025). For scholars working in multilingual or resource-constrained contexts, AI can lower linguistic and technical barriers to participation in global scholarly communication, potentially democratizing access to publication and collaboration (Ayyash & Salah, 2025).

Moreover, the incorporation of AI into research workflows established boundaries between assistance and authorship. While AI-generated outputs may support idea development or textual refinement, they raise unresolved ethical questions regarding originality, intellectual ownership, and epistemic responsibility. Existing academic norms and guidelines often lag behind practice, leading scholars to negotiate these dilemmas individually and informally (Di Plinio, 2025; Ghosh, 2025). As a result, research productivity becomes entangled with moral judgment and professional risk, particularly in institutional contexts where expectations for output are high but ethical guidance is ambiguous.

Moreover, AI-supported research practices risk standardizing scholarly expression and epistemic forms. The widespread use of similar generative tools may contribute to the homogenization of academic language, argumentation styles, and methodological approaches, potentially narrowing the diversity of scholarly voices and perspectives. This concern is especially salient in disciplines that value interpretive nuance, contextual sensitivity, and theoretical innovation.

Digital Research Infrastructures and Algorithmic Visibility

Beyond individual tools, AI operates within broader digital research infrastructures that shape scholarly visibility and evaluation. Bibliometric databases, journal indexing platforms, research information systems, and ranking mechanisms increasingly rely on algorithmic classification, comparison, and prediction. These infrastructures determine which publications are visible, how impact is calculated, and which research trajectories are institutionally rewarded (Bunduchi et al., 2025; Caamaño-Gordillo et al., 2025).

Algorithmic mediation introduces a layer of opacity into research evaluation. Metrics such as citation counts, h-indexes, journal impact factors, and altmetrics are frequently treated as objective indicators of quality, despite well-documented biases related to language, discipline, publication venue, and geographic location. AI amplifies these dynamics by accelerating data processing and reinforcing existing hierarchies of visibility. Consequently, research productivity becomes increasingly equated with alignment to algorithmically legible outputs rather than substantive intellectual contribution or societal relevance.

These infrastructures also shape research agendas by incentivizing particular topics, methods, and publication strategies that align with high-impact venues and ranking criteria. Scholars may strategically tailor research questions and outputs to maximize metric performance, potentially at the expense of intellectual risk-taking, interdisciplinarity, or locally grounded inquiry.

Metrication and the Reframing of the Scholarly Value

The integration of AI into research evaluation systems accelerates the measurement of scholarly output. AI-enhanced analytics enables real-time tracking of publications, citations, collaborations, and funding success, embedding performance measurement into everyday academic life. These metrics increasingly inform decisions related to promotion, tenure, and institutional reputation, shaping career trajectories and research agendas (Barus et al., 2025; Hadan et al., 2026).

From a critical perspective, metrication narrows the epistemic horizons of academic work by privileging standardized, internationally visible outputs over locally grounded, interdisciplinary, or pedagogically oriented research. Scholars may strategically align their work with dominant publication venues and research trends to maximize metric performance, potentially at the expense of intellectual risk-taking or social relevance (Babanoğlu et al., 2025; Gupta et al., 2024). These systems reinforce the growing emphasis on measurable research outputs.

Ethical Tensions and Professional Responsibility

The redefinition of research productivity through AI raises significant ethical and professional concerns. Issues of transparency, accountability, and bias permeate AI-supported research and evaluation systems. These challenges challenge the traditional norms of peer review and scholarly judgment (Araujo et al., 2020; Eke, 2023). Academics must navigate competing expectations to leverage AI for efficiency while upholding standards of integrity, originality, and responsibility.

Acceptance of AI-mediated research practices is thus contingent on institutional trust and governance. Where universities provide clear guidelines, training, and ethical frameworks, AI can support responsible research practices. In the absence of such structures, however, AI risks exacerbating uncertainty and inequality, undermining confidence in academic evaluation and professional legitimacy (Ahmad Malik et al., 2025; Bunduchi et al., 2025).

In summary, AI-supported academic work redefines research productivity in complex and contested ways. Generative AI tools and digital research infrastructures offer new capacities for scholarly production, yet they also intensify publication pressure and entrench metric-driven evaluation regimes. Research productivity increasingly reflects alignment with algorithmically legible outputs rather than sustained intellectual inquiry or societal contribution.

5. ACADEMIC WORKLOAD, PROFESSIONAL IDENTITY, AND AUTONOMY

The cumulative effects of artificial intelligence on teaching, research, and evaluation converge most visibly in the reconfiguration of academic workload, professional identity, and autonomy. While AI is frequently promoted as a means of reducing administrative burden and enhancing efficiency, a growing body of empirical and conceptual scholarship suggests that its integration into higher education often intensifies academic labor, reshapes professional roles, and introduces new forms of surveillance and ethical vulnerability. These dynamics must be understood within broader structural conditions characterized by managerial governance, audit cultures, and metric-driven accountability (Branda et al., 2025; Butson & Spronken-Smith, 2024).

Work Intensification and the Acceleration of Academic Time

AI-mediated academic environments are closely associated with work intensification rather than workload reduction. Although AI tools can automate or streamline specific tasks, such as grading support, literature synthesis, or administrative reporting, they simultaneously increase institutional expectations regarding output volume, speed, and responsiveness. Academics are increasingly required to redesign courses, update assessments, adapt research workflows, and engage in continuous professional learning to remain competent in rapidly evolving technological landscapes (Ayyash & Salah, 2025).

Digital connectivity and AI-enabled platforms further accelerate academic time. Learning management systems, communication platforms, and analytics dashboards normalize expectations of immediacy, continuous availability, and real-time performance visibility. As a result, boundaries between work and nonwork time become increasingly blurred, particularly for academics with heavy teaching loads, caregiving responsibilities, or precarious employment conditions (Adu, 2025; Alhwaiti, 2023). These pressures contribute to growing concerns about stress, fatigue, and professional sustainability.

Reskilling, Deskilling, and the Recomposition of Academic Expertise

The integration of AI into academic work reshapes professional expertise through parallel processes of reskilling and deskilling. Academics are increasingly expected to develop competences in AI literacy and prompt design, data ethics, digital pedagogy, and algorithmic awareness. These capacities are now framed as core indicators of professional competence and innovation, influencing perceptions of employability and relevance within academic labor markets (Baidoo-Anu et al., 2024; Habibi et al., 2023).

On the other hand, reliance on AI systems risks deskilling core aspects of academic practice. Tasks traditionally essential to scholarly expertise, such as critical literature engagement, conceptual synthesis, language refinement, and methodological judgment, may be partially delegated to AI tools, potentially diminishing scholars' direct engagement with foundational intellectual practices (Ghosh, 2025). This recomposition of expertise raises critical questions about which forms of knowledge and judgment remain distinctly human and how academic authority is maintained in AI-mediated environments.

The coexistence of reskilling and deskilling generates ambivalence within professional identity. Academics are positioned both as innovative knowledge workers expected to leverage AI and as custodians of disciplinary standards tasked with resisting excessive automation. Managing this tension demands sustained reflexivity, ethical judgment, and identity work. However, these forms of labor are seldom acknowledged or rewarded within formal workload models, promotion criteria, or appraisal systems.

Surveillance, Datafication, and the Erosion of Professional Autonomy

AI-enabled systems increasingly make academic activity more visible and measurable (Barus et al., 2025). Although these systems are often justified through claims of transparency, efficiency, and quality assurance, they also strengthen managerial control and limit professional discretion.

Surveillance in AI-mediated environments extends beyond direct monitoring to encompass algorithmic inference and prediction. AI systems may infer productivity, engagement, or risk from patterns of activity, thereby influencing decisions about workload allocation, performance appraisal, promotion, or institutional intervention. Such practices raise significant concerns about transparency, bias, explainability, and due process. These concerns are amplified when evaluative logics are embedded in proprietary or opaque systems that remain beyond meaningful academic scrutiny (Araujo et al., 2020; Bunduchi et al., 2025).

As surveillance becomes normalized, academic autonomy is progressively reshaped. Collegial governance is similarly weakened as evaluative authority shifts from peer-based deliberation to data-driven managerial oversight. This reconfiguration diminishes trust and constrains professional self-determination within academic institutions.

6. GOVERNANCE AND EVALUATION IN AI-MEDIATED ACADEMIC ENVIRONMENTS

As AI becomes embedded across teaching, research, and administrative systems, governance and evaluation function as key institutional mechanisms. Through them, transformations in academic work are stabilized, normalized, and enforced. AI-mediated infrastructures increasingly shape how academic performance is defined and evaluated. They also influence how career progression is regulated and how accountability is exercised within universities. These developments do not merely reflect technological innovation. They signal a deeper shift in governance logics from collegial self-regulation to data-driven, algorithmically informed management (Butson & Spronken-Smith, 2024; Caamaño-Gordillo et al., 2025).

Governance systems play a central role in institutionalizing AI-mediated academic practices. Governance and evaluation systems serve as the institutional nexus where these dynamics converge. Through performance metrics, analytics dashboards, and algorithmic decision-support systems, AI embeds assumptions about productivity, quality, and value into everyday academic life. Over time, these assumptions shift from contested norms to operational criteria.

Performance Appraisal and the Institutionalization of Datafied Academic Work

Performance appraisals in contemporary universities increasingly rely on digitally generated indicators of teaching, research, and service. AI-enhanced analytics aggregate data on publication output, citation impact, grant income, student evaluations, and teaching engagement. They produce standardized representations of academic performance. Such systems promise efficiency, comparability, and objectivity. Academic work is also redefined by privileging what is measurable over what is pedagogically, intellectually, or socially meaningful (Barus et al., 2025; Branda et al., 2025).

Important aspects of academic work, such as mentoring and interdisciplinary collaboration, are often difficult to capture through standardized metrics. Teaching quality, mentoring, interdisciplinary collaboration, and community engagement are key components of academic labor. However, they are often inadequately captured by algorithmic indicators. As AI systems operationalize these metrics, performance appraisal becomes increasingly detached from peer judgment and professional discretion. Managerial authority over academic careers is strengthened, reinforcing cultures of visibility, comparison, and compliance (Hadan et al., 2026).

Promotion, Tenure, and Algorithmic Mediation of Academic Careers

Promotion and tenure processes represent particularly consequential sites of AI-mediated governance. Career advancement decisions increasingly draw on algorithmically generated profiles that summarize research productivity, citation performance, and funding success. These profiles are often treated as neutral or objective representations of scholarly merit. However, extensive evidence shows structural bias related to discipline, language, gender, institutional prestige, and geographic location (Bunduchi et al., 2025; Caamaño-Gordillo et al., 2025).

AI amplifies these biases by accelerating standardization and comparison across diverse academic contexts. Early-career academics and scholars in teaching-intensive institutions are disproportionately disadvantaged by evaluation systems. The same applies to researchers engaged in locally relevant, interdisciplinary, or socially engaged work. These systems prioritize high-impact journal publications and internationally visible outputs (Adu, 2025; Alhwaiti, 2023). Algorithmic mediation obscures the normative and political judgments embedded in evaluation criteria. It presents stratified outcomes as technically neutral results.

Algorithmic Decision-Making and the Reconfiguration of Institutional Power

AI increasingly informs institutional decision-making beyond appraisal and promotion. It shapes workload allocation, resource distribution, strategic planning, and risk management. Predictive analytics may identify "high-performing" academics, forecast research impact, or assess teaching effectiveness, thereby influencing organizational priorities and investment decisions (Barus et al., 2025). Although these systems are justified through narratives of rationality and optimization, they fundamentally reconfigure power relations within universities.

Several universities have begun establishing AI ethics committees and faculty advisory groups to guide institutional decision-making related to AI use in teaching and research (Isaifan & Hasna, 2025; Jin et al., 2024). These initiatives recognize that AI governance cannot be treated solely as a technical issue managed by IT units or external vendors. Faculty participation remains essential because academics are directly affected by AI-related changes in assessment, workload, evaluation, and professional autonomy. Therefore, participatory governance approaches may strengthen institutional trust and reduce resistance to AI implementation.

Algorithm-based decision-making privileges those who design, procure, and interpret AI systems, such as senior management, IT units, or external vendors. Academics are positioned as subjects of algorithmic governance rather than as active participants in decision-making processes. Moreover, the opacity of many AI systems limits opportunities for explanation, contestation, or appeal. As a result, academic agency is constrained, and institutional trust may erode.

Toward Reflexive, Participatory, and Human-Centered Governance

Importantly, the governance of AI in higher education is not technologically predetermined. Institutions retain significant agency in shaping how AI systems are implemented, interpreted, and evaluated. Reflexive governance approaches emphasize the continuous scrutiny of AI impacts, alignment with academic values, and the active involvement of academics in decision-making processes (Gupta et al., 2024; Babanoğlu et al., 2025).

By restoring space for professional judgment, contextual evaluation, and ethical deliberation, participatory governance models can mitigate the risks of algorithmic overreach. Rather than treating AI as a managerial solution imposed upon academic work, such models recognize AI as a sociotechnical system whose effects depend on institutional choices, power relations, and normative commitments. Embedding AI governance within collegial structures—through academic senates, ethics committees, and transparent policy processes—is essential for sustaining autonomy, trust, and professional integrity.

Finally, governance and evaluation systems are central to how AI-mediated transformations in academic work become institutionalized. Through performance appraisal, promotion, and algorithmic decision-making, AI consolidates definitions of productivity, value, and legitimacy, reshaping academic careers and professional identities. The challenge for higher education lies not in whether AI will be used but in how it is governed. Without reflexive, participatory, and ethically grounded governance, AI risks entrenching managerial control, intensifying inequality, and undermining the normative foundations of the academic profession.

7. TOWARD SUSTAINABLE AND ETHICAL AI-MEDIATED ACADEMIC WORK

The rapid diffusion of artificial intelligence across higher education systems presents a dual imperative. On the one hand, AI offers opportunities to enhance pedagogical innovation, research capacity, and institutional efficiency. On the other hand, uncritical adoption may intensify managerial control, deepen inequalities, and weaken the ethical and professional foundations of academic work. As discussed earlier, AI-mediated transformations extend beyond discrete practices and are embedded in governance regimes that shape workload, identity, autonomy, and evaluation. Sustainable and ethical integration therefore requires systemic responses that align technological innovation with academic values, professional responsibility, and institutional accountability (Al-Emran et al., 2025; Dwivedi et al., 2023).

Governance Principles for Responsible AI in Higher Education

Sustainable AI-mediated academic work must be grounded in clear governance principles that recognize AI as a sociotechnical system rather than a neutral efficiency tool. The literature highlights core principles such as accountability for algorithmic decisions; transparency and explainability in evaluative systems; fairness in access and outcomes; and the protection of privacy, intellectual property, and academic freedom (Abdelwahab et al., 2022; Acosta-Enriquez et al., 2024; Alhumaid et al., 2025). These principles are especially critical in academic contexts where AI increasingly shapes assessment, research evaluation, and career progression.

Ethical AI governance requires explicit attention to equity and bias mitigation. Algorithmic systems trained on historically skewed data may reproduce linguistic, disciplinary, gendered, and geographic inequalities unless they are actively monitored and corrected (Aljabr & Al-Ahdal, 2024; Aristeidou et al., 2024; Avcı, 2024). From this perspective, sustainability is inseparable from justice. AI systems that enhance efficiency while reinforcing structural exclusion cannot be regarded as ethically viable within higher education.

Effective governance requires multilayered and participatory institutional structures. Establishing AI ethics committees, faculty advisory councils, and mechanisms for student representation allows institutions to incorporate diverse perspectives and address the normative tensions surrounding AI use (Bailey et al., 2021; Bashir & Lapshun, 2025; Gökçearslan et al., 2024). Empirical evidence indicates that participatory governance strengthens the trust, legitimacy, and acceptance of AI systems. This is particularly evident when academics perceive governance processes as transparent and procedurally fair (Anjulo Lambebo & Chen, 2025; Dwivedi et al., 2023).

Institutional Policies as Instruments of Ethical Alignment

Governance principles must be translated into coherent and enforceable institutional policies. Clear policy frameworks are necessary to define expectations for AI-assisted teaching, research, assessment, and data governance. Such policies should address intellectual authorship, the responsible use of generative AI in research writing, data ownership, student consent, and academic integrity. By doing so, they reduce uncertainty and lessen the ethical burden placed on individual academics (Al-Kfairy et al., 2024; Ghosh, 2025).

In assessment contexts, explicit guidelines are especially critical. Research shows that reliance on opaque AI detection or automated evaluation tools may undermine fairness and student trust, particularly when such systems exhibit bias or lack explainability (Bergdahl & Sjöberg, 2025; Y. Chen et al., 2023; Franco D'Souza et al., 2024). Ethical institutional policy should therefore prioritize human oversight, opportunities for contestation, and pedagogical coherence over purely technical solutions to academic integrity concerns.

Given the rapid evolution of AI capabilities, institutional policies must remain adaptive rather than static. Dynamic frameworks that include continuous monitoring, periodic review, and stakeholder feedback are better equipped to address emerging risks and regulatory changes (Al-Ali et al., 2025; Al-Rousan et al., 2025; Tavares & Pereira, 2024). Sustainability considerations are also becoming central to responsible AI policy in higher education. Issues such as energy consumption, data storage practices, and environmental impact must be integrated into governance strategies (Almogren et al., 2024; Bunduchi et al., 2025).

Professional development and the sustainability of academic identity

Sustainable AI integration ultimately depends on the capacity, agency, and ethical awareness of academic staff. Professional development initiatives therefore play a central role in enabling academics to navigate AI-mediated transformations without compromising professional identity or autonomy. Effective programs should move beyond technical training. They must also cultivate digital literacy, ethical reasoning, pedagogical redesign, and critical understanding of algorithmic systems (Abuadas & Albikawi, 2026; Al-Ali et al., 2025; Bashkirova & Krpan, 2024).

Research consistently shows that academics' willingness to engage with AI is influenced by self-efficacy, institutional support, and perceived alignment with professional values (Akman & Turhan, 2017; Alafnan et al., 2023; Arvai et al., 2025). Professional learning communities, mentoring structures, and interdisciplinary forums can support reflective engagement with AI. These spaces enable academics to share practices and voice concerns and collectively negotiate ethical boundaries.

Professional development must address the moral and identity dimensions of AI-mediated academic work. Scenario-based training, ethics modules, and deliberative workshops can help academics navigate dilemmas related to authorship, assessment fairness, data use, and professional accountability (Abulibdeh, 2025; Al-Rantisi et al., 2025). By recognizing ethical judgment as a core professional competence, institutions can enable academics to sustain responsible and meaningful professional identities amid technological change.

Context-Sensitive Pathways Toward Sustainable AI Practices

The pursuit of sustainable and ethical AI-mediated academic work must remain attentive to institutional and national contexts. In developing and transitional higher education systems, AI adoption unfolds amid constraints related to infrastructure, regulatory capacity, staff preparedness, and resource distribution. In these settings, sustainability depends less on technological sophistication than on alignment with national policy priorities, cultural expectations, and locally grounded pedagogical practices (Wu et al., 2025).

Context-sensitive approaches avoid importing governance models wholesale from the Global North. They emphasize gradual implementation, capacity-building, and inclusive dialog. Cross-institutional collaboration, regional knowledge sharing, and partnerships among policymakers, universities, and civil society can promote more equitable and sustainable AI integration (Fasano et al., 2025; Toker et al., 2024). In this view, ethical AI is not a fixed endpoint. It is an ongoing process of reflexive governance, institutional learning, and professional negotiation (Acosta-Enriquez et al., 2025; Alhumaid et al., 2025).

Sustainable and ethical AI-mediated academic work requires a holistic institutional strategy that integrates governance principles, adaptive policy frameworks, and robust professional development. AI should serve as a support for academic judgment and creativity rather than a substitute for professional autonomy or ethical responsibility.

8. CONCLUSION AND IMPLICATIONS

Conclusion

This chapter examines how AI increasingly influences teaching, research, governance, and professional life within contemporary universities. The rapid integration of artificial intelligence into higher education is reshaping the nature, organization, and meaning of academic work. It has been argued that AI is not merely an instrumental enhancement of teaching, research, and administration but also a sociotechnical force that reconfigures workload, professional identity, autonomy, and governance.

The chapter advances three interrelated insights. First, AI-mediated academic environments intensify and redistribute academic labor rather than simply reducing workload. Although AI creates efficiency in specific tasks, it also accelerates academic time, heightens performance expectations, and expands less visible forms of pedagogical, emotional, and ethical labor. These pressures raise concerns about sustainability and well-being within the profession, especially for early-career and precariously employed academics.

Second, professional identity is increasingly negotiated under conditions of algorithmic visibility and sociotechnical mediation. Academics are positioned both as innovators expected to adopt and leverage AI and as custodians of disciplinary standards responsible for ethical judgment and academic integrity. This dual expectation reshapes professional autonomy, shifting it away from collegial self-regulation toward individualized responsibility within managed and datafied systems.

Third, governance and evaluation function as the institutional mechanisms through which AI-mediated transformations are stabilized and normalized. Performance appraisal, promotion systems, and algorithmic decision-making embed specific definitions of productivity, quality, and legitimacy into everyday academic life. In the absence of reflexive and participatory governance, such systems risk entrenching managerial control, reinforcing inequality, and weakening trust in institutional processes. In conclusion, these insights demonstrate that the future of academic work is shaped not only by AI capabilities but also by the governance choices, policy frameworks, and professional cultures through which AI is enacted.

Implications for Higher Education Leadership and Policy

For higher education leadership, these findings point to the need for strategic and ethical foresight. University leaders should view academic work as a hybrid ecosystem in which human judgment, relational labor, and ethical responsibility remain central, even as AI capabilities expand. Leadership strategies must therefore emphasize transparent AI governance, meaningful faculty participation, and institutional cultures that value professional voice alongside innovation (Al-Emran et al., 2025).

At the policy level, national authorities and accreditation bodies play a critical role in establishing coherent frameworks for AI ethics, data governance, academic integrity, equity of access, and sustainability. Clear standards can strengthen institutional accountability and reduce the fragmentation of responsibility, which often shifts ethical risk onto individual academics (Tavares & Pereira, 2024). AI governance in higher education should thus be treated as a public policy issue rather than merely an institutional or technical concern.

Directions for Future Research

The transformation of academic work under AI-mediated conditions provides important directions for future research. Longitudinal studies are needed to explore how sustained engagement with AI reshapes academic identity, career trajectories, and well-being over time. Comparative and cross-cultural research can further clarify how AI governance, professional norms, and labor conditions differ across national and institutional settings, particularly between the Global North and Global South.

Future scholarship should also examine the pedagogical and epistemic implications of AI-assisted teaching and research, including their effects on the quality of learning, knowledge production, and disciplinary boundaries. Interdisciplinary approaches that bridge education, sociology, information systems, and AI ethics are essential for producing nuanced and policy-relevant insights (Abdelwahab et al., 2022; Acosta-Enriquez et al., 2025).

REFERENCES

Abdaljaleel, M., Barakat, M., Alsanafi, M., Salim, N. A., Abazid, H., Malaeb, D., Mohammed, A. H., Hassan, B. A. R., Wayyes, A. M., Farhan, S. S., El Khatib, S., Rahal, M., Sahban, A., Abdelaziz, D. H., Mansour, N. O., AlZayer, R., Khalil, R., Fekih-Romdhane, F., Hallit, R., & Sallam, M. (2024). A multinational study on the factors influencing university students' attitudes and usage of ChatGPT. *Scientific Reports, 14*(1), 1983. DOI: 10.1038/s41598-024-52549-8

Abdelwahab, H. R., Rauf, A., & Chen, D. (2022). Business students' perceptions of Dutch higher education institutions in preparing them for artificial intelligence work environments. *Industry and Higher Education, 37*(1), 22–34. DOI: 10.1177/09504222221087614

Abuadas, M., & Albikawi, Z. (2026). AI ethical awareness and academic integrity in higher education: Development and validation of a new scale. *Ethics & Behavior, 36*(2), 125–142. DOI: 10.1080/10508422.2025.2511336

Abulibdeh, A. (2025). A systematic and bibliometric review of artificial intelligence in sustainable education: Current trends and future research directions. *Sustainable Futures : An Applied Journal of Technology, Environment and Society, 10*, 101033. Advance online publication. DOI: 10.1016/j.sftr.2025.101033

Acosta-Enriquez, B. G., Arbulu Ballesteros, M., Vilcapoma Pérez, C. R., Huamaní Jordan, O., Martin Vergara, J. A., Martel Acosta, R., Arbulu Perez Vargas, C. G., & Arbulú Castillo, J. C. (2025). AI in academia: How do social influence, self-efficacy, and integrity influence researchers' use of AI models? *Social Sciences & Humanities Open, 11*, 101274. Advance online publication. DOI: 10.1016/j.ssaho.2025.101274

Acosta-Enriquez, B. G., Ramos Farroñan, E. V., Villena Zapata, L. I., Mogollon Garcia, F. S., Rabanal-León, H. C., Angaspilco, J. E. M., & Bocanegra, J. C. S. (2024). Acceptance of artificial intelligence in university contexts: A conceptual analysis based on UTAUT2 theory. *Heliyon, 10*(19), e38315. Advance online publication. DOI: 10.1016/j.heliyon.2024.e38315

Adiguzel, T., Kaya, M. H., & Cansu, F. K. (2023). Revolutionizing education with AI: Exploring the transformative potential of ChatGPT. *Contemporary Educational Technology, 15*(3), ep429. DOI: 10.30935/cedtech/13152

Adu, K. K. (2025). Artificial Intelligence in Academic Libraries: Threats, Opportunities, and Anxiety Levels. *Journal of Library & Information Services in Distance Learning, 19*(4), 175–194. Advance online publication. DOI: 10.1080/1533290X.2025.2534462

Ahmad Malik, I., Ahmyaw Adem, S., & Rasool, A. (2025). Understanding the adoption of educational AI tools in Sub-Saharan African higher education: A theory of planned behavior-based analysis. *Cogent Education, 12*(1), 2546126. Advance online publication. DOI: 10.1080/2331186X.2025.2546126

Akman, I., & Turhan, C. (2017). User acceptance of social learning systems in higher education: An application of the extended Technology Acceptance Model. *Innovations in Education and Teaching International, 54*(3), 229–237. DOI: 10.1080/14703297.2015.1093426

Al-Ali, A. A., Cherian, J., Farouk, S., & Al Nahyan, M. (2025). Prejob training factors, training effectiveness and graduate employability in support of sustainable development: Evidence from the SANAD program. *Management of Environmental Quality*, •••, 1–22. DOI: 10.1108/MEQ-04-2025-0280

Al-Emran, M., Al-Qaysi, N., Al-Sharafi, M. A., Khoshkam, M., Foroughi, B., & Ghobakhloo, M. (2025). Role of perceived threats and knowledge management in shaping generative AI use in education and its impact on social sustainability. *International Journal of Management Education, 23*(1), 101105. Advance online publication. DOI: 10.1016/j.ijme.2024.101105

Al-Kfairy, M., Mustafa, D., Al-Adaileh, A., Zriqat, S., & Sendaba, O. (2024). User acceptance of AI voice assistants in Jordan's telecom industry. *Computers in Human Behavior Reports, 16*, 100521. Advance online publication. DOI: 10.1016/j.chbr.2024.100521

Al-Rantisi, A. M., ElShanti, N. H., & Harb, S. A. (2025). Challenges of using artificial intelligence in social work education. *Social Work Education*. Advance online publication. DOI: 10.1080/02615479.2025.2483354

Al-Rousan, A. H., Ayasrah, M. N., Salih Yahya, S. M., & Khasawneh, M. A. S. (2025). Design and Psychometric Evaluation of the Artificial Intelligence Acceptance and Usage in Research Creativity Scale Among Faculty Members: Insights From the Network Analysis Perspective. *European Journal of Education, 60*(1), e12927. Advance online publication. DOI: 10.1111/ejed.12927

Alafnan, M. A., Dishari, S., Jovic, M., & Lomidze, K. (2023). ChatGPT as an Educational Tool: Opportunities, Challenges, and Recommendations for Communication, Business Writing, and Composition Courses. *Journal of Artificial Intelligence and Technology, 3*(2), 60–68. DOI: 10.37965/jait.2023.0184

Alhumaid, K., Ayoubi, K., Khalifa, M., & Salloum, S. (2025). Factors Determining Acceptance of Internet of Things in Medical Education: Mixed Methods Study. *JMIR Human Factors, 12*, e58377–e58377. DOI: 10.2196/58377

Alhwaiti, M. (2023). Acceptance of Artificial Intelligence Application in the Post-Covid Era and Its Impact on Faculty Members' Occupational Well-being and Teaching Self Efficacy: A Path Analysis Using the UTAUT 2 Model. *Applied Artificial Intelligence*, *37*(1), 2175110. Advance online publication. DOI: 10.1080/08839514.2023.2175110

Aljabr, F. S., & Al-Ahdal, A. A. M. H. (2024). Ethical and pedagogical implications of AI in language education: An empirical study at Ha'il University. *Acta Psychologica*, *251*, 104605. Advance online publication. DOI: 10.1016/j.actpsy.2024.104605

Almogren, A. S., Al-Rahmi, W. M., & Dahri, N. A. (2024). Exploring factors influencing the acceptance of ChatGPT in higher education: A smart education perspective. *Heliyon*, *10*(11), e31887. Advance online publication. DOI: 10.1016/j.heliyon.2024.e31887

Anjulo Lambebo, E., & Chen, H.-L. (2025). Chatbots in higher education: A systematic review. *Interactive Learning Environments*, *33*(4), 2781–2807. DOI: 10.1080/10494820.2024.2436931

Araujo, T., Helberger, N., Kruikemeier, S., & de Vreese, C. H. (2020). In AI we trust? Perceptions about automated decision-making by artificial intelligence. *AI & Society*, *35*(3), 611–623. DOI: 10.1007/s00146-019-00931-w

Aristeidou, M., Cross, S., Rossade, K. D., Wood, C., Rees, T., & Paci, P. (2024). Online exams in higher education: Exploring distance learning students' acceptance and satisfaction. *Journal of Computer Assisted Learning*, *40*(1), 342–359. DOI: 10.1111/jcal.12888

Arvai, N., Katonai, G., & Mesko, B. (2025). Health Care Professionals' Concerns About Medical AI and Psychological Barriers and Strategies for Successful Implementation: Scoping Review. *Journal of Medical Internet Research*, *27*(1), e66986. Advance online publication. DOI: 10.2196/66986

Avcı, Ü. (2024). Students' GAI Acceptance: Role of Demographics, Creative Mindsets, Anxiety, Attitudes. *Journal of Computer Information Systems*. Advance online publication. DOI: 10.1080/08874417.2024.2386545

Ayyash, M. M., & Salah, O. H. (2025). AI adoption in higher education: Advancing sustainable energy management in palestinian universities. *Journal of Open Innovation*, *11*(2), 100534. DOI: 10.1016/j.joitmc.2025.100534

Babanoğlu, M. P., Karataş, T. Ö., & Dündar, E. (2025). Ethical considerations of AI through a sociotechnical lens: Insights from ELT context as a higher education system. *Cogent Education*, *12*(1), 2488546. Advance online publication. DOI: 10.1080/2331186X.2025.2488546

Baidoo-Anu, D., Asamoah, D., Amoako, I., & Mahama, I. (2024). Exploring student perspectives on generative artificial intelligence in higher education learning. *Discover Education*, *3*(1), 98. Advance online publication. DOI: 10.1007/s44217-024-00173-z

Bailey, D., Southam, A., & Costley, J. (2021). Digital storytelling with chatbots: Mapping L2 participation and perception patterns. *Interactive Technology and Smart Education*, *18*(1), 85–103. DOI: 10.1108/ITSE-08-2020-0170

Barus, O. P., Hidayanto, A. N., Handri, E. Y., Sensuse, D. I., & Yaiprasert, C. (2025). Shaping generative AI governance in higher education: Insights from student perception. *International Journal of Educational Research Open*, *8*, 100452. DOI: 10.1016/j.ijedro.2025.100452

Bashir, S., & Lapshun, A. L. (2025). E-learning future trends in higher education in the 2020s and beyond. *Cogent Education*, *12*(1), 1–15. DOI: 10.1080/2331186X.2024.2445331

Bashkirova, A., & Krpan, D. (2024). Confirmation bias in AI-assisted decision-making: AI triage recommendations congruent with expert judgments increase psychologist trust and recommendation acceptance. *Computers in Human Behavior: Artificial Humans*, *2*(1), 100066. DOI: 10.1016/j.chbah.2024.100066

Be, B. (2026). AI in Higher Education: Attitudes and Acceptance Among University Students in Cambodia. In P. Chanty, J. Herzing, & M. I. Sean (Eds.), *The Future of AI for Development*. Konrad-Adenauer-Stiftung Cambodia. https://www.kas.de/en/web/kambodscha/digital-insights/detail/-/content/the-future-of-ai-for-development

Bergdahl, N., & Sjöberg, J. (2025). Attitudes, perceptions and AI self-efficacy in K-12 education. *Computers and Education: Artificial Intelligence*, *8*, 100358. Advance online publication. DOI: 10.1016/j.caeai.2024.100358

Branda, F., Ciccozzi, M., & Scarpa, F. (2025). Artificial intelligence in scientific research: Challenges, opportunities and the imperative of a human-centric synergy. *Journal of Informetrics*, *19*(4), 101727. Advance online publication. DOI: 10.1016/j.joi.2025.101727

Budhathoki, T., Zirar, A., Njoya, E. T., & Timsina, A. (2024). ChatGPT adoption and anxiety: A cross-country analysis utilizing the unified theory of acceptance and use of technology (UTAUT). *Studies in Higher Education*, *49*(5), 831–846. DOI: 10.1080/03075079.2024.2333937

Bunduchi, R., Sitar-Tăut, D.-A., & Mican, D. (2025). A legitimacy-based explanation for user acceptance of controversial technologies: The case of Generative AI. *Technological Forecasting and Social Change*, *215*, 124095. DOI: 10.1016/j.techfore.2025.124095

Butson, R., & Spronken-Smith, R. (2024). AI and its implications for research in higher education: A critical dialog. *Higher Education Research & Development*, *43*(3), 563–577. DOI: 10.1080/07294360.2023.2280200

Caamaño-Gordillo, D., Mula, J., & De La Torre, R. (2025). Impact of generative artificial intelligence on workload, efficiency and labor productivity. *IFAC-PapersOnLine*, *59*(10), 1408–1413. DOI: 10.1016/j.ifacol.2025.09.237

Chan, C. K. Y., & Hu, W. (2023). Students' voices on generative AI: Perceptions, benefits, and challenges in higher education. *International Journal of Educational Technology in Higher Education*, *20*(1), 1–18. DOI: 10.1186/s41239-023-00411-8

Chan, C. K. Y., & Tsi, L. H. Y. (2024). Will generative AI replace teachers in higher education? A study of teacher and student perceptions. *Studies in Educational Evaluation*, *83*, 101395. Advance online publication. DOI: 10.1016/j.stueduc.2024.101395

Chen, S., & Cheung, A. C. K. (2025). Effect of generative artificial intelligence on university students learning outcomes: A systematic review and meta-analysis. *Educational Research Review*, *49*, 100737. Advance online publication. DOI: 10.1016/j.edurev.2025.100737

Chen, Y., Jensen, S., Albert, L. J., Gupta, S., & Lee, T. (2023). Artificial intelligence (AI) student assistants in the classroom: Designing chatbots to support student success. *Information Systems Frontiers*, *25*(1), 161–182. DOI: 10.1007/s10796-022-10291-4

Cotton, D. R. E., Cotton, P. A., & Shipway, J. R. (2024). Chatting and cheating: Ensuring academic integrity in the era of ChatGPT. *Innovations in Education and Teaching International*, *61*(2), 228–239. DOI: 10.1080/14703297.2023.2190148

Di Plinio, S. (2025). Panta Rh-AI: Assessing multifaceted AI threats on human agency and identity. *Social Sciences & Humanities Open*, *11*, 101434. Advance online publication. DOI: 10.1016/j.ssaho.2025.101434

Dwivedi, Y. K., Kshetri, N., Hughes, L., Slade, E. L., Jeyaraj, A., Kar, A. K., Baabdullah, A. M., Koohang, A., Raghavan, V., Ahuja, M., Albanna, H., Albashrawi, M. A., Al-Busaidi, A. S., Balakrishnan, J., Barlette, Y., Basu, S., Bose, I., Brooks, L., Buhalis, D., & Wright, R. (2023). "So what if ChatGPT wrote it?" Multidisciplinary perspectives on opportunities, challenges and implications of generative conversational AI for research, practice and policy. *International Journal of Information Management*, *71*, 102642. Advance online publication. DOI: 10.1016/j.ijinfomgt.2023.102642

Eke, D. O. (2023). ChatGPT and the rise of generative AI: Threat to academic integrity? *Journal of Responsible Technology*, *13*, 100060. Advance online publication. DOI: 10.1016/j.jrt.2023.100060

Farrokhnia, M., Banihashem, S. K., Noroozi, O., & Wals, A. (2024). A SWOT analysis of ChatGPT: Implications for educational practice and research. *Innovations in Education and Teaching International*, *61*(3), 460–474. DOI: 10.1080/14703297.2023.2195846

Fasano, F., Bartoli, C., Cappa, F., & Boccardelli, P. (2025). Exploring the impact of AI on Web3 decentralized platform business model innovation. *Journal of Engineering and Technology Management - JET-M, 78*. DOI: 10.1016/j.jengtecman.2025.101911

Franco D'Souza, R., Mathew, M., Mishra, V., & Surapaneni, K. M. (2024). Twelve tips for addressing ethical concerns in the implementation of artificial intelligence in medical education. *Medical Education Online*, *29*(1), 2330250. Advance online publication. DOI: 10.1080/10872981.2024.2330250

Ghosh, M. (2025). Artificial intelligence (AI) and ethical concerns: A review and research agenda. *Cogent Business & Management*, *12*(1), 2551809. Advance online publication. DOI: 10.1080/23311975.2025.2551809

Gökçearslan, Ş., Yildiz Durak, H., & Atman Uslu, N. (2024). Acceptance of educational use of the Internet of Things (IoT) in the context of individual innovativeness and ICT competency of preservice teachers. *Interactive Learning Environments*, *32*(2), 557–571. DOI: 10.1080/10494820.2022.2091612

Grassini, S., Aasen, M. L., & Møgelvang, A. (2024). Understanding University Students' Acceptance of ChatGPT: Insights from the UTAUT2 Model. *Applied Artificial Intelligence*, *38*(1), 2371168. Advance online publication. DOI: 10.1080/08839514.2024.2371168

Guan, L., Lee, J. C. K., Zhang, Y., & Gu, M. M. (2025). Investigating the tripartite interaction among teachers, students, and generative AI in EFL education: A mixed-methods study. *Computers and Education: Artificial Intelligence*, *8*, 100384. Advance online publication. DOI: 10.1016/j.caeai.2025.100384

Gupta, P., Mahajan, R., Badhera, U., & Kushwaha, P. S. (2024). Integrating generative AI in management education: A mixed-methods study using social construction of technology theory. *International Journal of Management Education*, *22*(3), 101017. Advance online publication. DOI: 10.1016/j.ijme.2024.101017

Habibi, A., Muhaimin, M., Danibao, B. K., Wibowo, Y. G., Wahyuni, S., & Octavia, A. (2023). ChatGPT in higher education learning: Acceptance and use. *Computers and Education: Artificial Intelligence*, *5*, 100190. DOI: 10.1016/j.caeai.2023.100190

Hadan, H., Hadi Mogavi, R., Zhang-Kennedy, L., & Nacke, L. E. (2026). Who is Responsible When AI Fails? Mapping Causes, Entities, and Consequences of AI Privacy and Ethical Incidents. *International Journal of Human-Computer Interaction*, *42*(8), 5933–5977. DOI: 10.1080/10447318.2025.2549073

Isaifan, R. J., & Hasna, M. O. (2025). Artificial intelligence for quality assurance in higher education: A policy-to-practice model from Qatar with global relevance. *Quality in Higher Education*, *31*(3), 288–303. Advance online publication. DOI: 10.1080/13538322.2025.2576326

Jin, Y., Yan, L., Echeverria, V., Gašević, D., & Martinez-Maldonado, R. (2024). *Generative AI in Higher Education: A Global Perspective of Institutional Adoption Policies and Guidelines*. DOI: 10.1016/j.caeai.2024.100348

Kong, S. C., Yang, Y., & Hou, C. (2024). Examining teachers' behavioral intention of using generative artificial intelligence tools for teaching and learning based on the extended technology acceptance model. *Computers and Education: Artificial Intelligence*, *7*, 100328. Advance online publication. DOI: 10.1016/j.caeai.2024.100328

Lee, Y. F., Hwang, G. J., & Chen, P. Y. (2022). Impacts of an AI-based chabot on college students' after-class review, academic performance, self-efficacy, learning attitude, and motivation. *Educational Technology Research and Development*, *70*(5), 1843–1865. DOI: 10.1007/s11423-022-10142-8

Leonardi, P. M. (2025). Homo agenticus in the age of agentic AI: Agency loops, power displacement, and the circulation of responsibility. *Information and Organization*, *35*(3), 100582. Advance online publication. DOI: 10.1016/j.infoandorg.2025.100582

Madanchian, M., & Taherdoost, H. (2025). The impact of artificial intelligence on research efficiency. *Results in Engineering*, *26*, 104743. Advance online publication. DOI: 10.1016/j.rineng.2025.104743

Schmidt, D. A., Alboloushi, B., Thomas, A., & Magalhaes, R. (2025). Integrating artificial intelligence in higher education: Perceptions, challenges, and strategies for academic innovation. *Computers and Education Open*, *9*, 100274. Advance online publication. DOI: 10.1016/j.caeo.2025.100274

Tavares, J., & Pereira, F. V. (2024). Proof of concept: A practical approach to machine learning in video consultations' acceptance in higher education institutions. *Procedia Computer Science*, *239*, 1532–1538. DOI: 10.1016/j.procs.2024.06.328

Toker, S., Akay, C., Basmaci, F., Kilicarslan, M. A., Mumcu, E., & Cagiltay, N. E. (2024). Expectancy from, and acceptance of augmented reality in dental education programs: A structural equation model. *Journal of Dental Education*, *88*(9), 1277–1286. Advance online publication. DOI: 10.1002/jdd.13580

Wang, Z., & Wang, C. (2025). A posthumanist approach to AI literacy. *Computers and Composition*, *76*, 102933. Advance online publication. DOI: 10.1016/j.compcom.2025.102933

Wu, Q., Li, S., Xin, S., Hou, Q., & Li, P. (2025). A study on students' behavioral intention and use behavior of artificial intelligence-generated content in physical education: Employing an extended the unified theory of acceptance and use of technology model. *Journal of Hospitality, Leisure, Sport and Tourism Education*, *36*, 100547. Advance online publication. DOI: 10.1016/j.jhlste.2025.100547

Yurdunkulu, A., Bulut, M. A., & Göçen, A. (2025). From academics to Aidemics: Unpacking the human–AI symbiosis in higher education. *Acta Psychologica*, *261*, 105796. Advance online publication. DOI: 10.1016/j.actpsy.2025.105796

Chapter 2

Artificial Intelligence and the Transformation of Academic Work: A Policy Analysis and Institutional Case Study From India

Rajesh Prasad
http://orcid.org/0000-0002-3456-6980
Ajay Kumar Garg Engineering College, India

ABSTRACT

The study focuses on the topic of the artificial intelligence (AI) use in academic activity and faculty practice in Indian higher education, employing the mixed-method approach of policy analysis and a comprehensive case study. The analysis will also be based on the national policy documents as well as the information on the survey and interviews, collected via a chosen institution of higher learning. It examines how AI-led reforms can be perceived and experienced at different levels. The findings indicate that although the policy frameworks are very favourable to AI-enabled transformation, they are not yet fairly implemented, and are mediated by the institutional ability and readiness of the faculty. Empirical data shows that AI tools are used to teach and support research, but this application is associated with the increased demand on performance and the aggravation of academic labour. The research also indicates the differences in access to the digital infrastructure and reveals the new ethical issues regarding the surveillance, academic honesty and algorithmic discrimination.

DOI: 10.4018/979-8-2600-3204-6.ch002

1. INTRODUCTION

Artificial intelligence (AI) has evolved from a marginal technological advancement to a fundamental component of the core infrastructure of higher education. In India, AI is becoming a prescribed cure in admissions, analytical cabinets in the face of learning, content development, and research procedures. According to recent surveys and reports in the sector, the percentage of students and faculty who use AI-based learning support and academic writing, assessment, and literature review indicates a consistent increase in the rate of adoption of AI-based applications, thus indicating a strict change in the usual process of learning activities (Alifah & Hidayat, 2025). This new technological turn is occurring alongside a broader regulatory regime based on national reform. Although it is supported by policy instruments that encourage technology integration, interdisciplinarity, and flexibility, the reality of their execution is not simple. The reactions of institutions are highly differentiated by infrastructure, funding, and governance capacity. New regulatory frameworks around faculty recruitment and autonomy alongside other forms of academic work, including Professor of Practice, have increased the possibility of practice-oriented activity but have also brought about issues of quality assurance, accountability, and long-lasting sustenance of conventional academic career trajectories (Kulal et al., 2024; Narkhede et al., 2025; Burtch et al., 2023).

In this changing environment, there has been a significant change in the academic profession in India. The role of faculty is no longer limited to traditional teaching and research but is being increasingly extended to include AI-based pedagogy, data-driven student mentoring, cross-disciplinary teams, industry engagement, intellectual property development, and involvement in digital governance systems. These transitions are especially unbalanced across types of institutions, with central and private universities shifting faster than state institutions and colleges in Tier II and Tier III regions, where structural constraints remain important (Singh et al., 2025; Kumar Jain et al., 2025). Around the world, higher education systems are being transformed by AI development, specifically generative AI and machine learning. Universities are shifting to technology-mediated ecosystems in which decisions, curriculum design, and academic tests are increasingly mediated by intelligent systems. As a result, the faculty must develop not only disciplinary mastery but also digital mastery, the capacity for innovation, and the ability to adapt to new, more complex socioeconomic circumstances (Baig & Yadegaridehkordi, 2025; Buele & Llerena-Aguirre, 2025). The use of AI in teaching and learning practices is becoming more apparent in the Indian context. Learning management systems, automated evaluation systems, plagiarism detection systems, adaptive learning systems, and many others transform the interactions and teaching methods in the classroom. However, the adoption of these technologies is unequal, as it is usually limited by differences in digital infrastructure, institutional encouragement, and faculty training (Minja, 2024).

The practices of research are also transforming greatly. The tools that help with the literature review, data analysis, modeling, and manuscript preparation are efficient and use AI to make the research more productive. Moreover, such developments become acutely important in terms of academic integrity, responsible research practices, and excessive use of automated systems. The increasing adoption of AI-based metrics, citation analytics, and ranking-based evaluative systems further reestablishes the nature of academic performance measurement, specifically in those systems in which career promotion is directly linked to publication volume and institutional rankings (Khalifa & Albadawy, 2024). Alterations in faculty recruitment and model structures are indicative of a wider trend of performance-based and competency-based models. Colleges and universities are publicly placing greater emphasis on digital pedagogical skills, interdisciplinary studies, innovation and collaboration with industries among candidates. New appointment models such as short-term contracts and practice-oriented positions provide flexibility and integration in the industry but also present issues of job security and academic independence and endanger traditional tenure systems (Woelert et al., 2025).

On a governance level, AIs may introduce ethical and equity issues when implemented in institutional decision-making. Recruitment, evaluation, and monitoring algorithms can produce effects that are not intended to advance bias, decrease transparency, and aggravate inequalities. Such risks are especially acute in the highly heterogeneous system of higher education in India, where the differences between well-endowed institutions and underfunded colleges are still high (Mogoale et al., 2025). Overall, such academic profession change in India cannot be regarded solely as a form of technological change. It is a complex interaction between the issues of governance, institutional capacity and innovation. Integrating modernization induced by AI with preserving ethics, empowering faculty and equal opportunities and resources will aid in the next stage of Indian higher education (Zawacki-Richter et al., 2019).

This chapter is founded on the available empirical research that has been carried out on the integration of survey results and semistructured interviews in different areas of research at a single institution, Ajay Kumar Garg Engineering College, Ghaziabad (AKGEC), Ghaziabad, India. The findings presented in the current paper are therefore founded on quantitative information and qualitative observations that make it possible to provide a comprehensive analysis of how artificial intelligence affects the academic profession and recruitment processes of faculty personnel.

Given the sophistication of the AI-based change in higher education, the current research paper is based on a multilevel model of examination and a scope of macro (policy and regulatory frameworks), meso (institutional behaviors), and micro (faculty experiences). This framework facilitates a systematic review of the meaning, application and experiences of structural reforms in the entire academic system. The rest of the chapter is organized as follows. Section 2 presents a review of the literature, Section 3 presents the methodology, Section 4 presents the analysis, and finally, Section 5 concludes the chapter.

2. LITERATURE REVIEW

2.1 Search Strategy and Selection Criteria

The methodology of the current study is rigorous and structured, ensuring transparency and analytical accuracy in the literature. The key databases that are most common in the academic world, such as Scopus, Web of Science, and Google Scholar, were searched systematically. The search was limited to the years 2015 to 2025 to capture current trends in artificial intelligence in the higher education setting but also included seminal theoretical discussions when pertinent. The search strategy combined relevant keywords, including artificial intelligence in higher education, academic labor, digital labor, faculty work, platform governance, AI ethics in education, and the sociology of professions. True/false operators have been used to narrow the retrieved results and improve relevance.

The inclusion criteria were as follows:

i. high-quality peer-reviewed journal articles, monographs and conference proceedings;
ii. studies that are more educated in context;
iii. In the scholarly literature, articles and publications that address AI, digital technologies, or platformization in a timely manner; and
iv. those publications that are empirical, theoretical or policy relevant.

The exclusion criteria included nonacademic sources, studies that were not strictly connected with higher education, and articles that lacked conceptual/empirical depth. The process of selecting the titles, abstracts, and full texts was followed by a list of the relevant studies that were developed and examined.

This systematic treatment will see the review beyond being a descriptive overview but a more undertaking and analytically rooted synthesis of the scholarship that is available.

2.2 Theoretical Framework

Future research should focus on the interdisciplinary theoretical framework and apply the concepts of academic capitalism, digital labor theory, platform governance, the sociology of Professions, and AI ethics in education to explain the shift in academic labor. The concept of academic capitalism can be used to explain the development of a market-oriented orientation of colleges whereby the generation of knowledge is in tandem with economic worth, innovation, and international competitiveness. AI can be used to accelerate this trajectory by empowering the use of data in performance indicators, streamlining research deliverables and advancing university–industry connections.

On yet another critical approach to the reorganisation of academic work through digital systems, it is also possible to underscore digital labor theory. The application of AI tools in education and research redistributes labor, no longer focusing on overt intellectual work but rather on platform-mediated efficiency outputs to increase workload and conceal labor relations. People can be explained through platform governance, where academic decision-making processes are mediated by digital infrastructures and algorithmic systems, and learning management systems, AI-based assessment systems, and research analytics platforms are viewed as the governance tools through which outputs are standardized and institutional priorities are directed.

In terms of the sociology of professions, there are jurisdictional changes in the academic profession, where the competency in old expertise is being reconstructed in terms of technological proficiencies and interdisciplinary necessities. The influence of AI on professional authority goes beyond creating new lines of knowledge production that affect the authority of professionals because of the displacement of previously set limits between technology and humanity. Finally, the ethical concerns of AI in education anticipate the issues of transparency, bias, accountability, and academic integrity as critical points of concern in understanding the implications of AI adoption for the processes of governance, evaluation, and freedom.

2.3 AI in Higher Education: Global and Indian Contexts

AI has risen to prominence as a game changer in the sphere of higher education worldwide. They are AI-driven systems that are being increasingly implemented in universities to facilitate pedagogical, research, and administrative processes. These technologies make personalized learning possible, automate routine academic processes and allow decision-making in institutions on the basis of data, turning higher education institutions into digitally mediatized ecosystems and becoming efficiency-scale-responsiveness oriented.

The Indian context links the adoption of AI in a more general direction of digitalization and growth in higher education. The growing popularity of learning management systems, automated assessment systems and research support systems are signs of a sudden shift to technology-enabled educational scenarios. The introduction of AI is, however, an unequal process that relies on institutional capacity, financial resources and regional differences. Well-endowed universities have been able to implement digital infrastructures at high levels, and most institutions that are state-based and affiliate universities are grappling with issues of access, training and implementation.

2.4 AI and Transformation of Academic Work

The available literature tends to focus on the increasing role of AI in transforming academic work, particularly in the preparation of teaching and research. However, the findings are not always convergent or consistent. Major survey studies usually report a very high adoption rate and perceived efficiency growth of AI, and numerical values are especially concerned with the frequency of use of tools. Conversely, qualitative studies provide more information about details, such as faculty ambivalence, the fear of excessive reliance on AI, and the loss of critical thinking.

The survey-based methodology of study is more likely to use self-report data, which inflates actual use because of the biased nature of responses, whereas interview-based studies are more likely to access the richer nature of experiences, but their generalizability capabilities are lower. This is a difference in methodology, which suggests that the available literature may unnecessarily generalize adoption patterns or lack consideration of structural constraints. As a result, eliminating a more integrated approach that combines quantitative patterns with qualitative results is still necessary, thus providing a comprehensive projection of how AI is truly implemented in academic practice. The current research fills this gap by triangulating survey and interview data in a particular institutional setting.

2.5 Policy and Institutional Shifts in Academic Profession

Academic work is undergoing transformation, which is inextricably connected with changing policy environments and institutional structures and is focused on flexibility, innovation, and performance. Recent changes in the higher education sector have promoted the virtues of multidisciplinary practices, cooperation with industries, and outcome-driven evaluation systems, which have resulted in changes in staffing, career development, and staff expectations.

Organizations are now looking to hire candidates who have interdisciplinary skills, digital skills, and the ability to go to industry and innovation ecologies. Moreover, new types of contractual appointments and other forms of academic appointments are being developed as a result of a transition to a more flexible labor form. Although these changes present opportunities for the diversification and implementation of applied knowledge, they also raise questions about job security, the standardization of the quality of work and the prospective stability of academic jobs.

2.6 Professorial appointments, the NEP 2020 and UGC reforms

Recent changes in faculty hiring procedures and career outlines in Indian higher education are indicative of the cessation of qualification-based models and competency-based models that are more adaptable and versatile. Diversification of institutional hiring practices has been enabled through regulatory changes to incorporate interdisciplinary expertise, experience in the industry and digital skills, in addition to traditional academic qualifications. Although these reforms are supposed to make academic functions in line with the current technological and societal demands, they have been implemented with a manifest difference between institutions.

Recruitment is becoming more focused on applicants with the skills of digital pedagogy, AI-based teaching, interdisciplinary research, and industrial cooperation at the institutional level. This movement is notably eminent in both the centrally funded and the privately owned universities, where access to resources and the world has facilitated the embrace of such standards. On the other hand, numerous state universities and collaborating colleges (especially in Tier II and Tier III areas) still adhere to traditional recruitment standards because of infrastructural constraints, bureaucratic stiffness, and a lack of exposure to new academic patterns. As a result, a two-tier system will exist, as innovation-based employment will be concurrent with the application of conventional hiring, which will be based on compliance.

Another defining change in the structuring of the faculty is the introduction of alternative forms of appointment in academic practices, including practice-oriented appointments and short-term contracts. These two positions are meant to bridge academic and industry domains, imbuing practical knowledge into the classroom and research community. However, the claim of institutional practices indicates that such appointments are not always equally applied and do not have clear evaluative systems. In most instances, a gray area persists on expectations of roles and career growth and fits into the prevailing academic hierarchies.

2.7 Digital Labor

The digital labor literature provides a critical perspective for understanding AI-based changes in higher education. Although the initial research on educational technologies presented the use of digital tools as the process of minimizing workloads and promoting efficiency, more contemporary studies do not support this supposition. According to scholars, technological systems tend to redistribute, rather than to abolish labor, and this result, as termed by academics, is the intensification of labor.

Nevertheless, findings on this problem are inconclusive. Perceived improvements in productivity are often reported in quantitative studies, but in qualitative studies, these improvements are found to increase expectations of output, responsiveness and availability. This tension indicates a more general methodological gap: studies based on surveys are more likely to measure perceived efficiency, and studies based on ethnography and interviews will determine concealed labor processes.

Nevertheless, few studies in this area have analyzed how these dynamics emerge and whether such dynamics occur in any particular institutional setting, especially in the Global South. Placing digital labor theory in an institutional case study, the current study offers empirically supported facts about efficiency and intensification as coexisting factors of academic labor.

2.8 Institutional Inequality

Emerging literature suggests that AI implementation in higher education is not uniform and is directly linked to institutional resources. Studies concerning endow college institutions are more likely to document advanced usage of AI devices, which is supported by institutionalized learning programs and technological infrastructure. On the other hand, the literature concerning resource-constrained institutions indicates the existence of impediments such as a lack of access to technology, training and institutional inertia. However, the majority of such studies are not conducted comparatively; i.e., they are targeted at high-end or underprivileged institutions. The cross-national research methodology does not usually pay much attention to the differences within the country, particularly in environments such as India, where administrative diversity is a significant phenomenon.

2.9 Ethics and Governance

Data privacy and algorithmic bias as well as academic integrity are ethical problems in AI in the education field, and both are heavily covered in the literature. However, much of this is still rather conceptual and is not empirically validated by others or not at all. Research based on platform governance theory indicates that

AI systems are capable of expanding the boundaries of institutional control by creating mechanisms of information-based monitoring and assessment. However, few empirical studies have investigated the process of the perception and negotiation of these structures of governance by faculty. Current survey-based studies demonstrate general apprehensions regarding privacy and bias but have little or no depth in context, whereas qualitative research offers extensive descriptions but has a limited volume.

This gap highlights the significance of combining theoretical knowledge with research. The current research, which incorporates survey findings together with interview stories, provides more realistic insights into the ways in which ethical issues are realized in practice.

2.10 Multilevel Analytical Framework

The paper is based on a multilevel analytical approach that incorporates macro, meso, and micro levels to analyze changes in the academic profession with respect to AI.

i. Macrolevel analysis focuses on policies at the country level, such as regulatory principles and reform agendas, that enable digital transformation and the introduction of AI in higher education. These structures play out institutional priorities and create the overall direction of change for academics.
ii. At the meso level, the paper examines how the institutions interpret and translate to these policy directives. This dwells upon institutional policies and practices, organizational structures, and policies of governance through which AI technologies were mediated.
iii. On the micro level, the framework will portray the lived experiences of the faculty members, their dealing with AI tools, their experience with altered professional expectations, and their perceived ethical and practical dilemmas.

Through the combination of these three levels, the framework provides a delicate understanding of how the intent of policy can be transformed into an institutional practice and how it can eventually be felt by academic workers. The method is also useful for determining gaps, strains, and disparities at various tiers of the institution of a higher learning system.

2.11 Research Questions

Although this body of literature is growing, there are still a number of gaps. First, a significant part of the current literature focuses on concepts or policy, and little empirical research has discussed the experience of AI at the faculty practice level.

Second, integrated analysis involving the relation of macrolevel policy frameworks to meso-level institutional relations and microlevel lived experiences is nonexistent. Third, the context of Indian higher education is underresearched on the basis of grounded and evidence-based analysis.

The proposed work bridges a gap by applying a mixed-method institutional case study, a combination of policy analysis and a wafer-thin analysis of the AI-driven transformation at multiple levels. By applying theoretical knowledge and empirical data, this study provides more detailed insights into the way in which AI transforms academic work, professional identity, and institutional inequalities. To this end, the research questions that will guide the study encompass the following questions:

i. What is the influence of national policy frameworks on the use of AI in higher education?
ii. What is the implementation and introduction of AI to institutions?
iii. What are the experiences and perceptions of faculty members with respect to the effects of AI on their work and professional lives?

The literature, taken collectively, has valuable information, but it is still divided along the lines of methodology and theory. Whereas some researchers are concerned with efficiency and innovativeness, others emphasize labor intensification, the problem of institutional inequality and governance. These divisions increase the necessity of adhering to a multilevel model of analysis. Consistent with this, this paper summarizes various forms of scholarly capitalism, theories of digital labor, platform governance, and the sociology of professions to provide deeper insight into the changes caused by AI. Such integration of theory allows the research to go beyond descriptive narration and construct a more critically oriented analysis with an empirical basis.

3. METHODOLOGY

The research design used in this study was a mixed methods design that used a policy document analysis approach along with an institutional case study. The policy review considered major national systems that influence AI implementation among academics. The experimental part was carried out on a partially chosen higher education facility, allowing a thorough study of the way these policy orientations are implemented and finding their manifestations in practice (Rawat and Ashton-Bell, 2025). The research is founded on a given data collection and analysis, which means that all the findings provided are based on practical evidence but not on assumptions. The method used in the study is shown in Figure 1.

Figure 1. Methodology

3.1 Data collection

The empirical aspect of this research relies on the spread out of data gathered from one higher education organization (Ajay Kumar Garg Engineering College (AKGEC), Ghaziabad, India), which is assumed to constitute a detailed case study. The data collected during a survey are quantitative and provide an overview of the trends of using AI among faculty, whereas the results of semistructured interviews are qualitative and touch upon lived experiences. These findings are contextualized with the help of institutional and policy documents. The findings of the survey can therefore be considered context-specific and not indicative of the whole higher education system. This is a method that is consistent with the case study approach, where statistical generalization is not the object of the approach.

Sampling Strategy and Participant Profile

The research used a purposive method of sampling the faculty members of the case institution. One hundred and ninety faculty members were called to complete the survey, and 120 answered it, for a response rate of 63%. The sample consisted of representatives of various academic fields and different degrees of experience to provide representativeness in the institutional context. Although the sample size is relatively small, it is suitable for an exploratory case study design where the goal of the study is to produce context-specific knowledge to be generalized not statistically. Simple descriptive statistics were used to determine AI usage and perception trends among the respondents.

Data Triangulation

To improve validity, the survey results were triangulated with semistructured interviews of ten faculty members, which enabled further interpretation of the quantitative trends. Institutional and policy documents were also analyzed to provide a context (in the analysis of findings). Despite its small sample size, the multisource method is more robust and credible to the analysis.

Data Analysis

The quantitative data were examined through descriptive statistical operations to establish trends in the adoption of AI, frequency of use and its effects on academic practices. Interpretation was performed through thematic analysis of the qualitative data that were obtained from the interviews. Thematic areas were identified on the basis of academic labor, computer literacy, institutional support, and ethical issues. This allowed the paper to identify subtle interpretations of AI as experienced and perceived by the faculty members. Document analysis was applied to study the articulation of the role of AI in higher education in terms of policy frameworks and institutional strategies. This aided in establishing inconsistencies between policy objectives and the way they are implemented at the institutional level.

Survey Instrument

A survey questionnaire was created to address faculty experiences and perceptions of AI integration in three areas, namely, (i) teaching, content preparation, (ii) research support, and productivity, and (iii) perceptions of institutional expectations and ethical issues. The questionnaire was composed of 34 questions, comprising both closed-ended Likert-scale questions and few open-ended questions.

Scoring on a Likert scale was performed using a five-point scale, which was divided into strongly disagree (1) and strongly agree (5). To ensure transparency and replicability, the complete questionnaire is given in Appendix A.

3.2 Policy and document analysis

The analysis of policies and documents is among the key methodological tools of this research because the changes in the academic profession and faculty recruitment practices depend mainly on regulatory frameworks and institutional governance systems. Instead of repeating the policy stipulations, the discussion focuses on the impact of such structures on academic performance, the employment process, and organizational operations in colleges and universities. On this basis, a methodical review of policy texts, institutional accounts, and other documents is conducted to question the role of artificial intelligence (AI) not only as a technological resource but also as a governance process in the changing environment of higher learning (Rukadikar & Khandelwal, 2025).

The mentioned methodological position allows the identification of the prevailing policy discourses by which AI integration is defined and perceived in the context of higher education. It also enables an analysis of how faculty governance, academic labor and institutional priorities are conditioned by these discourses. Beyond the claims of the policy, the analysis also looks into how the institutional actors interpret and operationalize the rules of regulations and therefore provide information on the alignment of policy intention and institutional facts and, in other instances, the absence of such actions. As an increasing number of recruitment processes, career progression systems and performance evaluation systems move into the realm of digital transformation, a document analysis presents a keen insight through which to view the structural and operational changes that are occurring in the academic system.

3.3. Semi-structured interviews

A key qualitative approach in this research is semistructured interviews, which were used to study how AI transforms the structure of the academic profession and the system of appointing professors in Indian institutions of higher learning (HEIs). Since the changes in faculty roles, recruitment procedures, and administrative models are associated with human experience, perception, and institutional facts, semistructured interviews are especially appropriate in regard to tapping into delicate information, which might not be well covered in policy documents or as in quantitative surveys. In this way, researchers can investigate the interpretations of AI integration among different stakeholders, their reactions to policy change and their perceptions of changes in academic labor and professional identity.

The semistructured interview paradigm is based on an interpretive research paradigm whereby social realities are subject to construction by human understanding as well as the institutional context. Within the current research, the academic profession is founded as not only a series of administrative work tasks but also as a dynamic professional environment that is shaped by policy change, technology, and socioeconomic demands. As a result, interviews enable a crucial process of understanding how members of the faculty and academic administrators perceive the effects of AI in the actual institutional context (Hatch, 2023).

3.3.1 Interview Design and Structure

The interview guide is designed on the basis of the main themes associated with the research goals and wide literature coverage. The semistructured style ensures that all the interviews will touch on major themes and enable the participants to raise new points. The interview guide is usually composed of open-ended questions and is arranged in terms of the following themes:

(a) AI in Teaching and Pedagogy

The participants will be asked to share their views about the use of AI tools in the classroom, learning management systems, assessment, content generation and student interaction. These questions aim to determine whether AI is seen to improve teaching quality or to address the issues of authenticity and academic integrity.

(b) AI in Research and Scholarly Work

This section explores the use of AI by faculty members in the literature review, data analysis, research paper writing, and research publication and explores how AI has changed research productivity, collaboration, and scholarly output expectations.

(c) AI in Academic Administration and Governance

The participants expressed their opinions on the current state of AI use in the institutional administration, e.g., with the help of digital attendance tracking, biometric testing tools, automated admissions, or the decision-support machine, on its impact on their productivity or their apprehension of surveillance.

(d) Recruitment, Promotion, and Career Advancement

This theme blocks the question of how the standards of faculty recruitment and appointment are evolving depending on changes in the NEP 2020 and UGC reforms. The respondents are questioned about the emergence of new skills needed in recruitment and promotion, such as AI literacy, digital teaching capabilities and interdisciplinary research capability.

(e) Ethical, Equity, and Regional Issues

The participants explore whether the adoption of AI is fair at the institutional level, the presence of bias in AI applications and whether faculty and students in underresourced or rural institutions are at a disadvantage. There are also questions on the privacy of the data and the openness of AI-based decision-making.

(f) Future of the Academic Profession

The part dwells upon the anticipation of the faculty touching upon the future of academic activity, job supremacy, tenure, contractual teaching, and the prospective supersession or increase of academic labor by AI systems. This systematic thematic methodology is important to the data collected in interviews, as it allows them to be consistent with the research topic of the chapter and provides a rich compilation of qualitative accounts.

3.3.2 Data Analysis Approach

The data obtained in the interviews are thematically analyzed using a method that has become popular in qualitative research because of its ability to trace repetitive patterns and meaning that is embedded in textual data. The analysis process is conducted in a number of consecutive steps:

Step 1: Transcription

The interviews are recorded and transcribed verbatim to capture the originality of the participants' responses. The accuracy of the transcripts was subsequently checked.

Step 2: Coding

The researcher participates in open coding, which involves highlighting salient phrases, common ideas and salient statements. Some of the terms that could be included in codes are AI workload reduction, digital surveillance, research productivity, appointment flexibility, industry-academia collaboration, evaluation bias and training gap.

Step 3: Theme Development

The codes are divided into more general themes. As an example, the codes related to AI-based evaluation software and the issue of plagiarism can be grouped into the theme AI and academic integrity, whereas the codes related to recruitment reforms and new skills requirements can be the theme new competences in professional appointments.

Step 4: Interpretation

Themes have been understood within the context of research questions and hypotheses. This is analyzed to determine whether the faculty feel empowered by AI, threatened by AI, or both. It further criticizes the relevance of restructuring the meaning of academic professionalism and institutional autonomy through reforms. The interpretive reasoning that anchors the thematic analysis of the narratives of the stakeholders to more general policy and governance situations supports the thematic analysis.

3.3.3 Validity and Trustworthiness

To increase the authenticity of the results of the interviews, a range of methods are followed:

- **Triangulation:** The results of the interviews are channeled against policy analysis and survey data to establish consistency.
- **Diversity of participants:** Multiple categories of stakeholders make the presentation of views stronger.
- **Reflexivity:** The researcher does not forget that he/she is prone to bias and ensures that interpretations are based on data provided by participants.
- **Member checking (optional):** The major summaries of findings can be disseminated to selected members of the sample in a quest to verify accuracy.

These factors enhance the credibility and rigor of the qualitative results.

3.3.4 Ethical Considerations

This is because ethical principles are strictly adhered to in the interview process. An introduction to the participants is provided with detailed information about the goals of the study and the rights of a participant, including the right to discontinue their involvement at any time. Privacy is ensured by hiding the names and institutions in both the transcripts and the reporting. Given that the issues of recruitment policies, job security and performance appraisal are very sensitive, anonymity is maintained as a significant ethical requirement. The data are safely stored, and the interviews are recorded only to use them in the academic context.

3.4 Faculty survey

A faculty survey is also a critical quantitative element of the study, and it will be utilized to supplement qualitative methods of policy analysis and semistructured interviews. Since the integration of AI in the context of higher education is not balanced across all institutions and regions in India, survey-based research provides a systematic tool for including generic trends, perceptions, and adoption trends of AI usage among faculty members. The survey will help researchers collect empirical data on the level of AI application in teaching, research, and academic administration, as well as on faculty preparedness, training requirements, and ethical issues concerning governance. Surveys facilitate broad generalizability of findings and add credibility to the research by means of triangulation because of the large base of respondents (Tarhini et al., 2017).

3.4.1 Sampling and Data Collection

The survey applies purposive and convenience sampling to approach faculty members on a continuum of universities in India, that is, central universities, state universities, private universities, autonomous colleges, and technical institutions. Distribution is carried out through online channels through Google form or institutional email networks; hence, it is approached with accessibility and expanded coverage. An attempt is made to incorporate the faculty of both urban and rural institutions in an effort to capture regional differences in the adoption of AI. An adequate sample size is needed to ensure that the answers reflect different views in various fields, including engineering, sciences, management, humanities, and social sciences. Studies will be conducted as a voluntary exercise, and confidentiality and anonymity will be assured to the respondents (Yadav & Anubha, 2024)(Hwang & Tu, 2021)(Abuhassna et al., 2024)(Jiménez-García et al., 2025).

3.4.4 Data Analysis

The statistical procedures that were performed on the survey data were descriptive. The analytical process included a frequency distribution and percentual analysis to outline the patterns of AI adoption; calculation of the mean scores of the Likert-scale items to understand the attitudes of the faculty; a comparative analysis based on the types of institutions, geographic region, and academic designation; and cross tabulations to identify the correlation between AI utilization and other variables, including age, discipline, and institutional resources at hand. The quantitative results provide empirical data for supporting the qualitative themes obtained through interview data and policy review or polemicizing it.

3.5. Analytical framework

This paper follows a very rigorous analytical scheme to explore analytically in an organized manner how AI is transforming the academic profession and the processes involved in professorship appointments in Indian higher education institutions (HEIs). The framework is multidimensional and is founded on policy change, institutional execution and faculty-level experience, as it acknowledges that AI integration is not only a technological shift but also a significant change in organization and governance. It informs the understanding of how national regulations (e.g., the NEP 2020 and reforms issued by the UGC) impact academic practice, recruitment criteria, and professional responsibility in AI-driven governance situations.

The multilevel governance structure, which studies AI impacts on the macro, meso, and micro levels, also forms the basis of the analysis. The stratification approach is suitable since changes in academic labor occur at the convergence of the academic policy talk, organizational choices and local adjustment of individuals. In addition, it deploys the ideas of the scholarship of academic professionalism, digital labor theory and ethical governance to reconcile the complexity of the implications of adopting AI.

3.5.1 Macrolevel Analysis (Policy and Regulatory Context)

At the macro level, the research examines the national policy regimes and laws that influence the academic profession. Resourceful documents include the NEP 2020, the rules for the recruitment and promotion of UGC, the regulations of AICTE, and the initiatives of the country in the field of digital education and research innovations. Macrolevel analysis focuses on AI placement in policy discourse, especially in terms of quality improvement, global competitiveness, employability, interdisciplinary learning and technology-enabled governance. It also explores how academic excellence is reconceptualized in the form of innovation, outcome-driven education and the productivity of research and how the impact on professors and academic leaders is redefined under these policies (Vrabie, 2025).

3.5.2 Meso-level Analysis (Institutional Governance and Practices)

On the meso level, the framework examines the way universities and colleges implement policy changes and use AI-based systems. This would involve an analysis of the institutionalized approaches to incorporating AI in learning and teaching environments, e-governance solutions, recruitment systems, and performance appraisal systems. Meso-level research highlights the differences between central universities, state universities, private universities, and independent colleges. This tier is crucial for understanding the discrepancy in the implementation of AI in Indian HEIs and the role of institutional resources, leadership focus, and digital infrastructure in the process of implementing AI-related reforms. It also investigates new categories of appointment, such as Professor of Practice and contractual employment, and is indicative of moving academic labor formations.

3.5.3 Microlevel Analysis (Faculty Experience and Professional Identity)

On the micro level, AI reforms the experience of the faculty by changing the day-to-day practices of the academic, expectations, and professional identity. AI is being progressively used by faculty in teaching preparation, research assistance, and administration, making it more efficient but increasing workload and stress.

Continuous upskilling in digital and AI skills has become a must that is not always provided by institutions. Although a portion of the faculty view AI as a source of innovation and productivity, others state that it impacts academic integrity and autonomy and has created overdependence on technology. These ambivalent experiences point to a shift in which conventional academics are becoming digitally mediated and performance-oriented professionalities.

3.5.4 Ethical and Equity Lenses

We integrate an ethical and equity lens at all three levels of analysis to determine issues related to algorithmic bias, data privacy threats, surveillance issues and the unfair utilization of AI resources. In Indian society, regional and socioeconomic differences can affect the readiness of institutions and faculty members for AI, which is especially relevant to this lens. The ethical aspect also analyzes whether AI-based recruitment and evaluation systems contribute to the advancement of fairness and transparency or reinstate the inequalities that are present.

The research design is aligned with the multilevel framework of analysis, which encompasses policy document analysis at the macro level, institutional data and comparison level, and at the meso level and survey and interview data at the micro level. This mixed method will make the findings that come up inclusive of both the dynamics of structures and the experiences of the academics themselves.

4. ANALYSIS

4.1 Comparative framing

Although this research is based on the Indian context of higher education, placing the research findings within the scope of wider world trends is imperative. According to comparative studies of North America and Europe, institutional preparedness for AI incorporation is relative and in place because of developed digital infrastructure, institutional frameworks of formal governance, and specialized funding systems. In contrast, research in developing and emerging economies highlights issues related to infrastructural shortages, disparate access and reduced institutional capacity.

In comparison with these settings, the Indian system of higher education has a hybrid trend. On the one hand, national policy frameworks strongly support the practice of digital transformation and the adoption of AI; on the other hand, empirical data show that the practice has been disproportionately adopted in different institutions. This makes India an important case study in terms of comprehending the national adaptation of global technological trends using resource-constrained and institutionally diverse systems. The given study becomes part of this comparison because it provides empirically based knowledge derived from a particular institutional setting.

Table 1 shows a survey based on a quantitative survey of 120 faculty members at the institution of the author (AKGEC, India).

Table 1 (a): Quantitative Findings from the Faculty Survey on AI Adoption in AKGEC (Part 1)

Survey Indicator	**Response Category**	**Frequency (n)**	**Percentage (%)**
Awareness of AI tools (ChatGPT, Grammarly, Turnitin, LMS, etc.)	Yes	110	92%
	No	10	8%
Frequency of AI tool usage	Daily	73	61%
	Weekly	21	17%
	Occasionally	25	21%
	Never	1	1%
AI useful in preparing lecture notes and teaching material	Agree/Strongly Agree	101	84%
	Neutral	12	10%
	Disagree/Strongly Disagree	7	6%
AI used for preparing quizzes/assignments/ question banks	Yes	91	76%
	No	29	24%
AI improves classroom engagement	Agree/Strongly Agree	82	68%
	Neutral	21	18%
	Disagree/Strongly Disagree	17	14%
Trust in AI-assisted evaluation/grading	Agree/Strongly Agree	55	46%
	Neutral	34	28%
	Disagree/Strongly Disagree	31	26%
AI used for literature review and summarization	Yes	97	81%
	No	23	19%

Table 1(b): Quantitative Findings from the Faculty Survey on AI Adoption in AK-GEC (Part 2)

Survey Indicator	**Response Category**	**Frequency (n)**	**Percentage (%)**
AI improves research writing and manuscript structuring	Agree/Strongly Agree	89	74%
	Neutral	18	15%
	Disagree/Strongly Disagree	13	11%
AI reduces time required for drafting research papers	Agree/Strongly Agree	79	66%
	Neutral	23	19%
	Disagree/Strongly Disagree	18	15%
AI contributes significantly to originality and innovation in research	Agree/Strongly Agree	59	49%
	Neutral	31	26%
	Disagree/Strongly Disagree	30	25%
Institution provides digital infrastructure for AI-enabled learning	Yes	68	57%
	No	52	43%
Institution conducts AI training workshops regularly	Yes	49	41%
	No	71	59%
Faculty learned AI tools independently	Yes	76	63%
	No	44	37%
AI literacy will become important in faculty recruitment	Agree/Strongly Agree	86	72%
	Neutral	20	17%
	Disagree/Strongly Disagree	14	11%
AI-based productivity tools will influence promotion and appraisal	Agree/Strongly Agree	78	65%
	Neutral	24	20%
	Disagree/Strongly Disagree	18	15%

Table 1(c): Quantitative Findings from the Faculty Survey on AI Adoption in AK-GEC (Part 3)

Survey Indicator	Response Category	Frequency (n)	Percentage (%)
Concern about appointment becoming overly metric-based	Agree/Strongly Agree	65	54%
	Neutral	29	24%
	Disagree/Strongly Disagree	26	22%
Concern about data privacy and misuse	Agree/Strongly Agree	83	69%
	Neutral	20	17%
	Disagree/Strongly Disagree	17	14%
AI may create bias in recruitment and evaluation	Agree/Strongly Agree	74	62%
	Neutral	25	21%
	Disagree/Strongly Disagree	21	17%
AI may increase inequality between urban and rural institutions	Agree/Strongly Agree	85	71%
	Neutral	18	15%
	Disagree/Strongly Disagree	17	14%
Fear of AI-driven monitoring and institutional surveillance	Agree/Strongly Agree	70	58%
	Neutral	27	23%
	Disagree/Strongly Disagree	23	19%

The results show that faculty members (especially those working in the area of teaching preparation (84%) and research support (81%) are highly aware of and accepting and use AI tools. However, there is still little faith in AI-based grading (46%). Institutional preparedness is mediocre, with only 57% of the respondents saying they have sufficient infrastructure and 41% of the respondents saying they hold regular training workshops. Ethical issues also evidently echo, with 69% being concerned with data privacy and 71% being concerned with regional inequality.

4.2 Findings/Discussion

The results are analyzed using a macromeso-micro analytic framework to emphasize the way in which AI-based change occurs at various levels of the higher education system.

4.2.1 Macro level: Policy Frameworks and System-Level Transformation

The results of the current paper suggest that policy-driven transformation agendas influence the formation of artificial intelligence (AI) integration in Indian higher education at the macro level. The framework of national policies provides guidance in the embrace of digital and advanced AI-enabled innovation in teaching, research, and governance. Empirical data, however, support the idea that the overall effect of such policy measures is not uniform, as it is influenced by institutional capacity and local settings.

Although the discourse of policy focuses on the themes of innovation, readiness to use digital technologies and the ability to compete, the results suggest a discrepancy between policy intentions and practicality. It can be seen especially in the area of faculty hiring and appraisal, where policies promote interdisciplinary aptitudes, work with industry, and technological aptitudes. The research reveals that such expectations are slowly taking their toll on the structure of academic careers and is an indicator of a transition toward performance-based models of academic work. It shows a larger systematization of transitions linked to market-oriented reforms, where quantifiable deliverables and digital capacity are becoming increasingly important.

4.2.2 Meso Level: Institutional Practices and Structural Inequalities

At the meso level, the current paper depicts the role played by institutional context in the introduction of artificial intelligence (AI) as well as its effectiveness in the context of higher education. These disparities are also explained through interviews. This faculty associated with well-endowed institutions reported organized training programs, institutional membership in AI services and strategic support structures to support digital transformation. Conversely, researchers who worked in resource-constrained environments indicated that they relied on the use of freely available tools as well as self-directed learning methods. A single respondent noted that we are supposed to use AI, yet no specific assistance or training is offered, which is why the lack of alignment between institutional demands and the resource pool of the staff members was highlighted.

These results show that AI adoption is highly unequal and closely intertwined with organizational capability. As a result, the implementation of AI can provide more opportunities to address the existing disparities in the academic system because, in this way, well-endowed institutions can move faster in the areas of research productivity and pedagogical innovation and enhance their competitiveness in the global environment.

4.2.3 Micro level: Lived Academic Experience and Professional Transformation

At the micro level, the results provide insight into the predetermined experiences of faculty members, thus revealing the degree to which AI is embedded in the study of everyday academic activity. The statistics of the survey show that most faculty members who participated in the survey have applied AI solutions to pedagogical preparation, research support, and content generation. The narratives of the interviews provide clear examples of such practices, including writing lecture notes, synthesizing academic articles, and coming up with research outlines.

However, such experiences are heterogeneous. A prime example is one of the faculty members at a private university who said that the use of AI tools had decreased lecture preparation time; thus, increased attention was given to delivery. On the basis of this strategy, one respondent from a state university highlighted the inconsistency problem in accessing digital infrastructure, limiting effective AI use. These conflicting descriptions demonstrate that despite the ubiquity of AI implementation, the real-life advantages of the technology are dissimilar in the individual and institutional spheres.

One of the salient findings at this level is the amplification of academic labor. Despite seemingly being effective at improving efficiency, survey and interview results continue to show the growing expectations of an institution for faster content delivery, higher output of publications, and continued responsiveness to AI tools. According to one participant, what had taken one week before could now be delivered in two days, hence demonstrating that the amount of technological efficiency translated into increased pressure in performance. This finding shows that AI restructures but does not reduce academic work, which in turn affects the development of productivity standards.

A reconfiguration of academic identity is also revealed in the course of the study. Faculty members are increasingly viewing digital competence as an essential part of their work; however, according to the interview narratives, there are both positive and negative attitudes toward this change. On the one hand, some respondents hope that AI can be used as a means of innovation and professional growth, and on the other hand, some respondents are worried about the loss of classic academic values, including profound disciplinary interest and pedagogical freedom. These results imply that professional change is negotiated on a personal basis and is adjusted by different levels of approval and nonapproval.

Such issues as ethics and equity are especially relevant in terms of lived experiences. The results of the surveys reveal that a significant percentage of the faculty representatives are concerned about the problems of data privacy, academic honesty, and algorithmic bias. The participants of the interviews provided certain examples, such as the inability to confirm the work of the AI-generated students and the opportunity to use AI to track performance. Certain faculty members are complaining of increased monitoring and loss of autonomy, and one replied that there is a thin line between support and control. The lessons show that ethical issues are not abstract concepts but actually affect academic practice and perceptions in a practical way.

4.2.4 Synthesis across Levels

In general, the paper illustrates that AI-led transformation in Indian higher education is an interdependent multilevel process that is enacted at the macro, meso, and micro levels. Policy structures layout the path through which digital transformation should follow, institutional capacity dictates how much of such transformation should be implemented, and the impacts on digital transformation will be realized by faculty experience. Through their combination, the discussion provides a deliberate insight into the ways in which AI is transforming academic labor, professional identities, and institutional inequalities into a context-sensitive paradigm.

4.3 Limitations

Although the paper provides detailed results, they are based on a case study of one institution and hence are not entirely generalizable to the total body of the Indian higher education institution. However, the combination of policy analysis with empirical data increases the quality of the analysis and the relevance of the results.

This research focuses mainly on faculty experience as one of the key frames of AI-based transformation recognition. As much as this focus provides fascinating information about academic labor and professional change, it does not capture the views of other stakeholders, including students, administrators, or even policymakers. Therefore, the results can be interpreted only as faculty-based data of the larger systemic transformation but not as a complete depiction of all aspects of change.

5. CONCLUSION

This research contributes to the literature because it goes beyond the abstract theoretical resources of AI in higher education and provides empirically strong resources by adhering to a hybrid approach of policy analysis and an institutional case study.

The chapter can be in agreement that AI has not just been a technologically supplementary phenomenon but is also a structural phenomenon changing the concept of professoriality in India, including recruitment, workload, evaluation, and career paths. The changing requirements of the NEP 2020 and UGC, including new recruitment criteria, graded autonomy and the Professor of Practice model, provide a powerful but partial structure in which academic futures mediated by AI are negotiated.

From the opportunity perspective, AI holds the prospects of improving accessibility, alleviating administration, supporting high-quality investigations, and diversifying and practice-based university work, which is likely to occur under a well-developed digital framework and effective interactions involving the populace, companies, and academic institutions. On the other hand, the risks of increased inequalities, machine bias, loss of professional control, data mining and an overvaluation of measurable indicators require strong ethical protection, clarified policies and high levels of faculty participation in decision-making activities.

Indian policymakers should issue consistent models, within which AI ethics and data-protection principles are institutionalized in terms of recruitment, appraisal, and promotion; facilitating the ongoing training of AI-literate and AI pedagogist faculty; protecting academic freedom; establishing norms on the use of AI in education and research; and ensuring that AI adoption is inclusive across different regions and types of institutions by way of specific funding and capacity-building policies. In this way, Indian higher education can use AI to strengthen the social objectives of universities and colleges so that appointing professors are no longer deemed subordinate to order algorithmic logic.

In summary, this chapter confirms that artificial intelligence is a decisive factor in defining the Indian higher education academic profession and professorial appointment patterns. AI is no longer an assistant to teaching and research; it significantly influences institutional governance, recruiting expectations, performance appraisal systems, and the formation of professional identity. The results indicate that AI-based solutions increase the efficiency of academic performance, as they help professors develop content, research effectiveness, and administration. However, such productivity comes at a price of increased demands on improved academic output, better publication performance and measurable results, which can be seen as representative of the triumph of a metric-driven academic culture.

Another point brought out by the chapter is that the NEP 2020 and UGC reforms increase structural transformation through facilitating flexibility, interdisciplinarity, and alternative models of appointment, such as the Professor of Practice. Although reformation can strengthen innovation and collaboration between industries, it creates some issues related to job security, academic freedom and equity in evaluation procedures. Most importantly, the results of the analysis reveal that the adoption of AI has not yet become equal among Indian HEIs and that rural and underresourced schools face an infrastructural and training shortage that can provide an additional source of inequality in the region. In this context, the future of professorial governance in India will depend on the compromise between artificial intelligence-induced modernization and ethics, the inclusion approach, and the policy of strong faculty capacity building.

This paper provides various contributions to the current body of literature. First, it provides a combined theoretical approach that synthesizes academic capitalism, digital labor and platform governance to explain the intellectualization of academic labor. Second, it provides empirical information on the Indian context of higher education, thus filling an important research gap in modern research. Third, it further provides insights into how AI reinvents faculty recruitment, career development, and governance by the institution. This research connects technological change and professional and structural changes to the general discussion on the future of higher education in the digital age.

Future studies can add to the multistakeholder lens, which may include student experiences and the decision-making process by higher education administrations, and thus provide a more comprehensive understanding of AI-motivated change in higher education systems.

REFERENCES

Abuhassna, H., Awae, F., Adnan, M. A. B. M., Daud, M., & Almheiri, A. S. B. (2024). The Information Age for Education via Artificial Intelligence and Machine Learning: A Bibliometric and Systematic Literature Analysis. In *International Journal of Information and Education Technology* (Vol. 14, Issue 5). DOI: 10.18178/ijiet.2024.14.5.2095

Alifah, N., & Hidayat, A. R. (2025). Effectiveness of Artificial Intelligence-Based Learning Analytics Tool in Supporting Personalized Learning in Higher Education. *Jurnal Pendidikan Progresif, 15*(1), 74–84. Advance online publication. DOI: 10.23960/jpp.v15i1.pp74-84

Baig, M. I., & Yadegaridehkordi, E. (2025). Factors influencing academic staff satisfaction and continuous usage of generative artificial intelligence (GenAI) in higher education. *International Journal of Educational Technology in Higher Education, 22*(1), 5. Advance online publication. DOI: 10.1186/s41239-025-00506-4

Buele, J., & Llerena-Aguirre, L. (2025). Transformations in academic work and faculty perceptions of artificial intelligence in higher education. In *Frontiers in Education* (Vol. 10). DOI: 10.3389/feduc.2025.1603763

Burtch, G., Lee, D., & Chen, Z. (2023). The Consequences of Generative AI for UGC and Online Community Engagement. SSRN *Electronic Journal*. DOI: 10.2139/ssrn.4521754

Hatch, J. A. (2023). Doing Qualitative Research in Education Settings. In *Doing Qualitative Research in Education Settings*. DOI: 10.1515/9780791487945

Hwang, G. J., & Tu, Y. F. (2021). Roles and research trends of artificial intelligence in mathematics education: A bibliometric mapping analysis and systematic review. In *Mathematics* (Vol. 9, Issue 6). DOI: 10.3390/math9060584

Jiménez-García, E., Ruiz-Lázaro, J., Martínez-Requejo, S., & Redondo-Duarte, S. (2025). Artificial Intelligence and chatbots for sustainable higher education: A systematic review. *RIED-Revista Iberoamericana de Educacion a Distancia, 28*(2). Advance online publication. DOI: 10.5944/ried.28.2.43240

Khalifa, M., & Albadawy, M. (2024). Using artificial intelligence in academic writing and research: An essential productivity tool. In *Computer Methods and Programs in Biomedicine Update* (Vol. 5). DOI: 10.1016/j.cmpbup.2024.100145

Kulal, A. N. A., Dinesh, S., Bhat, D. C., & Girish, A. (2024). Evaluating the Promise and Pitfalls of India's National Education Policy 2020: Insights from the Perspectives of Students, Teachers, and Experts. *SAGE Open, 14*(4), 21582440241279367. Advance online publication. DOI: 10.1177/21582440241279367

Kumar Jain, V., Kumar Yadav, N., Professor, A., & Sharma, D. (2025). AI-Driven Pedagogy: Promoting Student Engagement, Intrinsic Motivation, and Self-Regulation. In *Journal of Informatics Education and Research* (Vol. 5).

Minja, L. (2024). The Role of Recruitment and Selection on Organisational Performance: A Case of National Housing Corporation in Tanzania. *Accounting and Business Review, 16*(5). Advance online publication. DOI: 10.59645/abr.v16i5.386

Mogoale, P., Pretorius, A., Mogase, R., & Segooa, M. (2025). Ethical considerations in artificial intelligence-driven environments for higher education. *South African Journal of Information Management, 27*(1), a2007. Advance online publication. DOI: 10.4102/sajim.v27i1.2007

Narkhede, G., Pasi, B., Dhamak, P., Mahalle, P., & Ambhore, N. (2025). In the pursuit of educational excellence: Investigating CSFs for implementing NEP 2020 to redefine the higher education ecosystem. *Journal of Applied Research in Higher Education*. Advance online publication. DOI: 10.1108/JARHE-09-2024-0454

Rawat, S., & Ashton-Bell, R. L. T. (2025). Responsible Ai-Readiness In Higher Education: Validating A Dual-Model Framework For Faculty Development. *Journal of Information Technology Education, 24*, 040. Advance online publication. DOI: 10.28945/5654

Rukadikar, A., & Khandelwal, K. (2025). Exploring perceptions of Indian graduates on the effectiveness of artificial intelligence in higher education campus hiring. *Discover Artificial Intelligence, 5*(1), 265. Advance online publication. DOI: 10.1007/s44163-025-00526-z

Singh, N., Kalam Khan, M., Dixit, A., & Jaiswar, K. (2025). NEP 2020 and Governance & Digital Infrastructure. *International Journal of Advanced Research in Science, Communication and Technology International Open-Access, Double-Blind, Peer-Reviewed, Refereed, Multidisciplinary Online Journal, 5*(16).

Tarhini, A., Hone, K., Liu, X., & Tarhini, T. (2017). Examining the moderating effect of individual-level cultural values on users' acceptance of E-learning in developing countries: A structural equation modeling of an extended technology acceptance model. *Interactive Learning Environments, 25*(3), 306–328. Advance online publication. DOI: 10.1080/10494820.2015.1122635

Vrabie, C. (2025). Improving Municipal Responsiveness Through Ai-Powered Image Analysis In E-Government. *Public Policy and Administration*, *24*(1), 9–23. Advance online publication. DOI: 10.5755/j01.ppaa.24.1.39756

Woelert, P., Croucher, G., & Hoang, S. (2025). The rise of a "casualised" workforce: A conceptual account of the institutional forces legitimizing contingent academic employment in Australia. *Higher Education*. Advance online publication. DOI: 10.1007/s10734-025-01405-3

Yadav, B., & Anubha, . (2024). A Bibliometric Review of Role of Artificial Intelligence In Education. *ShodhKosh: Journal of Visual and Performing Arts*, *5*(6). Advance online publication. DOI: 10.29121/shodhkosh.v5.i6.2024.3206

Zawacki-Richter, O., Marín, V. I., Bond, M., & Gouverneur, F. (2019). Systematic review of research on artificial intelligence applications in higher education – where are the educators? In *International Journal of Educational Technology in Higher Education* (Vol. 16, Issue 1). DOI: 10.1186/s41239-019-0171-0

Chapter 3

AI in Learning and Education:
Implications for Faculty Careers in Higher Education

Sanjeev Kumar
http://orcid.org/0000-0002-7375-7341
Lovely Professional University, India

Pardeep Kumar
http://orcid.org/0000-0003-0308-7634
Lovely Professional University, India

ABSTRACT

Artificial intelligence (AI) is transforming the learning and education, shapes teaching and learning methods, methods of evaluating learning, and the overall higher education. The AI provides opportunities and challenges to members of the faculty that have significant career growth implications, professional identity implications and instructional role implications. The effectiveness of the teaching process, adapting learning to the individual student, and stimulating research can be enhanced through artificial intelligence (intelligent tutoring systems), automated grading, adaptive learning, and data-driven analytics. However, there are other aspects of these developments, such as the faculty allowing new competencies in the context of AI literacy, digital pedagogy, and technology use ethics. The integration of AI may also be similar to the allocation of the ancient functions, where mentorship, the right to think critically, and the application of the human judgment can be put in the field where the AI devices will not be able to achieve the results of the complex thought.

DOI: 10.4018/979-8-2600-3204-6.ch003

INTRODUCTION

The reality of artificial intelligence has become one of the most significant technological forces shaping contemporary societies; its influence on the educational process and higher learning, in particular, has grown. The institutions of higher learning also underwent several technological changes over the past few decades, starting with the introduction of computers and the internet into learning management systems, online courses, and online assessment tools. Nevertheless, artificial intelligence is not the next stage in the development and use of previous technologies, but a qualitatively new one (Farooq et al., 2024). AI systems can use large volumes of data to identify trends, forecast, and even perform tasks that traditionally belong to human mental processes, in contrast with traditional digital solutions, which are useful only to the extent that they store and convey information to individuals. This disruptive feature has ensured that AI is at the center of change in teaching, learning, assessment, research, and academic administration, raising serious apprehensions about the technology's impact on faculty careers within the college industry. It is possible to trace the rise in AI's popularity in education to broader changes in computational power, data availability, and algorithmic development. The development of machine learning, natural language processing, and data analytics has also led to the creation of intelligent systems that can evolve with learners' needs, automate routine tasks, and provide real-time feedback. Meanwhile, the higher education sector has been experiencing mounting pressure associated with massification, demographic diversity, accountability, employability, and financial sustainability (Popenici & Kerr, 2017). The institutions are expected to provide high-quality instruction to a wider, more diverse group of learners, while maintaining school quality and responding to the rapidly changing demands of the workforce. In this regard, AI has been developed as a possible solution to numerous unsolvable problems, such as high student numbers, low student preparation rates, time-consuming reading and assessment systems, and the need for student-centered learning. The faculty members have been excited and anxious about such changes; they are still in the middle stage of technological development and traditional values among academicians.

AI is set to alter the structure of learning and teaching in pedagogy. Smart tutoring systems and adaptive learning platforms can provide instructional content in formats tailored to each student's performance, interests, and progress. This is because the assessment may be administration-intensive, and the rationale behind automated grading tools and AI-assisted feedback systems can make the administrative workload so great that teachers are unable to concentrate on higher-order teaching processes, such as mentoring, curriculum cultivation, and research management. Faculty can gain insight into student engagement, retention risk, and learning outcomes through learning analytics, which can lead to quicker, more efficient interventions (Lee et al., 2024). Meanwhile, these technologies can be viewed as challenging past notions of the faculty as the primary source of knowledge and the judge of student work. In addition to reconfiguring AI systems to embrace aspects of the teaching profession, the faculty will be compelled to renegotiate their roles and redefine the specific purpose of human knowledge in the teaching process. The process of introducing AI in higher education cannot be viewed through the prism of the technical component alone; it must be placed within broader institutional, cultural, and ethical contexts (Zhang et al., 2026). Colleges and universities are not merely sources of knowledge transmission but also social institutions, possessing well-established norms, values, and power structures. The academic profession is based on disciplinary career traditions, tenure and promotion systems, expectations for teaching, research, and service, and the tradition of professional autonomy associated with academic work. These arrangements can be disrupted by the introduction of AI technologies, which can change how teaching effectiveness is determined, the organization of academic labor, and the priorities in institutions (Kumar et al., 2025a). In performance evaluation, e.g., more data-driven approaches can affect performance evaluation and career progression, while using standard AI platforms can restrict pedagogical freedom of choice or favor one type of knowledge over another (Buele & Llerena-Aguirre, 2025). The dynamics mentioned above have demonstrated the need to study AI as both a tool system and a socio-technical phenomenon, with long-term implications for academic careers.

The area best equipped by artificial intelligence is higher education, which extends beyond the classroom. Apart from teaching and learning, AI is also actively applied in admissions, advising, library services, research analytics, and administrative decision-making. It is possible to forecast student achievement and dropouts using predictive analytics and to recommend students on the type of course and career to pursue with the aid of AI-driven recommendation systems. AI can be used in research to support literature reviews, data analysis, and even the formulation of research hypotheses. As applications have been developed to optimize efficiency and productivity, they have also raised issues related to academic honesty, intellectual property, and the boundaries between human- and machine-generated knowledge (Mah & Groß, 2024). The faculty members, in turn, will have to navigate the intricate ecosystem in which AI can be adopted as a source and a helpful tool, as a professional threat, and as an impetus to redefine academic work. Ethical questions, equity, and trust are among the most important issues to address AI-related problems within the context of higher education (Dhiraj & Kumar, 2023a). AI systems are over-reliant on data, and they reflect what has been assumed and favored in the facts used in the datasets and algorithms that produced the results. Bias algorithms have the potential to further amplify existing unfairness in the learning environment, as they can discriminate against groups of learners or exacerbate the biased views of success (Spathopoulou et al., 2025). Academics are also increasingly being compelled to study and critically assess the ethical aspects of AI tools in subjects and institutions as tools for academic integrity and social responsibility. The faculty's activity in this responsibility takes on a different dimension, and competencies in AI literacy, data ethics, and responsible use of technology must be involved. The problems associated with such competencies presuppose that the development of the faculty, workloads, and careers will be influenced specifically in spheres where technological knowledge was not a priority (Al-Zahrani & Alasmari, 2024).

The idea behind the research on AI in education and faculty careers is to shed light on how the specified development relates to professional development, professional identity, and the sustainability of career trajectories in higher education. Although a great portion of recent AI research in education has focused on student achievement, the quality of the educational facility, or technological progress, the experiences and professional implications of staff members have received relatively little attention. These are the implications that are critical to comprehend, as faculty play a significant role in mediating the introduction and impact of AI (Abbasi et al., 2025). Their mindset, expertise, and professional beliefs about them are significant factors in the implementation of AI to facilitate learning or to annihilate the very fabric of learning. Taking the faculty career as the case of analysis, the paper will aim to reveal the human aspect of technological change and even suggest the need to be vigilant about the most impactful implementation of AI in the academic profession. The other major aim of this study is to outline the trade-off between technological enhancement and human knowledge in higher education institutions. The topic of AI has been widely discussed regarding automation and efficiency, raising concerns about the risk of losing employment, becoming a deskilled employee, or losing academic control (Kumar, 2023). There, however, exists the other side of the coin in which AI is also capable of enhancing human abilities instead of ruining them. Through this model, the routine/large-volume activity will be addressed, so that the faculty will focus on the complex, creative, and interactive aspects of teaching and research that machines cannot provide. It is the balance that must be considered when calculating the potential sustainable patterns of faculty work, so that it may utilize the opportunities of AI while retaining the particular human aspects of the educational process, including moral judgment, empathy, and critical thinking (Fawaid et al., 2025). The applicability of the implications of AI for the faculty career of academic practice in this study is quite extensive. It also takes into consideration teaching roles, assessment practices, research activities, and career growth in the context of institutions of higher learning. The discussion does not take a particular technology or disciplinary specialization, but rather an integrative point of view that acknowledges the heterogeneity of institutional types, faculty roles, and educational cultures. Such an approach would allow for a less aggressive stance on how AI can impact faculty in different ways, depending on their career stage, discipline, institutional resources, and other factors. Meanwhile, the research also acknowledges that implementing AI is not a straightforward, dynamic process, and the impact of AI on faculty careers is underdeveloped (Omar et al., 2024).

In making the scope decision, one should also consider the limitations of analysing a quickly evolving technological environment. This trend of artificial intelligence tools and applications evolving continues to rise, surpassing policy-making and empirical inquiry. This means that this type of AI analysis in higher education needs to be viewed as temporary and conditional. However, with the synthesis of the available literature, theoretical perspectives, and the development of new practices, the current study will certainly provide a rational order of knowledge regarding the implications of AI for faculty members regarding their careers. This form of structure can be used to underpin institutional strategy, professional development programs, and policy-making as a means of getting faculty to adapt to technological change without damaging academic quality and integrity (Gedrimiene et al., 2024). Finally, the logic of the current study can be justified by the fact that the future of higher education is not just technological innovation but also individuals who will develop, implement, and critically handle the technologies (Kumar et al., 2025b). Faculty members who have close relations to the perception and use of AI in academic institutions play a central role in this process. In an effort to add a new dimension to the more open and anthropocentric AI debate on learning and education, the current study aims to contribute to the future of academic professionalism as a predictor of meaningful and equitable learning experiences, rather than radical changes in AI (Alnsour et al., 2025).

ARTIFICIAL INTELLIGENCE AS THEORETICAL FOUNDATION OF EDUCATION

An artificial intelligence in teaching can best be conceived by having a clear conceptual base that defines AI, its functioning in the learning environment, its development over the years, and its consistency with conventional theories of teaching and learning. Theoretically, AI can be described as computational systems intended to work, which usually involve human intelligence, e.g., reasoning, pattern recognition, decision-making, language comprehension, and adaptive problem-solving. The conceptualization of AI in education is not an autonomous technology but a collection of other technologies and systems that engage learners, teachers, and organizational processes (Ahmed, 2025). These technologies include machine learning algorithms to process learner data, natural language processing engines to read and write, or speak, intelligent agents to guide or provide feedback, and predictive analytics to predict learning outcomes. All of these applications, combined, constitute the foundations of AI-based educational innovation, which is realized through the delivery, assessment, and optimization of knowledge in higher education (Dhiraj & Kumar, 2023b).

Regarding learning issues, AI technologies can be grouped by function and role. AI systems exist and can be applied to support instruction by streamlining material to meet each learner's needs. An example of adaptive learning platforms is the analysis of student performance in real time, which, in turn, alters the difficulty, sequence, and shape of instruction. Intelligent tutoring systems recreate the tutor-to-student aspect, providing individual students with explanations, hints, and feedback (Ouyang & Jiao, 2021). The other uses of the AI include assessment and evaluation, which involve automated marking of objective tests, essays, or coding, and analysing student responses using pattern recognition and language models. The other well-known type of analytics device is learning analytics, which gathers and processes data on students' activities, including their participation and performance, with a view to providing responses that may be further disseminated to teachers and the institution. In addition, administrative and advisory services that AI provide aid in course recommendations, scholarly advising, and threat-of-risk student warning systems. Theoretically, the variety of applications has demonstrated that AI in education is not confined to the teaching aspect but extends across the entire academic ecosystem (Geada, 2024). The history of AI within the educational setting is also insightful,, as it enables one to observe how practices have transformed in the current context and why some issues persist. One can trace the idea of introducing AI into education to the middle of the twentieth century, when scholars began attempts to address the issue of computer-assisted education (Talukder, Kumar, et al., 2024). These early systems were more rule-based, based on set instructional tracks, and inflexible. The other monumental finding in the 70s and 80s was the invention of intelligent tutoring systems, which sought to package students' knowledge and provide individualized feedback. Nevertheless, the inability to measure their effectiveness and the complexity of a human thought model were factors that limited their effectiveness. The growth of the internet and online learning environments, and the beginning of the 2000s, shifted the focus to the online learning space and learning management systems, which did not emphasize intelligence and flexibility but were devoted to the provision of the content and communication (Chiu & Chai, 2020).

The modern renaissance in AI in education refers directly to the big data, machine learning, and cloud computing trends. Compared to older models, current AI services can process large amounts of learner data and even update their models with new data. This paradigm shift toward data-oriented methods has led to significant improvements in the AI tools used in higher education and their scalability. Meanwhile, it has raised new concerns about data confidentiality, algorithmic responsibility, and moral responsibility. AI history in teaching has shown that technology slowly evolved into a learning agent as an adjunct training device in instruction. This direction needed to be made known to institutions and the faculty since it does not just suggest the opportunity but the limitations of AI-based educational innovation. The theoretical principles of AI in education are accompanied by the theoretical lenses of technology-enhanced learning as well. Learning theories also provide the conceptual context for how learners are expected to take in information and how technology in teaching is known to limit or amplify this process. Early learning technologies, which are part of AI-based evaluation systems, may be defined by their adherence to the nature of reinforcement and feedback, where learning is facilitated by repetition and immediate feedback, as per the behaviorist approach (Chen et al., 2020). The automated quizzes, adaptive exercises, and feedback system describe this orientation and ensure that learners are given the right rewards and the means to achieve the desired outcome. Although it performs well in some forms of learning, such as learning skills or memorizing facts, practice under behaviorism is not effective for every problem of higher-order thinking (Zhai et al., 2021).

The learning theories in another field of cognitive studies are concerned with the activities of the mind, including memory, problem-solving, and metacognition, which can provide a more relevant role for AI in learning investigations. Cognitive approaches are highly correlated with AI systems that simulate learners' cognitive processes, address false beliefs, or are helpful for more complex tasks. For example, intelligent tutoring systems are designed to assist learners' internal thinking systems with targeted clarifications and tips. The cognitive support from this perspective is also the role of AI, which can help learners improve their information processing, observe their knowledge, and control their learning behaviours. In relation to the faculty, this theoretical compromise leads to the realization of the value of AI use in both the efficiency context and deep, holistic learning (Roll & Wylie, 2016). Social-constructivist theory and constructivist theory can also be relevant in the ideational background, which places learning within the context of a social, active, and contextual process. These perceptions concern interaction, cooperation, and problem-solving in knowledge building. Constructivist learning can be supported by AI technologies in the context of inquiry-based learning to facilitate a collaborative learning environment, simulate real-world contexts, or provide adaptive feedback on the learning process. Meanwhile, excessive reliance on automated systems may lead to the absence of social interaction and critical discussion if they are not properly designed. This counterargument highlights one of the key conceptual issues of AI-mediated, personalized learning: the trade-off between the social and relational aspects of academic life, which is particularly significant in higher education (Talukder, Khan, et al., 2024).

Recent concepts, including connectivism and human-centred learning, can be applied specifically to the issue of AI. It is assumed that the skill of navigating and sense-making information across networks of people, technologies, and resources is a key component of learning in connectivism. This opinion matches the AI systems that suggest content, redirect learners to the most advantageous materials, or analyze learning networks rather well. Conversely, humanistic models of learning are agency-oriented, moral and inclusive in the utilization of technology. In this perspective, AI must be designed and integrated in such a way that it can power learners, not think about them, but empower them (Xia et al., 2022). The theories put faculty and other institutions in a difficult position because they are tasked with critically analyzing the effects of AI on power relations, choice, and teaching values. Collectively, as a community, the philosophical underpinnings of AI in education have shown that AI is not an apolitical, purely technical phenomenon. Historical changes have influenced its definition, construction, and application through theories and institutional concerns. Faculty in higher education should be conversant with these foundations to become informed and thoughtful in their interactions with AI. As an alternative to viewing AI as an external force within academic practice, faculty members may locate AI within broader pedagogical terms and practices, thereby giving them the opportunity to make a more strategic choice about the essence and implications of AI in teaching and learning. On this conceptual basis, the potential of AI to improve the quality of education and protect the major human values on which the idea of higher education is founded can be considered (Yang, 2022).

AI-DRIVEN TRANSFORMATIONS IN TEACHING AND LEARNING

This application of artificial intelligence in education is changing how education is delivered and learned, how education is assessed and even how education choices are made. One of the most noticeable transformations should be the growing use of smart systems that make the learning process for students more individualized. AI-based applications can examine performance trends, specific behaviour during the learning process, and modify the information and the instructional course. It is this type of individualizing that disrupts the traditional concept of higher education as a one-size-fits-all and enables the instructors to better meet the needs of different learners. Consequently, the teaching process is slowly becoming less predetermined, with uniform content presentation, and more open and student-oriented, where the teacher becomes more of a guide, an assistant, and a facilitator of the learning process (Zootzky & Pfeiffer, 2024). The other significant change that is articulated is the field of assessment and feedback. Assignments, quizzes, essays, and even some complex issues can be evaluated with the help of AI systems, which will offer students extensive feedback in the near future. This positive feedback is applicable during the continuous learning process, and students can detect misconceptions as they occur and rectify them. Automation of faculty tasks saves time on tedious grade work, freeing up time that would otherwise be utilized for higher-level academic tasks such as curriculum development, research, archiving, and mentoring. Nevertheless, such a change should also allow the faculty to scrutinize this automated assessment critically and ensure that it is valid, fair, and aligned with learning objectives. The human factor is another factor that greatly contributes to the interpretation of results because it involves sensitive student work and the upholding of academic standards (Srivastava et al., 2025).

Another critical concern regarding the teaching and learning changes with AI is learning analytics. The AI systems generate insights for the educational process and the organization's policies by analyzing overwhelming data on students' participation, performance, and engagement. Faculty members can use this to identify students at risk, discuss the effectiveness of instructional methods, and improve course design. This evidence-based practice can contribute to the further evolution of higher education by enabling teaching and intervention to be grounded in data and making the educational process more adaptable and open to new visions. Simultaneously, it raises serious concerns about data privacy and surveillance, the ethical use of student data, and the ethical implications of big data. Faculty members need to learn to use technologies more responsibly and learn data literacy. AI-Driven Transformations in Teaching and Learning are shown in Table 1.

Table 1: AI-Driven Transformations in Teaching and Learning; Source: Author Contributions

AI Application Area	Key Features	Impact on Teaching Practices	Impact on Student Learning	Implications for Faculty
Intelligent Tutoring Systems & Adaptive Learning Platforms	Personalization, real-time adaptation, learner modeling	Supports differentiated instruction and targeted interventions	Enhances individualized learning pace and mastery	Shift from content delivery to mentoring and facilitation
Automated Assessment & Feedback Mechanisms	Automated grading, instant feedback, scalability	Reduces assessment workload and improves efficiency	Provides timely feedback and continuous improvement	Requires oversight, rubric design, and ethical judgment
Learning Analytics & Data-Driven Decision Making	Data collection, predictive analytics, dashboards	Informs instructional decisions and course redesign	Identifies learning gaps and engagement patterns	Demands data literacy and responsible data use

Collectively, these AI-driven transformations signify a fundamental shift in the teaching–learning relationship. Knowledge transmission is increasingly supported by intelligent systems, while the faculty role evolves to facilitate critical thinking, foster meaningful engagement, and apply human judgment where automation falls short. Teaching becomes more analytical, reflective, and strategic, relying on both technological insights and pedagogical expertise. For students, learning becomes more personalized, interactive, and feedback-rich, potentially enhancing motivation and academic success. These changes underscore that AI does not replace educators but redefines their role within a more complex, data-informed, and learner-centered educational ecosystem.

IMPLICATIONS OF AI FOR FACULTY ROLES AND PROFESSIONAL IDENTITY

The concept of artificial intelligence is changing the faculty role in higher education, not only by enabling the use of new tools and technologies that are radically altering the nature of professional identity, faculty roles, and the conceptualization of academic knowledge. The faculty members have historically been placed at the center stage in the imparting of knowledge, curriculum advancement, evaluation, and scholarly review. As teaching and learning processes are enabled by AI, intelligent systems, and human teachers, these systems share much of the load. Unchallenging learning activities, such as content delivery, assessment, and simple feedback, are gradually being assisted or even partially automated by an AI-based application (Leandro et al., 2024). This change disrupts the habitual order of the teaching process and prompts the faculty to rethink how their time, talents, and intellectual property can be used in the academic setting in the most optimal manner.

The alteration in the nature of instructional roles is one of the AI implications with the most profound effects on the faculty. With AI systems in place for personalization, assessment, and data analysis, the faculty members no longer have concerns about the repetitive or administrative nature of teaching, but are occupied with the larger matters of pedagogy. Education is becoming a process that involves learning analytics decoding, understanding student needs, creating valuable learning opportunities, and using AI tools in pedagogically practical ways. The faculty members must make conscious judgments about the use of AI, including when and how it will be used, to maintain alignment between learning outcomes and ethical considerations. New areas of knowledge emerge with this increased responsibility, such as AI literacy, digital pedagogy, and data ethics, which are added to academic professionalism. One of the major changes in professional identity is the faculty role shifting to become a facilitator of learning, a mentor, and a designer of learning. The faculty will instead direct students to more complex learning processes rather than engage them directly as lecturers or content experts, which they facilitate through AI-enhanced environments. Facilitation is an action that entails the creation of postulates of critical inquiry, discourse and reflection, in which the outside that is not capable of being generated in automated systems, students will be permitted to interact with the concepts. Mentorship becomes more confrontational when faculty members play a role in intellectual development, rational thinking, and self-development, requiring empathy, contextual perception, and human judgment. Meanwhile, the faculty members become the learning designers, which implies that they are particularly attentive to creating curricula, activities, and tests that make the most of AI without sacrificing human interaction or learning quality.

The redefinition of academic expertise in the AI era is another implication of major significance to faculty professional identity. Proficiency is no longer determined by the ability to master disciplinary knowledge, but rather by the capacity to inculcate the technology, pedagogy, and ethical rationale. Faculty knowledge is currently sufficient to critically evaluate AI tools, understand their flaws, and use them to facilitate learning rather than mediate it. This redefinition puts the old structures of knowledge and power into question, and (in certain instances) students may be less well informed or fed back by individual instructors than they themselves are capable of doing. As a reaction to this, faculty knowledge is reorganized as interpretive, integrative, judgmental, and focused on critical thinking, contextualization, and interdisciplinary synthesis of knowledge. The introduction of AI also affects faculty perceptions of their professional agency and autonomy. The mechanism by which AI technologies can provide educators with greater insights and efficiencies can also limit academic freedom, as it often occurs with minimal consultation of the faculty. Prescriptive or External.: There is a manner in which algorithms, standardized platforms, and data-based performance measures can intervene in teaching practice and the assessment process. Such dynamics can shape the morale and identity of the faculty and its sense of ownership of its work. In this way, the interaction among faculty in the planning, administration, and assessment of AI projects is significant in transforming technologies with academic values and, rather, leads to professional identity.

Overall, the implications of AI for faculty work and professional identity are part of a broader shift in academic work in higher education. AI does not encroach on the faculty's knowledge; instead, it transforms it and makes it more useful. Faculty are also increasingly being placed in a more reflective practitioner role, where they are capable of integrating disciplinary learning with pedagogical competency, technology awareness, and moral accountability. The transforming identity also underlines that the essential element of education, which is human judgment, human creativity/

interaction of relationships, will remain significant irrespective of the rise in the infiltration of intelligent systems in the academic life.

RESEARCH FACULTY DEVELOPMENT RESEARCH IN A FACULTY OF ARTIFICIAL INTELLIGENCE

The relentless impact of artificial intelligence on the faculty profession in colleges is massive, transforming the capabilities of the academic sector, the professional development culture, and the standards by which academic work is conducted and analyzed. The fields of disciplinary knowledge and the conventional indicators of teaching and research results will no longer define career development in an academic setting with the help of AI. Rather, it is expanding to connote greater technological fluency, adaptability, and the ability to engage intelligent systems critically and ethically. The faculty members have to grapple with an environment that is changing rapidly, where AI is affecting teaching, research, and institutional demands, and the nature of the academic career involves a lifelong learning process. The core of AI literacy and digital skills has been incorporated into faculty career development. AI literacy does not mean only basic technical knowledge, but also understanding the functionality of AI systems, how they process information, and how to read and analyze their results. The faculty members should be able to determine the pedagogical worth of AI tools, understand their drawbacks, and be aware of potential biases or ethical issues. The possibility to integrate AI technologies into the course material, assessment scheme, and research task is also supported by digital skills and can be used to enhance the learning process and educational efficiency. The competencies are progressively viewed as less optional and more and more talked of as the primary factors in academic professionalism in various fields, with the additional assimilation of AI in higher education.

The development of an AI-driven professional environment presupposes a transition to ongoing, flexible learning systems. The old methods of training, which are held once, are not always enough to keep up with the rapid development of AI technology. Rather, faculty development should be based on opportunities for continuous learning, peer experimentation, and innovation. Faculty can be assisted in gaining confidence and competence in the responsible use of AI through workshops, communities of practice, mentoring programs, and interdisciplinary collaborations. Institutional support makes up a significant percentage of this process, providing access to resources, time to learn professionally, and guidance on how much effort should be put into adapting to new technologies. In the absence of such support, inequities between faculty who can use AI and those who cannot can emerge due to workload, access, or prior experience issues. Career development, assessment, and reward systems are also evolving as AI becomes available in academic work. The traditional appraisal procedures used in higher education have long been obsessed with research publications and student scores in instruction, and less with pedagogy and the creation of technology integration. Examples of personnel contributions to an AI-enabled environment include designing AI-enhanced curricula, developing digital learning objects, teaching AI-inspired courses, or just joining an AI project within the institution. This type of work should be realized and paid in accordance with the career motivators to the organizational goals of innovation and good education. Concurrently, there is a risk that they may oversimplify and distort faculty performance unless data-driven evaluation tools are applied in a considerate and transparent manner.

Equity and inclusion are another critical issue in AI's impact on faculty career development. Different access to training, institutional resources, and technological infrastructure among faculty members can be the root cause of this difference in access to AI work and the resultant career advancement. Scholars in their initial employment, adjuncts, and those in teaching-intensive jobs might experience difficulties learning the skills associated with AI and meeting current professional demands. To correct these imbalances, they need to be consciously addressed by policy and practice that would not only bring equal access to the means of professional development, but also recognize the variety of forms of academic contribution. In this manner, the institutions will be in a position to facilitate more holistic and sustainable frameworks of faculty career development in the AI age. The profession of faculty working in an academic setting that utilizes AI has become more complicated, open, and accountable. AI also creates new opportunities for both innovation and professional development and requires flexibility and ethical consciousness, not least. The ability to create an organizational culture that supports the value of lifelong learning, the importance of academic work in its new manifestations, and provides faculty members with the chance to determine the role of AI in higher education is the key to successful career development. Through this approach, AI will be able to serve as an engine of career development in academia rather than a source of confusion and disruption.

ETHICAL, LEGAL, AND POLICY CONSIDERATIONS

The innovations in artificial intelligence in higher education are a trend with many ethical, legal, and policy-related questions at its heart, which constitute the basis for the responsible use of technology in education. As the use of AI systems in teaching, learning, evaluation, and administration continues to grow, the issues of integrity, fairness, accountability, and governance have become urgent. Faculty members who not only use AI technologies but also uphold academic values and norms are particularly worth considering. To solve such problems, it is better to strike a fine balance between innovation and responsibility so that AI is employed to improve the quality of education without compromising trust, equity, and academic freedom. One of the simplest AI ethical issues to notice in higher education is academic integrity. The uses of AI-driven technology, capable of producing text, tackling problems, or writing assignments, threaten the conventional perception of the work of an author, originality, and evaluation. The faculty should also find a fine line between using AI as a legitimate learning resource and ensuring it does not fall into the wrong hands and thereby jeopardize academic integrity. One option for using AI responsibly is to set boundaries between what is possible and what is not, create tests that require critical thinking and creativity, and teach students the importance of responsible use of AI technologies. The integrity-based approach to the problem is not grounded in detection and enforcement but is more focused on transparency, logical, ethical reasoning, and building students' responsibility toward the use of AI as an aspect of academic and professional development.

The other important group of ethical and legal issues is data privacy, surveillance and algorithmic prejudice. The AI systems applied in the education sphere are most dependent on the gathering and analysis of student and faculty information, such as performance, behavioural patterns, and personal data. Although the possibility of data can make the personalized learning process easier and provide early interventions, the issues are consent, data security, and over-surveillance. The opportunities include the ability to evaluate or trace faculty using data, and the fact that professionals have fewer opportunities to make decisions. Moreover, AI bias may be induced when inequalities are reflected in the training materials or in the design assumptions, and later manifest as biased outcomes detrimental to particular groups of students or teachers. These risks should be addressed through intensive legal protections, transparency in algorithmic decision-making, and the faculty's proactive participation in investigating the effectiveness and applicability of AI tools. The institutions governing systems and policies might also not be effective in how ethical and legal issues are actually resolved. It entails the adoption, use, and review of AI technologies in learning, research, and administration, which must be informed by clear policies. Such policies ought to manifest the principles of AI responsible use, encompassing accountability, transparency, inclusivity, and respect for academic freedom. The government bodies where the faculty members may be identified can be sure that the conclusions made regarding AI are not related to efficiency and cost-effectiveness, but are based on pedagogical outcomes and practising principles. Other effective governance practices include periodic revision and amendment of policies to ensure they do not lag behind technological developments and legal provisions.

The ethical and compliance section is closely connected to the legal one, especially in terms of disclosing data protection legislation, IP, and adherence to the regulatory architecture. The institutions should ensure that AI systems comply with applicable legal requirements and inform faculty of their rights and responsibilities. This involves defining topics such as who owns AI-generated content, where to stand in case of errors or damages caused by automated processes, and the legal issues surrounding the cross-border transfer of data on the platform of international education. The intent and expertise in these elements of practice in AI-enabled academic activities are needed to feel responsible and prepared to perform AI-enabled academic work. In general, the sustainable and trustworthy implementation of AI in higher education can be grounded in ethical, legal, and policy considerations. Constantly resolving such problems, as well as promoting the fundamental principles of academic honesty, equity, and intellectual freedom, could preserve the interests of students and faculty. When ethical reasoning, adherence to the law, and inclusive governance become the primary pillars of AI projects, colleges and universities can establish the conditions under which technological innovation serves, rather than substitutes for, the human and social objectives of education. Ethical, Legal, and Policy Considerations of AI in Higher Education are shown in Table 2.

Table 2: Ethical, Legal, and Policy Considerations of AI in Higher Education; Source: Author Contributions

Aspect	Key Concern	Faculty Implication
Academic Integrity	Misuse of AI tools in assessments	Redesign of evaluation methods
Data Privacy	Collection and monitoring of data	Protection of autonomy and trust
Algorithmic Bias	Unfair or biased AI outcomes	Ethical oversight of AI use
Legal Compliance	Data protection and IP rights	Awareness of legal responsibilities
Institutional Policy	Lack of clear AI guidelines	Need for faculty involvement

INSTITUTIONAL SUPPORT AND STRATEGIC IMPLEMENTATION

Artificial intelligence implementation in higher education ought to be strategic and institutionally supported to be successful and sustainable. The adoption of AI with high-level technologies is what determines its success, but it depends on the willingness of institutions to balance the leadership's vision, organizational structures, and valued academic colleges with technological change. During preparation, change management should also be considered, as when faculty are introduced to new technologies, they may experience uncertainty or resistance. Organisations that engage in significant communication and dialogue, and are conducive to experimentation, have a more comfortable, motivating environment in which faculty are more willing and motivated to engage with AI in a positive way.= The success of the implementation of AI is conditional on the sufficient number of infrastructures and resources, and technical assistance. A robust digital infrastructure, the use of appropriate AI tools, and continuous technical support should be available to faculty members to implement AI in teaching and research. Without this support, even well-planned programs would merely increase the burden and disappointment in the work, rather than making it productive. The investment in infrastructure should be accompanied by training and support mechanisms that enable the faculty to become competent enough to utilise AI effectively and responsibly. Access to resources should also be equal so that there are no inequalities among the different departments, disciplines, or faculty groups.

An innovative and ethical culture should also be developed to succeed in the long term. The culture of this type fosters experimentation, reflective practice, and self-managed learning, and bases innovation on common ethical values. The ways in which institutions could foster such a culture are by rewarding and acknowledging new pedagogical practices, fostering cross-disciplinary cooperation, and incorporating ethical considerations into the policies of AIs and career advancement programmes. Faculty are in a better position to discuss concerns about integrity, privacy, and fairness in day-to-day academic practice, in terms of moral thought. Combined with institutional support and implementation plans, AI will be installed as an instrument of learning and staff training rather than a machine of havoc and injustice.

FACULTY PROMOTION AND EVALUATION WORKLOAD

Faculty promotion and evaluation workload: It is the duties and tasks associated with evaluating teachers' performance and determining their promotion in educational institutions. This process is essential for ensuring the quality of education and promoting teachers' skill and performance improvement. Faculty evaluation responsibilities include the preparation of evaluation reports, the review of teaching approach, the monitoring of research activities and faculty's contributions to the institution. Teachers are judged on their classroom performance, student feedback, publications, seminars & administration. Colleges or universities make promotion decisions after a careful consideration of these factors by the committees set up by colleges or universities. In general, promotion to faculty is dependent on experience, qualifications, research and overall contribution to the institution. Rewards encourage educators to improve their performance and professional development. But it can add to the teacher's and administration's workload as they have to document, meet, and assess in detail. A clear and open promotion system must be provided to reward and offer opportunities to the worthy teacher. A proper evaluation and a balanced workload make education more effective and helps to build a positive education atmosphere for teachers and students.

HIGHER EDUCATION PROBLEMS AND ISSUES FACULTY

Artificial intelligence in higher education is a complex conglomeration of challenges and opportunities that not only shape the experience of higher education but also dictate its future. Resistance to change is one of the most troubling problems, and it is largely driven by technological anxiety, uncertainty, and fears of being irrelevant as a professional. The faculty can also believe that AI can reduce the cost of their experience, introduce additional surveillance, or create unrealistic productivity/availability expectations. Such fear is especially high among those with little prior experience with high-tech equipment or in institutional cultures that lack sufficient support for experimentation and learning. The resistance cannot simply be a personal complaint; it is representative of a broader structural concern about workload, power, and recognition, which makes understanding how to find complex, thorough ways to address technological transformation difficult. The other pertinent issue is the tension between automation and human judgment. Although AI systems are effective for grading, content recommendation, and data analysis, the ability to think within context, make ethical decisions, and express emotions is central to competent teaching. The downside of excessive automation is that education will become a mechanical process devoid of appreciation for art or the human element of learning. Professional discretion must therefore be exercised in a way that allows the faculty to determine when and how AI will be used, without making technology a substitute for human contact and critical questioning. This equilibrium should be constantly reconsidered within the context of pedagogic knowledge, with less institutional politics that tend to be more efficiency-oriented, and with a human-centred education.

Simultaneously, AI offers significant opportunities for innovation and improved teaching performance. Artificial intelligence will give faculty more time to practice creative curriculum design, conduct one-on-one mentoring, and pursue scholarship, as it will reduce the routine workload on the administration. The proposed AI-informed learning patterns can be implemented within evidence-based teaching practices, improving the learning process and student interactions and facilitating better learning outcomes. The faculty can test new pedagogical interventions (adaptive learning, flipped classes, and data-driven interventions) that were challenging to scale before. Professional satisfaction and faculty rebranding as the place where meaningful and successful learning experiences can be made possible can be promoted through such opportunities, when the right training and institutional support are in place. AI in higher education presents many issues and opportunities that are closely intertwined. Resistance and anxiety are also curable characteristics, since the realization of AI's benefits through wise integration without disruptive academic values is possible through the development of an inclusive and professional governance. Critically and creatively applying AI will empower faculty to tap into the possible distraction to create opportunities to enhance, innovate, and redefine professional purpose in a dynamic educational environment.

ARTIFICIAL INTELLIGENCE AND FACULTY CAREERS OF HIGHER EDUCATION

It is believed that artificial intelligence in the higher education sector will continue to redefine the learning process and the profession of teachers in the future. As AI technologies become more advanced and are increasingly applied, they will be used in teaching, research, and academic administration to reinvent the principles of how faculty work is organized and assessed. According to current trends, there is a movement toward more seamless, integrated AI systems that work with learning systems, evaluation instruments, and institutional decision-making systems. Changes of this kind ought to improve personalization, scalability, and educational efficiency, and raise major concerns about professional roles, autonomy, and accountability. Faculty will need to labour in a dynamic environment, and flexibility and on-the-job learning are the factors that determine a sustainable career. The most noticeable trend in AI applications in education is the increased adoption of generative AI and sophisticated analytics to support content development, instructional design, and research. As a matter of fact, AI tools may already be utilized to support the development of curricula, learning materials, and interdisciplinary research. The virtual teaching assistants and speaking agents can become popular and provide 24-hour service to students, leaving the faculty with the most frequently asked questions. Ethical and human AI is now gaining popularity, and more implications on transparency, fairness and inclusiveness are being considered. All these trends indicate that the further introduction of AI will not be limited to technological potential but will also address the need to align innovation with the value of education and social responsibility.

The implications for faculty in such developments are multi-dimensional and complex, particularly in terms of workload and job security. On the one hand, AI can be used to help decrease the administrative load and ease the routine so that the faculty members might spend more time teaching, mentoring, and researching. Conversely, there is always a fear that the working environment will get tough as a result of the efficiency drive, and this may lead to an increase in demand for productivity, responsiveness, and outcome measurement. Another area that could affect faculty is the displacement of jobs or the casualization of academic labour, especially in teaching-intensive or contingent positions. To overcome these anxieties, there is a need for specific institutional policies that aim to augment rather than substitute, ensuring that AI will never contribute to unsustainable workloads or that the traditional part of higher education involving human beings will not be lost.

Future research, policy, and practice areas should be recommended to ensure that AI becomes a career for one faculty member. The research will have to examine the long-term effects of AI on academic work and career self, as well as equity in another institution and discipline. Policymakers and the institution's leaders ought to develop methods to establish inclusive governance systems that integrate faculty into the decision-making process while maintaining academic freedom. In practice, institutions are expected to invest in professional development, recognize the contributions to AI evaluation systems, and develop ethical considerations for AI applications. A possible future with AI adding to faculty careers, providing high- and excellent-quality education, and cherishing the primary ideals of the academic profession, can be achieved through a more proactive, collaborative approach in higher education.

CONCLUSION

Artificial intelligence in learning and education is an important paradigm shift in higher education, and the impacts of AI in faculty jobs, professional identity, and institutional practice are incredibly broad. In this argument, AIs have not only been referred to as a technological breakthrough but also as a revolution transforming teaching, learning, assessment, and academic activities. The primary observation that emerges from this debate is that AI is radically altering the character of the distribution of educational roles between intelligent machines and human beings, and that faculty members would need to redefine their roles and restore the significance of human knowledge in higher education. One of the most significant lessons is that AI-based technologies could be introduced to facilitate education on personalization, timely feedback, and data-driven decision-making. To make education practices more responsive and efficient, learning analytics, smarter tutoring systems, and automated evaluation tools will be utilized. However, they are all directly associated with the faculty's capacity to be critical and ethical in the use of AI tools. Instead of replacing teaching staff, AI also transforms the role of faculty into a more facilitative, mentoring, curriculum-developing, and teaching role in terms of way of thinking and in learning how to acquire morality and moral reasoning. This redefinition underscores the need for faculty expertise, especially in areas where judgment, situational knowledge, and human relations cannot be overlooked. Both the practical and strategic implications for the institution and the faculty are significant. As far as the faculty is concerned, AI requires the emergence of new competencies, e.g. AI literacy, digital pedagogy, and ethical awareness. The most important element of career sustainability is continuous intellectual growth, since faculty members must be qualified to keep up with technological advances without a decline in the quality of the discipline. The successful implementation of AI will demand robust leadership, adequate infrastructure, inclusive governance, and policies that can appreciate and compensate for new types of academic work at the institutional level. The ethical and legal implications pertinent to institutions to be considered include academic integrity, data privacy, and algorithmic bias, as the implementation of AI should be organized in compliance with the values and social responsibility of the educational profession.

As far as the future is concerned, one can conclude that AI's efficiency in higher education will be based on a human and balanced approach. The technological growth per se will not assist, and the most radical change can be enabled when AI is consumed responsibly, with the faculty introduced as co-producers of the change, rather than an inactive consumer of it. Arguably, the commitment to teamwork, the encouragement of professional development, and the ethical reflection behind AI projects can also enable institutions of higher learning to embrace the transformative opportunities of AI without compromising the principal values of life in an academic environment. Finally, AI should be treated as a component that adds value and supplements faculty members' efforts, enabling them to create an inclusive, innovative, and thought-provoking learning experience in a setting that is more complex than ever.

REFERENCES

Abbasi, B. N., Wu, Y., & Luo, Z. (2025). Exploring the impact of artificial intelligence on curriculum development in global higher education institutions. *Education and Information Technologies, 30*(1), 547–581. DOI: 10.1007/s10639-024-13113-z

Ahmed, A.M (2025). Theoretical foundations of artificial intelligence and its applications in Arab e-learning. *Libyan Journal of Educational Research and E-Learning (LJERE)*, 31–41. DOI: 10.65417/ljere.v1i1.4

Al-Zahrani, A. M., & Alasmari, T. M. (2024). Exploring the impact of artificial intelligence on higher education: The dynamics of ethical, social, and educational implications. *Humanities & Social Sciences Communications, 11*(1), 912. DOI: 10.1057/s41599-024-03432-4

Alnsour, M. M., Qouzah, L., Aljamani, S., Alamoush, R. A., & AL-Omiri, M. K. (2025). AI in education: Enhancing learning potential and addressing ethical considerations among academic staff—a cross-sectional study at the University of Jordan. *International Journal for Educational Integrity, 21*(1), 16. DOI: 10.1007/s40979-025-00189-4

Buele, J., & Llerena-Aguirre, L. (2025). Transformations in academic work and faculty perceptions of artificial intelligence in higher education. *Frontiers in Education, 10*, 1603763. DOI: 10.3389/feduc.2025.1603763

Chen, L., Chen, P., & Lin, Z. (2020). Artificial Intelligence in Education: A Review. *IEEE Access : Practical Innovations, Open Solutions, 8*, 75264–75278. DOI: 10.1109/ACCESS.2020.2988510

Chiu, T. K. F., & Chai, C. (2020). Sustainable Curriculum Planning for Artificial Intelligence Education: A Self-Determination Theory Perspective. *Sustainability (Basel), 12*(14), 5568. DOI: 10.3390/su12145568

Dhiraj, A., & Kumar, P. D. S. (2023a). Impact of E-learning on the Higher Education Sector during the COVID-19 pandemic through Pedagogy tools: An observational Study. *Revista de Educación y Derecho*, (27). Advance online publication. DOI: 10.1344/REYD2023.27.40935

Dhiraj, A., & Kumar, P. D. S. (2023b). Impact of E-learning on the Higher Education Sector during the COVID-19 pandemic through Pedagogy tools: An observational Study. *Revista de Educación y Derecho*, (27). Advance online publication. DOI: 10.1344/REYD2023.27.40935

Farooq, U., Malik, S. A., & Syed, A. S. (2024). REVOLUTIONIZING HIGHER EDUCATION: THE TRANSFORMATIVE IMPACT OF ARTIFICIAL INTELLIGENCE ON TEACHING, LEARNING, AND CAREER PREPARATION. *ShodhKosh: Journal of Visual and Performing Arts*, *5*(3). Advance online publication. DOI: 10.29121/shodhkosh.v5.i3.2024.3239

Fawaid, A., Baharun, H., & Hamzah, M., Rohimah, Munawwaroh, I., & Putri, D. F. (2025). AI-based career management to improve the quality of decision making in higher education. *2025 IEEE Integrated STEM Education Conference (ISEC)*, 1–8. DOI: 10.1109/ISEC64801.2025.11147274

Geada, N. (2024). Artificial Intelligence: Theoretical Foundations, Applications, and Societal Implications. In Geada, N., Sood, R., & Sidana, A. (Eds.), (pp. 226–244). Advances in Finance, Accounting, and Economics. IGI Global., DOI: 10.4018/979-8-3693-1758-7.ch012

Gedrimiene, E., Celik, I., Kaasila, A., Mäkitalo, K., & Muukkonen, H. (2024). Artificial Intelligence (AI)-enhanced learning analytics (LA) for supporting Career decisions: Advantages and challenges from user perspective. *Education and Information Technologies*, *29*(1), 297–322. DOI: 10.1007/s10639-023-12277-4

Kumar, S. (2023). Impact of Digitalization in Higher Education and Smart Learning Techniques. In Nadda, V., Tyagi, P. K., Moniz Vieira, R., & Tyagi, P. (Eds.), *Advances in Hospitality, Tourism, and the Services Industry* (pp. 198–207). IGI Global., DOI: 10.4018/979-8-3693-0650-5.ch013

Kumar, S., Talukder, M. B., & Tyagi, P. K. (2025a). The Impact of Virtual Reality and Augmented Reality in TNE Learning. In Crawford, C. M., & Gee, T. T. (Eds.), *Motivating Engagement, Belonging, and Success in Higher Education Student Experience* (pp. 359–382). IGI Global., DOI: 10.4018/979-8-3693-8089-5.ch013

Kumar, S., Talukder, M. B., & Tyagi, P. K. (2025b). The Impact of Virtual Reality and Augmented Reality in TNE Learning. In Crawford, C. M., & Gee, T. T. (Eds.), *Motivating Engagement, Belonging, and Success in Higher Education Student Experience* (pp. 359–382). IGI Global., DOI: 10.4018/979-8-3693-8089-5.ch013

Leandro, G. D. S. M., Kumar, S., Jacinto Da Gama, M., Carvalho, H., & Leandro, E. (2024). Circular Economy Practices in the Hotel Sector in Luanda, Angola: Challenges and Future Perspectives. In P. K. Tyagi, V. Nadda, K. Kankaew, & K. Dube (Eds.), *Advances in Hospitality, Tourism, and the Services Industry* (pp. 54–66). IGI Global. DOI: 10.4018/979-8-3693-4042-4.ch004

Lee, D., Arnold, M., Srivastava, A., Plastow, K., Strelan, P., Ploeckl, F., Lekkas, D., & Palmer, E. (2024). The impact of generative AI on higher education learning and teaching: A study of educators' perspectives. *Computers and Education: Artificial Intelligence*, *6*, 100221. DOI: 10.1016/j.caeai.2024.100221

Mah, D.-K., & Groß, N. (2024). Artificial intelligence in higher education: Exploring faculty use, self-efficacy, distinct profiles, and professional development needs. *International Journal of Educational Technology in Higher Education*, *21*(1), 58. DOI: 10.1186/s41239-024-00490-1

Omar, A., Shaqour, A. Z., & Khlaif, Z. N. (2024). Attitudes of faculty members in Palestinian universities toward employing artificial intelligence applications in higher education: Opportunities and challenges. *Frontiers in Education*, *9*, 1414606. DOI: 10.3389/feduc.2024.1414606

Ouyang, F., & Jiao, P. (2021). Artificial intelligence in education: The three paradigms. *Computers and Education: Artificial Intelligence*, *2*, 100020. DOI: 10.1016/j.caeai.2021.100020

Popenici, S. A. D., & Kerr, S. (2017). Exploring the impact of artificial intelligence on teaching and learning in higher education. *Research and Practice in Technology Enhanced Learning*, *12*(1), 22. DOI: 10.1186/s41039-017-0062-8 PMID: 30595727

Roll, I., & Wylie, R. (2016). Evolution and Revolution in Artificial Intelligence in Education. *International Journal of Artificial Intelligence in Education*, *26*(2), 582–599. DOI: 10.1007/s40593-016-0110-3

Spathopoulou, F., Pitychoutis, K. M., & Papakonstantinidis, S. (2025). AI and higher education: Understanding faculty roles in teaching, research, and administration. *Contemporary Educational Technology*, *17*(4), ep600. DOI: 10.30935/cedtech/17406

Srivastava, A., Kumar, A. V. S., Maheshwari, D., & Ray, S. (2025). *Artificial Intelligence and Human Existence: Insights on Education, Technology, and Society* (1st ed.). CRC Press., DOI: 10.1201/9781003560463

Talukder, M. B., Khan, M. R., & Kumar, S. (2024). Socioeconomic Gaps and Foster Inclusive Growth: Sustainable Tourism Initiatives. In Hassan, V., Staszewska, A., & Bhartiya, S. (Eds.), *Advances in Hospitality, Tourism, and the Services Industry* (pp. 56–82). IGI Global., DOI: 10.4018/979-8-3693-5405-6.ch003

Talukder, M. B., Kumar, S., & Das, I. R. (2024). Mindful Consumers and New Marketing Strategies for the Restaurant Business: Evidence of Bangladesh. In Ramos, C. M. Q., Costa, T., Severino, F. S., & Calisto, M. D. L. (Eds.), *Advances in Hospitality, Tourism, and the Services Industry* (pp. 240–260). IGI Global., DOI: 10.4018/979-8-3693-0960-5.ch010

Xia, Q., Chiu, T. K. F., Lee, M., Sanusi, I. T., Dai, Y., & Chai, C. S. (2022). A self-determination theory (SDT) design approach for inclusive and diverse artificial intelligence (AI) education. *Computers & Education*, *189*, 104582. DOI: 10.1016/j.compedu.2022.104582

Yang, W. (2022). Artificial Intelligence education for young children: Why, what, and how in curriculum design and implementation. *Computers and Education: Artificial Intelligence*, *3*, 100061. DOI: 10.1016/j.caeai.2022.100061

Zhai, X., Chu, X., Chai, C. S., Jong, M. S. Y., Istenic, A., Spector, M., Liu, J.-B., Yuan, J., & Li, Y. (2021). A Review of Artificial Intelligence (AI) in Education from 2010 to 2020. *Complexity*, *2021*(1), 8812542. DOI: 10.1155/2021/8812542

Zhang, W., Guo, X., & Xie, J. (2026). Leveraging artificial intelligence and Big Data Analytics to model career progression and professional development pathways of higher education faculty. *Australian Journal of Electrical and Electronics Engineering*, 1–20. DOI: 10.1080/1448837X.2026.2614868

Zootzky, G., & Pfeiffer, A. (2024). Educational Transformation Through Ai: Preparing For A New Era Of Learning. 1202–1207. DOI: 10.21125/inted.2024.0382

Chapter 4
Can AI Improve Faculty Organisational Commitment and Reduce Turnover Intention?
Evidence From Private Higher Education Institutions

Ritu Arora
http://orcid.org/0009-0006-0148-4141
Chandigarh University, India

Azmee Zaheer
Chandigarh University, India

ABSTRACT

The fast adoption of Artificial Intelligence within private higher learning institutions has immensely changed the academic and administrative processes, thus impacting that of the faculty and organisational performance. This paper will discuss how perceptions of AI by the faculty members, in terms of perceived AI usefulness, perceived AI-driven workload reduction, perceived AI-based decision fairness, and perceived AI-enabled organisational support influence organisational commitment and turnover intention. Quantitative and cross-sectional research design was adopted and 520 respondents' private universities in India were sampled and primary data were obtained. Structural Equation Modeling was used to analyse the data to evaluate the measurement and structural relationships. The results reveal that the existence

DOI: 10.4018/979-8-2600-3204-6.ch004

of positive attitudes to AI as helpful, equitable, supporting, and workload-saving has a strong positive impact on the organisational commitment and indirectly on the turnover intentions of faculty members.

INTRODUCTION

The higher education sector is in the midst of radical change occasioned by rapid technological change, digitalization, and growing competition among institutions. Universities, especially private higher education institutions, are adopting sophisticated digital infrastructures and intelligent systems to improve academic efficiency, administration, and institutional performance. Within the changing academic ecosystem, technology is not merely about automating administration but is now deeply integrated into education, research administration, student analytics, and the institution's decision-making processes (Aithal & Maiya, 2023; Verboom et al., 2025). Technology-driven systems are therefore changing the way academic work and organizational environments are undertaken in universities.

One of these technological developments has been Artificial Intelligence (AI), which has become a game-changer in institutions of higher learning. Academic analytics, automated assessment, scheduling, communication, performance monitoring, and institutional management are also AI-based platforms that universities are deploying to enhance efficiency, transparency, and decision accuracy (Buele & Llerena-Aguirre, 2025; Robinson, 2025). Institutional portals, learning management systems, and data-driven academic tools are not alone; AI-integrated systems are also affecting the effectiveness of operations, faculty workload, professional autonomy, and interactions with institutional processes. Therefore, AI is slowly shifting from a technological innovation to a powerful organizational factor that shapes employees' perceptions and experiences at work.

Faculty members are a very important resource in higher education institutions, and their stability is critical to the quality of the institution, the quantity of research conducted, and the institution's sustainability. High faculty turnover disrupts academic continuity and increases recruitment and training expenses. Organizational commitment is a key factor in retention, as committed employees exhibit stronger attachment and lower turnover intentions (Guzeller & Celiker, 2020; Mensele & Coetzee, 2014). The growing performance demands and technological adaptation further emphasize the need to investigate the factors affecting commitment and turnover in higher education (Qiong et al., 2025; Parmar et al., 2022). In addition, the perceptions of usefulness, fairness, and support influence faculty reaction to AI and are important factors in trust, commitment, and behavioral intentions (Narayanan et al., 2024; Wang & Zhou, 2025; Sadeghi, 2024).

Based on the point of view of technology acceptance and organizational behavior, the perceived usefulness of AI is identified as a key predictor of positive attitudes of employees as technologies that increase the efficiency and performance of work are likely to promote organizational attachment and engagement (Mo et al., 2025; Rao et al., 2020). Similarly, AI-based workload reduction was associated with lower stress levels, better well-being, and greater organizational commitment, especially in demanding professional environments such as universities (Chuang et al., 2025; Deep et al., 2025). The perceived fairness of AI-based decisions is another important dimension, as transparency and objectivity in algorithmic systems play a major role in employees' trust, acceptance, and loyalty to the institution (Lee, 2018; Sari & Santosa, 2024). Moreover, AI-enabled organizational support, in the form of an institutional digital system and support mechanisms, helps employees feel that the organization appreciates their input and is attentive to their professional needs, which ultimately leads to increased commitment and decreased turnover intention (Babu & Kushwaha, 2024; Zeng et al., 2025).

Although the application of AI in higher education is increasing, the existing literature has, so far, predominantly focused on technological and performance aspects, with little attention to the psychological and organizational outcomes for faculty members. The majority of existing research focuses on adoption and performance of AI in corporate settings, and there is a dearth of empirical research on faculty perceptions and behavioral implications in universities (Obunge & Arannilewa, 2025; Verboom et al., 2025). Moreover, AI is often discussed as a single construct, overlooking its multidimensional nature of AI, including usefulness, workload reduction, fairness, and support for organizations. To fill this gap, the current study employs a multidimensional approach to investigate the impact of perceptions of AI on organizational commitment and turnover intention, drawing on technology acceptance, organizational support, and algorithmic fairness theories.

Therefore, the main idea of this chapter is that AI must not be perceived as a technological innovation but as an organizational and psychological process. Incorporating AI perception dimensions, organizational commitment, and turnover intention into the framework of personal higher education institutions, this chapter contributes to the developing discussion of human-centric AI adoption and provides actionable guidance on how supportive, ethical, and faculty-focused AI-mediated academic settings can be designed.

REVIEW OF LITERATURE AND HYPOTHESIS DEVELOPMENT

Theoretical Background

A theoretical perspective based on perception underlies the present study's conceptualization, which situates Artificial Intelligence (AI) as an organizational and technological factor that affects employee attitudes and behavioral intentions in higher learning institutions. In contrast to ancient technology research that views AI as an efficient means, recent organizational studies highlight that employees' perceptions of AI systems are determinants of psychological outcomes in the organizational context of technology use, including commitment, trust, and intention to leave.

Faculty members in higher education are exposed to AI-inclusive institutional solutions such as academic portals, evaluation tools, learning management platforms, and administrative automation systems, which directly affect their work experiences and organizational perceptions. Thus, the current research is based on a multidimensional perception of AI rather than a single-construct perspective of AI. This strategy is theoretically consistent with modern technology acceptance and organizational behavior viewpoints, which hold that employees evaluate technological systems in terms of their perceived utility, implications for workload, impartiality of decision-making processes, and the degree to which the systems demonstrate organizational backing.

In particular, perceived AI usefulness refers to the functional, performance-enhancing usefulness of AI in academic work, and perceived workload reduction refers to AI's role as a technological tool that decreases job demands in pressurized academic conditions. Perceived fairness of AI-driven decisions reflects the algorithmic transparency and justice in institutional processes such as evaluation and decision-making, which are pertinent in academic contexts characterized by the sensitivity of performance appraisals and professional autonomy. Also, perceived AI-based organizational support indicates the extent to which AI systems are perceived as supportive institutional processes that facilitate communication, efficiency, and faculty well-being.

All four of these dimensions together offer a holistic theoretical framework of the concept of AI as a socio-technical and organizational project and not a technological innovation. The study combines usefulness, workload reduction, fairness, and organizational support into a single framework, thereby assuming a central role in positioning AI perception as a primary antecedent of organizational commitment and turnover intention among faculty members. This integrative theoretical basis is especially applicable in the private institutions of higher learning, where the technologically intensive academic setting and performance demands of the academic environment, faculty perceptions on AI, become a determining factor of institutional attachment and retention behavior.

Perceived AI Usefulness and Organizational Commitment

The increased adoption of AI-driven academic platforms, learning management systems, and institutional analytics tools have had a profound impact on the work processes of the faculty in institutions of higher learning. According to previous empirical research, when employees believe AI systems are beneficial, productive, and performance-driven, they become increasingly positive about their organisation and have more positive attitudes of institutional trust and commitment. The level of utility presented by AI in technology-intensive academic settings promotes academic planning effectiveness, automated administrative management, and decision-making, which boost the productivity and job satisfaction of the faculty (Mo et al., 2025; Rao et al., 2020; Verboom et al., 2025). Moreover, AI-enhanced academic systems will minimise operational waste and enhance the quality of workflow, which enhances the psychological attachment and identification of employees with the organisation (Buele and Llerena-Aguirre, 2025; Moin et al., 2025). Research also indicates that perceived technological usefulness has a smaller influence on resistance to digital transformation, and provides a positive organisational climate in the long term that increases long-term organisational commitment (Robinson, 2025; Wang and Zhou, 2025). The more the faculty members are convinced that AI can be helpful to teaching, research, and academic management and the higher the rates of the development of emotional attachment and loyalty to the institution, the stronger the emotional attachment and loyalty to the institution in the context of the private higher education institution with the extensive application of the digital infrastructure and AI-enabled portals. Thus, on the empirical and theoretical evidence provided above, it is hypothesized that:

H1a: AI perceived usefulness has a positive impact on organisational commitment.

Reduction of perceived Workload and Organisational Commitment

Teaching, administrative, research pressure and institutional performance pressure are common in faculty members in a private higher education institution resulting in stress, burnout and low organisational attachment. The implementation of AI-powered services in schools has also played a significant role in automating the routine tasks of grading, scheduling, documentation, reporting, and monitoring the performance of students and decreased the cognitive and administrative load on faculty (Deep et al., 2025; Aithal and Maiya, 2023). By minimising stress and role overload, the Job Demands -Resources perspective states that technological resources that decrease job demands promote employee well-being, motivation, and organisational commitment (Chuang et al., 2025; Mishra et al., 2025). There is also empirical data that support of workload reduction with technological assistance enhances job satisfaction and loyalty to an institution, especially in high-request professional settings like academia (Parmar et al., 2022; Tongkachok et al., 2022). Also, AI-based academic management systems enable faculty to devote more time to the essential academic activities like teaching innovation and research productivity, thus, improving their sense of professional accomplishment and organisational identification (Wang and Zhou, 2025). As a result, organisational commitment among the faculty members of AI-integrated institutions of higher learning is greatly reinforced by the perception that AI is an effective method of workload reduction and task efficiency. Thus, based on the previous empirical literature and resource-based theoretical proposals, the hypothesised assumptions are as follows:

H1b: AI-related perceived workload reduction has a positive effect on organisational commitment.

Perceived Fairness of AI Decisions and Organizational Commitment

The growing role of AI in institutional decision-making, performance appraisal and academic analytics has heightened the significance of fairness, transparency and ethical governance in AI-based systems in institutions of higher learning. The concerns of the faculty members with regard to equity in AI-based evaluation and decision-making practices are especially strong because of the issues of academic autonomy, professional recognition, and institutional justice. Current sources on algorithmic fairness and organisational justice indicate that clear and impartial AI systems are regarded as an important factor to improve the trust of employees, their psychological safety, and the credibility of institutions (Narayanan et al., 2024; Lee, 2018). In case AI-based decision-making is viewed as objective and ethical, employees will be willing to embrace technological systems and become more connected to the organisation (Qin et al., 2023; Sari and Santosa, 2024). In addition, equitable AI management decreases the senses of technological bias, uncertainty, mistrust, and enhances institutional loyalty and commitment by employees (Hughes et al., 2019; Zekeriya, 2025). Considering that the concept of fairness in AI-driven systems is a primary predictor of organisational commitment in an academic environment, where the equity of evaluation and transparency of decisions is a very important factor of faculty morale and institutional involvement. Hence, based on the theoretical and empirical evidence regarding the concept of algorithmic fairness and organisational justice, the hypotheses are put forward as follows:

H1c: The perceived fairness of AI decision has a positive impact on organisational commitment.

Perceived Organizational Support using AI and Organizational Commitment

Perceived organisational support has since been known as a core predictor of employee commitment, engagement and retention in organisational settings. Technological systems in the AI-integrated higher education institutions serve as institutional support systems to improve communication on the inside, the accessibility of academic resources, responsiveness of the administrative process, and efficiency of services related to the faculty. Intuitive workplaces made by AI-enabled systems like institutional portals, digital communication, and academic decision-support systems build a sense of the organisation appreciating employees and their professional welfare (Yue et al., 2024; Tongkachok et al., 2022). Previously existing empirical data indicate that AI-based organisational practices are crucial in increasing employee loyalty, engagement at work, and, institutional commitment, through enhancing overall work experience and decreasing administrative pressure (Babu and Kushwaha, 2024; Al-Ayed, 2025; Obunge and Arannilewa, 2025). Moreover, the AI-based support systems contribute to the feeling of institutional care and professional empowerment, contributing to the emotional connection and commitment of academic employees in the long term (Zeng et al., 2025; Wang and Zhou, 2025). Perceived organisational support using AI is a very significant factor in influencing faculty attitudes and institutional loyalty in the case of private higher education institutions with technology-based governance and digital infrastructure adoption being very extensive. Thus, using the organisational support theory and AI-enabled workplace literature, it is supposed that:

H1d: The perceived organisational support with the help of AI has a positive impact on organisational commitment.

Organizational commitment and Employee turnover intentions

The topic of organizational commitment was one of the most acknowledged in organizational behavior literature as one of the strongest predictors of employee retention and turnover intention. Commitment indicates the feeling of emotional attachment, identification, and engagement of the employees at their organisation. Faculty commitment in institutions at higher learning is an important part of the continuity of the academics, research success, institutional stability, and long term viability in the institutions. When the members of the faculty feel attached emotionally to the institution and feel that their professional values are in line with the institutional goals, their desire to stay in the organisation rises considerably.

The evidence-based research shows that the negative relationship between organisational commitment and employee turnover intention exists in all industries, including higher education (Guzeller and Celiker, 2020; Mensele and Coetzee, 2014). Institutional attachment among faculty members reduces withdrawal behaviours or turnover intentions even in the high-pressure academic setting (Parmar et al., 2022; Qiong et al., 2025). Moreover, the study indicates that commitment can be seen as a psychological stabiliser that minimises job insecurity and enhances loyalty to the organisation, minimising turnover intentions (Xinbei and Kongruang, 2025; Wolle and Tuffa, 2025).

The organisational commitment in the context of the mitigation of faculty attrition is even more important in the area of the private higher learning institutions, where the technological integration and performance expectations are rather high. High commitment promotes resilience, job satisfaction and professional identification, which in turn decrease chances of voluntary turnover. Consequently, following the mass amount of empirical data and theoretical underpinnings in the book of organisational behaviour, it is hypothesised that:

H2: Organisational commitment has a negative impact on employee turnover intentions.

Intermediate Position of Organisational commitment between AI perceptions and employee turnover intentions

There is recent literature on AI-enabled workplaces that indicates that the psychological and attitudinal mediated mechanisms between technological perceptions and behavioural outcomes may be indirect in nature. Technology does not normally force employees to leave an organisation; instead, their perceived technology is what influences their organisational attitudes which in turn affect turnover intentions. Organisational commitment is a very important attitudinal mediator between experiences at the workplace and behavioural outcome.

Faculty attitudes towards the usefulness of AI in higher learning institutions that have adopted AI, workload reduction, fairness, and organisational support play an important role in influencing institutional attachment. Faculty members feel more trusted, content with their jobs and aligned to the institution when they are seen as having AI systems that are helpful, fair, supportive and workload reducing (Mo et al., 2025; Wang and Zhou, 2025). Such favourable views improve organisational commitment, and thus they decrease the chances of turnover intentions (Gessesse and Premanandam, 2023; Zeng et al., 2025).

On the other hand, the perceived unfairness, over-monitoring, or higher workload as a negative attitude towards AI may undermine commitment indirectly and lead to increased turnover tendencies (Sadeghi, 2024; Zulifiqar et al., 2025). Previous studies affirm the fact that organisational commitment mediates the connection between resources at workplace and employee retention in organisational settings (Babu and Kushwaha, 2024; Wang and Zhou, 2025).

Considering the context of the situation with private higher education institutions, organisational commitment is a key psychological process that explains how AI perception dimensions affect faculty retention behaviour. Therefore, the AI perceptions will indirectly decrease the turnover intentions through the increase in institutional commitment. That is why the mediation hypotheses below are put forward:

H3a: Organisational commitment is a mediating variable in the relationship between perceived AI usefulness and employee turnover intentions.
H3b: Organisational commitment has an indirect positive relationship between perceptions of workload reduction and employee turnover.
H3c: Organisational commitment mediates the connection between the perceived fairness of AI decisions and employee turnover intentions.

H3d: Organisational commitment is aided in the relation between perceived organisational support using AI and turnover intention among employees.

Research Gaps

Although the literature on the use of Artificial Intelligence (AI) in organisations and education is growing rapidly, there are a number of research gaps that cannot be filled, such as the perception-based behavioural outcomes in the field of a private higher education institution. To begin with, the body of research that has been conducted to date has largely been concerned with the technical adoption, efficiency, and performance implications of AI, whereas little consideration has been made on the psychological and organisational impacts of AI on employees. Majority of the previous research conceptualises AI as a technology of automation and productivity without looking at the impact of employees perceptions of AI on the major organisational attitudes such as commitment and turnover intention (Verboom et al., 2025; Buele and Llerena-Aguirre, 2025).

Second, there is a major contextual gap since most of the AI-related organisational research has been focused on corporate, hospitality, and general human resource management settings with comparatively limited empirical research studies being performed in the context of higher education institutions. The faculty members also work in a special professional context that is typified by academic freedom, pressure to conduct research and pressure to perform based on the performance of an organisation which is quite different to the conventional organisational environment. Nevertheless, the role of AI-driven organisational behaviour in academic staff (and especially in private institutions) has not been studied thoroughly (Rao et al., 2020; Obunge and Arannilewa, 2025).

Third, the existing literature has more or less represented AI as a one-dimensional or general explanation of technology, but not as a multidimensional interpretation of technology. The usefulness, fairness, implications of AI on workload, and organisational support mechanisms may make employees have varied perceptions of AI. The empirical and theoretical findings indicate that these unique dimensions of perception create different psychological and behavioural reactions in the workplaces that are aided by technology (Narayanan et al., 2024; Wang and Zhou, 2025). Lack of multidimensional AIs perception systems is a critical conceptual weakness of the literature.

Fourth, despite the established status of organisational commitment as one of the influential factors to employee turnover intention, only a few studies have investigated the concomitant nature of AI perceptions, organisational commitment, and turnover intention in an integrated broad framework. The current body of research will have a one-sided either attitudinal outcomes (including commitment) or behavioural outcomes (including turnover intention) interpretations and will lead to a patchy comprehension of employee retention in AI-enabled settings (Guzeller and Celiker, 2020; Zeng et al., 2025).

Fifth, institutional and geographical distance between higher education institutions is significant, with the empirical evidence regarding the subject of higher education at private institutions located in the emerging and technologically intensive academic environments being sparse. The technological integration, administrative burden, and performance expectations among faculty members in private universities are higher than in public ones, but research on AI perception and its organisational consequences in this particular environment remains few (Qiong et al., 2025; Aithal and Maiya, 2023).

Lastly, although recent literature has recognised the role of fairness and organisational support in technology acceptance, little literature has conceptualised AI-enabled organisational support as a perception-based construct in faculty commitment and turnover intention. In the majority of the previous researches, organisational support is viewed as a generic HR variable and is not considered an AI-added technology-mediated institutional process (Babu and Kushwaha, 2024; Al-Ayed, 2025).

Thus, the current research bridging these gaps in theoretical, contextual, and methodological aspects will employ a multidimensional framework of AI perception that will consider the perceived AI usefulness, reduction of workload, equity of AI-based decisions, and AI-driven organisational support to uncover the direct and indirect impacts that they have on the organisational commitment and employee turnover intention among faculty members in private higher education institutions. This strategy will offer a more integrated and situational contribution to the emerging literature on AI-based organisational behaviour in scholarly settings.

RESEARCH METHODOLOGY

Research Design

The research design that will be used in the current study is quantitative and cross-sectional, which will examine the hypothesis that the dimensions of AI perception as an independent variable have a meaningful effect on the dependent variables, which are organisational commitment and turnover intention among the faculty members of the Indian private Higher Education Institutions (HEIs). The research narrows down to examine four important dimensions of AI perception, namely, perceived usefulness of AI, perceived reduction in workload as a result of AI, perceived fairness of AI-driven decisions, and perceived organisational support by AI.

The chosen universities are Amity University (Noida), Lovely Professional University (Punjab), Chandigarh University (Punjab), SRM University (Delhi-NCR, Sonipat), and The NorthCap University (Gurugram) because the specified universities are progressive in using AI-based institutional portals and online academic platforms like AMIZONE, LPU UMS/LMS, CUIMS, E-Varsity ERP, and MyCampus. They are AI-based academic administration, performance tracking, internal communication, faculty management, and decision making tools that can offer suitable contextual environment in the analysis of the perceptions of AI-enabled institutional environment among the faculties.

Sample Design

The study population will include the teaching personnel working in the Indian private universities because these universities are quickly implementing AI-based academic and administrative processes. The respondents that were deemed suitable to respond to the research questions were faculty members that personally used institutional digital platforms and AI-supported systems. The purposive sampling method was used because it was necessary to assure that the respondents had a sufficient level of awareness and experience when it comes to the AI-enabled processes in the institution.

The information was gathered in the year 2025 using the structured questionnaires which were administered online and offline. The total responses received amounted to 550 with 520 questionnaires being found to be filled correctly, complete, and qualified as the ones to be analyzed. The number of 520 respondents used as the final sample is deemed sufficient to manage an adequate statistical power to conduct Confirmatory Factor Analysis (CFA) and Structural Equation Modeling (SEM)-based analysis.

Questionnaire Measurement Instrument and Sources

Standardized and validated scales that have been based on existing literature were used in measuring constructs to guarantee content validity and construct reliability. The independent variables characterising the dimensions of AI perception were operationalised in the following way: the items of perceived AI usefulness were adapted to the studies of the technology acceptance and AI perception (Robinson, 2025; Mo et al., 2025), perceived workload reduction under the influence of AI was at the same time adapted to the studies on AI and job demand-resource related

(Chuang et al., 2025; Deep et al., 2025), perceived fairness of AI-driven decisions was at the same time adapted to the studies on algorithmic fairness

The dependent variables were assessed on the basis of the existing scales of organisational commitment (Guzeller and Celiker, 2020; Mensele and Coetzee, 2014) and turnover intention (Li et al., 2019; Zeng et al., 2025). Everything was measured on a seven-point Likert scale with 1 (Strongly Disagree) to 7 (Strongly Agree). The questionnaire was firstly narrowed down by content validation and pilot screening and only clean, reliable and validated questions remained in the final CFA and SEM analysis.

DATA ANALYSIS AND DISCUSSION

This part of data analysis presents the structural relationships between perceived AI usefulness, perceived reduction in workload, perceived fairness of AI decisions, perceived support of AI to the organization, organizational commitment and intention to leave. The analysis of the data was performed with the help of SmartPLS 4. The process of testing the measurement and structural models used the Partial Least Squares Structural Equation Modeling (PLS-SEM) approach. The reliability, validity and significance of the proposed relationships was measured using the PLS algorithm and bootstrapping procedures. The approach is especially appropriate to analyse a complex model with multiple constructs and data based on perceptions.

Measurement Model

Measurement model was tested to test the reliability and validity of constructs employed in the study. Tables 1 to 4, which contain factor loadings, internal consistency reliability, convergent validity, and discriminant validity, present the results of the evaluation of the measurement model. All these findings prove that the measurement model is appropriate and corresponds to the recommended criteria to further conduct structural analysis. The results of the measurement model are shown in Figure 1 with the factor loading, path correlations and Cronbach's alpha of the proposed relationships.

Figure 1.

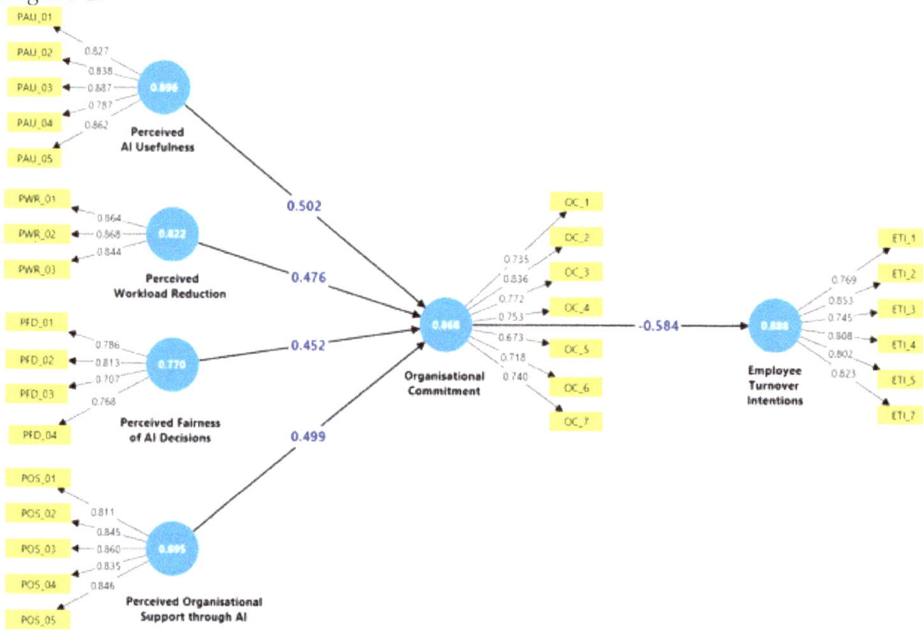

Table 1: Factor Loadings

	Outer loadings		Outer loadings
ETI_1 <- Employee_Turnover _Intentions	0.769	PAU_03 <- Perceived _AI Usefulness	0.887
ETI_2 <- Employee_Turnover _Intentions	0.853	PAU_04 <- Perceived _AI Usefulness	0.787
ETI_3 <- Employee_Turnover _Intentions	0.745	PAU_05 <- Perceived _AI Usefulness	0.862
ETI_4 <- Employee_Turnover _Intentions	0.808	PFD_01 <- Perceived Fairness _of AI Decisions	0.786
ETI_5 <- Employee_Turnover _Intentions	0.802	PFD_02 <- Perceived Fairness _of AI Decisions	0.813
ETI_7 <- Employee_Turnover _Intentions	0.823	PFD_03 <- Perceived Fairness _of AI Decisions	0.707
OC_1 <- Organisational_ Commitment	0.735	PFD_04 <- Perceived Fairness _of AI Decisions	0.768
OC_2 <- Organisational_ Commitment	0.836	POS_01 <- Perceived Organisational _Support through AI	0.811

continued on following page

Table 1: Factor Loadings

	Outer loadings		Outer loadings
OC_3 <- Organisational_ Commitment	0.772	POS_02 <- Perceived Organisational _Support through AI	0.845
OC_4 <- Organisational_ Commitment	0.753	POS_03 <- Perceived Organisational _Support through AI	0.86
OC_5 <- Organisational_ Commitment	0.673	POS_04 <- Perceived Organisational _Support through AI	0.835
OC_6 <- Organisational_ Commitment	0.718	POS_05 <- Perceived Organisational _Support through AI	0.846
OC_7 <- Organisational_ Commitment	0.74	PWR_01 <- Perceived_Workload Reduction	0.864
PAU_01 <- Perceived _AI Usefulness	0.827	PWR_02 <- Perceived_Workload Reduction	0.868
PAU_02 <- Perceived _AI Usefulness	0.838	PWR_03 <- Perceived_Workload Reduction	0.844

Source: Author

Table 1 shows the loading of the outer in all the measuring items, indicating the strength of the relationship between each indicator and the corresponding construct. The findings show that most of the factor loadings were above the recommended factor loading of 0.70, thus supporting satisfactory indicator reliability. Even though some of the items have a relatively lower loading, they are within a reasonable range of exploratory research. In general, the results indicate that the indicators have obtained good representation of their respective latent constructs.

Table 2: Reliability and Convergent Validity

	Cronbach's alpha	Composite reliability (rho_a)	Composite reliability (rho_c)	Average variance extracted (AVE)
Employee_Turnover _Intentions	0.888	0.893	0.915	0.641
Organisational_Commitment	0.868	0.874	0.899	0.560
Perceived Fairness _of AI Decisions	0.770	0.778	0.853	0.592
Perceived Organisational _Support through AI	0.895	0.897	0.923	0.705
Perceived _AI Usefulness	0.896	0.901	0.923	0.707
Perceived_Workload Reduction	0.822	0.822	0.894	0.737

Source: Author

Table 2 reports the results of internal consistency reliability and convergent validity. All constructs have a Cronbach alpha, composite reliability (rho a and rho c), and Average Variance Extracted (AVE) values that are larger than the recommended values (0.70 and 0.50, respectively). These findings show that a high degree of internal consistency is achieved and that the constructs capture the variance of the indicators of the constructs adequately. Therefore, the measurement model exhibits high reliability, and sufficient convergent validity.

Table 3: Discriminant Validity (HTMT criterion)

		1	2	3	4	5	6
1	Employee_Turnover _Intentions						
2	Organisational_Commitment	0.658					
3	Perceived Fairness _of AI Decisions	0.523	0.547				
4	Perceived Organisational _Support through AI	0.595	0.564	0.455			
5	Perceived _AI Usefulness	0.609	0.566	0.445	0.466		
6	Perceived_Workload Reduction	0.533	0.561	0.335	0.392	0.381	

Source: Author

Table 3 shows the discriminant validity test using the Heterotrait-Monomethod (HTMT) ratio. All the HTMT values are found to be below the conservative value of 0.85, which demonstrates that the constructs are empirically different to each other. This is a confirmation that there are no issues of multicollinearity and is a confirmation that the measurement model is discriminant valid.

Table 4: Model Fit Indices

	Saturated model	Estimated model
SRMR	0.042	0.080
d_ULS	0.836	3.002
d_G	0.276	0.335
Chi-square	841.226	963.216
NFI	0.899	0.884

Source: Author

Table 4 summarises the model fit measures, such as SRMR, d_ULS, d_G, Chi-square, and Normed Fit Index (NFI). The saturated model has a SRMR value less than the recommended value of 0.08 and a good model fit is noted. The value of the SRMR of the estimated model lies within the acceptable range, indicating that the model fits sufficiently. Additionally, NFI values are near the recommended level of

0.90 which is a satisfactory level of model fit. On the whole, these indices prove that the proposed model is sufficiently suitable to fit the data observed.

Structural Model

This part of data analysis reflects the analysis of the structural model, which will focus on the hypothesized relationships among the perceived AI usefulness, perceived workload reduction, perceived fairness of AI decisions, perceived organizational support through AI, organizational commitment, and employee turnover intentions. Path coefficients, the level of significance, (p-values), and coefficient of determination (R^2) were used to evaluate the structural model.

Figure 2.

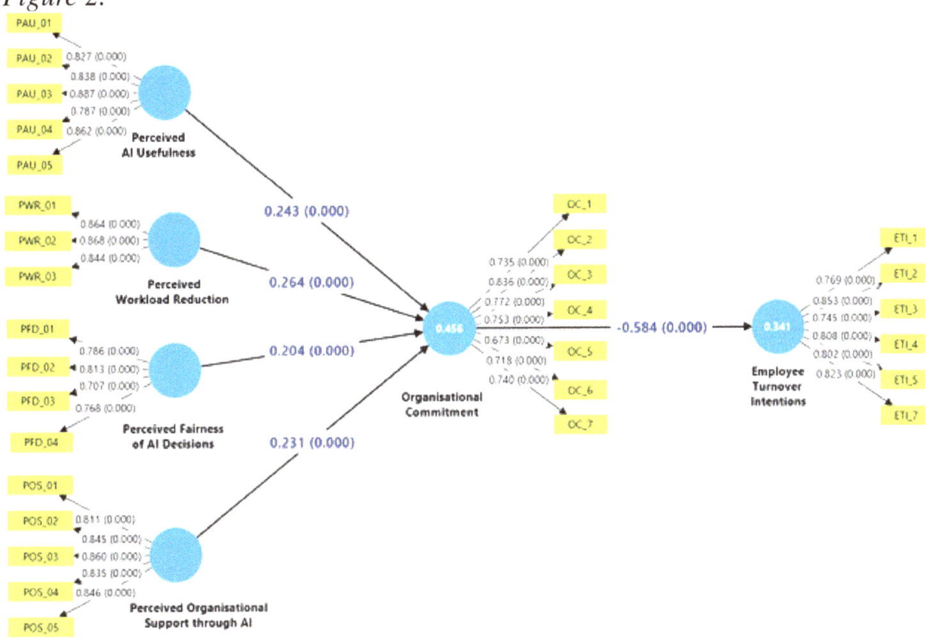

Table 5: Path Analysis and Hypothesis Results

	Path Coefficients	Standard deviation (STDEV)	T statistics	P values	Decision
Direct Effect					
Perceived _AI Usefulness -> Organisational_Commitment	0.243	0.036	6.773	0.000	*H_1a Supported*
Perceived_Workload Reduction -> Organisational_Commitment	0.264	0.035	7.541	0.000	*H_1b Supported*
Perceived Fairness _of AI Decisions -> Organisational_Commitment	0.204	0.034	5.920	0.000	*H_1c Supported*
Perceived Organisational _Support through AI -> Organisational_ Commitment	0.231	0.037	6.245	0.000	*H_1d Supported*
Organisational_Commitment -> Employee_Turnover _Intentions	-0.584	0.029	20.330	0.000	*H_2 Supported*
Indirect Effect					
Perceived _AI Usefulness -> Organisational_Commitment -> Employee_Turnover _Intentions	-0.142	0.023	6.183	0.000	*H_3a Supported*
Perceived_Workload Reduction -> Organisational_Commitment -> Employee_Turnover _Intentions	-0.154	0.022	6.974	0.000	*H_3b Supported*
Perceived Fairness _of AI Decisions -> Organisational_Commitment -> Employee_Turnover _Intentions	-0.119	0.021	5.553	0.000	*H_3c Supported*
Perceived Organisational _Support through AI -> Organisational_ Commitment -> Employee_Turnover _Intentions	-0.135	0.023	5.833	0.000	*H_3d Supported*

Source: Author

Findings

The findings of the structural model analysis have been provided in Table 5 with the direct and indirect impacts of AI perception dimensions on the organisational commitment and the turnover intentions of the employees using PLS-SEM at the 5% significance level. The results show that all the path coefficients are statistically significant since the p-values are 0.000 and t-statistics are greater than the threshold value of 1.96, which has a great empirical support of the suggested hypothesis.

There is a positive and statistically significant impact of Perceived AI Usefulness on Organisational Commitment with a path coefficient of 0.243, t-statistic of 6.773 and p-value of 0.000, which is lower than the 0.05 significant level; hence, the null hypothesis is accepted and the alternative hypothesis is rejected. The perception of Workload Reduction is also found to have a strong positive and significant impact on Organisational commitment with a coefficient of 0.264, t-value of 7.541 and p-value of 0.000, which indicates that H1b is accepted at the 5 per cent level of significance.

Perceived Fairness of AI Decisions also affects Organisational Commitment positively and significantly with path coefficient of 0.204, t-statistic of 5.920 and p-value of 0.000 supporting H1c and rejecting the null hypothesis. Likewise, with a coefficient of 0.231, t -value of 6.245 and p-value of 0.000, Perceived Organisational Support through AI, proves that H1d is not rejected. Additionally, the impact of Organisational Commitment on Employee Turnover Intentions is negative and statistically significant with a coefficient of -0.584, t-statistic of 20.330 and p-value of 0.000 meaning that H2 has been supported and the higher the commitment, the lower the turnover intentions.

As far as the indirect effects are concerned, the Organisational Commitment has a negative indirect impact on Employee Turnover Intentions, with a coefficient equal to -0.142, t-value equal to 6.183 and p-value equal to 0.000, which supports H3a as well as proves the mediating role of organisational commitment. Perceived Workload Reduction also has significant negative indirect effect on Employee Turnover Intentions through Organisational commitment with coefficient of -0.154, t-statistic of 6.974 and p-value of 0.000, resulting in the rejection of H3b.

Similarly, the Indirect Effect of Perceived Fairness of AI Decisions on Employee Turnover Intentions is significantly negative and its Organisational Commitment coefficient is -0.119, t-value is 5.553 and p-value of 0.000, that indicates that H3c is true. Finally, the Perceived Organisational Support via AI indirectly lowers the Employee Turnover Intentions by Organisational commitment at a coefficient of -0.135, t-statistic of 5.833 and p-value of 0.000; therefore, H3d is accepted and organisational commitment is proven to be a significant mediating variable between AI perception dimensions and turnover intentions.

Table 6: Model Summary

	R-square	R-square adjusted
Employee_Turnover _Intentions	0.341	0.339
Organisational_Commitment	0.456	0.451

Source: Author

The values of R-square in Table 6 show how many constructs were explained within the structural model of the endogenous constructs. The R-square of Organisational commitment is 0.456, and the adjusted R-square is 0.451 indicating that the four dimensions of AI perception including perceived AI usefulness, perceived workload reduction, perceived fairness of AI decisions, and perceived organisational support through AI accounted for an estimated 45.6 per cent variation in organisational commitment among faculty members.

On the same note, the R^2 of Employee Turnover Intentions is 0.341 and the adjusted R^2 of 0.339 shows that the organisational commitment explains 34.1% of turnover intentions. This indicates a medium strength of the model, which illustrates that the level of organisational commitment plays a significant role in reducing employee turnover intentions in the AI-enabled higher education institutions which are privately owned.

Discussion

The current research study investigated how the perception dimensions of AI affect organisational commitment and intention to leave among the faculty members of the private higher education institutions. The results indicate that perceived AI usefulness, perceived workload reduction, perceived fairness of AI decisions and perceived organisational support by AI have significant and positive impact on organisational commitment, which consequently has a significant negative impact on employee turnover intentions. These findings give good empirical evidence of the perception-based perspective on AI as an organisational and psychological element and not just a technological feature.

To begin with, the findings show that the perception AI usefulness influences the organisational commitment in a positive significant way. This result indicates that the emotional attachment and loyalty of the faculty towards the institution rise when they believe that AI systems can assist in enhancing efficiency, academic management, and work performance. This is consistent with the previous research that holds the view that performance-enhancing technologies enhance the engagement levels, trust, and organisational commitment of employees in technologically enabled work environments (Mo et al., 2025; Rao et al., 2020). Applying to the context of higher education, AI-based academic platforms and institutional systems are used to support teaching, research, and administrative activities, which improves faculty satisfaction and institutional identification (Verboom et al., 2025; Buele and Llerena-Aguirre, 2025).

Second, reduction of workload by AI was perceived to have a significant positive impact on organisational commitment. This observation aligns with the Job Demands Resources view of opinion that the technological resources that lessen job requirements enhance well-being and devotion. Professional work in private universities is usually physically and mentally demanding, and AI-based processes that rationalize repetitive activities help mitigate stress and mental load, increasing the levels of commitment (Deep et al., 2025; Chuang et al., 2025). The fact that the workload pressure is a major factor in burnout and declining commitment in institutions of higher education is also supported by previous studies (Parmar et al., 2022; Mishra et al., 2025), which confirms the value of AI systems that reduce workloads in academic institutions.

Third, perceived fairness of AI-driven decisions had a significant and positive impact on organisational commitment, as the findings of the study revealed. The outcome serves as a confirmation of the transparency, objectivity, and fair decision-making body of literature that highlights the importance of transparency, objectivity, and fairness in decision-making, which are factors that boost trust and institutional commitment among employees (Narayanan et al., 2024; Lee, 2018). Fairness A fair AI-based examination, performance tracking, and institutional decision system are also of special concern in a workplace context because faculty members are more associated with professional autonomy and evaluative sensitivity (Qin et al., 2023; Sari and Santosa, 2024). As AI systems become seen as just and clear, faculty tend to trust the institutional procedures and show greater commitment.

Fourth, the perceived organisational support by AI turned out to be a good predictor of organisational commitment. This observation is consistent with the organisational support theory that implies that employees tend to become more loyal and committed when they feel that the organisation appreciates their input and takes their professional needs into account (Zeng et al., 2025). AI-based institutionalized systems, including digital portals, communication platforms, and academic support tools, in turn contribute to increasing the perception of institutional care and responsiveness, thus facilitating the engagement of and retention of the faculty (Babu and Kushwaha, 2024; Yue et al., 2024). It has also been noted in other studies through similarly designed studies that AI-assisted HR and organisational practices are highly beneficial to increasing employee loyalty and workplace experience (Al-Ayed, 2025; Obunge & Arannilewa, 2025).

In addition, the findings show that the negative impact of organisational commitment on employee turnover intentions is an influential and eminent one. This affirms the fact that increased emotional attachment and institutional identification has a significant negative impact on faculty turnover intentions. The result aligns with the previous empirical studies that define organisational commitment as one of the most effective predictors of turnover intention in academic and organisational settings (Guzeller and Celiker, 2020; Xinbei and Kongruang, 2025). In the private institutions of higher education where there are high expectations of performance and integration of technology, commitment is a very important factor in the stability of faculty and continuity of the institution (Qiong et al., 2025).

The findings of the mediation also indicate that organizational commitment is a significant mediator of the relationship between AI perception dimensions and turnover intentions among employees. It means that positive attitudes toward AI can indirectly reduce turnover intentions by increasing organizational commitment. These results are also backed by past research studies that point out that increased perceived organizational support, technological value, and workplace resources affect turnover intentions using attitudinal processes of commitment and job satisfaction (Gessesse & Premanandam, 2023; Wang and Zhou, 2025). Likewise, studies of AI-supported workplaces indicate that supportive and equitable AI systems improve psychological attachment and reduce withdrawal behavior among employees (Zulifiqar et al., 2025; Li et al., 2019). Therefore, perceptions of AI significantly influence organizational commitment and reduce faculty turnover intentions, highlighting that successful AI implementation in higher education depends not only on technology adoption but also on faculty members' psychological and cognitive interpretations.

CONCLUSION

The current research focused on the effect of faculty views on Artificial Intelligence (AI) on organizational commitment and turnover intentions among private higher education institutions. The study involved a multidimensional perception-based method and considered the perceived use of AI to be useful, to reduce workload, to increase fairness in the decisions of AI, and to provide organizational support through AI, and their direct and indirect impacts on organizational commitment and turnover intentions. The results indicate that all dimensions of AI perception have a strong positive effect on organizational commitment, which, in turn, has a significant negative effect on turnover intentions. The findings show that faculty members who believe that AI systems are useful, fair, supportive, and capable of decreasing workload have a stronger emotional attachment and institutional loyalty. This shows that AI is not only useful for technological progress but also for creating positive psychological impressions. Moreover, the role of organizational commitment as an indirect factor that can decrease turnover intentions is also significant, indicating that perceptions of AI towards organizations may indirectly lower turnover intentions by enhancing faculty attachment to the organizations. Theoretically, the study fits within the literature on AI and organizational behavior by integrating perceptions of technology with commitment and turnover intention in a higher education setting. In practice, the results indicate that higher education institutions must implement clear, equitable, and faculty-focused AI systems to promote commitment and enhance faculty retention.

RECOMMENDED POLICY AND IMPLICATIONS FOR STAKEHOLDERS

Academic Institution (University Management and Administrators) Policy Recommendations

A human-focused approach to the deployment of AI in higher education institutions should be endorsed by the institutes and colleges that are privately owned instead of focusing on technological efficiency. As the results prove the perception of AI usefulness, fairness, reduction of workload, and organisational support as primary drivers of organisational commitment and decreased turnover intentions, university administrators need to guarantee that AI systems are set to support the faculty instead of surveilling and regulating them. To improve productivity within institutions, AI-based academic support systems should be invested in to help in automating routine administrative functions, which include scheduling, reporting, evaluation documentation, and academic analytics, to minimize the number of faculty members and increase their productivity.

Also, universities need to develop clear AI governance policies that specify how AI-driven decisions regarding performance assessment, workload distribution, and academic surveillance are made. Open and honest AI systems will boost faculty confidence, decrease resistance to technology adoption, and improve institutional commitment. Faculty orientation programs and AI literacy workshops should also be made a regular practice to enhance awareness and acceptance, as well as the useful application of AI-enabled institutional platforms. Moreover, the management must integrate AI, internal communication systems, and faculty support services to establish a conducive digital academic platform that promotes engagement, satisfaction, and long-term retention of academic staff.

Policymaker and Higher Education Regulation Body Policy Recommendations

Regulatory authorities and policymakers in higher education must devise systematic principles for the responsible and ethical use of AI in institutions of higher learning. Since AI integration is rapidly rising in private universities, policies should be established nationally to guarantee equity, transparency, data privacy, and responsibility in AI-driven academic systems. Regulations must require that AI-based institutional systems used to evaluate faculty performance and make decisions be based on the principles of algorithmic fairness and institutional justice.

Also, policymakers ought to promote funding and incentives for universities that implement AI systems that support faculty and minimize administrative workload, rather than prioritizing performance surveillance. AI capacity-building programs, the provision of digital infrastructure, and the development of faculty training programs can be part of national education policies to support fair and efficient AI application in higher education. These policy interventions will assist in the adoption of sustainable AI use, as well as the protection of faculty freedom, professional integrity, and trust.

Academic Researcher and Scholar Policy Recommendations

Scholars in higher education, organizational behavior, and educational technology should deepen AI-related research by focusing on multidimensional, perception-focused frameworks rather than treating AI as a single technological phenomenon. Future studies may conduct longitudinal and comparative research in public and private institutions to understand the psychological and behavioral implications of adopting AI amongst faculty members in the long term.

The scholars must also pay attention to the development of validated AI-perception scales in the academic context, since most current measurement tools are based on corporate or standard workplaces. Also, an interdisciplinary study of artificial intelligence, organizational psychology, and higher education management can provide more insight into faculty engagement, digital transformation, and institutional sustainability. Researchers are also advised to investigate moderating factors (e.g., age, academic experience, digital literacy, and institutional culture) to improve the strength and generalizability of AI-related academic studies.

Policy Recommendations on Institutional HR Department and Faculty Development Unit

AI-based systems should be used to create personalised faculty support programmes, training modules, and career development programmes using human resource departments and faculty development centres. Faculty workload trends, professional development requirements, and engagement can be detected with the help of AI analytics and allow institutions to make specific interventions to increase job satisfaction and organisational commitment.

HR policies must focus on positive AI incorporation where AI tools are tied to faculty mentoring, research support, and/or teaching innovation and not performance surveillance. Frequent feedback systems are to be developed to analyze how the faculty view AI systems and how these systems affect fairness, transparency, and the working load. In addition, faculty development departments are to arrange on-going professional development programmes on digital competence, the use of AI tools, and pedagogical innovation to reinforce the faculty flexibility in AI-enabled academic settings.

Technology Developers and EdTech Stakeholder Policy Recommendations

Faculty-centered and ethically-focused AI systems designed by AI developers and educational technology vendors should be specific to higher education institutions. The AI systems in universities must be designed to focus on usability, transparency, and explainability so that the communication can make the faculty members feel that the systems are fair, supportive, and beneficial to them. Clear decision-support systems, customisable dashboards, and user-friendly interfaces can go a long way in enhancing the levels of acceptance and trust of AI technologies within the faculty.

The stakeholders in EdTech must partner with universities to develop AI solutions together that help solve actual academic problems like workload, research support, student analytics, and institutional communication. In addition, institutional AI systems should integrate the ethical AI principles, data protection, and bias detection mechanisms into the systems of developers to increase the fairness and institutional credibility. The sustainable development of digital transformation and better retention of faculty in institutions of higher learning will be aided by such collaborative and responsible development of AI.

FUTURE RESEARCH DIRECTIONS AND LIMITATIONS

Limitations of the Study

Although the current study has been very instrumental in its theoretical and empirical contributions, it has some limitations. First, the study uses a cross-sectional design, which limits the ability to establish causal relationships regarding AI perception dimensions, organizational commitment, and turnover intention over time. The attitudes of the faculty towards AI can change with increased exposure to technology and an institution's digital maturity, which cannot be captured in a single data collection.

Second, the research is limited to private institutions of higher learning, which may limit the applicability of the study's results to public universities or other educational settings. There are important differences in the institutional governance structures, technological infrastructure, and organizational culture between government and private institutions, which could affect how faculty perceive AI systems.

Third, it is based on self-reported questionnaire data, which can be prone to common method bias and perceptual subjectivity. Given that the elements under measurement are perception-related (AI usefulness, fairness, workload reduction, and organizational support), the answers could be based on subjective cognitive explanations rather than on the existence of purely objective institutional facts. Fourth, the research uses four dimensions of AI perception and organizational commitment as a mediator, whereas other possible variables such as digital literacy, technological anxiety, organizational culture, and leadership support were not incorporated into the model, which could also play a role in turnover intentions in AI-enabled academic settings.

Future Research Directions

The current study can be expanded in future research by employing longitudinal designs to examine how faculty perceptions of AI and organizational commitment change over time in technology-driven higher education institutions. The longitudinal studies would provide more information on the long-term behavioral effects of AI integration on faculty retention and institutional stability.

Comparative analyses between the existing public and private universities and across countries could also be implemented in further research to increase the generalisability and contextual applicability of AI perception research in higher education. It would be possible to conduct cross-cultural inquiries that will provide a comprehensive explanation of how institutional contexts influence faculty reactions to AI-enabled systems.

It is also advisable for future scholars to consider moderating and mediating variables, such as digital competence, AI anxiety, organizational culture, leadership support, and job satisfaction, to develop more comprehensive models of AI-driven organizational behavior. Further discussion of other AI-related constructs, such as algorithmic transparency, ethical AI governance, and technological trust, can reinforce the conceptual framework. Lastly, the use of mixed-methods or qualitative research methods in the future could help gain deeper psychological insights into faculty members' lives as they interact with AI-enabled institutional systems, complementing quantitative results and offering more academic and policy-specific implications.

REFERENCES

Aithal, P. S., & Maiya, A. K. (2023). Innovations in higher education industry–Shaping the future. [IJCSBE]. *International Journal of Case Studies in Business, IT, and Education*, *7*(4), 283–311. DOI: 10.47992/IJCSBE.2581.6942.0321

Al-Ayed, S. (2025). Role of Artificial Intelligence Towards Employee Retention Via Mediation of Employee Loyalty: A Company Governance Study. *Journal of Governance and Regulation*, *14*(2), 363. DOI: 10.22495/jgrv14i2siart15

Babu, M. D., & Kushwaha, B. P. (2024). Does perceived organisational support reduce academicians turnover intention? A mediating role of perceived values of artificial intelligence. *International Journal of Learning and Change*, *16*(5), 508–528. DOI: 10.1504/IJLC.2024.140887

Buele, J., & Llerena-Aguirre, L. (2025, July). Transformations in academic work and faculty perceptions of artificial intelligence in higher education. [). Frontiers Media SA.]. *Frontiers in Education*, *10*, 1603763. DOI: 10.3389/feduc.2025.1603763

Chuang, Y. T., Chiang, H. L., & Lin, A. P. (2025). Insights from the Job Demands–Resources Model: AI's dual impact on employees' work and life well-being. *International Journal of Information Management*, *83*, 102887. DOI: 10.1016/j.ijinfomgt.2025.102887

Deep, P. D., Ghosh, N., & Chen, Y. (2025). Faculty burnout in higher education: Effects on student engagement, learning outcomes, and artificial intelligence-driven institutional responses. *Journal of Educational and Developmental Psychology*, *15*(1), 29–42. DOI: 10.5539/jedp.v15n1p29

Gessesse, K. T., & Premanandam, P. (2023). The mediating role of affective commitment on the relationship between job satisfaction and turnover intention using structural equation modeling: Empirical evidence from higher education institutions in Addis Ababa, Ethiopia. *Cogent Social Sciences*, *9*(1), 2202959. DOI: 10.1080/23311886.2023.2202959

Guzeller, C. O., & Celiker, N. (2020). Examining the relationship between organizational commitment and turnover intention via a meta-analysis. *International Journal of Culture, Tourism and Hospitality Research*, *14*(1), 102–120. DOI: 10.1108/IJCTHR-05-2019-0094

Hughes, C., Robert, L., Frady, K., & Arroyos, A. (2019). Artificial intelligence, employee engagement, fairness, and job outcomes. In *Managing technology and middle-and low-skilled employees* (pp. 61–68). Emerald Publishing Limited. DOI: 10.1108/978-1-78973-077-720191005

Lee, M. K. (2018). Understanding perception of algorithmic decisions: Fairness, trust, and emotion in response to algorithmic management. *Big Data & Society*, *5*(1), 2053951718756684. DOI: 10.1177/2053951718756684

Li, J. J., Bonn, M. A., & Ye, B. H. (2019). Hotel employee's artificial intelligence and robotics awareness and its impact on turnover intention: The moderating roles of perceived organizational support and competitive psychological climate. *Tourism Management*, *73*, 172–181. DOI: 10.1016/j.tourman.2019.02.006

Mensele, C., & Coetzee, M. (2014). Job embeddedness, organisational commitment and voluntary turnover of academic staff at a higher education institution in South Africa. *South African Journal of Labour Relations*, *38*(1), 9–30.

Mishra, A., Mohanty, A., & Sundaray, B. K. (2025). Can faculty job satisfaction reduce turnover intention s at management institutes in India? Analysing the mediation effect of organisational commitment. *Journal of Applied Research in Higher Education*, •••, 1–15.

Mo, Z., Liu, M. T., Chark, R., Zeng, S., & Song, X. (2025). How AI adoption in human resource management practices can enhance tourism employees' organizational commitment. *Journal of Hospitality and Tourism Management*, *63*, 54–67. DOI: 10.1016/j.jhtm.2025.03.003

Moin, M. F., Behl, A., Zhang, J. Z., & Shankar, A. (2025). AI in the organizational nexus: Building trust, cementing commitment, and evolving psychological contracts. *Information Systems Frontiers*, *27*(4), 1413–1424. DOI: 10.1007/s10796-024-10561-3

Narayanan, D., Nagpal, M., McGuire, J., Schweitzer, S., & De Cremer, D. (2024). Fairness perceptions of artificial intelligence: A review and path forward. *International Journal of Human-Computer Interaction*, *40*(1), 4–23. DOI: 10.1080/10447318.2023.2210890

Obunge, J. I., & Arannilewa, A. O. (2025). Artificial Intelligence Tools in Human Resource Management and Lecturers' Retention in Private Universities in Ekiti State. *International Journal of Advanced Research and Learning*, *4*(3), 9–19.

Parmar, V., Channar, Z. A., Ahmed, R. R., Streimikiene, D., Pahi, M. H., & Streimikis, J. (2022). Assessing the organizational commitment, subjective vitality and burnout effects on turnover intention in private universities. *Oeconomia Copernicana*, *13*(1), 251–286. DOI: 10.24136/oc.2022.008

Qin, S., Jia, N., Luo, X., Liao, C., & Huang, Z. (2023). Perceived fairness of human managers compared with artificial intelligence in employee performance evaluation. *Journal of Management Information Systems, 40*(4), 1039–1070. DOI: 10.1080/07421222.2023.2267316

Qiong, W., Li, M., & Chansongpol, T. (2025). A Study on the Factors Influencing Turnover Intention among Faculty in Chinese Private Higher Education Institutions. [JTCSS]. *Journal of Thai-Chinese Social Science*, *2*(2), 173–196.

. Rao, S., Chitranshi, J., & Punjabi, N. (2020). Role of artificial intelligence in employee engagement and retention. Journal of Applied Management-Jidnyasa, 42-60.

. Robinson, T. (2025). Generative Artificial Intelligence in Higher Education: Understanding Faculty Adoption through the Technology Acceptance Model. *i-Manager's Journal of Educational Technology, 22*(1).

Sadeghi, S. (2024). Employee well-being in the age of AI: Perceptions, concerns, behaviors, and outcomes. *arXiv preprint arXiv:2412.04796.*

Sari, I., & Santoso, A. (2024). Perceived AI Fairness and Organizational Commitment: The Mediating Role of Psychological Safety. *Future of Work and Digital Management Journal*, *2*(4), 44–54.

Tongkachok, K., Garg, S., Vemuri, V. P., Chaudhary, V., Koli, P. V., & Kumar, K. S. (2022). The role of artificial intelligence on organizational support programmes to enhance work outcome and employees behaviour. *Materials Today: Proceedings*, *56*, 2383–2387. DOI: 10.1016/j.matpr.2021.12.205

Verboom, A. D. P. R., Pais, L., Zijlstra, F. R., Oswald, F. L., & Santos, N. R. D. (2025). Perceptions of artificial intelligence in academic teaching and research: A qualitative study from AI experts and professors' perspectives. *International Journal of Educational Technology in Higher Education*, *22*(1), 46. DOI: 10.1186/s41239-025-00546-w

Wang, D., & Zhou, X. (2025). The Impact of AI Awareness on Employees' Job Burnout: A Chain Mediation of Perceived Organizational Support and Organizational Commitment. *SAGE Open*, *15*(4), 21582440251400532. DOI: 10.1177/21582440251400532

Wolle, G. S., & Tuffa, B. M. (2025). The mediating effect of organizational commitment on the relationship between teachers' job satisfaction and turnover intention. *Bahir Dar Journal of Education*, *25*(3), 112–128. DOI: 10.4314/bdje.v25i3.8

Xinbei, Y. A. O., & KONGRUANG, C. (2025). Predicting lecturer turnover intention in Chinese private universities: The roles of job satisfaction and organizational commitment. *Procedia of Multidisciplinary Research*, *3*(1), 6–6.

Yu, L., & Li, Y. (2022). Artificial intelligence decision-making transparency and employees' trust: The parallel multiple mediating effect of effectiveness and discomfort. *Behavioral Sciences (Basel, Switzerland)*, *12*(5), 127. DOI: 10.3390/bs12050127 PMID: 35621424

Yue, C. A., Men, L. R., Mitson, R., Davis, D. Z., & Zhou, A. (2024). Artificial intelligence for internal communication: Strategies, challenges, and implications. *Public Relations Review*, *50*(5), 102515. DOI: 10.1016/j.pubrev.2024.102515

. Zekeriya, N. A. S. (2025). Building Trust Between Humans And Artificial Intelligence: The Future of Perceived Justice in HR Management. *SOSYAL BİLİMLER*, 25.

Zeng, D., Swatdikun, T., Aujirapongpan, S., & Huang, S. Z. (2025). The influence of quality of work life and perceived organizational support on turnover intention in private higher education institutions. *Emerging Science Journal*, *8*, 335–357. DOI: 10.28991/ESJ-2024-SIED1-020

Zulifiqar, H., Fatima, L., Akhtar, M. S., & Akhtar, M. N. (2025). Artificial Intelligence in HR: Reducing Turnover Intentions with AI-Driven Employee Engagement Solutions. *International Research Journal of Social Sciences and Humanities*, *4*(1), 85–111.

Chapter 5
Professional Development for Academicians in the Age of Artificial Intelligence

Kritikka Kunte
http://orcid.org/0009-0002-4820-8831
Ajeenkya D.Y. Patil University, India

Sunil Sankathala
Ajeenkya D.Y. Patil University, India

Krutika Patre
http://orcid.org/0009-0001-7969-4409
Ajeenkya D.Y. Patil University, India

Susanta Das
http://orcid.org/0000-0002-9314-3988
Ajeenkya D.Y. Patil University, India

ABSTRACT

Intelligent tutoring systems, adaptive learning platforms, automated grading systems, & Gen AI applications are some of the tools used in universities to enhance educational practices. This chapter examines the connection between AI and higher education and puts the idea in its professional growth of academicians in the era of AI. It talks about the increasing applications of AI technologies in learning and teaching practices and how such tools can be used to facilitate data-driven decision making and customized learning. Another point that the chapter discusses is the changing of academic roles and the need to impart new digital competencies in ed-

DOI: 10.4018/979-8-2600-3204-6.ch005

ucators. Some of the most important aspects of professional growth are AI literacy, digital pedagogical skills, data literacy, ethical awareness, institutional training programs, and lifelong learning. The chapter concludes that effective implementation of AI in higher education is hinged on the constant learning and development of the institution and the capacity of the teachers to learn in fast changing technological environments.

INTRODUCTION

Artificial intelligence (AI) has become one of the most revolutionary technologies of the twenty-first century, touching various industries such as healthcare, finance, transportation, and education. Over the past few years, machine learning, natural language processing, and data analytics have advanced rapidly, enabling the creation of intelligent systems capable of performing tasks previously done by humans. The effects of these developments have been far-reaching, even in learning settings, especially in institutions of higher learning, where digital technologies are increasingly being integrated into teaching, learning, and administrative procedures. With the ongoing adoption of more sophisticated digital tools in universities to improve the learning process, AI has received significant attention as a technology capable of transforming how education is conducted and how institutions function (Chen et al., 2020; Zawacki-Richter et al., 2019).

The development of AI in education results from integrating it into educational systems. The field is interdisciplinary, drawing on knowledge from computer science, cognitive psychology, data science, and educational technology to develop intelligent systems that facilitate teaching and learning. Intelligent Tutoring Systems: AI technologies used in the education sector to analyze large amounts of student data and enhance educational outcomes. Adaptive Learning Systems: AI technologies used in education to process vast amounts of student data and drive better educational outcomes. Automated Grading Systems: Automated grading systems are AI technologies used in the education sector to process large volumes of student data to improve educational outcomes. Learning analytics tools: AI technologies used in the education sector to process large amounts of student data to positively impact learning. These technologies enable a customized learning experience, personalized instructional content, and feedback tailored to each student's needs, which improves learning and engagement. Consequently, AI has been identified by numerous researchers as a driving force in educational technology innovation and a significant element in the digitalization of higher education (Chen et al., 2020; Zawacki-Richter et al., 2019).

The adoption of AI technologies is gaining momentum in higher education and is being used to facilitate multiple academic and administrative processes. Universities are also using AI-based systems to automate routine administrative tasks, analyze student performance data, and provide customized academic assistance. For example, intelligent tutoring systems can provide students with personalized guidance and feedback, and predictive analytics tools can help institutions identify students at risk of failing or dropping out. Moreover, AI-based recommendation systems can propose suitable learning materials and courses based on students' profiles and performance. Such technological advances can make a substantial contribution to the efficiency of the teaching process, the increase in learning levels, and institutional decision-making. As a result, many colleges and universities are investing in AI technologies to enhance the quality of education and institutional performance (Zawacki-Richter et al., 2019).

The increased development of AI technologies has also been caused by the introduction of generative AI devices like ChatGPT and other large language models. These applications can produce human text, respond to questions, help in academic writing, and help in other learning processes. The ubiquity of generative AI technologies has generated strong debates in the academic community concerning their influence on education and their disadvantages. On the one hand, AI generative tools can help students master complexities, give them immediate feedback, and help educators create instructional aids. Conversely, there have been concerns about academic honesty, plagiarism, misinformation, and excessive reliance on computerized systems. Consequently, the innovation of more generative AI-based technologies has created opportunities as well as threats to educators and institutions globally (Kasneci et al., 2023).

Although AI technologies have great potential for the future in higher education, several challenges and ethical issues can be considered. AI-based systems require the use of large amounts of data, which raises important issues related to privacy, data security, and ethical governance. In addition, automated systems can be used in educational settings, but their implementation can result in algorithmic bias, transparency, and accountability problems. Another issue that has attracted scholars' attention is the possibility that AI might affect academic labor, as teachers may be too preoccupied by the risk of automated systems taking on some of their teaching duties. Nevertheless, many scholars argue that AI must not replace teachers but rather enhance their abilities by helping with the teaching process and lightening the administrative load. In this regard, the successful implementation of AI in learning institutions should be thoughtful about ethical standards, pedagogy, and institutional guidelines (Zawacki-Richter et al., 2019; Chen et al., 2020).

Another significant issue with AI integration in higher education is its impact on teaching practices and learning conditions. From an individualized learning perspective, collaborative learning, and data-oriented teaching, AI technologies are being applied to assist with these in the learning context. These systems enable educators to track the progress of students, detect learning problems, and offer specific interventions to enhance learning performance. Also, AI learning tools can facilitate adaptive learning classrooms, which vary teaching resources based on the needs of individual learners. These advancements highlight the potential of AI to improve teaching effectiveness and student interactions. Nevertheless, the effective adoption of AI in the educational sector will depend heavily on how educators learn and on the proper use of these new features in their teaching methods (Holmes et al., 2022). The work of academics is changing considerably as AI technologies rapidly evolve and gain increasing control over the educational system. It is assumed that the faculty members will be able to adjust to new digital settings, apply AI-related tools in their classroom experiences, and acquire new skills associated with digital literacy and data-informed decision-making. This change demands continuous professional growth to ensure that teachers have the knowledge and skills required to implement AI technologies in teaching and research. Lack of proper training and support can prevent educators from fully realizing the potential of AI technologies in educational settings. Hence, the career growth of academicians is now a burning problem in the era of artificial intelligence (Holmes et al., 2022).

While numerous studies have explored the use of artificial intelligence in higher education, much of the existing literature is devoted primarily to technological adaptation. There has been little attention paid to the professional development of academicians, nor to the skills needed to effectively operate in an AI-enabled academic setting. In addition, numerous studies discuss AI technologies without sufficiently linking them to changing work practices and roles, and to lifelong professional learning within institutions. This chapter attempts to address this gap with an integrated discussion on the ways in which AI is impacting academic work and why continuous professional development is a must-have for academics in modern institutions.

In this regard, the connection between the transformation of academic work and professional development by AI technologies is critical to the future of higher education. Institutions need to develop strategies that enable faculty members to adapt to rapidly changing technological conditions without violating the pedagogical and ethical principles of education. Effective ways of integrating AI technologies into teaching and research practices of educators can be offered by professional development programs on AI literacy, digital pedagogy, and ethical use of AI. To this end, the present chapter will analyze the changing role of academicians in the era of artificial intelligence and discuss the significance of professional development in enabling teachers to operate successfully in the context of AI-driven education.

ARTIFICIAL INTELLIGENCE IN HIGHER EDUCATION

The field of AI has gained prominence as a component of digital transformation in higher education institutions worldwide. Higher education institutions are incorporating AI technologies into their teaching methods to facilitate learning in students, as well as assisting the institution in making decisions. The ability of AI systems to process large amounts of data, conduct analysis, and make predictions will enable institutions to create more effective educational settings. Consequently, AI technologies are founding use in various fields of higher education, such as customized learning systems, intelligent tutoring platforms, learning analytics, and other automated administrative support systems. The developments show that AI is transforming the conventional model of higher education by proposing new ways of imparting knowledge and conducting education (Zawacki-Richter et al., 2019). An intelligent learning system that is used to facilitate individualized education is one of the most influential AI implementations in higher education. Educational technologies based on AI are used to improve student performance, learning behavior, and engagement patterns to offer personalized learning paths. With these systems, instructors can provide a delivery format that is responsive to students' learning styles. As an example, adaptive learning systems can be used where the difficulty level of learning materials can be varied based on the progress of the students, and the recommendation systems can also be used to recommend more learning materials in relation to the academic performance of the students. These technologies can assist teachers in determining the gaps in learning through machine learning algorithms and data analytics and then offer specific instructional support to learners. As a result, AI-driven customized learning platforms can enhance student interaction and academic accomplishments in institutions of higher education significantly (Nordgren et al., 2025).

Although AI technologies improve personalization and institutional efficiency, unequal access to digital infrastructure, technology resources and digital competencies may widen educational inequalities among institutions and learners. Furthermore, excessive dependence on automated system may reduce opportunities for fruitful human interactions.

The other significant use of AI in learning the pattern of institutions teaching is through intelligent tutoring systems and automated learning support systems. Intelligent tutoring systems refer to computer-based learning systems that emulate the functions of human tutors by providing instruction to the learners step-by-step and through feedback. Through such systems, AI algorithms are applied to track the progress of the students, detect mistakes and give recommendations on how to improve. These technologies come in handy, especially in big universities where it might be difficult to offer individualized support to each student. Giving students the opportunity to practice their problem-solving skills and provide immediate feedback on their learning performance, AI-based tutoring systems can provide constant support to students. Consequently, such systems can be used to supplement conventional teaching methods with supplementary assistance outside the classroom (Zawacki-Richter et al., 2019; Mah & Groß, 2024).

AI is also being instrumental in assisting teaching and assessment practices in higher education. Assessment tools based on AI are able to grade answers automatically, analyze written work, and identify trends in student answers. An automated scoring system for essays is a text-based response scoring system based on natural language processing methods that ranks the received texts based on specific criteria. Such technologies can save a lot of time and effort in grading assignments, especially in courses with a high number of students. Moreover, an AI-based feedback system based on AI can provide instant feedback to students, helping them learn from their mistakes and improve their learning outcomes. AI technologies can help educators reduce their time on repetitive assessment processes and nurture effective learning experiences, and offer students meaningful academic advice (Zawacki-Richter et al., 2019).

The use of AI technologies also facilitates the enhancement of student interaction and academic assistance in tertiary institutions. AI-driven learning analytics systems process information in learning management systems, online activities, and evaluation outcomes to learn how students behave and to what extent. These systems have the ability to identify the struggling students in their studies and warn the instructors to ensure necessary actions are taken in time. Immediate recognition of at-risk students is particularly important for enhancing retention rates and academic performance. Also, AI-based chatbots and virtual assistants are becoming increasingly popular among universities, and they are intended to provide students with immediate assistance with course registration, academic schedules, and institutional services. These technologies can minimize the number of people in the administration and enhance accessibility and responsiveness to student support services (Mah & Groß, 2024).

Institutional management and strategic decision-making are other significant fields in which AI is making a difference in the field of higher education. The universities produce large volumes of data on student registration, students' academic performance, and resource use. The data analytics tools developed using AI can assist institutions in analyzing these data to draw insights that support strategic planning and policy development. As an example, predictive analytics models can be used to forecast changes in enrolments and the factors that affect student success, and to help institutions better allocate funds. Technology can also help universities track institutional performance and measure the success of educational programs. With the assistance of data-driven insights, AI systems can help administrators to make well-informed decisions that increase the efficiency and sustainability of higher education institutions (Zawacki-Richter et al., 2019).

Although there are many positive aspects to using AI in higher education, its adoption faces several challenges and concerns. Data privacy and algorithmic bias, coupled with ethical governance, are some of the issues to be taken into consideration when implementing AI systems in learning institutions. It is also questioned how sensitive data of students can be protected when predictive analytics and learning analytics are used with large amounts of data. Also, AI algorithms can unintentionally reinforce existing prejudices when the information on which they are trained reflects discriminatory principles. The other issue is the potential impact of AI technologies on academicians' labor, as teachers fear that automated systems will take over some of their teaching roles. Nevertheless, most scholars stress that AI should be considered an aid to teachers rather than a replacement for them. Appropriately used AI technologies can improve teaching work and enable educators to concentrate on more significant pedagogical tasks (Zawacki-Richter et al., 2019). Moreover, AI tools should be successfully integrated into higher education, based on educators' digital skills and technological preparedness. The faculty needs to learn how to utilize AI-based tools in their practice. It involves knowledge of how AI systems function, interpretation of information produced by learning analytics systems, and the application of digital technologies in the instructional process. Institutional support systems, as well as professional training programs, are thus necessary to enable educators to successfully use AI technologies. Educators will not be able to successfully apply AI systems in their classrooms without proper training and support (Akgun & Greenhow, 2022).

All in all, AI is transforming higher education by creating new opportunities to enhance teaching, learning, and organizational management. Since intelligent tutoring systems and adaptive learning platforms with learning analytics and automated administrative tools are AI technologies that are changing the way knowledge is offered and administered in universities. Even though such technologies have tremendous advantages, ethical issues, institutional policies, and faculty training needs must be carefully considered upon their successful implementation. Since higher education has been shifting as a result of technological advancement, AI will become more instrumental in defining the future of teaching and learning in educational institutions.

CHANGING ACADEMIC ROLE IN THE AGE OF ARTIFICIAL INTELLIGENCE

The implementation of AI technologies in higher education has changed the conventional functions of academicians to a great extent. In the past, university teachers had the sole role of providing lectures, curriculum development and assessment of students. Nevertheless, with the advent of AI-based education technologies, these duties have been redefined by the system of automated mechanisms used to support a variety of teaching and administrative activities. Student learning patterns can now be analyzed using AI-powered tools, grades can now be automated, and students can now receive personalized learning recommendations. Consequently, the work of academicians is changing to being the main knowledge sender to one that facilitates the learning process and directs students in the technologically enriched learning settings (Mah & Groß, 2024; Zawacki-Richter et al., 2019).

Among the changes in academic functions that can be observed the most are the introduction of AI-based technologies into the educational process. The use of AI-based learning tools facilitates teaching practices by teachers which are more adaptive to the needs of individual students. Intelligent tutoring systems and adaptive learning platforms can examine the student progress, and give specific feedback according to the learning performance, as an example. These technologies enable the instructors to concentrate more on guidance and mentoring of the students and not just delivering the content. In turn, being an academician, one has to acquire new pedagogical skills to be able to use AI-driven tools in his or her teaching. The change shows the increased significance of digital literacy and technological competence in higher education institutions among educators (Crompton & Burke, 2023; Mah & Groß, 2024).

One more significant change is associated with the increasing focus on the use of data in teaching. Learning management systems, online learning platforms, and digital assessments are the sources of AI technologies that produce large amounts of educational information. Learning analytics technologies are used to process these datasets to find patterns of student engagement, academic performance, and learning behaviors. Academicians are also becoming obliged to read these implications and change their teaching approaches along those lines. As an example, predictive analytics models can be used to determine students who might be by risk of failing in school so that the educator can intervene early enough and offer them extra academic support. This increased dependency on data-driven decision-making imposes the necessity on academicians to gain analytical abilities that will allow them to comprehend and apply insights that were generated by AI-based education systems. Besides altering the teaching practices, artificial intelligence is also affecting research in the academic field (Qipeng & Jamaludin, 2026). The

AI technologies give researchers the opportunity to work with big data, discover patterns, and create forecasting models that can help to improve scientific research across different fields. Machine learning algorithms, natural language processing applications, and automated literature review systems have become a common tool used by many academic researchers to facilitate their research activities. Such technologies enable researchers to handle complex information more effectively and come up with new insights that cannot easily be identified in the conventional means of research. Consequently, academicians are facing an increased demand to learn interdisciplinary which will entail the integration of skills in their own fields with familiarity with the new digital technologies (Mah & Groß, 2024).

Mentoring and guidance activities of academicians are other areas that are influenced by the integration of AI technologies. Academic advising and mentorship have traditionally been offered by teachers by direct engagement with students. Nonetheless, AI-assisted products, including chatbots, virtual assistant, and automated advisory systems, are becoming more popular to assist student services in universities. These systems may offer students real-time answers to administrative and academic questions, which enhance the accessibility of assistance services within the institution. Although these technologies make teachers more efficient, they also compel teachers to reconsider the role of teachers' mentor and pay more attention to intellectual growth, critical thinking as well as ethical reasoning in the student community. In this context, academicians are important in making sure that technological advances in education are applied to facilitate meaningful learning experiences (Mbambo & Du Plessis, 2024; Mah & Groß, 2024).

Although AI technologies have established a wide variety of opportunities, the AI revolution of academic roles is not devoid of challenges as well. The problem is that many educators might be confused about how to introduce AI tools into their practice, as they do not have enough training or are not technologically skilled. Ethical issues have also been brought up when it comes to the use of AI in education such as the problem of data privacy, algorithm bias and academic dishonesty. Moreover, not all educators are sure that AI-technologies will never take away some of their activities. Nevertheless, most researchers state that AI must be perceived as an assistive technology that complements the features of teachers but not substitutes them. AI technologies empower academicians with more time to engage in tasks that involve human judgment, creativity, and mentorship as they can automate the routine tasks, as well as gather valuable insights into the student learning patterns (Kasneci et al., 2023; Holmes et al., 2022).

In general, the profession of academicians in universities is undergoing a change brought by artificial intelligence. Teachers are asked often to incorporate digital technologies into their lessons, analyze the data produced by AI systems, apply the methods of interdisciplinary research, and teach students how to work in the environment of the technologies. With these changing roles and responsibilities, there is the emergence of the need of continuous professional development as an academician should have the required skills and knowledge that would help them effectively interact with emerging technologies. Since institutions of higher learning are still adjusting in view of the fast-changing nature of artificial intelligence, academicians will be at the Centre stage in influencing the way these technologies are applied in learning, research and institutional growth.

PROFESSIONAL DEVELOPMENT FOR ACADEMICIANS IN THE AGE OF AI

The introduction of the AI technologies into college life has brought about a significant revolution in teaching, research and academic management. Since the use of AI-based systems like intelligent tutoring systems, learning analytics systems, and automated assessment systems continue to gain prominence in universities, academicians need to develop new skills that enable them to incorporate the systems into their professional careers. As a result, professional development has turned into an essential element in facilitating the ability of the educator to work within the changing digital learning environment. An effective professional system equips academicians with the knowledge, skills, and ethical awareness needed to work within AI-driven educational environments while still maintaining the core values of higher education pedagogy (Mbambo & Du Plessis, 2024; Tan et al., 2025). The future of professional development in the age of artificial intelligence extends beyond simple technical training. It includes a broad range of competencies such as AI literacy, digital pedagogy, data literacy, ethical consciousness, institutional training programs and lifelong learning practices among faculty members. These same skills help educators integrate AI technologies in educational institutions. (Crompton & Burke, 2023).

AI literacy for educators

Academician literacy in AI has become a fundamental requirement in contemporary institutions of higher learning set-ups. AI literacy can be defined as the level of knowledge of the educator about the main principles of artificial intelligence, such as machine learning, natural language processing, data-driven decision-making systems, etc. With the integration of AI technologies into the education platforms and the processes of the institutions, educators need to build a minimal knowledge base about the functionality of such systems and their impact on the teaching and learning processes (Chen et al., 2020).

Building AI literacy will help teachers see the power and drawbacks of the AI-based educational tools in a new light. Unless teachers have a proper knowledge of AI technologies, they might have difficulties in applying these systems to their teaching activities, or they might use them carelessly, not knowing fully what they imply. The studies have shown that teachers with a good level of AI literacy have an increased likelihood of using AI technologies successfully and integrating them into new instructional practices that can lead to improved learning experiences among students (Crompton & Burke, 2023). Besides, AI literacy also helps academicians to steer the students on its societal and technological consequences of artificial intelligence. With the increasing integration of AI in many fields of everyday life, universities can become critical in guiding students to be responsible and critical when dealing with AI systems. Teachers that are sufficiently AI literate can facilitate the discussion about the ethical, social, and economic consequences of AI technologies and can assist students in gaining the skills of critical thinking concerning the new technologies (Kasneci et al., 2023).

Digital pedagogical skills

Besides being AI literate, academicians should also acquire digital pedagogical literacy that would make them skilled to incorporate technology in education and learning contexts. Digital pedagogy implies that digital tools, platforms, and technologies are used to improve instructional strategies and design interesting learning experiences. The AI-based technologies offer new possibilities in using novel pedagogical models like adaptive learning systems, automated feedback systems, and intelligent tutoring systems (Crompton & Burke, 2023).

Digital pedagogical skills enable teachers to create learning environments by exploiting the potential of AI technologies and keeping the practices of teaching effective. As an example, adaptive learning systems powered by AI will be able to modify learning content based on the performance of each specific student to allow an educator to deliver a personalized learning experience. Correspondingly, automated feedback systems may also give students instant feedback on the assignments and assessments, giving educators more time to focus on student mentoring and guidance (Chen et al., 2020).

The use of AI technologies also promotes the application of more student-centered teaching models among educators. Instead of using only conventional examples of teaching by lectures, academicians may rely on AI assisted tools in designing interactive learning processes which promote collaborative learning, critical thinking and problem-solving. The establishment of digital pedagogical competencies, therefore, is a necessary solution in assuring that AI technologies complement but do not substitute effective teaching practices in higher education institutions.

Data Literacy for Academicians

In higher education the importance of data literacy among academicians has developed and increased along with the growing use of AI technologies. Data literacy refers to the ability to interpret, analyze and use data-driven insights to improve teaching and learning processes. AI driven learning analytic system generates large amounts of data related to student engagement, performance trends and behavior patterns (Mah & Groß, 2024). As an example, one can consider learning analytics tools that can be used to assess the risk of the student failing in the future or not engaging with the curriculum by examining the trends in attendance, assignment completion, and online engagement. Through the interpretation of these data insights, educators will be able to have early interventions to assist struggling students and enhance the overall academic results. Information literacy thus allows academicians to implement evidence-based instruction based on real-time student information (Zawacki-Richter et al., 2019). Nevertheless, to ensure a successful application of data analytics in education, educators must make themselves capable of data interpretation, visualization, and critical analysis. Awareness initiatives on data literacy can help academicians understand how AI driven analytics systems generate insights and how these insights can be used to improve teaching practices. Such training programs also enable educators to apply data driven decision making in their own teachings and activities (Crompton & Burke, 2023).

Ethical awareness and responsible AI use

As the use of AI technologies in higher education institutes continues to grow, ethical concerns have become an important part of professional development for academicians. Ai systems rely on large amounts of data and complex algorithms, which can raise issues related to data privacy, algorithmic bias, and lack of transparency. Teachers should be aware of the ethical considerations aligned with the use of AI technologies in teaching and research (Kasneci et al., 2023). Protecting student data is one of the significant ethical issues. AI-based learning platforms can easily gather data on student performance, behavior, and engagement patterns. In the absence of proper security measures, the data would be misused or put at risk of privacy. Teachers should thus take care that AI technologies are applied in a manner that guarantees student privacy and does not violate institutional and legal data protection regulations (Chen et al., 2020). The other ethical concern is algorithmic bias. The datasets used to train AI systems might have some level of inherent bias, which would result in unjust or even discriminatory results in the field of education. Academicians should know about these possible dangers and make sure that AI systems are introduced in the manner that fosters equity, transparency, and accessibility in the learning settings (George & Wooden, 2023).

Institutional training program

Higher education institutions are a vital part in facilitating academician's ability to learn in AI-supported learning settings. Incorporating AI into the teaching and academic governance process is not just about the skills of individual educators; it is also the responsibility of the institutions in place and structured professional development programs. Structured institutional training programs should thus be developed to equip educators with technical, pedagogical, and ethical skills to work with AI technologies in universities. Faculty development workshops, seminars should be held on the use of artificial intelligence in education, hands-on learning with digital learning platforms, and mentorship sessions for teachers to exchange knowledge and ideas about their learned experiences with AI in teaching. These various programs can help academics grasp the potential and concepts of AI tools, like learning analytics systems, adaptive learning platforms, and generative AI applications, in teaching and research fields (Kasneci et al., 2023; Tan et al., 2025; Mbambo & Du Plessis, 2024).

Moreover, universities should ensure that they have strong digital infrastructure, technical support services and institutional policies to guide the responsible and ethical use of AI technologies in higher education. Collaboration among teachers, engineers and administrators can make professional learning communities stronger and help encourage innovation in teaching methods. Therefore, institutional training program play an important role in improving institutional readiness and supporting the integration of AI in higher education institutions (Kasneci et al., 2023).

Lifelong learning for faculty

As AI technologies are continuously and rapidly evolving lifelong learning is becoming a critical part of the academic professional learning process. It is crucial for academicians to keep their knowledge and skills current to offer high-quality educational services to both students and researchers. Lifelong learning is a tool that can help educators stay relevant in the context of technological change in the area of interest of higher education. The faculty members are increasingly being encouraged to undertake continuous professional learning activities like online certification programmes, faculty development programmes, webinars, MOOCs, academic conferences and collaborative learning communities. These opportunities support the development of the competencies of academics in the areas of AI literacy, digital pedagogy, learning analytics and ethical practices of AI. Self-directed learning and collaborative peer learning also enable teachers to get creative with new teaching methods and to incorporate new technology into their teaching (Crompton & Burke, 2023; Tan et al., 2025).

Furthermore, lifelong learning encourages teachers to continuously reflect and improve their teaching practices, which is important in AI supported learning environments. Ongoing learning helps educators adapt to new technologies, use innovative teaching methods effectively, and respond to changing educational needs. In higher education institute building a culture that supports continuous professional learning among faculty members is essential for long term professional growth and for the successful integration of AI in teaching and learning (Mbambo & Du Plessis, 2024).

Conceptual framework for AI-driven professional development

As discussed in this chapter, a conceptual outline can be put forward on how a professional development for academicians does can be performed by using AI which is shown in Figure 1. The frameworks states that the integration of AI in higher education is a complex and sensitive area which requires the cooperation of several competency fields related to AI Literacy, digital pedagogical competence, data literacy with ethical awareness, support from institutions and develop lifelong learning. Together these skills can impact how well academics can integrate and fully use AI tools in teaching and administration.

The framework further emphasizes its attention towards institutional readiness and continuous professional development play a better role in supporting the integration of AI in higher education system. The framework also suggests the institutional readiness and ongoing professional development serves as facilitating conditions which gives sustainable embedding of AI in higher education institutes. AI literacy empowers educators to grasp and critically assess all AI technologies.

Figure 1: Hierarchical conceptual framework for AI-Driven professional development of academicians. (Developed based on reviewed literature).

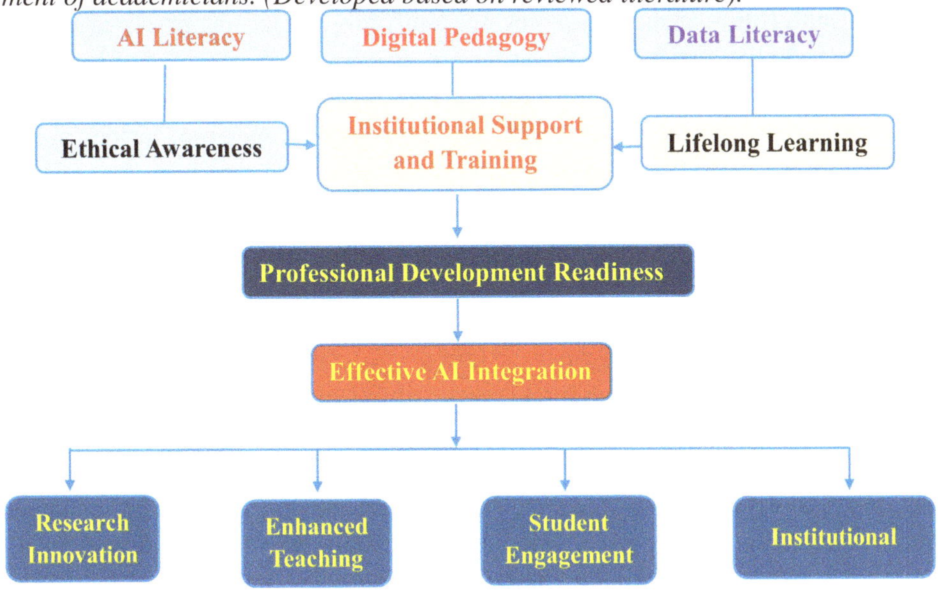

CHALLENGES AND OPPORTUNITIES IN AI DRIVEN PROFESSIONAL DEVELOPMENT

The fast work on the AI technologies has greatly redefined the idea of higher education as well as established new demands to professional growth of academicians. AI-powered systems are found in the teaching processes of university, assessment, administrative processes, and so on, which makes educators keep revising their skills and teaching strategies. The concept of AI-based professional development as such turns out to be an indispensable part of contemporary academic practice, providing educators with the ability to expand their pedagogical potential, embrace digital tools, and enhance the quality of teaching and learning outcomes. Nevertheless, on the one hand, AI can offer important prospects in enhancing professional development, on the other hand, there is a set of technical, institutional, and ethical concerns that need to be discussed by the academicians to be able to apply the technologies into their professional life (Zhang, 2025; Qipeng & Jamaludin, 2026; Zawacki-Richter et al., 2019).

The increase in teaching efficiency and teaching effectiveness is among the most valuable opportunities that AI can bring to the life of an academic professional. AI technology can be used to help an educator with repetitive academic issues like grading tasks, automatic feedback, and evaluating student performance information. Through automation of such processes, academicians can devote more time in high academic tasks like student mentoring, development of innovative educational plan, and research. The applications of AI-based learning analytics tools can also assist an educator with learning patterns among students and in which aspects they might need additional academic support. Such technologies allow the teacher to pursue data-driven instruction, which makes the learning process more effective and facilitates the more personalized learning process (Zhang, 2025; Holmes et al., 2019).

Initial AI technologies also open the door to everlasting online professional growth among academicians. As the number of online learning platforms, intelligent tutoring systems, and AI-enhanced training programs continue to expand their reach, educators are now introduced to the possibility of having unique professional development opportunities that will allow them to increase their digital literacy and pedagogical expertise. Professional development platforms of this type can examine the performance of teaching based on AI and suggest learning modules that will assist the educators to enhance their capabilities concerning digital pedagogy, data analysis, and utilizing educational technologies. These systems also help academicians to learn throughout their lives and enable them to be better suited to technological shifts in the higher education setting (Zhang, 2025; Chen et al., 2020). The possibility to facilitate innovative practice and curriculum planning is another opportunity that can be offered by AI technologies. The AI-powered content creation tools enable the academicians to develop dynamic learning content, simulators, and interactive learning experiences that make students more active. The generative AI technologies also would provide educators with the opportunity to create interdisciplinary learning experience involving the combination of knowledge in academic fields. Consequently, teachers are able to test an innovative teaching strategy that integrates both traditional pedagogical tools with advanced technological technologies and, consequently, enable a more flexible and interactive learner experience through the establishment of new and improved learning activities (Kasneci et al., 2023; Zhang, 2025).

Although there are all these advantages, AI-inspired professional development has several challenges which restrain successful implementation in institutions of higher learning. A major issue is the absence of relevant training and digital skills of teachers. Many academicians are not familiar with AI technologies and might not possess those technical abilities that they could use to implement AI tools in their instructional process. This problem is also enhanced by the increasing rate of technological development since teachers must continuously modernize themselves with digital innovations. Without the interventions of systematic training and institutional development few teachers may find it difficult to make good use of AI based learning system (Qipeng & Jamaludin, 2026; Tan et al., 2025).

Resistance to technological change among academics is also another crucial challenge. The implementation of AI technologies frequently demands radical changes in the teaching process, evaluation techniques and classroom management tools. There are some teachers who might not be comfortable implementing AI tools because of lack of knowledge using digital technologies or because confident that automated machines will work and be precise. There is also the worry that AI technologies would substitute some academic activities especially in various activities that involve grading, content production, and management. Such issues might cause opposition among teachers and hinder the implementation of AI-based professional development programs in higher educational institutions (Qipeng & Jamaludin, 2026; Crompton & Burke, 2023).

The issue of compatibility between AI-based technologies and the current academic practices poses another significant challenge to teachers as well. To be successfully incorporated in the higher educational setting, AI tools need to correspond with the organizational policies, educational programs, and pedagogical practices of educators. In case AI systems are not available to match the current teaching practice, academic staff can struggle to implement them into their practice. It has been argued that teachers are more inclined to use AI-based technologies when they believe that such technologies can fulfil their professional objectives and teaching methods. Hence, universities should make sure that professionally developed programs powered by AI are structured in such a way that they do not override the current pedagogical model of educators (Qipeng & Jamaludin, 2026).

Ethical issues also have an important role to play in professional development powered by AI. AI technologies can frequently work on big data and self-suggesting algorithms to process educational data and provide suggestions. As much as these capabilities provide effectiveness in analytical behavior in the same way they carry issues for data privacy, algorithmic prejudice, and decision-making transparency. Hence academicians need to develop ethical awareness, conciseness and critical thinking to analyze the outputs of AI and make sure that such technologies are applied with critical assistance in educational settings (Chen et al., 2020; Kasneci et al., 2023).

The success of AI-evoked professional development initiatives is also affected by institutional readiness. Universities need to invest in digital infrastructure, make AI-based learning platforms accessible, and have institutional policies that facilitate the responsible use of AI technologies. It is possible that educators cannot embrace AI tools when institutions do not offer sufficient technological infrastructure or training resources. Institutional encouragement is thus essential in helping the academicians go through AI-based professional development courses and apply these technologies within their learning systems (Zawacki-Richter et al., 2019).

To sum up, AI-based professional development is a field of opportunity and considerable difficulties to academicians in the academic sector. AI technologies can be used to make the teaching process more efficient, assist in shaping digital skills, and facilitate creative pedagogical activities that generate better student learning. Nevertheless, teachers should also address the problem of digital literacy, resistance to technology, issues of ethics, and institutional preparedness. To overcome these issues, universities, policymakers, and educators must work together to develop favorable training sessions, ethical systems, and technological systems that would allow academicians to integrate AI technologies into their practice successfully. The increasing use of AI based learning analytics systems may additionally raise concerns regarding surveillance, data privacy and institutional control over student and faculty activities (Zhang, 2025; Qipeng & Jamaludin, 2026; Zawacki-Richter et al., 2019).

CONCLUSION

AI is fast changing the institution, practices, and aspirations of higher learning. The increase in the application of AI technologies in the teaching and assessment processes and in the institutional management has produced new learning environments, which demand that academicians become technologically competent, digitally literate, and innovate in their instruction. This chapter has discussed how artificial intelligence and higher education are changing relationships and how the roles of academicians can evolve and the significance of professional development grows during the age of AI. AI technologies contribute to important opportunities in the teaching and learning process. Smart systems can be used to enable educators to process bulk learning data, learning trends of students, and facilitate individualised learning experiences. The repetitive duties involved in the processes of grading and feedback can be automated to enable academicians direct more attention to research supervision, curriculum development and student mentoring. Nonetheless, there are also a few disadvantages to integrating AI, such as the lack of technical skills, technological resistance, and the fear of ethical and transparent application of the AI systems. Universities and colleges therefore need to consider professional development initiatives which empower educators with digital literacy. Finally, although AI presents revolutionary possibilities towards enhancing the education process, it can only be effective when there has been a vigorous commitment to professional growth and development, enabling institutions to have supportive policies and regulate its use in the teaching and learning activity to make sure that academicians are at the core of the procedure.

REFERENCES

Akgun, S., & Greenhow, C. (2022). Artificial intelligence in education: Addressing ethical challenges in K-12 settings. *AI and Ethics*, *2*(3), 431–440. DOI: 10.1007/s43681-021-00096-7 PMID: 34790956

Chen, L., Chen, P., & Lin, Z. (2020). Artificial intelligence in education: A review. *IEEE Access : Practical Innovations, Open Solutions*, *8*, 75264–75278. DOI: 10.1109/ACCESS.2020.2988510

Crompton, H., & Burke, D. (2023). Artificial intelligence in higher education: The state of the field. *International Journal of Educational Technology in Higher Education*, *20*(1), 1–22. DOI: 10.1186/s41239-023-00392-8

George, B., & Wooden, O. (2023). Managing the strategic transformation of higher education through artificial intelligence. *Administrative Sciences*, *13*(9), 196. DOI: 10.3390/admsci13090196

Holmes, W. Centre for Curriculum Redesign, & Center for Curriculum Redesign. (2019). Artificial intelligence in Education. Promise and implications for teaching and learning. In *Artificial Intelligence in Education*. https://www.consorciosthem.com/wp-content/uploads/2025/02/sthem-ia-07-holmes-fadel-bialik-artificial-intelligence-in-education-promise-and-implications-for-teaching-and-learning-2019.pdf

Kasneci, E., Sessler, K., Küchemann, S., Bannert, M., Dementieva, D., Fischer, F., Gasser, U., Groh, G., Günnemann, S., Hüllermeier, E., Krusche, S., Kutyniok, G., Michaeli, T., Nerdel, C., Pfeffer, J., Poquet, O., Sailer, M., Schmidt, A., Seidel, T., & Kasneci, G. (2023). ChatGPT for good? On opportunities and challenges of large language models for education. *Learning and Individual Differences*, *103*, 102274. DOI: 10.1016/j.lindif.2023.102274

Mah, D. K., & Groß, N. (2024). Artificial intelligence in higher education: Exploring faculty use, self-efficacy, distinct profiles, and professional development needs. *International Journal of Educational Technology in Higher Education*, *21*(1), 58. DOI: 10.1186/s41239-024-00490-1

Mbambo, G. P., & Du Plessis, E. C. (2024). Impact of artificial intelligence on teacher training in open distance and electronic learning. *International Journal of Learning. Teaching and Educational Research*, *23*(5), 370–386. DOI: 10.26803/ijlter.23.5.19

Nordgren, C., Christensen, J., Spikol, D., & Tudorache, P. (2025). STUDENT EXPECTATIONS–AN ASPECT EASILY OVERLOOKED. *Journal of Teaching and Learning in Higher Education*, *6*(2). Advance online publication. DOI: 10.24834/jotl.6.2.1852

Qipeng, Y., & Jamaludin, K. A. B. (2026, January). The role of AI in higher education, teacher training, and professional development: Teachers' perspective. *International Journal of Academic Research in Progressive Education and Development, 15*(1), 496–508. https://hrmars.com/IJARPED/article/view/27522/The-Role-of-AI-in-Higher-Education-Teacher-Training-and-Professional-Development-Teachers-Perspective. DOI: 10.6007/IJARPED/v15-i1/27522

Tan, X., Cheng, G., & Ling, M. H. (2025). Artificial intelligence in teaching and teacher professional development: A systematic review. *Computers and Education: Artificial Intelligence, 8*, 100355. DOI: 10.1016/j.caeai.2024.100355

Zawacki-Richter, O., Marín, V. I., Bond, M., & Gouverneur, F. (2019). Systematic review of research on artificial intelligence applications in higher education – where are the educators? *International Journal of Educational Technology in Higher Education, 16*(1), 39. Advance online publication. DOI: 10.1186/s41239-019-0171-0

Zhang, S. (2025). Exploring challenges and opportunities in the AI-driven professional development of higher education faculty. *Lecture Notes in Education Psychology and Public Media, 113*(1), 22–29. DOI: 10.54254/2753-7048/2025.NS25886

KEY TERMS AND DEFINITIONS

Artificial Intelligence (AI): A subfield of computer science that deals with designing machines or systems that can execute activities that are traditionally performed by human intelligence, e.g., learning, reasoning, and decision-making.

Digital Literacy: The skill of using digital technologies, communication means, and networks to access, manage, evaluate, and create information successfully.

Machine Learning (ML): One of the branches of artificial intelligence that allows a system to learn patterns based on the data and then enhance its performance without explicit instructions.

Pedagogy: a method and practice of teaching that makes students understand easily, includes skills, strategies, and approaches utilized by educators for smooth learning.

Personalized Learning: A teaching model in which students have personalized and personalized teaching methods, teaching pace, and content.

Professional Development: The ongoing process by which teachers improve their knowledge, skills, and competencies in order to improve their teaching effectiveness and performance.

Chapter 6
Professional Development for Academicians in the Age of Artificial Intelligence:
A Multidimensional Framework for Academic Identity, Competence, and Institutional Transformation

Winter Seshoka
http://orcid.org/0000-0001-7832-2737
University of Limpopo, South Africa

ABSTRACT

AI is reshaping not only teaching and research in higher education but also academic identity, governance, and professional development. Yet little is known about AI-responsive professional development (PD) that addresses academic careers, appointments, and evaluation. This chapter develops a multidimensional, theoretically grounded PD framework based on TPACK, Human-AI Collaboration Theory, Transformational Learning Theory, and Digital Ethics. It analyses how AI transforms academic identities, institutional structures, and career pathways, with a comparative perspective on developed versus developing contexts. The chapter then identifies seven structural gaps in current PD models: fragmentation, techno-centrism, one-size-fits-all approaches, inequity, time constraints, policy-practice disconnects, and lack of collaboration. In response, the ACADEME-AI Professional Development Framework is introduced, integrating four dimensions: Knowledge & Competence, Relational & Agency, Identity & Transformation, and Digital Ethics.

DOI: 10.4018/979-8-2600-3204-6.ch006

1. INTRODUCTION

The advent of artificial intelligence (AI), more specifically, generative AI, is a significant development in modern higher education. Although digital tools have supported teaching, research, and administration for some time, developments in AI represent a step change. This shift is from technologies that simply support academic processes to those that exhibit competencies in knowledge production, pedagogy development, and institutional governance. This shift has profound implications for the practice, assessment and governance of academic work. Current research on AI in academia has tended to concentrate on technology integration, pedagogic development, and ethical issues. Although these are critical, the literature can be disjointed and disconnected from broader structures of academic careers. Specifically, there is little discussion of the relationship between AI and professional development, career progression, and professorial appointments, such as hiring, promotion, and evaluation. As AI is incorporated into institutional processes, these areas become more important to the future of the professoriate.

Despite the rising trend in research on AI and its relevance to higher education, the available literature still shows a fragmented pattern, which is divided into three separate discussions. First, the pedagogical application of AI in higher education has been explored (Batsaikhan & Correia, 2024; Dumitru, 2024; Nikolopoulou, 2024). While emphasising the integration of AI technology into educational planning and practice, they seldom consider the consequences of these developments in terms of their impact on the faculty member's career progression. Second, ethical and governance issues have been raised by the works of Marabelli et al. (2026) and Al-Kfairy et al. (2024). They shed light on the issues of bias, privacy, and accountability in using AI, yet they fail to identify any professional development strategy to tackle these issues in a manner that affects organisational structures. Finally, the third stream focuses on the identity and professional roles of academicians. However, this discussion fails to establish a connection between the evolution of the academician's identity and concrete mechanisms of career development, such as promotion, tenure, or evaluation systems.

Remarkably, there seems to be no systematic analysis of the intersection of the three previously discussed issues. No known study has provided an integrative model that considers how professional development can be strategically personalised to serve the purposes of career development, the appointment process of academicicians, and institutional evaluation systems. This chapter aims to fill this knowledge gap by suggesting a holistic framework to professional development for academicians, which should be considered a lifelong process embedded in the context of the institution.

2. RECONFIGURING THE ACADEMIC PROFESSION IN THE AGE OF AI

The emergence of AI is not just adding new tools to higher education; it is reshaping the academic profession. The shift is not simply about alterations in the way we teach and conduct research, but also about profound change in academic identity, institutional forms, and career paths. AI is a socio-technical actor that redefines the production, validation, and governance of knowledge. In so doing, it transforms what it is to be an academician in modern higher education. Therefore, in light of these developments, professional development cannot be considered as a marginal activity responsive to the need to enhance discrete skills but should be reconceptualised as a principal means through which academicians respond, engage with, and contribute to these changing structural dynamics.

2.1 AI and the evolving academic profession

Artificial intelligence is redefining the boundaries of the academic profession in higher education, thus transforming how knowledge is created, disseminated, assessed, and controlled. With the implementation of AI-powered systems in institutions of higher learning to teach, conduct research, administer, and perform quality assurance, the traditional roles and identities of academicians are being transformed substantively. This development is reflective of wider changes in higher education typified by digitalisation, massification, managerialism, and global competition, in which AI is both an agent of revolution and a source of new debates.

In higher institutions of learning, AI technologies in the domain of teaching and learning, including adaptive learning platforms, intelligent tutoring systems, and generative AI tools, are altering pedagogical approaches and practices (Batsaikhan & Correia, 2024; Dumitru, 2024; Nikolopoulou, 2024). Academicians are no longer solely content experts and transmitters of knowledge; they are increasingly expected to function as learning designers, facilitators, and critical mediators of AI-enhanced learning environments (Atabekova et al., 2025; Kotsis, 2025;Wu et al., 2024). Therefore, access to AI-generated materials threatens traditional understandings of authorship, originality, and integrity of assessment. This compels academicians to reconsider how curricula are designed, taught, and assessed. This shift requires academicians to develop pedagogical judgment that balances technological use with disciplinary epistemologies and learning outcomes, rather than adopting AI tools without critiquing them.

In addition to the teaching and learning task, AI is also transforming the research role of academicians. Machine-learning algorithms, data mining, and AI-assisted writing and analysis software have accelerated research processes, enabling large-scale data analysis, automated literature reviews, and predictive modelling across disciplines in higher education. Although these tools may improve the efficiency of the research process and introduce new methodological possibilities, they also evoke some significant questions related to research ethics, ownership of data, algorithmic bias, and integrity of the scholarly production of knowledge (Kim, 2024; Limongi, 2024; Qadhi et al., 2024). This means that academicians as researchers will have to find their way through a complicated terrain where AI can supplement intellectual work and, at the same time, transform the conventions of scholarly work, authorship, and evaluation.

Beyond teaching and research, AI is reshaping academic service and governance. AI in university governance has broadened the skill set demanded of academicians from teaching and research to include institutional leadership and governance. Academicians who are part of governance bodies - deans, heads of departments, senate members, chairs of committees - need to be familiar with how AI systems are used in decision-making, such as predictive analytics, performance dashboards, and decision support systems. This involves not only a basic understanding of AI, but also the critical analysis of how data are produced, analysed, and used, and how algorithmic predictions are interpreted, to avoid blind faith in algorithmic predictions. The subject also connects well with data literacy because data literacy helps academics understand how institutional data regarding students, scholarly publications, and staff can be interpreted while taking note of the inadequacies of relying on quantitative indicators to fully describe the complexities involved in academic activities (Esomonu, 2025; Shwedeh, 2024; George & Wooden, 2023).

On the same note, ethical literacy is critical because of issues surrounding governance involving AI. These include fairness, bias, accountability, and transparency. Academic professionals should be able to uncover any forms of bias that may arise from using algorithms for decision-making. The bias could affect some individuals who might lose out because of the bias, as well as affect the academic freedom of scholars. Therefore, academicians need to understand ethical principles such as fairness and human supervision in the use of algorithms. This aligns well with those in governance, as it adds up to policy and regulatory capacity for digital ethics. UNESCO (2023) states that it is necessary to transition from adopter-centric views of AI and its incorporation into the institution's operations to systemic methods that include three components, that is: ethical consideration, human involvement, and public responsibility in all stages of AI implementation.

The evolving academic profession in the age of AI is also marked by changing power relations and professional expectations. Academicians are supposed to continuously develop their digital competencies, engage in technology-enhanced innovation, and demonstrate adaptability in rapidly changing times, environments, and professions. However, access to AI tools, training, and institutional support seems to be uneven across institutions and their faculties globally (Alba et al., 2026; Mudenda, 2025). Such inequality may threaten and maintain existing disparities in the academic profession, especially between well-resourced and under-resourced institutions of higher education.

Importantly, AI does not necessarily introduce new tools into academic work, but it reshapes the values and assumptions underpinning academic professionalism (Nelson, 2025, 2024). The growing dependence on automation and datafication may challenge and support human-centred ideas of teaching, mentoring, and academic research. In reaction, academicians are expected to reaffirm the ethical, relational, and critical dimensions of their professional roles. This includes probing whose knowledge seems to be amplified through AI systems, whose voices are marginalised, and how AI may reproduce or address the existing social and epistemic inequalities within higher education epistemologies.

Within this changing environment, the academic profession may be defined as a struggle between opportunity and risk. AI can be used in the pedagogical process to make it more efficient, increase research possibilities, and enhance institutional responsiveness. Concurrently, it appears to present a threat to academic freedom, professional identity, and the social missions of higher education. Therefore, it is crucial to understand AI as a socio-technical phenomenon and not a neutral innovation. It is an insight that highlights the importance of professional development that not only prepares academicians with technical expertise but also with critical, ethical, and reflective abilities in order to inform the future of higher education in a manner that is socially responsible, inclusive, and in tandem with academic values. The ever-changing higher education milieu calls for the rethinking of professional development in the era of AI, an approach that acknowledges the dynamism of academia and supports academicians in exercising informed agency within higher education environments.

2.2 AI and academic identity

AI is not just reshaping academicians' roles. It is pushing them to reflect and rethink what it now means to be an academician. For a long time, academic identity hinged on deep expertise, independence, and a kind of personal authority in a specific field. However, AI seems to be disrupting all that. Now, academicians are dealing with knowledge that is scattered, algorithm-driven, and often hard to see through. Authority sits right at the heart of this shift. If AI can churn out detailed analyses, draft papers, or explain tough concepts, where does that leave the traditional academician as the go-to expert? Interestingly, this change does not erase academicians' importance. Instead, it rewires how authority works. Currently, with AI's use, the academician's job is not just about knowing their discipline. Academicians also must show that they can dissect what AI produces, put information in the right context, and steer the use of these tools in ethical directions. This means that the skill set has evolved; disciplinary expertise alone is not enough anymore.

Apart from authority, AI impacts the autonomy of the academician's work. The use of technological tools and algorithms becomes more prevalent, thus bringing changes related to monitoring and standardisation of activities. For example, learning analytics systems allow for monitoring teaching performance, whereas scientific metrics powered by AI may influence the publication techniques and funding processes. Such trends have the potential to limit the academician's independence, since they may lead to favouring particular approaches to the research practices and processes. On the other hand, they could also promote greater transparency and accountability within higher education institutions.

The issue of identity among academicians in relation to the development of AI technology is also associated with the growing trend of interdisciplinary and collaborative approaches among academicians. Technologies based on AI require expertise from different fields, such as computer science, data science, ethics, and specific knowledge in particular areas. As such, academicians from various disciplines may be forced to collaborate on various issues related to AI.

In addition to ethical and moral concerns regarding the use and deployment of AI, significant implementation issues arise because academia must not only be a user of AI technologies, but also a steward (in the sense of protecting the proper course and direction for the AI field) of the proper introduction and integration of these technologies into the broader higher education community. Issues of algorithmic, data privacy, and the social implications of AI are becoming more prevalent. Due to the increasing inclusion of ethical considerations in academic identity, there is a shift in responsibilities for academia from a single academician's identity to that of the academic community's collective impact on society.

So, professional development will continue to be critical in developing a new academic identity by providing opportunities for reflection, dialogue and critical engagement so that faculty at all levels (including individuals who are new to their fields) can renegotiate their roles and values concerning the use of AI in their respective fields and institutions. A professional development framework must establish a culture of agency so that all faculty members feel that they can contribute meaningfully to the use and implementation of AI in their respective fields and that they are not mere passive beneficiaries of technological change, such as AI use in academia.

2.3 AI and institutional transformation

It is difficult to assess the reconfiguration of the academic profession independently of other institutional changes occurring in higher education. As part of this process,

AI is driving massive transformation in how universities are structured, governed, and operated, with far-reaching implications for academic work and careers.

Institutions are maximising the benefits provided by implementing AI across a range of activities through data-driven decision-making. Data analytics are increasingly being used in higher education for functions related to the recruitment and retention of students, developing curricula, and assessing individual performance (Rodríguez-Ortiz et al., 2025). While a data analytics system can increase efficiency and provide institutions with opportunities for valuable insight, they also prompt worries about transparency, impartiality, and the simplification of complex educational processes into quantifiable metrics.

On an institutional level, AI has created major transformations in the work of evaluating individual academicians. So, the career path for each is based on the evaluation of the academicians based on metrics that are generated by AI. From hiring decisions, promotion criteria and allocation of resources, AI will significantly impact the career progression of academics. Algorithmic analyses, particularly when applied to metrics such as citation patterns or teaching evaluations, may inadvertently prioritise certain forms of academic output. For instance, if an AI-based promotion-support system is trained on past experiences from a department in which papers written by men had been cited more often in the past or where student evaluations showed correlation with gendered bias in language, then that bias will be embedded in and amplified by the algorithm. A woman researching feminist epistemology or critical race theory may find her work systematically ignored because the training set did not reflect topics such as these. Likewise, a younger researcher using alternative media or publishing formats (such as digital scholarship or open educational resources), would find themselves disadvantaged if the AI were basing its metric calculations on traditional journal impact factor metrics. In order to combat this form of bias, professional development must include teaching academicians about how AI systems encode historical biases as well as how they can demand transparency in terms of weights, training sets, and appeal processes. This practice can, in turn, potentially marginalise alternative or innovative approaches to scholarship.

AI is also having an influence on the governance and policy-making of institutions. Higher education institutions are creating policies and frameworks to guide how teaching, research, and administration can involve the use of AI. These policies cover areas like academic integrity, data privacy and responsible use of AI. However, the implementation of such policies relies on the professional development of academicians. Confused by a policy and without the required training and support to understand it, academicians can end up interpreting and enacting institutional policies in haphazard and contradictory ways.

In addition, AI also impacts higher education's globalisation and stratification. So, the ability of higher education institutions to invest in AI technology, infrastructure, and specialized professional development will continue to create disparities between different institutions globally. This will further perpetuate existing disparities in higher education academic opportunities and career progression. Despite these notable disadvantages, AI may also be advantageous as it may be a new model of collaboration among academicians as they connect internationally through global networks and find new ways to share resources.

The transformation in higher education institutions due to AI necessitates the development of coherent and well-thought-out professional development programmes. These should be in harmony with institutional goals and career progression. The need for such programmes to be flexible and cognisant of context must also be taken into consideration, as the challenges and possibilities of AI will not be identical across all disciplines, career stages, and geographical locations.

Therefore, the reconfiguration of the academic profession under AI is complex since it entails transformation into roles, identity, and institutional structures. The change in roles is interwoven with a change in identity, which in turn is inseparable from institutional reform. Hence, it requires a holistic approach to professional development, through which academicians can become active players in defining their future profession in a manner that is committed to its highest ideals.

3. COMPETENCIES FOR ACADEMICIANS IN THE AGE OF AI

The integration of artificial intelligence (AI) in the higher education sector has highlighted the need to reconceptualise the competencies required of academicians. In addition to technical skill, the modern AI age requires a multidimensional competency model that includes pedagogical, ethical, research, digital, and professional skills. Such competencies cannot be overlooked by academicians as these will be needed to critically interact with AI technologies, leverage their potential to improve scholarly work, and reduce the risks associated with them in complicated and diverse higher-education situations.

On the elementary level, AI and digital literacy have emerged as new competencies needed amongst academicians. This extends beyond basic technological skills to include an informed understanding of how AI systems function, their limitations, and their implications for teaching, assessment, research and governance. In their profession, academicians should be able to make pedagogically sound decisions about the implementation of AI tools in their practice by interpreting algorithmic outputs, assessing the trustworthiness of AI-generated content, and deciding when and how to integrate certain tools into their practice. This type of literacy will allow academicians to become more active and critical users of technology than passive users of technology, who can adjust the use of AI to the standards and learning goals of their disciplines.

Tightly connected with the idea of digital literacy is the concept of pedagogical competence. With AI changing curriculum design, teaching, assessment, and feedback, academicians should aim to create learning experiences that use AI to encourage student engagement, personalised learning, and formative assessment without compromising academic integrity (Ncube et al., 2026; Rao & Suhasini, 2025). This means that academicians should have the ability use AI tools in pedagogy and, most importantly, to design assessment activities that focus on higher-order thinking, creativity, and application, thereby reducing students' over-reliance on AI-generated outputs. Besides, academicians need to possess the ability to facilitate discussions about the ethical use of AI with students and promote transparency and shared responsibility in AI-mediated learning.

Ethical and critical reasoning constitutes another essential competency in the age of AI. The ethical issues of data privacy, surveillance, bias, intellectual property, and responsible use of generative AI continue to emerge as a challenge to academicians (Marabelli et al., 2026; Al-Kfairy et al., 2024). As such, academicians should develop ethical competence through an understanding of regulatory frameworks, institutional policies, and broader societal implications of AI in higher education. Importantly, it also involves cultivating a critical stance that questions whose knowledge is prioritised by AI systems, how power operates through algorithmic decision-making, and how AI may reproduce or challenge existing inequalities. This competency positions academicians as ethical stewards of AI use rather than mere implementers of institutional technologies.

In the research domain of academicians' profession, AI-assisted competence has become increasingly significant. Academicians should be able to use AI tools to analyse quantitative and qualitative data, model and communicate academically without compromising methodological rigour and research integrity. This comprises the ability to evaluate the appropriateness of AI methods to specific research inquiries, understand the epistemological consequences of AI-aided data analysis, and openly disclose the use of AI in the research process. Competence in this area also involves a critical interest in the new discussions of authorship, originality, and peer review in the age of AI-assisted scholarship.

The changing academic environment also demands strong adaptive and lifelong learning capabilities. Due to the dynamism of technological change, scholars should be capable of updating their knowledge and skills on a regular basis, participate in professional learning communities, and be adaptable to new AI applications. Such adaptability has not only been applied to technical learning but also covers the openness to pedagogical experimentation, reflective practice and responsiveness to student and societal needs. The concept of lifelong learning thus turns into the attribute of academic professionalism in the AI age.

Academicians should also note that collaborative and interdisciplinary competencies are also important in this AI age. The use of AI is not exclusive to intradisciplinary use. The integration of AI often goes across disciplinary boundaries, and academicians often have to work with colleagues in other disciplines, including computer science, education, ethics, social sciences, engineering, etc. Successful collaboration will enable joint problem-solving, curriculum co-design, and mutual response to AI-related ethical and pedagogical issues. The competencies assist in having a more integrated and institutionally coherent approach to the adoption of AI in higher education.

Lastly, leadership and agency in digital transformation become essential skills of academicians, especially those in senior or coordinating positions. Interestingly, academicians are increasingly expected to contribute to institutional decision-making on AI policies, professional development initiatives, and curriculum transformation. The academicians' leadership in this regard should be to advocate and promote human-centred, fair, and context-sensitive AI practices, and guide their peers and students in the responsible use of AI.

Collectively, these competencies signal a shift from a narrow focus of academicians possessing technical skills only and hint towards a holistic conception of academic capability in the age of AI. They emphasise that professional development strategies should be based on combining technical skills with pedagogical understanding, ethical use, critical thinking, and institutional participation. The development of these competencies is key to the continuity of the academic profession and the ability to make AI part of the educational mission of higher education instead of its devaluation.

4. PROFESSIONAL DEVELOPMENT AS A STRATEGIC RESPONSE TO AI: A COMPARATIVE GLOBAL PERSPECTIVE

As evident in the previous section, the competencies of academicians in higher education institutions are distinct. In many different parts of the world, higher education institutions such as universities have realised that the successful integration of AI into the academic domain depends on the ability of academicians to interact with this technology critically, ethically, and effectively. However, the nature and extent of professional development programmes vary significantly in universities in developed and developing countries. This comparison is particularly useful in understanding the changing role of professional development programmes as a reaction to AI-based transformation.

The global significance of using artificial intelligence in education can be noted by means of different strategy-based policies that are meant to improve the process of learning. For instance, China has already integrated AI technology into the existing education system as an important element of the country's modernisation process (Xia et al., 2022). In the United States (US), a lot of money and effort are invested into developing AI-powered platforms that help to adapt education to the specific needs of students (Williamson & Eynon, 2020). Moreover, international organisations like the Organisation for Economic Co-operation and Development (OECD) and the Jacobs Foundation-backed initiatives are funding projects aimed at preparing for the AI future as well as using data analytics for better results in education (Kuhl et al., 2019). In relation to the evaluation of teaching and research, universities in developed countries have adopted more proactive approaches to innovation, combining several types of advancements. In particular, one of the typical features is the adoption of an approach involving the use of AI in teaching through adaptive learning, generative AI, and the application of analytics-based assessment approaches (Ifenthaler & Gibson, 2020; Umer et al., 2023). AI systems have been widely integrated into European universities.

In Cyprus, one university as integrated AI into its teaching as AI is viewed to have great potential for learning improvement in terms of accessibility, scalability, effectiveness, and personalisation. Likewise, an institute in England use AI to support students. In a study by Yilmaz et al. (2026), based on feedback readability and reliability of assessments, the feedback provided through learning analytics and GenAI was rated significantly more readable than the feedback given by human tutors. Furthermore, the GenAI-generated feedback showed greater reliability than feedback given by tutors at an institute in the United Kingdom. Interestingly, formal strategic policy actions and initiatives like the U.S. and China in Europe aim at promoting the transition from traditional approaches to AI-based technologies in education. For example, the European Education Area (EEA) has a comprehensive policy initiative that promotes the adoption of AI and data-driven systems in education for responsible and ethical use. Such technologies may include personalised and adaptive AI systems that will foster the development of individualised education for students. Similarly, the Directorate-General for Education, Youth, Sport and Culture of the European Commission (2022) also promotes the exploitation and use of AI and data in education ethically with the aim of enhancing teaching and learning.

As presented above, AI innovations in developed countries are typically supported by well-developed institutional policies outlining the use of AI in teaching and research from the standpoint of effectiveness and ethics. Likewise, professional development of academicians in this context involves a structured and continuous process that enables academicians to develop skills related to the redesign of AI-based curricula, the creation of new assessment techniques, and the critical consideration of the current and future roles of AI in knowledge creation and dissemination (Sapawi & Yusoff, 2025; Zagkotas, 2025). Specifically, increased attention is paid to training academicians in designing authentic assessments as a means of limiting excessive reliance on AI-generated output while at the same time leveraging AI to make student learning and motivation more efficient (Mualla & Mualla, 2026). Notably, universities in the developed countries seem to be encouraging the incorporation of AI in academic activities. For this to happen ethically, they also have professional development initiatives for AI use for academicians.

In developing countries' universities, the integration of AI into academic activities is often in its early stages. There is an increasing recognition of the fact that AI could radically change not only the methods of instruction but also the process of assessment. Nonetheless, such processes are far from smooth and consistent, and more caution on the use of AI for academia still prevails. In different countries, much of the work currently undertaken by universities revolves around setting up rules for the use of AI (Maimela & Mbonde, 2025; Sangwa et al., 2025). There are a few efforts at creating a fully comprehensive system of incorporating AI technologies into the everyday practice of higher education. In different parts of Africa, there is a considerable variation in economic conditions, levels of technological adoption, and educational practices. Nonetheless, the implementation of technology is associated with certain problems common to most African countries. For example, previous studies have established issues related to infrastructure and access in connection with the incorporation of Information and Communication Technology (ICT) into teaching practice. So, the integration of AI technologies further exacerbates these issues. Specifically, inconsistent internet access throughout the continent poses barriers to the use of AI programmes. The expansion of the digital divide through AI technologies may increase educational inequality and widen the gap in these nations. So, as AI technologies are likely to become integral components of the economy of the future, the inability of African universities to incorporate them into academia will undermine their readiness to equip academicians with the needed AI skills for their work.

Apart from technical problems, financial constraints also represent a significant obstacle to the successful implementation of AI-based programmes in African universities. Implementation of new technologies requires substantial investments, which include licensing software, maintenance of computers, and continuous training of academicians. At present, many African countries experience shortages in textbooks, internet access, and personnel, and there is little money left for innovative solutions. Furthermore, due to a lack of skilled professionals who can develop, install, and manage AI-based technologies, the cost of implementation increases dramatically.

Consequently, many universities face serious difficulties in acquiring appropriate tools for improving institutional duties through artificial intelligence applications. Noticeably, in terms of professional development in AI, due to various challenges outlined above, academicians in this context may be offered general training on the introduction to AI technologies, as opposed to a more profound exploration of their application to teaching, research, and administrative practices.

The implementation of artificial intelligence in algorithmic decision-making clearly demonstrates disparities in different countries. As far as developed countries are concerned, universities are moving toward introducing data-driven systems which use AI for various purposes, including student analytics, optimizing financial decisions, and planning future development strategies. Such systems are supported by relatively advanced governance structures that include ethics, responsibility, and oversight. Thus, the professional development of academic staff includes not only technical skills but also the ability to analyse data, understand algorithms, critically engage with their results, and participate in the process of governance. The role of academicians includes knowledge about how AI can influence decisions and ensuring the ethical implementation of such systems.

In governance, developing countries' algorithmic decision-making in universities appear to be less developed and inconsistent. Many universities experiment with the implementation of AI-based systems; however, many of them are still working on prototypes or piloting projects (Sangwa et al., 2025). Thus, academicians have limited opportunities for developing competence in data-driven decision-making. Furthermore, as highlighted earlier, those who may need to use AI face difficulties associated with poor quality of data, lack of infrastructure, and institutional readiness. However, significant advancements can be seen in some countries when it comes to universities implementing innovation hubs focused on using AI for governance purposes. Even though these examples demonstrate potential for growth in the area, they cannot be generalised for all countries.

Professional development strategies practiced at institutional levels provide additional evidence of global differences. Universities in the developed world have implemented professional development programmes on an institutional level, integrating AI at all levels of university activities – from teaching and research to administrative functions. These types of approaches are always underpinned by effective and high-quality leadership, adequate financial backing, and team efforts in collaboration with different divisions in the organization. Academicians are motivated to use AI applications and become involved in pilot schemes, thereby acquiring practical knowledge and being part of innovative ventures. Learning processes are also a significant component of such programmes. It should be noted that evaluation strategies are often included in such professional development strategies, allowing for assessing their efficiency and improving them in the future.

Noticeably, in developing countries, professional development initiatives are more varied and often take the form of project-based or partnership-driven programmes. Universities may collaborate with industry partners, international organisations, or government agencies to provide training and resources for AI integration (Aleryani, 2025; Aderibigbe et al., 2023). While these initiatives can be innovative and impactful, they are often unevenly distributed and may lack long-term sustainability. In many cases, professional development is dependent on external funding or specific institutional projects, rather than being embedded within a coherent institutional strategy. Despite these challenges, such initiatives play a crucial role in building capacity and fostering innovation, particularly in these contexts where resources are limited.

In both developed and developing countries, professional development and AI in higher education include the common understanding that academicians' engagement with technologies is necessary for them to handle all the new aspects introduced with the rise of AI. However, these processes are influenced by various external factors, which determine their nature. For developed countries, the problem of AI implementation consists of sustaining ethical standards of operation and inclusiveness of technology, while avoiding any excessive use of data-driven approaches that would undermine academic values. For developing countries, the key aspect of professional development lies in creating sufficient infrastructure and capacities needed for dealing with AI in the most effective manner possible, and developing specific methods based on existing conditions unique to academicians at different universities. So, this discussion demonstrates the necessity for universities to design different frameworks of professional development for academicians depending on their needs. The application of the universal approach is not likely to produce the desired results since academicians are confronted with different AI issues in their positions.

It is worth noting that professional development serves as an important link between advancements in technology and the jobs of academicians. With the growing role of AI in higher education, the quality and nature of professional development will have significant effects on the overall adoption and implementation of AI in higher education institutions. Hence, the OECD (2023) stresses that capacity-building strategies at both the national and institutional level should have effective evaluation mechanisms in place that examine not only short-term learning outcomes but also the long-term changes in pedagogy and career progression.

5. GAPS AND CHALLENGES IN CURRENT PROFESSIONAL DEVELOPMENT FRAMEWORKS

An overview of the state of affairs within the framework of faculty professional development within the era of digital transformation, provided by Vreekamp et al. (2024), demonstrates the ongoing problematics: despite twenty years of technological advancements, the majority of the current professional development models of higher education remain sporadic, technocentric, and unable to provide a link between the activities proposed and career opportunities. Indeed, these statements correlate perfectly with the list of gaps identified further below. While Section 3 outlined the multidimensional competencies academicians require, that is: pedagogical, ethical, research, digital, and adaptive, professional development frameworks tend not to provide them systematically. Across the world of higher education, responses to AI have been reactive, inadequately resourced, and ill-suited to academicians' needs. This section identifies seven structural and design flaws accounting for this poor fit.

5.1 Fragmentation and reactivity

Professional development on AI is often ad hoc and reactive, appearing as sudden workshops in response to some breakthrough rather than being incorporated into more systematic plans. The absence of follow-up, contextualisation, and linkage to scaffolding results in shallow capacitation that is unlikely to be transferred into practice, as academicians in those workshops are not afforded enough time for reflection and experimentation, nor coaching (Polly et al., 2021). An academician attending a two-hour workshop about generative AI leaves their department without such support, leaving little hope that changes will occur. Moreover, such practices create professional development fatigue, the cynicism about yet another training, which discourages engagement.

5.2 Technocentrism at the expense of pedagogy and ethics

Existing models focus almost exclusively on using certain AI technologies, such as prompt engineering and formatting the output, and neglect other aspects, including why, when, and under what ethical considerations to employ them. This approach treats the academician like a client consuming technology rather than critical professionals reflecting on the ethical implications of algorithmic results or assessing whether an assessment question created by an AI tool is actually fair. In other words, technocentrism turns academicians into automating robots who are unable to think critically about a situation. Thus, the current technocentric approach to professional development stands in direct opposition to international policy recommendations.

UNESCO (2023) warns that technological proficiency alone is not enough; there must also be consideration of pedagogical judgement, privacy concerns, algorithmic biases, and human-centered educational values.

5.3 Standardised design neglecting discipline and career stage

Professional development is seldom tailored to AI's disciplinary variations or faculty at different career stages. The experience of a historian and a computational biologist is inherently dissimilar: one may be struggling with epistemological challenges of authorship and source criticism; the other with reproducibility and algorithmic automation. But standard professional development programmes are inadequate for either. Equally, an early-career lecturer on a fixed-term contract should receive professional development on how AI competencies will affect their probation assessment and provide safe spaces to experiment. Meanwhile, a full professor needs professional development that concentrates on strategy and policy design. However, most professional development fails to accommodate these variations by delivering a single programme of equal content to a mixed audience, generating disengagement on both ends.

5.4 Inequality of access

Access to professional development is radically unequal. Early career academicians, contingent faculty, and those at underfunded institutions are being left behind and pushed to the margins of the profession. Adjunct lecturers who are paid per course cannot afford to miss a single class. Internationally, not only does inequality have personal and social costs, but also epistemic ones, as views from under-resourced higher education institutions are systematically marginalised in global conversations on AI and higher education. The reality is, tools such as AI solutions developed elsewhere might not be suitable, may not work as desired, or may be harmful to use without local adaptation.

5.5 Time restrictions and excessive workload

Time limitations and excessive workload are consistent complaints among academicians regarding their lack of ability to pursue professional development (Haddock-Fraser, 2020; Kouritzin, 2019). This is not due to personal preferences but reflects the structural features of contemporary academic labour. Current professional development practices expect faculty to undertake additional tasks in addition to existing commitments. A lunch and learn workshop assume that faculty give up their lunch break; a self-directed module assumes faculty sacrifice their evenings or weekends. Such design choices burden faculty further. This is particularly the case for those already overworked, such as female and caregiving academicians. Structural solutions would require integrating professional development into faculty workload models, allotting them a percentage of their workload time for professional development, counting participation as professional service in promotion files, and paying contingent faculty for their professional development time.

5.6 Policy and practice disconnection

There has been a rush to develop policies on AI at institutions of higher education. However, the gap between the rhetoric of policies and academic practice has become very pronounced. What, for example, is meant by "academicians must use AI transparently" stated in one institutional policy? Is it disclosing one's use of AI in methodology, a simple footnote, a declaration to the editor of the journal? How is one supposed to do all this without proper professional development which provides a framework for implementing the policies? Overcoming this gap entails the need to design professional development alongside the policies, thus creating modules which will translate each of the principles of the policies into action via specific cases from various disciplines, while also treating the academicians as collaborators in the implementation of those policies.

5.7 Absence of reflective and collaborative methods

The prevalent type of professional development involves expert-led content delivery, positioning the faculty members in the roles of mere recipients of knowledge, not as co-creators of learning experiences. It is important to note that such a type of professional development is especially unsuitable for AI because it is characterised by rapid changes, uncertainties, and value conflicts. There cannot be any expert who could give a definite answer to the faculty questions on assessment redesign or the concept of fair use of AI in peer review. In order to overcome these challenges, there must be space for reflective and collaborative methods, communities of practice, peer observation, and discussion of AI cases in departments – practices that are seldom used.

All seven gaps listed above are indicative of a systemic design problem. The existing professional development model is fragmented, where it ought to be longitudinal, technocentric instead of being pedagogically and ethically focused, standardised instead of being differentiated, inequitable instead of being redistributive, workload-agnostic instead of being workload-aware, policy-unrelated instead of being policy-operationalising, and passive instead of being collaborative. All of these features are intertwined within an approach that considers AI to be a separate technical problem to be solved via episodic training, while it is more of a transformation of the academic profession.

6. THEORETICAL PERSPECTIVES INFORMING PROFESSIONAL DEVELOPMENT IN THE AGE OF AI

As evidenced by a series of case studies conducted on eleven institutions by Doria et al. (2026), the use of a standardised and uniform AI training programme proves to be inferior. Universities that succeeded in fostering substantial alterations in faculty practices did so because they offered multiple tracks for individualised development that academicians could choose based on their discipline, career level, and expertise. The gaps mentioned above cannot be solved only through technical training and additional workshops. Instead, what is needed is a shift in thinking based on well-established theories addressing issues associated with pedagogical, relational, transformative, and ethical issues in the context of AI-enhanced academic work. Hence, this chapter proposes a professional development framework that builds upon the following four different yet complementary theories: Technological Pedagogical Content Knowledge (TPACK), Theory of Human-AI Collaboration, Transformational Learning Theory, and Digital Ethics. By combining these theories, we obtain the proper conceptual framework for moving forward from the simple description of what needs to be known into action.

6.1 Technological Pedagogical Content Knowledge (TPACK)

The TPACK framework provides a conceptual framework that can be used to understand the increasing complexity of knowledge that is required to teach and learn in an institution of higher learning in the midst of AI usage by students. Initially developed to explain the dynamic interaction between content knowledge, pedagogical knowledge and technological knowledge (Li et al., 2022). TPACK is also relevant when AI technologies are no longer neutral tools but adaptive systems that can create content, analyse data and make pedagogical decisions. The intersections in TPACK are amplified by AI that brings technologies that can guide curriculum development, customise learning opportunities, and automate certain aspects of assessment.

For academicians, technological knowledge should be beyond operational proficiency. It should also include the knowledge of how AI systems work, what their assumptions are, and what pedagogical affordances and constraints exist in them. Therefore, professional development should help academicians to develop integrated knowledge that will empower them to make informed judgments on when, why, and how AI should be used to improve disciplinary learning as opposed to making disciplinary learning more efficient. In accordance with the TPACK approach, successful professional development in the era of AI should be discipline-sensitive, as the pedagogical consequences of AI differ across disciplines. This framework highlights the need to have professional development models that can help academicians to navigate the complex relationships between AI tools, disciplinary knowledge, and student learning in higher education.

6.2 Human-AI Collaboration Theory

In supplementing TPACK, the Human-AI Collaboration Theory provides a critical counter-narrative to discourse that presents AI as a substitute for academic labour. Instead, this school of thought imagines AI as a cooperative partner that can enhance academia instead of replacing human knowledge. In higher education, this theory may be useful for reframing academic roles in teaching, research, and assessment amid growing concerns about automation and academic precarity. In the context of professional development, Human-AI Collaboration Theory focuses on the development of competencies that would allow academicians to operate productively with AI systems. These capabilities encompass a sense of the respective capabilities and constraints of humans and machines, the creation of workflows that make use of AI to perform mundane or data-intensive tasks, and the preservation of human judgment in areas that demand ethical reasoning, contextual awareness, and pedagogical sensitivity. Academic growth based on this framework prompts academicians to perceive AI as a cognitive and pedagogical aid, i.e., facilitating feedback, learning analytics, and content generation, and maintain the primary role of human agency in academic decision-making. In addition, this view prefigures the relational and power relations in the adoption of AI, which makes it essential to critically reflect on who has access to AI systems, who is coded into their knowledge base, and how working with AI can transform academic identities and power. As such, the Human-AI Collaboration Theory provides a useful perspective on the development of professional development that makes the academic community more empowered, not as mere passive consumers of institutional technologies.

6.3 Transformational Learning Theory

Transformational Learning Theory also makes a strong contribution to comprehending how academicians make sense of, internalise, and react to the disruptive potential of AI in their profession. The implementation of AI in higher education often provokes certain beliefs about teaching, learning, assessment, authorship, and expertise (Awadallah Alkouk & Khlaif, 2024; Zawacki-Richter et al., 2019).

Transformational learning focuses on how adults revise their frames of reference through critical reflection, dialogue, and experience, making it highly relevant to AI-related professional development. In this view, professional development cannot be considered as a channel of acquiring skills only, but a mediator of the change in beliefs, values, and professional identities. AI can cause uneasiness, confusion, or opposition among academicians as it may be viewed as aiming to replace the traditional ways of academia. However, the Transformational Learning Theory emphasises the necessity of establishing safe, reflective environments in professional development programmes in which academicians are able to challenge their assumptions about knowledge, technology and their roles as teachers as well as researchers. The consideration and use of this theory in the design of professional development may highlight the need to have a long-term, reflective, and dialogic learning experience rather than a brief training experience. The aim should be to make academicians active meaning-makers who work critically with AI, negotiate its effects on the academic practice, and create new ethically-founded methods of teaching and research in higher education.

6.4 Digital Ethics frameworks

Digital Ethics frameworks offer a necessary normative basis of professional development in the era of AI. With the growing influence of AI systems on assessment practices, learning analytics, and research processes, academicians are faced with difficult ethical issues concerning data privacy, algorithmic bias, transparency, academic integrity, and responsible use of generative technologies (Holland, 2026; Kayyali, 2025). Making professional development based on digital ethics may change the perspective of what AI can do to what it should do in higher education. These frameworks underline the importance of such principles as fairness, accountability, transparency, and human oversight, which are essential in the maintenance of trust and equity within academic systems. For academicians, ethical competence is not only adherence to institutional policies but also the ability to critically assess AI tools, question their assumptions, and foresee their social and educational consequences. Digital ethics-informed professional development should thus be more than a compliance-based training and should encourage ethical thinking, critical digital literacy, and moral accountability. It is especially relevant in heterogeneous and unequal settings of higher education, where AI can alleviate or further deepen the current disparities. The implementation of digital ethics in professional development may guarantee that the implementation of AI is in accordance with the greater academic principles, such as social justice, inclusivity, and academic freedom.

Adopted and used collaboratively, these theoretical lenses provide a multidimensional approach to the concept of professional development among academicians in the era of AI in higher education. The chapter argues and provides a comprehensive and critical view of professional development in higher education by combining pedagogical knowledge (TPACK), collaborative human-machine relationships (Human-AI Collaboration Theory), deep professional learning processes (Transformational Learning Theory), and ethical responsibility (Digital Ethics frameworks). This integrated theoretical grounding supports the argument that effective professional development must not only equip academicians with new skills but also enable them to navigate the profound epistemic, pedagogical, and ethical transformations brought about by AI in higher education.

In light of the discussion, this chapter proposes the ACADEME-AI Professional Development Framework. This framework synthesises and integrates four main theoretical approaches to build an all-encompassing, multi-dimensional professional development framework. It incorporates the TPACK theory, Human-AI Collaboration Theory, Transformational Learning Theory, and Digital Ethics. The framework functions within the following interrelated dimensions:

- Dimension 1 (Knowledge and competence)

In this dimension, the TPACK framework is introduced into the picture as a way of allowing academicians to make reasoned and informed decisions about whether, why, and how to use artificial intelligence technologies to facilitate disciplinary knowledge learning and development. Thus, the focus of the technology adoption is made on enhancing pedagogical and subject knowledge rather than on increasing effectiveness, speed, or convenience of learning.

- Dimension 2 (Relational and agency)

AI technologies are viewed as partners that supplement academic expertise in the area in question rather than replacing it with some automated processes. This dimension gives rise to considerations about human agency as well as the necessity for academicians to apply critical thinking to issues of power relations, including questions related to control over AI use, amplification of particular perspectives through such use, and so forth.

- Dimension 3 (Identity and transformation)

Professional development is treated in terms of its reflexive and dialogic nature rather than as a one-shot workshop aimed at providing the necessary competencies. This dimension refers to transformational changes in academic identity and beliefs as well as value shifts associated with ongoing practice and professional dialogue.

- Cross-cutting dimension (Digital ethics)

This is incorporated into all three of these dimensions, serving as an unassailable cross-cutting basis. To be implemented successfully, it will need to incorporate disciplinary diversification, tracking of professional stages, reflective learning communities, and embedding evaluation. This combination of elements is meant to resolve fragmentation and inequity issues in the existing professional development models.

7. RECOMMENDATIONS FOR AI-RESPONSIVE PROFESSIONAL DEVELOPMENT FRAMEWORKS

When developing an AI-responsive framework, developers should note that a professional development system that responds to AI should be holistic, continuous, inclusive, and ethically based, guided by the frameworks discussed above. It should not only deal with technical competence but also with pedagogical innovation, research ability, and the development of professional identity. The framework is supposed to work on various levels of academia, that is, individual learning, collaboration, institutional policies and strategies, and global academic networks. This stratified approach is a guarantee of sustainability and contextual adaptability.

First, a fundamental problem with existing approaches to professional development is that they tend to have an overly generalised format and assume a one-size-fits-all principle. An AI-responsive framework would necessarily account for both career stage and disciplinary background of its participants. For early-career faculty members, such as doctoral candidates, postdoctoral researchers, and fixed-term lecturers, the focus of professional development should be on acquiring the basic AI literacy that would facilitate research (e.g., doing literature mining and analyzing big data), establishing pedagogical fundamentals, including drafting syllabi that include clear AI policies, and learning how the use of AI may impact their probation and/or reappointment decision. For mid-career faculty, professional development activities should involve integrating AI skills into their administrative portfolio, such as being a program director or a department chair, applying AI technology in the assessment of large classes, mentoring new hires on AI ethics, and understanding how it all will affect their promotion to an associate/full professor position. As for senior faculty and university administration members, their professional development activities should be concerned with developing AI-based policy design, university governance in the realm of AI, and the evaluation of AI instruments before implementation.

Similarly, there is a need for disciplinary differentiation. In the humanities, for example, professional development may focus on critical AI literacy (e.g., spotting potential AI bias in the analysed texts and engaging with algorithmic epistemology issues), addressing the issue of authorship and originality, and using AI tools for archival and discourse analysis. For sciences, the focus may be on AI-assisted reproducibility (including generation of codes and statistical tests), AI-integration into lab research processes, and ethical issues involved in the application of AI in human subjects' research. And for schools, such as medicine, law, and business, professional development topics may involve discipline-specific AI applications (diagnostic, legal research, or financial forecasting, respectively). Otherwise, professional development becomes irrelevant or even risky in that it will reinforce and further deepen the existing inequalities among the well-funded and less fortunate disciplines and career stages.

Academic institutions should go further than general ethical principles and turn them into practical policies. They need to implement the following practices: (a) an obligation to perform an algorithmic impact assessment before any deployment of an AI-based system that may have an impact on hiring, promotions, evaluations, and academic advancement; (b) a clear process for appeals against decisions made by AI algorithms, such as teaching evaluations and research metrics; (c) designated positions within the institution responsible for performing audits of AI-driven processes, halting them if necessary, and reversing their effects if necessary; and (d) annual transparency reports on the application of AI in personnel decisions in the academic environment, including statistics on demographic disparities in the outcomes of AI decisions. Furthermore, the training programme should provide academicians not only with the skills needed to operate with AI technologies but also with the ability to participate in decision-making regarding AI-based tools.

8. EVALUATING THE IMPACT OF AI-RESPONSIVE PROFESSIONAL DEVELOPMENT

Designing effective professional development will not suffice without conducting a comprehensive and long-term assessment of its impact. Institutions need to establish a hierarchical system of evaluating the impact of professional development on AI in higher education institutions. The first step would be to conduct pre- and post-assessments of academicians' competencies in using AI for education, including their AI literacy, ethical reasoning, and integration skills. For this purpose, researchers may utilise the existing TPACK-AI assessment instrument or devise other assessments, such as scenarios for testing ethical decision-making. In addition, institutions may engage in classroom observations, teaching portfolio evaluations, and assessment design analysis to ascertain whether the faculty members have incorporated AI in actual settings. On an institutional level, they may track indicators for long periods to assess the effect of AI professional development on the promotion rate, student performance (e.g., the number of completed courses using AI, academic dishonesty cases), and AI adoption within the discipline. Lastly, institutions need to evaluate whether proficiency in using AI through professional development leads to appointment and tenure decisions.

In terms of methodology, the framework developed by the OECD (2023) to examine the impacts of AI skill acquisition provides a practical model for the assessment of professional development, advocating for multi-dimensional methods that incorporate pre- and post-competency assessments, workplace observations, long-term career impact monitoring, and stakeholder interviews, in lieu of satisfaction surveys.

9. CONCLUSION

Artificial intelligence is redefining the sphere of higher education by changing the way teaching is conducted, research is done, and expectations are set in the institutions. For academicians, this change has become a challenge and an opportunity. Although AI tools can be used to increase productivity and open up learning opportunities, they also require new skills, ethical consciousness, and adaptable professional identities. The existing models of professional development seem not to be sufficient to meet these requirements since they are either fragmented, under-resourced or not linked to the institutional strategies. Institutions of higher learning need to embrace holistic and sustainable professional development models to equip academicians in the AI age, which entails the integration of technological literacy, pedagogical innovation, ethical responsibility, and collaborative learning cultures. Finally, professional development in the era of AI is not necessarily about technical competence but the maintenance and reinforcement of the academic mission. Higher education institutions can make sure that the advancement of technologies helps humanity, social accountability, and intellectual development by enabling academicians to be critical and creative in their interactions with AI.

REFERENCES

Aderibigbe, A. O., Ohenhen, P. E., Nwaobia, N. K., Gidiagba, J. O., & Ani, E. C. (2023). Artificial intelligence in developing countries: Bridging the gap between potential and implementation. *Computer Science & IT Research Journal*, *4*(3), 185–199. DOI: 10.51594/csitrj.v4i3.629

Al-Kfairy, M., Mustafa, D., Kshetri, N., Insiew, M., & Alfandi, O. (2024, August). Ethical challenges and solutions of generative AI: An interdisciplinary perspective. [). MDPI.]. *Informatics (MDPI)*, *11*(3), 58. DOI: 10.3390/informatics11030058

Alba, C., Mcilwain, C., & An, R. (2026). ChatGPT on campus: how top US universities govern generative AI across higher education. *Policy Reviews in Higher Education*, 1-30. https://doi.org/DOI: 10.1080/23322969.2026.2622674

Aleryani, A. Y. (2025). Roadmap: Empower researchers in AI skills in developing countries. *Artificial Intelligence*, *15*(1), 1–13. DOI: 10.14445/22492593/IJCOT-V15I1P301

Atabekova, A., Atabekov, A., & Shoustikova, T. (2025). AI-Facilitated Lecturers in Higher Education Videos as a Tool for Sustainable Education: Legal Framework, Education Theory and Learning Practice. *Sustainability (Basel)*, *18*(1), 40. DOI: 10.3390/su18010040

Awadallah Alkouk, W., & Khlaif, Z. N. (2024, December). AI-resistant assessments in higher education: Practical insights from faculty training workshops. [). Frontiers Media SA.]. *Frontiers in Education*, *9*, 1499495. DOI: 10.3389/feduc.2024.1499495

Batsaikhan, B. Z., & Correia, A. P. (2024). The effects of Generative Artificial Intelligence on Intelligent Tutoring Systems in higher education: A systematic review. *Studies in Technology Enhanced Learning*, *4*(1), 1–30. DOI: 10.21428/8c225f6e.33570bb1

Doria, B., Grion, V., Picasso, F., & Li, L. (2026). Faculty assessment development in higher education: The CRAFT framework emerging from a systematic literature review. *Assessment & Evaluation in Higher Education*, *51*(1), 16–40. DOI: 10.1080/02602938.2025.2584121

Dumitru, C. (2024). Future of learning: Adaptive learning systems based on language generative models in higher education. In *Impact of artificial intelligence on society* (pp. 31–42). Chapman and Hall/CRC. DOI: 10.1201/9781032644509-3

Esomonu, N. P. M. (2025). Utilizing AI and big data for predictive insights on institutional performance and student success: a data-driven approach to quality assurance. *AI and ethics, academic integrity and the future of quality assurance in higher education, 29.*

European Commission. (2022). *Ethical guidelines on the use of artificial intelligence (AI) and data in teaching and learning for educators, Directorate-General for Education, Youth, Sport and Culture.* https://data.europa.eu/doi/10.2766/153756

George, B., & Wooden, O. (2023). Managing the strategic transformation of higher education through artificial intelligence. *Administrative Sciences, 13*(9), 196. DOI: 10.3390/admsci13090196

Haddock-Fraser, J. (2020). 14. The unseen pressures of academia. *Modern day challenges in academia: Time for a change*, 211.

Holland, J. (2026). The Disclosure-Detection Nexus in Generative AI: An Integrated Analysis of Ethical Implications in Academia. *Int. J. Management and Data Analytics, 6*(1), 70–87. DOI: 10.5281/zenodo.18453863

Ifenthaler, D., & Gibson, D. (Eds.). (2020). *Adoption of data analytics in higher education learning and teaching*. Springer. DOI: 10.1007/978-3-030-47392-1

Kayyali, M. (2025). Ethical implications of generative AI in education: Privacy, bias, and integrity. In *Transformative AI practices for personalized learning strategies* (pp. 185–218). IGI Global Scientific Publishing. DOI: 10.4018/979-8-3693-8744-3.ch008

Kim, S. J. (2024). Research ethics and issues regarding the use of ChatGPT-like artificial intelligence platforms by authors and reviewers: A narrative review. *Science Editing, 11*(2), 96–106. DOI: 10.6087/kcse.343

Kotsis, K. T. (2025). Artificial intelligence as a catalyst for changes in university-level science education. *EIKI Journal of Effective Teaching Methods, 3*(3), 99–109. DOI: 10.59652/jetm.v3i3.618

Kouritzin, S. (2019). Extent and consequences of faculty members' workload creep in three Canadian faculties of education. *Canadian Journal of Education/Revue canadienne de l'éducation, 42*(4), 1092-1120.

Kuhl, P. K., Lim, S. S., Guerriero, S., & Damme, D. V. (2019). *Developing minds in the digital age*. OECD Publishing. DOI: 10.1787/562a8659-en

Li, S., Liu, Y., & Su, Y. S. (2022). Differential analysis of teachers' technological pedagogical content knowledge (TPACK) abilities according to teaching stages and educational levels. *Sustainability (Basel), 14*(12), 7176. DOI: 10.3390/su14127176

Limongi, R. (2024). The use of artificial intelligence in scientific research with integrity and ethics. *Future Studies Research Journal: Trends and Strategies*, *16*(1), e845–e845. DOI: 10.24023/FutureJournal/2175-5825/2024.v16i1.845

Maimela, C., & Mbonde, P. (2025). Artificial intelligence in South African universities: Curriculum transformation and decolonisation—aid or obstacle? *Frontiers in Sociology*, *10*, 1543471. DOI: 10.3389/fsoc.2025.1543471 PMID: 40697567

Marabelli, M., Davison, R. M., Gatti, G., Srivastava, A., & Tarafdar, M. (2026). Use of Generative AI in Scholarly Research: Challenges and Opportunities. *Communications of the Association for Information Systems*, *58*(1), 36.

Mualla, K. J., & Mualla, W. (2026). Leveraging AI in Higher Education: Contemporary Approaches for Teaching, Learning, and Assessment Design. In *Higher Education in the Arab World: Artificial Intelligence* (pp. 169-191). Springer Nature Switzerland.

Mudenda, S. (2025). Impact of Artificial Intelligence on College and University Students: A Global Transformation of the Education System. *Creative Education*, *16*(11), 1801–1828. DOI: 10.4236/ce.2025.1611112

Ncube, P. D., Dzvapatsva, G. P., Matobobo, C., & Ranga, M. M. (2026). Redefining student assessment in AI-infused learning environments: A systematic review of challenges and strategies for academic integrity. *AI and Ethics*, *6*(1), 68. DOI: 10.1007/s43681-025-00871-w

Nelson, R. (2024). *Academic identity in the age of AI: Higher education and the digital revolution*. Emerald Group Publishing.

Nelson, R. (2025). Academic Identity in the AI Era: Navigating Resistance, Adaptation and Traditional Values in Higher Education. In *AI-Powered Pedagogy and Curriculum Design* (pp. 153-168). Routledge.

Nikolopoulou, K. (2024). Generative artificial intelligence in higher education: Exploring ways of harnessing pedagogical practices with the assistance of ChatGPT. *International Journal of Changes in Education*, *1*(2), 103–111. DOI: 10.47852/bonviewIJCE42022489

OECD. (2023). *AI and the future of skills* (Volume 2: Methods for evaluating AI skill implications). OECD Publishing.

Polly, D., Martin, F., & Guilbaud, T. C. (2021). Examining barriers and desired supports to increase faculty members' use of digital technologies: Perspectives of faculty, staff and administrators. *Journal of Computing in Higher Education*, *33*(1), 135–156. DOI: 10.1007/s12528-020-09259-7

Qadhi, S. M., Alduais, A., Chaaban, Y., & Khraisheh, M. (2024). Generative AI, research ethics, and higher education research: Insights from a scientometric analysis. *Information (Basel)*, *15*(6), 325. DOI: 10.3390/info15060325

Rao, G. T., & Suhasini, N. (2025). Integrating artificial intelligence in higher education to enhance teaching and learning. *Computer Applications in Engineering Education*, *33*(6), e70085. DOI: 10.1002/cae.70085

Rodríguez-Ortiz, M. Á., Santana-Mancilla, P. C., & Anido-Rifón, L. E. (2025). Machine learning and generative AI in learning analytics for higher education: A systematic review of models, trends, and challenges. *Applied Sciences (Basel, Switzerland)*, *15*(15), 8679. DOI: 10.3390/app15158679

Sangwa, S., Ngobi, D., Ekosse, E., & Mutabazi, P. (2025). AI governance in African higher education: Status, challenges, and a futureproof policy framework. *Available at* SSRN *5386204. Artificial Intelligence and Education, 1*(1), 2054. https://doi.org/ DOI: 10.2139/ssrn.5386204

Sapawi, M. S. M., & Yusoff, N. M. R. N. (2025). Artificial Intelligence in Curriculum Development: A Global Systematic Review of Trends, Challenges, and Strategic Directions. *Journal of Curriculum Studies Research*, *7*(2), 466–497. DOI: 10.46303/jcsr.2025.30

Shwedeh, F. (2024). The integration of artificial intelligence (AI) into decision support systems within higher education institutions. *Nanotechnology Perceptions*, *20*(5), 331–357.

Umer, R., Susnjak, T., Mathrani, A., & Suriadi, L. (2023). Current stance on predictive analytics in higher education: Opportunities, challenges and future directions. *Interactive Learning Environments*, *31*(6), 3503–3528. DOI: 10.1080/10494820.2021.1933542

UNESCO. (2023). *Guidance for generative AI in education and research*. UNESCO Publishing.

Vreekamp, M., Gulikers, J. T., Runhaar, P. R., & Den Brok, P. J. (2024). A systematic review to explore how characteristics of pedagogical development programmes in higher education are related to teacher development outcomes. *The International Journal for Academic Development*, *29*(4), 446–462. DOI: 10.1080/1360144X.2023.2233471

Williamson, B., & Eynon, R. (2020). Historical threads, missing links, and future directions in AI in education. *Learning, Media and Technology*, *45*(3), 223–235. DOI: 10.1080/17439884.2020.1798995

Wu, D., Zhang, S., Ma, Z., Yue, X. G., & Dong, R. K. (2024). Unlocking potential: Key factors shaping undergraduate self-directed learning in AI-enhanced educational environments. *Systems*, *12*(9), 332. DOI: 10.3390/systems12090332

Xia, Q., Chiu, T. K., Lee, M., Sanusi, I. T., Dai, Y., & Chai, C. S. (2022). A self-determination theory (SDT) design approach for inclusive and diverse artificial intelligence (AI) education. *Computers & Education*, *189*, 104582. DOI: 10.1016/j.compedu.2022.104582

Yilmaz, M., Gauthier, A., & Cukurova, M. (2026). Supporting online learners' regulation skills with the help of learning analytics and generative artificial intelligence: M. Yilmaz et al. *Educational Technology Research and Development*, 1-30. https://doi.org/DOI: 10.1007/s11423-026-10595-1

Zagkotas, V. (2025). Artificial Intelligence and the Didactic Transposition of Knowledge: Implications for Curriculum Development and Knowledge Gatekeeping. *Futurity Education*, *5*(2), 44–66. DOI: 10.57125/FED.2025.06.25.03

Zawacki-Richter, O., Marín, V. I., Bond, M., & Gouverneur, F. (2019). Systematic review of research on artificial intelligence applications in higher education–where are the educators? *International Journal of Educational Technology in Higher Education*, *16*(1), 39. DOI: 10.1186/s41239-019-0171-0

KEY TERMS AND DEFINITIONS

Academic identity: the changing professional self-notion of academicians, which is influenced by technological progress, the necessity of lifelong learning, and the need to redefine the meaning of the academician roles in an AI-mediated setting.

Academic professional development: a series of institutional and individual processes that improve the skills of faculty in the areas of teaching, research, technology, and leadership in higher education.

AI literacy: the ability to read, critically evaluate, and ethically use the tools and products of artificial intelligence in academic research, pedagogy, and institutional practices.

AI Professional Development Framework: a comprehensive academic development framework that involves AI literacy, pedagogical innovation, ethical consciousness, collaborative learning, and institutional support mechanisms.

Artificial Intelligence in higher education: the application of AI technologies in teaching, learning, research, assessment, and administration of higher institutions.

Digital pedagogy: a set of teaching activities that combines digital and AI-driven technologies to support student-centred learning, interaction, and the development of critical knowledge.

Ethical use: involves the responsible use of AI technologies in academia, which takes care of issues of integrity, transparency, privacy, intellectual property, and algorithmic fairness.

Human-AI: a paradigm of the collaboration of researchers and AI systems, where they act as complementary partners, using computational efficiency and human judgment and pedagogical skills.

Chapter 7
Reimagining Doctoral Research in the Age of AI:
Strengthening Scholar-Supervisor Collaboration and Enhancing Research Quality

Kesavan Dhanapal
http://orcid.org/0000-0002-6208-4997
SRM Institute of Science and Technology, India

S. Sivaprakkash
http://orcid.org/0000-0003-4642-0660
Central University of Tamil Nadu, India

Rafia Banu
http://orcid.org/0000-0002-4143-1742
B.S. Abdur Rahman Crescent Institute of Sciences and Technology, India

Naveenraj Xavier
http://orcid.org/0000-0003-2681-5964
SRM Institute of Science and Technology, India

ABSTRACT

Doctoral research is increasingly shaped by the everyday presence of artificial intelligence, influencing how scholars think, write, manage uncertainty, and engage with supervision. This chapter examines the cognitive, emotional, and relational shifts that arise as doctoral students enter research with early clarity, structured thinking, and AI-supported confidence rather than prolonged ambiguity. While this transformation can reduce anxiety and sustain momentum, it also raises crit-

DOI: 10.4018/979-8-2600-3204-6.ch007

ical questions about independence, originality, and research quality. Drawing on doctoral education literature and supervisory perspectives, the chapter argues that fear-driven and prohibition-based institutional responses weaken trust and obscure learning processes. Instead, it reframes AI as part of the contemporary scholarly infrastructure requiring interpretive guidance. A collaborative research quality model is proposed to demonstrate how autonomy, methodological integrity, transparent supervision, and intellectual maturation can be strengthened through guided AI integration.

INTRODUCTION: THE AI-INFUSED DOCTORAL LANDSCAPE

The knowledge and organizational structures behind doctoral studies have undergone significant changes, meaning today's doctoral researchers may have perspectives that are completely different from those of previous generations. In fact, researchers can hardly imagine the research process without AI these days, from literature review and data gathering and management to analysis and synthesis, write-up, and peer feedback. Many of them have already been working with AI for some time, even before embarking on formal doctoral training. Therefore, it is not surprising that many cognitive skills related to critical thinking, information literacy, and problem-solving have already been shaped by regular interaction with AI-based assistance. That means that, merely through the use of AI, researchers can greatly alter not just their perception, connection, and interaction with knowledge but also their way of dealing with uncertainty and of forming self-confidence in their intellectual capacities. Scholars in higher education institutions witness a period of major transformation influenced by digital technologies (Selwyn, 2016; Williamson, 2017), including the integration of AI-based assistance that enhances critical thinking, information literacy, and problem-solving skills.

Although the topic of generative AI in higher education is gaining momentum, much of the current debate still focuses mainly on plagiarism detection, academic misconduct, surveillance, and institutional control. Then again, AI's impact on the intellectual, relational, and developmental aspects of doctoral research, particularly on the changing relationships among doctoral students, supervisors, and institutional research cultures, has received far less attention. First, this chapter suggests that, rather than viewing AI as simply a technical implement or an academic threat, it should be seen as a factor in the changing cognitive and organizational conditions of doctoral study. To this end, it offers the Collaborative Research Quality Model as a conceptualization of research quality, grounded in collaboration among doctoral candidates, supervisory connections, institutional structures, and AI-enabled research environments. This chapter also addresses the need to shift the focus of doctoral work toward a relational, progressive process within AI-influenced academic areas influenced by AI, discussing topics such as supervisory changes, the development of scholarly identity, research honesty, and the redefinition of academic progression and professorial work through the lens of AI-enhanced academic systems. Current debates on generative AI in higher education pay considerable attention to the dual nature of AI-supported learning: for one thing, they enhance the writing and knowledge production processes and feedback (Kasneci et al., 2023; Dwivedi et al., 2023), but they also involve certain risks. AI accountability, transparency, and human-centered academic monitoring have been the focus of the UNESCO (2023) and OECD (2019) reports. These authors emphasize that these are the key elements of any educational setting.

The modification is nuanced but substantial. Traditionally, during doctoral research, the first stage was characterized by the greatest uncertainty. Partial knowledge, lack of clear direction, and slow idea development handicapped researchers. Actually, periods of perplexity were training phases for scholars, supporting their gradual gaining of disciplinary judgment and intellectual identity (Lovitts, 2001; McAlpine & Amundsen, 2011). The contemporary doctoral students, meanwhile, generally perceive the initial phases of research as periods of rapid orientation. Through AI-facilitated interaction facilitated by AI, they can formulate initial conceptual outlines, working definitions, and provisional methodological structures much earlier in the research process. This acceleration in the building of coherence can not only facilitate continuous motivation and stress relief but also alter the very points of experience on which scholarly judgment has traditionally been based.

The doctoral program, educationally speaking, represents one of the major aspects of a person's career that can be shaped towards the academic field. The ways in which doctoral researchers are taught to understand, use, question, reveal, and control AI while pursuing their doctorates may determine their academic roles as supervisors, faculty members, and professors of the future. Therefore, AI supervision in doctoral education encompasses much more than just completing the issues related to the doctoral thesis. It influences the development of a scholarly person, research performance, supervisory ability, and principles of honesty in academia, as well as professional judgment for a career in academia. Taking AI as part of the doctoral training process, this chapter relates the quality of doctoral research to future work in academia and to a professor's responsibilities.

Such a change in mood completely transforms the whole doctoral journey. If the insight is activated instantly, the meaning of confusion will change. The mental struggle won't be completely eradicated; rather, it will be postponed, and in certain situations, doctoral students may even proceed smoothly to interpret, judge, and combine, just as they begin to familiarize themselves with the scholarly traditions that dictate the standards for such work. Because of these factors, a new form of doctoral education emerges, in which students are clearly yet ambiguously exposed to a great deal of uncertainty. To understand the essence of a contemporary Ph.D., one must look back at the historical development of such a pattern. Currently, the supervisory role, long considered the primary teacher-student relationship in doctoral education, is being redefined in this new climate. More precisely, this is the interaction point in academic writing at which the doctoral student, who has generated some content, a draft, and an outline and was in part assisted by AI, is when the supervisor nowadays comes to know his/her scholar. Most of the research to be discussed in the meeting has already been conducted separately. In addition to transforming the practical aspects of supervision, it also changes the unspoken elements that supervisors typically take for granted, such as the doctoral student's independence, originality, and research quality.

In the literature on doctoral supervision, it has repeatedly been noted that interpretive dialogue is at the very heart of a Ph.D. student's development and the growth of scholarly work. The emotional side of graduate school is also touched on. Over the years, graduate students have expressed feelings of vulnerability, self-doubt, and uncertainty about their future. Graduate students have always relied on finding several ways of support to deal with the emotional ups and downs of their graduate studies. Yet, they are in fact turning to AI for guidance in dealing with many of the same issues. Gardner (2009) and Lovitts (2001) have presented evidence that the emotional well-being of graduate students is a key factor not only in their success throughout their program but also in their persistence to graduation. Studies show that a student's emotional capacity to handle difficulties, their sense of being supported by faculty and colleagues, and their belief in their ability to accomplish scholarly work are main factors in staying in and ultimately graduating from their program (Gardner, 2009; Lovitts, 2001). As AI continues to develop, those same elements affect how resilience and scholarly identity are conferred on doctoral graduates.

The emergence of AI doesn't mean a reduced chance for graduate students to receive tuition and produce scholarly work; rather, it changes the way they do so. Earning a graduate degree still offers students the opportunity to master inquiry, interpretation, and scholarship throughout their studies. Yet the instruments and mental spaces used to carry out the tasks have changed. Graduate students establish their research-quality scholarly identity and academic integrity primarily through interactions with their instructional advisor, instructional assistant supervisor, institutional culture, and AI algorithms. These five elements are interconnected, and together they support the graduate experience in ways that differ from the past while remaining grounded in the traditional values of scholarship.

APPROACH

The chapter presented here is conceptual and interpretive, building on a selective synthesis of the literature. Rather than an empirical study, the chapter draws together the work of those involved in doctoral education, research supervision, academic integrity, AI governance, generative AI in higher education, and scholarly development to explore how artificial intelligence is transforming doctoral research environments. The literature was selectively reviewed with a focus on doctoral supervision, research quality, intellectual development, and responsible AI integration in academic contexts. From this synthesis, the chapter introduces the Collaborative Research Quality Model as a system for conceptualizing how research quality is emerging from the interactions among doctoral scholars' supervisors, institutional structures, and AI-assisted research practices.

OBJECTIVES

The increasing integration of artificial intelligence into doctoral research is reshaping how scholars engage with knowledge, develop research practices, and navigate academic environments. These changes extend beyond questions of technological adoption and require closer attention to the evolving relationships among doctoral scholars, supervisors, and institutional structures that influence research development and academic judgement.

This chapter aims to examine three interrelated concerns emerging within contemporary doctoral education. First, it explores the changing learning orientations of doctoral scholars, whose research practices are increasingly characterised by accelerated access to information, early conceptual structuring, and continuous feedback mechanisms. Such shifts have implications for scholarly development, intellectual independence, and the formation of doctoral identity.

The chapter considers the evolving nature of doctoral supervision. As supervisory interactions increasingly occur within technology-mediated research environments, supervisors face new challenges in interpreting scholarly reasoning, supporting intellectual growth, and sustaining disciplinary standards.

The chapter conceptualizes research quality as a systemic and collaborative outcome shaped through the interaction of scholars, supervisory practices, institutional environments, and emerging technological conditions. These objectives provide the foundation for developing an integrated understanding of doctoral research within contemporary academic contexts.

DOCTORAL SCHOLARS AS AI-NATIVE RESEARCHERS

Doctoral students entering research programmes today have developed their learning habits within digitally mediated environments where information, explanation, and feedback are readily available. As artificial intelligence becomes increasingly embedded within academic work, these technologies influence how scholars formulate problems, organize inquiry, and engage with knowledge production. Rather than functioning solely as research tools, AI systems are gradually becoming part of the environment within which scholarly work takes place.

Within this chapter, *AI-native researchers* refer to doctoral scholars whose learning practices, problem-solving approaches, and research habits have developed alongside AI-assisted educational technologies. Unlike earlier generations of researchers who encountered digital tools later in their academic careers, many contemporary doctoral students enter research programs already familiar with AI-supported systems for information retrieval, summarisation, conceptual clarification, and drafting support. Consequently, their experiences of uncertainty, research progress, and scholarly development increasingly occur in technology-mediated learning settings.

One noticeable shift concerns the expectation of early conceptual clarity. In earlier doctoral traditions, uncertainty and ambiguity were often considered important elements of scholarly development. Long periods of confusion, repeated reading, and gradual conceptual refinement frequently contributed to disciplinary judgment and intellectual growth (Lovitts, 2001; McAlpine & Amundsen, 2011). Current doctoral researchers often approach projects differently. AI tools can provide preliminary conceptual structures, working definitions, and alternative explanations at the beginning of the research process. Early clarity may support motivation and reduce anxiety, but it also changes how scholars experience the slower, less predictable processes traditionally associated with academic development.

Changes are also visible in how doctoral scholars engage with literature. Studies suggest that students increasingly rely on generative AI systems for conceptual clarification, summarisation, and writing assistance, reshaping learning practices and perceptions of scholarly work (Chan & Hu, 2023; Kasneci et al., 2023). AI-supported tools now assist researchers in constructing thematic overviews, identifying conceptual patterns, and developing initial research directions. While these functions may reduce the time required to navigate unfamiliar areas, reliance on summaries and conceptual maps may reduce sustained engagement with primary scholarly sources. Strong disciplinary understanding continues to depend on direct interaction with original texts and competing perspectives.

Writing practices have also evolved. Many doctoral scholars now use AI-assisted systems during drafting and revision processes to improve language, structure, and organisation. Such support can increase efficiency and clarity. At the same time, writing no longer functions solely as a process of gradual intellectual discovery; it increasingly becomes an iterative process involving revision, restructuring, and refinement. This shift alters how ideas develop and how scholars experience the relationship between thinking and writing.

The emotional dimensions of doctoral work are similarly affected. Doctoral research has long involved periods of uncertainty, self-doubt, and intellectual strain. AI systems increasingly provide forms of cognitive support through continuous feedback, alternative explanations, and guidance during difficult stages of research. Some scholars may begin associating progress and confidence with the availability of technological assistance. Consequently, the sources through which resilience and scholarly confidence develop may also be changing within contemporary doctoral environments.

These shifts also influence scholarly identity formation. Doctoral education has traditionally been viewed as a process of socialization into disciplinary values, norms, and scholarly practices (Gardner, 2009; McAlpine & Amundsen, 2011). Historically, scholars developed understanding through engagement with supervisors, peers, and disciplinary communities. AI-assisted environments introduce additional sources of explanation and interpretation into this process. As a result, doctoral scholars increasingly navigate multiple forms of authority as they develop their own academic judgment.

Such developments do not suggest a weakening of doctoral scholarship. Instead, they indicate changing conditions under which intellectual development occurs. Contemporary doctoral researchers increasingly operate within environments where knowledge, interpretation, and judgment are negotiated across both human and technological systems. Understanding these conditions is important for developing supervisory and institutional practices suited to present-day doctoral education.

SUPERVISOR PERSPECTIVES AND EMERGING TENSIONS

Supervisors are now working with doctoral students whose research methods illustrate the mental states as specified in the previous section. Initial drafts gradually show greater coherence, more structured arguments, and well-formulated methodological proposals, even at stages of inquiry where there was previously extended uncertainty and conceptual exploration. This change subtly but significantly affects the supervisory meeting. Supervision is no longer primarily about helping students find their way; it is about understanding the origins and depth of the direction already presented.

This development generates fresh varieties of evaluative tension. It is now a challenge for supervisors to decide whether students who explain things clearly at the beginning genuinely understand the work or are merely benefiting from AI-generated work. Earlier, immaculate writing was considered a reliable indicator of a student's progress, but in the current situation, it gives less of a clue about the learning process. Thus, supervisors are required to be more attentive to how students support their arguments, respond to criticism, and cope with complex ideas. The assessment's emphasis shifts from the physical product to the communicative process by which the product is challenged.

In this context, trust is a significant concern. Historically, the nature of the supervisory relationship has centered on openness and honesty about intellectual challenges, doubts, and successes within the context of an academic career, as documented in APA Style. When researchers use AI but are concerned about using it in front of others, they tend to communicate less about their research. Consequently, supervisors may notice a disconnect between the apparent success/progress of the researcher and the supervisor's understanding of the researcher's reasoning process for producing that success/progress. This disconnect can result in mutual uncertainty among participants, eroding one of the fundamental components of the doctoral educational experience—the collaborative development of research-based academic independence.

As relationships between scholars and supervisors develop, they evolve emotionally as well. Increasingly, supervisors are supervising scholars who exhibit confidence in some areas but appear anxious or insecure in others. AI-mediated development can lead to periods of strong self-confidence early in the developmental process, which can quickly diminish when scholars encounter additional theoretical, methodological, or conceptual barriers/difficulties. How the supervisor aids the scholar through the transition from the early clarity to the doubt stage requires significant, thoughtful ethical considerations of both supervisors and researchers. Supervisors need to support the researcher during times of disillusionment to ensure that the early confidence continues to develop.

Institutional pressures increase these effects. Expectations regarding timely completion, publication output, and research impact shape supervisory practice and influence how uncertainty is handled. If there are no clear institutional frameworks for AI use, supervisors must negotiate expectations on their own. This results in uneven practices across departments and programs, which, in turn, confuse scholars and put more pressure on individual supervisory relationships. Doctoral scholars' development still heavily depends on supervisory practice, even though the nature of supervision has changed. Several studies on doctoral supervision have regularly highlighted the relational and dialogic aspects of supervision (Lee, 2008; Grant, 2005). Now, within an AI-shaped research environment, this dialogic work is more challenging, calling for a new kind of awareness not only of how knowledge is constructed but also of how trust is built and scholarly identity is shaped over time.

Aside from these immediate supervisory issues, there are even greater questions about the nature of academic authority and responsibility. Supervisors are increasingly being asked to rethink what it means to lead a doctoral student to independence when algorithmic systems partly condition conceptual development. They are no longer the primary source and hence holders of knowledge; instead, they become those helping students interpret, evaluate, and contextualise the knowledge gained from different sources in a scholarly way.

The supervisor meeting continues to evolve, adapting its temporal patterns as the doctoral community works differently today than it did years ago. In the past, a doctoral student worked alone for long months at a time, and once every few months, there would be a consultation with the supervisor. Nowadays, supervisor-student consultations may occur more frequently (weekly) but for shorter periods, due to the rapid pace at which the doctoral student's intellectual contributions are generated and revised.

Supervisors must learn to adjust their supervision methods to establish appropriate standards for doctoral students' intellectual contributions within the compressed timeframes enabled by AI technologies. Supervisors must provide sufficient information and support to doctoral students. Hence, they know what they need to do to make an intellectual contribution, rather than relying on the quick pace of producing material without fully understanding it. Supervisors need to maintain high standards for the quality of discussion and conversation throughout the process of producing intellectual contributions, rather than focusing solely on output quantity.

Supervisors will face increasingly more complex questions regarding their students' originality. Research shows that students' early drafts often exhibit coherence in their thinking and reasoning, produced using AI technology. Supervisors must work with students to determine which parts of the draft demonstrate originality and how their original work builds on the previous body of knowledge. Supervisors will need to assist students in determining how to build their arguments through logical reasoning, connect their ideas, and contribute to their academic disciplinary conversations.

Power relations within supervision are also involuntarily changed. Scholars who bring in finished work can be seen as more confident, and their approach as more self-directed; thus, the interaction can be rebalanced accordingly. Meanwhile, supervisors can become uncertain about how far they can help and what forms of support they can legitimately provide. So, the supervisors and students must co-construct the relationship continuously and, as power dynamics change, place both students' and supervisors' roles and responsibilities under scrutiny.

In this changing context, supervisors experience different forms of professional insecurity. A good number of them were brought up in doctoral programs that emphasized single-mindedness and a holistic grasp of concepts, with very little technology involved. AI challenges long-standing assumptions about scholarly development, academic rigor, and the traditional pathways through which supervisors themselves pursued doctoral education. Their reflective process becomes a continual transformation of their academic practice.

Consequently, supervision becomes more multidimensional rather than straightforward at any level. It calls on supervisors to show greater awareness of their students' cognitive development, emotional resilience, ethical decision-making, and disciplinary standards. People can interpret inevitable tensions as signs of failure. However, they are markers of a supervisory role in transition, shaped by the same forces that are transforming doctoral scholarship more broadly.

WHY DOES PROHIBITION FAIL IN DOCTORAL RESEARCH?

Concerns about academic integrity, originality, and the scholarly standards for students and faculty typically prompt institutional responses to AI in doctoral education. Institutional concerns are warranted and accurate; however, when institutional structures that implement restrictions and prohibitions become the dominant means of governing AI use in doctoral education, they create ramifications that directly undermine the academic integrity, originality, and scholarly standards established by those restrictions and prohibitions. Due to technological developments that increase productivity and efficiency, it is nearly impossible to craft simple policies governing how scholars use AI, especially when scholars have already developed their cognitive processes and incorporated algorithmic systems before the commencement of their formal research training.

When institutions take prohibitive stances toward technology, many scholars will resort to concealing its use rather than engaging in reflection. Scholars who rely on AI for conceptual guidance, language enhancement, or methodological assistance will continue to do so in secret, even if their supervisors maintain the perception of compliance with institutional and supervisory expectations. Separating what is done in plain sight from what is done behind closed doors undermines the transparency that is a foundation of adequate supervision. Furthermore, studies on academic integrity demonstrate that environments that are founded on creating and participating in constructive dialogue, developing common expectations and fostering trust between supervisors and scholars support ethical behaviour much more effectively than environments where there is a focus on surveillance and punitive methods of compliance (Bretag et al., 2018) Therefore, the development of institutional practices must be based on an understanding of how doctoral scholars use AI, rather than merely developing institutional responses based on perceived or conceptual ideas about how doctoral scholars utilise AI.

The stress on control also limits the educational role of supervision. Instead of being facilitators of academic growth, supervisors are made to enforce the rules. This change significantly affects the atmosphere of doctoral education, shifting a situation in which one is free to inquire to one in which one is always cautious about one's performance. Students may focus on avoiding mistakes rather than on addressing the theoretical, methodological, and interpretive issues in depth. In fact, the creative process of generating original ideas, which involves intellectual risk, lies at its core and becomes much more difficult to sustain in an academic environment like this.

Moreover, fear-based forms of governance only add to the emotional strain that is already typical of a doctoral program. Engaging in doctoral research necessarily entails being vulnerable, experiencing self-doubt, and living with uncertainty. In situations where AI is largely seen as a threat, students may be deeply worried about being perceived as real researchers. It is this sort of distress that holds experimental work hostage, slows a person's intellectual development, and even damages the basis on which supervision is built in human relations.

Climate studies in doctoral education and separation from it have been an important focus for some time, and it has been established that a conducive environment and a good relationship with one's supervisor play a significant part in one's commitment to the program and eventual degree completion (Lovitts, 2001; Gardner, 2009). However, strict methods of handling things risk shaking the ground on which these conditions stand. Inconsistent institutional policies create an environment that leads to poor enforcement of the prohibition. Without consistent definitions for acceptable practice from all departments and their supervisors, there are many interpretations of what constitutes acceptable practice. Scholars must deal with these many interpretations of practice as they navigate through the various expectations of different departments and supervisors, which leads to confusion about where the boundaries are and when they have crossed them, which creates a lack of credibility within and for the institution and increases the ambiguity surrounding what constitutes acceptable scholar behavior. Ultimately, prohibition creates more confusion than it offers clarity.

The reasons for this dynamic illustrate the imperceptible gap between how regulators approach doctoral scholarship and how doctoral research occurs. The efforts undertaken through regulatory techniques address a lack of visible symptoms but do not focus on the change in how we think about structuring knowledge work. Understanding why prohibition has not worked enables us to create better systems for integrating and using AI within doctoral education that maintain research quality while accounting for the prevailing realities of doctoral scholarship.

REFRAMING AI IN DOCTORAL SCHOLARSHIP

AI is now one of the intellectual factors that influence a doctoral researcher's environment. Seeing it only as an external intrusion or a temporary disruption fails to capture its profound effect on how scholars think, organize their inquiries, and construct meaning. A more productive perspective considering AI as a component of the modern scholarly infrastructure changes the very conditions of knowledge production without displacing the pivotal role of human judgement.

In this narrated frame of reference, AI serves as a sort of cognitive scaffolding. It facilitates scholars in conceptual mapping, organizing complexity, and briefly visualizing ideas. Such inputs let research begin and provide initial trust in the results. However, the deciding factor in the final quality of the construction is not the mere presence of scaffolding. The development of scholarly judgment involves moving from clarity to interpretation, critical evaluation, and intellectual responsibility.

This evolving perspective is redefining how we think about independence in Doctoral Research. It is important to note that being independent as a researcher does not come from a lack of guidance on available technology, but instead from a researcher's ability to understand and reflect on how they use that technology to enhance their research and approach. Once researchers use AI resources to get started rather than as a product, they can use these tools effectively to evaluate evidence, challenge assumptions, and create something original. In addition, the concept of supervision will be instrumental in guiding the researcher in interpreting the output from these resources.

The supervision practice itself enables this change through a process of dialogue and critique. Supervisors create a space in which scholars learn to explore complexity deeply through ongoing conversation and support for their reasoning. Research on doctoral supervision has a long-standing tradition of describing this interpretive stewardship as the supervisor's role in supporting the scholar's development of the ability to think critically, judge objectively, and contribute successfully within the standards and constraints of their discipline (Lee, 2008; Grant, 2005). With the introduction of AI, a fundamentally different entry point into this process emerges, but, like interpretive stewardship, it does not change the reason the supervision process exists.

Rephrasing AI also makes its link to research quality clearer. Quality is not determined by the use of AI in the research process. It is determined by how the researcher engages with knowledge, how arguments are made and supported, and how the researcher situates their work within the discipline's dialogue. These activities remain rooted in human judgment, even as the tools that support them change.

Institutional culture plays a significant role in maintaining this reframing. If academic institutions promote openness, introspection, and co-responsibility for maintaining scholarly standards, then researchers and their supervisors will be better able to incorporate AI into their research without compromising integrity. This cultural harmony enables AI to be simply an element of the broader intellectual development mechanism, rather than a disruptive force to be kept at bay or hidden. As a result of this redefinition, AI is one element of the changing landscape of Ph.D. education. Recognizing this ecosystem thus paves the way for developing better collaboration models and reinforcing the conditions in which research quality and scholarly identity continue to evolve.

Also, through reframing AI, we must re-evaluate our fundamental beliefs about the epistemological foundations of doctoral education. A student does not just find knowledge through direct interaction (reading) with primary literature, datasets, and a scholarly community; this knowledge may also be filtered, organized, and altered by an algorithm. In other words, novice scholars will need to learn how to interpret the discipline they are studying, as well as the algorithmic systems that provide access to their discipline's body(ies) of knowledge. Learning to interpret both forms of access to disciplinary knowledge will become a fundamental element of being a scholar in today's academic climate.

Given this new understanding of the nature of Dialectical Judgment, scholars will have many opportunities to develop their ability to exercise Dialectical Judgment as they receive different forms of help from various sources, evaluate how different types of representations or expressions of knowledge and information may not be in agreement with their own perspective, and continue to seek answers to questions that arise from their own research and the knowledge that they have gained through their academic studies.

Figure 1. Reframing AI in doctoral scholarship: from intrusion to infrastructure

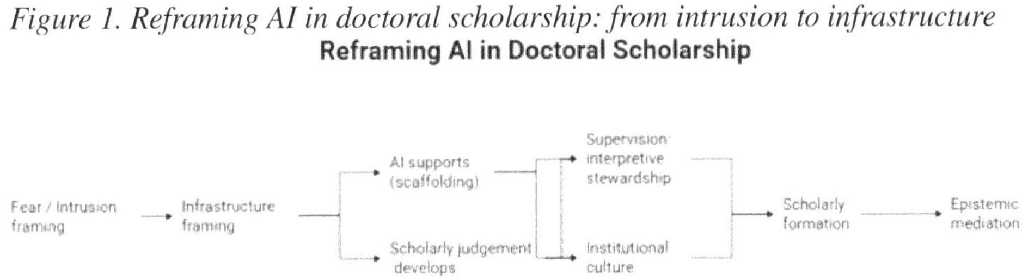

Source: Authors' work

The redefined function of artificial intelligence also changes how we understand error and correction. Traditionally, a doctoral student would discover errors through a slow, deep engagement with complex material. In AI, assisted processes can produce errors that are less obvious but more damaging, deeply embedded in seemingly logical arguments or beautifully structured texts. Recognizing, analyzing, and fixing such mistakes, therefore, requires a high level of understanding and supervision. Additionally, this space shapes how a scholar's voice develops. Doctoral candidates build their voice through the gradual adoption of the discipline's language, the positioning of concepts, and their personal intellectual commitment. When AI is involved in the initial writing and expression, scholars must be cautious to distinguish between external support and internal expression. Voice is something that has to be intentionally made and not something that is naturally acquired.

From an institutional standpoint, AI will be better acknowledged when it shifts how the academy shares and maintains its values. Instead of viewing AI as something separate from the normative functions of the academy, institutions should define how enduring scholarly values (roughly, rigor, transparency, accountability, and intellectual honesty) are incorporated into the evolving research environments we will see in the near future. This definition will facilitate the establishment and development of shared academic cultures that can adapt to technological evolution in the research environment while maintaining their essence and purpose as scholarly enterprises.

THE COLLABORATIVE RESEARCH QUALITY MODEL

Writing a doctoral-level thesis that is of high quality cannot be the output of a single scholar's work done in isolation. It results from a complex, interrelated network of the doctoral scholar, the supervisor, and the higher education institution in which both operate. The system that connects them is no longer dependent solely on disciplinary traditions and human interactions. Artificial Intelligence is now an integral part of the cognitive and organizational research infrastructure, influencing how knowledge is sought, structured, understood, and communicated. Thus, the notion of research quality from a present-day perspective demands a framework that captures the interaction between human and technological elements throughout the doctoral journey.

The Collaborative Research Quality Model conceptualizes doctoral research quality as a relational, developmental, and institutionally mediated process that emerges through interactions among doctoral scholars, supervisors, academic environments, and AI-supported research practices. Rather than treating research quality as the outcome of individual scholarly performance alone, the model positions quality as an evolving condition shaped by continuous negotiation among intellectual autonomy, methodological judgment, collaborative transparency, and long-term scholarly development. The framework further recognizes that AI does not operate outside doctoral education but increasingly functions within the cognitive, organizational, and interpretive structures through which contemporary research is conducted. Accordingly, the model provides a conceptual lens for understanding how high-quality doctoral research can be sustained within AI-infused academic environments while preserving scholarly integrity, disciplinary responsibility, and intellectual maturation.

The Collaborative Research Quality Model portrays doctoral research as a living organism that continually evolves through interactions among three main actors: the doctoral candidate, the supervisor, and the research environment, shaped by institutional norms, resources, and expectations. AI is part of this organism, not as a separate external instrument but as a mediating entity that determines how each character executes their role. The standard of research is determined by how well these characters carry out their duties and, throughout the temporal arc of doctoral study, how they manage to agree on the interpretation of the concepts.

The four interdependent dimensions described in the model above provide a framework for conducting high-quality research and require scholars to be autonomous, maintain methodological integrity, engage in transparent collaborations, and achieve intellectual maturity. Although these four dimensions are separate, they do not always proceed in a linear fashion (i.e., as a series of sequential steps or stages). Instead, the four dimensions interact as a doctoral student progresses through their doctoral research project, thereby creating a context for producing high-quality research output.

Figure 2. Collaborative Research Quality Model

Source: Authors' work

Scholarly Autonomy

Scholarly autonomy is about exercising independent judgment and creating, assessing, and defending original contributions. Today, a doctoral candidate is not considered autonomous because they lack access to technological tools. Instead, it is the scholar's intellectual control and capacity for reflection that determine their degree of autonomy. AI may provide guidance, summarisation, and formatting help. However, autonomy is achieved by the student continually immersing themselves in the subject matter, reflecting critically, and keeping the conversation with the supervisor going.

Autonomy emerges as researchers learn to recognise elements in their early drafts that do not quite fit, uncover the biases of AI-generated content, and accept the full range of decisions and research implementations they have made. We see that the presence of AI changes the first stage, but the fundamental requirement for the scholar to find and express his intellectual voice is the same. Technological mediation does not diminish the scholar's autonomy; rather, it is even more dependent on intentional development.

Methodological Integrity

Methodological integrity refers to the extent to which a researcher can support his/her research design, data collection, and data analysis through a statement of their methods. AI-enabled tools can help researchers create logical connections between their findings, develop models of how their work relates to the larger body of knowledge, provide insight into new analytical methods, and improve upon their existing processes. Thus, AI tools enhance the researcher's technical ability and make them more efficient. However, they do not eliminate the importance of one's expertise when justifying methodological choices, acknowledging limitations, and/or adapting to feedback/review from other scholars.

Methodological Integrity is part of a larger model that describes how researchers' creative/innovative work is maintained through ongoing conversations between the researcher and their supervisor(s). The supervisor/s can help ensure that the technological efficiencies gained from using AI tools do not lead to a loss of the methodological thought process that accompanies high-quality research methods. While many researchers believe that well-developed, sophisticated methodologies are key to quality research, the model indicates that a strong methodology entails multiple ways to justify the coherence of the research question, the research design, and the methods used to collect, analyze, and interpret the data.

Transparent Collaboration

Transparent collaboration is essentially the core element of the relational aspect of doctoral research. The key to successful supervision lies in open communication about the research process, including the role of AI in generating ideas, arguments, and texts. Being transparent makes it easier for supervisors to give more accurate feedback, spot where understanding is limited, and help the scholar move towards greater conceptual depth.

Collaboration at this level is not simply a matter of a joint venture or following a set of rules. It is based on the mutual construction of knowledge. Knowledge evolves through questioning, challenging, and agreeing. When researchers reveal their work methods, including the use of technology, supervision becomes a space where insights are unveiled and intellectual growth can be actively facilitated. The supervisory relationship is therefore the primary setting in which the quality of the research is continually assessed and enhanced.

Intellectual Maturation

Building a scholarly identity, confidence, and tolerance for ambiguity is the culmination of intellectual maturation, as this process evolves from repeatedly being exposed to complex problems over a long period of time through writing, revising, and responding to create constructive feedback. AI will further enhance quicker access to processes beyond that by providing earlier, more coherent development of the processes and by continuing to develop accurate, coherent knowledge after the individual has learned how to respond to ambiguity and revise their previously held assumptions. They must integrate all the knowledge into an integrated view of the world over time for themselves.

In the context of doctoral education, intellectual maturation refers to the gradual development of disciplinary judgement, conceptual depth, tolerance for ambiguity, independent reasoning, and scholarly identity through sustained engagement with complex intellectual problems. It involves more than technical competence or procedural knowledge. Instead, intellectual maturation reflects the scholar's evolving ability to critically evaluate assumptions, negotiate conflicting interpretations, integrate theoretical and methodological perspectives, and contribute responsibly to disciplinary knowledge. Within AI-mediated research environments, intellectual maturation becomes especially important because rapid access to information and early conceptual coherence may create the appearance of understanding before deeper interpretive judgement has fully developed.

The process of intellectual maturation is neither automatic nor uniformly progressive. The time each person spends will vary; therefore, the individual must work in an environment that allows for confusion, failure, reclassification of information, and conceptual development into a professional to prevent premature conclusions. The critical construct of intellectual maturation represents a timeline linking the various stages from the beginning of research activity to the final form of durable scholarly judgement.

Interdependence of the Four Dimensions

The interaction of the four dimensions creates the environment in which research quality can be maintained. If scholars have complete freedom but no emphasis on research methods, they may produce original work only in appearance but will be very fragile in substance. Similarly, focusing solely on methodological rigour while ignoring autonomy risks producing conceptually dependent and technically flawless studies. Collaboration without intellectual growth leads to well-managed projects but misses the development of a scholar's capacity for independent judgment over time. Intellectual growth without collaboration risks isolation and conceptual stagnation. Research-quality results come from the proper sealing and interaction of these dimensions, rather than from a single element taken separately.

The interaction among these dimensions is dynamic rather than sequential. Scholarly autonomy without methodological integrity may produce research that appears original but lacks analytical robustness and disciplinary coherence. Conversely, methodological integrity without intellectual maturation may result in technically competent research that remains conceptually dependent and limited in interpretive depth. Transparent collaboration without autonomy risks creating dependency on supervisors or technological systems, while intellectual maturation without collaborative engagement may lead to isolation, stagnation, and reduced critical reflexivity. The model therefore emphasises balance rather than dominance among dimensions. Research quality is sustained when doctoral scholars gradually develop the capacity to negotiate independence, methodological judgement, collaborative openness, and intellectual responsibility simultaneously within evolving AI-mediated research environments. In this sense, the four dimensions should not be interpreted as isolated categories, but as mutually reinforcing conditions that collectively shape the development of durable scholarly judgement and responsible research practice.

The Role of the Supervisor within the Model

Supervisors' roles in this system are not limited to assessment alone; they also actively develop each dimension. Supervisors help maintain scholarly autonomy by motivating scholars to express and defend their views clearly. They emphasise methodological integrity by questioning design choices and demanding rigorous justification. They support transparent collaboration by encouraging open discussion of the research, technology, and practices. They assist intellectual growth by leading scholars through the stages of confusion, modification, and theory change. It is through supervision that the four dimensions continuously stay in harmony over time.

AI as a Mediating Influence

The integration of artificial intelligence across all four dimensions of doctoral education will look different in each of those dimensions. AI will support and enhance the autonomy of scholarly work by providing access to ideas from a broader range of sources and opportunities for students to engage with ideas from other scholars' perspectives. The introduction of AI will aid researchers in maintaining their methodological integrity by assisting with data organization, modeling, and analysis throughout the iterative process. AI technologies will facilitate faster feedback cycles and the sharing of drafts, thereby promoting collaboration among researchers. AI will provide support to researchers in developing their ability to cope with the complexities and uncertainties of their research. How AI influences the quality of research will depend on how it is woven into the relational fabric of the doctoral education process, rather than on the technology itself.

Institutional Responsibilities Within the Model

The model further outlines the duties of these institutions in maintaining high research standards. Institutional rules, training schemes, and the overall academic environment are the main factors that will determine how the four aspects are understood and executed.

If institutions focus mainly on speed, output, and technical efficiency while ignoring judgment, integrity, collaboration, and maturation, then the research system will be imbalanced. Conversely, institutions that offer a nurturing environment for continuous research, open debate, and reflective practice can lay the conditions for high-quality doctoral research. The significance of each aspect will likely vary at different points in the Ph.D. journey. For example, the early stages of a Ph.D. program typically require the student to be more closely guided, methodologically supported, and collaboratively supported. In contrast, the final stages are more about student independence and intellectual integration. The framework is adaptable enough to accommodate these varying emphases while maintaining the unity of the entire research process.

STRENGTHENING SCHOLAR–SUPERVISOR COLLABORATION

The Ph.D. Researchers and Supervisors are no longer relying solely on uncertainty; they are working within contexts of coherence, structure, and several rapidly constructed arguments. Supervisors now do not provide feedback during meetings, instead Supervisors conduct meetings to initiate a collaborative process with materials that have already achieved some level of clarity and developed a sense of direction; rather than being a meeting where student draft writing included research questions, initial drafts of arguments, potential methods before the student had a comprehensive appreciation of their discipline's complexities, meetings are now opportunities for supervisors to help develop scholarly development using AI at a much earlier stage than previously possible. With AI, Supervisors can assist students in interpreting and using data without needing to judge how formal the student has been in meeting the conceptual complexities of their discipline, and more often than before Supervisors are likely exploring how the reasoning had been developed in the draft of the arguments, what sources of information were included in that reasoning, and where there may be gaps or inadequacies in conceptual understanding that require work to complete for the theoretical basis to be adequately understood and developed.

Thus, supervision work is more about interpretation than giving directions. The meetings involve less effort to fill gaps and more engagement in how the understanding is being created. Supervisors who prompt scholars to explain their choices allow the latter to reflect on their assumptions, consider alternatives, and foresee implications. Such interactions equip the scholar with stronger reasoning skills and the ability to see initial conclusions as only tentative. Eventually, the interpretive conversation between the two parties aids the development of intellectual habits that, besides being beneficial for the current research, also define the scholar's future inquiry style.

Feedback process changes, too. Whereas in the past a neat text was a sign of intellectual progress, now supervisors must pay close attention to the piece's conceptual structure. AI-assisted drafting can mask the lack of logic and unresolved theoretical tensions. Hence, good feedback delves more profoundly than surface clarity; it examines the soundness of arguments, how questions and methods correspond, and the reasoning that links evidence and interpretation. In this way, scholars become capable of differentiating between the attractive form and the rich content of a piece.

The emotional aspects of collaboration also need to be considered. Supervisors are finding that their students, who initially are very confident, later become unstable when they face complex problems, either conceptual or methodological. AI, preparation can make these mood changes even worse, leading to cycles of reassurance and doubts. Helping students through these changes becomes a significant part of supervisory work. Being emotionally sensitive, patient, and consistently providing intellectual guidance are some ways to help students maintain motivation and interest throughout the long doctoral period.

Gradually, these complex practices determine the nature of doctoral education. Researchers find that a high standard of research is not the result of hard work alone or technical perfection, but of the continuous working through of ideas, which are supported by relationships that provide guidance, take on responsibility, and ensure intellectual honesty. Collaboration is not simply a structural agreement; it is the primary setting in which scholarly identity and research quality are developed.

Transparency is imperative for encouraging effective collaborative working relationships. When scholars are allowed to openly discuss how they use AI to support their scholarly work, supervisors will gain greater insight into how scholars think and learn. In turn, this increased transparency helps supervisors better target their feedback to aid scholar development, reducing the possibility of confusion around originality and intellectual property. Transparency also creates a culture that normalises the new realities created by AI research, replacing suspicion with shared knowledge and understanding, and ultimately fostering improved scholarly relationships.

This practice generates conviction among academics in AI-infused research environments. Trust supports a culture of academic risk-taking and openness to uncertainty, and it diffuses the fear of judgment. It also allows supervisors to challenge assumptions and to support more thorough engagement with complexity. Throughout the doctoral supervision literature, trust has been cited as a key component of effective academic development (Lee, 2008; Grant, 2005). When considering the impact of an AI-infused research environment on trust, the significance of building trust in this context is magnified, as researchers experience new levels of dependency, independence, and accountability as they advance in their academic careers.

ENHANCING RESEARCH QUALITY THROUGH GUIDED AI INTEGRATION

Research quality in doctoral education depends not only on technical competence but also on a scholar's ability to engage critically with ideas, evidence, and disciplinary standards. Within contemporary research environments, this capacity increasingly develops through interactions among technological tools, supervisory guidance, and institutional support. AI can strengthen research processes by assisting scholars in organizing information, identifying relevant literature, and developing early conceptual direction. Such support may reduce initial uncertainty and allow greater attention to theoretical refinement, critical judgment, and deeper engagement with research problems.

Originality remains a central expectation of doctoral work. Its value lies not in avoiding technological support but in a scholar's ability to interpret information, develop insights, and construct meaningful contributions to knowledge. Supervisory dialogue plays an important role in this process. Through questioning, critique, and iterative discussion, scholars learn to distinguish borrowed coherence from genuine intellectual contribution and gradually strengthen their own academic voice.

AI-assisted tools also contribute to procedural organization and analytical efficiency. Yet methodological quality continues to depend on the scholar's capacity to justify research decisions, recognize limitations, and respond critically to alternative perspectives. As technological support becomes more common, supervisors increasingly need to focus on how scholars explain and defend methodological choices rather than simply evaluating procedural outcomes.

Writing practices are also changing. AI-supported systems can improve clarity, organisation, and linguistic expression. Even so, writing remains more than a process of presenting information; it continues to function as a space for developing and refining ideas. The quality of doctoral research therefore emerges not from technology alone but from interactions among scholarly judgement, supervisory engagement, and broader research environments.

Supervisory practices are similarly evolving. Rather than concentrating solely on completed drafts, supervisors increasingly examine how arguments are formed, where assumptions emerge, and how reasoning develops across revisions. This process highlights the importance of dialogue and constructive questioning in supporting intellectual growth and maintaining research quality.

Feedback itself becomes more subtle. Supervisors have to determine whether the fault lies in the student's wording or in their understanding. For instance, AI might help a student make a text more fluent, thereby missing the fact that it is entirely based on conceptual errors. Hence, the supervisor's feedback goes beyond the mere form and focuses on the internal logic of the arguments, conceptual coherence, and the correspondence between the research questions and the method choices. Gradually, students come to realize that just because the presentation looks fantastic, it does not mean that there is enough conceptual depth. There is also a transformation in collaborative writing practices. Redrafts are circulated more often and in a more complete form. During the iterative process, rounds of revision between supervisors and scholars may address both technical aspects and significant structural changes. So, the scholar gains a more profound understanding through the dialogue, and at the same time/their engagement with the work becomes stronger. Eventually, this collaborative rhythm becomes a training ground for intellectual habits needed in independent research.

To maximize effectiveness in navigating both research and study limits, scholars should consult others for guidance and advice to make their own independent decisions. Therefore, a supervisor needs to find the balance point at which to guide the scholar so that the scholar is given the best opportunity to make independent decisions promptly. Where AI offers the potential for greater efficiency in delivering timely guidance, its ability to provide prompt feedback on requests and concerns may reduce the need for a supervisory recommendation.

To ensure that supervisors and scholars understand the collaborative process during this time of rapid development, they need to continue to dialogue about their specific roles and responsibilities as they relate to it. Additionally, both supervisors and scholars need to continue the dialogue regarding the evolving nature of their respective responsibilities in decision-making and accountability. This ongoing discussion is critical for both supervisors and scholars to understand their respective roles in decision-making and responsibilities, and to be prepared for the ongoing collaborative transition.

As this collaborative transition is still a work in progress, supervisors must provide emotional support and encouragement to scholars. The doctoral process can be a time of vulnerability, uncertainty, and, at times, doubt for many scholars. Although

AI may help with some aspects of a scholar's research and study, it cannot replace the level of assurance and comfort that a supervisor can provide to help navigate through these feelings.

Supportive supervision provides a stabilizing influence for scholars by fostering continued engagement and perseverance during periods of conceptual impasse or low confidence. These interactions between scholars and supervisors result in collaborative partnerships that evolve from the supervisor's role as instructor to include mentorship and oversight of judgment, responsibility, and scholarly identity, while shifting the scholar from a passive recipient of guidance to an active participant in the construction of knowledge. The combined roles of both scholars and supervisors ensure that the conditions are in place for doctoral research to remain rigorous and original.

INSTITUTIONAL RESPONSIBILITIES IN DOCTORAL AI GOVERNANCE

Institutions establish the framework within which doctoral research is conducted. The researchers and research supervisors fulfill their duties and maintain the quality of the research over time, guided by policies, resources, training structures, and the academic cultures available to them. An AI-influenced research environment broadens the notion of institutional responsibility beyond mere compliance with the regulations and technical guidelines. It therefore involves fostering a consistent academic atmosphere in which new forms of scholarship can be practiced with integrity.

Providing clarity is one of the primary duties. Researchers and research supervisors need a shared understanding of how AI relates to other academic values, research integrity, and scholarly responsibility. If institutional directions are unclear or contradictory, then the entire doctoral program suffers from uncertainty. Supervisory methods change, expectations scatter, and the researchers are left to figure out the vague limits on their own. Therefore, clear and consistent institutional communication significantly reduces this confusion by establishing shared standards that support both research freedom and responsibility.

International policy frameworks such as UNESCO's Guidance for Generative AI in Education and Research (2023) and the OECD AI Principles (2019) similarly emphasize transparency, accountability, human oversight, and institutional responsibility in AI-integrated educational systems.

Training and professional development are yet another significant area in which institutions should take the lead. Both supervisors and doctoral students have the opportunity, through well-structured training events, to critically consider the impact of AI on research activities, whether through engagement with the literature, data analysis, or writing. The discussions should therefore not be limited to the technical features of AI, but also to the interpretive, ethical, and developmental aspects of research carried out with the help of AI. Universities, which provide such platforms for researchers to interact, will nurture the collective capability of academic staff to stay a step ahead of changes in their work environments and respond rationally.

Issues of equity add layers to the already complex institutional governance. Access to AI tools and digital infrastructure varies widely across social, economic, and geographic settings. Institutions that do not pay attention to these disparities may, without realizing it, be the ones to cause even more inequality in doctoral education. Ensuring regular access to resources, training, and support is therefore not merely a key step in protecting research opportunities but also a trust-building tool within academic systems.

The institution's culture shapes the integration of Artificial Intelligence into the academic community, which in turn determines how faculty and students experience it. A Culture that promotes values such as Transparency, Reflection, and Shared Responsibility has been proven to foster fruitful relationships between New Technologies (Howitt, 2015) and to provide security for supervisors and learners (Asraland et al., 2014). In contrast, a culture focused mainly on surveillance and control causes faculty and learners to hide what they are doing from each other or to distrust one another. Research on academic integrity supports the idea that positive, supportive environments, grounded in shared norms, are better able to sustain ethical conduct among researchers than punitive environments (Bretag et al., 2018). These two fundamental aspects (Coherent Governance and Thoughtful Leadership) are critical to creating an environment in which High-Quality Doctoral Research can flourish.

THE FUTURE OF DOCTORAL EDUCATION IN THE AI ERA

Doctoral education is still evolving alongside broader changes in how knowledge is produced, academic labor, and technological infrastructures. AI is definitely part of this progression, influencing how research problems are formulated, how evidence is interpreted, and how scholarly communities communicate and collaborate. Thus, the future of doctoral education will likely revolve around academic systems finding ways to develop human capacities that enable scholars to navigate increasingly complex intellectual environments, rather than on whether AI is present in academia.

One feature of doctoral education that is gaining prominence is the shift in understanding of scholarly expertise. Traditionally, expertise meant in-depth knowledge or familiarity with a disciplinary literature. However, it increasingly refers to one's skill in interpreting, evaluating, and integrating information derived from diverse, constantly changing sources. Since there will be much data, algorithms, and different knowledge representations competing, scholars have to learn to make judgments in such environments. This interpretative skill training will be the hallmark of advanced research development. The globalization of doctoral education will be a significant driver of change in these areas. The advancement of digital infrastructure is enabling collaborative partnerships between institutions worldwide, opening new opportunities for scholars to share information and collaborate. Nevertheless, disparities in technology and access to resources will remain a challenge for the sustainability of higher education institutions' initiatives to offer equitable, high-quality doctoral-level education.

Even as these trends evolve, Ph.D. education has always been, and will continue to be, grounded in timeless academic values. These values include a dedication to truth, a respect for evidence, a willingness to accept criticism, and a sense of duty towards knowledge production. AI will determine how these values are realized, but it will not be auxiliary to them. The fate of Ph.D. education depends mainly on academic communities' readiness to uphold these core values as they face an ever more complex research environment.

CONCLUSION

Doctoral education is undergoing a significant transformation. The use of artificial intelligence in research has changed, in various ways, the relationship between scholars and knowledge, the supervision process, and the assessment of research quality. It should be noted that these changes are not a sign of a decline in scholarly values but rather require a re-examination of how such values are maintained.

In the present chapter, doctoral research is conceived as a collaborative system whose components, scholars, supervisors, and institutions, interact in an academic environment permeated by AI. The quality of research can be understood as the outcome of this system delivered through the development of judgment, the negotiation of meaning, and the gradual formation of scholarly identity. If technological assistance is part of strong relational and institutional frameworks, then it may be used as a tool for these processes rather than as a replacement for them. As the future of doctoral education continues to evolve alongside new technologies and advancements in AI, academic communities must recognize the role of AI within the changing environment of scholarly activity, while also maintaining the importance of human involvement and engagement as defining characteristics of intellectual activity.

The main supports of supervisors' and supervisees' relationships, i.e., dialogue, trust, and interpretive responsibility, constitute the foundational elements for the creation of new knowledge and thus must be preserved regardless of changes in tools and environments. These main supports provide a structure for ongoing, logical coherence in the constantly changing scene of knowledge production.

The value of doctoral education as a place for new scholars not only to develop the skills necessary to conduct research effectively but also to become active participants in the ongoing development of new knowledge derives from the continued commitment to the principles outlined above.

REFERENCES

Bretag, T., Harper, R., Burton, M., Ellis, C., Newton, P., van Haeringen, K., Saddiqui, S., & Rozenberg, P. (2018). Contract cheating and assessment design: Exploring the relationship. *Assessment & Evaluation in Higher Education*, *44*(5), 676–691. DOI: 10.1080/02602938.2018.1527892

Chan, C. K. Y., & Hu, W. (2023). Students' voices on generative AI: Perceptions, benefits, and challenges in higher education. *Education and Information Technologies*, *28*, 1–22. DOI: 10.1007/s10639-023-12195-8

Dwivedi, Y. K., Kshetri, N., Hughes, L., Slade, E. L., Jeyaraj, A., Kar, A. K., Baabdullah, A. M., Koohang, A., Raghavan, V., Ahuja, M., Albanna, H., Albashrawi, M., Al-Busaidi, K. A., Balakrishnan, J., Barlette, Y., Basu, S., Bose, I., Brooks, L., Buhalis, D., & Wright, R. (2023). "So what if ChatGPT wrote it?" Multidisciplinary perspectives on opportunities, challenges and implications of generative conversational AI for research, practice and policy. *International Journal of Information Management*, *71*, 102642. DOI: 10.1016/j.ijinfomgt.2023.102642

Gardner, S. K. (2009). The development of doctoral students: Phases of challenge and support. *ASHE Higher Education Report*, *34*(6), 1–127. https://eric.ed.gov/?id=EJ835648

Grant, B. M. (2005). The pedagogy of graduate supervision: Figuring the relations between supervisor and student (Doctoral dissertation, University of Auckland).

Kasneci, E., Sessler, K., Küchemann, S., Bannert, M., Dementieva, D., Fischer, F., Gasser, U., Groh, G., Günnemann, S., Hüllermeier, E., Krusche, S., Kutyniok, G., Michaeli, T., Nerdel, C., Pfeiffer, F., Poquet, O., Sailer, M., Schmidt, A., Seidel, T., & Kasneci, G. (2023). ChatGPT for good? On opportunities and challenges of large language models for education. *Learning and Individual Differences*, *103*, 102274. DOI: 10.1016/j.lindif.2023.102274

Lee, A. (2008). How are doctoral students supervised? Concepts of doctoral research supervision. *Studies in Higher Education*, *33*(3), 267–281. DOI: 10.1080/03075070802049202

Lovitts, B. E. (2001). *Leaving the ivory tower: The causes and consequences of departure from doctoral study*. Bloomsbury Publishing PLC.

McAlpine, L., & Amundsen, C. (2011). *Doctoral education: Research-based strategies for doctoral students, supervisors, and administrators*. Springer. DOI: 10.1007/978-94-007-0507-4

OECD. (2019). *OECD principles on artificial intelligence*. OECD Publishing. https://oecd.ai/en/ai-principles

Selwyn, N. (2016). *Education and technology: Key issues and debates* (3rd ed.). Bloomsbury Publishing.

UNESCO. (2023). *Guidance for generative AI in education and research*. UNESCO Publishing. https://unesdoc.unesco.org/

Williamson, B. (2017). *Big data in education: The digital future of learning, policy and practice*. Sage Publications. DOI: 10.4135/9781529714920

Chapter 8

Enhancing Research Supervision in Cambodian Teacher Education:

The Academic Profession and Professorial Roles in the Age of AI

Da Bou
http://orcid.org/0009-0004-8971-9923
Graduate School, National University of Battambang, Cambodia

Chan Hum
http://orcid.org/0009-0007-8760-1966
National University of Battambang, Cambodia

Sopha Soeung
http://orcid.org/0000-0003-0569-3021
National Institute of Education, Cambodia

Rany Sam
http://orcid.org/0000-0003-3266-5974
National University of Battambang, Cambodia

ABSTRACT

This chapter investigates the impact of supervisory procedures used by Cambodian teacher educators on research outputs and student teachers' views within the framework of current educational changes in Cambodia. A quantitative survey was used to collect data from 106 teacher educators and 337 student teachers in

DOI: 10.4018/979-8-2600-3204-6.ch008

Teacher Education Colleges (TECs). The data collected were subjected to ANOVA and Regression analysis. The results reveal that CS has a major positive role in student teachers' research skills, as shown by a positive coefficient (β = 0.858, Sig. = 0.037) in the era of AI. On the other hand, MS has potential, although it shows a non-significant negative effect (β = -0.108, Sig. = 0.716). AS and TS, on the other hand, are not very satisfactory. In particular, TS has a substantial negative connection with research findings (β = -0.826, Sig. = 0.030). The results suggest the necessity to revise supervisory procedures and analyze transformative supervision to improve the effectiveness of instruction.

1. INTRODUCTION

1.1. Background of the study

The growing use of artificial intelligence (AI) in Cambodia is shifting the teacher's role from that of the primary source of information to an agent of AI-augmented research (Huot & Loch, 2025). We live in the era of artificial intelligence. Teacher educators still have a role to play in conventional supervision, but they need to be aware of the impact of AI-supported feedback and generative AI tools on the research processes of student teachers (Ba et al., 2025; Aldino et al., 2026; Wongvorachan et al., 2022). The technological transition requires rethinking supervision approaches such as mentoring, cooperation, autonomous, and transformative tactics to explore how they may complement AI to improve research outcomes in Teacher Education Colleges (TECs) (Sowa et al., 2025). Teacher educators play an important role in shaping the quality of the new generation of educators through their supervision and mentorship during the educational reform in Cambodia (Bou, 2025; Tep, 2024b; Yoeurng, 2024). While the country is struggling to improve its educational system, the Cambodian government and the Ministry of Education, Youth, and Sports are working in collaboration with the Japanese International Cooperation Agency (JICA) to reform the institutional structures and educational programs for Teacher Education Colleges (TECs).

TECs have been produced and processed from 2017 to present, aiming at the improvement of Cambodian teacher education reform (MoEYS, 2025). TECs have established a strategic plan to improve the development of successful educational programs, including the development of research abilities among teacher educators and student teachers (Sok & Heng, 2024; UNESCO, 2025). TECs see education as a driver of national development, and so the teacher training programs need to educate the prospective teachers with the necessary abilities to contribute to the profession and professional appointment (Sot et al., 2019; UNESCO, 2024). Thus, it is vital to understand the effect of research knowledge, research skills, and teacher educators' supervision style on student teachers' research outcomes and their perspectives in order to improve the teacher education programs in Cambodia. However, TEC's model has not yet produced a clear framework to inform the more effective supervision methods to improve the research outputs of student instructors (Huot et al., 2025; MoEYS, 2023).

Sequentially, Sengsoulintha (2025), Czerniawski et al. (2017), and Mercer et al. (2025) demonstrated that the challenges faced by teacher educators serving as supervisors in Teacher Education Colleges are multifaceted and significant, including in the Cambodian context. While various supervision frameworks—mentorship supervision (MS), collaborative supervision (CS), autonomous supervision (AS), and transformational supervision (TS)—offer valuable approaches to supervision, their implementation often runs into practical barriers (Chea, 2024a; Gordon, 2023; Pich, 2017; Tonna et al., 2017). Furthermore, CS promotes teamwork and peer engagement; however, the lack of a collegial culture and insufficient institutional support may hinder effective collaboration among educators and student teachers (Hoque et al., 2020; Lim, 2024). In addition, Bou et al. (2024) and Samoun and Pen (2025) explained that autonomous supervision encourages self-directed learning; however, many student teachers may lack the foundational skills and confidence necessary to engage in critical thinking and reflective practices independently. Lastly, Merdiaty and Sulistiasih (2024), Durksen et al. (2017), and Curran and Murray (2008) defined that transformational supervision aims to inspire and motivate student teachers to innovate in their research endeavors, but the prevailing educational climate may not always foster the intrinsic motivation and agency necessary for such transformative experiences. Consequently, addressing these challenges is crucial for advancing the effectiveness of teacher supervision and enhancing the overall quality of teacher training in Cambodia.

The supervision styles can be classified into four frameworks, which are mentoring supervision (MS), collaborative supervision (CS), autonomous supervision (AS), and transformative supervision (TS). Mentorship is a structured form of advice and feedback (Yuan, 2016; Parker et al., 2021). It is considered a requirement in developing students' academic writing skills in a fast-changing educational setting. This could be particularly useful in Cambodia, where student teachers may need more concrete orientation in dealing with the complexity of academic research. Collaborative supervision enhances cooperation and peer engagement, and builds a collegial climate that encourages collective learning (Lau et al., 2019; Wiyono et al., 2021). In Cambodia, where educational resources may be limited, co-operative efforts may provide a support network for student teachers and teachers. Autonomous supervision means that learners are self-directing which is an important aspect in the development of a generation of critical thinkers and reflective practitioners who will be able to encourage innovation in their communities (Ha et al., 2025; Tweed & Warrington, 2024). Transformational supervision is designed to motivate and inspire student teachers, thereby fostering a sense of agency and creativity in their research that is essential to the development of Cambodia's educational infrastructure (Em et al., 2025; Priyoherianto et al., 2025; Lambrecht et al., 2022).

The studies indicate a positive effect of effective supervision on students' performance and engagement in the context of Cambodian teacher education, especially in terms of the improvement of teacher practices and professional development (Casey et al., 2024; Sek, 2023; Tep, 2024a). Research has linked the quality of supervision with better instructional outcomes and student achievement. However, the implementation and outcomes of different supervision styles can considerably differ across the institutional contexts and educators' experience (Kini & Podolsky, 2016; Tan & Tee Ng, 2012; Wilson, 2006). In Cambodia, the move towards a more research-intensive teacher education program requires a more thorough examination of how different supervision styles affect student teachers' capacity to produce high-quality research reports (Bou et al., 2025; Pov & Kawai, 2025; Sharma & Sokal, 2015). Moreover, understanding student teachers' perspectives on these supervisory approaches is essential to enhance educator practices in this distinct context (Rahabav, 2016).

1.2. AI and the Reconfiguration of Professional Roles in Teacher Education

The academic profession is changing as generative AI and AI-enabled digital tools increasingly mediate teaching, research, and supervisory work (Flores & Mean, 2025). In Teacher Education Colleges (TECs), teacher educators monitor classroom-based practice and also guide student teachers' research writing, feedback cycles, and academic progress (Kumari et al., 2025). Here, AI-assisted writing tools, research support platforms, and digital collaboration environments are beginning to alter how professional roles are executed, especially in supervision practices where ongoing attention to structure, argumentation, scholarship, and research ethics is necessary (Paris et al., 2025). From the professional role perspective, AI tools have the potential to alter supervisory work in at least three ways. First, the feedback pipeline may change as supervisors evaluate AI-generated drafts more often, focus on the quality of argument rather than sentence-level form, and use AI-enabled tools to accelerate iterative revision (Omodan, 2025; Jensen et al., 2025). Second, the supervisory relationships and responsibilities may be modified, as supervisors will need to decide what sorts of help are suitable, how to teach transparency in AI aid, and how to deal with authorship and academic integrity (Bouzar & El Idrissi, 2025; Devine & Hunter, 2017). Third, the professional standards of research supervision may be affected as assessment parameters shift from superficial language output to critical thinking, originality, methodological coherence, and ethical compliance (Dzvapatsva et al., 2026; Naqvi et al., 2025; Madanchian & Taherdoost, 2025).

Crucially, AI could not deliver comparable gains for all types of monitoring. Mentor supervision might be "scaffolded" more, with supervisors assisting student teachers in using AI for outline and revision, but with human accountability still in place (Iatrellis et al., 2025; Helm & Hesse, 2026). According to Nicol and MacLeod (2005) and Thong et al. (2025), shared digital workplaces and co-editing with the use of artificial intelligence may also enable collaborative supervision and peer learning, respectively. AI technology can allow for autonomous supervision, overcoming procedural barriers (e.g., gaps in research, summaries). However, student teachers might have problems to develop independent thinking and research discernment (Dalky et al., 2025; Long, 2026). Transformative supervision is when the AI technologies are used by supervisors to create ideas and encourage creativity, but the teacher is still a central figure for injecting motivation and agency in genuine research practices (Sedkaoui & Benaichouba, 2024; Jia et al., 2025; Bekbolatova et al., 2024).

However, AI-enabled supervision introduces risks that directly concern the academic profession. These include uneven access to tools, the temptation of over-reliance or "outsourced writing," increased difficulty in verifying student teachers' authorship, potential bias in AI-generated suggestions, and confidentiality concerns when student teachers' data is processed through third-party platforms. Therefore, even where TECs have not fully integrated AI-related supervision policies, teacher educators' supervisory decisions are increasingly influenced by the opportunities and constraints AI introduces (Gulumbe et al., 2025). This makes it necessary to interpret supervision effectiveness not only as a function of supervision style, but also as a function of the changing professional environment in which supervision is practiced.

1.3. Research Problems

Previous studies have reported the role of supervision styles, but there is a lack of empirical evidence to show the relationship between specific styles and measurable research performance outcomes in Cambodia. The present research study seeks to fill this gap by exploring the impact of teacher educators' supervision styles on student teachers' writing of research reports and student teachers' perceptions of different supervisory methods. Despite the massive educational reforms in Cambodia, the effectiveness of the supervision styles used by teacher educators to develop student teachers' research capacity has not been fully investigated. The literature suggests that the interaction between supervision styles and student research output is important, but there is limited empirical evidence to support this relationship in the Cambodian context. This complexity is further complicated by the different perceptions that student teachers have regarding these different styles of supervision. For example, mentorship supervision and collaborative supervision are generally perceived to be in a positive light, yet their actual impacts on research are not well established. Moreover, the continued use of traditional supervision methods in Cambodian teacher education programs may be a barrier to the development of the research skills of future teachers. Autonomous supervision may not be appropriate for student teachers who may need more structured guidance. Similarly, transformational supervision, which is aimed at motivating student teachers, has produced mixed results in improving research outcomes and outputs, which casts doubt on its practical effectiveness.

There is a crucial lack of holistic assessment of the impact of different supervision approaches on the quality of research reports produced by student teachers in the TEC environment. This ambiguity raises questions about the overall effectiveness of teacher education programs in training future educators to fulfill the changing demands of education. Further, the absence of an in-depth investigation of the student teachers' viewpoints makes it impossible to make sound conclusions on what needs to be changed in the supervision methods. It is vital to examine the relationship between teacher educators' supervision approaches and student teachers' research results and perceptions in the setting of Cambodia. These problems will be addressed, which will increase the quality of teacher preparation and provide student teachers with the research skills they need for their future employment. This study aims to bridge these gaps by providing empirical facts and ideas to inform more effective supervision procedures in Teacher Education Colleges in Cambodia. To verify the research results, there were four main research questions as follows:

1. What are the teacher educators' supervision styles that enhance student teachers' writing of research reports?
2. How do student teachers perceive the supervision styles of teacher educators?
3. What is the relationship between teacher educators' supervision styles and student teachers' research outcomes?
4. What is the relationship between student teachers' research outcomes and their perceptions of teacher educators' supervision styles?

While this study does not directly measure AI tool use, it addresses supervision styles increasingly practiced in AI-mediated supervisory environments, making the findings relevant to how professional roles may be enacted under emerging technological conditions.

2. LITERATURE REVIEW

2.1. Theoretical Framework

The theoretical foundation of this research is based on the Constructivist Learning Theory, which states that knowledge is actively constructed through social interaction and engagement with the environment. This research correlates four specific supervision styles: Mentorship (M), Collaborative (C), Autonomous (A), and Transformational (T), to three core theoretical pillars to hypothesize their effect on student research outcomes:

- Vygotsky's Social Development Theory and MS/CS: MS and CS are based on Vygotsky's "Zone of Proximal Development" ("ZPD") (Vygotsky, 1978). MS is a more traditional form of scaffolding, in which a more knowledgeable teacher provides organized assistance, while CS takes this a step further to become a more horizontal social interaction in which learning occurs through peer participation (Fosnot & Perry, 1996; Narayan et al., 2013). This theoretical framework is in line with the study of styles of supervision as it points to the importance of teacher educators using strategies that promote active learning, critical thinking, and reflective practice among student teachers (Gusango et al., 2021; Kahyalar & Yazici, 2016; Vijaya Kumari, 2014).
- Wenger's Communities of Practice and CS: Wenger's theory is built on learning via membership and active engagement in a shared community. This approach is closely tied to the Collaborative Supervision (CS) style, which claims that the finest research skills are built through the unit of students and instructors (Christy, 2013; Kozulin, 2004; Usha, 2002).
- Shulman's Pedagogical Content Knowledge (PCK): Autonomous (AS) and Transformational Supervision (TS) both focus on the union of content knowledge and pedagogical practice. AS requires a strong background of PCK to enable students' full engagement in self-directed learning. TS is intended to inspire and motivate, and assumes that students acquire the basic information necessary to be creative (Reeve & Cheon, 2024; Holcomb et al., 2025; Hashweh, 2014).

According to Bjørndal et al. (2024) and Mok and Staub (2021), the framework supports the argument that effective research supervision should be adaptable, context-sensitive, and focused on building a supportive learning environment. It further advocates an approach that recognizes the diverse needs of student teachers in Cambodia, enabling tailored mentorship that can significantly enhance research outcomes and outputs, as well as overall educational outcomes (Kushwaha, 2022).

2.2. Implementation of Supervision Styles in a Particular Context

The use of different supervision methods in the Cambodian context offers both opportunities and challenges in the changing educational environment and the need to adequately prepare the future educators. The TECs in Cambodia have recognized the importance of using different supervision methods to develop students' research competency. Mentorship supervision (MS) is a common method used to provide structured guidance and constructive feedback, which are very important in an emerging educational system (Kemmis et al., 2014; Yuan et al., 2025). This style is especially helpful for student teachers who demand clear standards and support in developing their academic writing (Marshall et al., 2015). Assessment rubrics and logbooks are used routinely by the faculty members, and feedback is given iteratively to support student teachers in the development of their research skills (Grønli et al., 2025). On the other hand, collaborative supervision (CS) promotes collaboration among student instructors and cultivates a culture of peer participation and reciprocal learning. This strategy is very compatible with Cambodia's communal culture, where participation can improve the learning experience.

However, the implementation of autonomous supervision (AS) is not straightforward since it requires a tremendous change in the thinking and practices of teacher educators. Some student teachers may not be prepared for high autonomy levels. This highlights the role of teacher educators in mediating between guidance and autonomy (Bureau et al., 2022; Wang et al., 2025; Zheng & Xiao, 2026). Transformational supervision (TS) is intended to inspire and motivate, but its effectiveness is context dependent (Osman & Warner, 2020; Ronkainen et al., 2025). Teacher educators should seek ways to engage students in a meaningful way, adapting motivational strategies to students' needs (Dietrich et al., 2015; Karpudewan & Mohd Ali Khan, 2017; Lazarides et al., 2019). To conclude, the effective implementation of these supervisory styles depends on continuous professional development for teacher educators and a grasp of the contextual factors influencing student learning.

In the age of AI, the practical meaning of each supervision style may shift. Digital feedback tools, AI-assisted drafting and summarization, and AI-enabled literature support can intensify the supervisor's responsibility to guide student teachers toward research integrity, critical evaluation of sources, and transparent documentation of assistance. Consequently, supervision style may influence not only how guidance is delivered, but also how students learn to use tools responsibly in producing research outputs.

2.3. Previous Studies

Previous research has highlighted the importance of supervision approaches in relation to teacher education, particularly in terms of improving student teachers' capacity to undertake good research. Collaborative supervision strategies have been found to significantly improve student teachers' involvement and performance (Willegems et al., 2017; Strieker et al., 2016). Working together in groups gives future instructors an opportunity to improve their academic performance and practice their critical interpersonal skills.

The study by Dreer-Goethe (2025) on teacher education discusses mentorship supervision. The results show that systematic feedback and concrete goal setting considerably facilitate the development of research abilities of student teachers, which in turn results in a better quality of the submitted theses. However, the authors also note a potential drawback: too much reliance on this method may stifle creativity and autonomy in students who would prefer a more exploratory approach. However, Brandisauskiene et al. (2023) also studied the area of supervision and found that student instructors experience moments of unpreparedness and lack of support. The research indicates that students need to be provided with space for independence, but to be supported in their growth. Recently, Heng et al. (2020), Yang et al. (2026), and Li et al. (2026) did some research in Cambodia. They found that people are more aware of the impact of supervision styles on research production. The study showed that different institutions supervise in different ways. This is why there is a need for consistent procedures. This idea is also supported by other studies (Cardwell et al., 2024; Davidsson & Stigmar, 2023; Severinsson, 2012).

2.4. Research Gaps

There is a plethora of material on supervision styles, although there is a significant gap in the literature discussing the specific influence of these styles on research output in the Cambodian educational landscape. Most studies have been done in Western environments, and there is a need for more local studies to better understand the unique difficulties and potential in TEC's Cambodian context. Previous research has studied the effect of supervision approaches on student teacher performance, but there are many gaps, especially in the Cambodian setting. There is little empirical evidence that directly links different supervision styles to quantitative outcomes in student teachers' research output. In addition, there is a dearth of empirical studies into student teachers' views on different supervision styles, so their experiences and insights are mostly neglected. Furthermore, much of the previous research has been done.

2.5. Conceptual Framework

The theoretical foundations of this study are based on essential parts of the theoretical basis, and identify gaps in the existing literature. It depicts the relationships among the four supervision styles: Mentorship supervision (MS), Collaborative supervision (CS), Autonomous supervision (AS), and Transformational supervision (TS), and their effects on student teachers' research productivity and views.

Figure 1. The conceptual framework of the study

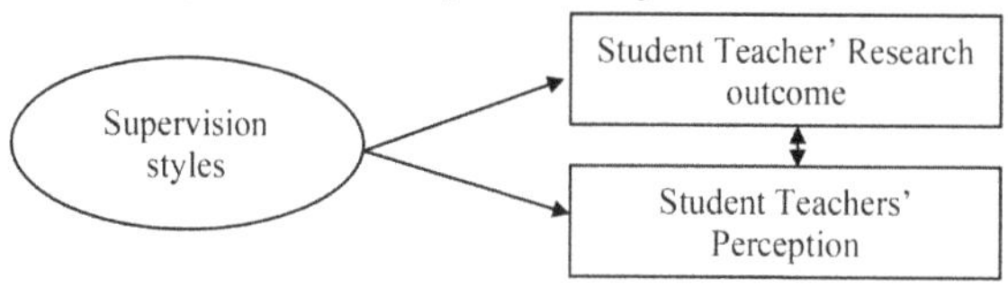

The framework was utilized to inform the methodology of the study, which was concerned with the interplay between supervision styles and student research outputs in the unique setting of Cambodian teacher education institutes. Understanding these linkages will help the study to contribute insight to improve supervisory procedures and the overall quality of education in Cambodia.

3. METHOD

3.1. Research Design

A quantitative research approach was adopted for the study, where survey questionnaires and assessment criteria were utilized together to examine the impact of supervision styles on student teachers' research output and perceptions. The research attempts to explore the complexities of educational supervision with this technique and to facilitate statistical analysis of tendencies and patterns. The surveys helped to understand individual experiences and perceptions that improved the understanding of the quantitative data on the teacher educators and the student teachers. The design is based on the rationale that it utilizes the strengths of the technique and thus enhances understanding of the influence of different supervision methods on teaching practices and outcomes.

3.2. Participants

Participants of this study were teacher educators and student teachers in a teacher education program at TECs. A target sample size of 106 teacher educators and 337 student teachers were randomly selected to get a representative sample of the varied backgrounds and experiences of the study. This was done so that a detailed analysis of the particular interactions between supervision styles and student teaching experiences could be performed. In the sampling process, demographic variables such as age, gender, previous teaching experience, etc., were taken into consideration to provide a valid and representative sample and to increase the validity of the results.

3.3. Research Tools

To collect data, survey questionnaires and evaluation criteria were employed. The survey instrument consisted of validated scales designed to determine teacher educators' supervision styles that guide student teachers' production of research reports and to measure perceptions of supervisory styles and self-efficacy among student teachers. Additionally, the tools were pre-tested in a pilot study to ensure validity by three experts, and their reliability is reported in Table 1.

Table 1. The table of reliability (Cronbach's Alpha)

Factors	Items	Cronbach's Alpha
Mentorship supervision (MS)	MS1-MS5	.864
Collaborative supervision (CS)	CS1-CS5	.858
Autonomous supervision (AS)	AS1-AS5	.910
Transformational supervision (TS)	TS1-TS5	.892

The reliability of the constructs of the study was checked by Cronbach's alpha. As shown in Table 1, Mentorship Supervision (MS1–MS5) had good internal consistency reliability ($\alpha = 0.864$), Collaborative Supervision (CS1–CS5) had good reliability ($\alpha = 0.858$), and Autonomous Supervision (AS1–AS5) had the highest internal consistency ($\alpha = 0.910$), indicating excellent reliability. Transformational Supervision (TS1–TS5) also showed strong dependability ($\alpha = 0.892$). In general, the Cronbach's alpha coefficients indicate that all measurement scales have satisfactory to high internal consistency, justifying the use of the instruments for the subsequent data analysis.

In addition, the assessment criteria for the research reports of student teachers were critically reviewed with specialists in educational research instruction, and these criteria were formally employed in TECs to evaluate the research reports of the student teachers. Table 2. The evaluation criteria were developed using a 5-point rating scale.

Table 2. The evaluation criteria are used to assess student teachers' research outcomes

Evaluation Criteria Scoring						
N⁰	**Introduction**	**1**	**2**	**3**	**4**	**5**
1	Explain how the background and the research problem have been solved.					
2	Write a proper research objective and a clear					
3	Write the right research questions and clear					
4	Write a valid research hypothesis. and clear (if any)					
5	Explain the importance of research clearly					
Literature Review						
6	Clearly explain the important rules related to the research problem.					
7	Reminder of the theory: Respond to the research problem/topic clearly					
8	The theoretical framework and/or the conceptual framework of the research are clear					
9	Clearly highlight research knowledge gaps					
Methodology						
10	Provide a reasonable research method that responds to the objectives and research questions					
11	Explain the reasons for choosing a clear research method					
12	Describe the participants and how to choose them participants					
13	Research tools have been found to be accurate and clear in confidence					
14	Describe the data collection tool clearly					
15	Clearly show the stages of the data collection procedure					
16	Clearly demonstrate how to analyze data					
17	Clearly describe the ethics of research					
Results and discussion						
18	The results answered the research questions and objectives					
19	Show results as a table and other graphics, follow APA format, and explain clearly					
20	A clear summary of the results					
21	The hypothesis is verified.					
22	Results can be discussed clearly and meet the objectives and research questions, theories, or previous research					
Conclusions and recommendations						
23	Make clear conclusions based on the results and discussion					
24	Provide clear recommendations for further research					
25	Recommendations provide concrete guidance for implementation. No conclusions are drawn based on the researcher's views or ideas.					
26	Revealed shortcomings in research					

Table 2 is a rubric for evaluating a research report. The rubric is a scale of 1-5 points in which higher points show better performance. The rubric consists of five main sections, which are Introduction, Literature Review, Methodology, Results and Discussion, and Conclusions and Recommendations. Evaluators assess the work according to each criterion, according to how well the student meets the expected academic requirements.

The Introduction section (Criteria 1–5) is dedicated to the development of a solid foundation for the study. The student teachers are to show their handling of the background and research problem, form a clear research objective, develop understandable research questions, propose a valid research hypothesis (if applicable), and convincingly justify the significance of the research with sufficient support. The second part, Literature Review (Criteria 6–9), assesses the student teachers' deep involvement in relevant scholarship by explaining key principles related to the problem, linking the theory directly to the research topic, developing a clear theoretical/conceptual framework, and identifying specific knowledge gaps that support the study.

The Methodology section (Criteria 10–17) assesses whether the study design is appropriate and scientifically sound. The student teachers should propose a reasonable research method that aligns with the objectives and questions, justify the rationale for choosing that method, and describe the participants and the sampling approach. The rubric also verifies if the research tools are accurate and clearly described, whether the data collection procedure is explained step-by-step, whether the data analysis is clearly demonstrated, and whether the work includes a transparent explanation of research ethics. The Results and Discussion section (Criteria 18–22) is evaluated on the basis of presentation of results that directly address the research questions and objectives, using tables and graphics in APA format with clear explanations, and a concise summary of results, with any hypothesis verified appropriately and discussion of results related to research objectives, relevant theories, and previous studies. The last academic output is the Conclusions and Recommendations section (Criteria 23-26), which is evaluated based on the strength of the final report. The student teachers must include clear conclusions based on the results and discussion and provide recommendations for future research, ensuring that recommendations are realistic and actionable and not based on personal opinion. The study should report the shortcomings or limitations identified in the research that show academic honesty and critical reflection.

3.4. Data Collection

Data were collected through online questionnaires utilizing Google Forms over a period of 2 months. Participants were recruited via email invitations and information sessions, and were fully informed about the study's purpose and procedures. During the data collection procedure, ethical problems were of vital relevance. Informed consent was obtained from all individual participants involved in the study. Data collection was carried out ensuring confidentiality and anonymity. An ethical framework was necessary to protect the rights and welfare of participants and to strengthen the trustworthiness and validity of study findings.

3.5. Data Analysis

The data analysis was performed using a quantitative method. The quantitative data that were gathered from the surveys were analyzed using statistical software such as SPSS. This made it possible to use descriptive (Mean, SD, etc.) and inferential statistics (ANOVA and Regression) to determine trends and correlations. The dual approach to data analysis enabled a comprehensive interpretation of the results, confirming the quantitative findings and providing a coherent understanding of the influence of supervision styles on student teachers' research outcomes and perceptions.

4. RESULTS

The results present the influence of teacher educators' supervision styles on student teachers' research outcomes and perceptions. The results were presented in accordance with the research questions.

RQ1. What teacher educator supervision styles enhance student teachers' writing of research reports?

Table 3. The descriptive analysis of Teacher Educators' Supervision Styles

SupervisionStyles	N	Minimum	Maximum	Mean	Std.
MS	106	5	25	18.40	3.676
CS	106	5	25	17.89	3.488
AS	106	5	25	17.46	3.802
TS	106	5	25	17.87	3.696
Valid N (listwise)	106				

Table 3 presents descriptive statistics for teacher educators' supervision styles (N=106) and provides insight into their perceptions of four supervisory approaches: mentorship supervision (MS), collaborative supervision (CS), autonomous supervision (AS), and transformational supervision (TS). The range of supervision styles was between 5 and 25, which shows a reliable scale of evaluation for the respondents. Mentorship supervision had the highest average score (M = 18.40, SD = 3.676). The mentoring style had the highest mean score of M=19.11 (SD = 3.505), suggesting teacher educators saw this as the most effective or preferred approach, followed by collaborative supervision (M=17.89, SD = 3.488). This points to a somewhat more positive but also less favourable perception. The autonomous supervision style had the lowest mean score of M = 17.46 (SD = 3.802), suggesting this aspect of supervision was perceived less favourably. The transformational supervision style had a mean score of 17.87 (SD = 3.696), which was perceived to be similar to the collaborative style but lower than the mentoring style. The standard deviations of all styles ranged from 3.488 to 3.802, which indicates moderate variation in responses. It indicates the general preference for mentoring and collaborative styles, but there is variation in the perception of the styles among teacher educators. These findings show the importance of supervision styles in educational settings, with mentoring and collaborative styles being particularly effective based on the participants' perceptions.

RQ2. How do student teachers perceive the supervision styles of teacher educators?

Table 4. The descriptive analysis of student teachers' perception of the teacher educators' supervision styles

Supervision Styles	N	Minimum	Maximum	Mean	Std.
MS	337	5	25	19.60	2.928
CS	337	5	25	19.40	2.886
AS	337	5	25	19.20	2.895
TS	337	5	25	19.41	2.910
Valid N (listwise)	337				

Descriptive statistics of four supervision styles (MS = mentorship supervision, CS = collaborative supervision, AS = autonomous supervision, and TS = transformational supervision) are presented in Table 4. The table presents the distributional and central tendency scores of the 337 participants of the study. The minimum and maximum scores in each of the four styles were 5 and 25, respectively, indicating that each of the four supervisory approaches was rated consistently across the spectrum. The mean scores indicated that mentorship supervision (M = 19.60, SD = 2.928) was rated the highest, indicating that the participants had a more favorable outlook on this style, while collaborative supervision was the second most favorable style with a mean of 19.40 (SD = 2.886). The mean scores for autonomous supervision were M = 19.20 (SD = 2.895) and transformational supervision were M = 19.41

(SD = 2.910), respectively, suggesting that the respondents generally rated all styles positively. The small standard deviations, which ranged between 2.886 and 2.928 for all styles, showed that there was a low degree of variability in responses. This showed that there was general agreement amongst participants on the effectiveness of these styles of supervision.

RQ3.What is the relationship between teacher educators' supervision styles and student teachers' research outcomes?

Table 5. The ANOVA analysis of teacher educators' supervision styles and student teachers' research outcomes

Model		Sum of Squares	df	Mean Square	F	Sig.
1	Regression	273.034	4	68.259	1.854	.126[b]
	Residual	3092.537	84	36.816		
	Total	3365.571	88			

a. Dependent Variable: Report

b. Predictors: (Constant), MS, CS, AS, TS, H_0 was accepted.

The analysis of ANOVA for regression model as shown in table 5 reveals that the predictors-mentorship supervision (MS), collaborative supervision (CS), autonomous supervision (AS), and transformational supervision (TS)—do not together account for a statistically significant proportion of the variance in the dependent variable, report scores (F (4, 84) = 1.854, Sig. = 0.126). The regression sum of squares (273.034) indicates some explanatory power; however, it is overshadowed by the residual sum of squares (3,092.537), which reflects substantial unexplained variation in report scores. Again, the regression mean square (68.259) is less than the residual mean square (36.816), indicating that the variance explained by the predictors is not enough to make meaningful conclusions. The analysis does not reject the null hypothesis at the conventional significance level of 0.05 or less, indicating that the combined effect of MS, CS, AS, and TS on report scores is not statistically significant. This suggests that other factors outside the scope of this model may be more important in determining report outcomes than the variables included in this model, and this points to the need to identify other variables relevant to student assessments.

Table 6. The coefficient analysis of the regression model

Model		Unstandardized Coefficients		Standardized Coefficients	t	Sig.	95.0% CI for B		Correlations		
		B	Std. Error	Beta			LB	UB	Zero-order	Partial	Part
1	(Constant)	45.340	3.597		12.606	.000	38.187	52.492			
	MS	-.108	.295	-.064	-.365	.716	-.695	.480	.067	-.040	-.038
	CS	.858	.404	.484	2.125	.037	.055	1.661	.145	.226	.222
	AS	.303	.268	.186	1.131	.261	-.230	.835	.118	.122	.118
	TS	-.826	.374	-.494	-2.206	.030	-1.571	-.081	.013	-.234	-.231

a. Dependent Variable: Report

Table 6 presents the coefficients, offering detailed insights into the relationships between the predictors—mentorship supervision (MS), collaborative supervision (CS), autonomous supervision (AS), and transformational supervision (TS)—and the dependent variable, report scores. The constant (45.340) is significant (t (84) = 12.606, Sig. < 0.001) and shows a baseline report score. Among the predictors, collaborative supervision shows a positive and significant relationship with report scores (β = 0.858, t (84) = 2.125, Sig. = 0.037), and this means that the higher the emphasis on collaboration in the learning environment, the higher the report scores. However, mentorship supervision has a non-significant negative effect (β = -0.108, t (84) = -0.365, Sig. = 0.716), and this means that it does not have a significant effect on the report outcomes. Autonomous supervision also has a non-significant positive effect (β = 0.303, t (84) = 1.131, Sig. = 0.261), suggesting that its effect on the report scores is negligible and inconclusive. However, transformational supervision has a significant negative effect (β = -0.826, t (84) = -2.206, Sig. = 0.030), which suggests that increased use of this style is associated with lower report scores. Overall, the results suggest that collaborative style has a positive effect on report results, while mentorship and autonomous supervision do not have a significant effect on scores, and supervisory style can be detrimental to performance, confirming the importance of educators considering the implications of these different instructional styles.

RQ 4. What is the relationship between student teachers' research outcomes and their perceptions of teacher educators' supervision styles?

Table 7. The ANOVA analysis of the relationship between student teachers' research outcomes and their perceptions

Model		Sum of Squares	df	Mean Square	F	Sig.
1	Regression	125.645	4	31.411	.839	.501[b]
	Residual	12435.795	332	37.457		
	Total	12561.440	336			

a. Dependent Variable: Report

b. Predictors: (Constant), TS, AS, MS, CS, H_0 was accepted.

The results of the ANOVA, as shown in Table 7, show that the regression model with mentorship supervision (MS), collaborative supervision (CS), autonomous supervision (AS), and transformational supervision (TS) as predictors could not significantly explain the variance in report scores (F (4, 332) = 0.839, Sig. = 0.501). The sum of squares for regression (125.645) shows that the predictors collectively explain some of the variance, but this contribution is modest relative to the residual variance (12,435.795), which reflects unexplained variability among report scores. The mean square for regression (31.411) is less than the mean square for the residuals (37.457), which shows the predictors' effect on report scores is not significant. Thus, since the significance is greater than the usual 0.05, we do not reject the null hypothesis and conclude that there is not enough statistical evidence to suggest that MS, CS, AS, and TS have a significant effect on report scores. This implies that there are other factors, not accounted for in this model, which might be more important in affecting the outcome variable.

Table 8. The coefficient analysis of the regression model

Model		Unstandardized Coefficients		Standardized Coefficients	t	Sig.	95.0%CI for B		Correlations		
		B	Std. Error	Beta			LB	UB	Zero-order	Partial	Part
1	(Constant)	49.536	2.470		20.059	.000	44.678	54.394			
	MS	-.287	.226	-.138	-1.271	.204	-.732	.157	.007	-.070	-.069
	CS	.399	.238	.188	1.675	.095	-.070	.868	.061	.092	.091
	AS	-.033	.200	-.016	-.165	.869	-.427	.361	.027	-.009	-.009
	TS	-.001	.202	-.001	-.006	.995	-.399	.397	.028	.000	.000

a. Dependent Variable: Report score

The coefficients are presented in Table 8, which provides insight into the relationships between the student teachers' perceptions about their teacher educators' supervision styles, such as mentorship supervision (MS), collaborative supervision

(CS), autonomous supervision (AS), and transformational supervision (TS), and the report scores. The constant term is significant (β = 49.536, t (332) = 20.059, Sig. < 0.001), which provides a baseline score for the reports. However, the individual predictors show varying levels of association with report scores. The MS has a negative but not significant effect (β = -0.287, t (332) = -1.271, Sig. = 0.204). A higher dependence on mentoring is weakly associated with lower report scores, but this is inconclusive as it is not statistically significant and needs further study. A collaborative style shows a positive trend (β = 0.399, t(332) = 1.675, Sig. = 0.095), approaching significance, suggesting that greater reliance on collaboration may positively affect report scores; however, the result is inconclusive at the traditional alpha level of 0.05. On the other hand, AS and TS have negligible effects on report scores (β = -0.033, t (332) = -0.165, Sig. = 0.869; β = -0.001, t (332) = -0.006, Sig. = 0.995), respectively, suggesting that neither of the variables has a significant effect on the report outcome. Taken together, these findings suggest that although there are signs of possible relationships, especially with collaborative style that made student teachers likely to increase their report scores and to be more satisfied with their teacher educators' supervision, the overall effect of these predictors on report scores is small, highlighting the need for further studies to investigate other factors that may affect student teachers' reports.

5. DISCUSSION

The results of this study provide useful information regarding the emerging professional roles at Cambodian Teacher Education Colleges (TECs) in the Age of AI. The analysis of supervision styles provides a subtle understanding of teacher educators' views on Mentorship supervision (MS), Collaborative supervision (CS), Autonomous supervision (AS), and Transformational supervision (TS). Descriptive statistics collected from a sample of 106 respondents revealed that the means of all four types of supervision were similar, with minimum and maximum scores ranging from 5 to 25. The means of the scores indicate that Mentorship supervision is the most preferred style (M = 18.40, SD = 3.676). It demonstrates that teacher educators regard this style as the most efficacious in their work. Mentorship was the most preferred style, with a mean score of (M= 18.05, SD = 3.579), indicating that it was overall considered effective. This was followed closely by collaborative supervision with a mean score of (M= 17.89, SD = 3.488). Autonomous and transformational supervision had mean scores of 17.46 (SD = 3.802) and 17.87 (SD = 3.696) respectively and these were lower than the other approaches. These results imply that these approaches may be perceived as less effective in the context of teacher education. The moderate standard deviations across the styles 3.488 to

3.802 indicate some variability in responses however the close proximity of the mean scores suggest consensus among teacher educators on the effectiveness of mentorship and collaborative approaches.

The coefficient analysis provides critical insights into the relationship between these supervisory styles and report scores. The significant positive correlation between collaborative supervision and report scores ($\beta = 0.858$, Sig. = 0.037) strongly supports the Constructivist Learning Theory, which suggests that in the Age of AI, the teacher educator's role is transitioning from a solitary "knowledge transmitter" to a "collaborative curator". The supervisors here do not just give the answers but work with student teachers to critically evaluate the AI-generated content to maintain the academic integrity and pedagogical richness of research reports (Dai et al., 2023). Through shared learning, student teachers are not passive recipients of knowledge but active participants who construct understanding through social interaction, a fundamental principle of Vygotsky's Social Development Theory. This shows that for Cambodian TECs, research competence is best cultivated when supervisors create a 'Zone of Proximal Development' in which peers and educators provide the necessary social scaffolding, and indicates that teacher educators who use collaborative approaches are likely to elicit higher report scores of student teachers, highlighting the potential benefit in promoting collaborative environments in educational contexts. Heng et al. (2020), Yang et al. (2022), and Wiyono et al. (2021) strongly supported the view that many university students preferred collaborative supervision, citing it as a motivating factor that enhanced their academic performance.

On the other hand, the mentorship supervision has a non-significant negative effect ($\beta = -0.108$, Sig. = 0.716), meaning that more dependence on this approach may not be associated with better report outcomes, and this too needs further exploration on why this may be the case (Chea, 2024b; Eby et al., 2008; Prabjandee, 2022; Turgut & Tasçi, 2024). To the international readership, this means that academic supervision competencies should now include "AI Literacy." Teacher educators should have the ability to guide student teachers in the use of AI tools for literature mapping or data organization, but they too must provide the necessary human scaffolding that is not possible at the moment with AI, and that is based on Vygotsky's ZPD (Jensen et al., 2025). Further, the success of collaborative approaches reflects Wenger's Communities of Practice. The results indicate that when student teachers feel a sense of belonging and engagement within a research community, their outcomes improve.

Equally, the significant negative relationship found with Transformational Supervision (TS) ($\beta = -0.826$, Sig.=0.030) may suggest that without the solid foundation of Shulman's Pedagogical Content Knowledge (PCK), high-level motivational strategies may overwhelm student teachers who still require foundational content and procedural expertise. In an AI-rich environment, a purely "visionary" or "transformational" approach that lacks procedural structure may lead students to over-rely on AI for "innovation" without the foundational Pedagogical Content Knowledge to verify its outputs. This suggests that "AI-enhanced supervision" should be grounded in Collaborative and Mentorship models rather than high-autonomy or purely motivational ones in the current Cambodian context. This suggests that the process of "transforming" a student teacher is difficult if the fundamental "content knowledge" and "teaching practices" have not yet been firmly embedded by more structured, collaborative means. The positive but non-significant impact of the former indicates little impact on report scores, while the significant negative impact of transformational supervision suggests a damaging association, and raises questions about its efficacy in practice. Taken together, these findings suggest that, while collaborative supervision shows promise in improving report scores, the effectiveness of mentorship and transformational approaches needs to be more closely examined.

In conclusion, the findings underscore the importance of supervisory styles in the educational context, emphasizing the significance of mentorship and collaborative approaches in achieving positive results. There is a need for a critical re-conceptualization and re-application of transformational supervision in teacher education. Future research should endeavor to more thoroughly examine the contextual factors that influence these supervisory styles and their impact on educational achievements, thus contributing to the construction of more effective supervisory models in the field.

6. CONCLUSION

6.1 Theoretical Reflections and International Relevance

This research adds to the existing theoretical perspectives by showing that while Constructivism and Communities of Practice are globally known, their application is context specific. In the Cambodian context, which is moving towards a research-intensive education, the 'social' aspect of learning (Vygotsky) seems more important for immediate research outcomes than 'autonomous' or 'transformational' models. For international readers, these findings suggest that in developing educational systems in rapid reform, supervisors should focus on Collaborative Supervision to build initial research efficacy. This refines Wenger's theory by suggesting that in emerging research cultures, the 'participation' in the community must be highly structured and collaborative to be effective. It warns against the universal application of Transformational Supervision without first ensuring that student teachers have reached a baseline of Pedagogical Content Knowledge as defined by Shulman.

6.2. Professional Roles

This study concludes that the professional role in Cambodian TECs in the Age of AI should be transformed into a more collaborative partnership. Supervisors should move away from the purely 'transformational' or 'autonomous' models, which often leave student teachers to wander the complex technological terrain without guidance, to a Collaborative Supervision model that offers the scaffolding that student teachers need to use AI tools in an ethical and effective fashion. Further research should explore how specific AI feedback tools can be incorporated into these collaborative structures to further improve Cambodian teacher education.

7. RECOMMENDATIONS

These insights give rise to a number of recommendations. Firstly, TECs should place greater emphasis on the development and implementation of collaborative and mentoring supervision practices, as these are perceived as most effective by student teachers and teacher educators. Training programs could be designed to equip teacher educators with the skills needed to create collaborative environments conducive to open communication and shared learning. Secondly, there is a need for a comprehensive redefinition of transformational supervision. This approach requires critical analysis and redefinition in order to uncover its shortcomings and to better tailor it to the realities of educational settings. Thirdly, the design of professional development programs should be explored in order to examine alternative models of transformational supervision that would better support student teachers and would be more in line with current pedagogical approaches. Lastly, future research should focus on qualitative investigations of the contextual factors affecting the effectiveness of these supervisory styles.

Understanding the specific dynamics at work would aid in customizing supervisory practices to better suit the needs of the educational context. This will not only enhance the supervisory models but will also enhance the overall teaching effectiveness and student teachers' learning outcomes. In light of the broader transformation of the academic profession in the era of AI, TECs should consider creating AI-responsive supervision guidelines. Such guidelines may include: (1) standards for transparency about AI assistance, (2) approaches to teach student teachers critical verification of AI-generated claims and references, (3) supervision practices that prioritize methodological reasoning and originality over language polishing, and (4) ethical and confidentiality procedures for any digital platforms used in supervision workflows.

8. ACKNOWLEDGMENTS

I would like to express my sincere gratitude to my main advisor, Dr. Chan Hum, whose unwavering support and insightful guidance have been instrumental throughout my research journey. His expertise not only provided clear direction but also motivated me to delve deeper into my study. I am also grateful to my co-advisor, Dr. Sopha Soeung, whose constructive feedback and encouragement substantially improved my work, allowing me to refine my ideas and approach. Additionally, I would like to acknowledge Dr. Rany Sam for helping edit this study, and I am also thankful to the administrators at the teacher education college for their logistical support and for fostering an environment that fosters academic inquiry. I am thankful to the teacher educators who shared their knowledge and experiences with me, which enriched the context of my research. Lastly, I extend my heartfelt gratitude to the student teachers who participated in this study. Their willingness to engage with the research process and share their insights has been invaluable in making this project possible. Together, their contributions have significantly influenced the outcomes of this research, and I am genuinely appreciative of their collaboration.

REFERENCES

Aldino, A. A., Maheshi, B., Li, Y., Zhou, Y., Tsai, Y.-S., Gašević, D., & Chen, G. (2026). Enhancing learner-centered feedback with AI: Teachers' practices and perceptions. *Assessment & Evaluation in Higher Education*, •••, 1–18. DOI: 10.1080/02602938.2026.2638920

Ba, S., Yang, L., Yan, Z., Looi, C. K., & Gašević, D. (2025). Unraveling the mechanisms and effectiveness of AI-assisted feedback in education: A systematic literature review. *Computers and Education Open*, *9*, 100284. DOI: 10.1016/j.caeo.2025.100284

Bekbolatova, M., Mayer, J., Ong, C. W., & Toma, M. (2024). Transformative potential of AI in healthcare: Definitions, applications, and navigating the ethical landscape and public perspectives. *Healthcare (Basel)*, *12*(2), 125. Advance online publication. DOI: 10.3390/healthcare12020125

Bjørndal, C., Mathisen, P., Wennergren, A.-C., & Thornberg, F. (2024). Challenges of the supervision process in the teacher education practicum – A qualitative research review. *Teaching and Teacher Education*, *146*, 104619. DOI: 10.1016/j.tate.2024.104619

Bou, D. (2025). Challenges and suggestions for improving the quality of higher education in Cambodia. *Cambodian Journal of Educational Research, 5*(1), 85–100. DOI: 10.62037/cjer.2025.05.01.03

Bou, D., Sran, L., & Phorn, P. (2025). Exploring Cambodian teacher educators' perspectives and challenges in conducting action research [Journal Article]. *Issues in Educational Research, 35*(3), 905–922. DOI: 10.3316/informit.T2025102900013190784088009

Bou, D., Sran, L., Teu, S., Tep, C., Kheuy, S., Vy, S., & Dul, V. (2024). Examining self-assessment of student teachers' self-directed learning: A case study at Battambang Teacher Education College, Cambodia. *Education Quarterly Eeview, 7*(4), 118–135. DOI: 10.31014/aior.1993.07.04.529

Bouzar, A., & El Idrissi, K. (2025). Supervisory feedback vs. AI: A comparative study on postgraduate student satisfaction. *Journal of Arts. Humanities and Social Sciences, 3*(1), 465–474. DOI: 10.5281/zenodo.14862530

Brandisauskiene, A., Buksnyte-Marmiene, L., Cesnaviciene, J., & Jarasiunaite-Fedosejeva, G. (2023). The relationship between teachers' autonomy-supportive behavior and learning strategies applied by students: The role of teacher support and equity. *SAGE Open, 13*(2), 1–16. DOI: 10.1177/21582440231181384

Bureau, J. S., Howard, J. L., Chong, J. X. Y., & Guay, F. (2022). Pathways to student motivation: A meta-analysis of antecedents of autonomous and controlled motivations. *Review of Educational Research, 92*(1), 46–72. DOI: 10.3102/00346543211042426

Cardwell, R., Nelson, K., Duncan, R., Copnell, B., & Moss, C. (2024). Being effective and supervising for thesis success in nursing coursework master's degrees: A qualitative descriptive study. *J Adv Nurs, 80*(12), 5050–5063. DOI: 10.1111/jan.16164

Casey, L., Sam, C., Seng, S., Pov, P., & Bo, C. (2024). The challenge of enhancing teacher professional identity and capability in Cambodian schools. *Schools, 21*(2), 348–367. DOI: 10.1086/732435

Chea, C. (2024a). Mentorship's role in shaping professional identity: Insights from Cambodian teaching practicums. *Cogent Education, 11*(1), 1–21. DOI: 10.1080/2331186X.2024.2419710

Chea, C. (2024b). Teaching practicum in the teacher education institutions in Cambodia: A cross-case analysis. *Journal of Teacher Education and Educators, 13*(1), 49–69. https://dergipark.org.tr/tr/download/article-file/3663332

Christy, T. C. (2013). Vygotsky, Cognitive Development and Language. *Historiographia Linguistica, 40*(1), 1–29. DOI: 10.1075/hl.40.1-2.07chr

Curran, E., & Murray, M. (2008). Transformative learning in teacher education: Building competencies and changing dispositions. *The Journal of Scholarship of Teaching and Learning*, *8*(3), 103–118. https://files.eric.ed.gov/fulltext/EJ854867.pdf

Czerniawski, G., Guberman, A., & MacPhail, A. (2017). The professional developmental needs of higher education-based teacher educators: An international comparative needs analysis. *European Journal of Teacher Education*, *40*(1), 127–140. DOI: 10.1080/02619768.2016.1246528

Dai, Y., Lai, S., Lim, C. P., & Liu, A. (2023). ChatGPT and its impact on research supervision: Insights from Australian postgraduate research students. *Australasian Journal of Educational Technology*, *39*(4), 74–88. https://ajet.org.au/index.php/AJET/article/view/8843/2026. DOI: 10.14742/ajet.8843

Dalky, A., Osaid Malkawi, R. M., Alrawashdeh, A., ALBashtawy, M., & Hani, S. B. (2025). Perceptions, barriers, and risk of artificial intelligence among healthcare professionals: A cross-sectional study. *Digital Health*, *11*, 20552076251360924. DOI: 10.1177/20552076251360924

Davidsson, E., & Stigmar, M. (2023). A literature review of content elements in supervision training courses. *London Review of Education*, *21*(1), 1–16. DOI: 10.14324/LRE.21.1.40

Devine, K., & Hunter, K. H. (2017). PhD student emotional exhaustion: The role of supportive supervision and self-presentation behaviours. *Innovations in Education and Teaching International*, *54*(4), 335–344. DOI: 10.1080/14703297.2016.1174143

Dietrich, J., Dicke, A.-L., Kracke, B., & Noack, P. (2015). Teacher support and its influence on students' intrinsic value and effort: Dimensional comparison effects across subjects. *Learning and Instruction*, *39*, 45–54. DOI: 10.1016/j.learninstruc.2015.05.007

Dreer-Goethe, B. (2025). The impact of mentor support and high-quality connections on student teachers' psychological safety and engagement during practicum [Original Research]. *Frontiers in Education*, *10*, 1499749. DOI: 10.3389/feduc.2025.1499749

Durksen, T. L., Klassen, R. M., & Daniels, L. M. (2017). Motivation and collaboration: The keys to a developmental framework for teachers' professional learning. *Teaching and Teacher Education*, *67*, 53–66. DOI: 10.1016/j.tate.2017.05.011

Dzvapatsva, G. P., Chinhamo, E., Matobobo, C., Ranga, M. M., & Ncube, P. D. N. (2026). Role of Generative Artificial Intelligence in Transforming Supervision Dynamics in Postgraduate Education: A Systematic Literature Review. In *Open Books and Proceedings* (pp. 1–16). ERRCD Forum. DOI: 10.38140/obp4-2026-01

Eby, L. T., Allen, T. D., Evans, S. C., Ng, T., & Dubois, D. (2008). Does mentoring matter? A multidisciplinary meta-analysis comparing mentored and non-mentored individuals. *Journal of Vocational Behavior, 72*(2), 254–267. DOI: 10.1016/j.jvb.2007.04.005

Em, S., Mok, S., & Sam, R. (2025). Exploring Cambodian teachers' views on transformational leadership of school directors. [JSKE]. *Journal of Social Knowledge Education, 6*(1), 76–89. DOI: 10.37251/jske.v6i1.1364

Flores, E., & Mean, U. (2025). Digital transformation in Cambodian higher education: Current trends and future directions. *Edelweiss Applied Science and Technology, 9*(1), 867–878. DOI: 10.55214/25768484.v9i1.4267

Fosnot, C. T., & Perry, R. S. (1996). Constructivism: A psychological theory of learning. *Constructivism: Theory, perspectives, and practice, 2*(1), 8–33. https://tinyurl.com/3jvv3krt

Gordon, S. P. (2023). Supervision, teaching, and learning in successful schools: A hall of mirrors. *Journal of Educational Supervision, 6*(3), 1–24. DOI: 10.31045/jes.6.3.1

Grønli, K. M., Walgermo, B. R., Uppstad, P. H., & McTigue, E. M. (2025). Transforming teacher feedback: A checklist for assessing and supporting reading skills, motivation, and student agency in oral reading. *Contemporary Educational Psychology, 82*, 102377. DOI: 10.1016/j.cedpsych.2025.102377

Gulumbe, B. H., Audu, S. M., & Hashim, A. M. (2025). Balancing AI and academic integrity: What are the positions of academic publishers and universities? *AI & Society, 40*(3), 1775–1784. DOI: 10.1007/s00146-024-01946-8

Gusango, E., Maani, J., & Ssetumba, J. (2021). The use of the constructivist approach in teacher preparation: a case of primary teachers' colleges of South Eastern Uganda. *American Journal of Education and Practice, 5*(1), 53–84. file:///c:/users/lenovo/downloads/705-article%20text-2364-2638-10-20210503.pdf

Ha, C., Pressley, T., & Marshall, D. T. (2025). Teacher voices matter: The role of teacher autonomy in enhancing job satisfaction and mitigating burnout. *PLoS One, 20*(1), e0317471. DOI: 10.1371/journal.pone.0317471

Hashweh, M. (2014). Pedagogical Content Knowledge: Lee Shulman. DOI: 10.4135/9781483346229.n248

Helm, G., & Hesse, F. (2026). Revising with AI: aligning feedback technologies with learners' revision processes [Hypothesis and Theory]. *Frontiers in Education, Volume 11 - 2026*. DOI: 10.3389/feduc.2026.1702406

Heng, K., Sol, K., Kaing, S., & Ros, V. (2020). Introduction: The need to promote a strong research and publication culture in Cambodia. *Cambodia Education Forum* 1–10. https://tinyurl.com/mr6j2yz7

Holcomb, D., Johnson, E., Vizina Roubal, J., & Thompson, C. (2025). Transformative supervision: A conceptual framework for relationally based, trauma-informed supervision in postpandemic practicum education. *Applied Learning in Social Work Education (ALSWE), 15*(1). https://alswe.simmons.edu/article/transformative-supervision-a-conceptual-framework-for-relationally-based-trauma-informed-supervision-in-postpandemic-practium-education/

Hoque, K. E., & Bt Kenayathulla, H. B., D/O Subramaniam, M. V., & Islam, R. (2020). Relationships between supervision and teachers' performance and attitude in secondary schools in Malaysia. *SAGE Open, 10*(2), 1–11. DOI: 10.1177/2158244020925501

Huot, S., & Loch, S. (2025). Educating in the Age of AI: Preparing Cambodian teachers and students for an AI-augmented learning future. *Journal of Educational Technology and E-Learning Innovations, 1*(2), 31–38. DOI: 10.54536/jeteli.v1i2.5170

Huot, S., Sam, R., & Nguon, T. (2025). Factors influencing teaching career choice among student teachers in cambodian teacher education colleges. *Education Quarterly Eeview, 8*(4), 1–17. DOI: 10.31014/aior.1993.08.04.226

Iatrellis, O., Bania, A., Samaras, N., Kosmopoulou, I., & Panagiotakopoulos, T. (2025). ChatGPT in doctoral supervision: Proposing a tripartite mentoring model for AI-assisted academic guidance. *International Journal of Doctoral Studies, 20*(9), 1–26. DOI: 10.28945/5579

Jensen, L. X., Bearman, M., Boud, D., & Konradsen, F. (2025). Feedback encounters in doctoral supervision: The role of generative AI chatbots. *Assessment & Evaluation in Higher Education*, •••, 1–14. DOI: 10.1080/02602938.2025.2478155

Jia, J., Zhang, Y., Bakar, L. J. A., & Ilyas, M. A. (2025). Transforming work in the digital era: AI-enhanced leadership and its effect on IT professional burnout. *Acta Psychologica, 260*, 105537. DOI: 10.1016/j.actpsy.2025.105537

Kahyalar, E., & Yazici, I. (2016). Supervision in language teaching: A supervisor's and three trainee teachers' perspectives. *The Reading Matrix: An International Online Journal, 16*(1), 78–90. https://readingmatrix.com/files/14-k5mwwz65.pdf

Karpudewan, M., & Mohd Ali Khan, N. S. (2017). Experiential-based climate change education: Fostering students' knowledge and motivation towards the environment. *International Research in Geographical and Environmental Education, 26*(3), 207–222. DOI: 10.1080/10382046.2017.1330037

Kemmis, S., Heikkinen, H. L. T., Fransson, G., Aspfors, J., & Edwards-Groves, C. (2014). Mentoring of new teachers as a contested practice: Supervision, support and collaborative self-development. *Teaching and Teacher Education*, *43*, 154–164. DOI: 10.1016/j.tate.2014.07.001

Kini, T., & Podolsky, A. (2016). *Does teaching experience increase teacher effectiveness? A review of the research* (Learning Policy Institute, Issue. L. P. Institution. https://files.eric.ed.gov/fulltext/ED606426.pdf

Kozulin, A. (2004). Vygotsky's theory in the classroom: Introduction. *European Journal of Psychology of Education*, *19*(1), 3–7. https://www.jstor.org/stable/23421397. DOI: 10.1007/BF03173233

Kumari, A., Begum, S., Paunikar, M. S., Kaur, A., & Verma, S. (2025). The role of artificial intelligence in teacher training: Enhancing pedagogical effectiveness. *Journal of Marketing & Social Research*, *2*, 116–122. DOI: 10.61336/jmsr/25-05-13

Kushwaha, A. (2022). Supervising teaching practice: Role perceptions and challenges. *Journal of Positive School Psychology*, *6*(11). https://journalppw.com/index.php/jpsp/article/view/13931/9030

Lambrecht, J., Lenkeit, J., Hartmann, A., Ehlert, A., Knigge, M., & Spörer, N. (2022). The effect of school leadership on implementing inclusive education: How transformational and instructional leadership practices affect individualised education planning. *International Journal of Inclusive Education*, *26*(9), 943–957. DOI: 10.1080/13603116.2020.1752825

Lau, J., Su, Y.-W., Chen, C.-C., & Dai, C.-L. (2019). Using a collaborative model in supervision with international counseling students. *The Journal of Humanistic Counseling*, *58*(2), 150–164. DOI: 10.1002/johc.12103

Lazarides, R., Dietrich, J., & Taskinen, P. H. (2019). Stability and change in students' motivational profiles in mathematics classrooms: The role of perceived teaching. *Teaching and Teacher Education*, *79*, 164–175. DOI: 10.1016/j.tate.2018.12.016

Li, R., Wang, X., Huang, G., Yang, W., Zhang, K., Gu, X., Tran, S. N., Garg, S., Alty, J., & Bai, Q. (2026). A comprehensive review of deep supervision in computer vision. *Neurocomputing*, *666*, 132193. DOI: 10.1016/j.neucom.2025.132193

Lim, R. R. (2024). Collaborative supervision of the master teachers and the teaching efficiency in selected junior high schools in Cavite. *International Journal for Multidisciplinary Research*, *6*(3), 1–15. https://www.ijfmr.com/papers/2024/3/22494.pdf

Long, Y. (2026). AI-Supervisor: Autonomous AI Research Supervision via a Persistent Research World Model. *arXiv preprint arXiv:2603.24402, 2*. /arXiv.2603.24402DOI: 10.48550

Madanchian, M., & Taherdoost, H. (2025). The impact of artificial intelligence on research efficiency. *Results in Engineering*, *26*, 104743. DOI: 10.1016/j.rineng.2025.104743

Marshall, J. H., Lawrence, E. C., Lee Williams, J., & Peugh, J. (2015). Mentoring as service-learning: The relationship between perceived peer support and outcomes for college women mentors. *Studies in Educational Evaluation*, *47*, 38–46. DOI: 10.1016/j.stueduc.2015.07.001

Mercer, S., Murillo-Miranda, C., & Smid, D. (2025). The invisible influencers: Understanding the motivation, emotions, and well-being of language teacher educators. *The Journal for the Psychology of Language Learning*, *7*(1), 27–44. DOI: 10.52598/jpll/7/1/3

Merdiaty, N., & Sulistiasih, S. (2024). Empowering learning: The mediating role of teachers in enhancing students' intrinsic motivation. *Al-Ishlah: Jurnal Pendidikan*, *16*(4), 5163–5172. DOI: 10.35445/alishlah.v16i4.6430

MoEYS. (2023). *Teacher policy action plan 2024-2030*. MoEYS. https://shorturl.at/WHuz3

MoEYS. (2025). *Strategic plan for teacher education reform in Cambodia 2024-2030*. https://shorturl.at/eS3S1

Mok, S. Y., & Staub, F. C. (2021). Does coaching, mentoring, and supervision matter for pre-service teachers' planning skills and clarity of instruction? A meta-analysis of (quasi-)experimental studies. *Teaching and Teacher Education*, *107*, 103484. DOI: 10.1016/j.tate.2021.103484

Naqvi, W. M., Ganjoo, R., Rowe, M., Pashine, A. A., & Mishra, G. V. (2025). Critical thinking in the age of generative AI: Implications for health sciences education. *Frontiers in Artificial Intelligence*, *8*, 1571527. DOI: 10.3389/frai.2025.1571527

Narayan, R., Rodriguez, C., Araujo, J., Shaqlaih, A., & Moss, G. (2013). Constructivism—Constructivist learning theory. In *The handbook of educational theories* (pp. 169–183). IAP Information Age Publishing., https://psycnet.apa.org/record/2013-11995-015

Nicol, D. J., & MacLeod, I. A. (2005). Using a shared workspace and wireless laptops to improve collaborative project learning in an engineering design class. *Computers & Education*, *44*(4), 459–475. DOI: 10.1016/j.compedu.2004.04.008

Omodan, B. I. (2025). Redefining the role of supervisors in the era of artificial intelligence: Implications for hybrid postgraduate research governance. *Cogent Education, 12*(1), 2536534. DOI: 10.1080/2331186X.2025.2536534

Osman, D. J., & Warner, J. R. (2020). Measuring teacher motivation: The missing link between professional development and practice. *Teaching and Teacher Education, 92*, 103064. DOI: 10.1016/j.tate.2020.103064

Paris, B., Conti-Cook, C., Greene, D., Jones, K. M., Justie, B., Kirschenbaum, M., Kresge, L., May, E., Nguyen, A., & Reynolds, R. (2025). Artificial intelligence and academic professions. *Available at* SSRN *5376147, 111*(3), 49–59. DOI: 10.2139/ssrn.5376147

Parker, A. K., Zenkov, K., & Glaser, H. (2021). Preparing school-based teacher educators: Mentor teachers' perceptions of mentoring and mentor training. *Peabody Journal of Education, 96*(1), 65–75. DOI: 10.1080/0161956X.2021.1877027

Pich, K. (2017). Challenges facing the implementation of teacher education policy and its impacts on teacher quality in Cambodia. *UC Occasional Paper Series, 1*(2), 39–59. https://tinyurl.com/er34hsan

Pov, S., & Kawai, N. (2025). Pre-service teachers' preparation for inclusive practices in Cambodia: Experience, self-efficacy, and concerns about inclusion. *Journal of Research in Special Educational Needs, 25*(1), 118–131. DOI: 10.1111/1471-3802.12715

Prabjandee, D. (2022). Inconvenient truth? How different mentoring approaches impact student–teacher identity development [Original Research]. *Frontiers in Education, 7*, 916749. Advance online publication. DOI: 10.3389/feduc.2022.916749

Priyoherianto, A., Mustaji, M., Roesminingsih, E., Hariyati, N., Rianto, Y., & Khamidi, A. (2025). The impact of organizational health and the levels of transformational leadership of school teachers in Indonesia: A systematic review. *International Journal of Current Educational Research, 4*(1), 25–45. DOI: 10.53621/ijocer.v4i1.47

Rahabav, P. (2016). The effectiveness of academic supervision for teachers. *Journal of Education and Practice, 7*(9), 47–55. https://files.eric.ed.gov/fulltext/EJ1095817.pdf

Reeve, J., & Cheon, S. H. (2024). Learning how to become an autonomy-supportive teacher begins with perspective taking: A randomized control trial and model test. *Teaching and Teacher Education, 148*, 104702. DOI: 10.1016/j.tate.2024.104702

Ronkainen, I., Vesterinen, V.-M., Lavonen, J., Järvinen, J., Malmberg, L.-E., Turkkila, M., & Salmela-Aro, K. (2025). Students' situational motivation in climate education: A multilevel profile approach. *Learning and Individual Differences*, *120*, 102698. DOI: 10.1016/j.lindif.2025.102698

Samoun, S., & Pen, D. (2025). A qualitative study of challenges faced by Cambodian teachers in implementing student-centered approaches. *Journal of General Education and Humanities*, *4*(2), 575–588. DOI: 10.58421/gehu.v4i2.426

Sedkaoui, S., & Benaichouba, R. (2024). Generative AI as a transformative force for innovation: A review of opportunities, applications and challenges. *European Journal of Innovation Management*. Advance online publication. DOI: 10.1108/EJIM-02-2024-0129

Sek, R. (2023). The effectiveness of transformational leadership in improving staff performance of private primary schools in Phnom Penh, Cambodia. *Journal As-Salam*, *7*(1), 26–41. https://www.ijtsrd.com/papers/ijtsrd97270.pdf. DOI: 10.37249/assalam.v7i1.554

Sengsoulintha, K. (2025). Teacher educators' challenges: Focusing on teacher training colleges in Laos [Original Research]. *Frontiers in Education*, *10*, 1–14. DOI: 10.3389/feduc.2025.1614060

Severinsson, E. (2012). Research supervision: Supervisory style, research-related tasks, importance, and quality - part 1. *Journal of Nursing Management*, *20*(2), 215–223. DOI: 10.1111/j.1365-2834.2011.01361.x

Sharma, U., & Sokal, L. (2015). The impact of a teacher education course on pre-service teachers' beliefs about inclusion: An international comparison. *Journal of Research in Special Educational Needs*, *15*(4), 276–284. DOI: 10.1111/1471-3802.12043

Sok, S., & Heng, K. (2024). Research on teacher education and implications for improving the quality of teacher education in Cambodia. *International Journal of Professional Development. Learners and Learning*, *6*(1), 1–9. DOI: 10.30935/ijpdll/14042

Sot, V., Sok, S., & Dickinson, G. (2019). Four decades of teacher development: Teacher preparation and teacher upgrading programs in Cambodia from 1979 to 2018. *Cambodia Education Review*, *3*(1), 115–139. https://shorturl.at/yEkEm

Sowa, S., Brown, C., Choi, T.-H., & Newman, R. (2025). Examining how generative AI tools benefit and challenge teachers' research-informed practice. *European Journal of Teacher Education*, *48*(5), 1036–1055. DOI: 10.1080/02619768.2025.2518193

Strieker, T., Adams, M., Cone, N., Hubbard, D., & Lim, W. (2016). Supervision matters: Collegial, developmental and reflective approaches to supervision of teacher candidates. *Cogent Education, 3*(1), 1–24. DOI: 10.1080/2331186X.2016.1251075

Tan, C., & Tee Ng, P. (2012). A critical reflection of teacher professionalism in Cambodia. *Asian Education and Development Studies, 1*(2), 124–138. DOI: 10.1108/20463161211240106

Tep, V. (2024a). Improving professional development: A case study on the influence of faculty evaluations in Cambodia. *SAGE Open, 14*(2), 1–13. DOI: 10.1177/21582440241241166

Tep, V. (2024b). Teacher educators as curriculum developers: A case study of teacher education colleges in Cambodia [Original Research]. *Frontiers in Education, 9*, 1–14. DOI: 10.3389/feduc.2024.1328023

Thong, C. L., Atallah, Z., Islam, S., Lim, W., & Cherukuri, A. K. (2025). AI-powered Tools for Doctoral Supervision in Higher Education: A Systematic Review. *Journal of Information & Knowledge Management, 24*(02), 2530001. DOI: 10.1142/S0219649225300013

Tonna, M. A., Bjerkholt, E., & Holland, E. (2017). Teacher mentoring and the reflective practitioner approach. *International Journal of Mentoring and Coaching in Education, 6*(3), 210–227. DOI: 10.1108/IJMCE-04-2017-0032

Turgut, S., & Tasçi, G. (2024). Learning to Hear Students' Voices: Teachers' Experiences on Student Mentoring. *International Education Studies, 17*(2), 1–14. https://files.eric.ed.gov/fulltext/EJ1421333.pdf. DOI: 10.5539/ies.v17n2p1

Tweed, A. D., & Warrington, S. (2024). Autonomous learning in Cambodia: A solution for problematic educational conditions? *Cambodian Journal of Educational Research, 4*(2), 64–78. https://cjerjournal.com/index.php/cjer/article/view/62. DOI: 10.62037/cjer.2024.04.02.04

UNESCO. (2024). *Strengthening teacher education programmes in Cambodia.* https://www.unesco.org/en/articles/strengthening-teacher-education-programmes-cambodia

UNESCO. (2025). *MoEYS and UNESCO launch the strategic plan for teacher education reform 2024–2030 at the national education congress 2025.* UNESCO. https://tinyurl.com/5an3tshc

Usha, G. (2002). Infancy: The Origins of Cognitive Development. In *Blackwell Handbook of Childhood Cognitive Development* (pp. 1–5). DOI: 10.1002/9780470996652.part1

Vijaya Kumari, S. (2014). Constructivist approach to teacher education: An integrative model for reflective teaching. *Journal of Educational Psychology*, *7*(4), 31–40. https://files.eric.ed.gov/fulltext/EJ1098640.pdf

Wang, G., Zhang, Q., Wang, L., & Liu, Y. (2025). The impact of teachers' autonomy support on students' academic performance from the perspective of hyperscanning: The mediating role of autonomy need satisfaction. *Social Cognitive and Affective Neuroscience*, *20*(1), nsaf115. Advance online publication. DOI: 10.1093/scan/nsaf115

Willegems, V., Consuegra, E., Struyven, K., & Engels, N. (2017). Teachers and pre-service teachers as partners in collaborative teacher research: A systematic literature review. *Teaching and Teacher Education*, *64*, 230–245. DOI: 10.1016/j.tate.2017.02.014

Wilson, E. K. (2006). The impact of an alternative model of student teacher supervision: Views of the participants. *Teaching and Teacher Education*, *22*(1), 22–31. DOI: 10.1016/j.tate.2005.07.007

Wiyono, B. B., Rasyad, A., & Maisyaroh, . (2021). The effect of collaborative supervision approaches and collegial supervision techniques on teacher intensity using performance-based learning. *SAGE Open*, *11*(2), 1–9. DOI: 10.1177/21582440211013779

Wongvorachan, T., Lai, K. W., Bulut, O., Tsai, Y.-S., & Chen, G. (2022). Artificial intelligence: Transforming the future of feedback in education. *Journal of Applied Testing Technology*, 95-116. http://jattjournal.net/index.php/atp/article/view/170387

Yang, B., Bao, S., & Xu, J. (2022). Supervisory styles and graduate student innovation performance: The mediating role of psychological capital and the moderating role of harmonious academic passion. *Frontiers in Psychology*, *13*, 1034216. DOI: 10.3389/fpsyg.2022.1034216

Yoeurng, S. (2024). Implementing a school-based mentoring program at a secondary resource school in Takeo province, Cambodia. [CJESS]. *Cambodian Journal of Educational and Social Sciences*, *1*(1), 67–88. DOI: 10.69496/cjess.v1i1.10

Yuan, E. R. (2016). The dark side of mentoring on pre-service language teachers' identity formation. *Teaching and Teacher Education*, *55*, 188–197. DOI: 10.1016/j.tate.2016.01.012

Yuan, X., Ironsi, C. S., & Liu, F. (2025). The role of group mentorship in supporting teachers across different developmental stages: A comparative study. *Studies in Educational Evaluation*, *86*, 101477. DOI: 10.1016/j.stueduc.2025.101477

Zheng, L., & Xiao, Y. (2026). Supervised or autonomous? Exploring the effect of instructional strategies on elementary school students' mathematics and science achievement. *Teaching and Teacher Education, 170*, 105315. DOI: 10.1016/j.tate.2025.105315

Chapter 9
AI-Enhanced Academic Careers in Cambodia:
Rethinking Professorial Roles, Evaluation, and Identity in a Digitally Transformed Higher Education

Sovanna Huot
http://orcid.org/0009-0006-8335-442X
Department of Education, National Institute of Education (NIE), Phnom Penh, Cambodia

Phearun Tep
http://orcid.org/0009-0000-2490-677X
Department of English, University of Delhi, New Delhi, India

ABSTRACT

This chapter investigates the impacts of AI on the transformation of academic evaluation, professorial roles, and professional identity within Cambodia's higher education system and beyond. Artificial intelligence (AI) impacts higher education systems around the world, from teaching and learning to research and assessment. In Cambodia, the modernization of higher education is intertwined with digitization and quality-assurance reforms, in which AI technologies strongly shape the academic profession. It reviews 136 articles on AI in higher education, labor, digital governance, and professional identity in Cambodia, using the PRISMA framework. The chapter discusses research, teaching, and administrative opportunities and challenges, as well as issues such as algorithmic bias, the digital divide, autonomy, reliance on metrics, and academic evaluation. This chapter offers a nuanced

DOI: 10.4018/979-8-2600-3204-6.ch009

and pragmatic approach to the integration of AI in Cambodia's higher education system, grounded in ethical policies and fair evaluation and academic governance that support capacity building and collaboration.

I. INTRODUCTION

Artificial intelligence has changed how higher education works globally. Bower et al. (2024) state that generative AI has enormous capabilities that are altering the way education is consumed, taught, and administered. Since ChatGPT arrived at the end of November 2022, the case for and against the benefits and detriments of AI on society has been hotly debated. Strzelecki et al. (2024) note that this situation has sparked a highly charged debate about the restrictions, benefits, and ethics of this technology. AI-based educational technology has rapidly changed how universities function. Kumar and Derawi (2025) suggest that AI has been applied across disciplines such as education, health sciences, business, and agriculture, and Ng (2012) shows that AI applications are interwoven with the fabric of modern educational systems. Gökçearslan et al. (2024) highlight that most studies on AI in education indicate that AI creates gray areas for institutions seeking to adopt it, as they balance the risks, gaps, and considerable benefits.

Universities around the globe have rapidly accelerated their digital transformation initiatives in the last couple of years. According to Naseer et al. (2024), AI supports new assessment methods through automated grading and rapid, adaptive feedback in formative assessments. Bae and Bozkurt (2024) claim that AI-driven assessments create opportunities for individualized learning at a scale previously impossible. According to Chan and Hu (2023), AI can assist students with idea generation and structuring academic writing, thereby changing how students and researchers think about productivity in an academic context. Bhat (2023) claims that AI enables better support for administrative tasks, thereby increasing efficiency within an institution and restructuring other academic activities. AI is becoming increasingly more evident in its role in teaching, researching, administration, and academic governance. Sok and Heng (2024) conducted a comprehensive review of 52 articles and noted that AI offered several advantages for higher education, including virtual learning support, innovative assessments and pedagogy, research support, academic writing support, and administrative and productivity support. Garzón et al. (2025), through their systematic scoping review of 118 articles, noted that, despite the integration of AI in education being beneficial, it posed several threats, such as low readiness, irreproducibility, lack of transparency, low beneficence, and privacy concerns.

The use of algorithms to manage academic activities marks a significant shift in how most university education systems and processes operate. Hussain et al. (2024)

argue that AI-based tools will be capable of more advanced interpretation, analysis, and the general use of human languages, thereby changing the nature of teaching, assessment, and research management in academic institutions. On the other hand, Garzón et al. (2025) identify potential problems, such as algorithmic biases and a lack of attention to ethics, as gaps in the new approach. Hoernig et al. (2024) provide a counterargument where heavy reliance on AI will eliminate creativity, critical thinking, and problem-solving skills, with dire effects on the academic profession and career advancement. The global use of AI in academic institutions combines both untapped prospects and a paradoxical challenge. Sullivan (2025) is the first to argue that the availability of AI-based systems has led to widespread cheating, while Delikoura et al. (2025) argue that such systems hurt education. Cambodia's higher education has evolved through stages influenced by political and economic factors, from the first institutions in the 1940s to the current focus on quality, access, internationalization, and governance as outlined in the Cambodia Higher Education Vision 2030. The system includes 132 institutions with over 209,000 students and emphasizes digital transformation, quality assurance, and research to meet labor market needs, despite ongoing challenges.

Cambodia has some of the most pronounced digital transformation challenges. Pum and Sok (2024) note that, despite improvements in systems in Cambodia, international research on educational technology, specifically AI in the Cambodian context, has developed very little. Huot et al. (2026) suggest that students have expressed deep concerns about the privacy and safety of using AI-based systems and about the lack of instruction on how to use them. The use of these systems has been ethically difficult to justify, as students have expressed discomfort with such advanced systems. Additionally, Hongseng (2023, May 19) cites a Cambodian academic forum's discussion of "*ChatGPT: Opportunities and Challenges*" and raises a copyright concern about the potentially unethical and illegal outputs that generative AI may produce. In the absence of the internet and digitized technologies, Cambodia's education system is one of the major drivers of the country's inequality (Teng, 2024). Khort et al. (2024) assert that the digital divide is socially divisive and, therefore, a socially responsive phenomenon that must be inclusive of social considerations. Changes to research and teaching responsibilities have reshaped the academic profession worldwide. Sok and Heng (2024) argue that the digital age has changed academic work, with teaching and research being automated and supported by AI, core parts of academics. According to Chan and Hu (2023), students' opinions on generative AI indicate clear advantages and disadvantages in higher education, and academic work is being redefined through human-AI partnerships. The Digital age has introduced more complex and demanding academic work. Bower et al. (2024) argue that even more advanced generative AI will create an even greater need for academics to change how they carry out their professional duties. Gökçearslan et al. (2024) argue that AI offers more advanced pedagogical practices, improved assessments through AI-supported grading, and more intelligent, real-time feedback, which is changing how academics do their work. Sullivan (2025) argue that academic work, critical thinking, and engagement will suffer as a result of an over-reliance on AI.

The demand for academic research and visibility has changed academic careers. Huot and Loch (2025) cite ChatGPT and similar AI tools as enabling students to develop writing, write paragraphs and essays, suggest academic vocabulary, check grammar, perform topic analyses, identify main ideas, and generate ideas. They show that Cambodian university students use Grammarly and similar AI tools for language translation and grammar checking to learn new languages more efficiently. However, Huot and Phin (2026) argue that the potential of AI tools to improve learning is undermined by the inequality faced by students who do not use AI for assignments. Academic evaluation and global rankings are becoming more metric- and algorithm-driven. Garzón et al. (2025) acknowledge the benefits of AI but highlight drawbacks, including limited preparedness and privacy concerns. The widespread adoption of bibliometric frameworks pushes academics to produce measurable research outputs, often at the expense of scholarly depth and local relevance. Limited digital preparedness hampers Cambodian higher education.

Pum and Sok (2024) highlight the need for structured AI training due to limited knowledge of ethical AI use. They found that students were concerned about data privacy and security due to limited AI training. Resource constraints and inequalities deepen digital transformation issues. Khort et al. (2024) emphasize the importance of a clear, socially aware digital policy that addresses gaps in students' digital skills and promotes equity. The World Bank (2024) reports a widening shortage of qualified STEM graduates in Cambodia. Relying on AI tools poses risks, with Teng (2024) noting that tools like ChatGPT may diminish students' creativity. Huot and Loch (2025) argue that AI reduces critical thinking, in which ethical and governance concerns grow with listing privacy, loss of critical skills, academic dishonesty, assessment problems, and biased information as key issues.

According to Tanveer et al. (2020), many students submit someone else's work as their own, which they argue is unethical and may infringe upon the Berne Convention copyright. Challenges to the establishment of professional identity and academic independence are serious. Heng and Sol (2024) encourage Cambodian higher education institutions to create or amend academic integrity policies and accompanying regulations to reflect changes in Artificial Intelligence (AI). The Cambodianess reports concern about the dangerous consequences of Artificial Intelligence (AI) in government and education; experts worry about the use of AI without limits (Teng, 2024). This chapter seeks to achieve four main objectives:

1. To explore how AI impacts teaching, academic appraisal, and professional self-conception in Cambodia's developing higher education system.
2. To develop a critical perspective on AI-based teaching, automated research assistance, digital metrics, governance, and institutional algorithms in relation to the teaching profession in the context of the Cambodian university system.
3. To combine the global and local literature on the role of AI in higher education, the transformation of academic labor, digital governance, and the reshaping of professional identity
4. To create a context-specific model for the introduction of AI to Cambodian higher education that balances consideration of ethics, adaptable policy frameworks, equitable evaluation mechanisms, and integrated systems with a focus on the augmentation of academic governance.

This chapter focuses on the following four research questions:

1. How does AI impact the roles of lecturers, teaching, and research within the context of Cambodian universities?
2. What are the pros and cons of AI-based research assessments and digital performance and program metrics, combined with AI-based governance in the context of Cambodian universities?
3. What is the impact of AI on professional academic identity and the autonomy and legitimacy of academics in a digitally modified Cambodian higher education system?
4. What is the appropriate balance of technology and academic human values in Cambodian higher education so that a framework for responsible, ethical, and context-sensitive artificial intelligence can be developed?

Cambodia-specific studies on AI in higher education are nearly nonexistent and underdeveloped. Huot and Such (2025) found that research on educational technologies, especially AI, is underexplored in the Cambodian context. They noted that, despite increased AI use among Cambodian educators and students, evidence-based studies remain scarce. The literature shows a gap regarding AI's impact on academic professions, evaluation systems, and professional identity in developing countries, especially in Southeast Asia. Garzón et al. (2025) highlighted issues such as insufficient readiness and privacy concerns regarding AI tools, but context-specific studies remain scarce. Sok and Heng (2024) suggest that while AI offers many benefits in higher education, most research is international and does not reflect Cambodian realities.

II. CONCEPTUAL FRAMEWORK AND LITERATURE REVIEW

2.1 Theoretical Foundations of AI in Higher Education

Transformations in AI and education represent a significant, fundamental shift in how universities perceive teaching, learning, and institutional management. According to Bower et al. (2024), given the immense power of generative AI to alter educational practice, there is a strong need to revise how teaching and assessment are conducted. In contrast, Naseer et al. (2024) argue that AI's rapid comment and grading systems, as well as rapid feedback mechanisms, facilitate new assessment practices that redefine the pace and quality of academic work. On the other hand, Garzón et al. (2025) note that, despite numerous advantages reported during the integration of AI-powered tools, several significant challenges, such as low levels of technological readiness and problems of non-reproducibility, opacity, and insufficient privacy, remain.

The theory of digital governance helps critically understand the integration of AI into higher education. A study by United Nations University Operating Unit on Policy-driven Electronic Governance (UNU-EGOV, 2026) claims that digital governance theory helps explain changes in how organizations behave in the new era of governance. It helps to understand how information technology and governance can be fused to create digital societies that are inclusive, transparent, and sustainable. According to Sun et al. (2024) and drawing on digital governance theory and collaborative governance theory, constructivists have articulated an institutional design in which institution is of greater significance than technology. Kunwar (2026) mentioned that new research employs digital governance theory and lifelong learning systems to provide a basis for understanding AI's role in organizations. The reconfiguration of the world of work is one of the major changes AI is bringing to academia. Alyasin and Shah (2026) contend that AI-assisted academic writing warrants an examination of university students' agency from a sociocultural perspective that focuses on the relationships and contexts surrounding technology. The UNESCO (2023) argues that institutions are designing programs that illustrate the models of human-AI collaboration. However, Santos (2024) states that the theory provides multiple frameworks for designing Human-AI collaboration in education.

Many theories have been developed to describe how universities adopt technology. According to Gökçearslan et al. (2024), research on the use of AI in education points to major shortcomings as well as important advantages, creating a challenging 'adoption' scenario. According to Kumar and Derawi (2025), the use of AI has spread across various disciplines, including education, the health sciences, business, and even agriculture, exemplifying its cross-disciplinary utility. According to Dimitriadou and Lanitis (2023), AI can support administrative tasks, assist with the overall functioning of institutions, and reconfigure academic labor.

2.2 The Academic Profession in the Digital Era

The digital era has brought significant changes to the sociology of academic professions. Archer (2008) notes that academic identity is, and always has been, plural rather than singular, and is differentiated by teaching, research, and service, including, increasingly, digital skills. Henkel (2005) argued that with the advance of digital technologies, the balance between individual and institutional goals has become more pronounced than in the past. Based on the findings of Povilaitis and Jõgi (2026), academic staff make sense of their academic identity in liminal spaces and through identity reconstruction within constantly changing universities. The digital era has made academic identity more tenuous, and Earl et al. (2026) suggest that professional stigma and identity are inextricably intertwined in complex ways, with academic identity extending beyond teaching and research alone. Jensen and Jetten (2015) reinforce the view that the constructs of identity, belonging, and collegiality are linked to confidence in teaching and are manifestations of social capital in the construction of professional identity. Lessky and Schiffecker (2024) caution that, for early-career academics, the construction of a consistent academic identity is crucial for belonging and for building a viable professional career in the long term.

Managerialism and neoliberalism have undergone massive shifts in academia. According to Morrish (2019), the emergence of neoliberalism in higher education can be viewed as the transformation of academia into its neoliberal variant, with significant consequences for all academicians who entered the profession after the 2000s. In the neoliberal university (Maisuria & Helmes, 2019), associated managerial practices reduce scholarship, teaching, and learning and denigrate and displace academic staff and students. Lia and Sunb (2024) illustrate that the reconfiguration of academic professional structures and their professional autonomy in the neoliberal university have been significant. The academic profession has been affected by the university's digital managerial practices. There has been a rapid shift in the digitalization of academic labor. According to Bower et al. (2024), a more powerful channel of generative artificial intelligence will require significant alterations to teaching and assessment and shift how academics fulfill their professional obligations. On the other hand, Sok and Heng (2024) argue that the integration of artificial intelligence in academic labor, teaching, and research has become a norm. The over-reliance on artificial intelligence for research has significantly compromised academic engagement, thereby impairing critical thinking and professional growth.

2.3 AI and Professorial Roles

The global integration of AI into teaching and curriculum design is altering the teaching and learning process. Naseer et al. (2024) state that better assessment and the introduction of automated grading and rapid adaptive feedback reshape the organization and management of teaching. Chan and Hu (2023) state that students' use of generative AI has both positive and negative aspects. Pedagogical relationships are being redesigned through human-AI partnerships. They suggest that AI will have a positive impact on the organization and construction of academic writing and on idea generation, which will change how academics design curricula and how scholars approach curriculum design.

Automated grading and assessment systems are an especially controversial subset of AI. Huot and Phin (2026) warn that the use of AI within educational contexts creates the potential for unfair, biased assessment. The validity of assessments is compromised when students who use AI to generate assignments receive higher grades than those who do not. Sullivan (2025) indicates that the potential for cheating, plagiarism, and AI-related misconduct is a serious threat to education and requires urgent policymaking. Concerns over data privacy and security in AI systems, and the lack of ethical and responsible training to ensure proper AI use, have caused concern among students. AI systems have improved research and publication efforts, increasing productivity, but they also pose a risk to academic integrity. Pum and Sok (2024) believe that AI tools, such as ChatGPT, can aid students in developing academic writing, paragraph and essay composition, suggestions for academic vocabulary, grammar checking, topic analysis, and idea generation. Huot et al. (2026) found that some Cambodian university students use AI-powered tools, such as Grammarly, to aid in grammar checking and translation, thereby supporting language learning. However, Tanveer et al. (2020) state that many students lack awareness of the ethical implications of their actions, and that submitting copied or pasted work can violate the Berne Treaty, for which they may face prosecution.

Changes to academic labor systems have been caused by the automation of administrative processes and the restructuring of workloads. Bhat (2023) claims AI effectively supports administrative tasks. As a result, it increases institutional efficiency, which in turn impacts the academic labor system. In their review of 52 articles, Sok and Heng (2024) found that the use of AI in higher education offered many benefits, including improved administrative efficiency and productivity, thereby reducing faculty members' administrative workload. Despite this, Hoernig et al. (2024) acknowledge that overreliance on AI could stifle creativity and undermine critical thinking and problem-solving skills, raising questions about the potential negative impact on academic staff's professional development in the long run.

2.4 AI-Driven Evaluation and Academic Metrics

The integration of bibliometric systems and research visibility into academic evaluation criteria is increasingly common worldwide. Garzón et al. (2025) noted the benefits of AI inclusion but also significant issues, such as low technological readiness and data privacy concerns, which affect bibliometric systems. Teymourifar (2026) explains how the ABS journal ranking clarifies the role of metric-driven evaluation and its impact on academic and institutional priorities. Meho (2025) warns that gaming metrics and anomalies threaten the integrity of evaluation systems, which are easily manipulated. A controversial aspect is the use of algorithms for evaluation and promotion. Fiesler et al. (2020) state that, despite barriers, these systems should promote equity and fairness. They highlight disciplinary blind spots, showing that not all computer scientists are interested in education or algorithms. Täuber (2026) suggests that scholarly evaluation results from techno-colonization, where scholars internalize metric-based approaches.

Data-oriented assessments have increased pressure on faculty. Khort et al. (2024) found that stakeholders viewed Digital Transformation in Cambodia's higher education positively, but called for more digital infrastructure, training, and leadership support. Conversely, the World Bank (2024) noted that Cambodia faces severe human resource constraints and a shortage of skilled STEM graduates, indicating that capacity-building cannot rely solely on metrics. The risks of measurement-based evaluation grow clearer. Meho (2025) reports metric manipulation and bibliometric anomalies undermine trust and system integrity. Täuber (2026) warns that an extreme focus on metrics causes symbolic violence, reducing academic freedom and autonomous thinking. Sullivan (2025) highlights that metric-driven systems fuel academic fraud and dishonesty.

2.5 Ethical and Governance Challenges

The main ethical issues with AI concern the absence of explanation and algorithmic bias/discrimination. According to Huot and Loch (2025), there are five main concerns regarding the deployment of AI in the education system of Cambodia: (1) issues of privacy and security, (2) the erosion of critical and creative thinking, (3) the potential for cheating, (4) issues concerning evaluations, and (5) underdeveloped or biased information. Furthermore, Huot and Phin (2026) suggest that the use of AI tools in education is likely the most profound cause of biased evaluations and thus the most significant concern regarding inequality. The issues of transparency and accountability remain unaddressed in AI governance frameworks. Garzón et al. (2025) highlight that insufficient replicability and transparency in AI-based educational solutions pose a significant obstacle to the construction of a trust-based system.

According to the United Nations Educational, Scientific and Cultural Organization, (UNESCO, 2025), Cambodia's AI Readiness Assessment Report reveals ongoing difficulties in the public's understanding of AI fundamentals.

The integration of AI increasingly challenges autonomy and independence of thought. Teng (2024) considers the integration of AI into Civil Service and Education, with unrestricted AI consequences, the greatest threat. Huot and Loch (2025) argue that deploying AI-based solutions does not enhance students' critical thinking skills, as students who use such solutions answer questions and therefore lose the desire to think critically. This trend may restrict educational practitioners' freedom to determine teaching and learning processes. Data privacy and surveillance issues have recently become more pronounced in education. They also show that students were very concerned about data in AI-based education and tools. This was due to insufficient training in ethics and the proper use of the tools. Pum and Sok (2024) identified privacy and security issues as one of the top five concerns related to the use of AI in Cambodian education, the impact of the digital divide results from inequity in AI integration. Khort et al. (2024) argue that persistent inequality in Internet access and unequal digital skills among students can only be eliminated through a consistent, socially inclusive digital approach to education that takes into account Cambodia's specific socio-economic conditions.

2.6 Higher Education and AI in Developing Countries

Some challenges to adopting AI in Global South universities are unique to those countries and regions. The United Nations Development Programme, (UNDP, 2025) notes that developing countries and regions also face limited data, a shortage of low-resource languages, privacy concerns, and insufficient governance frameworks. Radiya-Dixit and Christin (2025) argue that AI ethics and policies should be formulated in specific contexts rather than applying a one-size-fits-all approach across multiple contexts. The most important challenges in developing countries are infrastructure and institutional readiness. UNESCO (2025) reports that the AI Readiness Assessment for Cambodia identifies persistent challenges in developing the necessary infrastructure, training AI personnel, and raising awareness. The World Bank (2024) provides an account of Cambodia's higher education system, which is comprised of 132 institutions (48 of them public and 84 of them private) with approximately 209,059 students and 16,471 faculty members (31% of them hold a Bachelor's, 67.5% a Master's, and approximately 9% hold a PhD), illustrating that there are considerable gaps in terms of capacity. Huot and Such (2025) highlight that the literature on Educational Technology and AI in Education in the Cambodian context remains limited, despite recent improvements in Cambodian education.

As stated by UNU-EGOV (2026), digital governance frameworks emphasize integrating technology and governance, focusing on citizen empowerment, inclusivity, and the role of data in shaping policies. According to Archer (2008), the construction of academic identity has been disjointed and multifaceted, and cannot be divorced from the context of technology. The intersection of institutional governance and ethics determines outcomes of AI integration in society. Heng and Sol (2024) called on Cambodian higher education to demonstrate the highest ethical use of AI by creating academic integrity policies and supporting frameworks, signaling the importance of institutional governance. According to UNESCO (2025), the preparation of the assessment framework provides necessary support for the development of institutional policies. This model is inspired by digital governance UNU-EGOV (2026), sociology of academic professions (Archer, 2008; Henkel, 2005), and frameworks of human-AI collaboration (Alyasin & Shah, 2026). Numerous studies explore AI in higher education, but critical gaps remain, especially for Cambodia. Pum and Sok (2024) note minimal research on educational tech, despite improvements, and Huot et al. (2026) highlight the widespread use of AI among Cambodian educators without corresponding research. Sok and Heng (2024) review 52 articles, with few focusing on Cambodia and most on the international scene. Key limitations include a focus on technical adoption and barriers such as low technological readiness (Garzón et al., 2025), ignoring professional and regional perspectives, and neglecting digital governance and human-AI collaboration.

III. METHODOLOGY

3.1 Research Design

Using systematic literature review methodology and PRISMA 2020 principles, this research adopted a qualitative approach. The study examined how AI affects professors' roles, the academic evaluation system, and professional identities, using thematic analysis and contextual interpretation to understand the evolving state of higher education in Cambodia. The systematic approach, unlike the traditional narrative review, allowed for a thorough, clear, and repeatable synthesis of regional and global literature on AI in higher education, the academic labor continuum, digital governance, and the transformation of the professional self. The qualitative approach, particularly in contexts where AI's influence on academic professions is poorly documented and where slow-moving, developing countries lie on the periphery of quantitative metrics, was especially useful in balancing the dimensions of professional self and identity construction with the transformation of institutional structures and governance.

Three main reasons justify the use of the PRISMA approach in this work. Page et al. (2021) first described PRISMA 2020 as concerned with transparency and completeness of reporting in systematic reviews and related improvements in the rigor and replicability of reviews. Second, due to the multidisciplinary nature of the intersection of AI with educational research, layering and accommodating multiple dimensions of theory, structure, and context are all aspects of synthesis that must be considered. Third, the current body of work has established that PRISMA-based reviews in educational technology can provide an adequate mapping of the rapidly developing domain while adhering to a systematic selection framework. A PRISMA 2020-based review by Jaboob et al. (2026) on AI in higher education from 2014 to 2024 has shown that technology-related studies are amenable to this approach. The systematic review method complements the studies' aims by synthesizing the global body of work, situating the findings within Cambodia's institutional context, and integrating disparate global and local implementation challenges.

3.2 Data Sources and Literature Selection

To achieve the most comprehensive and systematic review of the pertinent literature, four major academic databases were employed: Scopus, Web of Science, ERIC (Education Resources Information Center), and Google Scholar. A thorough search of these databases ensured all areas of educational research, especially higher education and educational technology, as well as the intersection of AI and educational research, were covered. Scopus and Web of Science provided peer-reviewed publications and journals with good citation tracking; ERIC provided education literature; and Google Scholar provided gray and emerging literature that was previously unpublished. The inclusion and exclusion criteria were systematically applied throughout the screening process and are explained in Table 1.

Table 1. Inclusion and exclusion criteria for literature selection

Criterion	Inclusion	Exclusion
Publication Type	Peer-reviewed journal articles, original research, systematic reviews	Editorials, opinion pieces, conference abstracts without full text
Publication Years	2014–2026 (12-year span capturing AI evolution in education)	Before 2014 (pre-modern AI era in education)
Language	English language publications	Non-English publications (due to translation resource limitations)
Thematic Focus	AI in higher education, academic professions, academic identity, digital governance, Cambodia/Southeast Asia context	K-12 education, vocational training without higher education component, general technology without AI focus
Methodology	Empirical studies, conceptual papers, theoretical frameworks, systematic reviews	Book reviews, news articles, unpublished theses
Accessibility	Full-text available through institutional access	Full-text unavailable after interlibrary loan attempts

The publication years from 2014 to 2026 captured the evolution of AI in education, from early machine learning to the emergence of generative AI in 2022/2023. The scope of the six domains remained closely aligned to the AI in education movement: AI in higher education, academic professions and identity, digital governance, Cambodia, Southeast Asia, and higher education transformation. This broad thematic scope struck a balance between the movement's focus and the study's core research questions regarding professorial roles, evaluation systems, and professional identity. The search strategy involved iteratively combining keywords with Boolean operators. The main search strings were:

(*"artificial intelligence*" OR *"AI"* OR "*generative AI*" OR *ChatGPT*) AND ("*higher education*" OR "*university*" OR "*academic profession**") AND ("*academic identity*" OR "*professional identity*" OR "*academic labor*") AND ("*digital governance*" OR "*algorithmic*" OR "*metric**") AND ("*Cambodia*" OR "*Southeast Asia*" OR "*Global South*"). Other search strings contained specific reference to Cambodia: ("*Cambodia*" OR "*Cambodian*") AND ("*higher education*" OR "*university*") AND ("*digital transformation*" OR "*AI*" OR "*technology*").

Five databases were searched, and the following results were recorded in the referenced databases: Scopus returned 347 results; Web of Science returned 289 results; ERIC returned 156 results; and Google Scholar returned 412 potentially relevant results (including theses and institutional reports). Results were iteratively refined for relevance, with additional search terms added based on newly developed themes, such as "*generative AI*" and "*academic integrity*," following the development and release of ChatGPT in late 2022. Garzón et al. (2025) used the same method in their scoping review of 118 research articles on AI educational tools, illustrating the method's comprehensiveness.

3.3 Screening and Selection Procedures

The screening and selection process was conducted utilizing the PRISMA 2020 protocol, which includes the four steps of identification, screening, eligibility, and final inclusion. The identification process was first completed using the EndNote X9 reference management software to remove duplicates. Duplicate records were reduced by 187. The identification of unique records across all databases yielded 1,017 records.

The next step was screening, in which titles and abstracts were assessed against the inclusion criteria. Reviews of all records were conducted by two reviewers, with the option to discuss disagreements. This membership resulted in a reliable and bias-free process. Records clearly beyond the main themes of this review (K-12 education, general AI with no educational context, non-academic, etc.) were excluded during this process. From the total records (1,017), 683 were rejected during the review, and 334 potentially eligible records remained for full-text review. During the eligibility stage, we assessed 334 full-text articles. Each article was screened for methodological quality, relevance, thematic alignment, and contribution to understanding the impacts of AI on academic professions. Articles that lacked adequate theoretical framing, did not have elements of the academic profession, or only addressed the issues of integration of AI within academic professions at a cursory level were excluded. At this stage, 198 articles were excluded. Most articles were excluded due to insufficient treatment of dimensions of academic identity, evaluation mechanisms, and/or professional autonomy. As a result of the final inclusion process, 136 articles were retained for in-depth analysis. Table 2 shows the PRISMA flow chart for the selection process.

Table 2. PRISMA 2020 flow diagram for literature selection

Stage	Number of Records	Exclusions
Identification	1,017 unique records after duplicate removal	—
Records from Scopus	347	—
Records from Web of Science	289	—
Records from ERIC	156	—
Records from Google Scholar	412	—
Screening	334 advanced to eligibility	683 excluded (title/abstract screening)
Eligibility	136 included in final analysis	198 excluded (full-text assessment)
Final Inclusion	136 articles	—

To reduce duplicates, EndNote's deduplication function was used, followed by a manual review to check for the possible unintentional removal of relevant records. This manual review was conducted to ensure that the final corpus would provide a rich, relevant, and quality scholarship resource from various perspectives to answer the study's research questions.

3.4 Data Analysis Procedures

The data analysis relied on NVivo 14 to perform systematic qualitative data organization, coding, and thematic analysis. All 136 sample articles were imported into NVivo as PDFs and accompanied by bibliographic information. In NVivo, classification sheets were developed to capture the publication specifics of each sample article, including publication year, journal, research method, geography, theory, and key findings. Thematic analysis was conducted using Braun and Clarke's (2006) six-phase model, with modifications for this review. In the first phase, all the sample articles were read to gain an understanding, and NVivo memos were used to document initial impressions. In the second phase, the first codes were generated in NVivo based on the researcher's theory, the sample article framework, and the identification of patterns in the samples. Using NVivo, the researcher coded the sample articles, generating 47 codes after three coding iterations. The final coding framework used in NVivo was developed hierarchically (Table 3).

Table 3. NVivo coding framework: Final note on structure and code distribution

Parent Node	Child Nodes	Coded	Total Ref.
AI Transformation of Academic Work	AI-assisted teaching (n=89), Automated assessment (n=67), AI-supported research (n=94), Administrative automation (n=58)	136	1,847
Evaluation and Governance Mechanisms	Bibliometric systems (n=72), Algorithmic evaluation (n=81), Metric-driven culture (n=95), Promotion implications (n=54)	136	1,523
Professional Identity and Autonomy	Identity reconstruction (n=78), Academic legitimacy (n=63), Autonomy challenges (n=91), Expertise redefinition (n=69)	136	1,612
Ethical and Governance Challenges	Algorithmic bias (n=76), Transparency issues (n=68), Privacy concerns (n=84), Academic freedom (n=71)	136	1,489
Global South Context	Infrastructure constraints (n=92), Digital divide (n=87), Platform dependency (n=64), Regional patterns (n=53)	136	1,247
Cambodia-Specific Findings	Limited literature (n=23), Digital preparedness (n=31), Policy gaps (n=19), Institutional constraints (n=27)	48*	412

Note: *Cambodia-specific findings drawn from 48 articles containing Cambodia or Southeast Asia contextual references.*

Comparative synthesis used matrix coding queries in NVivo to determine the relationships between coding nodes and article classifications. Cross-tabulations were used to examine findings from different geographic contexts (Global North vs. Global South), publication years (before or after the 2022 onset of generative AI), and research methodology (empirical vs. conceptual). This approach highlighted temporal trends in the aftermath of the 2022 growing interest in generative AI research. Of the studies included in this review, 89% of articles (n=121) were published between 2023 and 2026, and only 11% of the articles (n=15) were published between 2014 and 2022. Contextual interpretation established Cambodia's institutional realities within the broader global context. Using NVivo, specific terms and Cambodia-focused contextual terminology and patterns were identified through text searches and word-frequency queries. Memos were used to record the interpretative and predictive choices about how global trends may affect Cambodia's resource-poor, complex, and institutionally structured higher education system. As part of the interpretative process, the AI Readiness Assessment report by UNES-

CO (2025) and the World Bank (2024) analysis were consulted to provide specific context for Cambodia's infrastructure, capacity, and policy development challenges.

3.5 Reliability, Validity, and Trustworthiness

Credibility of sources was ensured through a variety of mechanisms. To begin with, publication bias was minimized, and comprehensive coverage was ensured through a systematic search of four distinct databases. Additionally, the reliability of the selection process was enhanced by 91% inter-rater agreement during dual-reviewer screening. Finally, the inclusion criteria focused on peer-reviewed journal articles (89% of the final corpus, n=121). In contrast, the remaining 15 articles were systematic reviews and conceptual papers of equally high quality, published in reputable journals.

Selection process transparency was achieved through thorough PRISMA documentation. The PRISMA 2020 checklist was completed and provided as supplementary materials. It documented every selection decision and offered rationales for each. NVivo classification sheets documented every article attribute, allowing readers to follow the analysis from raw data to the developed themes. Page et al. (2021) argue that PRISMA 2020 enhances the completeness of reporting. They also helped with this research project.

The rigor of analysis was maintained through the triangulation of various analysis techniques. Thematic analysis was combined with word frequency, coding comparison, and cross-pattern matrix queries. Systematic checking of coding patterns was made possible with NVivo's query tools. 15% of the articles were randomly selected for double coding. Cohen's kappa measured 0.84, thereby demonstrating that the threshold for coding quality for qualitative research purposes was exceeded. Appropriate citation practices facilitated secondary data analysis for this research project. Intellectual property of the original authors was acknowledged. There were no primary human subjects. Thus, the issues of possible absence of informed consent, the likelihood of breach of confidentiality, and unanticipated adverse impact were removed. Scrupulous care was exercised to remain faithful to the original authors and to represent their findings.

3.6 Limitations of the Study

The most significant limitation of the study under review is the lack of literature focused on the Cambodian context. Of the reviewed articles, only 48 (35% of the total) cited Cambodia or Southeast Asia, and only 23 specifically included Cambodia's higher education system. According to Huot and Loch (2025), even when general references to educational improvement in Cambodia are provided, research and publications on educational technologies and Artificial Intelligence (AI) in education have been largely overlooked in the international literature on Cambodia. This study had to rely on literature from the Southeast Asia region and the Global South, which may overlook the distinctive dynamics of Cambodia's institutions.

Rapid AI developments add limitations. The emergence of Generative AI (2022-2023) has led to little literature on its long-term effects on academia and professions. Sok and Heng (2024) note their review of 52 articles focuses on the Cambodian context, though most are from other regions, highlighting the field's infancy. The 2014-2026 period includes AI's development, excluding pre-2014 publications. Reliance on secondary data limits causal inferences. As a systematic review, it offers detailed context analysis but cannot confirm causality between AI integration and academic changes. Regional data skew towards the Global North; 78% of 106 articles are from North America, Europe, or Australia, while only 22% from the Global South, including Southeast Asia. Radiya-Dixit and Christin (2025) emphasize that AI ethics and policy must consider regional nuances in the Global South. This study acknowledges these limitations and distinguishes between the Global North focus and the Cambodian context.

IV. RESULTS AND DISCUSSION

The introduction of generative AI in 2022 led to a rapid increase in the adoption of AI technologies in educational institutions. Sok and Heng (2024) illustrate the myriad benefits AI provides to higher education by documenting virtual learning aids, innovating new assessments and pedagogy, and providing administrative and academic writing assistance and research support. Huot and Loch (2025) suggest that although improvements were observed in Cambodia's education system, there was a critical delay in the adoption of AI technologies in educational research, demonstrating a significant AI research gap in the literature focused on Cambodia.

The digital transformation of teaching and research has become all-encompassing. Chan and Hu (2023) argue that generative AI has both positive and negative implications and has redefined pedagogical relationships by complementing the human-AI teaching partnership. They also argue that AI is leading to rapid changes in the skills and techniques required for teaching and learning. Cambodian students who participated in the research conducted by Huot et al. (2026) developed methods for using AI-based tools, such as Grammarly, to check grammar and improve translation, thereby improving their English-speaking skills. The participants also expressed concerns about the inadequate development of the ethical framework, due to critical gaps in data protection and security. Studies on institutions indicate that there are different methods of adoption. Khort et al. (2024) states that the digital transformations occurring in higher education in Cambodia receive a mostly positive assessment from stakeholders. However, they demand further improvements in the support systems for infrastructure, training, and especially leadership. The Ministry of Education, Youth, and Sport has invited all Cambodian teachers to use AI-based applications, indicating that Cambodian institutions have begun to recognize the relevance of AI. UNESCO (2025) states that Cambodia was the 4th country in South-East Asia to conduct a national AI Readiness Assessment for ethical and inclusive change.

Teaching obligations have changed dramatically. According to Bower et al. (2024), the use of large language models to generate learning simulations will require a complete restructuring of teachers' obligations, redefining the ethics of the profession. According to Naseer et al. (2024), AI has improved assessment through the innovation of instant, automated grading systems and the development of dynamic, iterative feedback, thereby restructuring the quality and efficiency of the assessment process. However, Tripathi and Thakar (2024) note that overreliance on AI will lead to a lack of engagement and critical thinking, raising issues for the profession. Teaching with AI has provided both an opportunity and a challenge. Dimitriadou and Lanitis (2023) claim that the digital age is a reconfiguration of teaching; AI provides better administrative support, improving efficiency and consequently reshaping the teaching load. Sok and Heng (2024) argue that the digital age is a reconfiguration of teaching and that AI has become central to the teaching load. Pum and Sok (2024) argue that tools such as ChatGPT promote academic writing and planning.

AI-assisted processes stimulated new levels of research productivity. Huot and Such (2025) argue that AI is changing the speed and saturation of writing and publishing tasks. However, Tanveer et al. (2020) argue that students performing copy-paste tasks are not only being unethical but also exposing themselves to potential lawsuits, as supported by the Berne Convention. This is a wider global issue of productivity versus integrity, and it is particularly challenging for Cambodian institutions. Changes in procedures affected how work was organized. AI reduced administrative workload and increased efficiency, according to Sok and Heng (2024). On the other hand, Hoernig et al. (2024) argue that if AI is let to take over administrative work, it may undermine our ability to think critically and creatively. The World Bank (2024) argues that workforce gaps in STEM in Cambodia are so severe that capacity needs cannot be met by automation alone. Digital tools make up the bulk of evaluation processes. Assessing bibliometrics is still in an early and anxious stage (Garzón et al., 2025).

The need to use metrics to evaluate work negatively impacts employees in academic institutions. Teymourifar (2026) argues that the ABS ranking is a clear example of the academic sector's adoption of a metrics-driven culture. Meho (2025) argues that

Cambodia's use of metrics provides an excellent example of how an integrity crisis develops. The World Bank (2024) argues that the 132 institutions in Cambodia have a faculty base of only 16,471, of whom only 9% hold a PhD, and shows that the use of metrics is not justified. The impact on the promotion process remains uncertain. Binns (2018) argues that valuation systems should prioritize fairness, whereas ECMF presents a different perspective. These cases are among the earliest examples of algorithmic governance. Täuber (2026) claims that techno-colonization results from categorization and algorithmic assessment. In such cases, 'symbolic violence' occurs when academics justify 'metric logics', which undermines their autonomy. Tripathi and Thakar (2024) suggest that relying on metrics can lead to unethical conduct, thereby increasing concerns about academic dishonesty. This can be seen critically in the redefinition of academic real expertise. Archer (2008) states that academic identity comprises teaching, research, and service, as well as digital skills. Teymourifar (2026) indicates that, in identifying liminality and Reconstruction, the staff focuses on structuring identity. Lessky and Schiffecker (2024) state that the challenges in shaping their identity led to early-career academics' difficulties with a sense of belonging and their career paths.

There is a fundamental friction between human-centric and automated work. Allen et al. (2018) state that a sense of belonging strengthens identity and confidence. On the contrary, Bower et al. (2024) state that the introduction of AI changes the scope of work and the profession's identity. There is still a lot to uncover on the emotional level. Earl et al. (2026) state that the interaction between professional identity and stigma is evident across all dimensions. Sullivan (2025) warns that AI is also a source of friction in engagement, dissipating satisfaction. There is increasing anxiety regarding the loss of academic independence.

Table 4. Transformation of academic profession dimensions

Dimension	Primary Changes	Key Concerns	Cambodian Context
Teaching	AI-assisted instruction, automated feedback	Reduced critical thinking, dependency	Limited training, infrastructure gaps
Research	Accelerated writing, AI-supported analysis	Academic integrity, plagiarism	Underexplored scholarship
Evaluation	Metric-driven, algorithmic systems	Bias, transparency, autonomy	Policy gaps, institutional constraints
Identity	Digital competence integration	Legitimacy, expertise redefinition	Lack of Cambodia-specific frameworks

V. CONCLUSION

The systematic review implemented PRISMA 2020 guidelines. Transparency and the overall quality of the methodology were considered critical, paving the way for a stepwise approach. A review protocol was designed and finalized, documenting the search strategy and inclusion criteria. A stepwise search was processed in four different databases. Scopus, Web of Science, ERIC, and Google Scholar were used to search, yielding a total of 1,017 unique records. Titles and abstracts were reviewed by two independent reviewers with a reported inter-rater agreement of 91%. During the eligibility stage, the full texts of 334 articles were reviewed, and 136 articles were selected for full qualitative analysis. The PRISMA flow process was completed as follows: 1,017 records were identified; 683 were excluded during screening; 198 were excluded during eligibility assessment; and 136 were included in the final analysis.

AI is replacing administrative, teaching, and research practices. While research and teaching practices are being complemented and increased by AI at a faster pace, this may reduce engagement and critical thinking within the academic community. The impact of AI can be seen in academic evaluation and in the administration of academic practices. The Algorithmic Promotion System in the academic community will influence the way academic practices are evaluated and promoted. The internalization of metric-driven logics leads to a loss of academic autonomy. It will lead to a loss of self and the destruction of academic practices that are not aligned with AI. The internalization of metric-driven logic leads to a loss of self and to academic practices that are not aligned with AI. Academic identity, which includes teaching, research, and digital competence, is significantly affected. There are considerable identity challenges for faculty resulting from the tension between human-centered values and automated efficiency. Institutional readiness hurdles are fundamental limits. Cambodia's higher education sector comprises 132 institutions across 16 ministries, with 209,059 students and 16,471 faculty members. Capacity constraints are apparent. Ongoing inequalities in access necessitate clear, socially responsive digital solutions. This chapter offers three contributions. First, it combines global literature with findings from Cambodia, filling the gaps in global/local literature. Second, it provides a critical assessment of algorithmic governance and academic autonomy, both of which are lacking in Global South literature. Third, it offers a context-oriented approach and emphasizes ethically informed policies and human-centric governance.

In the context of the academic profession, the contribution lies in a detailed assessment of the impact of AI technologies on academic practice and identity in the Global South. By bringing together digital governance, the sociology of academic professions, and human-AI collaboration frameworks, the current research sheds light on how AI is shaping academic professions and academic identity in the Global South. This is especially valuable for Cambodia and the Global South. This research addresses the significant gaps in Global South scholarship. By providing a Cambodia-centered assessment, the chapter responds to calls for country-specific AI ethics in developing countries. There is an urgent need for AI integration policies in Cambodian universities. The institutions must encourage responsible AI practices and maintain academic integrity. Clear boundaries need to be drawn regarding responsible AI use. Leadership needs to take digital infrastructure, faculty, and student support seriously.

AI governance must include multiple levels. First, UNESCO's Ethics of AI Readiness Assessment Methodology is a model that universities can adopt. Governance systems need to be built with many stakeholders and should include regular audits for algorithmic bias. Evaluation criteria must be made transparent, and academics must be encouraged to consider the implications of algorithms beyond outputs. Most capacity building focuses on concerns over the infrastructure, skills, and support gaps. Universities will need to support their communities through good infrastructure, including both hardware and software, as well as reliable internet access. Schools will need to develop staff by improving their pedagogical skills and knowledge, as well as ensuring reliable internet access. Community fogs and mentorship programs will further capacity soon. Reforming evaluation means balancing metrics with human capacity. Assessments should be multi-faceted, combining peer review and qualitative evaluation, with citation metrics as a backdrop. Promotion systems should recognize varied contributions beyond the sheer quantity of publications.

There is much to be studied. Starting with longitudinal studies of faculty in the region to track the evolution of the workforce and how it impacts professional identity and job satisfaction. Mixed-methods studies also seek to measure the emotional dimension of AI's rapid changes, combining metrics with interviews. The Comparative ASEAN studies will also be valuable. As Cambodia brings up the total number of AI Ethics Readiness Assessment completions in Southeast Asia to 4, it will be interesting to include Indonesia, the Philippines, and Thailand. Cross-national studies will focus on their unique institutional systems and will bring their understanding to a different level. As faculty members' perspectives in the region remain underexplored, it will be important to elucidate their understanding of AI's impact on academia. Also important will be longitudinal studies of governance frameworks to understand the impact of adapted governance on policy development.

This chapter highlights how AI is disrupting professional pathways, personal professional identity, and evaluation systems for Academia in Cambodia. AI will enable many benefits in education, research, and the academic profession. It can help the profession become more efficient by enabling it to do many things more quickly. It can enhance teaching methods and research, improve the administration of schooling, and promote readiness. However, some challenges arise, including algorithmic bias, the digital divide, academic autonomy, and dependence on metrics. The key requirement for the future is a balanced collaboration between humans and AI. AI must supplement academic knowledge rather than replace it. It must supplement human judgment, creativity, and teaching, not replace them. The Cambodia framework focuses on ethical governance, clear metrics, and professional and institutional support, while taking Cambodia's realities into account. The critical importance of ethical and context-aware AI cannot be overstated. Cambodia's history and institutional dynamics are unique. AI ethics must be based on specific regions instead of uniform cultures. The framework focuses on transformation, equity, and access.

The future of academic professionalism hinges on choices made by policymakers, leaders, faculty, and students. Balancing the human academic endeavor with technological innovation, this chapter contributes to professionalism and the governance of AI in developing countries. The task of universities is to harness the opportunities presented by AI while preserving the human aspects of academic excellence.

REFERENCES

Allen, K., Kern, M. L., Vella-Brodrick, D., Hattie, J., & Waters, L. (2018). What schools need to know about fostering school belonging: A meta-analysis. *Educational Psychology Review*, *30*(1), 1–34. DOI: 10.1007/s10648-016-9389-8

Alyasin, A., & Shah, M. A. (2026). Human-AI collaboration in academic writing: Exploring university students' agency through a sociocultural lens. *Ampersand (Oxford, UK)*, *16*, 1–11. DOI: 10.1016/j.amper.2026.100256

Archer, L. (2008). Younger academics' constructions of 'authenticity','success' and professional identity. *Studies in Higher Education*, *33*(4), 385–403. DOI: 10.1080/03075070802211729

Bae, H., & Bozkurt, A. (2024). The untold story of training students with generative AI: Are we preparing students for true learning or just personalization. *Online Learning : the Official Journal of the Online Learning Consortium*, *28*(3), 1–9. DOI: 10.24059/olj.v28i3.4689

Bhat, J. (2023). Automating higher education administrative processes with AI-powered workflows. *International Journal of Emerging Trends in Computer Science and Information Technology*, *4*(4), 147–157. DOI: 10.63282/3050-9246.IJETCSIT-V4I4P116

Binns, R. (2018). Fairness in machine learning: Lessons from political philosophy. In *Conference on fairness, accountability and transparency* (Vol. 81, pp. 149–159). PMLR. https://proceedings.mlr.press/v81/binns18a/binns18a.pdf

Bower, M., Torrington, J., Lai, J. W., Petocz, P., & Alfano, M. (2024). How should we change teaching and assessment in response to increasingly powerful generative Artificial Intelligence? Outcomes of the ChatGPT teacher survey. *Education and Information Technologies*, *29*(12), 15403–15439. DOI: 10.1007/s10639-023-12405-0

Braun, V., & Clarke, V. (2006). Using thematic analysis in psychology. *Qualitative Research in Psychology*, *3*(2), 77–101. DOI: 10.1191/1478088706qp063oa

Chan, C. K. Y., & Hu, W. (2023). Students' voices on generative AI: Perceptions, benefits, and challenges in higher education. *International Journal of Educational Technology in Higher Education*, *20*(1), 1–18. DOI: 10.1186/s41239-023-00411-8

Delikoura, I., Fung, Y. R., & Hui, P. (2025). From superficial outputs to superficial learning: Risks of large language models in education. *arXiv preprint arXiv:2509.21972, 1*(1), 1–35. https://doi.org//arXiv.2509.21972DOI: 10.48550

Dimitriadou, E., & Lanitis, A. (2023). A critical evaluation, challenges, and future perspectives of using artificial intelligence and emerging technologies in smart classrooms. *Smart Learning Environments*, *10*(1), 1–26. DOI: 10.1186/s40561-023-00231-3 PMID: 40478141

Earl, A., Raskovic, M. M., Iskhakova, M., & Iskhakov, F. (2026). Professional identity and stigma in the context of war. *Critical Perspectives on International Business*, •••, 1–27. DOI: 10.1108/cpoib-03-2025-0067

Fiesler, C., Garrett, N., & Beard, N. (2020). What do we teach when we teach tech ethics? A syllabi analysis. In *Proceedings of the 51st ACM technical symposium on computer science education* (pp. 289–295). Portland, OR, USA. DOI: 10.1145/3328778.3366825

Garzón, J., Patiño, E., & Marulanda, C. (2025). Systematic review of artificial intelligence in education: Trends, benefits, and challenges. *Multimodal Technologies and Interaction*, *9*(8), 1–19. DOI: 10.3390/mti9080084

Gökçearslan, S., Tosun, C., & Erdemir, Z. G. (2024). Benefits, challenges, and methods of artificial intelligence (AI) chatbots in education: A systematic literature review. *International Journal of Technology in Education*, *7*(1), 19–39. DOI: 10.46328/ijte.600

Heng, K., & Sol, K. (2024). The use of AI and ChatGPT for education and research in Cambodia: Current state and future directions. *Cambodian Journal of Educational Research*, *4*(2), 1–11. DOI: 10.62037/cjer.2024.04.02.01

Henkel, M. (2005). Academic identity and autonomy in a changing policy environment. *Higher Education*, *49*(1), 155–176. DOI: 10.1007/s10734-004-2919-1

Hoernig, S., Ilharco, A., Pereira, P. T., & Pereira, R. (2024). *Generative AI and higher education: Challenges and opportunities*. Institute of Public Policy. https://www.ipp-jcs.org/wp-content/uploads/2024/09/Report-AI-in-Higher-Education-IPP-1.pdf

Hongseng, R. (2023, May 19). *Generative AI: A threat to copyright?* Kiripost. https://kiripost.com/stories/cambodia-chatgpt-generative-ai-a-threat-to-copyright

Huot, S., & Loch, S. (2025). Educating in the age of AI: Preparing Cambodian teachers and students for an AI-augmented learning future. *Journal of Educational Technology and E-Learning Innovations*, *1*(2), 31–38. DOI: 10.54536/jeteli.v1i2.5170

Huot, S., Loch, S., Chheang, S., Hok, C., & Phin, K. (2026). The future of indexed research in Cambodia: Innovation, collaboration, and regional integration. In Em, S. (Ed.), *Digital leadership and innovation in ASEAN education* (pp. 455–486). IGI Global Scientific Publishing., DOI: 10.4018/979-8-2600-1142-3.ch013

Huot, S., & Phin, K. (2026). Transforming hybrid pedagogies: Harnessing AI and intercultural collaboration for global learning. In Nguyen, T.-P., Zhang, J., & Loseva, A. (Eds.), *Advancing hybrid pedagogies through AI and intercultural collaboration* (pp. 29–54). IGI Global Scientific Publishing., DOI: 10.4018/979-8-3373-7462-8.ch002

Huot, S., & Such, C. (2025). Leveraging social media for language learning: Opportunities and challenges. [JEILT]. *Journal of Education Innovation and Language Teaching*, *1*(2), 10–29. DOI: 10.63381/jeilt.v1i2.56

Hussain, S. M., Satti, S. M. J., & Khan, Z. (2024). AI-powered personalized learning: Advancing Language education in the digital era. *Journal of Social Signs Review*, *2*(4), 730–740. https://socialsignsreivew.com/index.php/12/article/view/71

Jaboob, M., Al-Ansi, A. M., & Riyadh, H. A. (2026). Artificial intelligence in higher education: A PRISMA 2020 review. *International Journal of Educational Management*, *40*(1–2), 113–132. DOI: 10.1108/IJEM-09-2024-0560

Jensen, D. H., & Jetten, J. (2015). Bridging and bonding interactions in higher education: Social capital and students' academic and professional identity formation. *Frontiers in Psychology*, *6*, 1–11. DOI: 10.3389/fpsyg.2015.00126 PMID: 25762954

Khort, M., Karimov, A., Murtazin, S., & Khayaleeva, A. (2024). Epistemic injustice of the digital divide. *Edelweiss Applied Science and Technology*, *8*(5), 1986–1996. DOI: 10.55214/25768484.v8i5.1939

Kumar, V., & Derawi, M. (2025). Applications and impact of Artificial Intelligence in the field of agriculture, education, healthcare, and administration. In Mishra, S., Gupta, N., & Goktas, P. (Eds.), *AI and ML Techniques in IoT-based Communication: A Path to Sustainable Development Goals* (pp. 97–118). The Institute of Electrical and Electronics Engineers, Inc., DOI: 10.1002/9781394337262.ch05

Kunwar, K. (2026). Algorithmic governance in lifelong learning systems: Artificial intelligence, educational policy transformation, and human development. *Artificial Intelligence in Lifelong and Life-Course Education*, *1*(2), 67–83. DOI: 10.66053/aillce.v1i2.31

Lessky, F., & Schiffecker, S. (2024). Academic identity crafting: How early-career women researchers in the United States and Austria form their professional identities. *Research in Comparative and International Education*, *21*(12), 157–175. DOI: 10.1177/17454999261417858

Lia, M., & Sunb, W. (2024). Research on the integration of ideological and political education into Chinese-English translation teaching. *Adult and Higher Education (2024) Clausius Scientific Press, Canada, 6*(7), 97–102. DOI: 10.23977/aduhe.2024.060714

Maisuria, A., & Helmes, S. (2019). *Life for the Academic in the Neoliberal University*. Routledge. DOI: 10.4324/9780429329951

Meho, L. I. (2025). Gaming the metrics? Bibliometric anomalies and the integrity crisis in global university rankings. *arXiv preprint arXiv:2505.06448, 1*, 1–51. https://doi.org//arXiv.2505.06448DOI: 10.48550

Morrish, L. (2019). *Pressure vessels: The epidemic of poor mental health among higher education staff*. Higher Education Policy Institute Oxford.

Naseer, F., Khalid, M. U., Ayub, N., Rasool, A., Abbas, T., & Afzal, M. W. (2024). Automated assessment and feedback in higher education using generative AI. In Sharma, R. C., & Bozkurt, A. (Eds.), *Transforming education with generative AI: Prompt engineering and synthetic content creation* (pp. 433–461). IGI Global Scientific Publishing., DOI: 10.4018/979-8-3693-1351-0.ch021

Ng, W. (2012). Can we teach digital natives digital literacy? *Computers & Education, 59*(3), 1065–1078. DOI: 10.1016/j.compedu.2012.04.016

Page, M. J., McKenzie, J. E., Bossuyt, P. M., Boutron, I., Hoffmann, T. C., Mulrow, C. D., Shamseer, L., Tetzlaff, J. M., Akl, E. A., & Brennan, S. E. (2021). The PRISMA 2020 statement: an updated guideline for reporting systematic reviews. *bmj, 372*, 1–9. DOI: 10.1136/bmj.n71

Povilaitis, K., & Jõgi, L. (2026). Understanding academic identity through liminality: Implications for leadership and academic development. *Frontiers in Education, 11*, 1–15. DOI: 10.3389/feduc.2026.1763425

Pum, M., & Sok, S. (2024). Leveraging AI in education in Cambodia: A review of perceived concerns and associated benefits. *Asian Journal of Distance Education, 19*(2), 157–167. DOI: 10.2139/ssrn.4932278

Radiya-Dixit, E., & Christin, A. (2025). Same stereotypes, different term? Understanding the "Global South" in AI ethics. In *Proceedings of the AAAI/ACM Conference on AI, Ethics, and Society* (Vol. 8, pp. 2081–2093). AAAI. DOI: 10.1609/aies.v8i3.36697

Santos, R. J. (2024). *Human-AI collaboration in education: Theoretical frameworks and pedagogical implications*. Digital Commons @ University of Nebraska – Lincoln. https://digitalcommons.unl.edu

Sok, S., & Heng, K. (2024). Opportunities, challenges, and strategies for using ChatGPT in higher education: A literature review. *Journal of Digital Educational Technology*, *4*(1), 1–11. DOI: 10.30935/jdet/14027

Strzelecki, A., Cicha, K., Rizun, M., & Rutecka, P. (2024). Acceptance and use of ChatGPT in the academic community. *Education and Information Technologies*, *29*(17), 22943–22968. DOI: 10.1007/s10639-024-12765-1

Sullivan, M. (2025). Collusion, plagiarism, or contract cheating? How generative AI fits into existing academic integrity policies. In Popenici, S., Rudolph, J., Ismail, F., & Tan, S. (Eds.), *Handbook of Artificial Intelligence in Higher Education* (pp. 72–386). Edward Elgar Publishing., DOI: 10.4337/9781035338764.00033

Sun, C., Jiang, G., & Zhang, J. (2024). An analysis of hotspots, subject structure, and emerging trends in digital governance research. *SAGE Open*, *14*(3), 1–19. DOI: 10.1177/21582440241268756

Tanveer, M., Hassan, S., & Bhaumik, A. (2020). Academic policy regarding sustainability and artificial intelligence (AI). *Sustainability*, *12*(22), 1–13. DOI: 10.3390/su12229435 PMID: 35136666

Täuber, S. (2026). Erasing critical scholarship: How attacks on academic freedom undermine democracy. *Organization*, •••, 1–19. DOI: 10.1177/13505084251392946

Teng, Y. (2024). *Cambodia needs to boost digital education*. Cambodianess. https://cambodianess.com/article/cambodia-needs-to-boost-digital-education

Teymourifar, A. (2026). Understanding the ABS journal ranking system: A critical review. *Frontiers in Education*, *11*, 1–20. DOI: 10.3389/feduc.2026.1773655

Tripathi, A., & Thakar, S. V. (2024). Ethical use of AI for academic integrity: Preventing plagiarism and cheating. In Kushwaha, R. K., Yadav, K., Yadav, P. K., & Yadav, M. K. (Eds.), *Ethical Frameworks in Special Education: A Guide for Researchers* (pp. 91–106). Blue Rose Publishers.

UNDP. (2025). *Human development report 2025: AI and global inequality*. United Nations Development Programme. https://hdr.undp.org

UNESCO. (2023). *Guidance for generative artificial intelligence (GenAI) in education and research: A human-centered approach*. United Nations Educational Scientific and Cultural Organization. https://policycommons.net/artifacts/6942367/guidance-for-generative-ai-in-education-and-research/7852269

UNESCO. (2025). *Cambodia: Artificial Intelligence readiness assessment report.* Paris: United Nations Educational Scientific and Cultural Organization. https://www.unesco.org/en/articles/cambodia-artificial-intelligence-readiness-assessment-report

UNU-EGOV. (2026). *UNU-EGOV Strategy 2025–2029: Developing digital governance for global justice, resilience, and sustainability.* United Nations University Operating Unit on Policy-driven Electronic Governance. https://unu.edu/egov/about/unu-egov-strategy-2025-2029

World Bank. (2024). *New World Bank supported project will improve the quality of thousands of students in Cambodia.* World Bank Group. https://www.worldbank.org/en/news/press-release/2024/09/24/new-world-bank-supported-project-will-improve-the-quality-of-thousands-of-students-in-cambodia

KEYWORD DEFINITIONS

Artificial Intelligence (AI): The use of computer simulation of human intelligence, including learning, understanding, and self-correction. In education, artificial intelligence refers to a combination of machine learning, natural language understanding, and tools like ChatGPT that generate human-like text and automate assessment or assist with learning, academic research, and administration, as a human would.

Academic Professions: Individuals engaged in the teaching profession in higher education institutions. Faculty and teaching staff, researchers, and professionals in higher education who are digital natives and capable of using artificial intelligence in the workplace.

Higher Education Transformation: Fundamental changes in structures, processes, cultures, and practices of post-secondary education. In the digital era, the transformation of higher education also encompasses the digitalization of teaching and learning, the adoption of advanced technologies, and the restructuring of educational governance and academic labor to meet global competition. In developing countries, this is linked to the internationalization of education, quality-assurance reforms, and the development of national digital (internet) infrastructure.

Academic Evaluation: This is a systematic approach to assessing students' academic performance and is used to determine grading, faculty promotions, recruitment, and other forms of accountability. It relies increasingly on digital metrics, bibliometric systems, citation metrics, and other related algorithmic mechanisms. Systematic approaches to academic evaluation are confronted with, among others, metric-driven cultures, algorithmic biases, accountability and transparency gaps, and the tension between quantitative and qualitative assessments in the age of artificial intelligence.

Professional Identity: Conceptualization of self and sense of belonging that results from participation in professional practices. For academics, this is an internalization of teaching, research, and scholarship, alongside a sense of expertise, entitlement, and autonomy. This is the result of negotiations between personal and professional goals and the institution's expectations. In the era of digital technology, this has been reshaped to include digital citizenship and collaboration with artificial intelligence, while the core of professional identity is intellectually maintained.

Chapter 10
The Moroccan Academic Profession in the Age of Rankings and AI-Driven Evaluation:
Professorial Appointments, Careers, and Daily Realities

Kenza Ennida
http://orcid.org/0000-0003-0884-6433
National School of Commerce and Management, Sidi Mohamed Ben Abdellah University, Morocco

Mehdi Chaoui Roqai
http://orcid.org/0009-0004-0034-4038
National School of Commerce and Management, Sidi Mohamed Ben Abdellah University, Morocco

Saif Allah Allouani
http://orcid.org/0000-0002-2848-169X
National School of Business and Management, Sidi Mohammed Ben Abdellah University, Fez, Morocco

ABSTRACT

This chapter proposes a theoretically grounded, empirically informed analysis of how successive waves of reform and the growing reliance on digital metrics and rankings are reshaping professorial appointments, academic careers and professional identities in Moroccan public universities. Framing Morocco as a Global South case of "AI-adjacent" and datafied governance, it draws on documentary

DOI: 10.4018/979-8-2600-3204-6.ch010

analysis, secondary survey data and bibliometric indicators to examine the incorporation of bibliometric measures into recruitment and promotion, the everyday consequences for teacher-researchers' workload, autonomy and status, and the scenarios this trajectory opens for the future integration of AI-based evaluation tools. The chapter contributes to debates on the academic profession in the age of AI by highlighting the specific vulnerabilities and opportunities of a middle-income, reform-oriented system.

1. INTRODUCTION

Across higher education systems worldwide, the academic profession is being reshaped by a convergence of powerful forces. Massification has increased student enrolments and diversified student populations, while new public management has introduced performance-based funding, accountability mechanisms and managerial logics borrowed from the private sector (Hood, 1991 ; Pollitt & Bouckaert, 2011). Digitalization has transformed research, teaching and administration, and the rise of artificial intelligence (AI) and data-driven systems has begun to affect how academic work is monitored, evaluated and rewarded (Williamson, 2017). In many systems, professorial appointments, promotion and tenure are increasingly governed by quantifiable indicators of productivity and impact generated and processed by digital platforms and, in some instances, algorithmic tools (Power, 1997 ; Wilsdon et al., 2015).

This international evolution has been documented in detail in North American, European and East Asian contexts (Altbach, 2004 ; Musselin, 2004), yet the ways in which systems in the Global South experience and negotiate these transformations remain comparatively under-researched. Morocco constitutes a strategically significant case for studying the intersection of metricization and academic work in the Global South for two reasons. First, it represents a hybrid governance model where traditional Francophone administrative structures are being rapidly overlaid with Anglo-Saxon managerial logics (New Public Management). Second, Morocco's position as a regional hub in the MENA and African research ecosystems makes it an 'early adopter' of international ranking pressures and digital data infrastructures, providing a window into how these global forces are domesticated in a middle-income context.

As illustrated in the timeline in Figure 1, the Moroccan public university has been characterized by 'permanent reform' since the late 1990s (Bourqia, 2009). Rather than discrete events, these policies—ranging from the LMD architecture (2003) to the recent Pacte ESRI 2030—represent cumulative layers of institutional change. Each layer has progressively shifted the academic profession away from traditional administrative oversight toward a managerial model that prioritizes international standards, modular efficiency, and quantifiable scientific output

Figure 1. Timeline of Key Policy Interventions in Moroccan Higher Education (1997–2023).

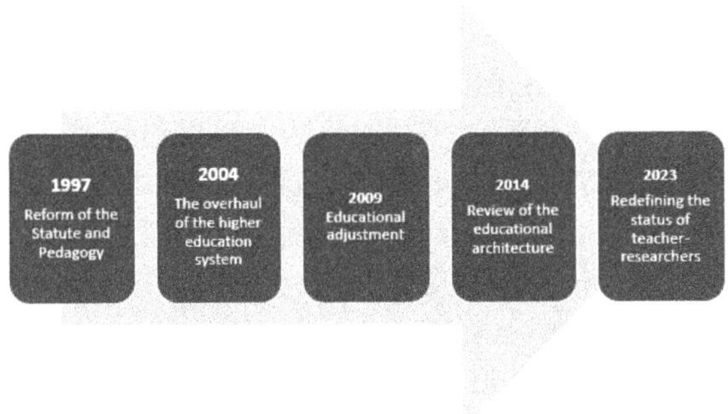

Source: Author's compilation based on official policy documents and legislation.

At the discursive level, these reforms are framed as necessary responses to the challenges of massification, the knowledge economy and international competitiveness (Marginson, 2008). The university is expected simultaneously to produce qualified graduates, generate research, support innovation and contribute to national development. At the same time, public debate often reduces higher education to a simplified and negative image: that of an institution that "produces unemployed graduates" and fails to adapt to labour market needs, a narrative recurrent in national media and policy discussions (Bourqia, 2009 ; Cherkaoui, 2011 ; Cherkaoui, 2015). Between the rhetoric of excellence and the stigma of inefficiency lies the daily reality of teacher-researchers, whose work and careers are profoundly shaped by these transformations but who remain relatively invisible in policy narratives.

Within this context, the notion of reform itself has been repeatedly mobilized. As Rahma Bourqia (2009) has noted, the frequent and sometimes ritualized invocation of *islah* risks emptying the concept of its mobilizing content: reform becomes a permanent condition rather than a clearly bounded process. The system is perpetually "under reform" without necessarily achieving stability, coherence or shared purpose. The academic profession is therefore required to adapt continuously to new rules, expectations and evaluation frameworks, often without clear temporal horizons or consolidated institutional support (Bourqia, 2009 ; Cherkaoui, 2011, Cherkaoui, 2015).

In parallel, digital metrics have acquired growing importance in the steering of higher education and research. National evaluation bodies produce reports comparing institutions through indicators of efficiency and effectiveness, while quality assurance procedures increasingly rely on standardized criteria and quantitative benchmarks (CSEFRS, 2019; INE, 2018). International bibliometric databases such as Web of Science and Scopus quantify scientific output and citation impact, and global rankings and specialized indices position Morocco and its universities in international hierarchies (INE, 2018). Promotion grids and institutional dashboards increasingly incorporate these numbers, making them central reference points in judgements about academic quality and productivity. In this sense, even before sophisticated AI tools are deployed in human resource management, the system already operates under a form of datafied governance that shapes academic careers and institutional trajectories (Beer, 2016 ; Williamson, 2017).

This research conceptualizes this transitional state as "AI-adjacent governance." In the Moroccan context, this is defined as a mode of institutional management where decision-making is not yet fully automated by Artificial Intelligence, but is strictly mediated by the digital and bibliometric infrastructures that enable it. This is operationalized through three key mechanisms: the use of metricized proxies (such as H-indices) as automated stand-ins for scientific "value"; the standardization of academic data through digital portals (e.g., CNRST-IMIST), which creates the machine-readable datasets required for future algorithmic sorting; and the shift toward "algorithmic legitimacy," where metrics generated by external platforms carry increasing weight relative to qualitative peer judgment.

Teacher-researchers stand at the intersection of these developments. Their missions have expanded to encompass not only teaching and research but also doctoral supervision, programme design, quality assurance, governance roles, external partnerships and innovation activities (Musselin, 2004 ; Enders & de Weert, 2009). They are asked to contribute simultaneously to mass education and high-level scientific production in a context of constrained resources, persistent massification and uneven infrastructure. Surveys and sectoral analyses point to high levels of dissatisfaction, significant levels of dual employment and a growing sense of contradiction between the expectations placed on academics and the conditions under which they work (Bourqia, 2009 ; Cherkaoui, 2011 ; Gaillard et al., 2017).

Against this backdrop, the growing emphasis on metrics and the prospective integration of AI-based tools raise critical questions about the future of the academic profession in Morocco. Given this hybrid configuration—where traditional administrative legacies meet new, data-driven managerial expectations—the Moroccan case allows for a precise examination of how global metricization is operationalized within a specific national context. By treating these digital and bibliometric infrastructures as 'AI-adjacent' precursors to more automated forms of governance, this research addresses four central questions:

1. In what ways have recent policy reforms and new statutes reshaped the roles, responsibilities and trajectories expected of teacher-researchers in Morocco?
2. How are bibliometric indicators, rankings and digital dashboards being integrated into recruitment, promotion and evaluation, and what weight do they carry relative to other criteria?
3. How do teacher-researchers describe the impact of these changes on their daily work, workload, autonomy and recognition?
4. Given the current trajectory of datafied governance, what possible futures can be envisaged for the integration of AI-based tools into academic human resource management, and what safeguards would be necessary to avoid exacerbating existing inequalities and tensions?"

The original contribution of this chapter lies in its conceptualization of 'AI-adjacent governance' within a middle-income context. While existing literature focuses either on historical reforms or future AI scenarios, this analysis bridges that gap by demonstrating how the 'reform-saturation' of the last two decades has created the data infrastructure necessary for algorithmic management, even in the absence of fully automated systems.

The structural evolution of this transition, from institutional reform to the current state of datafied governance, is synthesized in Figure 2. This model serves as the conceptual framework for the analysis that follows.

Figure 2. Conceptual Framework of the Pathway to AI-Adjacent Governance in Morocco.

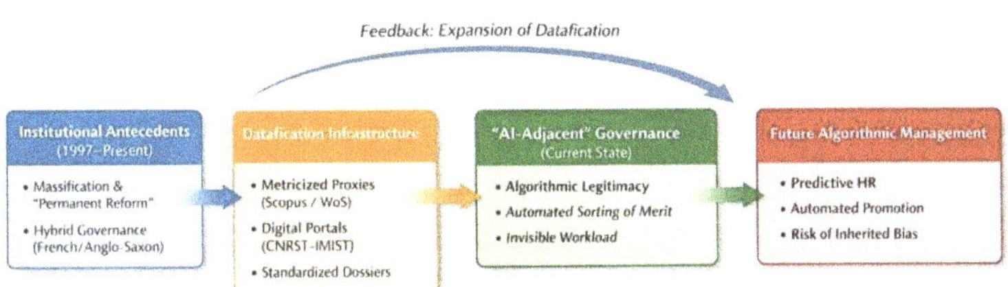

By addressing these questions, the chapter seeks to contribute to a better understanding of how data and metrics structure academic careers in a Global South context prior to the widespread adoption of sophisticated AI-based systems. The Moroccan case thus becomes an observatory for examining how existing cultures of metricized evaluation may shape the reception and effects of future AI tools in higher education.

2. METHODS

This chapter adopts a qualitative, interpretive research design that combines systematic documentary analysis with a synthesis of secondary empirical studies and descriptive quantitative indicators. The objective is not the generation of new primary data, but the reassembly and reinterpretation of existing evidence to produce a coherent analysis of academic work, metricization, and emergent AI-adjacent governance in Moroccan higher education. The research design is structured into three distinct analytic streams to ensure the findings are traced back to transparent procedures.

Methodologically, this study treats indicators with a dual analytic lens. Quantitatively, they are used as descriptive evidence of the system's growth (e.g., publication counts). Critically, however, they are analyzed as expressions of algorithmic governance—that is, as tools that do not merely 'count' work but actively 'reshape' the priorities of the teacher-researcher toward internationally indexed output.

2.1 Stream 1: Regulatory and Policy Mapping (Documentary Analysis)

The first component consists of a systematic analysis of the legal and regulatory framework governing the Moroccan academic profession.

- Corpus Boundaries: The corpus includes all major framework laws (e.g., Law 01-00), decrees defining the specific status of teacher-researchers (1975, 1997, 2023), and strategic reform programs such as the Emergency Plan 2009–2012 and the *Pacte ESRI 2030.*
- Selection and Appraisal: Documents were selected based on their role in defining missions, evaluation grids, and recruitment procedures. Official diagnostic reports from national bodies, such as the CSEFRS and the INE, were included as primary evidence of institutional discourse.
- Analytic Procedure: These texts are treated as "discursive artefacts" that construct representations of performance and the "ideal" academic. The research follows established protocols in documentary analysis, utilizing iterative coding to track the temporal layering of reforms and recurring problem frames, such as the ritualized invocation of *islah.*

2.2 Stream 2: Synthesis of Secondary Empirical Research

The second stream mobilizes empirical findings from prior research to anchor conceptual arguments in the professional reality of the Moroccan university.

- Corpus of Research: The synthesis integrates data from large-scale quantitative surveys (e.g., Bourqia, 2009; Cherkaoui, 2011; Gaillard et al., 2017) and qualitative studies on professional trajectories and perceptions of institutional justice.
- Analytic Procedure: These studies are re-analyzed with attention to narratives concerning workload, social status, and disengagement. Rather than merely re-reporting statistics, this research uses the findings to reconstruct how reforms are experienced from the standpoint of teacher-researchers. Where findings diverge across different studies, the analysis highlights these tensions rather than forcing a consensus.

2.3 Stream 3: Mapping of Descriptive Statistical and Bibliometric Indicators

A third component utilizes descriptive indicators to map the structural constraints of the academic environment.

- Data Sources: Structural data on staffing and age pyramids were extracted from the Ministry of Higher Education (ENSSUP) 2022–2023 statistics. Bibliometric time-series (1988–2017) were sourced from INE–CSEFRS and CNRST–IMIST reports based on Web of Science and Scopus.
- Functional Use: These indicators are utilized as contextual evidence rather than for inferential "causal story-telling". The research treats these metrics as both structural evidence and as "expressions of algorithmic governance," produced through specific computational data infrastructures.

2.4 Data Integrity and Limitations

The research acknowledges several limitations inherent in the available Moroccan datasets. Bibliometric comparisons (e.g., Table 2) rely on global databases that may under-represent Moroccan output in the humanities and social sciences due to linguistic and disciplinary biases. Consequently, productivity estimates (e.g., 0.54 articles per year) are interpreted as indicators of international visibility rather than absolute scientific production. Furthermore, demographic projections regarding retirements are based on ministerial estimates; actual figures may vary according to future regulatory changes in retirement age or voluntary departure schemes.

3. RESULTS

This section presents the main findings of the documentary analysis, secondary empirical material and statistical indicators. It focuses on four dimensions: the social status and collective mobilizations of teacher-researchers; the diffusion of new public management and metricized steering in Moroccan higher education; the role of algorithmic infrastructures and bibliometric indicators in the monitoring of scientific production ; and the career realities and institutional trajectories of academics.

3.1 Sociology of the Academic Profession: Social Status and Collective Mobilization

While the academic profession officially holds a high statutory position, the research identifies a disconnect in public discourse. An analysis of sectoral reports (e.g., CSEFRS, 2014) and recurring themes in national economic media (such as L'Économiste or Médias24) reveals a narrative that frequently reduces the public university to a 'crisis of employability' or a 'source of budgetary burden.' This discourse contributes to a perceived 'social devaluation' of the teacher-researcher, where the profession is increasingly scrutinized through the lens of immediate economic utility rather than its broader scientific or social contribution. This is consistent with empirical findings from a survey of 1,400 teacher-researchers in the humanities and social sciences shows that, across all positional dimensions considered—income, prestige and power—the status of the Moroccan university teacher is mediocre and the public image of the profession is clearly degraded (Cherkaoui & Bourqia, 2008). The academic profession appears relatively weak in economic terms, limited in institutional and political influence, and insufficiently valued in the social hierarchy (Talbi, 2018).

Beyond these indicators, the same survey and related studies point to the fragility of scientific communities, particularly in the humanities and social sciences. The academic community in these fields remains weakly institutionalised and little recognised, both by teacher-researchers themselves and by public authorities. This situation limits the capacity of academics to act collectively on issues such as evaluation, recruitment and promotion. Cherkaoui and Bourqia (2008) note that public authorities could significantly strengthen this community by granting it a formal role in the evaluation of project proposals and promotion dossiers, thus contributing to the professionalisation of the academic corps.

Faced with this combination of low status and weak recognition, teacher-researchers have resorted to various forms of expression and mobilization. They have voiced their dissatisfaction through public statements, press articles, social media and scientific meetings, and have organised collective actions and trade union struggles aimed at improving their financial and social situation. These mobilizations have included opposition to unilateral decisions by the ministry, such as the partial "Bachelor" reform, the centralised design and management of the university system, and draft legislation on the specific statute of teacher-researchers. In each case, demands have concerned both material aspects (salary scales, working conditions) and procedures (consultation, negotiation) (Ghouati, 2012).

Strikes and protest movements have been organised to defend what teacher-researchers call their "dignity", by seeking to improve salary scales that, according to union sources, have been frozen for more than two decades, to enhance their social and legal status, and to obtain better working conditions and more coherent mechanisms for scientific research and research allowances. These mobilizations have sometimes been accompanied by internal tensions. The Independent Coordination for the Dignity of Teacher-Researchers, for example, has criticised the national executive committee of the higher education union for insufficient efforts and has denounced a breakdown of dialogue and the emergence of conflict between teacher-researchers and their representatives. Together, these elements document a professional group that is simultaneously central in reform discourse and marginal in terms of resources and recognition, and that is engaged in ongoing collective action around status, working conditions and participation in decision-making.

3.2 New Public Management and the Metricization of Higher Education

Documentary analysis shows that Moroccan higher education has progressively adopted a managerial vocabulary and a set of steering instruments closely associated with new public management (NPM). Internationally, NPM has been characterised by an emphasis on efficiency, performance measurement, accountability and results-oriented governance in public services, including higher education (Hood, 1991 ; Pollitt & Bouckaert, 2011 ; Deem, 1998). Since the National Charter for Education and Training, Moroccan universities have been presented in policy texts as key levers for national competitiveness and socio-economic development, increasingly framed through the language of performance and effectiveness (Ma El Ainin et al., 2021 ; Ghouati, 2012). Law 01-00 on the organisation of higher education formalised university autonomy, but simultaneously tied this autonomy to mechanisms of evaluation, accreditation and performance-based steering, reflecting a classic NPM configuration in which decentralisation is accompanied by reinforced control through indicators (Marginson, 2008 ; Ozga, 2008).

Subsequent reform programmes, including the Emergency Plan (2009–2012) and the Pacte ESRI 2030, have reinforced this orientation. Official texts increasingly emphasise efficiency (efficience), effectiveness (efficacité), "results" and contractualisation between the State and higher education institutions. Strategic documents and evaluation reports produced by the Higher Council for Education, Training and Scientific Research (CSEFRS) and its National Evaluation Instance (INE) regularly assess universities—particularly open-access institutions—on the basis of quantitative indicators such as supervision ratios, graduation and success rates, programme accreditation status and research output (CSEFRS, 2014 ; INE, 2018). This mode of steering resonates with what Power (1997) conceptualises as the rise of an "audit society", in which evaluation devices become central tools of governance rather than neutral instruments of information.

At the institutional level, open-access universities are compared through dashboards of indicators that foreground overcrowding, low graduation rates and limited scientific production. Evaluation bodies repeatedly call for a closer alignment between allocated resources and measurable results, and for a more systematic use of indicators in planning, budgeting and funding decisions (INE, 2018). Quality assurance mechanisms have expanded accordingly: academic programmes, particularly at Licence and Master levels, are subject to assessment based on standardised criteria, and institutions are encouraged—or required—to establish internal quality assurance systems grounded in data collection and quantitative monitoring of teaching activities, student progression and employability outcomes. Similar dynamics have been observed in other higher education systems undergoing managerial reform, where quality assurance becomes a key vector for embedding metricized governance (Shore & Wright, 2015 ; Strathern, 2000).

Metricization also extends to the level of individual academic careers. Promotion grids and evaluation procedures increasingly weight scientific production, often operationalised through counts of publications and, implicitly or explicitly, through publication in indexed journals. While teaching, administrative responsibilities and community engagement are formally mentioned in evaluation frameworks, they are more difficult to quantify and therefore tend to be less visible and less decisive in practice (Wilsdon et al., 2015 ; Fochler & de Rijcke, 2017). Surveys and interview-based studies reported in sectoral analyses suggest that teacher-researchers perceive growing pressure to publish in specific outlets and to construct measurable research profiles, even though the structural conditions for research—time, funding, infrastructure and institutional support—remain limited, especially in mass open-access universities (Bourqia, 2009 ; Cherkaoui, 2011 ; Gaillard et al., 2017).

Overall, the findings point to a progressive and cumulative embedding of new public management logics in Moroccan higher education. Quantitative indicators, benchmarking exercises and performance-oriented language have become integral to policy discourse, institutional steering and, increasingly, individual evaluation and promotion. At the same time, the persistence of structural constraints—massification, limited resources and uneven research capacity—suggests that metricization operates in a context marked by significant tensions between managerial expectations and the material realities of academic work, a configuration widely documented in comparative studies of higher education reform (Altbach, 2004 ; Musselin, 2004 ; Marginson, 2008).

3.3 Algorithmic Governance, Scientific Production and AI-Adjacent Evaluation

Findings on scientific production and its monitoring show that Moroccan higher education operates within a strongly datafied and algorithmically mediated environment, even in the absence of fully fledged AI-based evaluation systems.

Policy discourse presents the National Research System (*Système national de recherche*, SNR) as a strategic lever for producing, transmitting and transferring knowledge, and as a key pillar of the "knowledge economy" (Lrhoul, 2017). Official documents emphasise the need to integrate information and communication technologies (ICTs) and open-access platforms in order to improve scientific productivity and international visibility, particularly in the context of the Global South.

Scientific activity is distributed across a range of institutions—public universities, non-university higher education institutions, public research centres, private universities, post-baccalaureate vocational institutes and certain private entities (companies, associations, foundations) —but public universities remain the main producers of indexed research outputs. National evaluations highlight the need to strengthen institutional capacities, improve research infrastructure and foster collaboration among these actors (INE, 2018).

The metricized and algorithmic dimension of this research system is evident in how scientific production is measured and valued. Indexed output in global databases such as Web of Science and Scopus is treated as a fundamental indicator of knowledge creation and diffusion, and as a marker of international recognition (INE, 2018). These databases classify journals, attribute citations and compute impact metrics according to proprietary algorithms, and national and institutional performance is increasingly perceived through the lens of these indicators.

Between 1988 and 2017, Morocco accumulated 45,911 publications indexed in Web of Science: 4,698 between 1988 and 1997; 12,333 between 1998 and 2007; and 28,880 between 2008 and 2017 (INE–CSEFRS, 2018). As shown in Table 1, this evolution over three decades reveals an overall upward trend. While these data are categorized into four identifiable phases for analytical clarity—an initial growth in the 1990s, a slowdown in the early 2000s, renewed growth from 2004, and acceleration from 2011—they represent a continuous evolution of the research ecosystem rather than discrete breaks. The implementation of the LMD reform (2004) and subsequent funding programs coincided with the significant upward trend in indexed publications. While this increase cannot be attributed solely to a single policy lever, these institutional changes provided the framework and the mandatory requirements for doctoral supervision that encouraged a shift toward indexed scientific production.

Table 1. Scientific production in Morocco (Web of Science, all document types), 1988–2017.

Period	1988-1997	1998-2007	2008-2017	Total
Number of publications	4.698	12.333	28.880	45.911

Source: Web of Science. Compilation and processing by INE–CSEFRS.

Source: Compiled by the research based on INE–CSEFRS (2018) and ENSSUP (2023). Productivity estimates (0.54) utilize the total permanent academic staff (N=15,880) as the denominator.

As illustrated in Table 2, international comparisons underline the modest scale of Moroccan production. Between 1998 and 2017, Malaysia's Web of Science output increased by more than 2,500%, Brazil's by over 500%, while Morocco's grew by 412% ; yet the absolute number of Moroccan articles in 2017 remained more than five times lower than Malaysia's (INE–CSEFRS, 2018). Average productivity per teacher-researcher is estimated at approximately 0.54 article per year, or just over one article every two years. National averages for universities are lower still, with some institutions recording only 0.22 publication per teacher-researcher per year; Scopus-based analyses converge on an average of around 0.47 publication per teacher-researcher per year (CNRST–IMIST, 2018).

Table 2. Growth of scientific production (Web of Science, all publication types), 1998–2017[1]

Country	1998	2017	Growth rate
Malaysia	1.045	27.354	2518%
South Africa	5.172	23.619	357%
Brazil	12.421	77.755	526%
Czech Republic	5.239	25.136	380%
Morocco	990	5.068	412%

Source: Web of Science, extracted 02/07/2020. Compilation and processing by INE–CSEFRS.

Disciplinary and geographical breakdowns reveal additional patterns. IMIST data for 1999–2010 indicate that more than half of Moroccan articles were in physics, with health sciences, life sciences and social sciences accounting for much smaller shares (Cherkaoui, 2009). For 2013–2017, Scopus data show that Moroccan researchers produced 17,689 articles, far fewer than Saudi Arabia (74,612), Tunisia (24,378) or Algeria (20,758) over the same period. Table 3 below compares scientific production by type of publication across selected countries. Rankings further shape perceptions: the Nature Index 2021 places Morocco fourth in Africa in terms of high-impact publications, but the country remains outside the top 50 worldwide (Ibrahimi, 2021). Morocco's position in global education indices is low (around 154th in an index based on university rankings and education spending), and Moroccan universities do not appear in the 2025 Shanghai Ranking of the top 1,000 universities worldwide (Shanghai Ranking Consultancy, 2025).

Table 3. Scientific production by type of publication

	Morocco	Algeria	Tunisia	Kenya	Saudi Arabia
Article	17689	20758	24378	10293	74612
Conference paper	5843	7953	9447	602	12167
Review	563	532	742	759	3959
Book chapter	565	502	715	895	1701
Note	718	53	346	210	460
Letter	426	83	714	126	733
Press article	33	74	57	16	147
Editorial	123	66	147	148	692
Book	36	20	35	58	195

Source: SCOPUS (2013-2017), CNRST- IMIST

These indicators play a prominent role in national debates on the state of higher education and research. Official reports, media coverage and institutional strategies frequently invoke Web of Science and Scopus figures, Nature Index scores and global rankings to characterise Morocco's relative position (Boujettou, 2016 ; Bouhalba et al., 2019). At the same time, surveys of researchers highlight structural constraints: limited resources and infrastructure, insufficient incentives for research, and promotion criteria that do not adequately reward scientific activity and international collaboration (Gaillard et al., 2017). Productive researchers contribute to the visibility of their laboratories and universities, but this contribution does not always translate into clear advantages compared to colleagues who concentrate mainly on teaching. Some teacher-researchers stop doing research altogether after obtaining their doctorate.

The results thus indicate a paradoxical configuration in which metrics and rankings derived from algorithmic infrastructures strongly influence representations and evaluations of Moroccan higher education, while the material and institutional conditions needed to respond to these metrics remain weak. Any future deployment of AI-based evaluation tools is likely to build on this existing data environment.

3.4 Career Realities and Institutional Trajectories of Teacher-Researchers

The analysis of statutory texts, ministerial data and empirical studies reveals career trajectories marked by expanding responsibilities, complex recruitment and evaluation procedures, staffing shortages, dual employment and frequent dissatisfaction. This subsection organises the main findings into six dimensions.

3.4.1 Regulatory Framework and Evolving Responsibilities

Statutory decrees define and progressively expand the missions of teacher-researchers. The 1975 statute and its 1997 revision assign core missions of teaching, supervision, research activities and tasks of general interest, and specify functions such as curriculum design, delivery of lectures and tutorials, collaboration with professional sectors, organisation of teaching loads, examination and assessment duties, promotion and dissemination of research, continuing education, outreach activities and supervision of final-year projects and fieldwork.

The draft decree of 2 August 2023 (Decree no. 2-23-545) further extends these missions by emphasising contributions to the advancement of research through publication and evaluation, collaboration with higher education institutions and territorial and civil society actors, teaching in initial and continuing education both in-person and online, and participation in the creation of printed and digital pedagogical resources.

The LMD reform and the Covid-19 pandemic have added layers of operational complexity. Teacher-researchers report having to assume new tasks, including programme coordination (Licence and Master), module coordination, leadership of research teams and management of doctoral centres, alongside emergency shifts to distance and blended teaching. Under the *Pacte ESRI 2030*, they are expected to elaborate integrated pedagogical strategies, foster innovation in curricula and valorise research through partnerships. Statutory teaching loads of around eight hours per week (approximately 240 hours per year) must be balanced with research, supervision and administrative responsibilities. The combined effect is an expanded professional profile and a workload that many consider difficult to reconcile with sustained research activity.

3.4.2 Career Management and Human Resource Constraints

Human resource management for teacher-researchers is heavily constrained by national regulations and ministerial control. Recruitment depends on budgetary posts allocated centrally, and involves several layers of approval, which makes procedures long and complex—often extending over many months or years. This delays responses to staffing needs and can hinder the capacity of institutions to recruit specialists in emerging fields or to attract international talent.

Promotion criteria are perceived as excessively formal and predominantly quantitative. Testimonies collected in prior studies indicate that counts of publications and listed activities weigh heavily, while qualitative aspects such as teaching quality, mentorship, innovation or community engagement are less systematically considered. This creates a significant disconnect between institutional requirements and professional reality. For instance, a teacher-researcher in the Social Sciences notes that while their local community impact—such as public policy advising or community outreach—is high, the current promotion grid exclusively rewards Scopus-indexed articles. This results in a perceived 'invisible' workload: essential academic contributions that are socially valuable but bibliometrically 'silent' and therefore professionally unrewarded. Opportunities for national and international mobility are limited by administrative barriers and lack of targeted support for exchanges and collaborations, which reduces academics' exposure to new research environments and networking possibilities.

These constraints contribute to feelings of frustration and a perception that bureaucratic requirements and rigid rules hinder professional development and autonomy. The available evidence suggests that many teacher-researchers perceive career management as cumbersome, insufficiently transparent and misaligned with the diverse realities of academic work.

3.4.3 Recruitment Modes, Staffing Shortages and Demographic Pressures

Recruitment procedures are governed by detailed decrees specifying conditions and processes for each cadre. For the Maître de conférences level, candidates generally need a doctorate and must be under 45 years of age, although this age limit does not apply to civil servants. Candidates for full professorship must present pedagogical and scientific dossiers evaluated by committees of experienced academics; recent reforms also envisage national lists of eligibility and minimum requirements in terms of years of service and experience in teaching, research and supervision.

In practice, evaluations are often based on extensive paper dossiers processed within short timeframes by committees that receive no additional remuneration.

This raises concerns about the depth and reliability of assessments. Essential competencies such as pedagogical skills, communication, digital literacy and language proficiency are not systematically evaluated. In the humanities and social sciences, studies report that a significant proportion of staff have not published research since their doctorate (Cherkaoui, 2009), and focus groups highlight the prevalence of mediocre teaching performance. Suspicions of favouritism and lack of objectivity in some recruitment and promotion decisions are recurrent themes in testimonies.

These qualitative issues are aggravated by a structural shortage of academic staff. In 2022–2023, public universities employed 15,880 permanent academic staff. However, the system faces a looming demographic shift: according to the Ministry of Higher Education (MESRSFC) sectoral projections, approximately 3,000 staff are expected to reach the age of retirement by 2026, and up to 5,000 by 2030. (MESRSFC, 2023). Table 4 summarises the distribution of permanent staff by age group and grade.

Table 4. Permanent academic staff by age group and grade, 2022–2023

Age group	Assistant Professor	Associate Professor	Full Professor	Non-research teaching & technical staff (engineers, secondary-cycle teachers, administrators, etc.)	Total
25–29	66	–	–	6	72
30–34	915	32	–	17	964
35–39	1,460	392	3	78	1,933
40–44	1,134	701	200	165	2,200
45–49	728	785	666	203	2,382
50–54	484	653	1,063	147	2,347
55–59	309	368	1,699	78	2,454
60–64	279	212	2,166	43	2,700
65+	98	49	679	2	828
Total	**5,473**	**3,192**	**6,476**	**739**	**15,880**

Source: ENSSUP.

The age structure reveals a significant concentration of staff in the 45–64 age brackets and very small cohorts of younger academics (only 72 in the 25–29 age group). Among the 15,880 permanent staff, 8,872 work in open-access institutions, 6,878 in selective institutions and 130 in scientific research institutes. Table 5 shows the uneven distribution of staff among universities, with Mohammed V and Hassan II universities employing the largest numbers.

Limited funding further constrains recruitment and retention. Salaries and social benefits are widely regarded as insufficiently attractive for young graduates, which reduces the pool of potential candidates. The integration of doctoral students as teaching assistants or "monitors" has been proposed as a stopgap solution, but the available documents and testimonies raise doubts about the sustainability of this approach and its implications for teaching quality and the future of the profession.

Table 5. Distribution of academic staff by type of institution and university

Type of institution	**Number of staff**
Open-access institutions	8 872
Selective institutions	6 878
Scientific research institutes	130
University	**Number of staff**
Mohammed V University	2 474
Hassan II University	2 303
Sidi Mohammed Ben Abdellah University	1 756
Cadi Ayyad University	1 678
Ibn Zohr University	1 495
Abdelmalek Essaadi University	1 317
Moulay Ismail University	1 123
Mohamed I University	1 025

Source: ENSSUP.

3.4.4 Academic Evaluation and the Experience of Assessment

Promotion and evaluation procedures rely heavily on documentation submitted by candidates and on evaluation grids whose criteria are defined in ministerial orders such as that of 4 June 2012. Teacher-researchers report that these grids often lack precision, particularly in the weighting of different activities. Cases are cited in which staff advance in their careers by submitting minimal pedagogical materials or by occupying positions (such as head of department) primarily to satisfy formal requirements. There are also reported instances of staff reaching full professorship with limited scientific production.

The standard six-year interval between promotions is frequently described as too long for productive academics. Proposals mentioned in testimonies include shorter intervals (for example, two years) combined with robust evaluation mechanisms. At the same time, the absence of a national, peer-based body for evaluating research and promotions is seen as a structural weakness. Faculty committees are often perceived as insufficiently independent and as constrained by bureaucratic rules that do not always align with academic norms based on scientific merit and fair competition.

3.4.5 Mobility, Dual Employment and Professional Disengagement

Studies by Bourqia (2009) and Cherkaoui (2011) report high levels of dissatisfaction and frequent dual employment among Moroccan academics. Many teacher-researchers supplement their income through activities in private schools and institutes, consultancy or informal teaching markets. According to one study, 89% of staff in private schools and institutes are temporary employees drawn mainly from public universities. Another survey cited by Bourqia indicates that 42% of teachers have another activity in addition to their work at their home university; 19% have a paid additional activity and 36% both paid and unpaid activities.

Academic staff express limited confidence in the non-selective public university system. In a survey on preferred higher education systems for their own children, 49% of respondents chose selective systems, 28% preferred studying abroad, 5% opted for private institutes and establishments, and only 6% selected the non-selective public system (Bourqia, 2009). Cherkaoui's (2011) study reports a 75% dissatisfaction rate among academics, a fragile sense of loyalty to institutions and a strong desire among many to leave higher education or research. Voluntary early retirement schemes have been seen favourably by a significant number of staff, and many do not recommend the profession to their children.

3.4.6 Promotion and Career Advancement

Promotion occurs either within grades (from step A to C) or through movement from assistant professor to *professeur habilité*, then to full professor. The criteria established in the 4 June 2012 order and related texts are widely criticised as vague and insufficiently operational, particularly regarding the balance between teaching, research, administration and other activities. Scientific committees and heads of department oversee the process using grids that record research and teaching activities and responsibilities, combined with oral presentations and discussions (Kaaouachi, 2010).

Progression by seniority typically requires eight years to move from one step to another. After six years, highly productive teacher-researchers may submit a dossier for accelerated advancement. Recent reforms have increased the quota of eligible candidates from 20% to 40%, benefiting smaller institutions and allowing more staff to access promotion. A new grade "D" and an exceptional grade have been created for staff with long seniority and documented excellence, as judged by a national commission.

Despite these measures, testimonies and evaluations indicate that many deserving academics feel blocked in their careers due to quota limits, ill-defined criteria and insufficient recognition of diverse forms of contribution. Promotion outcomes are perceived as uncertain and, in some cases, as influenced by procedural or relational factors rather than solely by merit. This contributes to frustration and can weaken motivation and engagement.

DISCUSSION

This chapter set out to analyse how successive reforms, metricized steering and emerging data-driven tools are reshaping the academic profession in Moroccan public universities. The results presented in Section 3 show a profession that is simultaneously central in reform discourse and fragile in terms of status, resources and recognition ; a university system increasingly governed through indicators and rankings; and academic careers marked by expanding responsibilities, structural shortages and uncertain promotion prospects. This section discusses these findings in light of the theoretical perspectives mobilised in the conceptual framework and reflects on their implications for the future integration of AI-based evaluation tools.

4.1 A Profession Between Centrality and Marginality

From the standpoint of the sociology of the academic profession, the Moroccan case exhibits a strong tension between normative centrality and practical marginality. Policy documents consistently position teacher-researchers as key actors in building a knowledge-based economy, enhancing competitiveness and supporting development. At the same time, empirical evidence documents low relative income, modest prestige and limited power when compared to other professional groups, as well as degraded public images of the academic profession (Cherkaoui & Bourqia, 2008).

This configuration resonates with international work on the erosion of academic status under conditions of massification, managerial reforms and public criticism (Altbach, 2004; Enders, 2000 ; Musselin, 2004), but the Moroccan context adds specific features. The weak institutionalisation and low visibility of scientific communities—particularly in the humanities and social sciences—limit the capacity of academics to act collectively as a recognised professional body. Professional associations and disciplinary communities do exist, but they have not yet acquired the kind of formal authority over evaluation and promotion that characterises more consolidated academic systems.

Collective mobilisations, strikes and the emergence of new coordinations such as the Independent Coordination for the Dignity of Teacher-Researchers indicate efforts to compensate for this structural weakness through contentious action. These movements articulate demands for salary reform, better working conditions and greater participation in decision-making around reforms and statutes. From a sociological perspective, they can be read as attempts to renegotiate the terms of professional autonomy and to reassert the value of academic work in a context where managerial and metricized logics tend to redefine what counts as legitimate performance.

However, internal tensions within representative structures, dissatisfaction with unions and a high propensity toward dual employment and voluntary early retirement suggest that professional cohesion is fragile. The high proportion of academics who would not recommend the profession to their children, and the prevalence of exit strategies (both literal and symbolic), point to a deeper crisis of attractiveness and identification with the academic role.

4.2 Governing by Numbers Under Structural Constraints

The results also show that new public management and metricization have become central features of Moroccan higher education governance. Reform programmes and evaluation bodies systematically mobilise indicators related to efficiency, effectiveness, supervision ratios, graduation rates and scientific output. Universities—especially open-access institutions—are compared using dashboards, and their "deficits" are framed in quantitative terms.

This reflects broader trends described in the international literature on "audit cultures" and "governing by numbers" (Power, 1997 ; Strathern, 2000; Shore & Wright, 2015). Indicators and performance contracts are not neutral ; they define the categories through which university performance is perceived and judged. In the Moroccan case, they contribute to constructing a persistent narrative of crisis: overcrowded lecture halls, low graduation rates, modest scientific production, weak international visibility.

Yet, the findings also reveal a persistent mismatch between metricized expectations and structural conditions. Average publication rates per teacher-researcher are low, and the age structure of the academic workforce indicates substantial looming retirements in a context of massification and constrained recruitment. Research infrastructure, funding and support structures (labs, incubation, project management) remain limited, and administrative and teaching loads are heavy. Under such conditions, the insistence on quantitative output indicators can be experienced less as an instrument of quality improvement and more as a source of pressure and symbolic devaluation (Boukhari, 2023 ; Aujourd'hui Le Maroc, 2024).

From the perspective of Goodhart's law ("when a measure becomes a target, it ceases to be a good measure"), there is a risk that publication counts and selected indicators become goals in themselves, potentially encouraging strategic behaviours—such as prioritising quantity over quality, focusing on easily indexable topics, or privileging disciplines and languages that are more visible in global databases—rather than holistic academic development. The Moroccan case illustrates how metricization can amplify existing inequalities between disciplines, institutions and individuals, particularly when the underlying structure of opportunities is uneven.

4.3 Datafication, Bibliometrics and AI-Adjacent Governance

The analysis of scientific production and rankings shows that Moroccan higher education is already deeply embedded in datafied and algorithmically mediated environments. Web of Science, Scopus, the Nature Index and global rankings provide the numbers through which national performance is narrated and compared (Barki, 2021). These infrastructures classify journals, compute impact metrics and produce indicators using proprietary algorithms, thereby shaping the visibility and evaluation of research long before explicit AI-based promotion tools are introduced (Beer, 2016 ; Williamson, 2017).

In this sense, the system described in this chapter can be characterised as "AI-adjacent": crucial decisions about policy and institutional reputation already depend on algorithmically generated indicators, even if formal AI systems for individual evaluation and promotion are not yet in place. These bibliometric profiles, impact factors, and institutional rankings constitute the pre-algorithmic infrastructure of the Moroccan university. They provide the standardized, machine-readable datasets required for the eventual integration of AI-driven analytics into academic human resource management. Consequently, the current reliance on these metrics creates a 'path dependency,' where future automated systems are likely to inherit the biases and disciplinary imbalances already embedded in today's data landscape.

The paradox documented in the results—strong reliance on algorithmic indicators combined with weak material conditions for research—raises important questions for the potential integration of AI. If AI-based evaluation systems are deployed in such a context without careful design, they are likely to reproduce and intensify existing biases. For instance, models that reward past publication patterns risk penalising disciplines, languages and institutions that are already under-represented in global databases. They may also reinforce short-term productivity metrics at the expense of long-term, locally relevant research and teaching contributions.

Conversely, the Moroccan case also highlights areas where data-driven tools could be used in more reflexive ways. AI could, in principle, help identify structural obstacles—such as extreme supervision ratios, disciplinary imbalances or bottlenecks in doctoral completion—and support more equitable resource allocation. It could also be used to recognise diverse forms of contribution if appropriate data are collected (e.g. on teaching innovation, community engagement, local impact). The precondition, however, is a shift from using metrics primarily as instruments of ranking and control to using them as diagnostic tools embedded in participatory governance.

4.4 Career Trajectories, Voice and Exit

The career realities documented in Section 3.4—expanded responsibilities, complex recruitment and promotion procedures, staffing shortages, dual employment and a strong desire to leave—can be interpreted through Albert Hirschman's (1970) framework of "voice" and "exit". When organisational members perceive deterioration or unaddressed problems, they may either express dissatisfaction (voice) or withdraw (exit).

In the Moroccan university system, both dynamics are visible. On the one hand, teacher-researchers mobilise collectively, negotiate through unions and new coordinations, and formulate detailed critiques of statutes, evaluation grids and promotion rules. These forms of voice indicate that academics are still invested in the institution and seek change from within. On the other hand, the high prevalence of dual employment, the attractiveness of opportunities outside the university and favourable attitudes towards early retirement demonstrate various forms of exit. Some academics withdraw from research, focusing on teaching or external activities; others leave the system altogether or discourage their children from entering the profession.

The combination of strong symbolic expectations—embodied in reform discourses, knowledge economy rhetoric and metricized targets—with limited career prospects and opaque evaluation processes risks further weakening commitment to the academic project. If promotion appears uncertain, if evaluation is seen as unfair or heavily procedural, and if working conditions remain challenging, incentives to invest in long-term academic trajectories diminish. This has direct consequences for the sustainability of the academic workforce, particularly given the ageing age structure and the relatively small cohorts of younger staff.

4.5 Morocco as a Global South Case of Reform-Saturated, Metricized and AI-Adjacent Governance

Taken together, the findings suggest that Moroccan public universities constitute a revealing Global South case of what might be termed "reform-saturated, metricized and AI-adjacent governance". Over more than two decades, the system has been subject to successive reforms, each adding new layers of objectives, structures and evaluation mechanisms. Metricization has become an integral part of governance, with national bodies and international databases providing a continuous flow of indicators and rankings. Teacher-researchers are expected to respond to these demands while coping with massification, limited resources and complex administrative requirements.

This configuration is not unique to Morocco, but the Moroccan case adds a specific combination of features:

- A long sequence of reforms with limited periods of consolidation ;
- Strong rhetorical emphasis on the knowledge economy and excellence, contrasted with constrained research conditions ;
- Weak institutionalisation of scientific communities in some disciplines ;
- Extensive reliance on global bibliometric infrastructures and rankings;
- And an emerging policy interest in digitalisation and AI.

For debates on the future of academic evaluation and AI in higher education, this case underscores the importance of context. Discussions on "responsible metrics" and "responsible AI" often originate in well-resourced systems, yet their application in settings marked by structural shortages, heavy teaching loads and fragile professional status raises distinct challenges. In such environments, the risk is high that AI will be used primarily as an additional layer of control and ranking, superimposed on existing bureaucratic and metricized frameworks, rather than as a means to address underlying structural problems.

The Moroccan case therefore invites a rethinking of AI-related reforms in higher education from a Global South perspective. It suggests that any move towards AI-enhanced evaluation must be preceded by a critical assessment of existing indicators, by efforts to strengthen academic communities and peer-based evaluation, and by reforms targeting working conditions, staffing and research infrastructure. Without these prerequisites, the promise of AI risks being absorbed into an already dense assemblage of reforms and numbers, with limited benefits for academic work and careers.

5. CONCLUSION

5.1. Main Contributions of the Chapter

This chapter has examined the transformation of the academic profession in Moroccan public universities under conditions of reform-saturated, metricized and AI-adjacent governance. By combining documentary and policy analysis, secondary empirical material and descriptive indicators, it has brought together strands of evidence that are often treated separately: legal statutes and reform programmes, bibliometric profiles and rankings, surveys of teacher-researchers, and staffing and demographic data.

A first contribution lies in the reconstruction of the reform trajectory that has shaped Moroccan higher education since the late 1990s. Rather than analysing individual reforms in isolation, the chapter has shown how successive laws, strategies and decrees have accumulated to produce a permanent state of reform, in which the missions, responsibilities and evaluation frameworks of teacher-researchers are continuously expanded and redefined. The notion of a "reform-saturated" system helps to capture the lack of consolidation and the resulting uncertainty for academic careers.

A second contribution concerns the integration of new public management, metricization and algorithmic governance perspectives in a Global South context. The analysis shows how performance indicators, bibliometric data and international rankings have become central instruments for steering universities and narrating their performance. It also demonstrates that Moroccan higher education is already deeply embedded in datafied environments—through Web of Science, Scopus, the Nature Index and global rankings—even before explicit AI-based evaluation tools are implemented. The concept of AI-adjacent governance captures this situation in which algorithmically generated indicators shape evaluation and decision-making in the absence of fully fledged AI systems.

A third contribution lies in the empirically grounded account of career realities and institutional trajectories of teacher-researchers. The chapter documents how statutory texts and reform programmes translate into expanding responsibilities, significant teaching loads, complex recruitment and promotion procedures, and constrained mobility. It highlights structural shortages and ageing staff, the prevalence of dual employment, high levels of dissatisfaction and weak attractiveness of the profession, as well as concerns about opacity and perceived injustice in recruitment and promotion. By mobilising Hirschman's concepts of "voice" and "exit", the chapter offers an interpretive lens to understand collective mobilisations, disengagement and early retirement strategies.

Finally, the chapter contributes to debates on AI and academic evaluation by arguing that any discussion of AI-based tools in higher education must be grounded in an understanding of existing metricized cultures and structural constraints. The Moroccan case serves as an observatory for the mechanisms of path dependency in digital governance. It demonstrates that future AI-driven systems do not emerge in a vacuum; rather, they are programmed to 'inherit' and potentially amplify the structural biases and disciplinary inequalities already encoded in current bibliometric regimes. Without deliberate corrective measures, the automation of academic evaluation risks formalizing existing 'blind spots'—such as the under-representation of local-language humanities—into the very architecture of university management.

5.2. Limitations of the Study

Several limitations of this chapter should be acknowledged.

First, the analysis is based primarily on documentary sources and secondary empirical studies, rather than on original fieldwork. Although the corpus is diverse—

encompassing legal texts, policy documents, evaluation reports, survey results and previous qualitative research—it does not provide the depth of insight that might be obtained through new interviews, ethnographic observation or large-scale quantitative surveys conducted specifically for this study. Teacher-researchers' voices are therefore mediated through existing studies and reports, and some dimensions of their experience may remain underexplored.

Second, the use of descriptive statistical and bibliometric indicators is constrained by the availability, quality and coverage of existing data. National datasets and international databases such as Web of Science and Scopus have known limitations: they privilege certain disciplines, languages and publication formats, and may not fully capture locally oriented or practice-based forms of knowledge production. The chapter treats these indicators both as evidence and as objects of critique, but it cannot fully correct for their inherent biases.

Third, the discussion of AI-adjacent governance and possible AI futures is necessarily speculative, given that large-scale AI-based evaluation systems are not yet deployed in Moroccan higher education. The scenarios envisaged are extrapolations based on current metricized practices and international debates about AI in education and research. They are intended as heuristic tools rather than predictions. Empirical research will be needed to document how specific AI tools are actually designed, introduced and used if and when they are implemented.

Finally, the chapter focuses primarily on public universities and teacher-researchers in Morocco. Private higher education institutions, non-university research organizations and other categories of academic and professional staff are not analysed in detail. The dynamics described here therefore do not exhaust the diversity of the Moroccan higher education and research landscape.

5.3. Future Perspectives for Policy, Practice and Research

Despite these limitations, the analysis points toward several avenues for future development in policy, institutional practice and research.

At the policy and governance level, the findings suggest that any move towards AI-enhanced evaluation in Moroccan higher education should be preceded by a critical review of existing metrics, evaluation grids and promotion procedures. Efforts to clarify criteria, strengthen peer-based assessment, and recognise the full range of academic activities—including teaching, supervision, administrative responsibilities and socially relevant research—appear essential. Without such reforms, AI tools risk automating and amplifying opaque or perceived-as-unfair practices rather than improving them.

A second policy priority concerns the structural conditions of academic work. The persistent combination of massification, staff shortages, heavy teaching loads, limited research infrastructure and frozen or relatively low salaries cannot be resolved through better indicators or smarter algorithms alone. Measures to renew the academic workforce, improve working conditions, support early-career researchers and strengthen research capacities are central to making any evaluation system—human or AI-assisted—credible and sustainable.

At the institutional practice level, universities could explore more reflexive uses of data and digital tools. Instead of relying solely on rankings and aggregate publication counts, institutions might use data analytics to identify structural bottlenecks (e.g. extreme supervision ratios, under-served disciplines, inequities in promotion patterns) and to inform targeted support measures. Participatory approaches in which teacher-researchers are involved in designing and interpreting indicators could help to build trust and enhance the legitimacy of evaluation practices.

For future research, several directions emerge. Empirical studies could:

- Investigate in greater depth how teacher-researchers in different disciplines and institutions experience metricized evaluation and how they anticipate the introduction of AI-based tools;
- Examine the specific effects of bibliometric indicators and rankings on research agendas, publication strategies and language choices in Moroccan universities;
- Compare the Moroccan case with other countries in the MENA region and the Global South, in order to develop more generalizable insights into reform-saturated and metricized higher education systems;
- And, as AI tools are progressively introduced, analyse their design, governance, and actual use in academic HR processes, including issues of bias, transparency, accountability and professional autonomy.

More broadly, the chapter points to the importance of developing context-sensitive frameworks for "responsible metrics" and "responsible AI" in higher education. In settings marked by structural constraints and fragile professional status, such as Morocco, responsible innovation in evaluation cannot be reduced to technical fixes or ethical guidelines at the level of algorithms. It requires attention to the broader institutional ecology in which data are produced and used, to the voices and capacities of academic actors, and to the material conditions under which academic work and careers are pursued (Ennida & Allouani, 2022 ; Ennida & Allah, 2024).

In this sense, the Moroccan academic profession offers not only a case to be analysed, but also a vantage point from which to rethink the promises and risks of AI in higher education globally.

REFERENCES

Altbach, P. G. (2004). Globalisation and the university: Myths and realities in an unequal world. *Tertiary Education and Management*, *10*(1), 3–25. DOI: 10.1080/13583883.2004.9967114

Aujourd'hui Le Maroc. (2024). Plus d'étudiants, moins de profs dans nos universités [More students, fewer professors in our universities]. *Aujourd'hui Le Maroc*. https://aujourdhui.ma

Barki, C. (2021). Recherche scientifique: Le Maroc, grand absent des classements prestigieux des universités [Scientific research: Morocco, largely absent from prestigious university rankings]. *L'Opinion*. https://www.lopinion.ma/Recherche-scientifique-Le-Maroc-grand-absent-desclassements-prestigieux-des-Universites_a17702.html

Beer, D. (2016). How should we do the history of Big Data? *Big Data & Society*, *3*(1), 2053951716646135. Advance online publication. DOI: 10.1177/2053951716646135

Bouhalba, S., ... (2019). Production scientifique nationale en comparaison avec d'autres pays – Scopus (2013–2017) [National scientific production in comparison with other countries – Scopus (2013–2017)]. Centre national pour la recherche scientifique et technique (CNRST). https://barometre.cnrst.ma/images/pdf/EtudeProductionScientifique.pdf

Boujettou, H. (2016). Le « ranking » comme mode de régulation de la performance des établissements de l'enseignement supérieur au Maroc ["Ranking" as a mode of regulating the performance of higher education institutions in Morocco]. *Revue marocaine de management, logistique et transport*.

Boukhari, M. (2023). Enseignement supérieur: des doctorants pour pallier le déficit de professeurs [Higher education: Doctoral students to compensate for the shortage of professors]. Finances News Hebdo. https://www.fnh.ma/article/actualite-education/enseignement-superieur-des-doctorants-pour-pallier-le-deficit-de-professeurs

Bourqia, R. (2009). Vers une sociologie de l'université marocaine [Towards a sociology of the Moroccan university]. *Al-Madrassa Al-Maghribiya*, *2*, 11–56.

Centre National pour la Recherche Scientifique et Technique (CNRST). (2018). *Production scientifique nationale en comparaison avec d'autres pays: Scopus (2013–2017)* [National scientific production compared with other countries: Scopus (2013–2017)]. Institut Marocain de l'Information Scientifique et Technique (IMIST). https://barometre.cnrst.ma/images/pdf/EtudeProductionScientifique.pdf

Cherkaoui, M. (2011). *Crise de l'université* [University crisis]. Librairie Droz. DOI: 10.3917/droz.cherk.2011.01

Cherkaoui, M. (2015). Entre recherche et crise des sciences sociales [Between research and the crisis of the social sciences]. *Economia.* http://economia.ma/fr/content/entre-recherche-et-crise-des-sciences-sociales

Cherkaoui, M., & Bourqia, R. (2008). Dilemmes de la recherche et crise des sciences sociales [Research dilemmas and social science crisis]. *La revue. Economía, 4*, 85–89.

Décret n° 2-23-545 du 15 moharrem 1445 (2 août 2023) portant statut particulier du corps des enseignants-chercheurs de l'enseignement supérieur [Decree no. 2-23-545 establishing the specific status of higher education teacher-researchers]. (2023). Bulletin officiel du Royaume du Maroc.

Décret n° 2-75-670 du 11 chaoual 1395 (17 octobre 1975) portant statut particulier du personnel enseignant-chercheur [Decree no. 2-75-670 establishing the specific status of academic teaching and research staff]. (1975). Bulletin officiel du Royaume du Maroc.

Décret n° 2-96-793 du 11 chaoual 1417 (19 février 1997) portant statut particulier des enseignants-chercheurs [Decree no. 2-96-793 establishing the specific status of teacher-researchers]. (1997). Bulletin officiel du Royaume du Maroc. http://bdj.mmsp.gov.ma/Fr/Document/243-D%C3%A9cret-n-2-96-793-du-11-chaoual-1417-19-f%C3%A9vrier-.aspx?KeyPath=

Deem, R. (1998). "New Managerialism" and Higher Education: The Management of Performances and Cultures in Universities in the United Kingdom. *International Studies in Sociology of Education, 8*(1), 47–70. DOI: 10.1080/0962021980020014

Enders, J., & De Weert, E. (Eds.). (2009). *The Changing Face of Academic Life: Analytical and Comparative Perspectives.* Palgrave Macmillan. DOI: 10.1057/9780230242166

Ennida, K., & Allah, A. S. (2024). The Moroccan teacher-researchers' organizational citizenship behavior as a predictor of university performance. *Global Journal of Business. Economics and Management: Current Issues, 14*(1), 70–74. DOI: 10.18844/gjbem.v14i1.9356

Ennida, K., & Allouani, S. A. (2022). L'enseignant-chercheur comme ressource humaine: Une approche par la citoyenneté organisationnelle [The teacher-researcher as a human resource: An organizational citizenship approach]. *Moroccan Journal of Business Studies*, *3*(2), 1–19. https://www.emaa.ma/mjbs/articles/pdfs/vol3issu2/L%E2%80%99enseignant%20chercheur%20comme%20ressource%20humaine%20%20une%20approche%20par%20la%20citoyennete%20organisationnelle.pdf

Fochler, M., & De Rijcke, S. (2017). Implicated in the indicator game? An experimental debate. *Engaging Science, Technology, and Society*, *3*, 21–40. DOI: 10.17351/ests2017.108

Gaillard, J., Tull, M., & Waast, R. (2017). Les défis de la recherche scientifique au Maroc [The challenges of scientific research in Morocco]. *Science, Technology & Society*, *22*(3), 345–366.

Ghouati, A. (2012). La dépossession. Réformes, enseignement supérieur et pouvoirs au Maghreb [Dispossession: Reforms, higher education and powers in the Maghreb]. *Revue du Monde Musulman et de la Méditerranée*, *131*(1), 65–90. DOI: 10.4000/remmm.7608

Higher Council for Education, Training and Scientific Research. (2014). Implementation of the national education and training charter 2000–2013: Acquisitions, deficits and challenges. Analytical report. Kingdom of Morocco. https://www.csefrs.ma/wp-content/uploads/2017/10/Rapport-analytique.pdf

Hirschman, A. O. (1970). *Exit, Voice, and Loyalty: Responses to Decline in Firms, Organizations, and States*. Harvard University Press.

Hood, C. (1991). A Public Management for All Seasons? *Public Administration*, *69*(1), 3–19. DOI: 10.1111/j.1467-9299.1991.tb00779.x

Ibrahimi, K. (2021). Recherche scientifique: Le Maroc classé quatrième en Afrique dans le "Nature Index 2021" [Scientific research: Morocco ranked fourth in Africa in the "Nature Index 2021"]. Le360. https://m.le360.ma/societe/recherche-scientifique-le-marocclasse-quatrieme-en-afrique-dans-le-nature-index-2021-244315

Instance Nationale d'Évaluation – Higher Council for Education, Training and Scientific Research. (2018). L'enseignement supérieur au Maroc: Efficacité, efficience et défis du système universitaire à accès ouvert [Higher education in Morocco: Effectiveness, efficiency and challenges of the open-access university system] (Sectoral report). https://www.csefrs.ma/wp-content/uploads/2018/10/Rapport-Enseignement-sup--rieur-Fr-03-10.pdf

Kaaouachi, A. (2010). L'évaluation dans le système d'enseignement supérieur au Maroc: Bilan des réalisations, limites et principaux défis. In Lamine, B. (Ed.), *Towards an Arab higher education space: International challenges and societal responsibilities* (pp. 409–422). UNESCO Regional Bureau for Education in the Arab States., https://search.shamaa.org/PDF/41452/KaaouachiEn41504.pdf

Lrhoul, H. (2017). La production scientifique des chercheurs de la faculté de médecine et de pharmacie de Casablanca: Mesures, cartographie et enjeux du libre accès [Scientific production of researchers at the Faculty of Medicine and Pharmacy of Casablanca: Measurement, mapping and open access challenges]. Unpublished manuscript.

Ma El Ainin, C. N., Janati Idrissi, F., & Nouib, A. (2021). L'enseignement à distance et la formation continue des enseignants au Maroc: Cas de la région Guelmim-Oued Noun [Distance learning and continuing teacher training in Morocco: The case of the Guelmim-Oued Noun region]. *Moroccan Journal of Business Studies*, 3.

Marginson, S. (2008). Global Field and Global Imagining: Bourdieu and Worldwide Higher *Education. British Journal of Sociology of Education*, *29*(3), 303–315. DOI: 10.1080/01425690801966386

Musselin, C. (2004). Towards a European academic labour market? Some lessons drawn from empirical studies on academic mobility. *Higher Education*, *48*(1), 55–78. DOI: 10.1023/B:HIGH.0000033770.24848.41

Ozga, J. (2008). Governing Knowledge: Research Steering and Research Quality. *European Educational Research Journal*, 7(3), 261 272. (Original work published 2008)DOI: 10.2304/eerj.2008.7.3.261

Pollitt, C., & Bouckaert, G. (2011). *Public Management Reform: A Comparative Analysis*—New Public Management, Governance, and the Neo-Weberian State (3th ed.). Oxford: Oxford University Press.

Power, M. (1997). *The Audit Society: Rituals of Verification*. Oxford University Press.

Shanghai Ranking Consultancy. (2025). 2025 *Academic Ranking of World Universities (ARWU)*. Shanghai Ranking Consultancy. https://www.shanghairanking.com

Shore, C., & Wright, S. (2015). Audit Culture Revisited: Rankings, Ratings, and the Reassembling of Society. *Current Anthropology*, *56*(3), 421–444. DOI: 10.1086/681534

Strathern, M. (2000). The Tyranny of Transparency. *British Educational Research Journal*, *26*(3), 309–321. https://www.jstor.org/stable/1501878. DOI: 10.1080/713651562

Talbi, M. (2018). Enseignement supérieur au Maroc: L'université à l'épreuve du développement économique de la société, Observatoire universitaire des politiques d'éducation et de formation. https://www.csmd.ma/documents/Observatoire%20 universitaire%20des%2 0politiques%20d'%C3%A9ducation%20et%20de%20formation%20- %20M.%20Talbi.pdf.

Williamson, B. (2017). *Big Data in Education: The Digital Future of Learning, Policy and Practice.* SAGE Publications Ltd., DOI: 10.4135/9781529714920

Wilsdon, J. (2015). *The metric tide.* SAGE Publications Ltd., DOI: 10.4135/9781473978782

ADDITIONAL READING

Bleiklie, I., Enders, J., & Lepori, B. (Eds.). (2017). *Managing universities: Policy and organizational change from a Western European comparative perspective.* Palgrave Macmillan. DOI: 10.1007/978-3-319-53865-5

Côme, T., & Rouet, G. (2016). How to evaluate academic staff? Efficacy and performance of the structures and schemes. *Gestion et Management Public, 5*(1), 57–80. DOI: 10.3917/gmp.051.0061

Duru-Bellat, M., Farges, G., & Van Zanten, A. (2018). *Chapitre 2. Les inégalités de carrières dans le système scolaire français. Sociologie de l'école: 5e édition.* Armand Colin., DOI: 10.3917/arco.zante.2018.01.0035

Enders, J. (Ed.). (2001). *Academic staff in Europe: Changing contexts and conditions.* Greenwood Press.

Gatignol, C. (2014). L'environnement professionnel des enseignants-chercheurs français explique-t-il leurs parcours de carrière? [Does the professional environment of French academics explain their career paths?]. @. *GRH, 11*(11), 51–80. DOI: 10.3917/grh.142.0051

Hicks, D., Wouters, P., Waltman, L., de Rijcke, S., & Rafols, I. (2015). Bibliometrics: The Leiden Manifesto for research metrics. *Nature, 520*(7548), 429–431. DOI: 10.1038/520429a

Horta, H., Jung, J., & Santos, J. M. (2018). Effects of mobilities on the research output and its multidisciplinarity of academics in Hong Kong and Macau: An exploratory study. *Higher Education Quarterly, 72*(3), 250–265. DOI: 10.1111/hequ.12161

Kleiche-Dray, M., & Belcadi, S. (2008). L'université marocaine en processus d'autonomisation [The Moroccan university in a process of autonomisation]. Conseil supérieur de l'enseignement.

Musselin, C. (2009). Les réformes des universités en Europe: Des orientations comparables, mais des déclinaisons nationales [University reforms in Europe: Comparable orientations but national variations]. *La Revue du MAUSS, 33*(1), 69–91. DOI: 10.3917/rdm.033.0069

Musselin, C. (2024). Les réformes de l'enseignement universitaire en tensions: Le cas de la France [Tension in reforms of university teaching: The case of France]. *Sociologie et Sociétés, 56*(1–2), 99–125. https://www.erudit.org/en/journals/socsoc/2024-v56-n1-2-socsoc010374/1121157ar/abstract/. DOI: 10.7202/1121157ar

Teichler, U. (2017). Internationalisation Trends in Higher Education And the changing Role of International Student Mobility. *Journal of international Mobility*, 5(1), 177-216. https://doi.org/.DOI: 10.3917/jim.005.0179

Whitley, R., & Glaeser, J. (Ed.), & Engwall, L. (Ed.) (2010). Reconfiguring the Public Sciences: The Impact of Governance Changes on Authority and Innovation in Public Science Systems. In *Reconfiguring Knowledge Production: Changing Authority Relationships in the Sciencesand their Consequences for Intellectual Innovation* (pp. 3-47). Oxford University Press.

KEY TERMS AND DEFINITIONS

Academic Profession: The community of university-based staff whose primary missions are teaching, research, supervision and service to society. In this chapter, the academic profession is analysed as a social group whose status, autonomy and working conditions are being reshaped by reforms, managerial logics and data-driven evaluation in Moroccan public universities.

AI-Adjacent Governance: A form of governance in which evaluation and decision-making in higher education rely heavily on data infrastructures, bibliometrics and rankings that are produced by opaque computational processes, even though fully fledged AI-based HR or promotion systems are not yet in place. The chapter uses "AI-adjacent governance" to describe the current Moroccan situation, where any future AI tools will build on existing metricized regimes.

Datafication and Algorithmic Governance: Datafication refers to the systematic transformation of academic activities into digital data, while algorithmic governance denotes the use of computational systems and metrics (such as Web of Science, Scopus, Nature Index and global rankings) to evaluate performance and guide decisions. Even before explicit AI tools are deployed, Moroccan higher education is governed through these algorithmically generated indicators.

Metricization of Higher Education: The process by which complex academic activities are translated into quantitative indicators (e.g., publication counts, supervision ratios, graduation rates, rankings) that are used to monitor, compare and steer universities and individual careers. Metricization in Morocco operates at both institutional and individual levels, increasingly influencing resource allocation, evaluation and promotion.

New Public Management (NPM): A set of managerial doctrines and policy instruments that apply private-sector logics—such as performance measurement, accountability, contractualisation and competition—to public services, including universities. In Moroccan higher education, NPM is reflected in performance contracts, quality assurance mechanisms and the widespread use of indicators to steer institutions and assess their results.

Reform-Saturated Higher Education System: A university system that has undergone successive waves of reform over a long period, with new laws, programmes and statutes being layered on top of each other without sufficient consolidation. Moroccan higher education since the late 1990s is characterised as reform-saturated, creating a permanent state of change that deeply affects academic work and careers.

Teacher-Researcher: A higher education academic whose duties formally combine teaching, research, supervision, administrative responsibilities and external engagement. In Morocco, teacher-researchers are subject to specific statutory decrees that define their missions, workloads and career paths, while also assigning them an expanding range of tasks in programme design, quality assurance and partnership-building.

Voice and Exit in Academic Careers: Concepts adapted from Hirschman to analyse how academics respond to dissatisfaction. "Voice" refers to collective action and protest to change the system (e.g., strikes, union mobilisation), whereas "exit" refers to withdrawal from research, dual employment outside the university or departure from the profession. The chapter shows how Moroccan teacher-researchers combine voice and exit strategies in response to perceived injustice, low recognition and uncertain career prospects.

ENDNOTES

1 The bibliometric data in Table 2 are sourced from the **Web of Science (WoS) Core Collection**, focusing specifically on 'Articles' and 'Review Papers' to ensure cross-national consistency. While absolute volumes are shown, these figures should be interpreted within the context of the Moroccan disciplinary landscape, which includes a high proportion of faculty in non-indexed local-language humanities, unlike the more STEM-concentrated output of Malaysia.

Chapter 11
The Dialectics of Digital Transformation AI Ethics, Academic Freedom:
Policy Praxis in Indonesian Universities

Amirul Mukminin
http://orcid.org/0000-0002-6806-1315
Universitas Jambi, Indonesia

Kasinyo Harto
http://orcid.org/0009-0002-3065-6046
Universitas Islam Negeri Raden Fatah, Palembang, Indonesia

Lenny Marzulina
http://orcid.org/0000-0002-1820-0161
Universitas Islam Negeri Raden Fatah, Palembang, Indonesia

Dian Erlina
http://orcid.org/0000-0001-5319-1662
Universitas Islam Negeri Raden Fatah, Palembang, Indonesia

Rina Antasari
http://orcid.org/0000-0002-9935-8859
Universitas Islam Negeri Raden Fatah, Palembang, Indonesia

Fridiyanto Fridiyanto
UIN Sulthan Thaha Saifuddin Jambi, Jambi, Indonesia

Edi Surya Negara
http://orcid.org/0000-0002-6387-2813
Universitas Bina Darma, Indonesia

Ella Masita
http://orcid.org/0009-0004-7829-9417
Universitas Jambi, Indonesia

ABSTRACT

The chapter critically assesses the dialectics of AI integration, ethical governance, and academic freedom in higher education institutions in Indonesia. Adopting the methodology of a systematic critical qualitative review informed by the PRISMA

DOI: 10.4018/979-8-2600-3204-6.ch011

principles, the paper brings together the analytical approaches of "What's the Problem Represented to Be?" and theories of algorithmic governance, digital colonialism, and epistemic justice. As results of analysis show, AI integration entails the emergence of opaque algorithmic governance undermining epistemic independence, entrenchment of digital colonial dependency, and, most importantly, a notable gap between regulatory aspirations and reality. In this regard, there is a need for the development of Pancasila-based AI governance models, Institutional AI Ethical Review Committees vested with powers from faculties, mandatory safeguards of data sovereignty, and AI literacy programs informed by local context.

INTRODUCTION

Artificial intelligence (AI) is a highly influential force in higher education worldwide. Through posing a challenge to traditional epistemology, pedagogy, and administration of university systems, it transforms the way higher education institutions function and produce and circulate knowledge (Kosbar, 2026; Jaldemark et al., 2025). In Indonesia, as elsewhere, there has been increasing attention toward the application of AI in various facets of academic work – from research to education and administrative activities (Haetami, 2025). This practice entails a dialectic of two equally vital aspects: the need for institutions to undergo digital transformation in response to changes on the world stage and preservation of epistemic autonomy needed for research. The paper provides an analysis of the relationship between these aspects of AI adoption within the Indonesian higher education system.

In recent years, there has been rapid growth in the literature on AI adoption in higher education (Holmes et al., 2022; Kosbar, 2026). On the one hand, AI is viewed as a tool that can promote learning opportunities by customizing individual academic journeys, performing administrative tasks, conducting research, and disseminating knowledge in underprivileged areas (Haetami, 2025; Ojha et al., 2024). On the other hand, scholars are increasingly concerned about issues such as biased algorithms, AI-based surveillance of students' behavior, violations of privacy, a lack of human judgment in academic processes, and the promotion of inequality (AAUP, 2025; Bozkurt et al., 2021). While this problem applies universally, the situation in Global South countries is even more pressing, since the institutional, regulatory, and epistemological infrastructure needed to address such problems as AI adoption in higher education is largely absent (Ahmed, 2026; Haetami, 2025).

The Indonesian case can be analyzed from several interesting angles, with strong arguments supporting this approach. First, as of now, the country boasts one of the largest higher education systems in Southeast Asia, including 4,586 institutions, with 953 offering courses related to AI or machine learning (UNESCO, 2024). Second, in 2023 alone, Indonesian scientists managed to publish 25,000 articles connected to AI, proving the significance of the problem under discussion (UNESCO, 2024). Lastly, there is a huge deficiency of IT specialists in the country – according to projections, in 2030, it will need to employ another 9 million workers in the sector (UNESCO, 2024)

One of the major steps toward regulating AI taken by the Government of Indonesia is the promulgation of Circular Letter No. 9/2023 on AI Ethical Guidelines by the Ministry of Communication and Informatics (KOMINFO) in December 2023 (HBT Law, 2024). Thus, according to the above guideline, the use of AI as the sole decision-making criterion regarding human welfare is prohibited, and it is to be used only in cases that do not entail racism or potential harm (HBT Law, 2024). The emergence of the above regulation was accompanied by another significant development. In 2024, UNESCO launched the AI Readiness Assessment Methodology for Indonesia, conducted in collaboration with KOMINFO, to assess the country's readiness to deploy AI responsibly across legal, socio-cultural, economic, scientific, and technical dimensions (UNESCO, 2024). At the same time, it is important to note that UNESCO's Recommendation on the Ethics of Artificial Intelligence, approved by 194 member states, including Indonesia, in November 2021, represents the normative international framework against which the national regulations on AI governance in Indonesia must be judged (UNESCO, 2023). While these initiatives represent an important step in AI governance, the relationship between the existing regulatory framework and its institutional practice has yet to be explored in the context of Indonesian higher education institutions.

Institutionally, Indonesian universities have failed to adopt a comprehensive approach to AI governance. For instance, recent research indicates that although numerous guidance documents have emerged regarding AI governance among major US-based research universities, fewer than one-quarter of faculty and staff are familiar with institutional AI policies (Robert, 2024; Wu et al., 2024). This governance problem is particularly relevant in the context of Southeast Asian higher education institutions, where the lack of standardized regulations, poor digital infrastructure, and the low levels of AI literacy among academics contribute to the uncritical acceptance of AI technology (Haetami, 2025). Importantly, the failure to adopt adequate governance measures has a negative impact not only on the management of AI systems but on the core of the university itself – the epistemic autonomy of its members. By making decisions about research workflow management, assessment, and knowledge generation using AI systems without transparent governance, the independence of scholars is at stake.

A key aspect that contributes to the above concern involves what scholars have referred to as algorithmic governance – an aspect of AI that refers to the process whereby the system makes, influences, or constrains certain decisions in ways that are non-transparent and difficult to contest by the individuals concerned (AAUP, 2025; Azevedo et al., 2025). Within the higher education environment, algorithmic governance can be observed in several dimensions, including admission screening that reproduces existing social inequalities; predictive algorithms that track, profile, and surveil both students and scholars compromising their privacy and consent; plagiarism detection systems that ignore culturally specific writing traditions; and research evaluation metrics based on algorithmically curated databases dominated by the Global North's publication practices (AAUP, 2025; Ahmed, 2026). Particularly for Indonesian universities, this problem is exacerbated by the structural aspects of digital colonialism, including the monopolization of AI technology and training data, as well as control over algorithmic governance by Global North countries (Ahmed, 2026; Couldry & Mejias, 2019).

First of all, the notion of digital colonialism offers a powerful theoretical tool to address this challenge. Indeed, recent literature has shown that universities located in the countries of the Global South increasingly depend on proprietary algorithms and software provided by major corporations of the Global North to perform plagiarism detection tests, engage in research analytics and manage cloud-based learning management systems (Ahmed, 2026). The use of proprietary systems raises a number of concerns regarding algorithmic governance and digital colonialism, as these systems are designed, trained, and managed by entities operating outside the country's legal jurisdiction (Ahmed, 2026). As a result, researchers and educators face the risk of epistemic injustice—systematic distortions of knowledge production and dissemination associated with their reliance on the Westernized epistemological conventions (Arora et al., 2023; Ahmed, 2026). Consequently, adopting proprietary algorithms threatens the research independence of Indonesian universities seeking to develop a distinct research agenda grounded in Pancasila values and Islamic educational philosophy.

It would be premature to consider reactionary approaches to AI use in Indonesian higher education that might ignore the benefits of enhancing the learning process and facilitating research. There are numerous issues affecting Indonesian higher education, and AI technology could help resolve them. First of all, the amount of money allocated to scientific research is rather low, at only 0.2% of GDP, compared with the worldwide average of 2% (UNESCO, 2024; Haetami, 2025). Second, Indonesia experiences significant inequality in access to education and in the quality of education across regions of the archipelago, while the development of digital competencies among both students and faculty members is required to support the country's economic growth (Haetami, 2025; Kosbar, 2026). Hence, the application of AI technologies, especially when used responsibly and effectively managed, might facilitate adaptive learning, enable AI-powered research, and lessen the burden of administration.

A dialectical analysis is crucial for finding a balance between the positive and negative perspectives on AI and developing potential approaches to it. To employ the dialectic method, it is necessary to determine the thesis, antithesis, and synthesis of the problem under discussion. According to the principles of Hegelian philosophy, critical theory, and the philosophy of education, the thesis (optimism regarding technology) and the antithesis (resistance to ethics) are two polarized viewpoints on AI in education (Hall, 2021; Jaldemark et al., 2025). Technological optimism implies that AI will bring progress to education, whereas ethical resistance warns about its potential risks and promotes ethical approaches to implementing the technology. Therefore, it is expected that the synthesis of these positions will provide an institutional framework to ensure compliance with Indonesian educational values and global research standards, and that research and academic freedom must be guaranteed within the suggested governance structure.

Based on the literature review presented above, it is clear that there is a considerable research gap regarding AI integration in Indonesian universities. Although a large body of scholarship has been published on AI technology in education, most research focuses on technological implementation and student outcomes, while ethical issues receive relatively little attention (Holmes et al., 2022; Kosbar, 2026; Jaldemark et al., 2025). Even though Indonesian scholarship discusses some general issues, such as faculty members' attitudes towards AI (Sariyasa & Monika, 2023), existing frameworks for ethical AI usage (Syaidina et al., 2024), or comparative studies of educational policy regarding AI technology (HBT Law, 2024; UNESCO, 2024), there has been no attempt to elaborate a theoretical framework for AI governance in relation to research autonomy. This gap is addressed in this paper. There is an evident need to explore the issue in greater detail, given the following trends in higher education policies. First, the number of AI solutions being adopted at Indonesian universities continues to grow, yet governance arrangements that ensure academic freedom have not been established (Robert, 2024; AAUP, 2025). Second, despite significant progress in AI regulation by the government, gaps between national and university policies persist (HBT Law, 2024). In other words, the ethical principles formulated in KOMINFO's Circular Letter No. 9/2023 and UNESCO's Recommendation might fail to operate in practice (KOMINFO, 2023; UNESCO, 2024). Third, there are numerous risks in adopting AI solutions without establishing proper control over them, as demonstrated by recent literature on algorithmic governance and digital colonialism (Ahmed, 2026; Arora et al., 2023). Finally, Indonesian universities are in a unique position to develop innovative models of integrating AI systems that align with Pancasila values and Islamic educational philosophy.

The paper makes three main contributions to the scholarship on AI, ethics, and higher education governance. First, it provides a detailed dialectical framework tailored to analyze the problems faced by Indonesian universities in the field of AI integration. Based on theories of critical philosophy and philosophy of education and the analysis of empirical data, it defines the three core dimensions (technological optimism, ethical resistance, and policy praxis) in relation to which the problem can be considered. Second, it outlines risks associated with algorithmic governance for academic freedom, paying special attention to the dimensions of data sovereignty, epistemic justice, and cultural responsiveness. Third, it suggests concrete policy recommendations that could help establish effective governance frameworks that promote academic freedom. The paper is structured as follows. Literature review analyzes the existing scholarship devoted to AI ethics in higher education, algorithmic governance, digital colonialism, and Indonesian educational policy. The conceptual framework introduces the dialectical methodology and discusses the dimensions along which the analysis is carried out. Analysis section explores current AI adoption and governance practices in Indonesian universities in the light of the established dialectical framework, highlighting both advantages and disadvantages. The discussion section synthesizes the analysis and provides a list of policy recommendations. Conclusion outlines philosophical implications of the paper's findings. Four research questions guide this inquiry:

> RQ1: In what ways does the current adoption of AI technologies in Indonesian universities generate forms of algorithmic governance that threaten the epistemic autonomy and research freedom of scholars?
> RQ2: How do the dynamics of digital colonialism and data sovereignty shape the ethical risks of AI integration for Indonesian higher education institutions operating within a Global South context?
> RQ3: What policy frameworks and institutional governance structures are required to establish ethically grounded AI integration in Indonesian universities that protect research autonomy while enabling educational innovation?
> RQ4: How can Indonesian universities draw on Pancasila values, Islamic educational philosophy, and indigenous pedagogical traditions to develop alternative models of AI governance that resist both technological determinism and epistemic subordination?

Algorithmic Governance and the Threat to Epistemic Autonomy in Indonesian Universities

The swift integration of artificial intelligence technologies into Indonesian tertiary education organizations has sparked a considerable body of academic literature not only about the efficiency of digitalization per se but also about the governance hazards inherent in the process. As Indonesian universities continue to adopt AI solutions for administrative management, research quality assessment, academic misconduct detection, and student performance analysis, an important but rarely considered issue arises: how does the integration of these technologies lead to forms of algorithmic governance that undermine researchers' autonomy and freedom? Algorithmic governance, defined as the ability of AI algorithms to influence, guide, or steer institutional decisions and researcher behavior in one way or another, presents a structural challenge to the fundamental tenets of academic life including independence, transparency, and freedom of intellect (Ahmed, 2026; AAUP, 2025). The current paper will consider five interrelated issues that are likely to cause algorithmic governance of scholars in Indonesian universities by the adoption of AI technologies.

Opacity and the Erosion of Scholarly Accountability

The core problem associated with the use of AI in universities in Indonesia is that of the opacity of AI decision-making mechanisms. When applying AI to research evaluation, grant evaluation, or checking the level of academic integrity, the criteria used for calculations, the weights assigned to these factors, and the logic behind these calculations remain unclear to the scholars (Azevedo et al., 2025; Wu et al., 2024). Such opaqueness leads to an epistemic injustice whereby the subject of evaluation does not have any way to challenge the decisions made about him/her and his/her research and professional performance (Ahmed, 2026; Kay et al., 2024).

In particular, the application of this type of opaqueness to the Indonesian situation makes it clear that there is an ethical issue with using AI in research and scholarship because this practice may be seen as another example of epistemic imperialism whereby certain standards and values prevail while others remain undervalued (UNESCO, 2026). When Indonesian research is evaluated on the basis of algorithms that operate on indexing databases following Western academic publishing norms and criteria, scholars in the country have limited means to challenge these rules as part of the ranking in SINTA. As stated in AAUP's (2025) report on AI and the professions, the adoption of AI in scholarly pursuits poses significant ethical challenges related to intellectual property, professional autonomy, and working conditions that influence research performance. It should be noted that the problems arise even more significantly when AI software is commercialized and developed by corporations operating in countries other than Indonesia.

Algorithmic Bias in Research Evaluation and Academic Integrity Monitoring

Another dimension is related to the pervasive risks of biases in AI systems used for assessing researchers' contributions as well as monitoring the integrity of their activities. Plagiarism checking tools using the algorithms that have been extensively employed at Indonesian universities after licensing programs such as Turnitin use training data sets containing primarily texts written in English language and according to the academic conventions prevailing in the West (Ahmed, 2026). It has been demonstrated in research that such software produces false-positive results much more frequently when dealing with non-English speaking authors or scholars whose rhetoric and style of citation differ from what is represented in the training set of data (Ahmed, 2026; Baker et al., 2022; Haetami, 2025). As a result, academic work written by Indonesian researchers in Indonesian or Javanese, or employing an indigenous style of rhetoric, can easily be classified by such AI tool as plagiarized, which constitutes a case of algorithmic discrimination detrimental to researchers' reputations.

This issue does not solely pertain to plagiarism detection. Various empirical studies focusing on assessing the performance of AI systems designed for grading, recommending actions and analyzing scholarly works across universities in Global South show that those tools produce worse results when employed to assess research conducted by authors representing the region (Ahmed, 2026; Haetami, 2025). Studies focused specifically on the case of Indonesian adoption of AI systems in higher education prove that AI tools developed for a specific country can lead to learning and assessment practices which are inapplicable in the context of linguistically diverse and resource-limited regions (Haetami, 2025). As a consequence, AI-mediated assessments of scholarly work contribute to the imposition of certain epistemological biases rather than provide an objective measure of a researcher's merit.

Algorithmic Surveillance and the Chilling of Intellectual Inquiry

In addition, another aspect through which AI integration threatens academic epistemological independence in Indonesian institutions pertains to the use of surveillance technologies for overseeing intellectual activity, including learning processes, research work, and other scholarly behaviors. The introduction of learning analytics software, AI-enabled library management software, and automatic monitoring of research works allows creating detailed personal profiles of each researcher's reading interests, research activities, and scholarly contacts—information that may pose a danger to intellectual freedom if available to university administration without proper governance structures (Azevedo et al., 2025; AAUP, 2025). In its investigation into predictive algorithms, higher education has found out that profiling and predicting academic activities poses a significant threat to scholars' trust in technology and freedom to think innovatively (Azevedo et al., 2025).

This aspect is particularly important within the Indonesian context, since the lack of comprehensive data protection laws covering higher education leaves room for unrestricted expansion of monitoring practices enabled through the use of AI. Indonesia's KOMINFO Circular Letter No. 9/2023 on AI Ethical Guidelines emphasizes that an AI system cannot be relied upon as the sole determinant in decision-making on matters that influence human well-being (HBT Law, 2024); yet, this requirement applies only to decisions themselves, rather than to the ways in which humans behave. Being aware of the fact that one's digital behavior is being constantly monitored and algorithmically analyzed would lead to an intellectual limitation—the result of internal censorship rather than an openly stated prohibitive policy. As noted in the AAUP 2025 report, monitoring scholarly activities by means of surveillance technologies without clear policies and control mechanisms violates principles of academic freedom (AAUP, 2025).

Epistemic Dependency and Digital Colonialism in Indonesian Research Infrastructure

Finally, there exists another dimension which refers to the epistemologies of AI use that emerge out of structural dependence of Indonesian universities on proprietary systems developed and owned by corporations in the Global North. As more and more universities across the Global South rely upon the AI-based infrastructure, such as plagiarism-detection systems, research analytics databases, and cloud-based management software, the designs of which as well as training data they have been using and governance models underpinning the systems correspond to the epistemological priorities of corporations and/or states behind them (Ahmed, 2026; Arora et al., 2023). Therefore, reliance on these systems may be viewed as yet another manifestation of digital colonialism as the concentration of ownership rights to key AI infrastructure among a limited number of actors from the Global North (Ahmed, 2026; Arora et al., 2023).

In the case of Indonesian institutions of higher learning, these dependencies manifest themselves in the following way. Scopus and Web of Science, which serve as the foundation of the national ranking system known as SINTA, value English language publications and Western academic disciplines, thus discriminating against local language literature and research programs that address regional issues. Analysis of dynamics of integration of AI into the practice of Indonesian higher education identifies the lack of standardization and localized development of the technology as critical factors contributing to inequality in the implementation process (Helmiatin et al., 2024). According to the UNESCO country profile on the ethics and governance of AI, curriculum study finds that imported materials cannot meet the demands of indigenous epistemology (UNESCO, 2026). Therefore, when the AI-driven infrastructure for research assessment, dissemination, and communication matches an epistemology other than that used in Indonesia, this creates a situation where knowledge generation is determined by algorithms alien to Indonesian scholarship.

The Governance Gap: Policy Aspiration Versus Institutional Practice

A fifth point pertains to the large discrepancy between Indonesia's policy commitments regarding ethical AI governance and the actual state of affairs at Indonesian universities. Even after the issuing of KOMINFO Circular Letter No. 9/2023 and the adoption of UNESCO Recommendation on the Ethics of Artificial Intelligence in 2021, the literature on AI use among Indonesian public universities continues to demonstrate a complete absence of any policy regulating the use of AI in research, assessment, and teaching (Helmiatin et al., 2024; UNESCO, 2026). As such a phenomenon is characteristic for global higher education trends more widely, the absence of policies at Indonesian institutions has been confirmed through EDUCAUSE's AI Landscape Survey, according to which, while 80% of all faculty and academic staff make use of AI tools in their work, only 21% report awareness of AI policy at their institutions (Robert, 2024). Additionally, it appears that due to the limited regulation enforcement abilities in Indonesia, along with the fragmented governance structure of Indonesian higher education institutions, it will be extremely difficult to implement such policies at universities.

This lack of institutional policy concerning the use of AI poses very serious risks to research freedom in practice. Indeed, without any formal regulations, academics do not have a way of contesting algorithmically made decisions regarding their research impact, publication activity, and overall academic performance (Azevedo et al., 2025; Wu et al., 2024). Research on AI governance in the Asian context confirms the absence of policies that would include relevant stakeholders (non-academic employees, in particular, as well as the existence of policy gaps pertaining to the use of evidence-based approaches. Consequently, Indonesian scholars face the threat of their research freedoms being affected by algorithmic decision-making, as the lack of governance framework prevents any possibility of addressing such issues effectively.

In conclusion, it may be suggested that AI adoption in Indonesian universities leads to the formation of several types of algorithmic governance that threaten epistemic autonomy and research freedom by means of five interrelated phenomena: lack of transparency in algorithmic decision-making processes; systematic bias of AI against non-Western languages and rhetorical traditions; scholarly surveillance under conditions of AI governance; epistemic dependencies resulting from dependence on Global North AI infrastructures; and the substantial difference between the Indonesian policy approach to AI ethics and the reality of its implementation. Clearly, overcoming the problem at hand necessitates a more proactive approach to formulating effective and institutionally enforceable policy that protects researchers' autonomy, ensures transparency of algorithms used, and promotes the development of locally appropriate AI technology.

DIGITAL COLONIALISM, DATA SOVEREIGNTY, AND THE ETHICAL RISKS OF AI INTEGRATION IN INDONESIAN HIGHER EDUCATION

The implementation of AI at the higher education institutions in Indonesia does not happen independently of the geopolitical circumstances. Rather, it happens against the backdrop of the unevenness and imbalance characteristic of the global digital order, which can be explored through the prism of the phenomenon of digital colonialism (Couldry & Mejias, 2019; Ahmed, 2026). In the case of Indonesian higher education institutions working in a Global South context, the ethical risks associated with the deployment of AI cannot be viewed in isolation from the larger context of digital colonialism and data sovereignty. Specifically, the domination of a small number of Global North companies and governments over the infrastructure and governance of AI as well as training datasets creates dependencies and epistemic subordination of those countries to the Global North actors, making the exercise of scholarly autonomy impossible. In this context, four interrelated dimensions of digital colonialism and data sovereignty emerge that affect the ethical risks of adopting AI in higher education institutions of Indonesia: infrastructural dependency and data extraction, the undermining of data sovereignty under Indonesian law, epistemic colonialism, and governance colonialism due to the importation of an external AI ethics framework.

Infrastructural Dependency and the Dynamics of Digital Colonialism

Digital colonialism refers to the process in which corporations based in the Global North monopolize critical infrastructure used for cloud computing, artificial intelligence technology, data storage and training, and academic databases utilized by universities throughout the world (Couldry & Mejias, 2019; Ahmed, 2026). Researchers, analyzing examples in Africa, Asia, and Latin America, show that digital platforms exploit people from the Global South in the same ways that colonial powers did, by gathering their data, passing it through infrastructure owned by Northern corporations and then analyzing it using algorithms biased toward Northern culture, with most benefits accruing to Global North companies and investors (Kwet, 2019; Bujnowska et al., 2026).

Indonesia's educational sector falls victim to the global structure of digital colonialism. Research analysis services are provided to Indonesian universities by such proprietary services as Elsevier's Scopus and Clarivate's Web of Science. Detection of plagiarism at Indonesian universities is carried out with the help of the software developed by Advance Publications, which operates in the United States. Cloud services for the management of Indonesian learning courses are provided mainly by Google and Microsoft (Ahmed, 2026). In all these cases, the use of corporate tools results in the export of data about the research work, scholarly publications, and intellectual practices of Indonesian scientists to corporations that operate within jurisdictions where Indonesian data protection regulations do not apply. Indonesia's share of visits to websites providing access to AI technologies was 1.4 billion in 2022-2023, which puts the country in third place in the global ranking (Helmiatin et al., 2024); however, most of the profit generated by these visits remains with foreign businesses. It illustrates the educational sphere's involvement in what is known as data colonialism – a new form of colonial exploitation of data resources (Couldry & Mejias, 2019; Bujnowska et al., 2026).

Data Sovereignty and the Limits of Indonesian Legal Protection

The issue of data sovereignty, namely the right of a country and its citizens to manage data originating from that country in terms of their collection, storage, processing, and transfer across borders, has become the focus of interest of many countries in the Global South in light of their growing reliance on AI technologies (Ahmed, 2026; Bujnowska et al., 2026). Among the most notable measures aimed at the implementation of a national data sovereignty framework is the recent introduction of the Law No. 27 of 2022 on Personal Data Protection (PDP Law) in Indonesia. Taking inspiration from the EU General Data Protection Regulation (GDPR), the PDP Law has put forward comprehensive requirements for all stages of data management and mandated the establishment of a body of national data protection (ICLG, 2025). In compliance with its provisions, this legislation will come into full effect on 17 October 2024, having gone through two years of transition period.

Despite its numerous benefits for the data sovereignty of the country, the applicability of the PDP Law to AI systems used in Indonesian universities remains practically unexplored. First of all, by 2025 Indonesia still lacked its own functional data protection body, and its regulations were under final drafting (ICLG, 2025). Therefore, the use of AI by universities does not fall under any official regulatory oversight at the moment, which implies that transfers of students' and researchers' personal data to foreign AI providers can occur without following the procedures mandated by the PDP Law. At the same time, such lack of regulatory oversight is critical in the field of higher education, in which the use of AI in learning analytics, academic monitoring tools, and libraries generates a large amount of data that are transferred abroad according to the terms of service drafted unilaterally by companies in the Global North. Researchers noted that the inability to enforce data protection regulations leaves personal data vulnerable to the exploitation of external actors and prevents countries from managing their digital resources independently (Akinyetun, 2023; Ahmed, 2026).

Epistemic Colonialism and the Marginalization of Indonesian Knowledge Systems

In addition to the legal and infrastructural components of digital colonialism, the use of AI at Indonesian universities raises the issue of epistemic colonialism, defined as the use of AI algorithms to privilege the knowledge system developed in the West through the selection of datasets, languages, writing styles, and other cultural indicators (Zembylas, 2023; Nemorin, 2024). AI-driven systems used at Indonesian universities for research evaluation, academic integrity management, language assessment, and scholarly recommendations are designed based on English-language datasets and Western writing and research traditions (Ahmed, 2026). As such, when Indonesian scholars' work is being evaluated using these systems, they become subject to epistemic governance that determines the boundaries of what counts as valid research according to criteria foreign to the scholars who submit their papers.

Empirical studies conducted in Indian and Brazilian contexts confirm that AI-driven translation, grading, and recommendations systems fail to deliver their promised functionality when applied to local languages, cultures, and rhetorical traditions (Ahmed, 2026). Research on AI in Indonesian educational context also reveals the persistent mismatch between AI content and Indonesian pedagogy and ethics, represented in the concepts of gotong royong, keadilan sosial, and Bhinneka Tunggal Ika which constitute the core of Indonesian pedagogical culture (Raharjo & Rohmadi, 2025; Wong-A-Foe, 2023). The mismatch between AI and pedagogy is not only a technical problem; it becomes an ethical problem as well because it results in epistemic injustice whereby the scholarship created by Indonesian researchers is consistently undervalued due to lack of relevant criteria in the algorithm (Zembylas, 2023; Sakhiyya & Mulya, 2023).

Furthermore, epistemic colonial practices associated with AI use at Indonesian universities are enabled by the existing research evaluation framework in which academic promotion and scholarly legitimacy depend on publication in journals indexed by Scopus and Web of Science – two databases dominated by Global North scholarship published in English (Adiprasetio, 2025; Sakhiyya & Mulya, 2023). Consequently, when AI-driven analytics apply the content of these databases as the basis for evaluation, a structural invisibility of Indonesian-language scholarship, locally oriented research, and interdisciplinarity enriched by Islamics is perpetuated (Zembylas, 2023; Ahmed, 2026). Scholars claim that such processes reproduce epistemic hierarchies in which global academic norms are defined by Western knowledge systems whereas alternative epistemologies are silenced or annihilated (epistemicide, per Santos, 2014).

Governance Colonialism and the Uncritical Importation of AI Ethics Frameworks

Another facet of digital colonialism that poses a threat to Indonesian higher education is governance colonialism, wherein developing countries adopt AI ethics, laws, and policies created in the West without considering the particular realities of those countries' environments and ethical issues specific to their national contexts (Ahmed, 2026; Zembylas, 2023). Both the United Nations Recommendation on the Ethics of Artificial Intelligence (2021) and the Principles on AI by the Organisation for Economic Co-operation and Development (2019) provide detailed normative guidance; however, these frameworks are largely based on European individualistic philosophy centered around liberalism and openness. Although there is nothing intrinsically incompatible about these philosophies and Indonesian educational ideology, the norms do not fully integrate the collective-oriented and religion-based values of Indonesia's Islamic education, which follows the principles of Pancasila philosophy (Wong-A-Foe, 2023; Udah, 2024).

This ethical dilemma is exacerbated by the processes that have been referred to as the 'ethical colony' dilemma: the necessity faced by developing countries to align themselves with foreign governance standards, possibly inconsistent with the socio-political context and research priorities in question, in order to maintain credibility and ensure access to research funds (Zhu et al., 2025). In particular, Indonesian Islamic universities—constitutionally defined through Pancasila values, and philosophically formed in the spirit of Nahdlatul Ulama and Muhammadiyah—adopting an AI ethics framework based on the secular liberal tradition runs the risk of establishing an approach to AI ethics governance misaligned with the very ethos of the university. Academics argue that in the Global South educational setting, frameworks for AI ethics governance should be developed alongside local communities and embedded in indigenous epistemologies, resistant to colonization by foreign governance models (Zembylas, 2023; Udah, 2024; Nemorin, 2024).

Dynamics associated with digital colonialism and data sovereignty govern the ethical risks arising from the incorporation of AI into Indonesian universities in four interrelated domains: (1) structural reliance on AI infrastructure developed in the Global North, which allows for exploitative practices involving the extraction of data; (2) inadequate provisions in the current Indonesian legal system for addressing issues related to the regulation of transborder data flows enabled through the use of AI; (3) epistemic colonial implications of AI systems used in Indonesian universities that exclude Indonesian languages, traditions, and scholarship; and (4) colonial-originated governance issues leading to the uncritical implementation of an AI ethics framework incompatible with Indonesian educational principles. It is crucial to adopt a governance strategy capable of supporting data sovereignty, epistemic diversity, and rootedness in philosophical and cultural resources of Indonesia. The development of research data infrastructure under local control, building Indonesian-language AI systems based on culturally relevant datasets, and creating AI ethics governance frameworks in collaboration with the Indonesian academic community and Islamic and indigenous educational systems would enable the overcoming of existing risks. Otherwise, the introduction of AI technologies will result in the reinforcement rather than deconstruction of colonial hierarchy that hindered the autonomous evolution of Indonesian universities.

Policy Frameworks and Institutional Governance for Ethically Grounded AI Integration in Indonesian Universities

The problem of what kinds of policies and governance regimes must be implemented to achieve an ethical implementation of AI into Indonesian universities is one that straddles the gap between the aspirations of national regulations, the capabilities of institutions, and the philosophical foundation that lies at the heart of Indonesian higher education systems. While Indonesian universities do not simply adopt global AI trends by chance, rather being active agencies that can choose how to incorporate these trends into their operations, the fact remains that poor governance could result in research freedom being compromised through unethical implementation of AI. This has been proven through current literature in that the failure to create effective governance regimes could lead to a situation in which university integrity and even public faith in leadership are harmed (Azevedo et al., 2025; Wu et al., 2024). At the same time, however, restrictive and externally-imposed governance could hinder the educational innovation that is possible with AI (Chan, 2023; Georgieva & Stuart, 2025). The proposed solution offers six such dimensions of governance.

A Nationally Coordinated, Pancasila-Grounded Policy Foundation

A crucial precondition for an ethical approach to the governance of AI systems in Indonesian universities is the creation of a unified policy framework at the national level, which would turn Indonesia's current AI regulatory regime into concrete institutional commitments related to higher education. The National Strategy for Artificial Intelligence 2020–2045 (Stranas KA) of Indonesia recognizes ethics and policy as one of the five strategic pillars and stipulates the mandatory alignment of all AI innovations with the values of Pancasila and Indonesia's Constitution of 1945, specifically highlighting the importance of inclusivity, human dignity, social justice, and national sovereignty (Digital Watch Observatory, 2024). Moreover, KOMINFO's Circular Letter No. 9/2023 on AI Ethical Guidelines identifies the key AI-related principles, including those of inclusivity, transparency, credibility, and accountability, applicable to all sectors of economy, including education (HBT Law, 2024). However, research into the current state of AI governance implementation in Indonesia indicates that there is an important gap between the above-named normative framework and actual institutional practice due to overlapping ministerial jurisdictions, low enforcement capacity, and lack of relevant technical standards, e.g., algorithmic auditing (Wadipalapa et al., 2024).

However, the problem described above could be resolved by setting clear guidelines for the implementation of AI in institutions of higher learning at the Ministry of Education, Culture, Research, and Technology (Kemendikbudristek) level according to the stipulations found in Stranas KA and Circular Letter No. 9/2023. Such guidelines will require Indonesian institutions of higher learning to develop an official statement on AI informed by the core values of Pancasila such as gotong royong, keadilan sosial, and Bhinneka Tunggal Ika. This AI statement needs to outline the AI applications in the institution and its data management system along with means of compensation for scholars whose work is conducted using AI research (Inayah et al., 2025; UNESCO, 2023). According to recent research in the field of AI governance among Indonesian higher learning institutions, having an official statement based on core values is an excellent starting point for effective operational governance (Smith et al., 2025).

Institutional AI Ethical Review Boards with Faculty Governance Authority

The next necessary aspect of effective university governance concerning AI is the creation of AI Ethical Review Boards (AIERBs) at Indonesian universities, which must follow the model of shared governance designed to protect researchers' autonomy. Evidence from research universities around the world has shown that AI governance works best when it is supported by an institutional committee composed of academic leaders, representative of the faculty members, research ethics officers, legal advisors, IT experts, and representatives of the students rather than delegated to administrative offices or the IT department (Georgieva & Stuart, 2025; Wu et al., 2024). Indeed, EDUCAUSE's survey of 2024 indicated that institutions with proper governance structures were much more capable of creating credible and enforceable AI policies compared to the institutions where AI was handled ad-hoc without formal frameworks in place (Robert, 2024).

Several key functions can be attributed to the AIERBs, and each is relevant to protecting researcher autonomy. First, the boards can be used as a venue of discussion where researchers can oppose any algorithmic decision made about their research productivity, publication record, and institutional performance. Second, procurement and implementation of AI tools can be governed to ensure that any platform used by the university, whether a plagiarism detection system, a research analytics system, or administrative AI, is reviewed to rule out algorithmic bias and data sovereignty issues and that it aligns with the institution's values. Third, feedback mechanisms for addressing academic freedom concerns caused by AI use can be implemented. In particular, a study of generative AI governance conducted at Universitas Pelita Harapan (Indonesia) demonstrated strong support among students for implementing ethical governance structures for AI usage in the university (Barus et al., 2025).

Enforceable Data Governance and Sovereignty Protections

The third governance requirement is in relation to the implementation of data sovereignty provisions through institutions' AI governance framework. Under the Personal Data Protection Law No. 27 of 2022 (PDP Law), Indonesia has established strict rules governing the collecting, processing, and transferring of personal data including AI-assisted academic data (ICLG, 2025). Nonetheless, according to legal analysis, implementing regulations under the Personal Data Protection Law are yet to be finalized, and Indonesia's national data protection agency has yet to fully develop its capability (ICLG, 2025; Law Asia, 2025). In this respect, institutions adopting an AI-powered platform from countries outside of the Global South, such as Turnitin or Scopus, will essentially export the research work of Indonesian scholars to a country whose data protection regulation is ineffective in protecting the same scholars.

Hence, Indonesian universities need to formulate their data governance mechanisms irrespective of the state of the national implementation mechanism. These must involve the following elements: conducting DPIAs before rolling out any AI system capable of collecting and processing scholar or student data; requiring that AI platform providers respect cross-border transfer restrictions; clearly establishing data minimization and purpose limitation principles; allowing scholar access to and challenge against any algorithmically processed data held against them; and having procurement policies that favor AI tools based out of Indonesia or the region

(Haetami, 2025; Ahmed, 2026). The ASEAN Guide on AI Governance and Ethics provides a regionally informed guide that universities in Indonesia may consult.

AI Literacy, Capacity Building, and Critical Pedagogy

The fourth governance condition relates to the human element of integration with AI, referring specifically to a systematic cultivation of critical literacy of AI amongst Indonesian academics, administration, and students, in addition to technical knowledge skills. Studies have revealed that governance structures remain deficient when the academic community is not literate enough to be able to understand algorithmic threats and recognize the need for AI governance in order to participate constructively in policy-making efforts (Azevedo et al., 2025; Borenstein & Howard, 2021). A study carried out in 2025 by MDPI on AI governance in higher education revealed that knowledge-focused leadership is strongly correlated with stronger and more active governance culture amongst institutions that consider AI to be an object of critical discussion as opposed to merely a tool of increased efficiency (Oncioiu & Bularca, 2025).

For Indonesian universities, the implementation of such programs will require contextualization and alignment with the philosophy of Pancasila. A UNESCO training program on AI governance for academics held at Universitas Gadjah Mada in collaboration with UNESCO Jakarta in 2023 showed that capacity building exercises which address global principles of AI ethics in light of the Pancasila philosophy are institutionally appropriate and effectively cultivate critical AI literacy amongst Indonesian lecturers (UNESCO, 2023). A scholarly discussion on the concept of Pancasila ethics and AI shows that the introduction of an academic curriculum which considers moral value and principles of AI ethics, including but not limited to benefits, fairness, autonomy, responsibility, and explainability, can help increase the capacity for moral criticism of algorithmic systems within Indonesia's institutional setting (Inayah et al., 2025; Daffana, 2024).

Adaptive, Participatory Governance Through Continuous Review

The fifth aspect of AI governance highlights the inherent dynamics of AI technology and the associated need for flexible and adaptive governance mechanisms. According to global findings regarding policies in higher education, governance mechanisms without review, faculty engagement, and impact assessments will quickly become redundant and obsolete (Chan, 2023; Smith et al., 2025). Among the best practices in AI governance include an annual audit of deployed AI applications, faculty/student surveys on AI governance, regular quarterly reviews of vendor relations, and constant monitoring of high-risk applications (Robert, 2024; Georgieva

& Stuart, 2025). In addition, findings regarding the decentralized approach to AI governance in Indonesia reveal the problem of the mismatch between the central government's goals and institutional capacity, indicating the need for continuous stakeholder consultation in order to effectively implement AI governance (Wadipalapa et al., 2024).

In addition, the implementation of adaptive participatory AI governance in the Indonesian Islamic university setting would require engaging Islamic scholars, indigenous epistemology, and other stakeholders who do not have significant representation in global AI governance discourses. In this context, the vision outlined in the Stranas KA 2020–2045 of collaboration among government, academia, business, and civil society organizations is highly significant because it gives national legitimacy to stakeholder-driven and multi-level governance of AI technology (Digital Watch Observatory, 2024). To actualize the vision, Indonesian universities need to adopt participatory approaches to governance and see it as an ongoing dialogue on the values, risks, and opportunities related to AI deployment within their institutions.

Five governance dimensions should be simultaneously activated to achieve ethically sound AI integration in Indonesian higher education institutions: national governance frameworks based on the Pancasila principles and translating Indonesia's AI regulation into institutional practices; Institutional AI Ethical Review Boards that support shared governance and research freedom through the deliberative approach to ethical evaluation; enforceable data governance mechanisms translating Indonesia's Personal Data Protection law into concrete institutional governance measures before the establishment of the national infrastructure of enforcement; institution-specific AI literacy programs allowing academic communities to reflect on the ethical issues; and participatory adaptive mechanisms to ensure ongoing accountability.

PANCASILA, ISLAMIC EDUCATIONAL PHILOSOPHY, AND INDIGENOUS PEDAGOGICAL TRADITIONS AS FOUNDATIONS FOR ALTERNATIVE AI GOVERNANCE IN INDONESIAN UNIVERSITIES

The international discourse on AI governance in higher education institutions has been dominated by the frameworks from Western liberal philosophical traditions, such as UNESCO's Recommendation on the Ethics of Artificial Intelligence (2021), OECD AI Principles (2019), and the European Union's AI Act (2024). Although there are some valuable normative guidelines provided in those frameworks, implementing them in the context of Indonesian universities would be an act of governance colonialism, where the application of ethical norms developed in other contexts might not necessarily resonate with the country's unique philosophical, religious, and cultural tradition (Ahmed, 2026; Zembylas, 2023). The purpose of the analysis is to suggest that Indonesian universities have enough resources in indigenous philosophical thought (Pancasila) and local knowledge to come up with the alternative framework for AI governance, which will resist technodeterminism and epistemic subordination in the process of developing the policy in higher education institutions. Technodeterminism refers to the idea that the introduction of artificial intelligence in universities is an inevitable and positive trend towards which all educational institutions should adapt without resistance (Sethy, 2026; Zembylas, 2023).

Pancasila as a Philosophical Foundation for Humanistic AI Governance

Pancasila, the basic philosophy of Indonesia enshrined in the country's Constitution of 1945, is made up of five principles, namely: faith in one God (Ketuhanan Yang Maha Esa); the principle of humanity, which entails justice and civilization (Kemanusiaan yang Adil dan Beradab); unity of Indonesia (Persatuan Indonesia); representative democracy under the guidance of deliberative wisdom (Kerakyatan yang Dipimpin oleh Hikmat Kebijaksanaan dalam Permusyawaratan Perwakilan); and social justice for all Indonesians (Keadilan Sosial bagi Seluruh Rakyat Indonesia). Various pieces of research on the subject matter suggest that the five principles form an ethically sound system and can offer a unique Asian perspective on the regulation of AI (Irawan, 2024; Inayah et al., 2025; Daffana, 2024).

The second principle of Pancasila, the just and civilized humanity, lays out the requirement that all technological advancement must serve human needs, rather than transform human beings into mere tools of algorithms. In the context of university AI systems, this requirement implies certain specific requirements for AI governance. Specifically, it would mean that AI would not become the only determining factor of scholars' professional reputation; all algorithmic systems used in university decision-making would have to be explainable to people using them; and any research evaluation via AI tools should remain open to human deliberation (HBT Law, 2024). Another important principle that provides the philosophical foundation for sharing governance over AI is the fourth principle, which is democracy based on wisdom. This means that decisions about implementing AI technology in universities should come out of musyawarah, consultation between all parties involved in the process (Irawan, 2024; Daffana, 2024). The fifth principle of Pancasila, the idea of social justice, means that AI implementation should neither worsen inequalities in educational resources distribution nor make marginalized scholars even more marginalized due to working with regional languages or following different intellectual traditions.

Several empirical studies performed within Indonesian educational frameworks have shown that, by teaching Pancasila values, educators can develop a specific ability in their students and fellow scholars to reflect critically on the issues related to AI ethics (Daffana, 2024). Additionally, empirical findings indicate that curricular frameworks based on Pancasila values, such as the Merdeka Belajar (freedom to learn) approach, provide for successful integration of AI technologies while maintaining epistemological diversity and cultural responsiveness (Setyawan et al., 2025).

Islamic Educational Philosophy and Maqasid Al-Shariah as an Ethical Framework for AI

In Indonesia, Islamic universities including UIN, IAIN, and STAIN utilize Islamic educational philosophy as a valuable resource in AI governance. Specifically, the framework of Maqasid al-Shariah, which identifies the basic goals of Islamic laws as the preservation of religion (hifz al-din), life (hifz al-nafs), intellect (hifz al-aql), lineage (hifz al-nasl), and property (hifz al-mal), has been identified in recent academic literature as one of the most useful approaches to evaluating the moral challenges of integrating AI into Islamic educational institutions (Mohadi & Tarshany, 2023; Mustapha & Malkan, 2025). Among all the above-mentioned goals, it is hifz al-aql (the preservation of intellect) that becomes the main factor influencing the use of AI in Islamic universities. Hifz al-aql assumes that human ability to think rationally needs to be preserved because its development and nurturing is an important moral goal. In this regard, scholars note a conflict between this aspect of Maqasid al-Shariah and the current trend towards delegating intellectual tasks to artificial intelligence. Although it is clear that AI could help improve cognitive abilities of humans, its excessive use is likely to create dependence on technologies that will impede human understanding and rationality – both of which are highly valued in Islamic tradition (Mustapha & Malkan, 2025). Such an opposition raises the importance of governance and ensures that artificial intelligence in Islamic universities is used not for the replacement of scholar's rational thinking but for the support of it, which opposes technological determinism assuming that universities will inevitably change under the influence of AI regardless of their willingness (Hakim & Anggraini, 2023).

Furthermore, as any technological innovation should be beneficial to its community, the concept of maslaha (public welfare) should be applied when using AI in university context. It means that the introduction of new technologies should promote common good and provide some benefits to everyone involved. Besides, the philosophical approach to AI governance in Islamic universities is based on the concept of khilafah (stewardship or trusteeship), which implies that individuals acting as scholars and leaders of educational institution bear certain responsibilities in relation to knowledge that they are supposed to be custodians of and not owners of the technology (Raquib et al., 2022). According to contemporary studies, the application of khilafah in the context of Islamic university ethics can be instrumental in identifying specific governance demands in regards to AI governance, which include such aspects as algorithm transparency, accountability, and non-violation of social justice and human dignity (Raquib et al., 2022; Mustapha & Malkan, 2025).

Indigenous Pedagogical Traditions and Local Wisdom as Epistemic Resistance

In addition to the philosophical approach and Islamic educational ethics, the diversity of native pedagogies in Indonesia that includes local wisdom (kearifan lokal) in hundreds of different cultural communities, ethnopedagogical principles based on Javanese, Sundanese, Minangkabau, Acehnese, Batak, Dayak, and other traditions, as well as unique pedagogic principles of pesantren institutions is another resource to build resistance against epistemic domination. According to research, local knowledge systems are not passive elements of culture but powerful sources of epistemological knowledge that offer alternative perspectives on technology, knowledge, and community (Sethy, 2026; Tella et al., 2025).

In a qualitative study of innovations in the university curriculum in Aceh, Indonesia, researchers found that universities introducing the concept of local knowledge such as adat (traditional law), local folklore, and traditional ecological knowledge through the use of Merdeka Belajar's localized curriculum model were able to effectively reject the hierarchization of curriculums in favor of the idea that international curriculums cannot be regarded as the only valid source of academic knowledge (Ramli et al., 2025). The challenge to knowledge hierarchies raised by local knowledge systems is especially important in terms of building AI governance since the implementation of algorithms that rely on specific data sets, training protocols, and evaluation criteria that embody Global North epistemological values can only be identified and challenged using the perspective offered by the local wisdom. Studies on ethnopedagogy in Indonesian educational settings show that ethnopedagogical approaches help students and scholars develop cultural knowledge necessary for AI governance (Sakti et al., 2024).

Furthermore, the traditional model of pesantren schools' governance presents a unique model of technology governance that involves ethical selection and not the blind adoption of technology. All studies investigating the application of technologies in these institutions reveal that these institutions implement a selective approach towards technology and regard it as an opportunity to preserve scholarly traditions and ensure religious moderation, paying special attention to the importance of integrating religious values in technological innovations (Azzukhruf, 2025). Thus, the implementation of value-based technology in Indonesia can be achieved through the selective approach when AI is selected by community itself according to its needs (Setyawan et al., 2025).

Toward a Synthesized Alternative Model of AI Governance

Combining Pancasila philosophy, Islamic educational ethics, and the rich pedagogical tradition of the archipelago, Indonesian universities are well-placed to create a synthesized alternative AI governance model, which would serve as a valid counter to the pitfalls of either technocriticism or technocracy. Such a governance model will have four distinguishing characteristics. First, it will be communitarian in nature, with institutional decision-making based on deliberative consultation, or musyawarah, according to the principles laid out by Pancasila philosophy. Second, this model will be spiritually and ethically responsible: the act of governing an artificial intelligence will be treated as an exercise in khilafah, with accountability of institutional authorities both to their scholarly communities and to the ethical imperatives of Islamic and Pancasila philosophies. Third, the governance of AI will involve an explicit epistemological pluralism, protecting local linguistic and knowledge traditions from homogenization through AI systems trained on Global North material. Fourth, it will be characterized by selective adoption, where institutions will choose to implement AI systems only after a critical analysis of their performance with regards to the institution's philosophical mission and effect on its research and learning conditions (Irawan, 2024; Inayah et al., 2025; Sethy, 2026).

Indonesian universities enjoy unique philosophical, religious, and cultural advantages in the form of Pancasila philosophy, Islamic educational philosophy, and indigenous pedagogical traditions, respectively, which could become the basis for an alternative model of AI governance that is more nuanced than simple rejection or uncritical acceptance. The fact is that the latter two approaches cannot be seen as obstacles to AI integration but, rather, preconditions for such integration and a guarantee against technological determinism and epistemic hegemony. To make use of the identified advantages, it is necessary to embrace three complementary strategies. The first is embedding the principles of Pancasila ethics in the operational aspects of AI governance in universities. The second involves assessing AI tools using the criteria of Maqasid al-Shariah, i.e. determining the extent to which the adoption of such tools would preserve human intellect and integrity. The third is making indigenous pedagogy and knowledge traditions a central component of the governance framework, thus ensuring the validity and recognition of the former amidst AI-mediated research evaluation.

CONCLUSION

The present study attempts to fill the existing research gap that was mostly neglected in the fast-growing literature on the application of artificial intelligence in higher education. This research gap lies in exploring the dialectical relationship between policy, research freedom, and AI in the context of the institutional, cultural, and legal particularities of higher education in Indonesia. Previous studies did not explore the exact ways in which algorithmic governance could affect the epistemic autonomy of researchers or the resources available to Indonesian universities to conduct contextualized research based on AI technologies. Instead, academic literature explored AI ethics in the universalist and Eurocentric Western philosophical tradition or discussed AI technology adoption in Indonesia in general terms. The use of a dialectical approach across four dimensions allowed filling the identified gap.

The conducted analysis revealed five mutually reinforcing forms of algorithmic governance in Indonesian universities that structurally undermine research freedom. They include: 1) lack of transparency in algorithmic decision-making in research assessment; 2) systemic bias against non-Western languages and rhetorical styles in AI systems; 3) chilling effect associated with AI-based scholarly surveillance and the lack of proper governance; 4) epistemic dependency related to the dependence of Indonesian universities on algorithmic infrastructures in the Global North; and 5) significant AI governance gap between policies formulated by the government and implemented in Indonesian universities. Thus, it is evident that the threat to epistemic autonomy is not an incidental result of introducing AI systems but is an inherent property of such integration. In addition to this structural aspect, the analysis revealed the problem of data sovereignty and digital colonialism associated with the extraction of the value generated from Indonesian scholars' intellectual work. The latter is caused by the fact that Indonesian universities use proprietary algorithms developed in the Global North, including plagiarism checking software, research information systems, and scholarly communication platforms. At the same time, the Personal Data Protection Law (No. 27/2022) in Indonesia provides grounds for data sovereignty. Epistemic colonialism is more severe because AI algorithms are trained using exclusively Western-centric data sources, disadvantaging non-Western scholarly products. In addition, the rapid rate of adoption and algorithmic governance makes the issue even more urgent.

The identified risks require adopting a set of governance mechanisms tailored specifically for the Indonesian context. In total, the study suggested five dimensions forming a framework for managing the risks associated with AI governance in Indonesian universities: 1) nationally coordinated and Pancasila-centered policy foundation using existing regulatory instruments; 2) AI Ethical Review Boards with true faculty governance powers; 3) enforceable data governance and data sovereignty provisions that do not depend on the development of national law enforcement capacities; 4) culturally and socially relevant AI literacy training programs; and 5) adaptively designed participatory governance systems allowing ongoing reviews. All proposed strategies have a common aim to protect epistemic autonomy, the main goal of research conducted by Indonesian universities, while providing educational opportunities offered by AI technologies.

Finally, the analysis identified several valuable resources available to Indonesian universities that allow developing alternative forms of governance resisting the deterministic nature of technology and epistemic domination: 1) Pancasila philosophy; 2) Maqasid al-Shariah-inspired Islamic ethics of education; and 3) indigenous pedagogy. The principles of Pancasila such as democratic deliberation, social justice, and being just and civilized provide specific and philosophically justified governance requirements. The concept of epistemic accountability in the Islamic context includes hifz al-'aql (preservation of intellect), khilafah (trusteeship), and maslaha (public welfare), forming the basis for ethically assessing AI tools in Islamic institutions. Finally, value filtering and ethnopedagogy used in pesantren schools represent valuable practices for AI governance.

This study adds new insights into the discussion about how higher education systems can adopt AI governance in order to avoid negative consequences while benefiting from innovations. Specifically, the key contribution of this research includes the identification of an important resource base that can be used by Indonesian universities to establish innovative governance systems resistant to epistemic subordination. More importantly, Indonesia's case study shows that countries in the Global South are not passive recipients of AI governance solutions shaped according to Western standards. On the contrary, Indonesia provides a valuable experience of developing an AI governance framework based on local philosophies and cultural traditions.

REFERENCES

Adiprasetio, J. (2025). Epistemic bias and the rise of qualitative dominance in post-authoritarian Indonesian communication research. *Frontiers in Communication, 10*, 1602567. Advance online publication. DOI: 10.3389/fcomm.2025.1602567

Ahmed, S. A. (2026). Algorithmic dependence and digital colonialism: A conceptual framework for artificial intelligence in education and knowledge systems of the Global South. *Frontiers in Education, 11*, 1720563. Advance online publication. DOI: 10.3389/feduc.2026.1720563

Akinyetun, T. S. (2023). Digital colonialism, data sovereignty, and Africa's quest for technological independence. *African Journal of Science, Technology, Innovation and Development, 15*(4), 489–501. DOI: 10.1080/20421338.2022.2116579

American Association of University Professors (AAUP). (2025). *Artificial intelligence and academic professions.* https://www.aaup.org/reports-publications/aaup-policies-reports/topical-reports/artificial-intelligence-and-academic

Arora, A., Barrett, M., Lee, E., Oborn, E., & Prince, K. (2023). Risk and the future of AI: Algorithmic bias, data colonialism, and marginalization. *Information and Organization, 33*(3), 100478. Advance online publication. DOI: 10.1016/j.infoandorg.2023.100478

ASEAN. (2024). *ASEAN guide on AI governance and ethics (2nd ed.).* ASEAN Secretariat. https://asean.org/asean-guide-on-ai-governance-and-ethics/

Azevedo, R., Gašević, D., Pavlik, P., Scheines, R., & Smith, H. (2025). Institutional policies on artificial intelligence in higher education: Frameworks and best practices for faculty. *New Directions for Adult and Continuing Education, 2025*(188), 70–78. Advance online publication. DOI: 10.1002/ace.70013

Azzukhruf, M. W. (2025). Mapping research trends on technology and artificial intelligence in Islamic education: A bibliometric analysis of Scopus Database (2019–2025). *Edu Cendikia: Jurnal Ilmiah Kependidikan, 5*(3), 1155–1169. DOI: 10.47709/educendikia.v5i03.7604

Baker, R. S., & Hawn, A. (2022). Algorithmic Bias in Education. *International Journal of Artificial Intelligence in Education, 32*(4), 1052–1092. DOI: 10.1007/s40593-021-00285-9

Barus, O. P., Hidayanto, A. N., Handri, E. Y., Sensuse, D. I., & Yaiprasert, C. (2025). Shaping generative AI governance in higher education: Insights from student perception. *International Journal of Educational Research Open*, *8*, 100452. Advance online publication. DOI: 10.1016/j.ijedro.2025.100452

Borenstein, J., & Howard, A. (2021). Emerging challenges in AI and the need for AI ethics education. *AI and Ethics*, *1*(1), 61–65. DOI: 10.1007/s43681-020-00002-7 PMID: 38624388

Bozkurt, A., Karadeniz, A., Baneres, D., Guerrero-Roldan, A. E., & Rodríguez, M. E. (2021). Artificial intelligence and reflections from educational landscape: A review of AI studies in half a century. *Sustainability (Basel)*, *13*(2), 800. DOI: 10.3390/su13020800

Bujnowska, A., Nguyen, H., & Tran, L. (2026). Data colonialism and digital sovereignty in the Global South. *Development in Practice*, 1–8. Advance online publication. DOI: 10.1080/09614524.2025.2609155

Chan, C. K. Y. (2023). A comprehensive AI policy education framework for university teaching and learning. *International Journal of Educational Technology in Higher Education*, *20*(1), 38. DOI: 10.1186/s41239-023-00408-3

Couldry, N., & Mejias, U. A. (2019). *The costs of connection: How data is colonizing human life and appropriating it for capitalism*. Stanford University Press.

Daffana, I. (2024). Rediscovering Pancasila-based civic education through artificial intelligence: A conceptual framework. [INJOSER]. *Indonesian Journal of Social Education and Research*, *3*(1). Advance online publication. DOI: 10.58260/injoser.v3i1.504

Digital Watch Observatory. (2024). *The Indonesian National Strategy on Artificial Intelligence*. Digital Watch Observatory https://dig.watch/resource/the-indonesian-national-strategy-on-artificial-intelligence

Georgieva, M., & Stuart, J. (2025). *Ethics is the edge: The future of AI in higher education*. EDUCAUSE Review. https://er.educause.edu/articles/2025/6/ethics-is-the-edge-the-future-of-ai-in-higher-education

Haetami, M. (2025). AI-driven educational transformation in Indonesia: From learning personalization to institutional management. *Al-Ishlah: Jurnal Pendidikan*, *17*(2), 1819–1832. DOI: 10.35445/alishlah.v17i2.7448

Hakim, A., & Anggraini, P. (2023). Artificial intelligence in teaching Islamic studies: Challenges and opportunities. *Molang: Journal of Islamic Education*, *4*(1), 1–15.

Hall, R. (2021). *The hopeless university: Intellectual work at the end of the end of history*. MayFly Books.

Helmiatin, H., Hidayat, A., & Kahar, M. R. (2024). Investigating the adoption of AI in higher education: A study of public universities in Indonesia. *Cogent Education, 11*(1), 2380175. Advance online publication. DOI: 10.1080/2331186X.2024.2380175

Holmes, W., Bialik, M., & Fadel, C. (2022). *Artificial intelligence in education: Promises and implications for teaching and learning*. Center for Curriculum Redesign.

ICLG. (2025). *Data protection laws and regulations report 2025–2026: Indonesia*. International Comparative Legal Guides. https://iclg.com/practice-areas/data-protection-laws-and-regulations/indonesia

Inayah, M., Musyarofah, S., Az Zahra, A. F. Z., & Agrariyanti, Y. (2025). Pancasila and artificial intelligence: Ethical analysis of AI regulations in Indonesia. *LITERA: Jurnal Ilmiah Multidisiplin, 4*(3). Advance online publication. DOI: 10.62307/litera.v4i3.217

Irawan, I. (2024). Penerapan etika Pancasila dalam pengembangan kecerdasan buatan yang bertanggung jawab di Indonesia [Application of Pancasila ethics in responsible AI development in Indonesia]. *bit-Tech, 7*(2), 263–271. https://doi.org/DOI: 10.32877/bt.v7i2.1740

Jaldemark, J., Lundin, J., Säljö, R., Edwards, J., Gegenfurtner, A., Holmes, W., Järvelä, S., de Laat, M., Lindberg, Y., Littlejohn, A., Seufert, S., Specht, M., Svensson, L., Rapanta, C., Hayes, S., & Zeivots, S. (2025). A multidisciplinary research agenda for artificial intelligence, education, learning, and instruction. *Postdigital Science and Education, 7*(4), 1414–1450. DOI: 10.1007/s42438-025-00602-8

Kay, J., Brereton, M., & Oviatt, S. (2024). Generative epistemic injustice: Four ways AI systems misrepresent and marginalise. *AI & Society*. Advance online publication. DOI: 10.1007/s00146-024-01966-4

Kay, J., Kasirzadeh, A., & Mohamed, S. (2024). Epistemic injustice in generative AI. *Proceedings of the AAAI/ACM Conference on AI, Ethics, and Society, 7*(1), 684–697. https://doi.org/DOI: 10.1609/aies.v7i1.31671

Kosbar, Y. (2026). TransformED futures: Towards human-centred, ethical and inclusive use and governance of AI in higher education. *Policy Futures in Education*. Advance online publication. DOI: 10.1177/19467567251406292

Kwet, M. (2019). Digital colonialism: US empire and the new imperialism in the Global South. *Race & Class, 60*(4), 3–26. DOI: 10.1177/0306396818823172

Law, H. B. T. (2024, February). *Ethical guidelines on use of artificial intelligence (AI) in Indonesia*. https://www.hbtlaw.com/insights/2024-02/ethical-guidelines-use-artificial-intelligence-ai-indonesia

Law Asia. (2025). *Building trust in the algorithm: Indonesia's emerging AI framework*. https://law.asia/indonesia-ai-governance-framework/

Ministry of Communication and Informatics Indonesia (KOMINFO). (2023). *Surat Edaran No. 9/2023 tentang Etika Kecerdasan Artifisial [Circular Letter No. 9/2023 on AI Ethical Guidelines]*. Kementerian Komunikasi dan Informatika Republik Indonesia.

Mohadi, M., & Tarshany, Y. (2023). Maqasid al-Shari'ah and the ethics of artificial intelligence. *Journal of Contemporary Maqasid Studies*, *2*(2), 79–102. DOI: 10.52100/jcms.v2i2.107

Mustapha, R., & Malkan, S. N. A. (2025). Maqasid al-Shariah in the AI era: Balancing innovation and Islamic ethical principles. *International Journal of Islamic Theology & Civilization*, *3*(3), 1–21. DOI: 10.5281/zenodo.15381828

Nemorin, S. (2024). Towards decolonising the ethics of AI in education. *Globalisation, Societies and Education*, *22*(3), 411–426. DOI: 10.1080/14767724.2024.2333821

Ojha, B., Agrawal, A., & Arya, A. (2024). Artificial intelligence integration in higher education. In *Integrating AI into higher education* (pp. 1–20). CRC Press., DOI: 10.1201/9781003469315-1

Oncioiu, I., & Bularca, A. R. (2025). Artificial intelligence governance in higher education: The role of knowledge-based strategies in fostering legal awareness and ethical artificial intelligence literacy. *Societies (Basel, Switzerland)*, *15*(6), 144. Advance online publication. DOI: 10.3390/soc15060144

Raharjo, R. S., & Rohmadi, S. H. (2025). Artificial intelligence in indonesian education: A critical review of ethical considerations, implementation challenges, and educational management perspectives. *At-Tarbawi. Jurnal Kajian Kependidikan Islam*, *10*(1), 50–68. DOI: 10.22515/attarbawi.v10i1.12141

Ramli, R., Razali, R., Gadeng, A. N., Diana, N., & Hariadi, J. (2025). Integrating local knowledge into higher education: A qualitative study of curriculum innovation in Aceh, Indonesia. *Education Sciences*, *15*(9), 1214. DOI: 10.3390/educsci15091214

Raquib, A., Channa, B., Zubair, T., & Qadir, J. (2022). Islamic virtue-based ethics for artificial intelligence. *Discover Artificial Intelligence*, *2*(1), 11. Advance online publication. DOI: 10.1007/s44163-022-00028-2

Robert, J. (2024). *2024 EDUCAUSE AI landscape study*. EDUCAUSE Center for Analysis and Research. https://library.educause.edu/resources/2024/2/2024-educause-ai-landscape-study

Sakhiyya, Z., & Mulya, T. W. (Eds.). (2023). *Education in Indonesia: Critical perspectives on equity and social justice*. Springer., DOI: 10.1007/978-981-99-1878-2

Sakti, S. A., Endraswara, S., & Rohman, A. (2024). Revitalizing local wisdom within character education through ethnopedagogy approach: A case study on a preschool in Yogyakarta. *Heliyon*, *10*(10), e31370. Advance online publication. DOI: 10.1016/j.heliyon.2024.e31370 PMID: 38803959

Santos, B. de S. (2014). *Epistemologies of the South: Justice against epistemicide*. Routledge.

Sariyasa, S., & Monika, K. A. L. (2023). Artificial intelligence and academic ethics in the era of Merdeka Belajar: How are students' responses? *Jurnal Kependidikan: Jurnal Hasil Penelitian dan Kajian Kepustakaan di Bidang Pendidikan, Pengajaran dan Pembelajaran, 9*(3). https://e-journal.undikma.ac.id/index.php/jurnalkependidikan/article/view/8720

Sethy, M. (2026). Artificial intelligence and epistemic justice: A decolonial turn through indigenous knowledge systems. *AI & Society*, *41*(5), 5401–5410. Advance online publication. DOI: 10.1007/s00146-026-02936-8

Setyawan, M. B., Dewi, D. A., Hidayah, Y., & Hamid, M. A. (2025). Assessing students' readiness for artificial intelligence-based project learning to strengthen local wisdom values in Indonesia. *Cogent Education*, *12*(1), 2582948. Advance online publication. DOI: 10.1080/2331186X.2025.2582948

Smith, S., Tate, M., Freeman, K., Walsh, A., Ballsun-Stanton, B., Hooper, M., & Lane, M. (2025). A university framework for the responsible use of generative AI in research. *Journal of Higher Education Policy and Management*, *47*(1), 17–36. DOI: 10.1080/1360080X.2025.2509187

Syaidina, M. O., Fahrudin, R., & Mutiara, I. A. (2024). Implementation of ethics of using artificial intelligence in the education system in Indonesia. *Blockchain Frontier Technology*, *4*(1), 63–71. Advance online publication. DOI: 10.34306/bfront.v4i1.571

Tella, A., Jatto, E. O., & Ajani, Y. A. (2025). Preserving indigenous knowledge: Leveraging digital technology and artificial intelligence. *IFLA Journal*, *51*(3), 703–721. DOI: 10.1177/03400352251342505

Udah, H. (2024). Decolonising research for justice: Ethical imperatives and practical applications. *International Journal of Qualitative Methods, 23*, 16094069241294040. Advance online publication. DOI: 10.1177/16094069241294040

UNESCO. (2021). *Recommendation on the ethics of artificial intelligence.* United Nations Educational, Scientific and Cultural Organization. https://unesdoc.unesco.org/ark:/48223/pf0000381137

UNESCO. (2023). *UNESCO trains Indonesian teachers on AI ethics.* https://www.unesco.org/en/articles/unesco-trains-indonesian-teachers-ai-ethics

UNESCO. (2024). *Leading AI ethics: UNESCO and KOMINFO launch AI readiness assessment methodology in Indonesia.* UNESCO. https://www.unesco.org/en/articles/leading-ai-ethics-unesco-and-kominfo-launch-ai-readiness-assessment-methodology-indonesia

UNESCO. (2024). *Indonesia: artificial intelligence readiness assessment report.* UNESCO. https://unesdoc.unesco.org/ark:/48223/pf0000392317?posInSet=1&queryId=7060cf11-7d11-4ca1-bc7d-fdfb04af70f8

Wadipalapa, R. P., Katharina, R., Nainggolan, P. P., Aminah, S., Apriani, T., Ma'rifah, D., & Anisah, A. L. (2024). An ambitious artificial intelligence policy in a decentralised governance system: Evidence from Indonesia. *Journal of Current Southeast Asian Affairs, 32*(1), 67–89. DOI: 10.1177/18681034231226393

Wong-A-Foe, D. (2023). Navigating the implications of AI in Indonesian education: Tutors, governance, and ethical perspectives. In Anutariya, C., & Bonsangue, M. M. (Eds.), *Data Science and Artificial Intelligence: DSAI 2023. Communications in Computer and Information Science* (Vol. 1942, pp. 333–346). Springer., DOI: 10.1007/978-981-99-7969-1_26

Wu, C., Zhang, H., & Carroll, J. M. (2024). AI governance in higher education: Case studies of guidance at Big Ten universities. *Future Internet, 16*(10), 354. DOI: 10.3390/fi16100354

Zembylas, M. (2023). A decolonial approach to AI in higher education teaching and learning: Strategies for undoing the ethics of digital neocolonialism. *Learning, Media and Technology, 48*(1), 25–37. DOI: 10.1080/17439884.2021.2010094

Zhu, Y., Zhu, Z., Xu, W., & Zhu, Y. (2025). Cross-border higher education cooperation under the dual context of artificial intelligence and geopolitics: Opportunities, challenges, and pathways. *Frontiers in Education, 10*, 1656518. Advance online publication. DOI: 10.3389/feduc.2025.1656518

Chapter 12
An Empirical Study From Odisha State of India for Studying the Knowledge and AI Literacy of Pre-Service Teachers

Arakhita Behera
http://orcid.org/0000-0002-6761-9313
Regional Institute of Education (NCERT), Ajmer, India

Ajay Kumar Singh
http://orcid.org/0000-0003-0429-0925
Department of Humanities and Social Sciences, Graphic Era (Deemed to be) University, Dehradun, India

Rahul Ranjan
RIE (NCERT), Mysuru, India

Kiranbala Behera
http://orcid.org/0009-0000-7196-5203
Department of Rural Development, Ravenshaw University, Cuttack, India

ABSTRACT

Artificial Intelligence (AI) is used by all stakeholders in most educational organizations. AI is thought to improve student engagement, personalize the learning process, and increase administrative effectiveness in educational processes. This paper explores and examines the awareness of AI and its different approaches among pre-service teachers (PSTs) in Odisha state of India. A systematic evaluation process

DOI: 10.4018/979-8-2600-3204-6.ch012

is undertaken to achieve the mentioned objective. It conducts a survey of 150 PSTs who were randomly selected from three public B.Ed. colleges in Khordha district of this state. The descriptive analysis and Chi-square test were used to investigate AI literacy scale. It noted that PSTs pursue different programmes to increase their efficiency in AI application at institute level. There appeared an insignificant gap in the AI competency literacy among PSTs. It demonstrates the value of in-person group instruction and experiential, hands-on training for improving PSTs' AI literacy.

INTRODUCTION

AI has significant implications for social, economic, industrial, technological, environmental, skill development, education, and the digital revolution (Khare et al., 2018; Celik, 2023). Therefore, the scope and breadth of AI are very broad. AI refers to mechanical and computer systems that can replicate human cognitive functions such as reasoning, learning, and problem-solving (Russell & Norvig, 2016). Many sectors, such as education, healthcare, business, banking, tourism, and government, use AI for various purposes. For instance, the banking and business sectors are using AI for automation and to increase customer satisfaction (De & Singh, 2025; Singh et al., 2025). The government is applying AI to maintain processes and monitor and implement ongoing policies. AI is used by common people to track their geographical location. Other sectors also rely on AI to improve their services. However, AI has multiple definitions that vary across disciplines. For example, AI can generate repetitive text on a specific topic using multiple language-tool approaches, and it can function as a large language model (Kasneci et al., 2023). Although some differences in terminology exist, most people agree that AI systems try to mimic human thought processes and learn from mistakes (Obschanka & Audretsch, 2020) and increase humans' ability to reduce mistakes.

Recently, AI has been employed by educational organizations and other sectors (Zhang et al., 2023; Celik, 2023). Furthermore, it improves the instruction and learning aspects of educational processes and enhances students' engagement in academic activities and learning ability (Verganti et al., 2020; BaHammam, 2023). A separate AI course in schools improves students' understanding. AI training for students across diverse fields, such as computer science, arithmetic, and statistics, is improving their progress and developing new skills. Moreover, AI courses help academics learn about the ethical application of AI. Given its active interaction with teachers, the development of educational technology settings is projected to be profoundly affected by AI (USDE, 2023). However, technological advancements resulting from the online transformation of the education system are creating many challenges for teachers and students (Singh et al., 2024a). AI-based tools are highly useful for increasing learning and teaching opportunities (Popenici & Kerr, 2017; Celik, 2023). This shows that educators must be more aware of the demands and repercussions of the extensive use of AI in academic activities. Extensive application of AI is leading to new learning processes for academics in the real world. AI is also posing new challenges and problems for academics. Therefore, teachers' specific knowledge to apply AI is highly essential before it is used in the education system (Celik, 2023). Hence, primary information is needed to understand the role of teachers in AI literacy in educational organizations.

Furthermore, critical thinking and the customization of AI in education are mentioned, but these topics are often treated as incidental in existing research. However, PSTs need to critically assess the ethical bias and dependability of the tools they utilize in addition to using AI for academic work, such as research, presentations, and lesson preparation (Helvacı, 2025). Awareness of PSTs toward AI applications would be helpful for increasing the skills of students in the future (Zhang et al., 2023). There is a gap in practice and research because despite being confronted with AI in their academic and daily lives, teachers may not receive structured, reflective training, which is needed to increase their understanding of AI. Accordingly, teachers and students can follow the ethical practices of AI in academics. This is an emerging research area on whether or not educators are willing to employ AI technologies in their activities. What are the practical implications of AI for the skills of teachers? How well AI is incorporated into education? What are the negative implications of AI application for academics?

Previous studies on AI literacy have been carried out both domestically and internationally. However, research on preservice teachers in the state of Odisha has been less extensive. This chapter, therefore, seeks to further the body of knowledge on AI literacy among preservice teachers in the Khordha district of Odisha and elsewhere by providing insights into the present situation and suggesting a framework for incorporating AI education into teacher preparation programs. This research aims to close the knowledge gap and advance a thorough understanding of the role of AI in education by investigating AI literacy among preservice teachers, taking into account both technical and ethical factors. The results have the potential to provide revolutionary learning opportunities that use AI to promote student achievement, equality, and creativity. Thus, this study identifies the AI literacy of PSTs in three B.Ed. institutions in the district of Khordha in Odisha state of India. This research uses the chi-square test to address subclassifying patterns of AI awareness among participants and to obtain a deeper understanding of various groups in the context of teacher education.

This study also investigated the degree of AI literacy among PSTs. Therefore, this research examines the differences in AI literacy at the department level and the usage of AI devices using a mixed-methods approach. The results are anticipated to influence curriculum development, teacher training regulations, and educational technology design in this research. As the profile, the knowledge and skills of teachers are technologically practical, socially and culturally viable in the twenty-first century. Accordingly, this study aims to answer the following research questions:

- What is the awareness of teachers toward AI in B.Ed? institutes in the Khordha district of Odisha state of India?
- What is the perspective of teachers about the application of AI in education?
- Does a preservice teacher's degree of AI literacy vary according to their course of study?
- What primary challenges are faced by PSTs because of the application of AI in academic activities?
- Which policy actions are required to minimize the challenges of PSTs due to the advancement and use of AI among academics?
- What are the future perspectives of AI in educational organizations in India?

LITERATURE REVIEW

Numerous benefits and issues related to the incorporation of AI in teacher education have been identified in the literature. For instance, AI can be applied to create educational content and enhance the engagement of students (Kasneci et al., 2023). AI also improves teaching and learning practices in educational organizations (Popenici & Kerr, 2017; Kundu et al., 2025). The use of AI is found to increase the success of students and teachers (Khare et al., 2018). This process requires additional knowledge and skills for teachers and students. Furthermore, it looks at how the behavioral intentions of PSTs integrate AI into academic activities. It focuses on the preparation of PSTs for integrating AI into future teaching methods. It explains the AI literacy of PSTs. Finally, the problems associated with using AI in the learning process among academics are discussed. This review section summarizes the various perspectives of AI and identifies the gaps in the existing body of knowledge.

Theoretical Framework

AI and its related technologies play significant roles in many common areas, such as chat bots, spam filters, robotic vacuum cleaners, and social media algorithms. Even though AI is widely used and incorporated into every item, the majority of people still interact with AI without a complete understanding of its underlying principles and the ethical implications of its use (Jordan 2019). Despite its ubiquitous usage, this misunderstanding highlights the need for AI literacy, which includes critical understanding and ethical engagement.

The ability to read and write by which individuals acquired and shared information among themselves was formally considered literacy. Later, as technology advanced, the concept of digital literacy emerged, in which an individual could have the capacity to operate a computer and navigate digital settings (Willinsky 2006). This concept has further advanced with the emergence of AI, which is called AI literacy, in which the individual requires proficiency not only in applying AI technology but also in understanding its capabilities, function and ethical repercussions.

A subfield of computer science known as artificial intelligence (AI) gives computers the ability to make choices on their own by imbuing technical instruments with intelligence that replicates and expands human cognitive capacity (McCarthy 2004). AI includes a number of technological domains, including deep learning, machine learning, and natural language processing (Zawacki-Richter et al. 2019). According to McCarthy (2004) and Zawacki-Richter et al. (2019), these technologies allow computers to analyze enormous volumes of data, identify patterns, and make judgments with growing autonomy, often matching or surpassing human skills.

The use of AI technology is becoming more favorable for people. Thus, AI literacy and proficiency are highly useful for people. AI literacy involves people's understanding and ability to apply the best utilization of AI technologies in different activities. The capacity to comprehend, assess, and use AI systems in an ethical and efficient manner is known as AI literacy (Wang et al., 2022). AI literacy, efficiency and proficiency are highly beneficial for people to gain more knowledge and skills. It also increases people's awareness of the ethical, educational, and societal consequences of AI in their lives (Elçiçek, 2024; Behera et al., 2025). For instance, the application of AI in people's lives would be helpful for them to a certain extent. Extensive utilization of AI is harmful to human skills and knowledge. For instance, extensive use of AI may reduce students' and teachers' thinking and logical capacity.

The crucial part of AI literacy is its ethical concern. Users must manage the ethical implications of AI technology, such as algorithmic bias, privacy concerns, and the social repercussions of automation. By being aware of these issues, citizens may encourage the responsible use of AI and demand transparency from lawmakers and developers (Hermann 2022). Educational programs play a major role in the development of AI literacy. Initiatives should be taken to include AI education in the K-12 curriculum to provide students with the basic knowledge and skills required to operate in an AI-driven future (Ng et al., 2021). These programs enable the next generation to engage with AI technology responsibly by emphasizing ethical awareness, critical thinking, and technical skills. Research on AI literacy is continuously evolving in an attempt to identify core competencies and effective training strategies. Awareness, utilization, evaluation, and ethics are the four pillars of AI literacy (Wang et al., 2023).

Technology acceptance model (TAM)

A framework named the TAM is effective at describing the variables that impact the inclusion of information systems (Davis, 1989). The foundation of the TAM is the theory of reasoned action by Fishbein and Ajzen (1997), which describes the behavioral intention that is influenced by the attitudes of people (Fishbein & Ajzen 1975). It is a framework used by most researchers to understand the inclusion of new technology by users. The major determinants of the behavioral intention to use new technology are perceived utility and ease of implementation (Davis, 1989). Additionally, the mindset influences the behavioral intention of the person, which mirrors the actual use of new technology.

Thus, the perception of PSTs on AI is strongly affected by its usability and utility, which fosters PSTs' AI literacy. Since its creation, the TAM has been widely used to characterize the factors that influence the inclusion of new technology of the user in their work. It is mostly used in education to predict how PSTs can adopt new technology in their learning activities. A recent study by Zhang et al. (2023) revealed that the main reasons for adopting AI by PSTs are its perceived utility and usability.

PSTs' Digital Skills and AI Literacy

Future educators will need to be highly proficient in both AI and general digital abilities, according to recent studies. Although many preservice teachers easily use common AI technologies, they do not have a basic understanding of AI (Yang et al., 2024). This disparity suggests that new teachers may not be prepared, increasing the likelihood that they would be impacted by AI in the classroom in unexpected ways. To help teachers understand, use, and evaluate AI technologies in a critical and ethical manner, researchers have requested that AI literacy be included in teacher education curricula (Guan et al., 2025). For example, a three-week narrative inquiry with 141 preservice teachers using ChatGPT revealed that while AI may facilitate lesson preparation and make learning more individualized, participants were concerned about data security and academic integrity (Karataş & Yüce, 2024).

A conceptual readiness framework pertaining to digital citizenship, perceived AI threats, and AI-supported innovation should be used to address the AI literacy of prospective teachers; education programs should incorporate ethical, competency, vision, and cognitive dimensions (Özüdoğru & Durak, 2025). These results are consistent with those of a study from Nigeria that revealed that understanding AI is a major predictor of positive results in the domains of AI usage, detection, ethics, invention, and problem-solving using structural equation modeling on 529 PSTs (Ayanwale et al., 2024a). This combination of opportunity and risk highlights how crucial it is for teacher preparation programs to include ethics in their AI literacy instruction. In response, initiatives such as UNESCO's AI Competency Framework for Teachers (UNESCO, 2024) have begun to outline the knowledge, skills, and values that educators must possess in the era of artificial intelligence. In fact, new data show that test integrity, security, and privacy are major concerns for teacher candidates and that these issues need to be specifically addressed for the safe integration of AI in education (Özüdoğru & Durak, 2025).

The familiarity of AI technologies and AI literacy has become a fundamental concept for analyzing the AI usability of teachers. Understanding the guiding principles of AI systems and the moral ramifications of their application go beyond the mechanical application of technology (Hornberger et al., 2023). AI literacy is a collection of skills that includes communication, critical analysis, and the actual use of these technologies in the education system (Long & Magerko, 2020). Given how AI technologies are developing, it is important to identify AI literacy as a dynamic concept that changes in response to educational demands and technical advancements (Laupichler et al., 2022). Three essential components of AI competences must be developed by educators, i.e., pedagogical approaches for incorporating AI into instructional design, technical proficiency for using AI tools, and conceptual knowledge of AI (Kim & Kwon, 2023). Kim and Kwon (2023) reported that AI competency is highly essential for increasing the AI teaching practices of teachers. These components could work as revolutionary tools to increase the application of AI in academic systems. Singh and Singh (2025) argued that digital technologies are working as creative tools to increase the learning and knowledge of students. Brianza et al. (2024) investigated the knowledge and beliefs of PSTs with respect to teaching and technology. A significant impact of technological knowledge on technological pedagogical knowledge was noted.

AI literacy is the capacity of an individual to employ AI to critically assess and to interact and cooperate with AI in an efficient manner (Long & Magerko, 2020; Černý, 2024). Few efforts have been made to include AI literacy in teacher-education programs, despite it having many significant effects on the education system (Ng et al., 2023). Ayanwale et al. (2024) argued that AI literacy includes proficiency in AI detection, application, ethics, and problem-solving. The AI literacy of preservice instructors and students is crucial for increasing their survival in an AI-driven world. However, we have a poor understanding of how PSTs use AI technology for professional development using SDL because of the inadequacy of the research.

PSTs' Perceptions of and Experiences with AI Applications

PST teachers also encounter and play with it more often as future educators and higher education students. Teachers and educators should develop more knowledgeable, moral, and pedagogically sound solutions and viewpoints for integrating Gen AI in academic tasks. According to the findings of prior research, teachers' perceptions—beliefs, attitudes, and familiarity with digital technologies, especially in relation to knowledge and confidence—are crucial in determining how they adopt and use AI in the classroom (Huang et al., 2024). Otherwise, it diminishes the ability, critical thinking, reasoning and decision-making capacity of teachers.

AI is defined as the capacity of an educator to comprehend, assess, and use AI technology in educational settings (Long & Magerko, 2020). Conceptual knowledge of AI operations is a component of AI literacy, and its applications are strongly influenced by familiarity, beliefs, and attitudes (Ng et al., 2021). PSTs' perceptions of Gen AI as a disruptive force or as a tool for meaningful teaching might be influenced by teacher educators' embrace or skepticism of the technology. Few studies have investigated how teachers' perspectives and experiences differ from or coincide with those of PSTs. Research has investigated how educators individually react to evolving technology among academics. Designing responsive and forward-thinking teacher education programs requires increasing teachers' understanding of AI applications.

Many studies have consistently investigated how PSTs' instructional beliefs affect their use of technology in the classroom and emphasize how deeply ingrained pedagogical frameworks influence their academic activities. Moreover, earlier studies also observed how digital tools are seen and used in instructional settings, technical expertise, and tool availability or familiarity (Abedi, 2024; Singh et al., 2024a). Academicians realized that any significant technological change in education needed to be accompanied by a change in instruction and their duties and responsibilities at the time of the introduction of computers in classrooms. That time, more focus was given to the belief systems of teachers on technological uses among academics (Dexter et al., 1999).

Instructors are more likely to embrace strategies that encourage deeper, more meaningful learning when they believe that technology has educational value. Technological applications are useless and inappropriate without creating educational value in educational organizations. As a result, research into how educators use AI should concentrate on belief systems that essentially influence how these technologies are seen and used in academics. However, users should place relatively low importance on the infrastructure or training of AI. However, the main takeaway from this corpus of work is that educators do not use new technology in an academic system. The responses of technological users are heavily influenced by their professional and personal beliefs about technologies. Many users have developed personal experiences during PST education and classroom practices over a long period of time (Abedi, 2024). Therefore, taking into account teachers' attitudes about AI and the academic environment that influence their ideas in academics is crucial. In a research context, we should examine the new opportunities for teachers that enhance their knowledge and experience with existing technologies in educational organizations. GoI also introduced NEP2020, which prioritizes digital technologies and digital tools to increase the digital literacy and digital skills of students (Singh et al., 2024b).

Finding institutional and personal characteristics that either facilitate or hinder PSTs' ability to integrate technology into their educational experiences must be the main focus of research (Starkey, 2010). It would be highly fruitful for policy makers to adopt AI in educational organizations worldwide. PST opinions about AI and its use in the education system are the main concern of recent studies (Kohnke et al., 2025). Nevertheless, less information is available on how the attitudes of PSTs toward AI are influenced by instructional decisions and modeling at the institutional level. It is necessary to examine the connection between the acceptability of GenAI by educators and their involvement in the future. GenAI is the current need for PSTs to develop technological pedagogical content knowledge (Kohnke et al., 2025). Therefore, it is also necessary to observe the acceptance and rejection ability of academics when they apply GenAI.

Existing research has mostly looked at PSTs as distinct groups, while little attention has been given to examining the application of AI in PST education (Celik et al., 2022). For instance, Lindfors et al. (2021) reported that a large number of teachers have low confidence in developing digital role models for students in Sweden. This means that a lack of confidence among teachers creates a barrier to the application of AI among academics. Moorhouse and Kohnke (2024) acknowledged the importance of GenAI in PSTs in Hongkong. GenAI has the potential to increase the revolution in educational techniques in PSTs. Singh et al. (2024a) investigated the problems faced by teachers and students by online transformation educational organizations after COVID-19 in India. However, a study by Moorhouse and Kohnke (2024) also reported that most teachers have low confidence and capacity to apply GenAI in academic activities.

The significance of developing strong AI-related competencies in teacher education was further highlighted by Heine and Konig (2025) in Germany. Kim and Kwon (2023) also examined the AI competency of teachers in South Korea. Teachers have less confidence in generating text and content knowledge. Although these studies provide insightful information on the viewpoints of each group, they only partially explain the ways in which experiences and perceptions interact in teacher education. PSTs' perceptions and interactions with technology are directly influenced by the modeling and adoption of digital practices (Gudmundsdottir & Hatlevik, 2018). A comparison of the two groups in the same research will aid in understanding how teachers' perspectives coincide with or vary with respect to AI. The purpose of our study is to fill the abovementioned research needs. PSTs and their perspectives and experiences with AI and its various practices at primary and lower secondary education levels are empirically investigated in this paper. Using the technology acceptance model (TAM), Davis (1989) emphasized that perceived utility and perceived ease of use are important factors in the adoption of information technology.

This study contributes to previous research in national and international contexts by examining PSTs' awareness of the use of AI in the same institutional environment. At the local level, it expands upon past Norwegian research on ICT integration and digital competency in teacher education (e.g., Gudmundsdottir & Hatlevik, 2018). On a global scale, it contributes to an expanding quantity of research that has generally examined teachers or PSTs separately. Furthermore, it contributes a body of knowledge on generative AI in teaching and education systems worldwide. It also offers statistically supported data to guide the development of AI literacy programs and frameworks for teacher training across the globe. The next subsection expands on this basis by placing the research in the Norwegian educational setting and describes the institutional framework and national initiatives that support the incorporation of AI in the teaching and education ecosystem.

The Preparedness of PSTs to Include AI in Their Future Teaching Methods

To succeed in today's classrooms, PSTs must improve their core teaching skills, which include a solid understanding of AI and its usability (Salas-Pilco et al., 2022). Other resources, such as the student edition of MagicSchoolAI, enable children to take control of their education and develop their digital literacy, problem-solving capacity, and teamwork ability (Miao & Shiohira, 2024). These talents can be cultivated, and activities that motivate children to interact meaningfully with AI can be created. Teachers play a critical role in building the abovementioned abilities among students (Seo et al., 2024). Educators should gain confidence and the ability to use AI in the classroom to achieve the abovementioned target.

Moreover, many teacher-preparation programs do not provide adequate opportunities for developing AI skills among students (Park & Son, 2022). Furthermore, the knowledge and abilities of PSTs that are required to increase their proficiency in AI tools and how GenAI has an impact on education are unclear. As technology advances and its impact on people's actions, attitudes, and behaviors becomes more apparent, academics and the demands of AI and technologies shift (Starkey, 2020). Without this preparation, PSTs may use inconsistent teaching strategies, which can be harmful to the student. Hence, PSTs should gain more knowledge, skills and practical viability of AI to avoid the abovementioned issues.

It is imperative that instructors acquire AI literacy throughout their training since they will need to integrate these technologies into their everyday lessons. PSTs cannot develop the digital skills and usability of technological advancement among students without having an appropriate understanding of AI literacy (Moorhouse, 2024). Additionally, the recognition that students from underprivileged families could not be exposed to AI outside of the classroom was neglected. Moreover, teachers with low AI literacy may unintentionally contribute to increasing inequalities in access to digital literacy among students (Karan & Angadi, 2024).

Most researchers have argued that more research in this field would be creative to avoid all the issues related to the appropriate application of AI in teaching and learning processes in educational institutions. According to some authors, more studies are necessary on this topic, as existing researchers cannot suggest an authentic solution for resolving different issues that have emerged because of the application of AI in academics (Sperling et al., 2024). Frimpong (2025) examined the role of AI in the PSTs of Ghana. The author reported that AI training had a favorable effect on teachers' desire to study and spread AI-related knowledge effectively. Ayanwale et al. (2024) reported that attitudes, anxiety, preparedness, self-transcendence, aspirations, and confidence affect PSTs' participation in AI learning in Ghana. Hence, these variables are worthy of enhancing the acceptability of teachers to apply AI in classroom teaching and increasing the skills of students. Zhang et al. (2023) reported that the main determinants of teachers' readiness to utilize AI are their perceived utility and simplicity of use in PSTs in Germany. Therefore, a simple process for the utilization of AI is helping teachers adopt AI tools in the teaching and learning process of educational organizations. AI readiness helps people understand the application of AI (Luckin et al., 2022).

Ayanwale et al. (2024) reported a correlation between PSTs' knowledge of AI and their comprehension of its use. However, neither active AI usage nor understanding of AI was shown to be related to emotional control. Moorhouse (2024) examined the intention of the first language to apply AI techniques and looked at how ready Hong Kong's first language instructors were to employ generative AI techniques in Hong Kong. It is suggested that the teacher's experience motivates them to apply for ChatGPT. However, new instructors have a limited understanding of ChatGPT and low use efficiency (Helvaci, 2025). Otherwise, diversity in AI literacy may increase the diversity in teaching learning practices among academics. Thus, an appropriate understanding of how teachers can apply AI tools is highly essential for academics.

However, most studies provide insightful information about this topic. Existing studies could apply robust data and empirical models to examine the relationships among many elements that can influence PSTs' preparedness to use AI. In addition, most researchers could include one institution of a nation to observe the perceptions of teachers toward AI. Existing studies could not include teacher education policies pertaining to the digital competency of teachers. For instance, the preparedness of PSTs to incorporate AI into their future instruction has not yet been examined in the particular settings of Portugal and Spain. Furthermore, it is unclear whether PSTs are receiving significant benefits from continuing curricular revisions and advancements in digital competency among academics.

Concerns and difficulties with integrating AI in educational institutions

Teachers also point out a number of issues and difficulties with integrating AI in the classroom, ranging from applicability in certain learning environments to dependability constraints, particularly with AI-generated material (Haenlein & Kaplan, 2019; Celik et al., 2022). Additionally, while new AI tools are being developed, teachers' expectations and viewpoints are sometimes overlooked, which may restrict their applicability in circumstances unique to education (Celik et al., 2022). According to research, instructors with low AI-related competencies—that is, knowledge and skills related to AI technologies in the classroom—may become more anxious about using these tools, which further hinders their acceptance in classrooms (Wang et al., 2024). The ethical issues surrounding AI in educational settings, such as those pertaining to what Chounta et al. (2022) refer to as FATE, or "fairness, accountability, transparency, and ethics", further amplify educators' worries (Sobaih et al., 2024).

MATERIALS AND METHODS

Study Area and Survey Design

Three B.Ed. colleges in the Khordha district—Regional Institute of Education (RIE), College of Teacher Education (CTE), and Nalini Devi Women's College of Teacher Education—are included in this study. The Khordha district is the state capital and hub of teacher training institutions. Therefore, this district is selected for field visits. Moreover, these institutions are purposely selected. These colleges are located in the Khordha district of Odisha state of India. This study assesses PSTs' comprehension of AI using descriptive methods. Thus, the required data are taken from the PSTs of the three teacher preparation programs. A cross-sectional approach is used to finalize these institutions for further primary surveys. Quantitative approaches are utilized for data collection and analysis.

Instrument

Data are gathered by means of a standardized, self-administered questionnaire. PSTs' knowledge of AI and respondents' sociodemographic traits are the subjects of closed-ended survey questions. The frequency of diverse levels of AI literacy among PSTs from different programs is measured through a Likert scale, i.e., 1–5.

Population and Sample

The required information is gathered from 150 PSTs who are enrolled in three Khordha district teacher education schools. A convenience sampling technique is applied to select respondents. Using the convenience sampling strategy, data are collected from a sample that a researcher can access easily (Büyüköztürk, 2024). The researcher may obtain information from the local surroundings by using this sampling technique. PSTs in programs in the fields of science, social science, and language are considered the main respondents to collect the required information. The data are collected from 1st September, 2025, to 6th November, 2025.

AI literacy scale

Wang et al. (2022) and Ng et al. (2022) developed the "AI literacy scale". This scale is used to measure how well the preservice instructors understood AI in this study. This scale has 18 items or questions or elements that are further divided into four subdimensions or constructs (i.e., the use and application of AI, knowledge and comprehension of AI, the detection of AI, and the ethics of AI). The 1st and 2nd constructs have six and six elements or items, respectively. The 3rd and 4th constructs have three and three elements or items, respectively. The constructs are also categorized as "use and apply", "knowledge and understanding", "detection of AI", and "ethics of AI."

Methods of Data Collection and Analysis

Thirty students at three teacher training colleges had taken a pretest about the study in the Odisha district of Khordha. The pretest was administered in accordance with the methods of Czaja (1998). Czaja's (1998) advice to address issues pertaining to four important topics: sampling, coding analysis, problem and interest, investigators' obligations, questionnaire issues, and respondents' awareness. The pretest used an undisclosed arrangement, which meant that the survey was conducted similarly to how the main survey was intended. Unfinished response sets and respondents' inability to understand some questions due to improper wording were identified as the main issues with the questionnaire during the pretest. The questionnaire is gradually modified as per the feedback received from the pretest. Therefore, real data from the respondents were collected.

Nevertheless, descriptive analysis is used to achieve the objectives of this research. SPSS statistical software was used for data analysis, data coding and descriptive and inferential statistics. The χ^2 test for independence was applied to evaluate whether there was a significant association between the AI literacy scale and the different programs that PSTs undertake. There was a 0.05 significance level according to the two-tailed χ^2 test. The correlation value shows how two category variables are related to each other. The values are also included in the cross-tabulation of this study. For example, χ^2 and contingency tables are used to investigate how people with different mental problems react differently to a certain rehabilitation program (Bhat, 1996). Thus, the following hypothesis is tested in this research:

H_0: PSTs enrolled in different programs have the same level of AI literacy.

H_1: Different PSTs have different levels of AI literacy that also depend on the program in which they are enrolled.

RESULTS AND ANALYSIS

Demographic Profile of the Respondents

The demographic characteristics of the PSTs who participated in this study are shown in Table 1. Table 1 also explores the frequencies and percentage values of all the elements. In a sample of 150 PSTs, 70.7% ($f = 106$) were female, and 29.3% ($f = 44$) were male. The participants' age distribution revealed that 18.0% ($f = 27$) of the respondents were between the ages of 17 and 19 years, 44.7% ($f = 67$) of the respondents were between the ages of 20 and 22 years, and 25.3% ($f = 38$) of the respondents were between the ages of 23 and 25 years. Educationally, 16.7% ($f = 25$) of respondents were enrolled in B.A. and B.Ed. In contrast, 39.3% ($f = 59$) of respondents were enrolled in B.Sc. and B.Ed. A total of 10.7% ($f = 16$) of respondents were enrolled in B.Ed. and Science Group, and 9.3% ($f = 14$) of respondents were enrolled in B.Ed. A total of 16.7% ($f = 25$) of the respondents were pursuing M.Ed. program. Only 7.3% ($f = 11$) of respondents had pursued M.Ed. This reveals that the sample of 150 PSTs belongs to different age groups.

Table 1. Demographic Details of the Sample's PSTs

Variable	*Feature*	*F*	*%*
Gender	Male	44	29.3
	Female	106	70.7
Age	17-19	27	18.0
	20-22	67	44.7
	23-25	38	25.3
	Above 25	18	12
Program Type	B.A.B.Ed	25	16.7
	B.Sc.B.Ed	59	39.3
	B.Ed. Science Group	16	10.7
	B.Ed. Social Science and Language Group	14	9.3
	M.Ed. Science Group	25	16.7
	M.Ed. Social Science and Language Group	11	7.3
Education of Mother	Primary	10	6.7
	Middle	57	38.0
	Secondary	32	21.3
	Higher Secondary	27	18.0
	Undergraduate or Graduate	17	11.3
	Post Graduate	7	4.7
Education of Father	Primary	3	2.0
	Middle	11	7.3
	Secondary	33	22.0
	Higher Secondary	37	24.7
	Undergraduate or Graduate	41	27.3
	Post Graduate	25	16.7
Do you have any AI apps on your Smartphone?	Yes	107	71.3
	No	43	28.7
Have you had any technological training?	Yes	60	40
	No	90	60
Is AI a part of your work?	Yes	111	74
	No	39	26
Total		150	100

Source: Author's estimate based on the field survey (2025).

With respect to the participants' mothers' education level, 6.7% (f=10) had completed primary education, while 38.0% (f=57) had completed middle, 21.3% (f=32) had completed secondary school, 18% (f = 27) had completed higher secondary,

11.3% (f=17) had a degree of undergraduate or graduate, and only 4.7% (f = 7) had completed university studies or above. A total of 27.3% (f = 41) of the fathers of PSTs had a bachelor's degree, whereas 24.7% (f = 37) had higher secondary, 22.0% (f = 33) had secondary school, 16.7% (f = 25) had postgraduate, 7.3% (f=11) had middle, and only 2% (f=3) had primary education qualifications. This means that the mothers and fathers of 150 PSTs had different levels of education.

The majority of participants, i.e., 71.3% (f = 107), reported that they are using AI apps on their mobile devices, and 74% (f = 111) of respondents agreed that they use AI for personal or academic research. These findings demonstrate that AI technologies are now widely deployed and actively used by PSTs to increase learning and skills. Nonetheless, 60% (f = 90) of respondents reported not receiving any technological training, while 40% (f = 60) of respondents had received professional training in the use of AI. The results show that the sample group is mostly composed of young female students who have a high level of exposure to technology, particularly artificial intelligence (AI) applications.

AI Literacy Scale of Respondents

Table 2. Summary of the AI literacy scale scores of PSTs

Items	Construct	SD	D	N	A	SA	χ^2 Test
I am able to employ AI applications in my everyday life.	Using and Application of AI	4	5.3	14.7	36.0	40.0	21.564
I can simplify my daily life using AI apps.		7.3	9.3	7.3	33.3	42.7	29.647***
I can employ AI significantly to attain my daily aims.		9.3	10.7	6.0	34.0	40.0	26.253
I can work with AI in my daily life to enhance my productivity.		8.0	8.7	10.0	35.3	38.0	13.099
I can collaborate profitably with an artificial intelligence in my daily life.		10.0	5.3	8.7	40.0	36.0	18.968
I am able to use artificial intelligence to communicate profitably in my daily life.		9.3	8.0	11.3	34.0	37.3	29.941***

continued on following page

Table 2. Continued

Items	Construct	SD	D	N	A	SA	χ^2 Test
I know key ideas in the area of AI.	Knowledge and comprehension of AI	7.3	8.7	14.7	33.3	36.0	21.426
I am aware of what artificial intelligence is.		8.7	11.3	8.7	34.7	36.7	29.113***
I am able to analyze the pros and downsides of adopting AI.		11.3	5.3	6.0	38.0	39.3	26.065
I am able to evaluate the benefits and drawbacks of using AI.		7.3	2.0	6.7	40.0	44.0	19.551
I can come up with novel applications for AI.		6.0	3.3	9.3	39.3	42.0	15.456
I can see potential applications for AI in the future.		8.0	10.7	10.0	35.3	36.0	24.575
I can detect whether the application I'm using is based on AI.	Detection of AI	7.3	8.7	10.7	33.3	40.0	12.909
I am able to tell the difference between AI-enabled and non-AI equipment.		5.3	8.7	9.3	34.0	42.7	16.164
I can tell whether I'm interacting with a "real human" or an AI.		4.0	9.3	11.3	32.0	43.3	22.703
I am able to assess how employing AI would affect society.	Ethics of AI	11.3	6.7	7.3	32.7	42.0	24.695
When determining whether to utilize data supplied by an AI, I am able to take ethical factors into account.		8.0	3.3	8.7	36.0	44.0	13.440
I am able to assess the ethical implications of AI-based applications.		4.7	5.3	16.7	33.3	40.0	32.700*

Source: Author's estimation as per the field survey (2025). **Note:** *Measured on a five-point Likert scale: (SD= Strongly Disagree, D= Disagree, N= Neutral, A= Agree, SA=Strongly Agree. *p<0.05, **p<0.01, ***p<0.10).*

Most of the PSTs had various levels of knowledge of AI literacy (Table 2). With respect to the usability and application of AI, 40% of respondents had used AI in their daily life, whereas 42.7% of respondents had strongly agreed that they had used AI to make their life easier. Forty percent of PSTs strongly agreed that they utilized AI significantly to accomplish their daily objectives, whereas 38% of respondents strongly agreed that AI made their lives simpler. Thirty-six percent of PSTs strongly feel that they work with AI gainfully, and 37.3% interact with AI gainfully in daily life.

In terms of knowing and comprehending AI, 36% of PSTs strongly agreed that they understood the main essential ideas of the AI, whereas 36.7% of PSTs strongly agreed that they recognized the definition of AI. A total of 39.3% of PSTs strongly agreed that they could analyze the limits and possibilities of using AI, while 40% of PSTs strongly agreed that they could determine the benefits and drawbacks of

AI. Forty-two percent of PSTs strongly agreed that they can conceive of novel applications of AI, whereas 36.0% of PSTs strongly agreed that they can envision potential future use of AI. Information about the application of AI through apps indicates that 40% of PSTs strongly agreed that they are using AI through an app. When asked if they could determine the difference between devices that use AI and those that do not, 42.7% of the PSTs strongly agreed. When asked if they could explain the difference between interacting with an AI and a "real human," 43.3% of the PSTs strongly agreed. Forty-two percent of PSTs strongly agreed that they could think about the effects of using AI on society, 42% strongly agreed that they could think about ethical issues when deciding whether to use data from an AI, and 40% of PSTs strongly agreed that they could look at AI-based applications to see what ethical issues they might have.

The results of the chi-square test demonstrated the link between various programs of PSTs and their AI literacy level. The chi-square results show that all of the AI literary skill items are not statistically significant (accepting H_0), except for using AI applications to make life easier, talking to AI in a useful way every day, knowing what artificial intelligence is, and looking at AI-based applications to see how they affect ethics. The main conclusions of the research indicate that PSTs' levels of AI literacy do not vary much. In other words, even if they are in various programs, the level of AI literacy among PSTs is the same.

Scale Reliability of Items and Construct

Table 3. Scale reliability of the items

Item	Item-test correlation	Item-rest correlation	Average interitem correlation	Alpha
Item1	0.1463	-0.0329	0.0501	0.4728
Item2	0.3157	0.1427	0.0431	0.4339
Item3	0.3561	0.1864	0.0415	0.4239
Item4	0.3114	0.1381	0.0433	0.435
Item5	0.2392	0.062	0.0463	0.4521
Item6	0.3208	0.1483	0.0429	0.4327
Item7	0.1825	0.0038	0.0486	0.4649
Item8	0.2563	0.0798	0.0456	0.4481
Item9	0.4304	0.2685	0.0384	0.4045
Item10	0.3086	0.1351	0.0434	0.4357
Item11	0.4519	0.2927	0.0375	0.3988

continued on following page

Table 3. Continued

Item	Item-test correlation	Item-rest correlation	Average interitem correlation	Alpha
Item12	0.225	0.0474	0.0469	0.4554
Item13	0.3239	0.1515	0.0428	0.4319
Item14	0.5151	0.3652	0.0349	0.3811
Item15	0.1602	-0.0189	0.0495	0.4698
Item16	0.3966	0.2309	0.0398	0.4135
Item17	0.4242	0.2616	0.0387	0.4062
Item18	0.2275	0.0499	0.0468	0.4548
Test scale			0.0434	0.4493

Source: Author's estimation

The Cronbach's alpha test is applied to check the overall and scale reliability of an individual item. The statistical value of the Cronbach's alpha test is reported to be less than 0.5 for each item (Table 3). This means that further statistical tests, such as CFA and EFA, cannot be applied to the collected data set. The low value of this test may be due to low variation in the academic patterns of these institutions. Moreover, most respondents were teachers at these institutions. Most specifically, all the teachers have a similar ecosystem in these institutions. Therefore, all the teachers received similar training to increase their understanding of AI tools. Therefore, further studies should include larger sample sizes with diverse institutions across Indian states to resolve the abovementioned issues. Accordingly, *CFA* and *EFA* can be applied to obtain a better understanding of teachers' attitudes toward AI.

DISCUSSION

The findings of this chapter are significant because the students who use AI have greater knowledge of AI. The outcome of the study reveals that PSTs with different programs do not have any effect on their AI literacy due to the easy accessibility of digital technology. This finding indicates that using technology in teaching and learning processes has advanced their learning skills, which is in line with the findings of Mishra and Koehler (2006). It also reveals the active use of AI by PSTs, which discuss their practical approach to the new technology by understanding the potential of integrating AI in their learning process (Luckin, 2017). They also discovered how AI could be helpful for saving their time, making them find the information in a very easy way, helping them very quickly in searching for any particular information, and advancing their learning process. It is apparent that some PSTs, who prepare teaching curricula, have low proficiencies in the preparation of new and interesting studies in AI. This situation compels PSTs to develop competences beyond technical skills with AI tools.

The results also demonstrated a very complex system in which students interrelate AI according to their needs. This finding is significant in addition to the increasing body of empirical research. The outcomes of the study demonstrated that PSTs have different views on AI. Our findings revealed that PSTs have different programs with different outlooks on the use of AI in teaching and learning processes. The results of the field study revealed that some PSTs actively apply AI in their learning process, while others do not. Those who have very deep knowledge about AI might integrate it into their teaching and learning methods in a very effective manner (Starkey, 2010; Gamlem et al., 2025). Another finding of the study illustrated that the actual knowledge of AI is still very low among PSTs, while they claim that they are quite familiar with AI. These findings are consistent with those of another study that reported the overestimation of AI knowledge by PSTs (Luckin et al., 2017). Finally, most of the students had mixed views about AI. However, they acknowledged that AI may improve the efficiency of lesson preparation and resource collection. The results were in line with research showing AI's ability to assist with administrative and teaching duties (Susnjak & McIntosh, 2024). However, there were widespread concerns about reliability, moral application, and the decline of human-centered education methods. These concerns align with broader discussions in the literature on the dangers of overreliance on AI and its effects on one's professional identity (Selwyn, 2019).

IMPLICATIONS FOR TEACHERS AND EDUCATIONAL ORGANIZATIONS

There are significant ramifications for teachers and education in terms of the differences in PSTs' attitudes and methods. First, the results emphasize the need to include AI literacy in the curriculum as part of pedagogical and ethical competence, not only as a technological talent (Creely et al., 2025; Ng et al., 2021). Second, the use of AI is influenced by students' attitudes and behavior (Tondeur et al., 2017). In addition, the use of AI should be subject-specific and permitted by institutions, guided by professional ethics, rather than a one-size-fits-all approach. They may use AI more effectively and with greater confidence if they have a proper opportunity for collaborative study. PSTs should gain more knowledge of AI applications. More training programs must be organized to increase the awareness of PSTs to apply AI.

LIMITATION AND FUTURE WORK

Several limitations must be acknowledged since they may impact the interpretability and generalizability of the findings. First, since the PSTs were chosen from a particular demographic and geographic area of the Indian state of Odisha, the results may not be as applicable to a larger cohort of PSTs in India. Differences in educational frameworks and cultural environments may have influenced AI adoption, while these associations were not identified in this research. As a result, determining causal linkages among the constructs is difficult, as this study is cross-sectional. Longitudinal approaches need to be used in future studies to provide a more thorough investigation of the development of AI literacy. In addition, a more nuanced understanding of the causal relationships between different aspects of AI literacy and competency would result from such an approach. Furthermore, social desirability bias may be introduced by depending only on self-reported data, which might jeopardize the veracity of the participants' stated skills and actions. We are also aware of the limitations of employing survey data. In particular, the small sample size limits the generalization of the qualitative findings, especially in regard to PSTs. Moreover, the statistical values of the Cronbach's alpha test are less than 0.5 for all the items in this research. This value for all the items is beyond the accepted range for further statistical investigations, such as CFA and EFA. Our sample size was 150 respondents from the three colleges in the same district. These colleges have a uniform academic ecosystem. Moreover, PSTs have attended similar programs and training to improve their understanding of AI. This means that all the items have less variation in magnitude. Therefore, the statistical values of the Cronbach's alpha test for all the items are reported to be less than 0.5. Hence, this study suggested that a larger sample size from different colleges across Indian states is needed to analyze the real implications of AI for improving the knowledge of PSTs in India.

Furthermore, subsequent studies might enhance the validity of its findings by integrating objective evaluations and observational techniques. Furthermore, the main focus of this research was on the personal characteristics that affect the AI literacy of PSTs. Future studies should include contextual elements, curriculum design, institutional support, and teaching strategies to provide a more systematic understanding of the evolution of the AI literacy of PSTs. More research should be undertaken on how quickly AI technology is developing in an educational context. Given these limitations, future research initiatives should focus on filling these gaps and expanding on the current results. As a result, this approach provides a better understanding of the complex process of PSTs' growth in AI literacy and provides useful information for practitioners and policy makers.

POLICY RECOMMENDATIONS

AI literacy is a multidisciplinary approach that depends on multiple activities, such as behavioral intention and the perception of an individual. Professional development training programs, AI knowledge and skills, etc., are essential for increasing the intention of an individual to apply AI in educational organizations. Thus, educational organizations should organize regular training programs for PSTs to increase their awareness of AI usage and its practical implications. AI trainers should also inform the negative consequences of AI in educational organizations. For instance, the extensive use of AI will reduce the thinking and logical capacity of teachers and students in educational organizations. Thus, teachers and students should pursue ethical practices for using AI in educational organizations. To foster critical thinking, educational institutions should provide course materials to use AI from the perspective of users and creators. For that, the curriculum must emphasize the ethics, data protection and proof of authenticity within the AI system.

Practical, hands-on training may be crucial to achieving these goals. In addition, project-based learning and pedagogical approaches must be introduced in educational organizations. AI must be applied to solve existing problems in educational organizations. These initiatives encourage young students and teachers to apply AI to increase their innovative skills and make them intellectual in educational organizations. Moreover, requirement-based applications of AI would be more fruitful for students and teachers in educational organizations. Educational organizations should increase the digital competency and literacy of PSTs to motivate them to apply AI. Educational organizations should increase the AI competency of teachers to further utilize AI in education (Kim & Kwon, 2023). AI readiness is also required to increase the usability and practicability of teachers (Luckin et al., 2022). Educational organizations must develop appropriate ICT ecosystems and e-platforms to increase the practice of digital technologies (Singh et al., 2024a).

CONCLUSION

This study concluded that the use of technology helps improve PST teaching and learning. The use of AI appears to increase consistency and access to the materials required for PSTs. PSTs have attended various programs on the use of AI in teaching and learning. There is little knowledge about AI among PSTs in the survey area. PSTs have mixed opinions about the use of AI in academic work. There is also significant variation in AI literacy among PSTs. PSTs face multiple challenges, such as limited knowledge, low literacy, and limited ability to use AI. PSTs are perceived as widespread worries about using AI. The use of AI would improve the efficacy of PSTs in preparing lesson plans and delivering lectures in the classroom.

The results also provide insights into the consistency of PSTs' AI knowledge. It may help to provide guidance and targeted interventions in teacher education programs to improve PSTs' AI competence. This study provides a basic overview of PSTs' perceptions and experiences of using AI in their academic activities, such as conducting research, preparing lecture materials, and delivering lectures in the classroom. The paper's findings reveal both agreement and disagreement among PSTs regarding the pedagogical use of AI. The application of AI is also affected by PSTs' comfort and confidence levels. Nevertheless, concerns remain about the reliability, ethical use, and upholding of human-centered educational principles in AI applications within educational organizations. PSTs require structural support, institutional guidance, and targeted professional development for the further application of AI in educational organizations.

Most importantly, this study highlights that successful AI integration requires not only technical training but also pedagogical modeling, ethical awareness, and critical reflection among educational organizations. AI advancements and teacher education programs need to take proactive measures to address these problems by incorporating AI literacy into their curricula. It establishes collaborative spaces where students and teachers can work together to analyze the benefits and drawbacks of AI and other emerging technologies in educational organizations.

REFERENCES

Abedi, E. A. (2024). Tensions between technology integration practices of teachers and ICT in education policy expectations: Implications for change in teacher knowledge, beliefs and teaching practices. *Journal of Computers in Education, 11*(4), 1215–1234. DOI: 10.1007/s40692-023-00296-6

Ayanwale, M. A., Adelana, O. P., Molefi, R. R., Adeeko, O., & Ishola, A. M. (2024). Examining artificial intelligence literacy among preservice teachers for future classrooms. *Computer Education Open, 6*, 100179. . caeo.2024.100179DOI: 10.1016/j

Ayanwale, M. A., Adelana, O. P., Molefi, R. R., Adeeko, O., & Ishola, A. M. (2024a). Examining artificial intelligence literacy among preservice teachers for future classrooms. *Computers and Education Open, 6*, 100179. Advance online publication. DOI: 10.1016/j.caeo.2024.100179

BaHammam, R. (2023). Artificial intelligence in education: Opportunities, challenges, and future directions. *Educational Technology Research Journal, 41*(2), 105–124. DOI: 10.1234/edtech.2023.41.2.105

Behera, A., Trivedi, P., Patra, S. K., & Makeni, C. (2025). Artificial intelligence and higher education: A systematic review. *American Journal of STEM Education, 11*(1), 27–52. DOI: 10.32674/0x43s107

Bhat, M. (1996). Outcome of rehabilitation programme: Is there a differential response? *European Psychiatry : the Journal of the Association of European Psychiatrists, 11*(4), 281–295. DOI: 10.1016/0924-9338(96)88851-1

Brianza, E., Schmid, M., Tondeur, J., & Petko, D. (2024). The digital silver lining of the pandemic: The impact on preservice teachers' technological knowledge and beliefs. *Education and Information Technologies, 29*(2), 1591–1616. DOI: 10.1007/s10639-023-11801-w

Büyüköztürk, Ş. KılıçÇakmak, E., Akgün, Ö. E., Karadeniz, Ş., & Demirel, F. (2024). Sampling methods. In Scientific Research Methods in Education (pp. 82-103). Pegem Academy.

Celik, I. (2023). Toward intelligent-TPACK: An empirical study on teachers' professional knowledge to ethically integrate artificial intelligence (AI)-based tools into education. *Computers in Human Behavior, 138*, 107468. DOI: 10.1016/j.chb.2022.107468

Celik, I., Dindar, M., Muukkonen, H., & J¨arvel, S. (2022). The promises and challenges of artificial intelligence for teachers: A systematic review of research. *TechTrends*, *66*(1), 616–630. DOI: 10.1007/s11528-022-00715-y

Černý, M. (2024). University students' conceptualization of AI literacy: Theory and empirical evidence. *Social Sciences (Basel, Switzerland)*, *13*(3), 1–26. DOI: 10.3390/socsci13030129

Chounta, I. A., Bardone, E., Raudsep, A., & Pedaste, M. (2022). Exploring teachers' perceptions of artificial intelligence as a tool to support their practice in Estonian K-12 education. *International Journal of Artificial Intelligence in Education*, *32*(3), 725–755. DOI: 10.1007/s40593-021-00243-5

Creely, E., Barnes, M., Tour, E., Henderson, M., Waterhouse, P., Pena, M. A., & Patel, S. V. (2025). Exploring attitudes to generative AI in education for English as an additional language (EAL) adult learners. *ReCALL*, *37*(2), 1–17. DOI: 10.1017/S0958344024000314

Czaja, R. (1998). Questionnaire pretesting comes of age. *Marketing Bulletin*, *9*(1), 52–66.

Davis, F. D. (1989). Perceived usefulness, perceived ease of use, and user acceptance of information technology. *Management Information Systems Quarterly*, *13*(3), 319–340. DOI: 10.2307/249008

De, D., & Singh, A. K. (2025). A global perspective on impact of digitalization on business development. In Yıldırım, D., Yıldırım, S., & Kandpal, V. (Eds.), *Sustainable Digitalization Strategies in Business and Healthcare* (pp. 1–32). IGI Global Scientific Publishing., DOI: 10.4018/979-8-3373-5087-5.ch001

Dexter, S. L., Anderson, R. E., & Becker, H. J. (1999). Teachers' views of computers as catalysts for changes in their teaching practice. *Journal of Research on Computing in Education*, *31*(3), 221–239. DOI: 10.1080/08886504.1999.10782252

Elçiçek, M. (2024). An investigation on students' artificial intelligence literacy. *Journal of Information and Communication Technologies*, *6*(1), 24–35.

Fishbein, M., & Ajzen, I. (1975). *Belief, attitude, intention, and behavior: An introduction to theory and research*. Addison-Wesley.

Frimpong, V. (2025). Artificial intelligence investment in resource-constrained African economies: Financial, strategic, and ethical trade-offs with broader implications. *WORLD (Oakland, Calif.)*, *6*(2), 1–17.

Gamlem, S. M., McGrane, J., Brandmo, C., Moltudal, S., Sun, S. Z., & Hopfenbeck, T. N. (2025). Exploring preservice teachers' attitudes and experiences with generative AI: A mixed methods study in Norwegian teacher education. *Educational Psychology*, *46*(1), 27–51. DOI: 10.1080/01443410.2025.2528663

Guan, L., Zhang, Y., & Gu, M. M. (2025). Preservice teachers preparedness for AI-integrated education: An investigation fromperceptions, capabilities, and teachers' identity changes. *Computers and Education: Artificial Intelligence*, *8*, 100341. Advance online publication. DOI: 10.1016/j.caeai.2024.100341

Gudmundsdottir, G. B., & Hatlevik, O. E. (2018). Newly qualified teachers' professional digital competence: Implications for teacher education. *European Journal of Teacher Education*, *41*(2), 214–231. DOI: 10.1080/02619768.2017.1416085

Haenlein, M., & Kaplan, A. (2019). A brief history of artificial intelligence: On the past, present, and future of artificial intelligence. *California Management Review*, *61*(4), 5–14. DOI: 10.1177/0008125619864925

Heine, S., & K¨onig, J. (2025). Applying artificial intelligence in teacher education: Preservice teachers' attitudes and reflections in using ChatGPT for teaching and learning. *European Journal of Teacher Education*, *48*(5), 934–963. DOI: 10.1080/02619768.2025.2540791

Helvaci, İ. (2025). Preparing teachers for a ChatGPT-influenced workforce. *Kastamonu Education Journal*, *33*(2), 401–410.

Hermann, E. (2022). Artificial intelligence and mass personalization of communication content—An ethical and literacy perspective. *New Media & Society*, *24*(5), 1258–1277. DOI: 10.1177/14614448211022702

Hornberger, M., Bewersdorff, A., & Nerdel, C. (2023). What do university students know about Artificial Intelligence? Development and validation of an AI literacy test. *Computers and Education: Artificial Intelligence*, *5*, 100165. DOI: 10.1016/j.caeai.2023.100165

Huang, F., Wang, Y., & Zhang, H. (2024). Modeling generative AI acceptance, perceived teachers' enthusiasm and self-efficacy to English as a foreign language learners' wellbeing in the digital era. *European Journal of Education*, *59*(4), e12770. DOI: 10.1111/ejed.12770

Jordan, M. I. (2019). Artificial intelligence—The revolution hasn't happened yet. *Harvard Data Science Review*, *1*(1), 1–9.

Karan, B., & Angadi, G. R. (2024). Potential risks of artificial intelligence integration into school education: A systematic review. *Bulletin of Science, Technology & Society, 43*(3–4), 67–85. Advance online publication. DOI: 10.1177/02704676231224705

Karataş, F., & Yüce, E. (2024). AI and the future of teaching: Preservice teachers' reflections on the use of artificial intelligence inopen and distributed learning. *International Review of Research in Open and Distance Learning*, *25*(3), 304–325. Advance online publication. DOI: 10.19173/irrodl.v25i3.7785

Kasneci, E., Sessler, K., Küchemann, S., Bannert, M., Dementieva, D., Fischer, F., Gasser, U., Groh, G., Günnemann, S., Hüllermeier, E., Krusche, S., Kutyniok, G., Michaeli, T., Nerdel, C., Pfeffer, J., Poquet, O., Sailer, M., Schmidt, A., Seidel, T., & Kasneci, G. (2023). ChatGPT for good? On opportunities and challenges of large language models for education. *Learning and Individual Differences*, *103*, 102274. DOI: 10.1016/j.lindif.2023.102274

Khare, K., Stewart, B., & Khare, A. (2018). Artificial intelligence and the student experience: An institutional perspective. *IAFOR Journal of Education, 6*(3), 63-78. https://files.eric.ed.gov/fulltext/EJ1198691.pdf

Kim, K., & Kwon, K. (2023). Exploring the AI competencies of elementary school teachers in South Korea. *Computers and Education: Artificial Intelligence*, *4*, 100137. DOI: 10.1016/j.caeai.2023.100137

Kohnke, L., Zou, D., & Xie, H. (2025). Microlearning and generative AI for preserviceteacher education: A qualitative case study. *Education and Information Technologies*, *30*(1), 21221–21248. DOI: 10.1007/s10639-025-13606-5

Kundu, A., Bej, T., & Mondal, R. (2025). Exploring teachers' AI literacy: Cognitive, pedagogical, ethical, and contextual insights from Indian schools. *Teaching Education*, •••, 1–21. DOI: 10.1080/10476210.2025.2570227

Laupichler, M. C., Aster, A., Schirch, J., & Raupach, T. (2022). Artificial intelligence literacy in higher and adult education: A scoping literature review. *Computers and Education: Artificial Intelligence*, *3*, 100101. DOI: 10.1016/j.caeai.2022.100101

Lindfors, M., Pettersson, F., & Olofsson, A. D. (2021). Conditions for professional digitalcompetence: The teacher educators' view. *Education Inquiry*, *12*(4), 390–409. DOI: 10.1080/20004508.2021.1890936

Long, D., & Magerko, B. (2020). What is AI literacy? Competencies and design considerations. In *Proceedings of the 2020 CHI conference on human factors in computing systems* (pp. 1–16). DOI: 10.1145/3313831.3376727

Luckin, R. (2017). Toward artificial intelligence-based assessment systems. *Nature Human Behavior*, 1(3), 0028. DOI: 10.1038/s41562-016-0028

Luckin, R., Cukurova, M., Kent, C., & du Boulay, B. (2022). Empowering educators to be AI-ready. *Computers and Education: Artificial Intelligence*, *3*, 1–11. DOI: 10.1016/j.caeai.2022.100076

McCarthy, J. (2004). *What is artificial intelligence.* [Online]. http://www-formal .standford.edu/jmc/whatisai.html

Miao, F., & Shiohira, K. (2024). *AI competency framework for students* [Online]. UNESCO., DOI: 10.54675/JKJB9835

Mishra, P., & Koehler, M. J. (2006). Technological pedagogical content knowledge: A framework for teacher knowledge. *Teachers College Record*, *108*(6), 1017–1054. DOI: 10.1111/j.1467-9620.2006.00684.x

Moorhouse, B. L. (2024). Beginning and first-year language teachers' readiness for the generative AI age. *Computers and Education: Artificial Intelligence*, *6*, 100201. DOI: 10.1016/j.caeai.2024.100201

Moorhouse, B. L., Wan, Y., Wu, C., Kohnke, L., Ho, T. Y., & Kwong, T. (2024). Developing language teachers' professional generative AI competence: An intervention study in an initial language teacher education course. *System*, *125*, 103399. DOI: 10.1016/j.system.2024.103399

Ng, D. T. K., Leung, J. K. L., Chu, S. K. W., & Qiao, M. S. (2021). Conceptualizing AI literacy: An exploratory review. *Computers and Education: Artificial Intelligence*, *2*, 100041. DOI: 10.1016/j.caeai.2021.100041

Ng, D. T. K., Leung, J. K. L., Su, J., Ng, R. C. W., & Chu, S. K. W. (2023). Teachers' AI digital competencies and twenty-first century skills in the postpandemic world. *Education Technology Research and Development, 71*(1), 137–161. , 023-10203-6DOI: 10.1007/s11423-023-10203-6

Obschanka, M., & Audretsch, D. B. (2020). Artificial intelligence and big data in entrepreneurship: A new era has begun. *Small Business Economics*, *55*(1), 529–539. DOI: 10.1007/s11187-019-00202-4

Park, M., & Son, J. B. (2022). Preservice EFL teachers' readiness in computer-assisted language learning and teaching. *Asia Pacific Journal of Education*, *42*(2), 320–334. DOI: 10.1080/02188791.2020.1815649

Popenici, S. A. D., & Kerr, S. (2017). Exploring the impact of artificial intelligence on teaching and learning in higher education. *Research and Practice in Technology Enhanced Learning*, *12*(1), 22. DOI: 10.1186/s41039-017-0062-8

Russell, S. J., & Norvig, P. (2016). *Artificial intelligence: a modern approach* (3rd ed.). Pearson Education Limited.

Salas-Pilco, S. Z., Xiao, K., & Hu, X. (2022). Artificial intelligence and learning analytics in teacher education: A systematic review. *Education Sciences*, *12*(8), 569. DOI: 10.3390/educsci12080569

Selwyn, N. (2019). *Should robots replace teachers? AI and the future of education*. John Wiley & Sons.

Seo, K., Yoo, M., Dodson, S., & Jin, S.-H. (2024). Augmented teachers: K-12 teachers' needs for artificial intelligence's complementary role in personalized learning. *Journal of Research on Technology in Education*, *57*(4), 876–893. DOI: 10.1080/15391523.2024.2330525

Singh, A. K., Ashraf, S. N., & Gupta, M. (2025). Digital transformation and customer's problems in banking industry of India. In Tunio, M. (Ed.), *Applications of Career Transitions and Entrepreneurship* (pp. 1–34). IGI Global Scientific Publishing., DOI: 10.4018/979-8-3693-4163-6.ch001

Singh, A. K., & Singh, R. (2025). Digital infrastructure and sustainable development goals in G20 countries. In Popescu, C. (Ed.), *Building Inclusive Global Knowledge Societies for Sustainable Development* (pp. 363–408). IGI Global Scientific Publishing., DOI: 10.4018/979-8-3693-6298-3.ch014

Singh, A. K., Singh, R., & Thapliyal, C. (2024b). Current challenges and future prospective of new education policy 2020 in higher educational institutions of India. In R. Kumar, E. Ong, S. Anggoro, T. Toh, & M. Fukui (Ed.), *Transdisciplinary Teaching and Technological Integration for Improved Learning: Case Studies and Practical Approaches* (pp. 269-301). IGI Global. DOI: 10.4018/979-8-3693-8217-2.ch013

Singh, A. K., Singh, S., & Shamra, S. K. (2024a). Importance and challenges of online learning in higher educational institutions during COVID-19 in Uttarakhand state of India. In Hossain, S. (Ed.), *Cases on Social Media and Entrepreneurship* (pp. 193–212). IGI Global., DOI: 10.4018/979-8-3693-1781-5.ch012

Sobaih, A. E. E., Elshaer, I. A., & Hasanein, A. M. (2024). Examining students' acceptance and use of ChatGPT in Saudi Arabian higher education. *European Journal of Investigation in Health, Psychology and Education*, *14*(3), 709–721. DOI: 10.3390/ejihpe14030047

Sperling, K., Stenberg, C.-J., McGrath, C., Åkerfeldt, A., Heintz, F., & Stenliden, L. (2024). In search of artificial intelligence (AI) literacy in teacher education: A scoping review. *Computers and Education Open*, *6*, 100169. DOI: 10.1016/j.caeo.2024.100169

Starkey, L. (2010). Supporting the digitally able beginning teacher. *Teaching and Teacher Education*, *26*(7), 1429–1438. DOI: 10.1016/j.tate.2010.05.002

Starkey, L. (2020). A review of research exploring teacher preparation for the digital age. *Cambridge Journal of Education*, *50*(1), 37–56. DOI: 10.1080/0305764X.2019.1625867

Susnjak, T., & McIntosh, T. R. (2024). ChatGPT: The end of online exam integrity? *Education Sciences*, *14*(6), 656. DOI: 10.3390/educsci14060656

Tondeur, J., Van Braak, J., Ertmer, P., & Ottenbreit-Leftwich, A. (2017). Understanding the relationship between teachers' pedagogical beliefs and technology use in education: A systematic review of qualitative evidence. *Educational Technology Research and Development*, *65*(3), 555–575. DOI: 10.1007/s11423-016-9481-2

UNESCO. (2024). *AI competency framework for teachers*. UNESCO Digital Library., DOI: 10.54675/ZJTE2084

US Department of Education (USDE). (2023). Artificial intelligence and the future of teaching and learning. [Online]. https://www.ed.gov/sites/ed/files/documents/ai-report/ai-report.pdf

Verganti, R., Vendraminelli, L., & Iansiti, M. (2020). Innovation and design in the age of artificial intelligence. *Journal of Product Innovation Management*, *37*(3), 212–227. DOI: 10.1111/jpim.12523

Wang, B., Rau, P. L. P., & Yuan, T. (2022). Measuring user competence in using artificial intelligence: Validity and reliability of artificial intelligence literacy scale. *Behaviour & Information Technology*, *42*(9), 1324–1337. DOI: 10.1080/0144929X.2022.2072768

Wang, B., Rau, P. L. P., & Yuan, T. (2023). Measuring user competence with artificial intelligence: Validity and reliability of the artificial intelligence literacy scale. *Behaviour & Information Technology*, *42*(9), 1324–1337. DOI: 10.1080/0144929X.2022.2072768

Wang, K., Ruan, Q., Zhang, X., Fu, C., & Duan, B. (2024). Preservice teachers' GenAI anxiety, technology self-efficacy, and TPACK: Their structural relations with behavioral intention to design GenAI-assisted teaching. *Behavioral Sciences (Basel, Switzerland)*, *14*(5), 373. DOI: 10.3390/bs14050373

Willinsky, J. (2006). *The access principle: The case for open access to research and scholarship*. MIT Press.

Y. (2025). Conceptualizing preservice teachers' artificial intelligence readiness and examining its relationship with various variables: The role of artificial intelligence literacy, digital citizenship, artificial intelligence-enhanced innovation and perceived threats from artificial intelligence. *Information Development, 41*(3), 916-932. DOI: 10.1177/02666669251335657

Yang, Y.-F., Tseng, C. C., & Lai, S.-C. (2024). Enhancing teachers' self-efficacy beliefs in integrating AI-based technology into English-language teaching through a professional development program. *Teaching and Teacher Education, 144*, 104582. Advance online publication. DOI: 10.1016/j.tate.2024.104582

Zawacki-Richter, O., Marín, V. I., Bond, M., & Gouverneur, F. (2019). Systematic review of research on artificial intelligence applications in higher education–where are the educators? *International Journal of Educational Technology in Higher Education, 16*(1), 39. DOI: 10.1186/s41239-019-0171-0

Zhang, J., Zhang, M., & Liu, X. (2023). Acceptance of artificial intelligence among preservice teachers: A multigroup analysis. *International Journal of Educational Technology in Higher Education, 20*(1), 49. DOI: 10.1186/s41239-023-00420-7

KEY TERMS AND DEFINITIONS

Artificial Intelligence (AI): AI helps improve learning, reasoning, decision-making, and problem-solving and increases humanity's intellectual capacity.

AI Knowledge and Skills: AI knowledge and skills ensure the ability and efficiency of a person to understand the usability of AI, understand its utilization, and follow appropriate guidelines for further utilization.

AI Literacy: AI literacy refers to an individual's adaptability, knowledge, and skills to apply AI in an academic organization.

Behavioral Intention (BI): BI includes the personal attitude of an individual to perceive or engage in an activity to achieve a certain task. It is a person's intention to behave in a certain way to handle existing problems and finalize solutions.

Digital Competency and Literacy: Digital competency measures the ability of a person to apply digital technologies with confidence and responsibility in their life. Digital literacy encompasses an individual's reading, writing, technical application, and critical thinking in the use of digital technologies.

Educational Organizations: These are academic institutions where teachers, trainers, and students work together to create knowledge, learning, skills, talent, technology, and innovation for further social, economic, technological, and human development.

Technology: It is the practical and scientific application of knowledge, skills, mechanical processes, and methods for producing new products, improving production processes, and reducing human effort to achieve success.

Compilation of References

Abbasi, B. N., Wu, Y., & Luo, Z. (2025). Exploring the impact of artificial intelligence on curriculum development in global higher education institutions. *Education and Information Technologies*, *30*(1), 547–581. DOI: 10.1007/s10639-024-13113-z

Abdaljaleel, M., Barakat, M., Alsanafi, M., Salim, N. A., Abazid, H., Malaeb, D., Mohammed, A. H., Hassan, B. A. R., Wayyes, A. M., Farhan, S. S., El Khatib, S., Rahal, M., Sahban, A., Abdelaziz, D. H., Mansour, N. O., AlZayer, R., Khalil, R., Fekih-Romdhane, F., Hallit, R., & Sallam, M. (2024). A multinational study on the factors influencing university students' attitudes and usage of ChatGPT. *Scientific Reports*, *14*(1), 1983. DOI: 10.1038/s41598-024-52549-8

Abdelwahab, H. R., Rauf, A., & Chen, D. (2022). Business students' perceptions of Dutch higher education institutions in preparing them for artificial intelligence work environments. *Industry and Higher Education*, *37*(1), 22–34. DOI: 10.1177/09504222221087614

Abedi, E. A. (2024). Tensions between technology integration practices of teachers and ICT in education policy expectations: Implications for change in teacher knowledge, beliefs and teaching practices. *Journal of Computers in Education*, *11*(4), 1215–1234. DOI: 10.1007/s40692-023-00296-6

Abuadas, M., & Albikawi, Z. (2026). AI ethical awareness and academic integrity in higher education: Development and validation of a new scale. *Ethics & Behavior*, *36*(2), 125–142. DOI: 10.1080/10508422.2025.2511336

Abuhassna, H., Awae, F., Adnan, M. A. B. M., Daud, M., & Almheiri, A. S. B. (2024). The Information Age for Education via Artificial Intelligence and Machine Learning: A Bibliometric and Systematic Literature Analysis. In *International Journal of Information and Education Technology* (Vol. 14, Issue 5). DOI: 10.18178/ijiet.2024.14.5.2095

Abulibdeh, A. (2025). A systematic and bibliometric review of artificial intelligence in sustainable education: Current trends and future research directions. *Sustainable Futures : An Applied Journal of Technology, Environment and Society*, *10*, 101033. Advance online publication. DOI: 10.1016/j.sftr.2025.101033

Acosta-Enriquez, B. G., Arbulu Ballesteros, M., Vilcapoma Pérez, C. R., Huamaní Jordan, O., Martin Vergara, J. A., Martel Acosta, R., Arbulu Perez Vargas, C. G., & Arbulú Castillo, J. C. (2025). AI in academia: How do social influence, self-efficacy, and integrity influence researchers' use of AI models? *Social Sciences & Humanities Open*, *11*, 101274. Advance online publication. DOI: 10.1016/j.ssaho.2025.101274

Acosta-Enriquez, B. G., Ramos Farroñan, E. V., Villena Zapata, L. I., Mogollon Garcia, F. S., Rabanal-León, H. C., Angaspilco, J. E. M., & Bocanegra, J. C. S. (2024). Acceptance of artificial intelligence in university contexts: A conceptual analysis based on UTAUT2 theory. *Heliyon*, *10*(19), e38315. Advance online publication. DOI: 10.1016/j.heliyon.2024.e38315

Aderibigbe, A. O., Ohenhen, P. E., Nwaobia, N. K., Gidiagba, J. O., & Ani, E. C. (2023). Artificial intelligence in developing countries: Bridging the gap between potential and implementation. *Computer Science & IT Research Journal*, *4*(3), 185–199. DOI: 10.51594/csitrj.v4i3.629

Adiguzel, T., Kaya, M. H., & Cansu, F. K. (2023). Revolutionizing education with AI: Exploring the transformative potential of ChatGPT. *Contemporary Educational Technology*, *15*(3), ep429. DOI: 10.30935/cedtech/13152

Adiprasetio, J. (2025). Epistemic bias and the rise of qualitative dominance in post-authoritarian Indonesian communication research. *Frontiers in Communication*, *10*, 1602567. Advance online publication. DOI: 10.3389/fcomm.2025.1602567

Adu, K. K. (2025). Artificial Intelligence in Academic Libraries: Threats, Opportunities, and Anxiety Levels. *Journal of Library & Information Services in Distance Learning*, *19*(4), 175–194. Advance online publication. DOI: 10.1080/1533290X.2025.2534462

Ahmad Malik, I., Ahmyaw Adem, S., & Rasool, A. (2025). Understanding the adoption of educational AI tools in Sub-Saharan African higher education: A theory of planned behavior-based analysis. *Cogent Education*, *12*(1), 2546126. Advance online publication. DOI: 10.1080/2331186X.2025.2546126

Ahmed, A.M (2025). Theoretical foundations of artificial intelligence and its applications in Arab e-learning. *Libyan Journal of Educational Research and E-Learning (LJERE)*, 31–41. DOI: 10.65417/ljere.v1i1.4

Ahmed, S. A. (2026). Algorithmic dependence and digital colonialism: A conceptual framework for artificial intelligence in education and knowledge systems of the Global South. *Frontiers in Education, 11*, 1720563. Advance online publication. DOI: 10.3389/feduc.2026.1720563

Aithal, P. S., & Maiya, A. K. (2023). Innovations in higher education industry–Shaping the future. [IJCSBE]. *International Journal of Case Studies in Business, IT, and Education*, *7*(4), 283–311. DOI: 10.47992/IJCSBE.2581.6942.0321

Akgun, S., & Greenhow, C. (2022). Artificial intelligence in education: Addressing ethical challenges in K-12 settings. *AI and Ethics*, *2*(3), 431–440. DOI: 10.1007/s43681-021-00096-7 PMID: 34790956

Akinyetun, T. S. (2023). Digital colonialism, data sovereignty, and Africa's quest for technological independence. *African Journal of Science, Technology, Innovation and Development*, *15*(4), 489–501. DOI: 10.1080/20421338.2022.2116579

Akman, I., & Turhan, C. (2017). User acceptance of social learning systems in higher education: An application of the extended Technology Acceptance Model. *Innovations in Education and Teaching International*, *54*(3), 229–237. DOI: 10.1080/14703297.2015.1093426

Alafnan, M. A., Dishari, S., Jovic, M., & Lomidze, K. (2023). ChatGPT as an Educational Tool: Opportunities, Challenges, and Recommendations for Communication, Business Writing, and Composition Courses. *Journal of Artificial Intelligence and Technology*, *3*(2), 60–68. DOI: 10.37965/jait.2023.0184

Al-Ali, A. A., Cherian, J., Farouk, S., & Al Nahyan, M. (2025). Prejob training factors, training effectiveness and graduate employability in support of sustainable development: Evidence from the SANAD program. *Management of Environmental Quality*, •••, 1–22. DOI: 10.1108/MEQ-04-2025-0280

Al-Ayed, S. (2025). Role of Artificial Intelligence Towards Employee Retention Via Mediation of Employee Loyalty: A Company Governance Study. *Journal of Governance and Regulation*, *14*(2), 363. DOI: 10.22495/jgrv14i2siart15

Alba, C., Mcilwain, C., & An, R. (2026). ChatGPT on campus: how top US universities govern generative AI across higher education. *Policy Reviews in Higher Education*, 1-30. https://doi.org/DOI: 10.1080/23322969.2026.2622674

Aldino, A. A., Maheshi, B., Li, Y., Zhou, Y., Tsai, Y.-S., Gašević, D., & Chen, G. (2026). Enhancing learner-centered feedback with AI: Teachers' practices and perceptions. *Assessment & Evaluation in Higher Education*, •••, 1–18. DOI: 10.1080/02602938.2026.2638920

Al-Emran, M., Al-Qaysi, N., Al-Sharafi, M. A., Khoshkam, M., Foroughi, B., & Ghobakhloo, M. (2025). Role of perceived threats and knowledge management in shaping generative AI use in education and its impact on social sustainability. *International Journal of Management Education*, *23*(1), 101105. Advance online publication. DOI: 10.1016/j.ijme.2024.101105

Aleryani, A. Y. (2025). Roadmap: Empower researchers in AI skills in developing countries. *Artificial Intelligence*, *15*(1), 1–13. DOI: 10.14445/22492593/IJCOT-V15I1P301

Alhumaid, K., Ayoubi, K., Khalifa, M., & Salloum, S. (2025). Factors Determining Acceptance of Internet of Things in Medical Education: Mixed Methods Study. *JMIR Human Factors*, *12*, e58377–e58377. DOI: 10.2196/58377

Alhwaiti, M. (2023). Acceptance of Artificial Intelligence Application in the Post-Covid Era and Its Impact on Faculty Members' Occupational Well-being and Teaching Self Efficacy: A Path Analysis Using the UTAUT 2 Model. *Applied Artificial Intelligence*, *37*(1), 2175110. Advance online publication. DOI: 10.1080/08839514.2023.2175110

Alifah, N., & Hidayat, A. R. (2025). Effectiveness of Artificial Intelligence-Based Learning Analytics Tool in Supporting Personalized Learning in Higher Education. *Jurnal Pendidikan Progresif*, *15*(1), 74–84. Advance online publication. DOI: 10.23960/jpp.v15i1.pp74-84

Aljabr, F. S., & Al-Ahdal, A. A. M. H. (2024). Ethical and pedagogical implications of AI in language education: An empirical study at Ha'il University. *Acta Psychologica*, *251*, 104605. Advance online publication. DOI: 10.1016/j.actpsy.2024.104605

Al-Kfairy, M., Mustafa, D., Al-Adaileh, A., Zriqat, S., & Sendaba, O. (2024). User acceptance of AI voice assistants in Jordan's telecom industry. *Computers in Human Behavior Reports*, *16*, 100521. Advance online publication. DOI: 10.1016/j.chbr.2024.100521

Al-Kfairy, M., Mustafa, D., Kshetri, N., Insiew, M., & Alfandi, O. (2024, August). Ethical challenges and solutions of generative AI: An interdisciplinary perspective. [). MDPI.]. *Informatics (MDPI)*, *11*(3), 58. DOI: 10.3390/informatics11030058

Allen, K., Kern, M. L., Vella-Brodrick, D., Hattie, J., & Waters, L. (2018). What schools need to know about fostering school belonging: A meta-analysis. *Educational Psychology Review*, *30*(1), 1–34. DOI: 10.1007/s10648-016-9389-8

Almogren, A. S., Al-Rahmi, W. M., & Dahri, N. A. (2024). Exploring factors influencing the acceptance of ChatGPT in higher education: A smart education perspective. *Heliyon, 10*(11), e31887. Advance online publication. DOI: 10.1016/j.heliyon.2024.e31887

Alnsour, M. M., Qouzah, L., Aljamani, S., Alamoush, R. A., & AL-Omiri, M. K. (2025). AI in education: Enhancing learning potential and addressing ethical considerations among academic staff—a cross-sectional study at the University of Jordan. *International Journal for Educational Integrity*, *21*(1), 16. DOI: 10.1007/s40979-025-00189-4

Al-Rantisi, A. M., ElShanti, N. H., & Harb, S. A. (2025). Challenges of using artificial intelligence in social work education. *Social Work Education*. Advance online publication. DOI: 10.1080/02615479.2025.2483354

Al-Rousan, A. H., Ayasrah, M. N., Salih Yahya, S. M., & Khasawneh, M. A. S. (2025). Design and Psychometric Evaluation of the Artificial Intelligence Acceptance and Usage in Research Creativity Scale Among Faculty Members: Insights From the Network Analysis Perspective. *European Journal of Education*, *60*(1), e12927. Advance online publication. DOI: 10.1111/ejed.12927

Altbach, P. G. (2004). Globalisation and the university: Myths and realities in an unequal world. *Tertiary Education and Management*, *10*(1), 3–25. DOI: 10.1080/13583883.2004.9967114

Alyasin, A., & Shah, M. A. (2026). Human-AI collaboration in academic writing: Exploring university students' agency through a sociocultural lens. *Ampersand (Oxford, UK)*, *16*, 1–11. DOI: 10.1016/j.amper.2026.100256

Al-Zahrani, A. M., & Alasmari, T. M. (2024). Exploring the impact of artificial intelligence on higher education: The dynamics of ethical, social, and educational implications. *Humanities & Social Sciences Communications*, *11*(1), 912. DOI: 10.1057/s41599-024-03432-4

American Association of University Professors (AAUP). (2025). *Artificial intelligence and academic professions.* https://www.aaup.org/reports-publications/aaup-policies-reports/topical-reports/artificial-intelligence-and-academic

Anjulo Lambebo, E., & Chen, H.-L. (2025). Chatbots in higher education: A systematic review. *Interactive Learning Environments*, *33*(4), 2781–2807. DOI: 10.1080/10494820.2024.2436931

Araujo, T., Helberger, N., Kruikemeier, S., & de Vreese, C. H. (2020). In AI we trust? Perceptions about automated decision-making by artificial intelligence. *AI & Society*, *35*(3), 611–623. DOI: 10.1007/s00146-019-00931-w

Archer, L. (2008). Younger academics' constructions of 'authenticity','success' and professional identity. *Studies in Higher Education*, *33*(4), 385–403. DOI: 10.1080/03075070802211729

Aristeidou, M., Cross, S., Rossade, K. D., Wood, C., Rees, T., & Paci, P. (2024). Online exams in higher education: Exploring distance learning students' acceptance and satisfaction. *Journal of Computer Assisted Learning*, *40*(1), 342–359. DOI: 10.1111/jcal.12888

Arora, A., Barrett, M., Lee, E., Oborn, E., & Prince, K. (2023). Risk and the future of AI: Algorithmic bias, data colonialism, and marginalization. *Information and Organization*, *33*(3), 100478. Advance online publication. DOI: 10.1016/j.infoandorg.2023.100478

Arvai, N., Katonai, G., & Mesko, B. (2025). Health Care Professionals' Concerns About Medical AI and Psychological Barriers and Strategies for Successful Implementation: Scoping Review. *Journal of Medical Internet Research*, *27*(1), e66986. Advance online publication. DOI: 10.2196/66986

ASEAN. (2024). *ASEAN guide on AI governance and ethics (2nd ed.)*. ASEAN Secretariat. https://asean.org/asean-guide-on-ai-governance-and-ethics/

Atabekova, A., Atabekov, A., & Shoustikova, T. (2025). AI-Facilitated Lecturers in Higher Education Videos as a Tool for Sustainable Education: Legal Framework, Education Theory and Learning Practice. *Sustainability (Basel)*, *18*(1), 40. DOI: 10.3390/su18010040

Aujourd'hui Le Maroc. (2024). Plus d'étudiants, moins de profs dans nos universités [More students, fewer professors in our universities]. *Aujourd'hui Le Maroc*. https://aujourdhui.ma

Avcı, Ü. (2024). Students' GAI Acceptance: Role of Demographics, Creative Mindsets, Anxiety, Attitudes. *Journal of Computer Information Systems*. Advance online publication. DOI: 10.1080/08874417.2024.2386545

Awadallah Alkouk, W., & Khlaif, Z. N. (2024, December). AI-resistant assessments in higher education: Practical insights from faculty training workshops. [). Frontiers Media SA.]. *Frontiers in Education*, *9*, 1499495. DOI: 10.3389/feduc.2024.1499495

Ayanwale, M. A., Adelana, O. P., Molefi, R. R., Adeeko, O., & Ishola, A. M. (2024). Examining artificial intelligence literacy among preservice teachers for future classrooms. *Computer Education Open, 6*, 100179. . caeo.2024.100179DOI: 10.1016/j

Ayanwale, M. A., Adelana, O. P., Molefi, R. R., Adeeko, O., & Ishola, A. M. (2024a). Examining artificial intelligence literacy among preservice teachers for future classrooms. *Computers and Education Open*, *6*, 100179. Advance online publication. DOI: 10.1016/j.caeo.2024.100179

Ayyash, M. M., & Salah, O. H. (2025). AI adoption in higher education: Advancing sustainable energy management in palestinian universities. *Journal of Open Innovation*, *11*(2), 100534. DOI: 10.1016/j.joitmc.2025.100534

Azevedo, R., Gašević, D., Pavlik, P., Scheines, R., & Smith, H. (2025). Institutional policies on artificial intelligence in higher education: Frameworks and best practices for faculty. *New Directions for Adult and Continuing Education*, *2025*(188), 70–78. Advance online publication. DOI: 10.1002/ace.70013

Azzukhruf, M. W. (2025). Mapping research trends on technology and artificial intelligence in Islamic education: A bibliometric analysis of Scopus Database (2019–2025). *Edu Cendikia: Jurnal Ilmiah Kependidikan*, *5*(3), 1155–1169. DOI: 10.47709/educendikia.v5i03.7604

Babanoğlu, M. P., Karataş, T. Ö., & Dündar, E. (2025). Ethical considerations of AI through a sociotechnical lens: Insights from ELT context as a higher education system. *Cogent Education*, *12*(1), 2488546. Advance online publication. DOI: 10.1080/2331186X.2025.2488546

Babu, M. D., & Kushwaha, B. P. (2024). Does perceived organisational support reduce academicians turnover intention? A mediating role of perceived values of artificial intelligence. *International Journal of Learning and Change*, *16*(5), 508–528. DOI: 10.1504/IJLC.2024.140887

Bae, H., & Bozkurt, A. (2024). The untold story of training students with generative AI: Are we preparing students for true learning or just personalization. *Online Learning : the Official Journal of the Online Learning Consortium*, *28*(3), 1–9. DOI: 10.24059/olj.v28i3.4689

BaHammam, R. (2023). Artificial intelligence in education: Opportunities, challenges, and future directions. *Educational Technology Research Journal*, *41*(2), 105–124. DOI: 10.1234/edtech.2023.41.2.105

Baidoo-Anu, D., Asamoah, D., Amoako, I., & Mahama, I. (2024). Exploring student perspectives on generative artificial intelligence in higher education learning. *Discover Education, 3*(1), 98. Advance online publication. DOI: 10.1007/s44217-024-00173-z

Baig, M. I., & Yadegaridehkordi, E. (2025). Factors influencing academic staff satisfaction and continuous usage of generative artificial intelligence (GenAI) in higher education. *International Journal of Educational Technology in Higher Education, 22*(1), 5. Advance online publication. DOI: 10.1186/s41239-025-00506-4

Bailey, D., Southam, A., & Costley, J. (2021). Digital storytelling with chatbots: Mapping L2 participation and perception patterns. *Interactive Technology and Smart Education, 18*(1), 85–103. DOI: 10.1108/ITSE-08-2020-0170

Baker, R. S., & Hawn, A. (2022). Algorithmic Bias in Education. *International Journal of Artificial Intelligence in Education, 32*(4), 1052–1092. DOI: 10.1007/s40593-021-00285-9

Barki, C. (2021). Recherche scientifique: Le Maroc, grand absent des classements prestigieux des universités [Scientific research: Morocco, largely absent from prestigious university rankings]. *L'Opinion*. https://www.lopinion.ma/Recherche-scientifique-Le-Maroc-grand-absent-desclassements-prestigieux-des-Universites_a17702.html

Barus, O. P., Hidayanto, A. N., Handri, E. Y., Sensuse, D. I., & Yaiprasert, C. (2025). Shaping generative AI governance in higher education: Insights from student perception. *International Journal of Educational Research Open, 8*, 100452. DOI: 10.1016/j.ijedro.2025.100452

Ba, S., Yang, L., Yan, Z., Looi, C. K., & Gašević, D. (2025). Unraveling the mechanisms and effectiveness of AI-assisted feedback in education: A systematic literature review. *Computers and Education Open, 9*, 100284. DOI: 10.1016/j.caeo.2025.100284

Bashir, S., & Lapshun, A. L. (2025). E-learning future trends in higher education in the 2020s and beyond. *Cogent Education, 12*(1), 1–15. DOI: 10.1080/2331186X.2024.2445331

Bashkirova, A., & Krpan, D. (2024). Confirmation bias in AI-assisted decision-making: AI triage recommendations congruent with expert judgments increase psychologist trust and recommendation acceptance. *Computers in Human Behavior: Artificial Humans, 2*(1), 100066. DOI: 10.1016/j.chbah.2024.100066

Batsaikhan, B. Z., & Correia, A. P. (2024). The effects of Generative Artificial Intelligence on Intelligent Tutoring Systems in higher education: A systematic review. *Studies in Technology Enhanced Learning, 4*(1), 1–30. DOI: 10.21428/8c225f6e.33570bb1

Be, B. (2026). AI in Higher Education: Attitudes and Acceptance Among University Students in Cambodia. In P. Chanty, J. Herzing, & M. I. Sean (Eds.), *The Future of AI for Development*. Konrad-Adenauer-Stiftung Cambodia. https://www.kas.de/en/web/kambodscha/digital-insights/detail/-/content/the-future-of-ai-for-development

Beer, D. (2016). How should we do the history of Big Data? *Big Data & Society*, *3*(1), 2053951716646135. Advance online publication. DOI: 10.1177/2053951716646135

Behera, A., Trivedi, P., Patra, S. K., & Makeni, C. (2025). Artificial intelligence and higher education: A systematic review. *American Journal of STEM Education*, *11*(1), 27–52. DOI: 10.32674/0x43s107

Bekbolatova, M., Mayer, J., Ong, C. W., & Toma, M. (2024). Transformative potential of AI in healthcare: Definitions, applications, and navigating the ethical landscape and public perspectives. *Healthcare (Basel)*, *12*(2), 125. Advance online publication. DOI: 10.3390/healthcare12020125

Bergdahl, N., & Sjöberg, J. (2025). Attitudes, perceptions and AI self-efficacy in K-12 education. *Computers and Education: Artificial Intelligence*, *8*, 100358. Advance online publication. DOI: 10.1016/j.caeai.2024.100358

Bhat, J. (2023). Automating higher education administrative processes with AI-powered workflows. *International Journal of Emerging Trends in Computer Science and Information Technology*, *4*(4), 147–157. DOI: 10.63282/3050-9246.IJETCSIT-V4I4P116

Bhat, M. (1996). Outcome of rehabilitation programme: Is there a differential response? *European Psychiatry : the Journal of the Association of European Psychiatrists*, *11*(4), 281–295. DOI: 10.1016/0924-9338(96)88851-1

Binns, R. (2018). Fairness in machine learning: Lessons from political philosophy. In *Conference on fairness, accountability and transparency* (Vol. 81, pp. 149–159). PMLR. https://proceedings.mlr.press/v81/binns18a/binns18a.pdf

Bjørndal, C., Mathisen, P., Wennergren, A.-C., & Thornberg, F. (2024). Challenges of the supervision process in the teacher education practicum – A qualitative research review. *Teaching and Teacher Education*, *146*, 104619. DOI: 10.1016/j.tate.2024.104619

Borenstein, J., & Howard, A. (2021). Emerging challenges in AI and the need for AI ethics education. *AI and Ethics*, *1*(1), 61–65. DOI: 10.1007/s43681-020-00002-7 PMID: 38624388

Bou, D. (2025). Challenges and suggestions for improving the quality of higher education in Cambodia. *Cambodian Journal of Educational Research*, *5*(1), 85–100. DOI: 10.62037/cjer.2025.05.01.03

Bou, D., Sran, L., & Phorn, P. (2025). Exploring Cambodian teacher educators' perspectives and challenges in conducting action research [Journal Article]. *Issues in Educational Research*, *35*(3), 905–922. DOI: 10.3316/informit.T2025102900013190784088009

Bou, D., Sran, L., Teu, S., Tep, C., Kheuy, S., Vy, S., & Dul, V. (2024). Examining self-assessment of student teachers' self-directed learning: A case study at Battambang Teacher Education College, Cambodia. *Education Quarterly Eeview*, *7*(4), 118–135. DOI: 10.31014/aior.1993.07.04.529

Bouhalba, S., ... (2019). Production scientifique nationale en comparaison avec d'autres pays – Scopus (2013–2017) [National scientific production in comparison with other countries – Scopus (2013–2017)]. Centre national pour la recherche scientifique et technique (CNRST). https://barometre.cnrst.ma/images/pdf/EtudeProductionScientifique.pdf

Boujettou, H. (2016). Le « ranking » comme mode de régulation de la performance des établissements de l'enseignement supérieur au Maroc ["Ranking" as a mode of regulating the performance of higher education institutions in Morocco]. *Revue marocaine de management, logistique et transport*.

Boukhari, M. (2023). Enseignement supérieur: des doctorants pour pallier le déficit de professeurs [Higher education: Doctoral students to compensate for the shortage of professors]. Finances News Hebdo. https://www.fnh.ma/article/actualite-education/enseignement-superieur-des-doctorants-pour-pallier-le-deficit-de-professeurs

Bourqia, R. (2009). Vers une sociologie de l'université marocaine [Towards a sociology of the Moroccan university]. *Al-Madrassa Al-Maghribiya*, *2*, 11–56.

Bouzar, A., & El Idrissi, K. (2025). Supervisory feedback vs. AI: A comparative study on postgraduate student satisfaction. *Journal of Arts. Humanities and Social Sciences*, *3*(1), 465–474. DOI: 10.5281/zenodo.14862530

Bower, M., Torrington, J., Lai, J. W., Petocz, P., & Alfano, M. (2024). How should we change teaching and assessment in response to increasingly powerful generative Artificial Intelligence? Outcomes of the ChatGPT teacher survey. *Education and Information Technologies*, *29*(12), 15403–15439. DOI: 10.1007/s10639-023-12405-0

Bozkurt, A., Karadeniz, A., Baneres, D., Guerrero-Roldan, A. E., & Rodríguez, M. E. (2021). Artificial intelligence and reflections from educational landscape: A review of AI studies in half a century. *Sustainability (Basel)*, *13*(2), 800. DOI: 10.3390/su13020800

Branda, F., Ciccozzi, M., & Scarpa, F. (2025). Artificial intelligence in scientific research: Challenges, opportunities and the imperative of a human-centric synergy. *Journal of Informetrics*, *19*(4), 101727. Advance online publication. DOI: 10.1016/j.joi.2025.101727

Brandisauskiene, A., Buksnyte-Marmiene, L., Cesnaviciene, J., & Jarasiunaite-Fedosejeva, G. (2023). The relationship between teachers' autonomy-supportive behavior and learning strategies applied by students: The role of teacher support and equity. *SAGE Open*, *13*(2), 1–16. DOI: 10.1177/21582440231181384

Braun, V., & Clarke, V. (2006). Using thematic analysis in psychology. *Qualitative Research in Psychology*, *3*(2), 77–101. DOI: 10.1191/1478088706qp063oa

Bretag, T., Harper, R., Burton, M., Ellis, C., Newton, P., van Haeringen, K., Saddiqui, S., & Rozenberg, P. (2018). Contract cheating and assessment design: Exploring the relationship. *Assessment & Evaluation in Higher Education*, *44*(5), 676–691. DOI: 10.1080/02602938.2018.1527892

Brianza, E., Schmid, M., Tondeur, J., & Petko, D. (2024). The digital silver lining of the pandemic: The impact on preservice teachers' technological knowledge and beliefs. *Education and Information Technologies*, *29*(2), 1591–1616. DOI: 10.1007/s10639-023-11801-w

Budhathoki, T., Zirar, A., Njoya, E. T., & Timsina, A. (2024). ChatGPT adoption and anxiety: A cross-country analysis utilizing the unified theory of acceptance and use of technology (UTAUT). *Studies in Higher Education*, *49*(5), 831–846. DOI: 10.1080/03075079.2024.2333937

Buele, J., & Llerena-Aguirre, L. (2025). Transformations in academic work and faculty perceptions of artificial intelligence in higher education. In *Frontiers in Education* (Vol. 10). DOI: 10.3389/feduc.2025.1603763

Bujnowska, A., Nguyen, H., & Tran, L. (2026). Data colonialism and digital sovereignty in the Global South. *Development in Practice*, 1–8. Advance online publication. DOI: 10.1080/09614524.2025.2609155

Bunduchi, R., Sitar-Tăut, D.-A., & Mican, D. (2025). A legitimacy-based explanation for user acceptance of controversial technologies: The case of Generative AI. *Technological Forecasting and Social Change, 215*, 124095. DOI: 10.1016/j.techfore.2025.124095

Bureau, J. S., Howard, J. L., Chong, J. X. Y., & Guay, F. (2022). Pathways to student motivation: A meta-analysis of antecedents of autonomous and controlled motivations. *Review of Educational Research, 92*(1), 46–72. DOI: 10.3102/00346543211042426

Burtch, G., Lee, D., & Chen, Z. (2023). The Consequences of Generative AI for UGC and Online Community Engagement. SSRN *Electronic Journal*. DOI: 10.2139/ssrn.4521754

Butson, R., & Spronken-Smith, R. (2024). AI and its implications for research in higher education: A critical dialog. *Higher Education Research & Development, 43*(3), 563–577. DOI: 10.1080/07294360.2023.2280200

Büyüköztürk, Ş. KılıçÇakmak, E., Akgün, Ö. E., Karadeniz, Ş., & Demirel, F. (2024). Sampling methods. In Scientific Research Methods in Education (pp. 82-103). Pegem Academy.

Caamaño-Gordillo, D., Mula, J., & De La Torre, R. (2025). Impact of generative artificial intelligence on workload, efficiency and labor productivity. *IFAC-PapersOnLine, 59*(10), 1408–1413. DOI: 10.1016/j.ifacol.2025.09.237

Cardwell, R., Nelson, K., Duncan, R., Copnell, B., & Moss, C. (2024). Being effective and supervising for thesis success in nursing coursework master's degrees: A qualitative descriptive study. *J Adv Nurs, 80*(12), 5050–5063. DOI: 10.1111/jan.16164

Casey, L., Sam, C., Seng, S., Pov, P., & Bo, C. (2024). The challenge of enhancing teacher professional identity and capability in Cambodian schools. *Schools, 21*(2), 348–367. DOI: 10.1086/732435

Celik, I. (2023). Toward intelligent-TPACK: An empirical study on teachers' professional knowledge to ethically integrate artificial intelligence (AI)-based tools into education. *Computers in Human Behavior, 138*, 107468. DOI: 10.1016/j.chb.2022.107468

Celik, I., Dindar, M., Muukkonen, H., & J¨arvel, S. (2022). The promises and challenges of artificial intelligence for teachers: A systematic review of research. *TechTrends, 66*(1), 616–630. DOI: 10.1007/s11528-022-00715-y

Centre National pour la Recherche Scientifique et Technique (CNRST). (2018). *Production scientifique nationale en comparaison avec d'autres pays: Scopus (2013–2017)* [National scientific production compared with other countries: Scopus (2013–2017)]. Institut Marocain de l'Information Scientifique et Technique (IMIST). https://barometre.cnrst.ma/images/pdf/EtudeProductionScientifique.pdf

Černý, M. (2024). University students' conceptualization of AI literacy: Theory and empirical evidence. *Social Sciences (Basel, Switzerland), 13*(3), 1–26. DOI: 10.3390/socsci13030129

Chan, C. K. Y. (2023). A comprehensive AI policy education framework for university teaching and learning. *International Journal of Educational Technology in Higher Education, 20*(1), 38. DOI: 10.1186/s41239-023-00408-3

Chan, C. K. Y., & Hu, W. (2023). Students' voices on generative AI: Perceptions, benefits, and challenges in higher education. *Education and Information Technologies, 28*, 1–22. DOI: 10.1007/s10639-023-12195-8

Chan, C. K. Y., & Hu, W. (2023). Students' voices on generative AI: Perceptions, benefits, and challenges in higher education. *International Journal of Educational Technology in Higher Education, 20*(1), 1–18. DOI: 10.1186/s41239-023-00411-8

Chan, C. K. Y., & Tsi, L. H. Y. (2024). Will generative AI replace teachers in higher education? A study of teacher and student perceptions. *Studies in Educational Evaluation, 83*, 101395. Advance online publication. DOI: 10.1016/j.stueduc.2024.101395

Chea, C. (2024a). Mentorship's role in shaping professional identity: Insights from Cambodian teaching practicums. *Cogent Education, 11*(1), 1–21. DOI: 10.1080/2331186X.2024.2419710

Chea, C. (2024b). Teaching practicum in the teacher education institutions in Cambodia: A cross-case analysis. *Journal of Teacher Education and Educators, 13*(1), 49–69. https://dergipark.org.tr/tr/download/article-file/3663332

Chen, L., Chen, P., & Lin, Z. (2020). Artificial Intelligence in Education: A Review. *IEEE Access : Practical Innovations, Open Solutions, 8*, 75264–75278. DOI: 10.1109/ACCESS.2020.2988510

Chen, S., & Cheung, A. C. K. (2025). Effect of generative artificial intelligence on university students learning outcomes: A systematic review and meta-analysis. *Educational Research Review, 49*, 100737. Advance online publication. DOI: 10.1016/j.edurev.2025.100737

Chen, Y., Jensen, S., Albert, L. J., Gupta, S., & Lee, T. (2023). Artificial intelligence (AI) student assistants in the classroom: Designing chatbots to support student success. *Information Systems Frontiers*, *25*(1), 161–182. DOI: 10.1007/s10796-022-10291-4

Cherkaoui, M. (2015). Entre recherche et crise des sciences sociales [Between research and the crisis of the social sciences]. *Economia*. http://economia.ma/fr/content/entre-recherche-et-crise-des-sciences-sociales

Cherkaoui, M. (2011). *Crise de l'université* [University crisis]. Librairie Droz. DOI: 10.3917/droz.cherk.2011.01

Cherkaoui, M., & Bourqia, R. (2008). Dilemmes de la recherche et crise des sciences sociales [Research dilemmas and social science crisis]. *La revue. Economía*, *4*, 85–89.

Chiu, T. K. F., & Chai, C. (2020). Sustainable Curriculum Planning for Artificial Intelligence Education: A Self-Determination Theory Perspective. *Sustainability (Basel)*, *12*(14), 5568. DOI: 10.3390/su12145568

Chounta, I. A., Bardone, E., Raudsep, A., & Pedaste, M. (2022). Exploring teachers' perceptions of artificial intelligence as a tool to support their practice in Estonian K-12 education. *International Journal of Artificial Intelligence in Education*, *32*(3), 725–755. DOI: 10.1007/s40593-021-00243-5

Christy, T. C. (2013). Vygotsky, Cognitive Development and Language. *Historiographia Linguistica*, *40*(1), 1–29. DOI: 10.1075/hl.40.1-2.07chr

Chuang, Y. T., Chiang, H. L., & Lin, A. P. (2025). Insights from the Job Demands–Resources Model: AI's dual impact on employees' work and life well-being. *International Journal of Information Management*, *83*, 102887. DOI: 10.1016/j.ijinfomgt.2025.102887

Cotton, D. R. E., Cotton, P. A., & Shipway, J. R. (2024). Chatting and cheating: Ensuring academic integrity in the era of ChatGPT. *Innovations in Education and Teaching International*, *61*(2), 228–239. DOI: 10.1080/14703297.2023.2190148

Couldry, N., & Mejias, U. A. (2019). *The costs of connection: How data is colonizing human life and appropriating it for capitalism*. Stanford University Press.

Creely, E., Barnes, M., Tour, E., Henderson, M., Waterhouse, P., Pena, M. A., & Patel, S. V. (2025). Exploring attitudes to generative AI in education for English as an additional language (EAL) adult learners. *ReCALL*, *37*(2), 1–17. DOI: 10.1017/S0958344024000314

Crompton, H., & Burke, D. (2023). Artificial intelligence in higher education: The state of the field. *International Journal of Educational Technology in Higher Education, 20*(1), 1–22. DOI: 10.1186/s41239-023-00392-8

Curran, E., & Murray, M. (2008). Transformative learning in teacher education: Building competencies and changing dispositions. *The Journal of Scholarship of Teaching and Learning, 8*(3), 103–118. https://files.eric.ed.gov/fulltext/EJ854867.pdf

Czaja, R. (1998). Questionnaire pretesting comes of age. *Marketing Bulletin, 9*(1), 52–66.

Czerniawski, G., Guberman, A., & MacPhail, A. (2017). The professional developmental needs of higher education-based teacher educators: An international comparative needs analysis. *European Journal of Teacher Education, 40*(1), 127–140. DOI: 10.1080/02619768.2016.1246528

Daffana, I. (2024). Rediscovering Pancasila-based civic education through artificial intelligence: A conceptual framework. [INJOSER]. *Indonesian Journal of Social Education and Research, 3*(1). Advance online publication. DOI: 10.58260/injoser.v3i1.504

Dai, Y., Lai, S., Lim, C. P., & Liu, A. (2023). ChatGPT and its impact on research supervision: Insights from Australian postgraduate research students. *Australasian Journal of Educational Technology, 39*(4), 74–88. https://ajet.org.au/index.php/AJET/article/view/8843/2026. DOI: 10.14742/ajet.8843

Dalky, A., Osaid Malkawi, R. M., Alrawashdeh, A., ALBashtawy, M., & Hani, S. B. (2025). Perceptions, barriers, and risk of artificial intelligence among healthcare professionals: A cross-sectional study. *Digital Health, 11*, 20552076251360924. DOI: 10.1177/20552076251360924

Davidsson, E., & Stigmar, M. (2023). A literature review of content elements in supervision training courses. *London Review of Education, 21*(1), 1–16. DOI: 10.14324/LRE.21.1.40

Davis, F. D. (1989). Perceived usefulness, perceived ease of use, and user acceptance of information technology. *Management Information Systems Quarterly, 13*(3), 319–340. DOI: 10.2307/249008

Décret n° 2-23-545 du 15 moharrem 1445 (2 août 2023) portant statut particulier du corps des enseignants-chercheurs de l'enseignement supérieur [Decree no. 2-23-545 establishing the specific status of higher education teacher-researchers]. (2023). Bulletin officiel du Royaume du Maroc.

Décret n° 2-75-670 du 11 chaoual 1395 (17 octobre 1975) portant statut particulier du personnel enseignant-chercheur [Decree no. 2-75-670 establishing the specific status of academic teaching and research staff]. (1975). Bulletin officiel du Royaume du Maroc.

Décret n° 2-96-793 du 11 chaoual 1417 (19 février 1997) portant statut particulier des enseignants-chercheurs [Decree no. 2-96-793 establishing the specific status of teacher-researchers]. (1997). Bulletin officiel du Royaume du Maroc. http://bdj.mmsp.gov.ma/Fr/Document/243-D%C3%A9cret-n-2-96-793-du-11-chaoual-1417-19-f%C3%A9vrier-.aspx?KeyPath=

De, D., & Singh, A. K. (2025). A global perspective on impact of digitalization on business development. In Yıldırım, D., Yıldırım, S., & Kandpal, V. (Eds.), *Sustainable Digitalization Strategies in Business and Healthcare* (pp. 1–32). IGI Global Scientific Publishing., DOI: 10.4018/979-8-3373-5087-5.ch001

Deem, R. (1998). "New Managerialism" and Higher Education: The Management of Performances and Cultures in Universities in the United Kingdom. *International Studies in Sociology of Education*, *8*(1), 47–70. DOI: 10.1080/0962021980020014

Deep, P. D., Ghosh, N., & Chen, Y. (2025). Faculty burnout in higher education: Effects on student engagement, learning outcomes, and artificial intelligence-driven institutional responses. *Journal of Educational and Developmental Psychology*, *15*(1), 29–42. DOI: 10.5539/jedp.v15n1p29

Devine, K., & Hunter, K. H. (2017). PhD student emotional exhaustion: The role of supportive supervision and self-presentation behaviours. *Innovations in Education and Teaching International*, *54*(4), 335–344. DOI: 10.1080/14703297.2016.1174143

Dexter, S. L., Anderson, R. E., & Becker, H. J. (1999). Teachers' views of computers as catalysts for changes in their teaching practice. *Journal of Research on Computing in Education*, *31*(3), 221–239. DOI: 10.1080/08886504.1999.10782252

Dhiraj, A., & Kumar, P. D. S. (2023a). Impact of E-learning on the Higher Education Sector during the COVID-19 pandemic through Pedagogy tools: An observational Study. *Revista de Educación y Derecho*, (27). Advance online publication. DOI: 10.1344/REYD2023.27.40935

Di Plinio, S. (2025). Panta Rh-AI: Assessing multifaceted AI threats on human agency and identity. *Social Sciences & Humanities Open*, *11*, 101434. Advance online publication. DOI: 10.1016/j.ssaho.2025.101434

Dietrich, J., Dicke, A.-L., Kracke, B., & Noack, P. (2015). Teacher support and its influence on students' intrinsic value and effort: Dimensional comparison effects across subjects. *Learning and Instruction, 39*, 45–54. DOI: 10.1016/j.learninstruc.2015.05.007

Digital Watch Observatory. (2024). *The Indonesian National Strategy on Artificial Intelligence*. Digital Watch Observatory https://dig.watch/resource/the-indonesian-national-strategy-on-artificial-intelligence

Dimitriadou, E., & Lanitis, A. (2023). A critical evaluation, challenges, and future perspectives of using artificial intelligence and emerging technologies in smart classrooms. *Smart Learning Environments, 10*(1), 1–26. DOI: 10.1186/s40561-023-00231-3 PMID: 40478141

Doria, B., Grion, V., Picasso, F., & Li, L. (2026). Faculty assessment development in higher education: The CRAFT framework emerging from a systematic literature review. *Assessment & Evaluation in Higher Education, 51*(1), 16–40. DOI: 10.1080/02602938.2025.2584121

Dreer-Goethe, B. (2025). The impact of mentor support and high-quality connections on student teachers' psychological safety and engagement during practicum [Original Research]. *Frontiers in Education, 10*, 1499749. DOI: 10.3389/feduc.2025.1499749

Dumitru, C. (2024). Future of learning: Adaptive learning systems based on language generative models in higher education. In *Impact of artificial intelligence on society* (pp. 31–42). Chapman and Hall/CRC. DOI: 10.1201/9781032644509-3

Durksen, T. L., Klassen, R. M., & Daniels, L. M. (2017). Motivation and collaboration: The keys to a developmental framework for teachers' professional learning. *Teaching and Teacher Education, 67*, 53–66. DOI: 10.1016/j.tate.2017.05.011

Dwivedi, Y. K., Kshetri, N., Hughes, L., Slade, E. L., Jeyaraj, A., Kar, A. K., Baabdullah, A. M., Koohang, A., Raghavan, V., Ahuja, M., Albanna, H., Albashrawi, M. A., Al-Busaidi, A. S., Balakrishnan, J., Barlette, Y., Basu, S., Bose, I., Brooks, L., Buhalis, D., & Wright, R. (2023). "So what if ChatGPT wrote it?" Multidisciplinary perspectives on opportunities, challenges and implications of generative conversational AI for research, practice and policy. *International Journal of Information Management, 71*, 102642. Advance online publication. DOI: 10.1016/j.ijinfomgt.2023.102642

Dzvapatsva, G. P., Chinhamo, E., Matobobo, C., Ranga, M. M., & Ncube, P. D. N. (2026). Role of Generative Artificial Intelligence in Transforming Supervision Dynamics in Postgraduate Education: A Systematic Literature Review. In *Open Books and Proceedings* (pp. 1–16). ERRCD Forum. DOI: 10.38140/obp4-2026-01

Earl, A., Raskovic, M. M., Iskhakova, M., & Iskhakov, F. (2026). Professional identity and stigma in the context of war. *Critical Perspectives on International Business*, •••, 1–27. DOI: 10.1108/cpoib-03-2025-0067

Eby, L. T., Allen, T. D., Evans, S. C., Ng, T., & Dubois, D. (2008). Does mentoring matter? A multidisciplinary meta-analysis comparing mentored and non-mentored individuals. *Journal of Vocational Behavior*, *72*(2), 254–267. DOI: 10.1016/j.jvb.2007.04.005

Eke, D. O. (2023). ChatGPT and the rise of generative AI: Threat to academic integrity? *Journal of Responsible Technology*, *13*, 100060. Advance online publication. DOI: 10.1016/j.jrt.2023.100060

Elçiçek, M. (2024). An investigation on students' artificial intelligence literacy. *Journal of Information and Communication Technologies*, *6*(1), 24–35.

Em, S., Mok, S., & Sam, R. (2025). Exploring Cambodian teachers' views on transformational leadership of school directors. [JSKE]. *Journal of Social Knowledge Education*, *6*(1), 76–89. DOI: 10.37251/jske.v6i1.1364

Enders, J., & De Weert, E. (Eds.). (2009). *The Changing Face of Academic Life: Analytical and Comparative Perspectives*. Palgrave Macmillan. DOI: 10.1057/9780230242166

Ennida, K., & Allah, A. S. (2024). The Moroccan teacher-researchers' organizational citizenship behavior as a predictor of university performance. *Global Journal of Business. Economics and Management: Current Issues*, *14*(1), 70–74. DOI: 10.18844/gjbem.v14i1.9356

Ennida, K., & Allouani, S. A. (2022). L'enseignant-chercheur comme ressource humaine: Une approche par la citoyenneté organisationnelle [The teacher-researcher as a human resource: An organizational citizenship approach]. *Moroccan Journal of Business Studies*, *3*(2), 1–19. https://www.emaa.ma/mjbs/articles/pdfs/vol3issu2/L%E2%80%99enseignant%20chercheur%20comme%20ressource%20humaine%20%20une%20approche%20par%20la%20citoyennete%20organisationnelle.pdf

Esomonu, N. P. M. (2025). Utilizing AI and big data for predictive insights on institutional performance and student success: a data-driven approach to quality assurance. *AI and ethics, academic integrity and the future of quality assurance in higher education, 29*.

European Commission. (2022). *Ethical guidelines on the use of artificial intelligence (AI) and data in teaching and learning for educators, Directorate-General for Education, Youth, Sport and Culture*. https://data.europa.eu/doi/10.2766/153756

Farooq, U., Malik, S. A., & Syed, A. S. (2024). REVOLUTIONIZING HIGHER EDUCATION: THE TRANSFORMATIVE IMPACT OF ARTIFICIAL INTELLIGENCE ON TEACHING, LEARNING, AND CAREER PREPARATION. *ShodhKosh: Journal of Visual and Performing Arts*, *5*(3). Advance online publication. DOI: 10.29121/shodhkosh.v5.i3.2024.3239

Farrokhnia, M., Banihashem, S. K., Noroozi, O., & Wals, A. (2024). A SWOT analysis of ChatGPT: Implications for educational practice and research. *Innovations in Education and Teaching International*, *61*(3), 460–474. DOI: 10.1080/14703297.2023.2195846

Fasano, F., Bartoli, C., Cappa, F., & Boccardelli, P. (2025). Exploring the impact of AI on Web3 decentralized platform business model innovation. *Journal of Engineering and Technology Management - JET-M, 78*. DOI: 10.1016/j.jengtecman.2025.101911

Fawaid, A., Baharun, H., & Hamzah, M., Rohimah, Munawwaroh, I., & Putri, D. F. (2025). AI-based career management to improve the quality of decision making in higher education. *2025 IEEE Integrated STEM Education Conference (ISEC)*, 1–8. DOI: 10.1109/ISEC64801.2025.11147274

Fiesler, C., Garrett, N., & Beard, N. (2020). What do we teach when we teach tech ethics? A syllabi analysis. In *Proceedings of the 51st ACM technical symposium on computer science education* (pp. 289–295). Portland, OR, USA. DOI: 10.1145/3328778.3366825

Fishbein, M., & Ajzen, I. (1975). *Belief, attitude, intention, and behavior: An introduction to theory and research*. Addison-Wesley.

Flores, E., & Mean, U. (2025). Digital transformation in Cambodian higher education: Current trends and future directions. *Edelweiss Applied Science and Technology*, *9*(1), 867–878. DOI: 10.55214/25768484.v9i1.4267

Fochler, M., & De Rijcke, S. (2017). Implicated in the indicator game? An experimental debate. *Engaging Science, Technology, and Society*, *3*, 21–40. DOI: 10.17351/ests2017.108

Fosnot, C. T., & Perry, R. S. (1996). Constructivism: A psychological theory of learning. *Constructivism: Theory, perspectives, and practice*, *2*(1), 8–33. https://tinyurl.com/3jvv3krt

Franco D'Souza, R., Mathew, M., Mishra, V., & Surapaneni, K. M. (2024). Twelve tips for addressing ethical concerns in the implementation of artificial intelligence in medical education. *Medical Education Online*, *29*(1), 2330250. Advance online publication. DOI: 10.1080/10872981.2024.2330250

Frimpong, V. (2025). Artificial intelligence investment in resource-constrained African economies: Financial, strategic, and ethical trade-offs with broader implications. *WORLD (Oakland, Calif.)*, *6*(2), 1–17.

Gaillard, J., Tull, M., & Waast, R. (2017). Les défis de la recherche scientifique au Maroc [The challenges of scientific research in Morocco]. *Science, Technology & Society*, *22*(3), 345–366.

Gamlem, S. M., McGrane, J., Brandmo, C., Moltudal, S., Sun, S. Z., & Hopfenbeck, T. N. (2025). Exploring preservice teachers' attitudes and experiences with generative AI: A mixed methods study in Norwegian teacher education. *Educational Psychology*, *46*(1), 27–51. DOI: 10.1080/01443410.2025.2528663

Gardner, S. K. (2009). The development of doctoral students: Phases of challenge and support. *ASHE Higher Education Report*, *34*(6), 1–127. https://eric.ed.gov/?id=EJ835648

Garzón, J., Patiño, E., & Marulanda, C. (2025). Systematic review of artificial intelligence in education: Trends, benefits, and challenges. *Multimodal Technologies and Interaction*, *9*(8), 1–19. DOI: 10.3390/mti9080084

Geada, N. (2024). Artificial Intelligence: Theoretical Foundations, Applications, and Societal Implications. In Geada, N., Sood, R., & Sidana, A. (Eds.), (pp. 226–244). Advances in Finance, Accounting, and Economics. IGI Global., DOI: 10.4018/979-8-3693-1758-7.ch012

Gedrimiene, E., Celik, I., Kaasila, A., Mäkitalo, K., & Muukkonen, H. (2024). Artificial Intelligence (AI)-enhanced learning analytics (LA) for supporting Career decisions: Advantages and challenges from user perspective. *Education and Information Technologies*, *29*(1), 297–322. DOI: 10.1007/s10639-023-12277-4

George, B., & Wooden, O. (2023). Managing the strategic transformation of higher education through artificial intelligence. *Administrative Sciences*, *13*(9), 196. DOI: 10.3390/admsci13090196

Georgieva, M., & Stuart, J. (2025). *Ethics is the edge: The future of AI in higher education*. EDUCAUSE Review. https://er.educause.edu/articles/2025/6/ethics-is-the-edge-the-future-of-ai-in-higher-education

Gessesse, K. T., & Premanandam, P. (2023). The mediating role of affective commitment on the relationship between job satisfaction and turnover intention using structural equation modeling: Empirical evidence from higher education institutions in Addis Ababa, Ethiopia. *Cogent Social Sciences*, *9*(1), 2202959. DOI: 10.1080/23311886.2023.2202959

Ghosh, M. (2025). Artificial intelligence (AI) and ethical concerns: A review and research agenda. *Cogent Business & Management, 12*(1), 2551809. Advance online publication. DOI: 10.1080/23311975.2025.2551809

Ghouati, A. (2012). La dépossession. Réformes, enseignement supérieur et pouvoirs au Maghreb [Dispossession: Reforms, higher education and powers in the Maghreb]. *Revue du Monde Musulman et de la Méditerranée, 131*(1), 65–90. DOI: 10.4000/remmm.7608

Gökçearslan, S., Tosun, C., & Erdemir, Z. G. (2024). Benefits, challenges, and methods of artificial intelligence (AI) chatbots in education: A systematic literature review. *International Journal of Technology in Education, 7*(1), 19–39. DOI: 10.46328/ijte.600

Gökçearslan, Ş., Yildiz Durak, H., & Atman Uslu, N. (2024). Acceptance of educational use of the Internet of Things (IoT) in the context of individual innovativeness and ICT competency of preservice teachers. *Interactive Learning Environments, 32*(2), 557–571. DOI: 10.1080/10494820.2022.2091612

Gordon, S. P. (2023). Supervision, teaching, and learning in successful schools: A hall of mirrors. *Journal of Educational Supervision, 6*(3), 1–24. DOI: 10.31045/jes.6.3.1

Grant, B. M. (2005). The pedagogy of graduate supervision: Figuring the relations between supervisor and student (Doctoral dissertation, University of Auckland).

Grassini, S., Aasen, M. L., & Møgelvang, A. (2024). Understanding University Students' Acceptance of ChatGPT: Insights from the UTAUT2 Model. *Applied Artificial Intelligence, 38*(1), 2371168. Advance online publication. DOI: 10.1080/08839514.2024.2371168

Grønli, K. M., Walgermo, B. R., Uppstad, P. H., & McTigue, E. M. (2025). Transforming teacher feedback: A checklist for assessing and supporting reading skills, motivation, and student agency in oral reading. *Contemporary Educational Psychology, 82*, 102377. DOI: 10.1016/j.cedpsych.2025.102377

Guan, L., Lee, J. C. K., Zhang, Y., & Gu, M. M. (2025). Investigating the tripartite interaction among teachers, students, and generative AI in EFL education: A mixed-methods study. *Computers and Education: Artificial Intelligence, 8*, 100384. Advance online publication. DOI: 10.1016/j.caeai.2025.100384

Guan, L., Zhang, Y., & Gu, M. M. (2025). Preservice teachers preparedness for AI-integrated education: An investigation fromperceptions, capabilities, and teachers' identity changes. *Computers and Education: Artificial Intelligence*, *8*, 100341. Advance online publication. DOI: 10.1016/j.caeai.2024.100341

Gudmundsdottir, G. B., & Hatlevik, O. E. (2018). Newly qualified teachers' professional digital competence: Implications for teacher education. *European Journal of Teacher Education*, *41*(2), 214–231. DOI: 10.1080/02619768.2017.1416085

Gulumbe, B. H., Audu, S. M., & Hashim, A. M. (2025). Balancing AI and academic integrity: What are the positions of academic publishers and universities? *AI & Society*, *40*(3), 1775–1784. DOI: 10.1007/s00146-024-01946-8

Gupta, P., Mahajan, R., Badhera, U., & Kushwaha, P. S. (2024). Integrating generative AI in management education: A mixed-methods study using social construction of technology theory. *International Journal of Management Education*, *22*(3), 101017. Advance online publication. DOI: 10.1016/j.ijme.2024.101017

Gusango, E., Maani, J., & Ssetumba, J. (2021). The use of the constructivist approach in teacher preparation: a case of primary teachers' colleges of South Eastern Uganda. *American Journal of Education and Practice, 5*(1), 53–84. file:///c:/users/lenovo/downloads/705-article%20text-2364-2638-10-20210503.pdf

Guzeller, C. O., & Celiker, N. (2020). Examining the relationship between organizational commitment and turnover intention via a meta-analysis. *International Journal of Culture, Tourism and Hospitality Research*, *14*(1), 102–120. DOI: 10.1108/IJCTHR-05-2019-0094

Habibi, A., Muhaimin, M., Danibao, B. K., Wibowo, Y. G., Wahyuni, S., & Octavia, A. (2023). ChatGPT in higher education learning: Acceptance and use. *Computers and Education: Artificial Intelligence*, *5*, 100190. DOI: 10.1016/j.caeai.2023.100190

Ha, C., Pressley, T., & Marshall, D. T. (2025). Teacher voices matter: The role of teacher autonomy in enhancing job satisfaction and mitigating burnout. *PLoS One*, *20*(1), e0317471. DOI: 10.1371/journal.pone.0317471

Hadan, H., Hadi Mogavi, R., Zhang-Kennedy, L., & Nacke, L. E. (2026). Who is Responsible When AI Fails? Mapping Causes, Entities, and Consequences of AI Privacy and Ethical Incidents. *International Journal of Human-Computer Interaction*, *42*(8), 5933–5977. DOI: 10.1080/10447318.2025.2549073

Haddock-Fraser, J. (2020). 14. The unseen pressures of academia. *Modern day challenges in academia: Time for a change*, 211.

Haenlein, M., & Kaplan, A. (2019). A brief history of artificial intelligence: On the past, present, and future of artificial intelligence. *California Management Review*, *61*(4), 5–14. DOI: 10.1177/0008125619864925

Haetami, M. (2025). AI-driven educational transformation in Indonesia: From learning personalization to institutional management. *Al-Ishlah: Jurnal Pendidikan*, *17*(2), 1819–1832. DOI: 10.35445/alishlah.v17i2.7448

Hakim, A., & Anggraini, P. (2023). Artificial intelligence in teaching Islamic studies: Challenges and opportunities. *Molang: Journal of Islamic Education*, *4*(1), 1–15.

Hall, R. (2021). *The hopeless university: Intellectual work at the end of the end of history*. MayFly Books.

Hashweh, M. (2014). Pedagogical Content Knowledge: Lee Shulman. DOI: 10.4135/9781483346229.n248

Hatch, J. A. (2023). Doing Qualitative Research in Education Settings. In *Doing Qualitative Research in Education Settings*. DOI: 10.1515/9780791487945

Heine, S., & K¨onig, J. (2025). Applying artificial intelligence in teacher education: Preservice teachers' attitudes and reflections in using ChatGPT for teaching and learning. *European Journal of Teacher Education*, *48*(5), 934–963. DOI: 10.1080/02619768.2025.2540791

Helm, G., & Hesse, F. (2026). Revising with AI: aligning feedback technologies with learners' revision processes [Hypothesis and Theory]. *Frontiers in Education, Volume 11 - 2026*. DOI: 10.3389/feduc.2026.1702406

Helmiatin, H., Hidayat, A., & Kahar, M. R. (2024). Investigating the adoption of AI in higher education: A study of public universities in Indonesia. *Cogent Education*, *11*(1), 2380175. Advance online publication. DOI: 10.1080/2331186X.2024.2380175

Helvaci, İ. (2025). Preparing teachers for a ChatGPT-influenced workforce. *Kastamonu Education Journal*, *33*(2), 401–410.

Heng, K., Sol, K., Kaing, S., & Ros, V. (2020). Introduction: The need to promote a strong research and publication culture in Cambodia. *Cambodia Education Forum* 1–10. https://tinyurl.com/mr6j2yz7

Heng, K., & Sol, K. (2024). The use of AI and ChatGPT for education and research in Cambodia: Current state and future directions. *Cambodian Journal of Educational Research*, *4*(2), 1–11. DOI: 10.62037/cjer.2024.04.02.01

Henkel, M. (2005). Academic identity and autonomy in a changing policy environment. *Higher Education, 49*(1), 155–176. DOI: 10.1007/s10734-004-2919-1

Hermann, E. (2022). Artificial intelligence and mass personalization of communication content—An ethical and literacy perspective. *New Media & Society, 24*(5), 1258–1277. DOI: 10.1177/14614448211022702

Higher Council for Education, Training and Scientific Research. (2014). Implementation of the national education and training charter 2000–2013: Acquisitions, deficits and challenges. Analytical report. Kingdom of Morocco. https://www.csefrs.ma/wp-content/uploads/2017/10/Rapport-analytique.pdf

Hirschman, A. O. (1970). *Exit, Voice, and Loyalty: Responses to Decline in Firms, Organizations, and States*. Harvard University Press.

Hoernig, S., Ilharco, A., Pereira, P. T., & Pereira, R. (2024). *Generative AI and higher education: Challenges and opportunities*. Institute of Public Policy. https://www.ipp-jcs.org/wp-content/uploads/2024/09/Report-AI-in-Higher-Education-IPP-1.pdf

Holcomb, D., Johnson, E., Vizina Roubal, J., & Thompson, C. (2025). Transformative supervision: A conceptual framework for relationally based, trauma-informed supervision in postpandemic practicum education. *Applied Learning in Social Work Education (ALSWE), 15*(1). https://alswe.simmons.edu/article/transformative-supervision-a-conceptual-framework-for-relationally-based-trauma-informed-supervision-in-postpandemic-practium-education/

Holland, J. (2026). The Disclosure-Detection Nexus in Generative AI: An Integrated Analysis of Ethical Implications in Academia. *Int. J. Management and Data Analytics, 6*(1), 70–87. DOI: 10.5281/zenodo.18453863

Holmes, W. Centre for Curriculum Redesign, & Center for Curriculum Redesign. (2019). Artificial intelligence in Education. Promise and implications for teaching and learning. In *Artificial Intelligence in Education*. https://www.consorciosthem.com/wp-content/uploads/2025/02/sthem-ia-07-holmes-fadel-bialik-artificial-intelligence-in-education-promise-and-implications-for-teaching-and-learning-2019.pdf

Holmes, W., Bialik, M., & Fadel, C. (2022). *Artificial intelligence in education: Promises and implications for teaching and learning*. Center for Curriculum Redesign.

Hongseng, R. (2023, May 19). *Generative AI: A threat to copyright?* Kiripost. https://kiripost.com/stories/cambodia-chatgpt-generative-ai-a-threat-to-copyright

Hood, C. (1991). A Public Management for All Seasons? *Public Administration, 69*(1), 3–19. DOI: 10.1111/j.1467-9299.1991.tb00779.x

Hoque, K. E., & Bt Kenayathulla, H. B., D/O Subramaniam, M. V., & Islam, R. (2020). Relationships between supervision and teachers' performance and attitude in secondary schools in Malaysia. *SAGE Open*, *10*(2), 1–11. DOI: 10.1177/2158244020925501

Hornberger, M., Bewersdorff, A., & Nerdel, C. (2023). What do university students know about Artificial Intelligence? Development and validation of an AI literacy test. *Computers and Education: Artificial Intelligence*, *5*, 100165. DOI: 10.1016/j.caeai.2023.100165

Huang, F., Wang, Y., & Zhang, H. (2024). Modeling generative AI acceptance, perceived teachers' enthusiasm and self-efficacy to English as a foreign language learners' wellbeing in the digital era. *European Journal of Education*, *59*(4), e12770. DOI: 10.1111/ejed.12770

Hughes, C., Robert, L., Frady, K., & Arroyos, A. (2019). Artificial intelligence, employee engagement, fairness, and job outcomes. In *Managing technology and middle-and low-skilled employees* (pp. 61–68). Emerald Publishing Limited. DOI: 10.1108/978-1-78973-077-720191005

Huot, S., & Loch, S. (2025). Educating in the Age of AI: Preparing Cambodian teachers and students for an AI-augmented learning future. *Journal of Educational Technology and E-Learning Innovations*, *1*(2), 31–38. DOI: 10.54536/jeteli.v1i2.5170

Huot, S., Loch, S., Chheang, S., Hok, C., & Phin, K. (2026). The future of indexed research in Cambodia: Innovation, collaboration, and regional integration. In Em, S. (Ed.), *Digital leadership and innovation in ASEAN education* (pp. 455–486). IGI Global Scientific Publishing., DOI: 10.4018/979-8-2600-1142-3.ch013

Huot, S., & Phin, K. (2026). Transforming hybrid pedagogies: Harnessing AI and intercultural collaboration for global learning. In Nguyen, T.-P., Zhang, J., & Loseva, A. (Eds.), *Advancing hybrid pedagogies through AI and intercultural collaboration* (pp. 29–54). IGI Global Scientific Publishing., DOI: 10.4018/979-8-3373-7462-8.ch002

Huot, S., Sam, R., & Nguon, T. (2025). Factors influencing teaching career choice among student teachers in cambodian teacher education colleges. *Education Quarterly Eeview*, *8*(4), 1–17. DOI: 10.31014/aior.1993.08.04.226

Huot, S., & Such, C. (2025). Leveraging social media for language learning: Opportunities and challenges. [JEILT]. *Journal of Education Innovation and Language Teaching*, *1*(2), 10–29. DOI: 10.63381/jeilt.v1i2.56

Hussain, S. M., Satti, S. M. J., & Khan, Z. (2024). AI-powered personalized learning: Advancing Language education in the digital era. *Journal of Social Signs Review*, *2*(4), 730–740. https://socialsignsreivew.com/index.php/12/article/view/71

Hwang, G. J., & Tu, Y. F. (2021). Roles and research trends of artificial intelligence in mathematics education: A bibliometric mapping analysis and systematic review. In *Mathematics* (Vol. 9, Issue 6). DOI: 10.3390/math9060584

Iatrellis, O., Bania, A., Samaras, N., Kosmopoulou, I., & Panagiotakopoulos, T. (2025). ChatGPT in doctoral supervision: Proposing a tripartite mentoring model for AI-assisted academic guidance. *International Journal of Doctoral Studies*, *20*(9), 1–26. DOI: 10.28945/5579

Ibrahimi, K. (2021). Recherche scientifique: Le Maroc classé quatrième en Afrique dans le "Nature Index 2021" [Scientific research: Morocco ranked fourth in Africa in the "Nature Index 2021"]. Le360. https://m.le360.ma/societe/recherche-scientifique-le-marocclasse-quatrieme-en-afrique-dans-le-nature-index-2021-244315

ICLG. (2025). *Data protection laws and regulations report 2025–2026: Indonesia*. International Comparative Legal Guides. https://iclg.com/practice-areas/data-protection-laws-and-regulations/indonesia

Ifenthaler, D., & Gibson, D. (Eds.). (2020). *Adoption of data analytics in higher education learning and teaching*. Springer. DOI: 10.1007/978-3-030-47392-1

Inayah, M., Musyarofah, S., Az Zahra, A. F. Z., & Agrariyanti, Y. (2025). Pancasila and artificial intelligence: Ethical analysis of AI regulations in Indonesia. *LITERA: Jurnal Ilmiah Multidisiplin*, *4*(3). Advance online publication. DOI: 10.62307/litera.v4i3.217

Instance Nationale d'Évaluation – Higher Council for Education, Training and Scientific Research. (2018). L'enseignement supérieur au Maroc: Efficacité, efficience et défis du système universitaire à accès ouvert [Higher education in Morocco: Effectiveness, efficiency and challenges of the open-access university system] (Sectoral report). https://www.csefrs.ma/wp-content/uploads/2018/10/Rapport-Enseignement-sup--rieur-Fr-03-10.pdf

Irawan, I. (2024). Penerapan etika Pancasila dalam pengembangan kecerdasan buatan yang bertanggung jawab di Indonesia [Application of Pancasila ethics in responsible AI development in Indonesia]. *bit-Tech*, *7*(2), 263–271. https://doi.org/ DOI: 10.32877/bt.v7i2.1740

Isaifan, R. J., & Hasna, M. O. (2025). Artificial intelligence for quality assurance in higher education: A policy-to-practice model from Qatar with global relevance. *Quality in Higher Education, 31*(3), 288–303. Advance online publication. DOI: 10.1080/13538322.2025.2576326

Jaboob, M., Al-Ansi, A. M., & Riyadh, H. A. (2026). Artificial intelligence in higher education: A PRISMA 2020 review. *International Journal of Educational Management, 40*(1–2), 113–132. DOI: 10.1108/IJEM-09-2024-0560

Jaldemark, J., Lundin, J., Säljö, R., Edwards, J., Gegenfurtner, A., Holmes, W., Järvelä, S., de Laat, M., Lindberg, Y., Littlejohn, A., Seufert, S., Specht, M., Svensson, L., Rapanta, C., Hayes, S., & Zeivots, S. (2025). A multidisciplinary research agenda for artificial intelligence, education, learning, and instruction. *Postdigital Science and Education, 7*(4), 1414–1450. DOI: 10.1007/s42438-025-00602-8

Jensen, D. H., & Jetten, J. (2015). Bridging and bonding interactions in higher education: Social capital and students' academic and professional identity formation. *Frontiers in Psychology, 6*, 1–11. DOI: 10.3389/fpsyg.2015.00126 PMID: 25762954

Jensen, L. X., Bearman, M., Boud, D., & Konradsen, F. (2025). Feedback encounters in doctoral supervision: The role of generative AI chatbots. *Assessment & Evaluation in Higher Education*, •••, 1–14. DOI: 10.1080/02602938.2025.2478155

Jia, J., Zhang, Y., Bakar, L. J. A., & Ilyas, M. A. (2025). Transforming work in the digital era: AI-enhanced leadership and its effect on IT professional burnout. *Acta Psychologica, 260*, 105537. DOI: 10.1016/j.actpsy.2025.105537

Jiménez-García, E., Ruiz-Lázaro, J., Martínez-Requejo, S., & Redondo-Duarte, S. (2025). Artificial Intelligence and chatbots for sustainable higher education: A systematic review. *RIED-Revista Iberoamericana de Educacion a Distancia, 28*(2). Advance online publication. DOI: 10.5944/ried.28.2.43240

Jin, Y., Yan, L., Echeverria, V., Gašević, D., & Martinez-Maldonado, R. (2024). *Generative AI in Higher Education: A Global Perspective of Institutional Adoption Policies and Guidelines*. DOI: 10.1016/j.caeai.2024.100348

Jordan, M. I. (2019). Artificial intelligence—The revolution hasn't happened yet. *Harvard Data Science Review, 1*(1), 1–9.

Kaaouachi, A. (2010). L'évaluation dans le système d'enseignement supérieur au Maroc: Bilan des réalisations, limites et principaux défis. In Lamine, B. (Ed.), *Towards an Arab higher education space: International challenges and societal responsibilities* (pp. 409–422). UNESCO Regional Bureau for Education in the Arab States., https://search.shamaa.org/PDF/41452/KaaouachiEn41504.pdf

Kahyalar, E., & Yazici, I. (2016). Supervision in language teaching: A supervisor's and three trainee teachers' perspectives. *The Reading Matrix: An International Online Journal, 16*(1), 78–90. https://readingmatrix.com/files/14-k5mwwz65.pdf

Karan, B., & Angadi, G. R. (2024). Potential risks of artificial intelligence integration into school education: A systematic review. *Bulletin of Science, Technology & Society, 43*(3–4), 67–85. Advance online publication. DOI: 10.1177/02704676231224705

Karataş, F., & Yüce, E. (2024). AI and the future of teaching: Preservice teachers' reflections on the use of artificial intelligence inopen and distributed learning. *International Review of Research in Open and Distance Learning, 25*(3), 304–325. Advance online publication. DOI: 10.19173/irrodl.v25i3.7785

Karpudewan, M., & Mohd Ali Khan, N. S. (2017). Experiential-based climate change education: Fostering students' knowledge and motivation towards the environment. *International Research in Geographical and Environmental Education, 26*(3), 207–222. DOI: 10.1080/10382046.2017.1330037

Kasneci, E., Sessler, K., Küchemann, S., Bannert, M., Dementieva, D., Fischer, F., Gasser, U., Groh, G., Günnemann, S., Hüllermeier, E., Krusche, S., Kutyniok, G., Michaeli, T., Nerdel, C., Pfeffer, J., Poquet, O., Sailer, M., Schmidt, A., Seidel, T., & Kasneci, G. (2023). ChatGPT for good? On opportunities and challenges of large language models for education. *Learning and Individual Differences, 103*, 102274. DOI: 10.1016/j.lindif.2023.102274

Kay, J., Brereton, M., & Oviatt, S. (2024). Generative epistemic injustice: Four ways AI systems misrepresent and marginalise. *AI & Society*. Advance online publication. DOI: 10.1007/s00146-024-01966-4

Kay, J., Kasirzadeh, A., & Mohamed, S. (2024). Epistemic injustice in generative AI. *Proceedings of the AAAI/ACM Conference on AI, Ethics, and Society, 7*(1), 684–697. https://doi.org/DOI: 10.1609/aies.v7i1.31671

Kayyali, M. (2025). Ethical implications of generative AI in education: Privacy, bias, and integrity. In *Transformative AI practices for personalized learning strategies* (pp. 185–218). IGI Global Scientific Publishing. DOI: 10.4018/979-8-3693-8744-3.ch008

Kemmis, S., Heikkinen, H. L. T., Fransson, G., Aspfors, J., & Edwards-Groves, C. (2014). Mentoring of new teachers as a contested practice: Supervision, support and collaborative self-development. *Teaching and Teacher Education, 43*, 154–164. DOI: 10.1016/j.tate.2014.07.001

Khalifa, M., & Albadawy, M. (2024). Using artificial intelligence in academic writing and research: An essential productivity tool. In *Computer Methods and Programs in Biomedicine Update* (Vol. 5). DOI: 10.1016/j.cmpbup.2024.100145

Khare, K., Stewart, B., & Khare, A. (2018). Artificial intelligence and the student experience: An institutional perspective. *IAFOR Journal of Education, 6*(3), 63-78. https://files.eric.ed.gov/fulltext/EJ1198691.pdf

Khort, M., Karimov, A., Murtazin, S., & Khayaleeva, A. (2024). Epistemic injustice of the digital divide. *Edelweiss Applied Science and Technology*, *8*(5), 1986–1996. DOI: 10.55214/25768484.v8i5.1939

Kim, K., & Kwon, K. (2023). Exploring the AI competencies of elementary school teachers in South Korea. *Computers and Education: Artificial Intelligence*, *4*, 100137. DOI: 10.1016/j.caeai.2023.100137

Kim, S. J. (2024). Research ethics and issues regarding the use of ChatGPT-like artificial intelligence platforms by authors and reviewers: A narrative review. *Science Editing*, *11*(2), 96–106. DOI: 10.6087/kcse.343

Kini, T., & Podolsky, A. (2016). *Does teaching experience increase teacher effectiveness? A review of the research* (Learning Policy Institute, Issue. L. P. Institution. https://files.eric.ed.gov/fulltext/ED606426.pdf

Kohnke, L., Zou, D., & Xie, H. (2025). Microlearning and generative AI for preserviceteacher education: A qualitative case study. *Education and Information Technologies*, *30*(1), 21221–21248. DOI: 10.1007/s10639-025-13606-5

Kong, S. C., Yang, Y., & Hou, C. (2024). Examining teachers' behavioral intention of using generative artificial intelligence tools for teaching and learning based on the extended technology acceptance model. *Computers and Education: Artificial Intelligence*, *7*, 100328. Advance online publication. DOI: 10.1016/j.caeai.2024.100328

Kosbar, Y. (2026). TransformED futures: Towards human-centred, ethical and inclusive use and governance of AI in higher education. *Policy Futures in Education*. Advance online publication. DOI: 10.1177/14782103251406292

Kotsis, K. T. (2025). Artificial intelligence as a catalyst for changes in university-level science education. *EIKI Journal of Effective Teaching Methods*, *3*(3), 99–109. DOI: 10.59652/jetm.v3i3.618

Kouritzin, S. (2019). Extent and consequences of faculty members' workload creep in three Canadian faculties of education. *Canadian Journal of Education/Revue canadienne de l'éducation, 42*(4), 1092-1120.

Kozulin, A. (2004). Vygotsky's theory in the classroom: Introduction. *European Journal of Psychology of Education, 19*(1), 3–7. https://www.jstor.org/stable/23421397. DOI: 10.1007/BF03173233

Kuhl, P. K., Lim, S. S., Guerriero, S., & Damme, D. V. (2019). *Developing minds in the digital age*. OECD Publishing. DOI: 10.1787/562a8659-en

Kulal, A. N. A., Dinesh, S., Bhat, D. C., & Girish, A. (2024). Evaluating the Promise and Pitfalls of India's National Education Policy 2020: Insights from the Perspectives of Students, Teachers, and Experts. *SAGE Open, 14*(4), 21582440241279367. Advance online publication. DOI: 10.1177/21582440241279367

Kumar Jain, V., Kumar Yadav, N., Professor, A., & Sharma, D. (2025). AI-Driven Pedagogy: Promoting Student Engagement, Intrinsic Motivation, and Self-Regulation. In *Journal of Informatics Education and Research* (Vol. 5).

Kumari, A., Begum, S., Paunikar, M. S., Kaur, A., & Verma, S. (2025). The role of artificial intelligence in teacher training: Enhancing pedagogical effectiveness. *Journal of Marketing & Social Research, 2*, 116–122. DOI: 10.61336/jmsr/25-05-13

Kumar, S. (2023). Impact of Digitalization in Higher Education and Smart Learning Techniques. In Nadda, V., Tyagi, P. K., Moniz Vieira, R., & Tyagi, P. (Eds.), *Advances in Hospitality, Tourism, and the Services Industry* (pp. 198–207). IGI Global., DOI: 10.4018/979-8-3693-0650-5.ch013

Kumar, S., Talukder, M. B., & Tyagi, P. K. (2025a). The Impact of Virtual Reality and Augmented Reality in TNE Learning. In Crawford, C. M., & Gee, T. T. (Eds.), *Motivating Engagement, Belonging, and Success in Higher Education Student Experience* (pp. 359–382). IGI Global., DOI: 10.4018/979-8-3693-8089-5.ch013

Kumar, V., & Derawi, M. (2025). Applications and impact of Artificial Intelligence in the field of agriculture, education, healthcare, and administration. In Mishra, S., Gupta, N., & Goktas, P. (Eds.), *AI and ML Techniques in IoT-based Communication: A Path to Sustainable Development Goals* (pp. 97–118). The Institute of Electrical and Electronics Engineers, Inc., DOI: 10.1002/9781394337262.ch05

Kundu, A., Bej, T., & Mondal, R. (2025). Exploring teachers' AI literacy: Cognitive, pedagogical, ethical, and contextual insights from Indian schools. *Teaching Education*, •••, 1–21. DOI: 10.1080/10476210.2025.2570227

Kunwar, K. (2026). Algorithmic governance in lifelong learning systems: Artificial intelligence, educational policy transformation, and human development. *Artificial Intelligence in Lifelong and Life-Course Education, 1*(2), 67–83. DOI: 10.66053/aillce.v1i2.31

Kushwaha, A. (2022). Supervising teaching practice: Role perceptions and challenges. *Journal of Positive School Psychology*, *6*(11). https://journalppw.com/index.php/jpsp/article/view/13931/9030

Kwet, M. (2019). Digital colonialism: US empire and the new imperialism in the Global South. *Race & Class*, *60*(4), 3–26. DOI: 10.1177/0306396818823172

Lambrecht, J., Lenkeit, J., Hartmann, A., Ehlert, A., Knigge, M., & Spörer, N. (2022). The effect of school leadership on implementing inclusive education: How transformational and instructional leadership practices affect individualised education planning. *International Journal of Inclusive Education*, *26*(9), 943–957. DOI: 10.1080/13603116.2020.1752825

Lau, J., Su, Y.-W., Chen, C.-C., & Dai, C.-L. (2019). Using a collaborative model in supervision with international counseling students. *The Journal of Humanistic Counseling*, *58*(2), 150–164. DOI: 10.1002/johc.12103

Laupichler, M. C., Aster, A., Schirch, J., & Raupach, T. (2022). Artificial intelligence literacy in higher and adult education: A scoping literature review. *Computers and Education: Artificial Intelligence*, *3*, 100101. DOI: 10.1016/j.caeai.2022.100101

Law Asia. (2025). *Building trust in the algorithm: Indonesia's emerging AI framework*. https://law.asia/indonesia-ai-governance-framework/

Law, H. B. T. (2024, February). *Ethical guidelines on use of artificial intelligence (AI) in Indonesia*. https://www.hbtlaw.com/insights/2024-02/ethical-guidelines-use-artificial-intelligence-ai-indonesia

Lazarides, R., Dietrich, J., & Taskinen, P. H. (2019). Stability and change in students' motivational profiles in mathematics classrooms: The role of perceived teaching. *Teaching and Teacher Education*, *79*, 164–175. DOI: 10.1016/j.tate.2018.12.016

Leandro, G. D. S. M., Kumar, S., Jacinto Da Gama, M., Carvalho, H., & Leandro, E. (2024). Circular Economy Practices in the Hotel Sector in Luanda, Angola: Challenges and Future Perspectives. In P. K. Tyagi, V. Nadda, K. Kankaew, & K. Dube (Eds.), *Advances in Hospitality, Tourism, and the Services Industry* (pp. 54–66). IGI Global. DOI: 10.4018/979-8-3693-4042-4.ch004

Lee, A. (2008). How are doctoral students supervised? Concepts of doctoral research supervision. *Studies in Higher Education*, *33*(3), 267–281. DOI: 10.1080/03075070802049202

Lee, D., Arnold, M., Srivastava, A., Plastow, K., Strelan, P., Ploeckl, F., Lekkas, D., & Palmer, E. (2024). The impact of generative AI on higher education learning and teaching: A study of educators' perspectives. *Computers and Education: Artificial Intelligence*, *6*, 100221. DOI: 10.1016/j.caeai.2024.100221

Lee, M. K. (2018). Understanding perception of algorithmic decisions: Fairness, trust, and emotion in response to algorithmic management. *Big Data & Society*, *5*(1), 2053951718756684. DOI: 10.1177/2053951718756684

Lee, Y. F., Hwang, G. J., & Chen, P. Y. (2022). Impacts of an AI-based chabot on college students' after-class review, academic performance, self-efficacy, learning attitude, and motivation. *Educational Technology Research and Development*, *70*(5), 1843–1865. DOI: 10.1007/s11423-022-10142-8

Leonardi, P. M. (2025). Homo agenticus in the age of agentic AI: Agency loops, power displacement, and the circulation of responsibility. *Information and Organization*, *35*(3), 100582. Advance online publication. DOI: 10.1016/j.infoandorg.2025.100582

Lessky, F., & Schiffecker, S. (2024). Academic identity crafting: How early-career women researchers in the United States and Austria form their professional identities. *Research in Comparative and International Education*, *21*(12), 157–175. DOI: 10.1177/17454999261417858

Lia, M., & Sunb, W. (2024). Research on the integration of ideological and political education into Chinese-English translation teaching. *Adult and Higher Education (2024) Clausius Scientific Press, Canada*, *6*(7), 97–102. DOI: 10.23977/aduhe.2024.060714

Li, J. J., Bonn, M. A., & Ye, B. H. (2019). Hotel employee's artificial intelligence and robotics awareness and its impact on turnover intention: The moderating roles of perceived organizational support and competitive psychological climate. *Tourism Management*, *73*, 172–181. DOI: 10.1016/j.tourman.2019.02.006

Limongi, R. (2024). The use of artificial intelligence in scientific research with integrity and ethics. *Future Studies Research Journal: Trends and Strategies*, *16*(1), e845–e845. DOI: 10.24023/FutureJournal/2175-5825/2024.v16i1.845

Lim, R. R. (2024). Collaborative supervision of the master teachers and the teaching efficiency in selected junior high schools in Cavite. *International Journal for Multidisciplinary Research*, *6*(3), 1–15. https://www.ijfmr.com/papers/2024/3/22494.pdf

Lindfors, M., Pettersson, F., & Olofsson, A. D. (2021). Conditions for professional digitalcompetence: The teacher educators' view. *Education Inquiry*, *12*(4), 390–409. DOI: 10.1080/20004508.2021.1890936

Li, R., Wang, X., Huang, G., Yang, W., Zhang, K., Gu, X., Tran, S. N., Garg, S., Alty, J., & Bai, Q. (2026). A comprehensive review of deep supervision in computer vision. *Neurocomputing*, *666*, 132193. DOI: 10.1016/j.neucom.2025.132193

Li, S., Liu, Y., & Su, Y. S. (2022). Differential analysis of teachers' technological pedagogical content knowledge (TPACK) abilities according to teaching stages and educational levels. *Sustainability (Basel)*, *14*(12), 7176. DOI: 10.3390/su14127176

Long, Y. (2026). AI-Supervisor: Autonomous AI Research Supervision via a Persistent Research World Model. *arXiv preprint arXiv:2603.24402, 2.* /arXiv.2603.24402DOI: 10.48550

Long, D., & Magerko, B. (2020). What is AI literacy? Competencies and design considerations. In *Proceedings of the 2020 CHI conference on human factors in computing systems* (pp. 1–16). DOI: 10.1145/3313831.3376727

Lovitts, B. E. (2001). *Leaving the ivory tower: The causes and consequences of departure from doctoral study*. Bloomsbury Publishing PLC.

Lrhoul, H. (2017). La production scientifique des chercheurs de la faculté de médecine et de pharmacie de Casablanca: Mesures, cartographie et enjeux du libre accès [Scientific production of researchers at the Faculty of Medicine and Pharmacy of Casablanca: Measurement, mapping and open access challenges]. Unpublished manuscript.

Luckin, R. (2017). Toward artificial intelligence-based assessment systems. *Nature Human Behavior*, 1(3), 0028. DOI: 10.1038/s41562-016-0028

Luckin, R., Cukurova, M., Kent, C., & du Boulay, B. (2022). Empowering educators to be AI-ready. *Computers and Education: Artificial Intelligence*, *3*, 1–11. DOI: 10.1016/j.caeai.2022.100076

Ma El Ainin, C. N., Janati Idrissi, F., & Nouib, A. (2021). L'enseignement à distance et la formation continue des enseignants au Maroc: Cas de la région Guelmim-Oued Noun [Distance learning and continuing teacher training in Morocco: The case of the Guelmim-Oued Noun region]. *Moroccan Journal of Business Studies*, 3.

Madanchian, M., & Taherdoost, H. (2025). The impact of artificial intelligence on research efficiency. *Results in Engineering*, *26*, 104743. Advance online publication. DOI: 10.1016/j.rineng.2025.104743

Mah, D.-K., & Groß, N. (2024). Artificial intelligence in higher education: Exploring faculty use, self-efficacy, distinct profiles, and professional development needs. *International Journal of Educational Technology in Higher Education*, *21*(1), 58. DOI: 10.1186/s41239-024-00490-1

Maimela, C., & Mbonde, P. (2025). Artificial intelligence in South African universities: Curriculum transformation and decolonisation—aid or obstacle? *Frontiers in Sociology*, *10*, 1543471. DOI: 10.3389/fsoc.2025.1543471 PMID: 40697567

Maisuria, A., & Helmes, S. (2019). *Life for the Academic in the Neoliberal University*. Routledge. DOI: 10.4324/9780429329951

Marabelli, M., Davison, R. M., Gatti, G., Srivastava, A., & Tarafdar, M. (2026). Use of Generative AI in Scholarly Research: Challenges and Opportunities. *Communications of the Association for Information Systems*, *58*(1), 36.

Marginson, S. (2008). Global Field and Global Imagining: Bourdieu and Worldwide Higher *Education. British Journal of Sociology of Education*, *29*(3), 303–315. DOI: 10.1080/01425690801966386

Marshall, J. H., Lawrence, E. C., Lee Williams, J., & Peugh, J. (2015). Mentoring as service-learning: The relationship between perceived peer support and outcomes for college women mentors. *Studies in Educational Evaluation*, *47*, 38–46. DOI: 10.1016/j.stueduc.2015.07.001

Mbambo, G. P., & Du Plessis, E. C. (2024). Impact of artificial intelligence on teacher training in open distance and electronic learning. *International Journal of Learning. Teaching and Educational Research*, *23*(5), 370–386. DOI: 10.26803/ijlter.23.5.19

McAlpine, L., & Amundsen, C. (2011). *Doctoral education: Research-based strategies for doctoral students, supervisors, and administrators*. Springer. DOI: 10.1007/978-94-007-0507-4

McCarthy, J. (2004). *What is artificial intelligence*. [Online]. http://www-formal .standford.edu/jmc/whatisai.html

Mensele, C., & Coetzee, M. (2014). Job embeddedness, organisational commitment and voluntary turnover of academic staff at a higher education institution in South Africa. *South African Journal of Labour Relations*, *38*(1), 9–30.

Mercer, S., Murillo-Miranda, C., & Smid, D. (2025). The invisible influencers: Understanding the motivation, emotions, and well-being of language teacher educators. *The Journal for the Psychology of Language Learning*, *7*(1), 27–44. DOI: 10.52598/jpll/7/1/3

Merdiaty, N., & Sulistiasih, S. (2024). Empowering learning: The mediating role of teachers in enhancing students' intrinsic motivation. *Al-Ishlah: Jurnal Pendidikan*, *16*(4), 5163–5172. DOI: 10.35445/alishlah.v16i4.6430

Miao, F., & Shiohira, K. (2024). *AI competency framework for students* [Online]. UNESCO., DOI: 10.54675/JKJB9835

Ministry of Communication and Informatics Indonesia (KOMINFO). (2023). *Surat Edaran No. 9/2023 tentang Etika Kecerdasan Artifisial [Circular Letter No. 9/2023 on AI Ethical Guidelines].* Kementerian Komunikasi dan Informatika Republik Indonesia.

Minja, L. (2024). The Role of Recruitment and Selection on Organisational Performance: A Case of National Housing Corporation in Tanzania. *Accounting and Business Review*, *16*(5). Advance online publication. DOI: 10.59645/abr.v16i5.386

Mishra, A., Mohanty, A., & Sundaray, B. K. (2025). Can faculty job satisfaction reduce turnover intention s at management institutes in India? Analysing the mediation effect of organisational commitment. *Journal of Applied Research in Higher Education*, •••, 1–15.

Mishra, P., & Koehler, M. J. (2006). Technological pedagogical content knowledge: A framework for teacher knowledge. *Teachers College Record*, *108*(6), 1017–1054. DOI: 10.1111/j.1467-9620.2006.00684.x

MoEYS. (2023). *Teacher policy action plan 2024-2030.* MoEYS. https://shorturl .at/WHuz3

MoEYS. (2025). *Strategic plan for teacher education reform in Cambodia 2024-2030.* https://shorturl.at/eS3S1

Mogoale, P., Pretorius, A., Mogase, R., & Segooa, M. (2025). Ethical considerations in artificial intelligence-driven environments for higher education. *South African Journal of Information Management*, *27*(1), a2007. Advance online publication. DOI: 10.4102/sajim.v27i1.2007

Mohadi, M., & Tarshany, Y. (2023). Maqasid al-Shari'ah and the ethics of artificial intelligence. *Journal of Contemporary Maqasid Studies*, *2*(2), 79–102. DOI: 10.52100/jcms.v2i2.107

Moin, M. F., Behl, A., Zhang, J. Z., & Shankar, A. (2025). AI in the organizational nexus: Building trust, cementing commitment, and evolving psychological contracts. *Information Systems Frontiers*, *27*(4), 1413–1424. DOI: 10.1007/s10796-024-10561-3

Mok, S. Y., & Staub, F. C. (2021). Does coaching, mentoring, and supervision matter for pre-service teachers' planning skills and clarity of instruction? A meta-analysis of (quasi-)experimental studies. *Teaching and Teacher Education*, *107*, 103484. DOI: 10.1016/j.tate.2021.103484

Moorhouse, B. L. (2024). Beginning and first-year language teachers' readiness for the generative AI age. *Computers and Education: Artificial Intelligence*, *6*, 100201. DOI: 10.1016/j.caeai.2024.100201

Moorhouse, B. L., Wan, Y., Wu, C., Kohnke, L., Ho, T. Y., & Kwong, T. (2024). Developing language teachers' professional generative AI competence: An intervention study in an initial language teacher education course. *System*, *125*, 103399. DOI: 10.1016/j.system.2024.103399

Morrish, L. (2019). *Pressure vessels: The epidemic of poor mental health among higher education staff.* Higher Education Policy Institute Oxford.

Mo, Z., Liu, M. T., Chark, R., Zeng, S., & Song, X. (2025). How AI adoption in human resource management practices can enhance tourism employees' organizational commitment. *Journal of Hospitality and Tourism Management*, *63*, 54–67. DOI: 10.1016/j.jhtm.2025.03.003

Mualla, K. J., & Mualla, W. (2026). Leveraging AI in Higher Education: Contemporary Approaches for Teaching, Learning, and Assessment Design. In *Higher Education in the Arab World: Artificial Intelligence* (pp. 169-191). Springer Nature Switzerland.

Mudenda, S. (2025). Impact of Artificial Intelligence on College and University Students: A Global Transformation of the Education System. *Creative Education*, *16*(11), 1801–1828. DOI: 10.4236/ce.2025.1611112

Musselin, C. (2004). Towards a European academic labour market? Some lessons drawn from empirical studies on academic mobility. *Higher Education*, *48*(1), 55–78. DOI: 10.1023/B:HIGH.0000033770.24848.41

Mustapha, R., & Malkan, S. N. A. (2025). Maqasid al-Shariah in the AI era: Balancing innovation and Islamic ethical principles. *International Journal of Islamic Theology & Civilization*, *3*(3), 1–21. DOI: 10.5281/zenodo.15381828

Naqvi, W. M., Ganjoo, R., Rowe, M., Pashine, A. A., & Mishra, G. V. (2025). Critical thinking in the age of generative AI: Implications for health sciences education. *Frontiers in Artificial Intelligence*, *8*, 1571527. DOI: 10.3389/frai.2025.1571527

Narayanan, D., Nagpal, M., McGuire, J., Schweitzer, S., & De Cremer, D. (2024). Fairness perceptions of artificial intelligence: A review and path forward. *International Journal of Human-Computer Interaction*, *40*(1), 4–23. DOI: 10.1080/10447318.2023.2210890

Narayan, R., Rodriguez, C., Araujo, J., Shaqlaih, A., & Moss, G. (2013). Constructivism—Constructivist learning theory. In *The handbook of educational theories* (pp. 169–183). IAP Information Age Publishing., https://psycnet.apa.org/record/2013-11995-015

Narkhede, G., Pasi, B., Dhamak, P., Mahalle, P., & Ambhore, N. (2025). In the pursuit of educational excellence: Investigating CSFs for implementing NEP 2020 to redefine the higher education ecosystem. *Journal of Applied Research in Higher Education*. Advance online publication. DOI: 10.1108/JARHE-09-2024-0454

Naseer, F., Khalid, M. U., Ayub, N., Rasool, A., Abbas, T., & Afzal, M. W. (2024). Automated assessment and feedback in higher education using generative AI. In Sharma, R. C., & Bozkurt, A. (Eds.), *Transforming education with generative AI: Prompt engineering and synthetic content creation* (pp. 433–461). IGI Global Scientific Publishing., DOI: 10.4018/979-8-3693-1351-0.ch021

Ncube, P. D., Dzvapatsva, G. P., Matobobo, C., & Ranga, M. M. (2026). Redefining student assessment in AI-infused learning environments: A systematic review of challenges and strategies for academic integrity. *AI and Ethics*, *6*(1), 68. DOI: 10.1007/s43681-025-00871-w

Nelson, R. (2025). Academic Identity in the AI Era: Navigating Resistance, Adaptation and Traditional Values in Higher Education. In *AI-Powered Pedagogy and Curriculum Design* (pp. 153-168). Routledge.

Nelson, R. (2024). *Academic identity in the age of AI: Higher education and the digital revolution*. Emerald Group Publishing.

Nemorin, S. (2024). Towards decolonising the ethics of AI in education. *Globalisation, Societies and Education*, *22*(3), 411–426. DOI: 10.1080/14767724.2024.2333821

Ng, D. T. K., Leung, J. K. L., Su, J., Ng, R. C. W., & Chu, S. K. W. (2023). Teachers' AI digital competencies and twenty-first century skills in the postpandemic world. *Education Technology Research and Development, 71*(1), 137–161. , 023-10203-6DOI: 10.1007/s11423-023-10203-6

Ng, D. T. K., Leung, J. K. L., Chu, S. K. W., & Qiao, M. S. (2021). Conceptualizing AI literacy: An exploratory review. *Computers and Education: Artificial Intelligence*, *2*, 100041. DOI: 10.1016/j.caeai.2021.100041

Ng, W. (2012). Can we teach digital natives digital literacy? *Computers & Education*, *59*(3), 1065–1078. DOI: 10.1016/j.compedu.2012.04.016

Nicol, D. J., & MacLeod, I. A. (2005). Using a shared workspace and wireless laptops to improve collaborative project learning in an engineering design class. *Computers & Education*, *44*(4), 459–475. DOI: 10.1016/j.compedu.2004.04.008

Nikolopoulou, K. (2024). Generative artificial intelligence in higher education: Exploring ways of harnessing pedagogical practices with the assistance of ChatGPT. *International Journal of Changes in Education*, *1*(2), 103–111. DOI: 10.47852/bonviewIJCE42022489

Nordgren, C., Christensen, J., Spikol, D., & Tudorache, P. (2025). STUDENT EXPECTATIONS–AN ASPECT EASILY OVERLOOKED. *Journal of Teaching and Learning in Higher Education*, *6*(2). Advance online publication. DOI: 10.24834/jotl.6.2.1852

Obschanka, M., & Audretsch, D. B. (2020). Artificial intelligence and big data in entrepreneurship: A new era has begun. *Small Business Economics*, *55*(1), 529–539. DOI: 10.1007/s11187-019-00202-4

Obunge, J. I., & Arannilewa, A. O. (2025). Artificial Intelligence Tools in Human Resource Management and Lecturers' Retention in Private Universities in Ekiti State. *International Journal of Advanced Research and Learning*, *4*(3), 9–19.

OECD. (2019). *OECD principles on artificial intelligence*. OECD Publishing. https://oecd.ai/en/ai-principles

OECD. (2023). *AI and the future of skills* (Volume 2: Methods for evaluating AI skill implications). OECD Publishing.

Ojha, B., Agrawal, A., & Arya, A. (2024). Artificial intelligence integration in higher education. In *Integrating AI into higher education* (pp. 1–20). CRC Press., DOI: 10.1201/9781003469315-1

Omar, A., Shaqour, A. Z., & Khlaif, Z. N. (2024). Attitudes of faculty members in Palestinian universities toward employing artificial intelligence applications in higher education: Opportunities and challenges. *Frontiers in Education*, *9*, 1414606. DOI: 10.3389/feduc.2024.1414606

Omodan, B. I. (2025). Redefining the role of supervisors in the era of artificial intelligence: Implications for hybrid postgraduate research governance. *Cogent Education*, *12*(1), 2536534. DOI: 10.1080/2331186X.2025.2536534

Oncioiu, I., & Bularca, A. R. (2025). Artificial intelligence governance in higher education: The role of knowledge-based strategies in fostering legal awareness and ethical artificial intelligence literacy. *Societies (Basel, Switzerland)*, *15*(6), 144. Advance online publication. DOI: 10.3390/soc15060144

Osman, D. J., & Warner, J. R. (2020). Measuring teacher motivation: The missing link between professional development and practice. *Teaching and Teacher Education, 92*, 103064. DOI: 10.1016/j.tate.2020.103064

Ouyang, F., & Jiao, P. (2021). Artificial intelligence in education: The three paradigms. *Computers and Education: Artificial Intelligence, 2*, 100020. DOI: 10.1016/j.caeai.2021.100020

Ozga, J. (2008). Governing Knowledge: Research Steering and Research Quality. *European Educational Research Journal*, 7(3), 261 272. (Original work published 2008)DOI: 10.2304/eerj.2008.7.3.261

Page, M. J., McKenzie, J. E., Bossuyt, P. M., Boutron, I., Hoffmann, T. C., Mulrow, C. D., Shamseer, L., Tetzlaff, J. M., Akl, E. A., & Brennan, S. E. (2021). The PRISMA 2020 statement: an updated guideline for reporting systematic reviews. *bmj, 372*, 1–9. DOI: 10.1136/bmj.n71

Paris, B., Conti-Cook, C., Greene, D., Jones, K. M., Justie, B., Kirschenbaum, M., Kresge, L., May, E., Nguyen, A., & Reynolds, R. (2025). Artificial intelligence and academic professions. *Available at* SSRN *5376147, 111*(3), 49–59. DOI: 10.2139/ssrn.5376147

Parker, A. K., Zenkov, K., & Glaser, H. (2021). Preparing school-based teacher educators: Mentor teachers' perceptions of mentoring and mentor training. *Peabody Journal of Education, 96*(1), 65–75. DOI: 10.1080/0161956X.2021.1877027

Park, M., & Son, J. B. (2022). Preservice EFL teachers' readiness in computer-assisted language learning and teaching. *Asia Pacific Journal of Education, 42*(2), 320–334. DOI: 10.1080/02188791.2020.1815649

Parmar, V., Channar, Z. A., Ahmed, R. R., Streimikiene, D., Pahi, M. H., & Streimikis, J. (2022). Assessing the organizational commitment, subjective vitality and burnout effects on turnover intention in private universities. *Oeconomia Copernicana, 13*(1), 251–286. DOI: 10.24136/oc.2022.008

Pich, K. (2017). Challenges facing the implementation of teacher education policy and its impacts on teacher quality in Cambodia. *UC Occasional Paper Series, 1*(2), 39–59. https://tinyurl.com/er34hsan

Pollitt, C., & Bouckaert, G. (2011). *Public Management Reform: A Comparative Analysis*—New Public Management, Governance, and the Neo-Weberian State (3th ed.). Oxford: Oxford University Press.

Polly, D., Martin, F., & Guilbaud, T. C. (2021). Examining barriers and desired supports to increase faculty members' use of digital technologies: Perspectives of faculty, staff and administrators. *Journal of Computing in Higher Education, 33*(1), 135–156. DOI: 10.1007/s12528-020-09259-7

Popenici, S. A. D., & Kerr, S. (2017). Exploring the impact of artificial intelligence on teaching and learning in higher education. *Research and Practice in Technology Enhanced Learning, 12*(1), 22. DOI: 10.1186/s41039-017-0062-8 PMID: 30595727

Povilaitis, K., & Jõgi, L. (2026). Understanding academic identity through liminality: Implications for leadership and academic development. *Frontiers in Education, 11*, 1–15. DOI: 10.3389/feduc.2026.1763425

Pov, S., & Kawai, N. (2025). Pre-service teachers' preparation for inclusive practices in Cambodia: Experience, self-efficacy, and concerns about inclusion. *Journal of Research in Special Educational Needs, 25*(1), 118–131. DOI: 10.1111/1471-3802.12715

Power, M. (1997). *The Audit Society: Rituals of Verification*. Oxford University Press.

Prabjandee, D. (2022). Inconvenient truth? How different mentoring approaches impact student–teacher identity development [Original Research]. *Frontiers in Education, 7*, 916749. Advance online publication. DOI: 10.3389/feduc.2022.916749

Priyoherianto, A., Mustaji, M., Roesminingsih, E., Hariyati, N., Rianto, Y., & Khamidi, A. (2025). The impact of organizational health and the levels of transformational leadership of school teachers in Indonesia: A systematic review. *International Journal of Current Educational Research, 4*(1), 25–45. DOI: 10.53621/ijocer.v4i1.47

Pum, M., & Sok, S. (2024). Leveraging AI in education in Cambodia: A review of perceived concerns and associated benefits. *Asian Journal of Distance Education, 19*(2), 157–167. DOI: 10.2139/ssrn.4932278

Qadhi, S. M., Alduais, A., Chaaban, Y., & Khraisheh, M. (2024). Generative AI, research ethics, and higher education research: Insights from a scientometric analysis. *Information (Basel), 15*(6), 325. DOI: 10.3390/info15060325

Qin, S., Jia, N., Luo, X., Liao, C., & Huang, Z. (2023). Perceived fairness of human managers compared with artificial intelligence in employee performance evaluation. *Journal of Management Information Systems, 40*(4), 1039–1070. DOI: 10.1080/07421222.2023.2267316

Qiong, W., Li, M., & Chansongpol, T. (2025). A Study on the Factors Influencing Turnover Intention among Faculty in Chinese Private Higher Education Institutions. [JTCSS]. *Journal of Thai-Chinese Social Science, 2*(2), 173–196.

Qipeng, Y., & Jamaludin, K. A. B. (2026, January). The role of AI in higher education, teacher training, and professional development: Teachers' perspective. *International Journal of Academic Research in Progressive Education and Development, 15*(1), 496–508. https://hrmars.com/IJARPED/article/view/27522/The-Role-of-AI-in-Higher-Education-Teacher-Training-and-Professional-Development-Teachers-Perspective. DOI: 10.6007/IJARPED/v15-i1/27522

Radiya-Dixit, E., & Christin, A. (2025). Same stereotypes, different term? Understanding the "Global South" in AI ethics. In *Proceedings of the AAAI/ACM Conference on AI, Ethics, and Society* (Vol. 8, pp. 2081–2093). AAAI. DOI: 10.1609/aies.v8i3.36697

Rahabav, P. (2016). The effectiveness of academic supervision for teachers. *Journal of Education and Practice, 7*(9), 47–55. https://files.eric.ed.gov/fulltext/EJ1095817.pdf

Raharjo, R. S., & Rohmadi, S. H. (2025). Artificial intelligence in indonesian education: A critical review of ethical considerations, implementation challenges, and educational management perspectives. *At-Tarbawi. Jurnal Kajian Kependidikan Islam, 10*(1), 50–68. DOI: 10.22515/attarbawi.v10i1.12141

Ramli, R., Razali, R., Gadeng, A. N., Diana, N., & Hariadi, J. (2025). Integrating local knowledge into higher education: A qualitative study of curriculum innovation in Aceh, Indonesia. *Education Sciences, 15*(9), 1214. DOI: 10.3390/educsci15091214

Rao, G. T., & Suhasini, N. (2025). Integrating artificial intelligence in higher education to enhance teaching and learning. *Computer Applications in Engineering Education, 33*(6), e70085. DOI: 10.1002/cae.70085

Raquib, A., Channa, B., Zubair, T., & Qadir, J. (2022). Islamic virtue-based ethics for artificial intelligence. *Discover Artificial Intelligence, 2*(1), 11. Advance online publication. DOI: 10.1007/s44163-022-00028-2

Rawat, S., & Ashton-Bell, R. L. T. (2025). Responsible Ai-Readiness In Higher Education: Validating A Dual-Model Framework For Faculty Development. *Journal of Information Technology Education, 24*, 040. Advance online publication. DOI: 10.28945/5654

Reeve, J., & Cheon, S. H. (2024). Learning how to become an autonomy-supportive teacher begins with perspective taking: A randomized control trial and model test. *Teaching and Teacher Education, 148*, 104702. DOI: 10.1016/j.tate.2024.104702

Robert, J. (2024). *2024 EDUCAUSE AI landscape study*. EDUCAUSE Center for Analysis and Research. https://library.educause.edu/resources/2024/2/2024-educause-ai-landscape-study

Rodríguez-Ortiz, M. Á., Santana-Mancilla, P. C., & Anido-Rifón, L. E. (2025). Machine learning and generative AI in learning analytics for higher education: A systematic review of models, trends, and challenges. *Applied Sciences (Basel, Switzerland)*, *15*(15), 8679. DOI: 10.3390/app15158679

Roll, I., & Wylie, R. (2016). Evolution and Revolution in Artificial Intelligence in Education. *International Journal of Artificial Intelligence in Education*, *26*(2), 582–599. DOI: 10.1007/s40593-016-0110-3

Ronkainen, I., Vesterinen, V.-M., Lavonen, J., Järvinen, J., Malmberg, L.-E., Turkkila, M., & Salmela-Aro, K. (2025). Students' situational motivation in climate education: A multilevel profile approach. *Learning and Individual Differences*, *120*, 102698. DOI: 10.1016/j.lindif.2025.102698

Rukadikar, A., & Khandelwal, K. (2025). Exploring perceptions of Indian graduates on the effectiveness of artificial intelligence in higher education campus hiring. *Discover Artificial Intelligence*, *5*(1), 265. Advance online publication. DOI: 10.1007/s44163-025-00526-z

Russell, S. J., & Norvig, P. (2016). *Artificial intelligence: a modern approach* (3rd ed.). Pearson Education Limited.

Sadeghi, S. (2024). Employee well-being in the age of AI: Perceptions, concerns, behaviors, and outcomes. *arXiv preprint arXiv:2412.04796.*

Sakhiyya, Z., & Mulya, T. W. (Eds.). (2023). *Education in Indonesia: Critical perspectives on equity and social justice*. Springer., DOI: 10.1007/978-981-99-1878-2

Sakti, S. A., Endraswara, S., & Rohman, A. (2024). Revitalizing local wisdom within character education through ethnopedagogy approach: A case study on a preschool in Yogyakarta. *Heliyon*, *10*(10), e31370. Advance online publication. DOI: 10.1016/j.heliyon.2024.e31370 PMID: 38803959

Salas-Pilco, S. Z., Xiao, K., & Hu, X. (2022). Artificial intelligence and learning analytics in teacher education: A systematic review. *Education Sciences*, *12*(8), 569. DOI: 10.3390/educsci12080569

Samoun, S., & Pen, D. (2025). A qualitative study of challenges faced by Cambodian teachers in implementing student-centered approaches. *Journal of General Education and Humanities*, *4*(2), 575–588. DOI: 10.58421/gehu.v4i2.426

Sangwa, S., Ngobi, D., Ekosse, E., & Mutabazi, P. (2025). AI governance in African higher education: Status, challenges, and a futureproof policy framework. *Available at* SSRN *5386204. Artificial Intelligence and Education, 1*(1), 2054. https://doi.org/ DOI: 10.2139/ssrn.5386204

Santos, R. J. (2024). *Human-AI collaboration in education: Theoretical frameworks and pedagogical implications*. Digital Commons @ University of Nebraska – Lincoln. https://digitalcommons.unl.edu

Santos, B. de S. (2014). *Epistemologies of the South: Justice against epistemicide*. Routledge.

Sapawi, M. S. M., & Yusoff, N. M. R. N. (2025). Artificial Intelligence in Curriculum Development: A Global Systematic Review of Trends, Challenges, and Strategic Directions. *Journal of Curriculum Studies Research*, *7*(2), 466–497. DOI: 10.46303/jcsr.2025.30

Sari, I., & Santoso, A. (2024). Perceived AI Fairness and Organizational Commitment: The Mediating Role of Psychological Safety. *Future of Work and Digital Management Journal*, *2*(4), 44–54.

Sariyasa, S., & Monika, K. A. L. (2023). Artificial intelligence and academic ethics in the era of Merdeka Belajar: How are students' responses? *Jurnal Kependidikan: Jurnal Hasil Penelitian dan Kajian Kepustakaan di Bidang Pendidikan, Pengajaran dan Pembelajaran, 9*(3). https://e-journal.undikma.ac.id/index.php/jurnalkependidikan/article/view/8720

Schmidt, D. A., Alboloushi, B., Thomas, A., & Magalhaes, R. (2025). Integrating artificial intelligence in higher education: Perceptions, challenges, and strategies for academic innovation. *Computers and Education Open*, *9*, 100274. Advance online publication. DOI: 10.1016/j.caeo.2025.100274

Sedkaoui, S., & Benaichouba, R. (2024). Generative AI as a transformative force for innovation: A review of opportunities, applications and challenges. *European Journal of Innovation Management*. Advance online publication. DOI: 10.1108/EJIM-02-2024-0129

Sek, R. (2023). The effectiveness of transformational leadership in improving staff performance of private primary schools in Phnom Penh, Cambodia. *Journal As-Salam*, *7*(1), 26–41. https://www.ijtsrd.com/papers/ijtsrd97270.pdf. DOI: 10.37249/assalam.v7i1.554

Selwyn, N. (2016). *Education and technology: Key issues and debates* (3rd ed.). Bloomsbury Publishing.

Selwyn, N. (2019). *Should robots replace teachers? AI and the future of education*. John Wiley & Sons.

Sengsoulintha, K. (2025). Teacher educators' challenges: Focusing on teacher training colleges in Laos [Original Research]. *Frontiers in Education*, *10*, 1–14. DOI: 10.3389/feduc.2025.1614060

Seo, K., Yoo, M., Dodson, S., & Jin, S.-H. (2024). Augmented teachers: K-12 teachers' needs for artificial intelligence's complementary role in personalized learning. *Journal of Research on Technology in Education*, *57*(4), 876–893. DOI: 10.1080/15391523.2024.2330525

Sethy, M. (2026). Artificial intelligence and epistemic justice: A decolonial turn through indigenous knowledge systems. *AI & Society*, *41*(5), 5401–5410. Advance online publication. DOI: 10.1007/s00146-026-02936-8

Setyawan, M. B., Dewi, D. A., Hidayah, Y., & Hamid, M. A. (2025). Assessing students' readiness for artificial intelligence-based project learning to strengthen local wisdom values in Indonesia. *Cogent Education*, *12*(1), 2582948. Advance online publication. DOI: 10.1080/2331186X.2025.2582948

Severinsson, E. (2012). Research supervision: Supervisory style, research-related tasks, importance, and quality - part 1. *Journal of Nursing Management*, *20*(2), 215–223. DOI: 10.1111/j.1365-2834.2011.01361.x

Shanghai Ranking Consultancy. (2025). 2025 *Academic Ranking of World Universities (ARWU)*. Shanghai Ranking Consultancy. https://www.shanghairanking.com

Sharma, U., & Sokal, L. (2015). The impact of a teacher education course on pre-service teachers' beliefs about inclusion: An international comparison. *Journal of Research in Special Educational Needs*, *15*(4), 276–284. DOI: 10.1111/1471-3802.12043

Shore, C., & Wright, S. (2015). Audit Culture Revisited: Rankings, Ratings, and the Reassembling of Society. *Current Anthropology*, *56*(3), 421–444. DOI: 10.1086/681534

Shwedeh, F. (2024). The integration of artificial intelligence (AI) into decision support systems within higher education institutions. *Nanotechnology Perceptions*, *20*(5), 331–357.

Singh, A. K., Singh, R., & Thapliyal, C. (2024b). Current challenges and future prospective of new education policy 2020 in higher educational institutions of India. In R. Kumar, E. Ong, S. Anggoro, T. Toh, & M. Fukui (Ed.), *Transdisciplinary Teaching and Technological Integration for Improved Learning: Case Studies and Practical Approaches* (pp. 269-301). IGI Global. DOI: 10.4018/979-8-3693-8217-2.ch013

Singh, N., Kalam Khan, M., Dixit, A., & Jaiswar, K. (2025). NEP 2020 and Governance & Digital Infrastructure. *International Journal of Advanced Research in Science, Communication and Technology International Open-Access, Double-Blind, Peer-Reviewed, Refereed, Multidisciplinary Online Journal, 5*(16).

Singh, A. K., Ashraf, S. N., & Gupta, M. (2025). Digital transformation and customer's problems in banking industry of India. In Tunio, M. (Ed.), *Applications of Career Transitions and Entrepreneurship* (pp. 1–34). IGI Global Scientific Publishing., DOI: 10.4018/979-8-3693-4163-6.ch001

Singh, A. K., & Singh, R. (2025). Digital infrastructure and sustainable development goals in G20 countries. In Popescu, C. (Ed.), *Building Inclusive Global Knowledge Societies for Sustainable Development* (pp. 363–408). IGI Global Scientific Publishing., DOI: 10.4018/979-8-3693-6298-3.ch014

Singh, A. K., Singh, S., & Shamra, S. K. (2024a). Importance and challenges of online learning in higher educational institutions during COVID-19 in Uttarakhand state of India. In Hossain, S. (Ed.), *Cases on Social Media and Entrepreneurship* (pp. 193–212). IGI Global., DOI: 10.4018/979-8-3693-1781-5.ch012

Smith, S., Tate, M., Freeman, K., Walsh, A., Ballsun-Stanton, B., Hooper, M., & Lane, M. (2025). A university framework for the responsible use of generative AI in research. *Journal of Higher Education Policy and Management, 47*(1), 17–36. DOI: 10.1080/1360080X.2025.2509187

Sobaih, A. E. E., Elshaer, I. A., & Hasanein, A. M. (2024). Examining students' acceptance and use of ChatGPT in Saudi Arabian higher education. *European Journal of Investigation in Health, Psychology and Education, 14*(3), 709–721. DOI: 10.3390/ejihpe14030047

Sok, S., & Heng, K. (2024). Opportunities, challenges, and strategies for using ChatGPT in higher education: A literature review. *Journal of Digital Educational Technology, 4*(1), 1–11. DOI: 10.30935/jdet/14027

Sok, S., & Heng, K. (2024). Research on teacher education and implications for improving the quality of teacher education in Cambodia. *International Journal of Professional Development. Learners and Learning, 6*(1), 1–9. DOI: 10.30935/ijpdll/14042

Sot, V., Sok, S., & Dickinson, G. (2019). Four decades of teacher development: Teacher preparation and teacher upgrading programs in Cambodia from 1979 to 2018. *Cambodia Education Review, 3*(1), 115–139. https://shorturl.at/yEkEm

Sowa, S., Brown, C., Choi, T.-H., & Newman, R. (2025). Examining how generative AI tools benefit and challenge teachers' research-informed practice. *European Journal of Teacher Education*, *48*(5), 1036–1055. DOI: 10.1080/02619768.2025.2518193

Spathopoulou, F., Pitychoutis, K. M., & Papakonstantinidis, S. (2025). AI and higher education: Understanding faculty roles in teaching, research, and administration. *Contemporary Educational Technology*, *17*(4), ep600. DOI: 10.30935/cedtech/17406

Sperling, K., Stenberg, C.-J., McGrath, C., Åkerfeldt, A., Heintz, F., & Stenliden, L. (2024). In search of artificial intelligence (AI) literacy in teacher education: A scoping review. *Computers and Education Open*, *6*, 100169. DOI: 10.1016/j.caeo.2024.100169

Srivastava, A., Kumar, A. V. S., Maheshwari, D., & Ray, S. (2025). *Artificial Intelligence and Human Existence: Insights on Education, Technology, and Society* (1st ed.). CRC Press., DOI: 10.1201/9781003560463

Starkey, L. (2010). Supporting the digitally able beginning teacher. *Teaching and Teacher Education*, *26*(7), 1429–1438. DOI: 10.1016/j.tate.2010.05.002

Starkey, L. (2020). A review of research exploring teacher preparation for the digital age. *Cambridge Journal of Education*, *50*(1), 37–56. DOI: 10.1080/0305764X.2019.1625867

Strathern, M. (2000). The Tyranny of Transparency. *British Educational Research Journal*, *26*(3), 309–321. https://www.jstor.org/stable/1501878. DOI: 10.1080/713651562

Strieker, T., Adams, M., Cone, N., Hubbard, D., & Lim, W. (2016). Supervision matters: Collegial, developmental and reflective approaches to supervision of teacher candidates. *Cogent Education*, *3*(1), 1–24. DOI: 10.1080/2331186X.2016.1251075

Strzelecki, A., Cicha, K., Rizun, M., & Rutecka, P. (2024). Acceptance and use of ChatGPT in the academic community. *Education and Information Technologies*, *29*(17), 22943–22968. DOI: 10.1007/s10639-024-12765-1

Sullivan, M. (2025). Collusion, plagiarism, or contract cheating? How generative AI fits into existing academic integrity policies. In Popenici, S., Rudolph, J., Ismail, F., & Tan, S. (Eds.), *Handbook of Artificial Intelligence in Higher Education* (pp. 72–386). Edward Elgar Publishing., DOI: 10.4337/9781035338764.00033

Sun, C., Jiang, G., & Zhang, J. (2024). An analysis of hotspots, subject structure, and emerging trends in digital governance research. *SAGE Open*, *14*(3), 1–19. DOI: 10.1177/21582440241268756

Susnjak, T., & McIntosh, T. R. (2024). ChatGPT: The end of online exam integrity? *Education Sciences*, *14*(6), 656. DOI: 10.3390/educsci14060656

Syaidina, M. O., Fahrudin, R., & Mutiara, I. A. (2024). Implementation of ethics of using artificial intelligence in the education system in Indonesia. *Blockchain Frontier Technology*, *4*(1), 63–71. Advance online publication. DOI: 10.34306/bfront.v4i1.571

Talbi, M. (2018). Enseignement supérieur au Maroc: L'université à l'épreuve du développement économique de la société, Observatoire universitaire des politiques d'éducation et de formation. https://www.csmd.ma/documents/Observatoire%20 universitaire%20des%2 0politiques%20d'%C3%A9ducation%20et%20de%20formation%20- %20M.%20Talbi.pdf.

Tan, C., & Tee Ng, P. (2012). A critical reflection of teacher professionalism in Cambodia. *Asian Education and Development Studies*, *1*(2), 124–138. DOI: 10.1108/20463161211240106

Tanveer, M., Hassan, S., & Bhaumik, A. (2020). Academic policy regarding sustainability and artificial intelligence (AI). *Sustainability*, *12*(22), 1–13. DOI: 10.3390/su12229435 PMID: 35136666

Tan, X., Cheng, G., & Ling, M. H. (2025). Artificial intelligence in teaching and teacher professional development: A systematic review. *Computers and Education: Artificial Intelligence*, *8*, 100355. DOI: 10.1016/j.caeai.2024.100355

Tarhini, A., Hone, K., Liu, X., & Tarhini, T. (2017). Examining the moderating effect of individual-level cultural values on users' acceptance of E-learning in developing countries: A structural equation modeling of an extended technology acceptance model. *Interactive Learning Environments*, *25*(3), 306–328. Advance online publication. DOI: 10.1080/10494820.2015.1122635

Täuber, S. (2026). Erasing critical scholarship: How attacks on academic freedom undermine democracy. *Organization*, •••, 1–19. DOI: 10.1177/13505084251392946

Tavares, J., & Pereira, F. V. (2024). Proof of concept: A practical approach to machine learning in video consultations' acceptance in higher education institutions. *Procedia Computer Science*, *239*, 1532–1538. DOI: 10.1016/j.procs.2024.06.328

Tella, A., Jatto, E. O., & Ajani, Y. A. (2025). Preserving indigenous knowledge: Leveraging digital technology and artificial intelligence. *IFLA Journal*, *51*(3), 703–721. DOI: 10.1177/03400352251342505

Teng, Y. (2024). *Cambodia needs to boost digital education*. Cambodianess. https://cambodianess.com/article/cambodia-needs-to-boost-digital-education

Tep, V. (2024a). Improving professional development: A case study on the influence of faculty evaluations in Cambodia. *SAGE Open*, *14*(2), 1–13. DOI: 10.1177/21582440241241166

Tep, V. (2024b). Teacher educators as curriculum developers: A case study of teacher education colleges in Cambodia [Original Research]. *Frontiers in Education*, *9*, 1–14. DOI: 10.3389/feduc.2024.1328023

Teymourifar, A. (2026). Understanding the ABS journal ranking system: A critical review. *Frontiers in Education*, *11*, 1–20. DOI: 10.3389/feduc.2026.1773655

Thong, C. L., Atallah, Z., Islam, S., Lim, W., & Cherukuri, A. K. (2025). AI-powered Tools for Doctoral Supervision in Higher Education: A Systematic Review. *Journal of Information & Knowledge Management*, *24*(02), 2530001. DOI: 10.1142/S0219649225300013

Toker, S., Akay, C., Basmaci, F., Kilicarslan, M. A., Mumcu, E., & Cagiltay, N. E. (2024). Expectancy from, and acceptance of augmented reality in dental education programs: A structural equation model. *Journal of Dental Education*, *88*(9), 1277–1286. Advance online publication. DOI: 10.1002/jdd.13580

Tondeur, J., Van Braak, J., Ertmer, P., & Ottenbreit-Leftwich, A. (2017). Understanding the relationship between teachers' pedagogical beliefs and technology use in education: A systematic review of qualitative evidence. *Educational Technology Research and Development*, *65*(3), 555–575. DOI: 10.1007/s11423-016-9481-2

Tongkachok, K., Garg, S., Vemuri, V. P., Chaudhary, V., Koli, P. V., & Kumar, K. S. (2022). The role of artificial intelligence on organizational support programmes to enhance work outcome and employees behaviour. *Materials Today: Proceedings*, *56*, 2383–2387. DOI: 10.1016/j.matpr.2021.12.205

Tonna, M. A., Bjerkholt, E., & Holland, E. (2017). Teacher mentoring and the reflective practitioner approach. *International Journal of Mentoring and Coaching in Education*, *6*(3), 210–227. DOI: 10.1108/IJMCE-04-2017-0032

Tripathi, A., & Thakar, S. V. (2024). Ethical use of AI for academic integrity: Preventing plagiarism and cheating. In Kushwaha, R. K., Yadav, K., Yadav, P. K., & Yadav, M. K. (Eds.), *Ethical Frameworks in Special Education: A Guide for Researchers* (pp. 91–106). Blue Rose Publishers.

Turgut, S., & Tasçi, G. (2024). Learning to Hear Students' Voices: Teachers' Experiences on Student Mentoring. *International Education Studies*, *17*(2), 1–14. https://files.eric.ed.gov/fulltext/EJ1421333.pdf. DOI: 10.5539/ies.v17n2p1

Tweed, A. D., & Warrington, S. (2024). Autonomous learning in Cambodia: A solution for problematic educational conditions? *Cambodian Journal of Educational Research, 4*(2), 64–78. https://cjerjournal.com/index.php/cjer/article/view/62. DOI: 10.62037/cjer.2024.04.02.04

Udah, H. (2024). Decolonising research for justice: Ethical imperatives and practical applications. *International Journal of Qualitative Methods, 23*, 16094069241294040. Advance online publication. DOI: 10.1177/16094069241294040

Umer, R., Susnjak, T., Mathrani, A., & Suriadi, L. (2023). Current stance on predictive analytics in higher education: Opportunities, challenges and future directions. *Interactive Learning Environments, 31*(6), 3503–3528. DOI: 10.1080/10494820.2021.1933542

UNDP. (2025). *Human development report 2025: AI and global inequality*. United Nations Development Programme. https://hdr.undp.org

UNESCO. (2021). *Recommendation on the ethics of artificial intelligence*. United Nations Educational, Scientific and Cultural Organization. https://unesdoc.unesco.org/ark:/48223/pf0000381137

UNESCO. (2023). *Guidance for generative AI in education and research*. UNESCO Publishing.

UNESCO. (2023). *Guidance for generative AI in education and research*. UNESCO Publishing. https://unesdoc.unesco.org/

UNESCO. (2023). *Guidance for generative artificial intelligence (GenAI) in education and research: A human-centered approach*. United Nations Educational Scientific and Cultural Organization. https://policycommons.net/artifacts/6942367/guidance-for-generative-ai-in-education-and-research/7852269

UNESCO. (2023). *UNESCO trains Indonesian teachers on AI ethics*. https://www.unesco.org/en/articles/unesco-trains-indonesian-teachers-ai-ethics

UNESCO. (2024). *AI competency framework for teachers*. UNESCO Digital Library., DOI: 10.54675/ZJTE2084

UNESCO. (2024). *Indonesia: artificial intelligence readiness assessment report*. UNESCO. https://unesdoc.unesco.org/ark:/48223/pf0000392317?posInSet=1&queryId=7060cf11-7d11-4ca1-bc7d-fdfb04af70f8

UNESCO. (2024). *Leading AI ethics: UNESCO and KOMINFO launch AI readiness assessment methodology in Indonesia.* UNESCO. https://www.unesco.org/en/articles/leading-ai-ethics-unesco-and-kominfo-launch-ai-readiness-assessment-methodology-indonesia

UNESCO. (2024). *Strengthening teacher education programmes in Cambodia.* https://www.unesco.org/en/articles/strengthening-teacher-education-programmes-cambodia

UNESCO. (2025). *Cambodia: Artificial Intelligence readiness assessment report.* Paris: United Nations Educational Scientific and Cultural Organization. https://www.unesco.org/en/articles/cambodia-artificial-intelligence-readiness-assessment-report

UNESCO. (2025). *MoEYS and UNESCO launch the strategic plan for teacher education reform 2024–2030 at the national education congress 2025*. UNESCO. https://tinyurl.com/5an3tshc

UNU-EGOV. (2026). *UNU-EGOV Strategy 2025–2029: Developing digital governance for global justice, resilience, and sustainability*. United Nations University Operating Unit on Policy-driven Electronic Governance. https://unu.edu/egov/about/unu-egov-strategy-2025-2029

US Department of Education (USDE). (2023). Artificial intelligence and the future of teaching and learning. [Online]. https://www.ed.gov/sites/ed/files/documents/ai-report/ai-report.pdf

Usha, G. (2002). Infancy: The Origins of Cognitive Development. In *Blackwell Handbook of Childhood Cognitive Development* (pp. 1–5). DOI: 10.1002/9780470996652.part1

Verboom, A. D. P. R., Pais, L., Zijlstra, F. R., Oswald, F. L., & Santos, N. R. D. (2025). Perceptions of artificial intelligence in academic teaching and research: A qualitative study from AI experts and professors' perspectives. *International Journal of Educational Technology in Higher Education*, *22*(1), 46. DOI: 10.1186/s41239-025-00546-w

Verganti, R., Vendraminelli, L., & Iansiti, M. (2020). Innovation and design in the age of artificial intelligence. *Journal of Product Innovation Management*, *37*(3), 212–227. DOI: 10.1111/jpim.12523

Vijaya Kumari, S. (2014). Constructivist approach to teacher education: An integrative model for reflective teaching. *Journal of Educational Psychology*, *7*(4), 31–40. https://files.eric.ed.gov/fulltext/EJ1098640.pdf

Vrabie, C. (2025). Improving Municipal Responsiveness Through Ai-Powered Image Analysis In E-Government. *Public Policy and Administration, 24*(1), 9–23. Advance online publication. DOI: 10.5755/j01.ppaa.24.1.39756

Vreekamp, M., Gulikers, J. T., Runhaar, P. R., & Den Brok, P. J. (2024). A systematic review to explore how characteristics of pedagogical development programmes in higher education are related to teacher development outcomes. *The International Journal for Academic Development, 29*(4), 446–462. DOI: 10.1080/1360144X.2023.2233471

Wadipalapa, R. P., Katharina, R., Nainggolan, P. P., Aminah, S., Apriani, T., Ma'rifah, D., & Anisah, A. L. (2024). An ambitious artificial intelligence policy in a decentralised governance system: Evidence from Indonesia. *Journal of Current Southeast Asian Affairs, 32*(1), 67–89. DOI: 10.1177/18681034231226393

Wang, B., Rau, P. L. P., & Yuan, T. (2022). Measuring user competence in using artificial intelligence: Validity and reliability of artificial intelligence literacy scale. *Behaviour & Information Technology, 42*(9), 1324–1337. DOI: 10.1080/0144929X.2022.2072768

Wang, D., & Zhou, X. (2025). The Impact of AI Awareness on Employees' Job Burnout: A Chain Mediation of Perceived Organizational Support and Organizational Commitment. *SAGE Open, 15*(4), 21582440251400532. DOI: 10.1177/21582440251400532

Wang, G., Zhang, Q., Wang, L., & Liu, Y. (2025). The impact of teachers' autonomy support on students' academic performance from the perspective of hyperscanning: The mediating role of autonomy need satisfaction. *Social Cognitive and Affective Neuroscience, 20*(1), nsaf115. Advance online publication. DOI: 10.1093/scan/nsaf115

Wang, K., Ruan, Q., Zhang, X., Fu, C., & Duan, B. (2024). Preservice teachers' GenAI anxiety, technology self-efficacy, and TPACK: Their structural relations with behavioral intention to design GenAI-assisted teaching. *Behavioral Sciences (Basel, Switzerland), 14*(5), 373. DOI: 10.3390/bs14050373

Wang, Z., & Wang, C. (2025). A posthumanist approach to AI literacy. *Computers and Composition, 76*, 102933. Advance online publication. DOI: 10.1016/j.compcom.2025.102933

Willegems, V., Consuegra, E., Struyven, K., & Engels, N. (2017). Teachers and pre-service teachers as partners in collaborative teacher research: A systematic literature review. *Teaching and Teacher Education, 64*, 230–245. DOI: 10.1016/j.tate.2017.02.014

Williamson, B. (2017). *Big data in education: The digital future of learning, policy and practice*. Sage Publications. DOI: 10.4135/9781529714920

Williamson, B., & Eynon, R. (2020). Historical threads, missing links, and future directions in AI in education. *Learning, Media and Technology*, *45*(3), 223–235. DOI: 10.1080/17439884.2020.1798995

Willinsky, J. (2006). *The access principle: The case for open access to research and scholarship*. MIT Press.

Wilsdon, J. (2015). *The metric tide*. SAGE Publications Ltd., DOI: 10.4135/9781473978782

Wilson, E. K. (2006). The impact of an alternative model of student teacher supervision: Views of the participants. *Teaching and Teacher Education*, *22*(1), 22–31. DOI: 10.1016/j.tate.2005.07.007

Wiyono, B. B., Rasyad, A., & Maisyaroh, . (2021). The effect of collaborative supervision approaches and collegial supervision techniques on teacher intensity using performance-based learning. *SAGE Open*, *11*(2), 1–9. DOI: 10.1177/21582440211013779

Woelert, P., Croucher, G., & Hoang, S. (2025). The rise of a "casualised" workforce: A conceptual account of the institutional forces legitimizing contingent academic employment in Australia. *Higher Education*. Advance online publication. DOI: 10.1007/s10734-025-01405-3

Wolle, G. S., & Tuffa, B. M. (2025). The mediating effect of organizational commitment on the relationship between teachers' job satisfaction and turnover intention. *Bahir Dar Journal of Education*, *25*(3), 112–128. DOI: 10.4314/bdje.v25i3.8

Wong-A-Foe, D. (2023). Navigating the implications of AI in Indonesian education: Tutors, governance, and ethical perspectives. In Anutariya, C., & Bonsangue, M. M. (Eds.), *Data Science and Artificial Intelligence: DSAI 2023. Communications in Computer and Information Science* (Vol. 1942, pp. 333–346). Springer., DOI: 10.1007/978-981-99-7969-1_26

Wongvorachan, T., Lai, K. W., Bulut, O., Tsai, Y.-S., & Chen, G. (2022). Artificial intelligence: Transforming the future of feedback in education. *Journal of Applied Testing Technology*, 95-116. http://jattjournal.net/index.php/atp/article/view/170387

World Bank. (2024). *New World Bank supported project will improve the quality of thousands of students in Cambodia*. World Bank Group. https://www.worldbank.org/en/news/press-release/2024/09/24/new-world-bank-supported-project-will-improve-the-quality-of-thousands-of-students-in-cambodia

Wu, C., Zhang, H., & Carroll, J. M. (2024). AI governance in higher education: Case studies of guidance at Big Ten universities. *Future Internet, 16*(10), 354. DOI: 10.3390/fi16100354

Wu, D., Zhang, S., Ma, Z., Yue, X. G., & Dong, R. K. (2024). Unlocking potential: Key factors shaping undergraduate self-directed learning in AI-enhanced educational environments. *Systems, 12*(9), 332. DOI: 10.3390/systems12090332

Wu, Q., Li, S., Xin, S., Hou, Q., & Li, P. (2025). A study on students' behavioral intention and use behavior of artificial intelligence-generated content in physical education: Employing an extended the unified theory of acceptance and use of technology model. *Journal of Hospitality, Leisure, Sport and Tourism Education, 36*, 100547. Advance online publication. DOI: 10.1016/j.jhlste.2025.100547

Xia, Q., Chiu, T. K. F., Lee, M., Sanusi, I. T., Dai, Y., & Chai, C. S. (2022). A self-determination theory (SDT) design approach for inclusive and diverse artificial intelligence (AI) education. *Computers & Education, 189*, 104582. DOI: 10.1016/j.compedu.2022.104582

Xinbei, Y. A. O., & KONGRUANG, C. (2025). Predicting lecturer turnover intention in Chinese private universities: The roles of job satisfaction and organizational commitment. *Procedia of Multidisciplinary Research, 3*(1), 6–6.

Y. (2025). Conceptualizing preservice teachers' artificial intelligence readiness and examining its relationship with various variables: The role of artificial intelligence literacy, digital citizenship, artificial intelligence-enhanced innovation and perceived threats from artificial intelligence. *Information Development, 41*(3), 916-932. DOI: 10.1177/02666669251335657

Yadav, B., & Anubha, . (2024). A Bibliometric Review of Role of Artificial Intelligence In Education. *ShodhKosh: Journal of Visual and Performing Arts, 5*(6). Advance online publication. DOI: 10.29121/shodhkosh.v5.i6.2024.3206

Yang, B., Bao, S., & Xu, J. (2022). Supervisory styles and graduate student innovation performance: The mediating role of psychological capital and the moderating role of harmonious academic passion. *Frontiers in Psychology, 13*, 1034216. DOI: 10.3389/fpsyg.2022.1034216

Yang, W. (2022). Artificial Intelligence education for young children: Why, what, and how in curriculum design and implementation. *Computers and Education: Artificial Intelligence, 3*, 100061. DOI: 10.1016/j.caeai.2022.100061

Yang, Y.-F., Tseng, C. C., & Lai, S.-C. (2024). Enhancing teachers' self-efficacy beliefs in integrating AI-based technology into English-language teaching through a professional development program. *Teaching and Teacher Education, 144*, 104582. Advance online publication. DOI: 10.1016/j.tate.2024.104582

Yilmaz, M., Gauthier, A., & Cukurova, M. (2026). Supporting online learners' regulation skills with the help of learning analytics and generative artificial intelligence: M. Yilmaz et al. *Educational Technology Research and Development*, 1-30. https://doi.org/DOI: 10.1007/s11423-026-10595-1

Yoeurng, S. (2024). Implementing a school-based mentoring program at a secondary resource school in Takeo province, Cambodia. [CJESS]. *Cambodian Journal of Educational and Social Sciences, 1*(1), 67–88. DOI: 10.69496/cjess.v1i1.10

Yuan, E. R. (2016). The dark side of mentoring on pre-service language teachers' identity formation. *Teaching and Teacher Education, 55*, 188–197. DOI: 10.1016/j.tate.2016.01.012

Yuan, X., Ironsi, C. S., & Liu, F. (2025). The role of group mentorship in supporting teachers across different developmental stages: A comparative study. *Studies in Educational Evaluation, 86*, 101477. DOI: 10.1016/j.stueduc.2025.101477

Yue, C. A., Men, L. R., Mitson, R., Davis, D. Z., & Zhou, A. (2024). Artificial intelligence for internal communication: Strategies, challenges, and implications. *Public Relations Review, 50*(5), 102515. DOI: 10.1016/j.pubrev.2024.102515

Yu, L., & Li, Y. (2022). Artificial intelligence decision-making transparency and employees' trust: The parallel multiple mediating effect of effectiveness and discomfort. *Behavioral Sciences (Basel, Switzerland), 12*(5), 127. DOI: 10.3390/bs12050127 PMID: 35621424

Yurdunkulu, A., Bulut, M. A., & Göçen, A. (2025). From academics to Aidemics: Unpacking the human–AI symbiosis in higher education. *Acta Psychologica, 261*, 105796. Advance online publication. DOI: 10.1016/j.actpsy.2025.105796

Zagkotas, V. (2025). Artificial Intelligence and the Didactic Transposition of Knowledge: Implications for Curriculum Development and Knowledge Gatekeeping. *Futurity Education, 5*(2), 44–66. DOI: 10.57125/FED.2025.06.25.03

Zawacki-Richter, O., Marín, V. I., Bond, M., & Gouverneur, F. (2019). Systematic review of research on artificial intelligence applications in higher education – where are the educators? In *International Journal of Educational Technology in Higher Education* (Vol. 16, Issue 1). DOI: 10.1186/s41239-019-0171-0

Zembylas, M. (2023). A decolonial approach to AI in higher education teaching and learning: Strategies for undoing the ethics of digital neocolonialism. *Learning, Media and Technology*, *48*(1), 25–37. DOI: 10.1080/17439884.2021.2010094

Zeng, D., Swatdikun, T., Aujirapongpan, S., & Huang, S. Z. (2025). The influence of quality of work life and perceived organizational support on turnover intention in private higher education institutions. *Emerging Science Journal*, *8*, 335–357. DOI: 10.28991/ESJ-2024-SIED1-020

Zhai, X., Chu, X., Chai, C. S., Jong, M. S. Y., Istenic, A., Spector, M., Liu, J.-B., Yuan, J., & Li, Y. (2021). A Review of Artificial Intelligence (AI) in Education from 2010 to 2020. *Complexity*, *2021*(1), 8812542. DOI: 10.1155/2021/8812542

Zhang, W., Guo, X., & Xie, J. (2026). Leveraging artificial intelligence and Big Data Analytics to model career progression and professional development pathways of higher education faculty. *Australian Journal of Electrical and Electronics Engineering*, 1–20. DOI: 10.1080/1448837X.2026.2614868

Zhang, J., Zhang, M., & Liu, X. (2023). Acceptance of artificial intelligence among preservice teachers: A multigroup analysis. *International Journal of Educational Technology in Higher Education*, *20*(1), 49. DOI: 10.1186/s41239-023-00420-7

Zhang, S. (2025). Exploring challenges and opportunities in the AI-driven professional development of higher education faculty. *Lecture Notes in Education Psychology and Public Media*, *113*(1), 22–29. DOI: 10.54254/2753-7048/2025.NS25886

Zheng, L., & Xiao, Y. (2026). Supervised or autonomous? Exploring the effect of instructional strategies on elementary school students' mathematics and science achievement. *Teaching and Teacher Education*, *170*, 105315. DOI: 10.1016/j.tate.2025.105315

Zhu, Y., Zhu, Z., Xu, W., & Zhu, Y. (2025). Cross-border higher education cooperation under the dual context of artificial intelligence and geopolitics: Opportunities, challenges, and pathways. *Frontiers in Education*, *10*, 1656518. Advance online publication. DOI: 10.3389/feduc.2025.1656518

Zootzky, G., & Pfeiffer, A. (2024). Educational Transformation Through Ai: Preparing For A New Era Of Learning. 1202–1207. DOI: 10.21125/inted.2024.0382

Zulifiqar, H., Fatima, L., Akhtar, M. S., & Akhtar, M. N. (2025). Artificial Intelligence in HR: Reducing Turnover Intentions with AI-Driven Employee Engagement Solutions. *International Research Journal of Social Sciences and Humanities*, *4*(1), 85–111.

About the Contributors

Rany Sam has been a dedicated civil servant with the Cambodian Ministry of Education, Youth, and Sport since 2007. Since 2017, he has served as the Vice-Rector of the National University of Battambang (NUBB), a prominent public university in northwest Cambodia. In this capacity, he oversees the Graduate School, Faculty of Arts, Humanities, and Education, the Institute of Foreign Languages, and the Confucius Institute. Previously, he served as Director of the Institute of Foreign Languages from 2010 to 2017. He has served as the Director of the Confucius Institute at NUBB in Cambodia since 2019. Dr. Sam is an active member of several academic organizations, including the Southeast Asia Research Academy (SEARA), the Society of Transnational Academic Researchers (STAR) as a country director, and Responsible Borneo (REBORN). He earned his PhD in Education from the School of Educational Studies at the University of Science Malaysia in 2016. Additionally, he completed diplomas in public administration, leadership, and innovation programs at the Royal School of Administration in Cambodia in 2017 and 2022. He holds a Bachelor's and Master's degree in Law (LL.B. and LL.M.) from the Royal University of Law and Economics, completed in 2004 and 2007, respectively. Dr. Sam has authored approximately 100 academic papers and book chapters. He serves as project coordinator for multiple initiatives, including Erasmus+ Capacity Building in Higher Education, Korean ODA, USAID, and the World Bank-funded Higher Education Improvement Project (HEIP). His editorial roles include associate editor of Frontiers in Education (Higher Education) and Frontiers in Political Science, as well as editor for IGI Global book chapters. He has peer-reviewed over 100 manuscripts and book chapters published by leading academic publishers, including Springer Nature, Sage, Taylor & Francis, and Routledge. His research interests encompass legal studies, public policy and administration, educational history and cooperation, educational leadership and management, and various social research areas.

***

Saif Allah Allouani is an Accredited Professor of Intercultural Management and Organizational Behavior at the Business School in Sidi Mohammed Ben Abdellah University of Fez, Morocco. His teaching and research focus on Human flourishing, particularly emphasizing Well-being, Practical Wisdom, and Character Education. A seasoned counselor and trainer, he leverages his experience to craft specific coaching and training programs with a broad societal outreach. His latest book, "You Shall not Languish, an anti-guide for Wisdom and Well-being," features some of his key ideas about the ailment of our educational system and some directions for corrective actions. He works with the Wisdom and Culture Lab of the University of Waterloo to develop a culturally grounded understanding and measurement of constructs related to wisdom, character, and culture.

Rina Antasari is a Professor in the field of Civil Law and Constitutional Law at the Faculty of Sharia and Law, Raden Fatah State Islamic University (UIN) Palembang.

Ritu Arora is a dedicated research scholar specializing in internal marketing and employee turnover intentions. Her research focuses on understanding how organizational practices shape employee behavior, satisfaction, and retention. She has presented and published her research papers in international conferences, reflecting the quality and relevance of her academic contributions.

Rafiya Banu Syed, Position: Assistant Professor and Research Supervisor, Institution: B.S. Abdur Rahman Crescent Institute, Chennai; Expertise: Dr. Rafiya Banu Syed is a distinguished academic with profound expertise in Human Capital Management (HCM). Her substantial knowledge and experience also encompass auditing, banking, e-commerce, and digital marketing. Research Focus: Dr. Syed's research primarily investigates the impact of HCM practices on employee performance, productivity, and satisfaction across various sectors, including banking and education. Her work contributes significantly to creating engaging learning environments and advancing the academic community. Academic Contributions: Dr. Syed has a robust portfolio of publications in Scopus-indexed journals and has presented her research at numerous international conferences. Her scholarly activities have cemented her reputation as a prominent figure in HCM. Professional Development: Dr. Syed holds a Ph.D. and has actively participated in workshops on research methodology and academic publishing. Her dedication to professional growth aligns with themes of employee development, organizational effectiveness, and HRM best practices.

Borey Be is an independent researcher and lecturer at various universities in Cambodia. He holds a master's degree in educational leadership and policy from Beijing Normal University. His research centers on teaching and teacher education, special and inclusive education, online teaching and learning, educational technology, and parental involvement.

Arakhita Behera Assistant Professor in Economics, Department of Social Science and Humanities Regional Institute of Education (NCERT), Ajmer, Rajasthan -305004 (India).

Da Bou is a PhD student at the National University of Battambang in Cambodia. He was appointed as vice dean of the Faculty of Social Science Education at Battambang Teacher Education College.

Mehdi Chaoui Roqai is a Doctor from the Sidi Mohamed Ben Abdellah University (National School of Business and Management of Fez, Morocco), a training manager in entrepreneurship, a certified coach in IBA (Authentic Well-being Engineering) and PracWise (practical wisdom). Passionate about character education, virtues and values.

Susanta Das is a seasoned educator with a proven record of teaching and mentoring diverse students, working at multiple institutions, and providing service to the various initiatives of organizations. He received his Ph.D. and M.A. degrees from Western Michigan University (WMU), USA, and M.Sc. degree from Banaras Hindu University (BHU), India all in Physics. He continued his research as a Marie-Curie post-doctoral fellow at Stockholm University, Stockholm, Sweden on beam diagnostics for the DESIREE (Double ElectroStatic Ion Ring ExpEriment) in the project DITANET (Diagnostic Techniques for particle Accelerators – a Marie-Curie initial training NETwork), at the Indian Institute of Science Education and Research-Kolkata, India on high-pressure physics as a Project Scientist-B, and at the University of Electro-Communications, Tokyo, Japan on ion-surface interactions as a Post-doctoral fellow. Throughout his career, Dr. Das worked and collaborated with many researchers, Ph.D., master, and visiting students from different countries. He further visited many countries to discuss research and an international conference participant (UK, Italy, Germany, Greece, Belgium, Bulgaria, Romania, Brazil etc.). He worked at several institutions before assuming his current role at Ajeenkya D Y Patil University. He received the Marie-Curie post-doctoral fellowship in Sweden, Science Academies' Summer Research Fellowship in India, Gowen Frostic Doctoral Fellowship, Department Graduate Research and Creative Scholar Award by WMU, and Leo R. Parpart Doctoral Fellowship by Dept. of Physics, WMU, among many others, throughout his academic journey. He co-authored several research articles in

WoS/Scopus indexed international journals, conference proceedings, and scholarly book chapters and co-edited several books published by renowned international publishing houses (IGI-Global, Springer Nature, Nova Science Publishers, Wiley, Scrivener-Wiley, Notion Press). At present, Dr. Das continues to delve into cutting-edge fields, with a keen interest in nanotechnology, UN SDGs, and data science. His multifaceted contributions, spanning teaching, research, and administrative leadership, showcase a dedicated professional who is instrumental in advancing the vision and mission of the institutions he serves.

D. Kesavan presently working as Assistant Professor at SRMIST: Faculty of Management, Chennai. He has 8 Years of Industrial experience in Banking and IT sector and 5 years of teaching experience. He has published nearly 47 articles in various reputed UGC, Peer reviewed and Scopus journals. Has published 2 International Book Chapters and 2 National level book chapters and authored 2 Books. He has won Young Researcher award and Excellence in Research award from reputed academic agencies. He is also an approved faculty at University of Madras. He has been editor for International Book on Crypto Currency in association with IGI global, USA. He is the Chief Editor of International Journal of Advanced Research in Commerce, Management and Finance: He is also reviewer for International Journal of Management and AKINIK journal. His areas of interest are Renewable Energy, International Business, Banking and Financial Management. He has also got a funded project with Ministry of Education, India in the field of Sustainable Financial Management for Entrepreneurs

Ennida Kenza, PhD student at the Sidi Mohamed Ben Abdellah University (National School of Business and Management of Fez, Morocco) and human resources professional in the public sector. Member of the Moroccan Interuniversity Research Initiative for Character Education (MIRICE) and the American Psychological Association. Passionate about and certified in the fields of work psychology and organizational behavior.

Dian Erlina is a Professor of English Education in the Department of English Education, Faculty of Tarbiyah and Teaching Sciences (Fakultas Ilmu Tarbiyah dan Keguruan), Universitas Islam Negeri (UIN) Raden Fatah Palembang, South Sumatra, Indonesia. She earned her Doctor of Philosophy in Language Education from Universitas Negeri Jakarta (2015), her Master of Humanities in Linguistics from Universitas Gadjah Mada (2003), and her Bachelor of Education in English Education from Universitas Sriwijaya (1996). Her research interests span language education, applied linguistics, English teacher professional development, and instructional materials development, with an extensive publication record in international peer-reviewed journals. Beyond her scholarly contributions, she has served as Dean of the Faculty of Science and Technology, led international educational development projects, and serves on the editorial boards of multiple academic journals. She also contributes as a national assessor for academic promotions in Indonesia.

Fridiyanto is an academic figure at Sultan Thaha Saifuddin State Islamic University (UIN STS) Jambi. He was born in Muara Bungo, Jambi, and currently holds a strategic position as Head of the Institute for Research and Community Service (LPPM) of UIN Jambi. He is particularly interested in EDUCATION. His research and teaching focus on higher education including educational management and planning, educational change, educational administration.

Kasinyo Harto is a Professor of Islamic Religious Education at Raden Fatah State Islamic University (UIN) Palembang. He is known as an academic and prominent figure on campus, with a research focus on multicultural-based Islamic learning and education methodologies.

Chan Hum is a Director of the Graduate School at the National University of Battambang, located in Battambang, Cambodia. He holds a PhD degree in Educational Management from the Education University of Hong Kong, China.

Sovanna Huot is a PhD candidate in political science at the University of Delhi, New Delhi, India. He oversees academic and administrative operations as vice principal at a Cambodian Government Public High School. His master's degrees are a highly competitive TEFL scholarship program and a Master of Education in High School Principalship from the National Institute of Education (NIE) in Phnom Penh, Cambodia, in 2021. He investigates educational reform, the practice-policy nexus of digital pedagogy, and global (global-national-local) educational systems. He educates and publishes in political science and education, including Scopus-indexed works (Author ID: 59316244400).

Nayheak Khun is a lecturer at various universities and a government official at the Ministry of Labor and Vocational Training (MLVT), Cambodia. She is currently a PhD candidate in Law at Southwest University of Political Science and Law, China. Her research interests focus on labour law, labour market governance, vocational education and training (TVET), and employment policy.

Pardeep Kumar Assistant Professor, Department of Mathematics, Lovely Professional University, Phagwara, Punjab, India Dr. Pardeep Kumar holds a Ph.D. in Mathematics from Lovely Professional University (2021). His research expertise lies in Stochastic Processes, with a specialized focus on Markov Models,

Engineering System Reliability, and Reliability Theory. He actively contributes to the modeling and reliability analysis of IoT-enabled and sensor-integrated systems for next-generation engineering applications. Dr. Kumar has a profound command of Stochastic Modelling, Reliability Testing, and advanced analytical methods for complex system behavior under uncertainty. His work emphasises practical implementations in smart technologies and cyber-physical systems. He has an exceptional academic track record, having qualified the prestigious CSIR-UGC NET twice, securing All India Ranks (AIR) of 15 and 32, respectively. To date, Dr. Kumar has published 26 high-quality research papers in reputed national and international journals, reflecting his continued contribution to the advancement of mathematical reliability and its engineering applications.

Sanjeev Kumar Is a Professor in Lovely Professional University Punjab India. He received Undergraduate in Hotel Management from Osmania University, Postgraduate in Tourism Management from Madurai Kamaraj University. He completed Doctor of Philosophy in Hospitality Management in 2019 from Amity University Jaipur India. His research areas lies in food Service Industry, his research focuses on Alcoholic beverages, Event management and Sustainable Management Practices, Metaverse, AI Machine Learning and Artificial Intelligence. He published more than 80 research papers, articles and chapters in Scopus Indexed, UGC Approved and peer reviewed Journals and books. Dr. Sanjeev Kumar participated and acted as resource person in various National and International conferences, seminars, session chair, research workshops and industry talks and his work has been widely cited. Dr. Sanjeev also edited more than 20 books with various International Publishers such as IGI Global, Cambridge Scholars, Emerald, CABI, Bentham Science, Taylor & Francis. Dr Sanjeev is an active researcher and has published numerous research articles in prestigious National and International journals and books.

Kritikka Kunte is a third-year undergraduate student pursuing a Bachelor of Technology in Artificial Intelligence and Data Science at the School of Engineering, Ajeenkya DY Patil University, Pune, Maharashtra, India. With a strong academic orientation toward data-driven problem solving, she has developed a focused interest in the domains of data analytics and data science, supported by both theoretical foundations and applied project experience. Throughout her academic journey, Kritikka has cultivated proficiency in core programming and analytical competencies, including Python, SQL, and Java, along with essential data science methodologies such as data preprocessing, exploratory data analysis (EDA), and machine learning techniques. She is proficient in industry-relevant tools and platforms, including Advanced Microsoft Excel, Matplotlib, Tableau, and Power BI, to derive insights from complex datasets and present them in a structured and interpretable manner. Her practical exposure includes the successful completion of projects such as Ocean Salinity Analysis, which involved analyzing environmental datasets to identify patterns and trends, and Speech Recognition and Translation, where she explored applied machine learning concepts in natural language processing. These projects reflect her ability to translate conceptual knowledge into functional, real-world solutions. Kritikka has further strengthened her technical profile through professional certifications, including the AWS re/Start Graduate credential from Amazon Web Services, a certification in Software Development, and Python training certified by Google. Her engagement in competitive and collaborative academic environments is demonstrated by her participation in the Smart India Hackathon (SIH) and by securing Second Runner-Up in an inter-collegiate Tableau competition, highlighting her analytical aptitude and visualization skills. With a growing interest in advanced transportation systems and data-centric engineering solutions, Kritikka brings a multidisciplinary perspective to the GHC Hyperloop Project Competition hosted at IIT Madras. She aspires to contribute meaningfully to innovative, technology-driven initiatives that integrate artificial intelligence, data science, and sustainable engineering to address complex global challenges.

Lenny Marzulina works as a lecturer researcher and head of English education study program in the State Islamic University of Raden Fatah, Palembang, Indonesia. She obtained her undergraduate and graduate degrees in English Education from Sriwijaya University, Indonesia. Her research interests are on the area of education, language teaching, material development, and TEFL.

Ella Masita is an academic and lecturer in the English Language Education Study Program, Faculty of Teacher Training and Education (FKIP), Unversitas Jambi. Her main research focus and expertise include Language Teaching Pedagogy & TESOL (Teaching English for Speakers of Other Languages), Applied Linguistics and Literacy Teaching, and Curriculum & Syllabus Development (including the implementation of the Independent Curriculum).

Amirul Mukminin is a professor of educational policy in the Graduate School/Faculty of Education, Universitas Jambi, Indonesia and Head of Research and Community Services Center, Universitas Jambi, Indonesia. He holds a PhD from Florida State University in Educational Leadership and Policy Studies with a specialization in sociocultural and international development education studies, an MS in educational sciences from Groningen University, the Netherlands, and BA in English Education from Universitas Jambi. He received a Fulbright scholarship to pursue his PhD and was an Erasmus Mundus postdoctoral researcher at the

University of Groningen, the Netherlands. He also received a 2016–2017 Fulbright Senior Research at Claremont Graduate University, California. He is particularly interested in EDUCATION. His research and teaching focus on Pre-K to higher education in Indonesia and other countries: bilingual/multilingual education policy, Religious Education, international and national educational policy, language and educational technology, curriculum policy, teacher policy reforms, English/ Indonesian language policy reforms which will influence educational outcomes for underachieving student populations and family.

Edi Surya Negara Harahap is a Professor and the youngest Professor in Indonesia in the field of Informatics Engineering. He is an accomplished academic from Bina Darma University who currently serves as Vice Rector for Research, Technology, and Innovation. Research Focus and Expertise: Data Science, Artificial Intelligence, and Informatics.

Krutika Patre, is an aspiring programmer and technology enthusiast, currently pursuing Engineering in Artificial Intelligence and Data Science. With a passion for learning, she is building experience in a variety of programming languages and technologies, including C, C++, Python, Data Structures (DS), HTML, CSS, and JavaScript, DBMS (My SQL). After learning this programming language, she has created interest in Full Stack Development. She had also attended an Arduino-Based Automation course at Dolphin Labs to improve my software knowledge. There, she learned how to work with sensors, microcontrollers, and circuit design. She has written review paper on Sustainable engineering on build environment. She is doing researching and learning many topics related to AI, Policy and governance and related to my interest. She has taken part in hackathons, workshops, and tech events to explore many fields. She is also working with a group on Hyperloop. Being part of this project has really helped her grow, especially in areas like teamwork, innovation, and systems thinking.

Rajesh Prasad is currently working as Professor in the Department of Computer Science and Engineering at Ajay Kumar Garg Engineering College, Ghaziabad, India. He received the M.Tech. degree in Software Engineering and the PhD degree in Computer Science and Engineering from the Motilal Nehru National Institute of Technology, Allahabad, India. He has more than 23 years of teaching experience in various universities and higher Institutions. He has published more than 70 research papers in various journals and conferences. He is a reviewer of various reputed journals. His research interests include data mining, artificial intelligence, data compression, algorithms, and bioinformatics

Rahul Ranjan is an Assistant Professor in Economics at Regional Institute of Education Mysuru, a constituent unit of National Council of Educational Research and Training. His academic interests include digital financial inclusion, labour economics, financial literacy, and development economics. He is actively engaged in research on mobile banking adoption, digital finance, employment quality, and structural equation modelling using large-scale datasets such as the Global Findex and PLFS. He has contributed to interdisciplinary discussions on digital transformation, financial access, and inclusive development, with a particular focus on emerging and developing economies

S. Sivaprakkash has done all his degrees from Loyola College, Chennai. He is a Gold Medalist in M.Com. and M.Phil. Currently working as an Assistant Professor in the Department of Commerce at Central University of Tamil Nadu. To his credit, he has published 5 articles in Scopus-listed journals and 20 articles in UGC-listed journals. He is a recipient of the Rajiv Gandhi National Fellowship for Persons with Disabilities for the year 2016-17. He has completed a Minor Research Project (M.R.P.) sponsored by the Indian Council of Social Science Research (I.C.S.S.R.). His areas of interest include Sustainable Development, Global Marketing Perspective, Investment Management, and Human Resource Management.

Sunil Sankathala is pursuing B. Tech. in Computer Science and Engineering at Ajeenkya D Y Patil University, with a diverse range of interests that bridge technology, sustainability, and innovation. His academic focus lies in computer science fundamentals like programming, data structures, algorithms, and software development. He actively supplements this with hands-on experience in web development and robotics. Beyond the core curriculum, He has a strong research inclination in emerging and impactful fields. His current research interests include Artificial Intelligence in Healthcare, bioplastics, nano bioplastics, e-waste management, and solid waste management—areas where he believes technology can make a meaningful difference in solving real-world problems. He has been publishing research articles and book chapters in reputed national and international journals and books. He is also part of an ambitious Hyperloop project, which involves interdisciplinary collaboration and cutting-edge engineering aimed at revolutionizing transportation. Working on this project has enhanced his skills in teamwork, innovation, and systems thinking. In the tech domain, he has developed proficiency in web development using technologies such as HTML, CSS, JavaScript, and React. His interests in robotics further reflect building smart, responsive systems that interact with the physical world. Throughout his course, he has helped strengthen problem-solving and collaborative skills. He is proficient in languages such as Python, C, C++, MySQL, Ubuntu, Machine Learning and familiar with frameworks and tools like React, Git. He actively participates in hackathons, coding competitions, and tech events to challenge himself and learn from peers. He is also a quick learner and highly adaptable, with an eagerness to stay updated with the latest trends in the tech world. He aspires to become a skilled software engineer and contribute to building innovative solutions that have a positive impact on society. The long-term goal is to work in a dynamic environment where knowledge, grow professionally, and make meaningful contributions to the field of technology. Driven by a spirit of exploration and sustainability, he aims to contribute to technological solutions that address both human and environmental needs. The long-term goal is to become a versatile engineer and researcher, working at the intersection of computer science, environmental innovation, and human well-being.

Matome Winter Seshoka is a Senior Lecturer in the Department of Educational Studies at the University of Limpopo in South Africa. He holds a Doctor of Philosophy (PhD) in Education (Curriculum Studies).

Ajay K. Singh is working as an Associate Professor (Research) in the Department of Humanities and Social Science, Graphic Era (Deemed to be University) Dehradun. He has worked as Assistant Professor (Economics) in the School of Liberal Arts & Management, DIT University Dehradun for 6 years. He did Post-Doctorate Research with EDI of India, Ahmedabad, Gujarat (India). He received MPhil (Economics) from DAVV Indore (India), and PhD (Economics) from IIT Indore (India. He has published several research papers in the diversified area such as climate change, agricultural productivity, assessment of food security; estimation of GFSI, development of environmental sustainability index (ESI) and its association with socio-economic indicators; measurement and determinants of entrepreneurship ecosystem, and dimension of sustainable development and its interlinkages with economic development.

Sopha SOEUNG is a Teacher Educator at the National Institute of Education (NIE), Cambodia. He holds a Doctoral Degree in Educational Research from Hiroshima University, Japan.

Phearun Tep is from the Department of English at the University of Delhi. With his extensive experience in teaching English literature, working as a translator, and authoring scholarly works in Cambodia. He is a committed researcher with interests in South Asian and Southeast Asian literature, Translation Studies, Indian Literary Theory & Criticism, Fiction, cultural and post-conflict studies, and identity representation. His research examines how historical trauma, cultural memory, and narrative imagination inform the human experience, contributing to the broader discourse of literary scholarship and interdisciplinary studies.

X. Naveenraj is an Assistant Professor in the Faculty of Management at SRM Institute of Science and Technology, Vadapalani Campus. He has several years of academic and professional experience in the field of management education and research. His research interests include organizational psychology, workplace environment, strategic management, customer loyalty, and service quality. With a strong background in teaching and mentoring, he focuses on how leadership and organizational behavior influence employee performance and business outcomes. Before joining SRMIST, he gained valuable experience through academic coordination, corporate interactions, and consultancy-related activities that enhanced his practical understanding of business management. Dr. Naveenraj actively encourages students to engage in research, critical thinking, and industry-oriented learning. He also organizes industrial visits, workshops, and extension activities to bridge the gap between theory and practice. Through his teaching, research, and professional involvement, he aims to develop competent and responsible management professionals equipped with analytical, ethical, and leadership skills.

Azmee Zaheer is an Assistant Professor at the University School of Business (USB), Chandigarh University, India. He holds a Ph.D. and M.Phil. in Management and has over a decade of experience in academia, research, and industry. His research interests include marketing, digital marketing, services marketing, sustainability, consumer behavior, and business management. Dr. Zaheer has published research in peer-reviewed journals and actively contributes to interdisciplinary research, innovation, and higher education.

Index

A

academic careers 15, 17, 53, 63, 137, 138, 172, 188, 231, 234, 261, 264, 265, 270, 279, 284, 293
academic evaluation 2, 12, 231, 234, 239, 241, 251, 259, 277, 283, 284
academic freedom 18, 56, 71, 74, 79, 94, 140, 141, 156, 239, 258, 295, 299, 300, 303, 311
academic identity 19, 21, 54, 137, 139, 141, 142, 157, 163, 165, 235, 237, 241, 243, 244, 250, 252, 255, 256, 257
Academic Profession 1, 2, 3, 6, 17, 32, 33, 35, 36, 39, 42, 43, 44, 47, 48, 56, 63, 64, 79, 139, 140, 141, 142, 144, 146, 154, 197, 200, 201, 218, 231, 233, 237, 243, 244, 251, 252, 253, 261, 262, 263, 264, 266, 268, 279, 283, 286, 292
Academic professional development 165
academic professions 226, 235, 237, 241, 243, 244, 252, 259, 320
Academic Workload 6, 12
AI Ethics 3, 6, 16, 18, 21, 22, 34, 35, 56, 158, 240, 248, 252, 253, 257, 295, 300, 304, 305, 308, 309, 312, 315, 318, 321, 325
AI Knowledge and Skills 348, 357
AI literacy 6, 9, 13, 30, 44, 51, 61, 64, 70, 72, 80, 107, 116, 118, 124, 125, 128, 158, 159, 165, 216, 296, 297, 312, 313, 319, 327, 328, 329, 330, 331, 332, 333, 334, 336, 337, 339, 340, 342, 343, 344, 345, 346, 347, 348, 349, 351, 352, 353, 354, 357
AI Professional Development Framework 137, 157, 165
AI tools 4, 6, 7, 8, 10, 12, 13, 24, 31, 35, 39, 44, 50, 51, 52, 54, 64, 66, 70, 71, 72, 74, 75, 76, 78, 80, 108, 109, 121, 123, 127, 128, 130, 131, 139, 140, 144, 145, 155, 156, 159, 160, 172, 183, 191, 198, 200, 216, 218, 227, 234, 235, 238, 239, 264, 265, 285, 286, 292, 293, 302, 304, 311, 314, 317, 319, 333, 336, 337, 338, 345, 346
Algorithmic governance 16, 250, 252, 256, 266, 267, 271, 284, 293, 296, 297, 298, 299, 300, 301, 304, 318
Artificial Intelligence 1, 2, 4, 7, 10, 12, 17, 20, 23, 24, 25, 26, 27, 28, 29, 30, 31, 32, 33, 34, 42, 53, 56, 57, 58, 59, 60, 61, 62, 63, 65, 68, 70, 72, 73, 75, 77, 78, 79, 81, 82, 83, 84, 85, 86, 88, 94, 106, 108, 111, 112, 113, 114, 115, 116, 118, 119, 122, 123, 124, 125, 127, 132, 134, 135, 137, 138, 139, 144, 147, 149, 157, 160, 161, 162, 163, 164, 165, 167, 171, 172, 179, 180, 185, 191, 192, 195, 198, 201, 221, 224, 225, 226, 229, 231, 232, 234, 235, 237, 243, 248, 254, 255, 256, 258, 259, 260, 262, 264, 296, 297, 300, 304, 305, 308, 310, 313, 314, 315, 317, 318, 320, 321, 322, 323, 324, 325, 327, 331, 333, 342, 343, 344, 350, 351, 352, 353, 354, 355, 356, 357
Artificial Intelligence in higher education 26, 30, 34, 58, 59, 73, 77, 81, 83, 111, 113, 118, 119, 134, 163, 164, 165, 256, 258, 318, 320

D

dialectical analysis 299
Digital competency and literacy 348, 357
digital pedagogy 13, 37, 61, 70, 80, 118, 124, 125, 128, 130, 166
digital transformation 39, 43, 49, 53, 55, 89, 108, 109, 119, 146, 151, 222, 232, 233, 234, 239, 243, 248, 295, 296, 355

E

Educational organizations 327, 328, 329, 330, 334, 335, 337, 341, 346, 348, 349, 358
Educational Technology 2, 23, 27, 29, 58,

60, 83, 108, 109, 113, 116, 134, 135, 165, 221, 223, 232, 233, 241, 242, 254, 255, 258, 321, 328, 330, 350, 356, 357
Ethical use 69, 107, 118, 127, 145, 146, 147, 166, 241, 258, 349

F

faculty development 59, 72, 108, 127
Faculty Retention 93, 107, 110

G

Governance and Ethics 241, 312, 320

H

Higher Education 1, 2, 3, 4, 5, 6, 7, 8, 9, 10, 12, 17, 18, 19, 20, 21, 23, 24, 25, 26, 27, 29, 30, 31, 32, 33, 34, 35, 36, 37, 38, 39, 40, 41, 42, 46, 47, 49, 50, 53, 55, 56, 57, 58, 59, 60, 61, 62, 63, 64, 65, 66, 67, 68, 69, 70, 71, 72, 73, 74, 75, 77, 78, 79, 80, 81, 82, 83, 84, 85, 86, 87, 88, 89, 91, 92, 93, 94, 95, 104, 105, 106, 107, 108, 109, 110, 111, 112, 113, 114, 115, 116, 117, 118, 119, 120, 121, 122, 124, 126, 127, 128, 129, 130, 132, 134, 135, 137, 138, 139, 140, 141, 142, 143, 144, 145, 146, 148, 150, 151, 152, 153, 155, 156, 157, 159, 160, 161, 162, 163, 164, 165, 168, 169, 171, 180, 192, 194, 219, 220, 221, 222, 223, 228, 231, 232, 233, 234, 235, 236, 237, 238, 239, 240, 241, 242, 243, 246, 247, 248, 249, 252, 254, 255, 256, 257, 258, 259, 262, 263, 265, 266, 267, 268, 269, 270, 271, 272, 273, 274, 276, 278, 280, 281, 283, 284, 285, 286, 287, 288, 289, 290, 291, 292, 293, 295, 296, 297, 298, 299, 300, 302, 303, 304, 305, 307, 308, 309, 310, 312, 313, 314, 318, 319, 320, 321, 322, 323, 324, 325, 334, 350, 355, 357
Higher education reform 271
higher education transformation 243, 259
Human-AI 137, 154, 155, 157, 166, 233, 236, 238, 241, 248, 252, 254, 257

I

Indian Higher Education 31, 33, 37, 40, 47, 53, 55, 56
Indonesian higher education 296, 297, 298, 300, 303, 304, 305, 308, 309, 313

M

Morocco 261, 262, 264, 265, 271, 272, 273, 282, 285, 286, 287, 289, 290, 293

N

NEP 2020 37, 44, 47, 48, 56, 59
New public management 262, 268, 269, 270, 280, 284, 290, 293

O

Organisational Commitment 85, 86, 89, 90, 91, 92, 93, 94, 95, 97, 102, 103, 104, 105, 107, 108, 112

P

policy praxis 295, 300
Private Higher Education Institutions 85, 86, 91, 93, 95, 104, 106, 113, 114, 285
Professional Development 1, 3, 6, 7, 19, 20, 64, 65, 72, 73, 74, 77, 79, 80, 83, 84, 108, 115, 118, 124, 126, 127, 128, 129, 130, 131, 132, 134, 135, 137, 138, 139, 141, 142, 143, 144, 146, 147, 148, 149, 150, 151, 152, 153, 154, 155, 156, 157, 158, 159, 160, 165, 190, 200, 204, 218, 226, 227, 228, 238, 275, 333, 348, 349, 357
Professional Identity 1, 3, 5, 6, 9, 12, 14, 19, 20, 40, 43, 48, 56, 61, 64, 70, 71, 79, 141, 158, 220, 231, 234, 235, 237, 243, 250, 253, 254, 255, 256, 260, 346
Professional Roles 13, 78, 138, 141, 200,

202, 215, 218
Professorial Appointments 37, 138, 261, 262

S

Supervision Styles 199, 200, 201, 202, 203, 204, 205, 206, 207, 210, 211, 212, 214, 215
Sustainable AI Integration 19, 20

T

Turnover Intention 85, 87, 88, 92, 94, 95, 97, 105, 106, 109, 111, 112, 113, 114

www.ingramcontent.com/pod-product-compliance
Lightning Source LLC
LaVergne TN
LVHW080910300926
849162LV00003B/627
* 9 7 9 8 2 6 0 0 3 2 0 4 6 *